REAL-TIME SYSTEMS

McGraw-Hill Series in Computer Science

Senior Consulting Editor

C. L. Liu, University of Illinois at Urbana-Champaign

Consulting Editor

Allen B. Tucker, Bowdoin College

Fundamentals of Computing and Programming
Computer Organization and Architecture
Computers in Society/Ethics
Systems and Languages
Theoretical Foundations
Software Engineering and Database
Artificial Intelligence
Networks, Parallel and Distributed Computing
Graphics and Visualization
The MIT Electrical and Computer Science Series

Systems and Languages

*Abelson and Sussman: *Structure and Interpretation of Computer Programs*
Appleby: *Programming Languages, Paradigm and Practice*
Cohen: *Ada as a Second Language*
Friedman, Wand, and Haynes: *Essentials of Programming Languages*
Kant: *Introduction to Computer System Performance Evaluation*
Krishna and Shin: *Real-Time Systems*
Madnick and Donovan: *Operating Systems*
Milenkovic: *Operating Systems: Concepts and Design*
Singhal and Shivaratri: *Advanced Concepts in Operating Systems: Distributed, Multiprocessor, and Database Operating Systems*
*Springer and Friedman: *Scheme and the Art of Programming*

*Co-published by the MIT Press and McGraw-Hill, Inc.

REAL-TIME SYSTEMS

C. M. Krishna
University of Massachusetts

Kang G. Shin
The University of Michigan

The McGraw-Hill Companies, Inc.
New York   St. Louis   San Francisco   Auckland   Bogotá   Caracas
Lisbon   London   Madrid   Mexico City   Milan   Montreal   New Delhi
San Juan   Singapore   Sydney   Tokyo   Toronto

McGraw-Hill
*A Division of The **McGraw·Hill** Companies*

REAL-TIME SYSTEMS

1 2 3 4 5 6 7 8 9 0 DOC DOC 9 0 9 8 7 6

ISBN 0-07-057043-4

This book was set in Times Roman by ETP Harrison.
The editor was Eric M. Munson;
the production supervisor was Annette Mayeski.
The cover was designed by Karen K. Quigley.
Cover photo: Charles Daniels/Photonica.
Project supervision was done by ETP Harrison (Portland, Oregon).
R. R. Donnelley & Sons Company was printer and binder.

Library of Congress Cataloging-in-Publication Data

Krishna, C. M.
    Real-time systems / C.M. Krishna, Kang G. Shin.
      p.   cm.
    Includes bibliographical references and index.
    ISBN 0-07-057043-4 (acid-free paper)
    1. Real-time data processing.   2. Real-time control.   I. Shin,
Kang G.
QA76.54.K75   1997
004'.33—DC20   96-39004

http://www.mhcollege.com

ABOUT THE AUTHORS

C. M. KRISHNA

C. M. Krishna has been on the faculty of the University of Massachusetts since 1984. He has published in the areas of distributed processing, real-time systems, and fault tolerance, edited two volumes of readings for the IEEE Computer Society Press, and been Co-Guest-Editor of special issues of *IEEE Computer* and the *Proceedings of the IEEE* on real-time systems. Professor Krishna's current research deals with the reliability and performance modeling of real-time systems, fault-tolerant synchronization, distributed real-time operating systems, and real-time networks.

KANG G. SHIN

Kang G. Shin is Professor and Director of the Real-Time Computing Laboratory, Department of Electrical Engineering and Computer Science, The University of Michigan, Ann Arbor. He has authored and coauthored over 360 technical papers (about 150 of these in archival journals) and numerous book chapters in the areas of distributed real-time computing and control, fault-tolerant computing, computer architecture, robotics and automation, and intelligent manufacturing. Professor Shin is an IEEE Fellow, was the Program Chairman of the 1986 IEEE Real-Time Systems Symposium (RTSS), the General Chairman of the 1987 RTSS, the Guest Editor of the 1987 August special issue of *IEEE Transactions on Computers* on real-time systems, and an Editor of IEEE Transactions on Parallel and Distributed Systems from 1991–1995.

To our parents and family

CONTENTS

PREFACE

Real-time systems have proliferated over the past few years. Today, computers are found embedded in almost everything, from toasters to cars to fly-by-wire aircraft. The computational workload of such embedded systems varies widely, from machines expected to do a few arithmetic operations every second to computers executing complex calculations at tremendous rates. The consequences of computer failure also vary widely, from burnt toast at the one extreme to the loss of life in an air crash or a chemical plant explosion at the other.

The objective of this book is to introduce readers to design and evaluation issues in such systems. We cover a wide range of topics; both hardware and software issues are treated in some detail. We expect this book to be used by both practicing engineers and graduate or final-year undergraduate students.

Some of the discussion is mathematical. Wherever possible, we have separated the more mathematical portions from the descriptive. This enables the text to be read at multiple levels. The more advanced sections are starred (⋆); these require additional perseverance or ability to understand them, and can be skipped if necessary. However, we urge the reader to avoid skipping the mathematical portions. Most often, avoidance of mathematics is grounded on nothing more substantial than a primitive fear of and negative associations with mathematical symbols. A true understanding of many of the issues covered here cannot be achieved without understanding their mathematical underpinnings.

This book contains far more material than can comfortably be covered in a one-semester course. Instructors may decide to concentrate on particular topics, for example, task assignment and scheduling, or fault-tolerance. Alternatively, they may decide to present a wide-ranging survey of the various topics of interest to the real-time systems engineer. To enable both approaches to be used, we have tried to make the chapters as independent of one another as possible. In addition, this allows the book to be used as a reference handbook by the practicing engineer. Typographical or other errors should be reported to the authors at

rtbook@tikva.ecs.umass.edu

We plan to maintain a page of errata on the World Wide Web at

http://www.ecs.umass.edu/ece/gradfac/krishna.html

ACKNOWLEDGMENTS

Many people have contributed to making this book a reality. We would like to thank Eric Munson of McGraw-Hill for commissioning it, and for being willing to countenance a delay of over a year beyond our original deadline. It is perhaps ironic that the authors of a book that deals largely with tasks meeting deadlines were themselves unable to meet their contracted deadline!

A number of our colleagues and students have read through this book, either in part on in its entirety, and provided valuable suggestions or pointed out mistakes. We list them below in random order.

Y.-H. Lee	C. Ravishankar	N. Soparkar
A. Ansari	J. Rexford	S. H. Son
N. Suri	J. Strosnider	F. Zhou
A. Mehra	W. Feng	A. Shaikh
T. Abdelzaher	A. Indiresan	E. Atkins
P. Ramanathan	S. Daniel	T. Koprowski
S. Wilson	K. Ramamritham	W. Preska

Beverly Monaghan of The University of Michigan and June Daehler of the University of Massachusetts provided valuable secretarial assistance. Julie F. Nemer of ETP Harrison was the copyeditor, and her comments helped improve the readability of the text. Thanks are also due to Michael J. Kolibaba for coordinating our interactions with the copyeditor and to the following reviewers: Wei Zhao, In-Sup Lee, William Marcy, and Borko Furht.

C. M. Krishna
Kang G. Shin

CHAPTER
1

INTRODUCTION

After writing a book on real-time systems, you might think that we would be able to give you a precise, cogent statement of what a real-time system is. Unfortunately, we cannot. If pressed for a definition, we might say something like this:

> Any system where a timely response by the computer to external stimuli is vital is a real-time system.

The above statement is true, but only because it is almost content-free. If you take a second look at it, you will find that it raises as many questions as it answers. If you decide to dig a little deeper by taking apart the above definition, you might have the following dialogue with us:

You: What do you mean by "timely"?

Us: It means a real-time system runs tasks that have deadlines.

You: By "deadlines" do you mean that the task *must* be done by then?

Us: Not necessarily. Sometimes, yes: If you are controlling an aircraft by computer and you miss a sequence of deadlines as the aircraft comes in to land, you risk crashing the plane. Sometimes, no: If you are playing a video game and the response takes a mite longer than specified, nothing awful will happen.

You: What do you mean by a task being "done"? Is there a sharp distinction between when a task is "done" and when it is not?

Us: Not necessarily. Sometimes, yes: If you have a banking application that needs to total some figures before it will let you draw a million dollars from your checking account, then yes. Sometimes, no: If your application needs to calculate the value of π, it can decide either to stop early and accept a less accurate value, or to continue calculating and make the estimate more and more accurate.

1

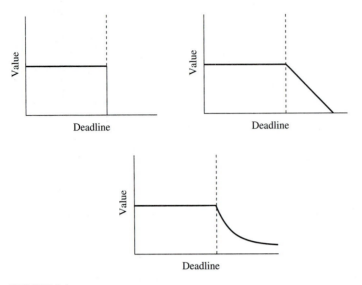

FIGURE 1.1
Examples of task value functions.

You: What do you do with a real-time task that misses its deadline? Do you drop it or complete it anyway?

Us: It depends. If you are on the aircraft that has crashed because a series of deadlines has been missed, neither you nor the computer is in a position to care. If, on the other hand, you have a video-conferencing application that encounters a minor delay in processing a voice packet, you may decide not to drop that packet. In any case, a task's value will drop to a certain level after the deadline has been missed. In some cases, it will be reduced abruptly to zero; in others, it will decline more gradually. Figure 1.1 shows some examples.

You: Does this make every computer a real-time computer by your definition?

Us: Unfortunately, yes. If you read our definition too legalistically, the general-purpose workstation or personal computer is also a real-time system: if you hit the key and the computer takes an hour to echo the character onto the screen, you will not be very happy. Everything is "real-time" in the sense of our needing the result within a finite time. So, our definition covers all computers and is therefore worthless.

You: Do you want to change your definition of real-time systems?

Us: Yes. The new definition is fuzzier, less sweeping, and not as clear-cut, but it has the inestimable virtue of ending this argument.

A real-time system is anything that we, the authors of this book, consider to be a real-time system. This includes embedded systems that control things like aircraft, nuclear reactors, chemical power plants, jet engines, and other objects where Something Very Bad will happen if the computer does not deliver its output in time. These are called *hard* real-time systems. There is another category called (not surprisingly) *soft* real-time systems, which are systems such as multimedia, where nothing catastrophic happens if some deadlines are missed, but where the performance will be degraded below what is generally considered acceptable. In general, a real-time system is one in which a substantial fraction of the design effort goes into making sure that task deadlines are met.

1.1 A CAR-AND-DRIVER EXAMPLE

To understand the major issues of real-time computing, consider a familiar problem of human control—driving a car. The driver is the real-time controller, the car is the controlled process, and the other cars together with the road conditions make up the operating environment. By understanding what is required of the driver, we can understand something of the major issues in real-time computing.

The main actuators in a car are the wheels, the engine, and the brakes. The controls are the accelerator, the steering wheel, the brake-pedal, and other elements (such as the switches for the lights, radio, wipers, etc.).

What are the constraints that the driver must meet? She must get from her starting point to the destination without colliding with other vehicles or stationary objects and keep her speed within designated limits. Let us translate this into the terms used in real-time computing.

The driver may be said to be performing a *mission*—that of getting to her destination while satisfying the constraints mentioned above. How can we quantify the driver's performance? We measure the outcome of the driver's actions, taken in the context of the operating environment. One obvious outcome is getting to the destination; a secondary consideration is the time it takes to get there. However, our assessment of the time taken must be weighted by a consideration of the road conditions: A driver may be performing very well if she maintains an average speed of 15 mph in a snowstorm (and gets to her destination without killing or maiming herself or anyone else); if the weather is dry and the roads are clear, however, the same speed of 15 mph represents an abject failure.

Suppose the driver fails to get to her destination and instead ends up unhurt in a ditch by the side of the road. Once again, our assessment of the driver's performance depends not just on the outcome—her landing in the ditch—but also on what caused her to get there. If she was forced into the ditch to avoid a head-on collision with someone driving on the wrong side of the road, we count that as a success; if she went into the ditch by taking a turn too quickly and skidding, we count that as a failure.

The point is that performance is not an absolute commodity. Performance must be measured instead in terms of what the conditions allow. In other words, *performance* measures the goodness of the outcome relative to the best outcome possible under the circumstances. This is an important point, and we shall return to it in Chapter 2.

Let us consider now the tasks that the driver must perform. Some of them are critical to the success of the mission, and some are not. Steering and braking are critical tasks; tuning the radio is a noncritical task. Steering and braking are real-time tasks with varying deadlines that depend on the operating environment. The deadlines associated with driving down a quiet street at 6 o'clock on a Sunday morning are very different from those associated with driving along a busy highway at the height of the rush hour. *Task deadlines* in real-time systems are not constant; they vary with the operating environment.

What information do we need about the driver's physical condition in order to predict her performance? It is not sufficient to know that the driver will be awake for 99.99% of her trip. If she falls asleep for more than a second or two at a stretch, she will fail catastrophically. If, on the other hand, there are many periods of "micro-sleep" along the way, each lasting no more than half a second, the chances are high that she will not fail. Simple average measures are useless to predict the performance of a real-time controller.

Even if she gets to her destination safely, it is possible that the micro-sleeping driver has cause to brake and accelerate abruptly. This can increase her fuel consumption; so even if she completes her mission successfully, her micro-sleep has not been free of cost. It is possible to discriminate on the basis of secondary factors, such as fuel consumption or time taken, among missions that have been successfully completed.

Suppose we try to precisely specify the responsibilities of the driver. The overall goal of the mission is clear: get to the destination safely, without committing any traffic violations. But what of the details? Suppose we are to include in the specifications precisely what the driver must do in each conceivable eventuality. How would we write such specifications and then ensure that the specifications were complete? The reader might, as an exercise, try writing out a set of specifications in plain English. A few minutes of this activity will be sufficient to convince him that to write a complete and correct set of specifications for even so well understood a task as driving a car is extremely difficult. Writing out formal specifications and validating them are perhaps the most difficult tasks in real-time systems. They are also the tasks about which researchers know the least.

With this background, we now turn to listing some major issues in real-time computing.

1.2   ISSUES IN REAL-TIME COMPUTING

A real-time computer must be much more reliable than its individual hardware and software components. It must be capable of working in harsh environments, rich in electromagnetic noise and elementary-particle radiation, and in the face of rapidly changing computation loads.

The field of real-time computing is especially rich in research problems because all problems in computer architecture, fault-tolerant computing, and operating systems are also problems in real-time computing, with the added complexity that real-time constraints must be met.

For example, take task scheduling. The purpose of task scheduling in a general-purpose system is fairness, by which we mean that the computer's resources must be shared out equitably among the users. This end is usually achieved by using round-robin scheduling. Each process is associated with a time-slice. The computer executes a process until one of the following happens: it is done, it has to stop for something like a disk access or interrupt, or its allotted time-slice has expired. The computer then switches context to another process. There may be variations on this basic theme; for example the time-slice could be varied according to how much execution time has already been spent on that task.

Round-robin scheduling ensures that one user does not get a disproportionate share of the computer's services. Such an approach does not work in a real-time application. Why? See Example 1.1.

Example 1.1. Consider a computer controlling an aircraft. Among its tasks are maintaining stability and keeping the cabin temperature within acceptable limits. Suppose the aircraft encounters turbulence that makes it momentarily unstable. The computer is then supposed to adjust the control surfaces to regain stability. If we use round-robin scheduling for this application, the computer may switch context partway through making the control adjustments in order to spend time making sure the cabin temperature is just right. The result may well be a crash, and the fact that the cabin is being maintained at optimum temperature will be scant consolation to the passengers as the airliner falls out of the sky. What we want is to give the stability-maintenance task a very high *priority*, which ensures that when stability is threatened, all other interfering tasks are elbowed out of the way to allow this all-important task enough computer cycles.

Let us take a second example where the solution to a design problem is different because of real-time deadlines. Caches are commonplace in computers; they reduce the effective memory-access time and increase the average through-put. There are two ways to allocate cache space. One is to allow the process currently executing the right to use the entire cache area. This keeps the miss rate (and hence the effective memory-access time) low and is the approach adopted by general-purpose systems. However, from a real-time engineer's standpoint, this approach has the unpleasant side effect of making task run times less predictable.

Example 1.2. Suppose process A takes t_1 seconds to execute when it is not interrupted by any other process. Consider what happens if A is preempted by another process, B, and then takes up from where it left off when B gets done. See Figure 1.2. Is $t_{2.1} + t_{2.2} = t_1$? Not necessarily! This is because when B was executing it might have displaced some of A's lines from the cache to make room for its own working set. When A resumes and accesses one of these displaced lines, a cache miss results and the access time is greater than it would have been if B had not come along and disrupted things. As a result, $t_{2.1} + t_{2.2}$ is very likely to be greater than t_1. The execution time of A will depend (among many other things) on the number of times A is preempted and on what happens to the cache upon each preemption.

It is important that the task execution time be predictable to allow the designer to figure out if all critical tasks will meet their deadlines. If the effect of the cache is to make task run times very unpredictable, it may actually do more harm than good from the designer's point of view.

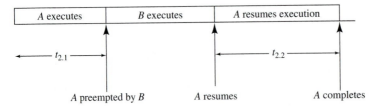

FIGURE 1.2
Preemption of process *A* by process *B*.

Real-time computer systems differ from their general-purpose counterparts in two important ways. First, they are much more specific in their applications, and, second, the consequences of their failure are more drastic.

A real-time computer is typically designed for a specific application, for example, to control a particular aircraft. The advantage of this is that the characteristics of the application and its operating environment are more precisely known than for general-purpose machines. As a result, it is possible to fine-tune real-time systems more precisely for optimum performance.

Since the consequences of failure are more severe in real-time systems than in their general-purpose counterparts, such systems need to be specified more carefully and their performance better validated; that is, we need specification languages and performance measures that are capable of expressing timing requirements. We require, among other things, means by which to predict the execution times of programs; to model the reliability of software and of hardware; to assign tasks to processors and schedule them so that deadlines are met; and to develop mechanisms by which the system can quickly recover from the failure of an individual component. We shall look at these and other issues in detail.

Example 1.3. Contrast the situation of an engineer designing a computer to control a jet engine with that of someone designing a general-purpose workstation. The engine-control designer knows precisely the workload that must be executed by the system. He knows, for example, roughly how many times a second the computer must adjust the engine settings, as well as roughly how long it takes to compute each setting. The workstation designer, in contrast, has a general application area in mind (e.g., the machine may be projected for use in mostly graphical or multimedia applications), but she has no idea of exactly what software the machine will be running. Even if she magically acquired the power of the oracle and could foresee what each copy of her machine would be running, it wouldn't do her much good—adjusting the design to suit one user type may make it worse for another user type. This underlines what we said about the real-time designer (especially the hard real-time designer) having more information about the general operating conditions of his products than does the general-purpose workstation designer.

However, the real-time engineer has a greater burden of meeting performance goals than his general-purpose counterpart. If a variable-cycle jet engine does not get its control inputs on time, it may explode. If the workstation turns out to be a few milliseconds slower than projected for a given application, the consequences will not be as drastic.

1.3 STRUCTURE OF A REAL-TIME SYSTEM

Figure 1.3 shows a schematic block diagram of a real-time system in control of some process. The state of the controlled process and of the operating environment (e.g., pressure, temperature, speed, and altitude) is acquired by sensors, which provide inputs to the controller, the real-time computer. The data rate from each sensor depends on how quickly the measured parameters can change; it is usually less than 1 kilobyte/second (KB/s).

There is a fixed set of application tasks or jobs,[1] the "job list" in Figure 1.3. The software for these tasks is preloaded into the computer. If the computer has a shared main memory, then the entire software is loaded into that. If, on the other hand, it consists of a set of private memories belonging to individual processors, the question arises as to which memories each job should be loaded into. This question relates to the allocation and scheduling of jobs that we discuss in detail in this book.

The "trigger generator" is a representation of the mechanism used to trigger the execution of individual jobs. It is not really a separate hardware unit; typically it is part of the executive software. Many of the jobs are periodic (i.e., they execute regularly). The schedule for these jobs can be obtained offline and loaded as a lookup table to be used by the scheduler. Jobs can also be initiated depending on the state of the controlled process or on the operating environment. For example, when the pressure of a boiler is greater than the preset threshold in a chemical

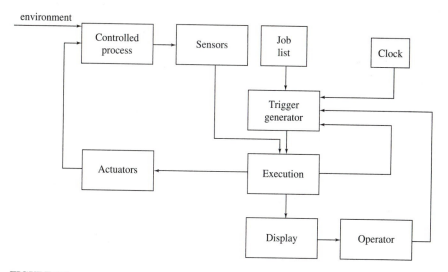

FIGURE 1.3
A schematic block diagram of a real-time system.

---

[1]In this book, we use the terms "tasks" and "jobs" interchangeably. This set is the union of all tasks associated with different operation modes.

plant or the altitude is less than the threshold in an aircraft, it may be necessary to run some task every x ms. Finally, jobs can be initiated on command from the operator input panel.

The output of the computer is fed to the actuators and the displays. Fault-tolerant techniques (which we discuss in detail in Chapter 7) ensure that, despite a small number of erroneous outputs from the computer, the actuators are set correctly. The actuators typically have a mechanical or a hydraulic component, and so their time constants are quite high. As a result, the data rates to the actuators are quite low; one command per 25 ms, on average, is not uncommon.

A control computer exhibits a dichotomy in terms of the data rates. The sensors and actuators run at relatively low data rates. The computer itself must be fast enough to execute the control algorithms, and these can require throughputs in excess of 50 million instructions per second (MIPS). As a result, the system separates into three areas: an outer low-rate area consisting of the sensors, actuators, displays, and input panels; a middle or *peripheral* area consisting of the processing that is necessary to format the data from and to this layer properly; and the *central* cluster of processors where the control algorithms are executed. Figure 1.4 depicts this logical decomposition. Quite frequently, the controlled process can go through distinct *phases*, each of which defines the required set of control tasks, task priorities, and deadlines. For example, there are the following four phases in a civilian aircraft:

1. Takeoff and cruise until VHF omnirange VOR/DME (distance measuring equipment) is out of range.
2. Cruise until VOR/DME is in range again.
3. Cruise until landing is to be initiated.
4. Land.

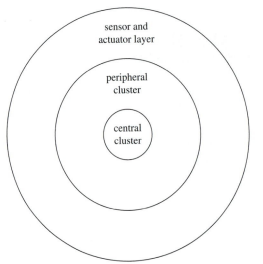

FIGURE 1.4
Schematic decomposition of a real-time control computer.

1.4 TASK CLASSES

Tasks can be classified in two ways: by the predictability of their arrival and by the consequences of their not being executed on time.

Periodic and aperiodic tasks: There are many tasks in real-time systems that are done repetitively. For example, one may wish to monitor the speed, altitude, and attitude of an aircraft every 100 ms. This sensor information will be used by periodic tasks that control the control surfaces of the aircraft (e.g., the ailerons, elevator, rudder and engine thrusts), in order to maintain stability and other desired characteristics. The periodicity of these tasks is known to the designer, and so such tasks can be prescheduled.

In contrast, there are many other tasks that are *aperiodic*, that occur only occasionally. For instance, when the pilot wishes to execute a turn, a large number of subtasks associated with that action are set off. By their very nature, aperiodic tasks cannot be predicted and sufficient computing power must be held in reserve to execute them in a timely fashion. Aperiodic tasks with a bounded interarrival time are called *sporadic* tasks.

Critical and noncritical tasks: Real-time tasks can also be classified according to the consequences of their not being executed on time. *Critical* tasks are those whose timely execution is critical; if deadlines are missed, catastrophes occur. Examples include life-support systems and the stability control of aircraft. Despite their critical nature, it is not always essential that every iteration of the critical tasks be executed successfully and within a given deadline. Critical tasks are often executed at a higher frequency than is absolutely necessary. This constitutes time redundancy and ensures one successful computation every n_i iterations of critical periodic task i, which is sufficient to keep the system alive. Of course, the actual value of n_i will depend on the application, the nature of the task itself, and the number of times the task is invoked over a given interval.

Noncritical real-time (or soft real-time) tasks are, as the name implies, not critical to the application. However, they do deal with time-varying data and hence they are useless if not completed within a deadline. The goal in scheduling these tasks is thus to maximize the percentage of jobs successfully executed within their deadlines.

1.5 ISSUES COVERED IN THIS BOOK

1.5.1 Architecture Issues

Processor architecture: Since, for reasons of economy, off-the-shelf processors are preferred, real-time designers seldom (if ever) design their own processors. For this reason, we do not treat processor architecture in detail here; the interested reader should consult one of the many excellent texts on the subject. However, a real-time engineer is frequently faced with the need to estimate task execution times and it is important to know how to analyze how long a particular architecture takes to execute a given stretch of code. Much work remains to be done on this topic, but Section 2.3 contains a few ideas.

Network architecture: To make systems reliable and provide sufficient processing capacity, most real-time systems are multiple-processor machines. The designer is faced with deciding the topology of the network and how much of the network-accessing function to offload from the core processors to special-purpose network interface engines. Both issues have implications for what communication protocols can be supported and the fault-tolerance of the network, as well as the magnitude, predictability, and controllability of network delays. We discuss these issues in Chapter 6.

Architectures for clock synchronization: In order to facilitate the interaction between the multiple units of a real-time system, the clocks of these units must be synchronized fairly tightly. The clock synchronization mechanism must be fault-tolerant; if a few individual clocks fail, the rest must remain synchronized. A low-overhead, low-skew synchronization architecture based on phase-locked clocks is presented in Chapter 9.

Fault-tolerance and reliability evaluation: People can die when real-time systems fail. Such systems must therefore be highly fault-tolerant. The use and evaluation of redundancy in real-time architectures to maintain high reliability are discussed in Chapters 7 and 8.

1.5.2   Operating System Issues

Task assignment and scheduling: The scheduling of tasks to ensure that real-time deadlines are met is central to the mission of a real-time operating system. This has been a very active research area and many of the available results are of practical interest to the designer. Chapter 3 provides a fairly detailed survey of this area.

Communications protocols: It is important to have interprocessor communication that has predictable delays and is controllable. While much remains to be done in this field, there are many algorithms already in existence that can be used to control interprocessor communication. See Chapter 6.

Failure management and recovery: When a processor or software module fails, the system must limit such failure and recover from it. Techniques for this are covered in Chapter 7.

Clock synchronization algorithms: We mentioned in Section 1.5.1 a hardware synchronization architecture built out of phase-locked clocks. There are also software implementations of fault-tolerant clock synchronization, and these are covered in Chapter 9.

1.5.3   Other Issues

Programming languages: Real-time engineers need much greater control over timing and need to interface to special-purpose devices (e.g., sensors, actuators, etc.) more often than do general-purpose programmers. General-purpose languages such as Pascal or C do not provide such control. In Chapter 4, we explore some issues relating to real-time programming languages.

Databases: There are many real-time database applications, such as the stock market, airline reservations, and artificial intelligence. While some research into soft real-time databases has been reported, little has been done for hard real-time applications. Real-time databases are covered in Chapter 5.

Performance measures: Commonly used performance measures such as conventional reliability and throughput are useless for real-time systems. Measures are required that accurately convey the needs of the application and accurately characterize the computer's ability to meet such needs. While this area has not received much attention, some useful results are available; these are described in Chapter 2.

CHAPTER
2

CHARACTERIZING
REAL-TIME
SYSTEMS
AND TASKS

2.1 INTRODUCTION

In this chapter, we consider two questions:

- Which performance measures are the most appropriate for real-time systems? Do these have to be different from those used for general-purpose computers (such as throughput and reliability)?
- How can engineers estimate the worst-case run time of a program, given the source code and the target architecture? (In order to determine whether a real-time computer can meet task deadlines, we must be able to estimate how long individual programs take to run.)

Neither of these crucial issues has received the attention that it deserves from the research community, and the results described here are far from being the last word on the subject. Much work remains to be done in this area, especially in accurately obtaining worst-case task run times.

2.2 PERFORMANCE MEASURES FOR REAL-TIME SYSTEMS

Real-time systems are often used in critical applications, and must therefore be carefully designed and validated before being put into operation. The validation process includes checking design correctness using formal and informal methods and characterizing performance and reliability. This section is concerned with a preparatory step that needs to be completed before performance or reliability can be characterized, the choice of performance measures.

The choice of appropriate performance measures is crucial to the correct characterization of performance. Performance measures are yardsticks by which performance is expressed. They are, in a very real sense, languages through which we convey system performance. Our experience with natural languages suggests that not only does language determine how our thoughts are expressed, but also which ideas arise and get expressed. Through the richness or poverty of the vocabulary available to describe certain things, as well as the associations that humans create between words, natural languages act partially as mechanisms of idea generation and idea communication, reinforcing certain ideas and suppressing others. We will see that performance measures, too, act as filters, imposing a scale of values on performance.

To be useful, a performance measure must be concise. That is, it must encapsulate in very few numbers (preferably a single number) the performance of a system. In other words, it must convey what is important about the performance of a system and leave out what is not. If, for instance, we use the mean response time of a computer for a given task as a performance measure, we are, deliberately or unwittingly, laying down that it is the average that is important, not the variance.

Example 2.1. Consider two systems A and B. A and B have system response times with the probability density functions[1] shown in Figure 2.1. System A is clearly

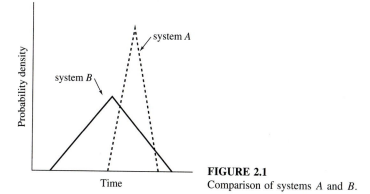

FIGURE 2.1
Comparison of systems A and B.

---

[1] See the Appendix for a definition of probability density functions.

more predictable than system B and is only slightly slower. However, if the mean response time is our performance measure, we rank B higher than A.

Suppose we wish to change the measure so that it is a weighted sum of the mean M and variance V of the response time, that is, $a_1 M + a_2 V$. Now comes the task of picking values for a_1 and a_2. These parameters will be chosen based on our assessment of the relative impacts of M and V on the user's view of performance. There is no formal way to do this, but the choice will determine how the systems are ranked in performance.

Suppose we decide to avoid the problem of picking a_1 and a_2 and define the performance measure as a vector of the mean and the variance, (M, V). How then do we compare A and B on this basis? We cannot, except to say that if the means of A and B are equal, the system with the lower variance will rank higher, and vice versa.

Example 2.2. Sometimes the performance perceived by a user depends in a complex way on the system response time. Consider a user typing at a terminal. He sees the echo on the display. If the delay between typing a character and seeing it on the display is not noticeable, the system is performing perfectly as far as the user is concerned. For instance, the user cannot distinguish between a delay of 5 μs and 10 μs, so both response times yield the same performance from his point of view.

As the delay in echoing a character to the terminal becomes more pronounced, the performance perceived by the user becomes worse. One might posit the performance-response time characteristic shown in Figure 2.2. As the response time becomes increasingly noticeable, the performance degrades. Beyond a point, the performance degrades to essentially zero. The actual curve will vary from one user to the next; some people are more patient than others.

Example 2.3. Computers used in pocket pagers have relatively simple functions, so speed of response is not the critical performance determinant. Rather, since pagers operate on battery power, the computer's power consumption becomes a more important performance measure.

Quite often, even if there is a good performance measure that accurately represents performance as the user perceives it, the application determines how systems are ranked.

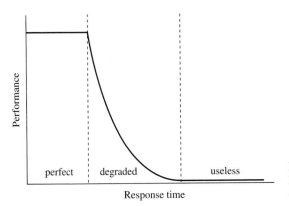

FIGURE 2.2
Performance from the point of view of a typist.

Example 2.4. Consider two systems, C and D. System C has a special array-processing unit that makes it possible to multiply two matrices of up to 256×256 in size in four clock cycles; System D, on the other hand, has no such unit. The cycles per instruction are the same on both machines for all other instructions. However, System D has a clocking frequency of 10 MHz, which is twice that of System C. Both systems cost roughly the same. We have chosen mean response time as our measure of performance.

There is, in this case, no "better" system in an absolute sense; which system is better depends on the application. If the application software consists of a large number of array multiplications, system C is better, despite having a much slower clock rate than D; if the software is largely scalar, D is better.

It is frequently possible for a reasonable-sounding performance measure to be misleading.

Example 2.5. Many people use the number of instructions executed per second as a performance measure. Computers are popularly rated according to their MIPS (the millions of instructions that they execute in a second). Consider two systems E and F. System E has a very simple instruction set, while F has a typical mainframe instruction set with dozens of complex instructions. Because of the simplicity of E's instruction set, its architects have been able to design the instruction pipeline so that, on average, each instruction takes 1.2 clock cycles. On the other hand, for System F the average instruction takes 1.8 clock cycles. Both systems have the same clock frequency.

On the face of it, System E is 1.5 times faster than System F. However, let us suppose that, due to the additional complexity of the System-F instruction set, an average program when translated into machine code is twice as long in System E as it is in System F. From the user's point of view, therefore, System E is slower than F.

The trap that we have fallen into is in not taking into account the power of an instruction set.

Performance as perceived by the user depends on so many factors that it is difficult in most cases to find a measure that is perfect in all respects.

2.2.1   Properties of Performance Measures[2]

A good performance measure must:

1. Represent an efficient encoding of relevant information.
2. Provide an objective basis for the ranking of candidate controllers for a given application.
3. Provide objective optimization criteria for design.
4. Represent verifiable facts.

---

[2]Section 2.2.1 is largely drawn from C. M. Krishna and K. G. Shin, "Performance Measures for Control Computers," *IEEE Trans. Automatic Control*, Vol. AC-32, No. 6, June 1987. © IEEE. Used with permission.

EFFICIENT ENCODING. One of the problems of dealing with complex systems is the volume of information that is available about them and their interactions with the environment. Determining the relevance of individual pieces of data is impossible unless the data are viewed within a certain context or framework. Such a context suppresses the irrelevant and highlights the relevant.

To be an efficient encoding for what is relevant about a system, the measures must be congruent to the application. The application is as important to performance as the computer itself—while it is the computer that is being assessed, it is the application that dictates the scale of values used to assess it.

If the performance measure is congruent to the application, that is to say if it is in a language natural to the application, then specifications can be written concisely and without contortion. This not only permits one to write specifications economically, but also to write specifications correctly and check for accuracy. The simpler a set of specifications, the more likely it is in general to be correct and internally consistent.

OBJECTIVE BASIS FOR RANKING. Performance measures must, by definition, quantify the goodness of computer systems in a given application or class of applications. It follows from this that they should permit the ranking of computers for the same application. It should be emphasized that the ranking must always depend on the application for the reasons given above.

OBJECTIVE OPTIMIZATION CRITERIA. The more complex a system, the more difficult it is to optimize or to fine-tune its structure. There are numerous side effects of even simple actions, for example, changing the number of buses in the computer. So, intuition applied to more and more complex computers becomes less and less dependable as an optimization technique. Multiprocessors are among the most complex computers. They provide, due to their complexity, a wealth of configurations of varying quality; this complexity can be used to advantage or ignored with danger.

Multiprocessors that adapt or *reconfigure* themselves (e.g., by changing their structure) in response to their current environment (e.g., current job mix, expected time-to-go in a mission-oriented system, etc.) to enhance productivity are likely to become feasible soon. All the impressive sophistication of such a reconfigurable system will come to naught if good, application-sensitive optimization criteria are unavailable.

VERIFIABLE FACTS. A performance measure that is impossible to derive is of no use to anybody. To be acceptable, a performance measure should hold out some prospect of being estimated reasonably accurately. What constitutes "reasonably accurate" depends on the purpose for which the performance characterization is carried out. Sometimes, when the requirements are too stringent (e.g., an extremely low failure probability) to be validated to the required level of accuracy, it is difficult to decide which, if either, is to blame: the performance measure itself or the mathematical tools used to determine it.

In the remainder of Section 2.2, we will look at various performance measures. We will begin by considering the traditional measures of reliability, availability, and throughput. Then, we will consider the *performability* and *cost function* approaches, which are tailored more specifically for real-time systems. We will provide examples of how to obtain these measures. Finally, we will discuss hard deadlines.

2.2.2 Traditional Performance Measures

Reliability, availability, and throughput, together with related measures, are the focus of this section. These measures are widely used for general-purpose systems.

Reliability is the probability that the system will not undergo failure over any part of a prescribed interval. *Availability* is the fraction of time for which the system is up. *Throughput* is the average number of instructions per unit time that the system can process.

These measures require us to define what is meant by the system being up or down. For simple systems, this is obvious. When the system is gracefully degradable, however, we have to define a set of failed system states. The system will be *up* whenever it is outside this set of failure states. The set of failure states depends on the application, since different applications require different capabilities on the part of the computer. The probability of the system being outside the failure states throughout some interval of time is the *capacity reliability* over that period. Related measures include the *expected capacity survival time*, which is the expected time for the capacity reliability to drop to a specific value, and the *mean computation before failure*, which is the mean amount of computation done before failure. The *computational reliability* $R^*(s, t, T)$ is the probability that the system can start a task T at time t and successfully execute it to completion. The system state at time t is s, which is assumed to be a functional state. Related to this is the *computational availability*, which is the expected value of the system computation capacity at any given time.

> **Example 2.6.** Consider a reconfigurable fault-tolerant system composed of processor triads. A *triad* (also called a *triplex*) is a group of three processors that independently run exactly the same software and do exactly the same tasks in parallel. When they finish a job, the outputs of the processors in a triad are voted on. If all the processors are functional, all their outputs will be exactly the same. If one processor is faulty, and the others nonfaulty, then two of the three processors will agree and the output of the faulty processor will be suppressed as a result of the voting. (We elaborate on this fault-tolerance technique in Chapter 7.)
>
> Our system begins with a total of eight functional processors, that is, two triads plus two spare processors. It is reconfigurable, which means that when failure happens, the triads can be reconstituted by switching in any available functional processors. For example, if we have seven functional processors, we have two triads, plus one spare functional processor. If a processor in one of the triads fails, it can be switched out of the triad and replaced by the spare, thus reconstituting the triad. Clearly, we can keep two triads operating only as long as we have at least six functional processors in the system.

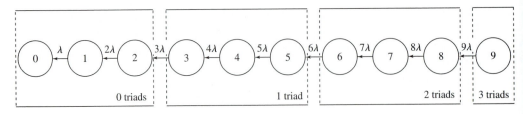

FIGURE 2.3
Markov diagram for a gracefully degradable system.

For the purposes of this example, we will assume that all failures are permanent, the processors fail independently of one another, and the failure process per processor is a Poisson process with rate λ. For simplicity, only processor failures are considered; the failures of the voters, the interprocessor network, and so on are excluded from consideration. There is no repair for this system.

Figure 2.3 contains a Markov diagram for this system.[3] The states are the number of functional processors, which can range from 0 to 9. As far as the user is concerned, however, the performance of the system depends on how many triads are functional; these are shown by the dashed boxes, which group together states into triads. Denote by $\pi_i(\xi)$ the probability that the system is in state i at time ξ.

The reliability of the system over a given period of operation t is then given by

$$p_{\text{fail}} = \sum_{i \in \text{FAIL}} \pi_i(t)$$

where the set FAIL consists of all the system states that are defined as failure. If the system is said to fail when not even one triad is available, FAIL = $\{0, 1, 2\}$; if it fails when both triads are unavailable, FAIL = $\{0, 1, 2, 3, 4, 5\}$.

If each triad has a throughput of x instructions per unit time, the throughput of the system at time ξ is given by

$$x \sum_{i=3}^{5} \pi_i(\xi) + 2x \sum_{i=6}^{8} \pi_i(\xi)$$

The drawback of these measures is that they do not provide a mechanism to study the interplay among the hardware, the system software, and the applications software. Reliability typically focuses on either the hardware or the software, independently of each other. Availability is practically useless as a measure of the ability to meet execution deadlines; the long-term fraction of time for which the system is up tells us nothing about the length of the individual down times. Throughput is an average measure; it conveys the raw computing capacity of the computer, but tells us nothing about the response time of the various control jobs.

These traditional measures work well so long as the set of failed states can be unambiguously defined in terms of just the hardware. For complex systems,

---

[3]Readers unfamiliar with Markov modeling should consult the Appendix.

this set depends not only on the state of the hardware but also on the current allocation of tasks to the processors, and the way in which these are scheduled. There is no clean way to incorporate these effects in traditional measures. For these reasons, traditional reliability, availability, and throughput are not suitable performance measures for real-time computers.

2.2.3 Performability

Performability improves upon the traditional measures by explicitly and formally accounting for the fact that the performance of a real-time computer should be tied to the consequent performance of the process that it controls. The controlled process is defined as having several *accomplishment levels*, which are different levels of performance as seen by the user. Every such level of performance is associated with the execution of a certain set of control tasks. To accomplish each control task requires the real-time computer to run a set of control algorithms. The performability of the real-time computer is defined as the probability that the computer system will allow each accomplishment level to be met. More formally, if there are n accomplishment levels $A_1, A_2, \ldots A_n$, the performability of the real-time system is given by the vector $(P(A_1), P(A_2), \ldots, P(A_n))$, where $P(A_i)$ is the probability that the computer functions in such a way as to have the controlled process reach accomplishment level A_i. Thus, the quality of performance of the controlled process as seen by the user is linked to the performance of the real-time system.

Figure 2.4 shows four views of a hierarchical view of performability. Each view is driven by the requirements of the one above it and receives input from the one below it. Each view is more detailed than the one above it. View 0 specifies in terms of the state variables of the controlled process just what enables the user to distinguish one grade of performance from another. View 1 is more detailed in specifying the controlled-process tasks that must be run (together with their

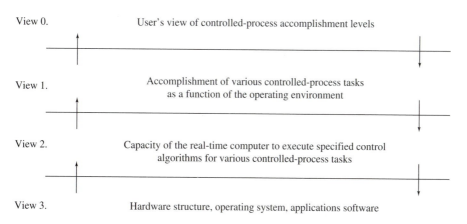

FIGURE 2.4
Hierarchical view of performance.

associated timing constraints) to meet each such grade of performance, and View 2 is even more detailed in specifying which algorithms must be run to meet each of the controlled-process tasks in View 1. Finally, View 3 considers the hardware structure, the operating system, and the applications software attributes needed to meet the requirements of View 2.

Performability takes the operating environment into account in Views 1 and 2. The controls that must be applied and the algorithms that must be run in order to achieve certain user-defined grades of performance are functions of the operating environment.

By suitably defining the accomplishment levels, we can reduce performability to any of the traditional performance measures. For example, if we define the accomplishment level to be the number of jobs processed per unit time, this reduces performability to throughput. However, performability's advantage lies not in this, but in its ability to express performance in the only measure that truly matters—the user's perception of it.

Example 2.7.   Consider the landing portion of the flight of a civilian aircraft. The aircraft has an automatic landing system, which allows it to land even in zero-visibility weather at suitably equipped airports. If the automatic-landing feature on the aircraft is not working when the landing phase begins, and if the destination airport has low-visibility weather, the aircraft is diverted to another airport. It is assumed that an alternative airport with sufficient visibility to permit a manual landing can always be found within the range of the aircraft. We assume that whenever a manual landing is possible, the automatic-landing feature is dispensed with and the aircraft is landed manually. If the automatic-landing feature fails during automatic landing, there is a crash. Pilot errors are not accounted for.

As far as the user is concerned, the accomplishment levels are:

A_0 Safe arrival at the designated destination

A_1 Diversion to another airport, but safe landing there

A_2 Crash

We have assumed here that the user considers crashing at the designated destination just as bad as crashing at some other airport, and so have specified just one accomplishment level, A_2, to take care of both cases.

This can be translated into a two-tuple *state description* at View 0: (a_0, b_0), where

$$a_0 = \begin{cases} 0 & \text{if the aircraft is not diverted} \\ 1 & \text{if the aircraft is diverted} \end{cases}$$

$$b_0 = \begin{cases} 0 & \text{if the aircraft does not crash} \\ 1 & \text{if the aircraft crashes} \end{cases}$$

Table 2.1 indicates which View-0 states correspond to which accomplishment levels.

We now turn to View 1. The operating environment is the weather at the designated airport. The control task that needs to run is the automatic-landing (AL) feature. The View-1 state is expressed through a three-tuple (a_1, b_1, c_1), where

$$a_1 = \begin{cases} 0 & \text{if the visibility is good at the designated airport} \\ 1 & \text{if the visibility is poor at the designated airport} \end{cases}$$

TABLE 2.1
Mapping of View-0 states to accomplishment levels

Accomplishment level	Corresponding View-0 states
A_0	(0,0)
A_1	(1,0)
A_2	(0,1), (1,1)

TABLE 2.2
Mapping of View-1 states to View-0 states

View-0 state	Corresponding View-1 states
(0,0)	(0,0,0), (0,1,0), (0,2,0), (1,0,0)
(0,1)	(0,0,1), (0,1,1), (0,2,1), (1,0,1), (1,2,0), (1,2,1)
(1,0)	(1,1,0)
(1,1)	(1,1,1)

$$b_1 = \begin{cases} 0 & \text{if the AL feature is functional during the landing phase} \\ 1 & \text{if the AL feature fails before the landing phase begins} \\ 2 & \text{if the AL feature fails during the landing phase} \end{cases}$$

$$c_1 = \begin{cases} 0 & \text{if all the flight-critical mechanical parts work correctly} \\ 1 & \text{if there is a flight-critical mechanical failure} \end{cases}$$

We now decide which View-1 states map to which View-0 states. By inspection, we arrive at Table 2.2. The probability of being in each of these states depends on the weather, on the state of the mechanical components, and on the state of the computer system. The weather and the state of the mechanical components are outside the control of our computer; hence View 2 can be described by a single state variable

$$a_2 = \begin{cases} 0 & \text{if the computer has sufficient resources to run the AL job} \\ & \text{throughout the landing phase} \\ 1 & \text{if the computer does not have sufficient resources to run the} \\ & \text{AL job at any time during the landing phase} \\ 2 & \text{if the computer has sufficient resources at the beginning} \\ & \text{of the landing phase, but suffers failures which} \\ & \text{make it impossible to run the AL job some time} \\ & \text{during the landing phase} \end{cases}$$

The mapping between the View-1 and View-2 states is easy, and left to the reader.

It only remains for us to specify states to describe the weather at the designated airport. Let the weather state variable be:

$$w = \begin{cases} 0 & \text{if the visibility at the designated airport is good} \\ 1 & \text{otherwise} \end{cases}$$

What is the performability of the computer? It is the vector $(P(A_1), P(A_2), P(A_3))$ where, as before, $P(A_i)$ is the probability of the computer being able to function sufficiently well to ensure that accomplishment level A_i is attained. This can be done by tracing through the mappings of the states in Tables 2.1 and 2.2, and the mapping between View 1 and View 2.

For example, accomplishment level A_0 is attained whenever the system is in View-0 state $(0, 0)$, which happens whenever the system is in any of the set of View-1 states $\{(0, 0, 0), (0, 1, 0), (0, 2, 0), (1, 0, 0)\}$. This in turn happens whenever the states of the weather and the computer are $(w, a_2) \in \{(0, 0), (0, 1), (0, 2), (1, 0)\}$, and when $c_1 = 0$. So,

$$P(A_0) = \text{Prob}\{w = 0\}\text{Prob}\{c_1 = 0\} + \text{Prob}\{w = 1\}\text{Prob}\{b_1 = 0\}\text{Prob}\{c_1 = 0\}$$

We can write $P(A_2)$ and $P(A_3)$ in a similar way. This is left as an easy exercise for the reader.

Let us now examine the qualities of performability. To begin with, note that it uses *information hiding*; each view is more detailed than the previous one and is directed to a different set of people. View 0 is meant for the user to specify. Based on this, in View 1 we list the set of environmental conditions, controlled-process performance, and computer performance that maps onto each accomplishment level in View 0. View 1 is meant essentially for the control engineer, who knows what control tasks need to be run and what the deadlines of such tasks are. View 1 says nothing about how the tasks are going to be allocated, scheduled, and run on the processors. In View 2, we concern ourselves with the capacity of the computer to meet each of the demands specified in View 1. This, in turn, is driven by View 3, which focuses on the hardware (including such things as hardware failure rates), the operating system (including the scheduling algorithms), and the applications software (including the software failure rate). Views 2 and 3 are the domain of the computer architect.

Notice how the views are arranged in such a way that the user needs to know nothing about the dynamics of the controlled process or the design and operation of the real-time computer; the control engineer needs to know nothing about the hardware, executive software, and applications software used to execute the control algorithms; and the computer engineer needs to know little or nothing about the control dynamics of the controlled process—all he cares about is the rate at which various jobs will be initiated and what the hard deadlines of each of the critical jobs will be.

Turning now to the four requirements that we listed in Section 2.2.1, we can see how the information-hiding property of the measure allows an efficient encoding of relevant information (requirement **1**). Because it is ultimately driven by user-specified accomplishment levels, it provides an objective basis for comparison between different real-time systems (requirements **2** and **3**). Whether it represents verifiable facts (requirement **4**) depends on the modeling techniques used.

Note that the performability of the computer depends not just on the computer system but also on factors over which it has no control. The computer has, for example, no control over any flight-critical mechanical failures that may happen; however, the probability of such failures affects its performability. It has no control over the weather either, but that also affects its performability. This is because the accomplishment levels are at a level that are meaningful to the user.

What causes an accomplishment level to be reached is irrelevant to the user; it is just as bad for the user to have the aircraft crash because of a mechanical failure as it is to have it crash because the computer failed during an automatic landing in low-visibility weather.

In Example 2.7, the accomplishment levels were discrete. This is not always the case, as we see in Example 2.8 below.

2.2.4 Cost Functions and Hard Deadlines

Real-time tasks frequently have *hard deadlines*, the time by which they must finish executing if catastrophic failure of the controlled process is to be avoided. They also have *cost functions* of the response time. These functions are obtained by comparing the performability of a real-time system with a zero response time to a system with given positive response times.[4]

We can make this more formal as follows. The controlled process is meant to operate within a given *state space*. If it leaves this state space, it suffers failure. The hard deadline of any task is defined as the maximum computer response time that will still allow the process to be kept within the designated state space. The cost function of a particular task execution is given by

$$\mathcal{P}(\xi) - \mathcal{P}(0)$$

where $\mathcal{P}(x)$ is the performability associated with a response time of ξ. Cost functions and hard deadlines are best explained through a simple and idealized example.

> **Example 2.8.** Consider a body of mass m, constrained to move only along one dimension and subject to impacts that change its velocity. Its state vector $\Sigma = (x, v, a)$, consists of its current position x, velocity v, and acceleration a. The job of the real-time computer controlling m is to use thrusters that can exert a thrust of magnitude up to H in either a positive or negative direction to keep the body at a given ideal point for as much of the time as possible. If the body leaves a designated allowed state space S_A, consisting of an interval of length $2b$ centered at the ideal point (which we can define as the origin), we say that the controlled process has failed. See Figure 2.5.

FIGURE 2.5
The body must be kept in the allowed state space $S_A = [-b, +b]$.

---

[4]Readers without much exposure to control theory may omit the remainder of this section.

What is the hard deadline associated with this process? Let us assume for simplicity that the controller delay (i.e., the computer response time) is solely in recognizing that an impact has occurred and that the other reaction times are zero (e.g., that the thrusters can be turned on instantaneously). If this delay is too long, the controller may not be able to stop the body from moving out of the allowed state space.

What is the cost function associated with this process? Let us define the accomplishment level as the energy expended by the system in getting the body back to the ideal point as soon as possible. The longer the controller takes to respond to the change in velocity, the more work ultimately needs to be done in getting the body back to rest at the ideal point and the more energy is expended.

There is a further observation that is worth making. The hard deadline and cost functions are functions of the current state of the controlled process, that is, of the current position, velocity, and acceleration of the body. In general, the closer the body is to the boundary of the allowed state space or the faster it is moving away from the ideal point, the shorter the hard deadline.

Let us make these intuitive points more concrete by computing the hard deadlines and cost functions at several points in the allowed state space. Recall that the state of the process is defined by a three-tuple (x, v, a), where x, v, and a are its current position, velocity and acceleration, respectively.

Consider the process in state $(0, 0, 0)$—the body is already at the ideal point, has zero velocity, and is not accelerating. In such a case, the controller has nothing to accomplish; the body is already where it is supposed to be. Consequently, the hard deadline is infinity and the cost function is zero throughout. This is a formal way of saying that as long as the body is where it is supposed to be, the controller does not have to do anything.

Consider the process in state $(x, 0, 0)$—the body is stationary at point x in the allowed state space. The controller brings it back to rest at the ideal point. Since the body is not moving, no amount of controller delay will cause it to move out of the allowed state space. Consequently, the hard deadline is infinity. The energy that the controller expends in bringing back the body to rest at the ideal point is also not a function of how long the controller takes to react; the energy expended when the controller delay is ξ is exactly the same as that when it is 0. Hence, the cost function is zero in this case also.

Consider the process in state $(x, v, 0)$—the body is in position x, has velocity v, and is not accelerating. Assume for this example that both x and v are positive. The controller response time is ξ; that is, it takes ξ time for the real-time computer to realize that an impact has occurred and must be responded to. By this time, the body is in state $(x + v\xi, v, 0)$. The controller first must stop the movement of the body in the positive direction. This it can do by deploying a thrust of H in the negative direction, which will yield an acceleration of $-a = -H/m$. The basic equations of motion can be used to show that the body will come to rest at position $x_1 = x + v\xi + v^2/2a$. If $x_1 > b$, then the controlled process fails. This happens whenever

$$x + v\xi + v^2/2a > b \Rightarrow \xi > \frac{b - x - v^2/2a}{v}$$

That is, the hard deadline is

$$t_d(x, v, 0) = \frac{b - x - v^2/2a}{v}$$

What is the cost function? This can be computed by studying the distance over which the thrust has to be maintained. The body is stopped at x_1, which means that it has been decelerated over the interval $x_1 - x$. From this point, the body is accelerated towards the origin at maximal thrust until position $x_1/2$, and then it is decelerated at maximal thrust until it comes to rest at the origin. That is, the thrust of H has to be maintained over a distance of $d_\xi = x_1 - x + x_1 = 2x_1 - x$, which corresponds to an energy expenditure of $d_\xi H$. What is the energy expenditure if the response time is zero? In such a case, as the reader can easily check, the expended energy is $H(x + v^2/a)$. The cost function of this task is then given by the difference in the energies

$$C_{x,v,0}(\xi) = H(2x_1 - x) - H\left(\frac{x + v^2}{a}\right)$$

$$= v\xi H$$

The preceding example shows that the cost functions and hard deadlines depend on the state of the controlled process, but it is a simplified example. In most instances, cost functions and hard deadlines are almost impossible to calculate in closed form and numerical methods must be used instead. In Section 2.4, we provide references to the literature on this subject.

2.2.5   Discussion

The correct choice of performance measures is vital to the ability to accurately and concisely represent the performance of any system. Performance measures are not just a means to convey to the user or the buyer the relative goodness of a computer for a particular application. If properly chosen, they can also provide efficient interfaces between the worlds of the user and the control engineer, and between the worlds of the control engineer and the computer engineer. Performability and cost functions are particularly attractive in this respect.

2.3   ESTIMATING PROGRAM RUN TIMES

Since real-time systems should meet deadlines, it is important to be able to accurately estimate program run times. Estimating the execution time of any given program is a very difficult task and is the focus of current research. It depends on the following factors:

Source code: Source code that is carefully tuned and optimized takes less time to execute.

Compiler: The compiler maps the source-level code into a machine-level program. This mapping is not unique; the actual mapping will depend on the actual implementation of the particular compiler that is being used. The execution time will depend on the nature of the mapping.

Machine architecture: Many aspects of the machine architecture have an effect on the execution time that is difficult to quantify exactly. Executing a program may require much interaction between the processor(s) and the memory and I/O devices. Such an interaction can take place over an interconnection network (e.g., a bus) that can be shared by other processors. The time spent waiting to gain access to the network affects the execution time. The number of registers per processor affects how many variables can be held in the CPU. The greater the number of registers and the cleverer the compiler is in managing these registers, the fewer the number of accesses that need to go out of the CPU. This results in reducing the memory-access time, and hence the instruction-execution time. The size and organization of the cache (if any) will also affect the memory-access time, as will the clock rate. Also, many machines use dynamic RAM for their main memory. To keep the contents of these memories, we need to periodically *refresh* them; this is done by periodically reading the contents of each memory location and writing them back. The refresh task has priority over the CPU and thus affects the memory-access time.

Operating system: The operating system determines such issues as task scheduling and memory management, both of which have a major impact on the execution time. Along with the machine architecture, it determines the interrupt-handling overhead.

These factors can interact with one another in complex ways. In order to obtain good execution-time bounds, we need to account for these interactions precisely. Such accounting is very hard to do since it requires the analysis of every aspect of the execution of the program and of any interactions of that task with others.

Ideally, we would like to have a tool that would accept as inputs the compiler, the source code, and a description of the architecture, and then produce a good estimate of the execution time of the code. Unfortunately, such a tool does not exist. In this section, we look at partial solutions to the problem of execution-time estimation.

Some readers may wonder why an experimental approach to estimating the execution time is not followed, that is, actually running the program on the target architecture for a large number of input sets and gathering statistics on the run time. This is not feasible for two reasons. First, the actual number of potential input sets is very large and it would take too long to try them all. Second, individual programs are not run in isolation; their run times are affected by the rest of the workload (including interrupts). We therefore need a more analytical approach to estimating execution time.

We begin by considering what information can be extracted from the source code. This is followed by a discussion of how to make estimates for code running on pipelined architectures using a case study of a two-stage pipeline. Finally, we discuss how instruction and data caches affect the run time estimates.

2.3.1 Analysis of Source Code

Let us begin by considering a very simple stretch of code.

```
L1: a := b * c;
L2: b := d + e;
L3: d := a - f;
```

This is straight-line code. Once control is transferred to the first of these statements, execution will continue sequentially until the last statement has been completed. *Straight-line code* is thus a stretch of code with exactly one entry point and exactly one exit point. Let us consider how to make a timing estimate for this stretch of code.

The total execution time is given by

$$\sum_{i=1}^{3} T_{\text{exec}}(Li) \tag{2.1}$$

where $T_{\text{exec}}(Li)$ is the time needed to execute Li.

The time needed to execute L1 will depend on the code that the compiler generates for it. For example, L1 could be translated into the following sequence:

```
L1.1  Get the address of c
L1.2  Load c
L1.3  Get the address of b
L1.4  Load b
L1.5  Multiply
L1.6  Store into a
```

The time needed to execute these instructions will depend on the machine architecture. If the machine is very simple, does not use pipelining, and has only one I/O port to the memory, then the execution time is given by the sum $\sum_{i=1}^{6} T_{\text{exec}}(L1.i)$. This assumes that the machine is devoted during that time to just these instructions; for example, that there are no interrupts. However, there are two factors that could make this bound rather loose. First, we are implicitly assuming that the variables b and c are not already in the CPU registers and have to be fetched from the cache or the main memory. This overlooks the possibility that some preceding code might have already loaded these variables into the registers and that they are still there. Second, the bounds on the execution times of individual instructions could be loose because they are data-dependent. For example, the multiply operation does not take a deterministic time on most machines—the time it takes to multiply two numbers depends on the numbers themselves. If we do not know in advance what these numbers are, we can only write loose bounds on the multiplication time.

Suppose that we have the following loop.

```
L4.  while (P) do
L5.       Q1;
L6.       Q2;
L7.       Q3;
L8.  end while;
```

where P is a logical statement and Q1, Q2, and Q3 are instructions. It is obvious that unless we know how many times this loop is going to be executed, we have no way of estimating the execution time. So, at the very least, we need upper and lower bounds on the number of loop iterations. These bounds may be derived either from an analysis of P, Q1, Q2, and Q3, or from some other user-derived input. The difficulty of deriving such bounds is why while loops are forbidden in the Euclid real-time programming language.

Consider the following if-then-else construct.

```
L9. if B1 then
        S1;
    else if B2 then
        S2;
    else if B3 then
        S3;
    else
        S4;
    end if;
```

The execution time will depend on which of the conditions B1, B2, B3 are true. In the case where B1 is true, the execution time is

$$T(\text{B1}) + T(\text{S1}) + T(JMP) \tag{2.2}$$

where $T(JMP)$ is the time it takes to jump to the end of the if-then-else construct.

In the case where B1 is false but B2 is true, the execution time is

$$T(\text{B1}) + T(\text{B2}) + T(\text{S2}) + T(JMP) \tag{2.3}$$

The equations for the other two cases are written similarly.

If $t_{\text{lower}}(i)$ and $t_{\text{upper}}(i)$ are the lower and upper bounds of the estimates of case i, then (since there are four cases in all) the lower and upper execution-time bounds for this construct are given by

$$\min_{i \in \{1,2,3,4\}} t_{\text{lower}}(i) \qquad \text{and} \qquad \max_{i \in \{1,2,3,4\}} t_{\text{upper}}(i) \tag{2.4}$$

respectively.

This becomes considerably more complex if we allow interrupts. The execution-time bound is then a function of the rates at which the interrupts occur and on the bounds on the time taken to service each interrupt.

Figure 2.6 shows the schematic of an experimental estimation system developed at the University of Washington for programs written in C. The preprocessor produces compiled assembly-language code and marks off blocks of code to be analyzed. For example, it might mark off the code associated with a single source-level instruction or a straight-line stretch of code as a block. The *parser* analyzes the input source program. The *procedure timer* maintains a table of procedures and their execution times. The *loop bounds* module obtains bounds on the number of iterations for the various loops in the system. The *time schema* is independent of the system; it depends only on the language. It computes the execution times of each block using the execution time estimates computed by the code prediction module. The *code prediction* module does this by using the code generated by the preprocessor and using the architecture analyzer to include the influence of the architecture.

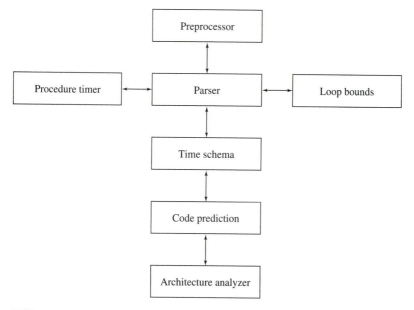

FIGURE 2.6
Schematic of a timing estimation system. (From C. Y. Park and A. Shaw, "Experiments with a Program Timing Tool Based on Source-Level Timing Schema," *IEEE Computer*, Vol. 24, No. 5, May 1991. © IEEE. Reprinted with permission.)

Take, for example, the `if-then-else` construct that we considered earlier in this section. The timing schema will come up with bounds such as Equation (2.4). The code prediction module will look at the assembly-level output of the preprocessor and obtain the parameters in Equation (2.4) by interacting with the architecture analyzer.

2.3.2 Accounting for Pipelining

The traditional von Neumann model of computers assumes sequential execution. An instruction is fetched, decoded, and executed. Only after that has been done does work begin on the next instruction. Under such conditions, computing the execution time of a straight-line stretch of code (in the absence of interrupts) consists, as we have seen above, of adding up the execution times of the individual instructions. The instruction execution-time is itself computed by simply adding up the times taken to fetch the instruction, decode it, fetch any operands that are required, execute the instruction, and, finally, carry out any store operations that are called for. The time taken for each of these steps can be obtained by examination of the machine architecture.

Most modern computers do not follow the von Neumann model exactly. They use *pipelining*, which involves the simultaneous handling of different parts of different instructions. To make programming easier, the machine still looks to the programmer as if it were following the von Neumann model.

Much of the complexity in dealing with pipelined machines arises from dependencies between instructions simultaneously active in the computer. For example, if instruction I_i requires the output of I_j, I_i must wait for I_j to produce that output before it can execute. Two other sources of complexity are conditional branches and interrupts.

The condition of a conditional branch has to be evaluated before the processor can tell whether the branch will be taken. Such an evaluation typically takes place in the execute stage. After the unconditional branch has been uncovered, but before the system knows whether or not it will be taken, the fetch unit has the following options.

- Stop prefetching instructions until the condition has been evaluated.
- Guess whether or not the branch will be taken and fetch instructions according to this guess.

The first alternative degrades performance, and so systems usually implement the second. In the worst case, there will be an incorrect guess. In such an event, the incorrectly prefetched instructions must be discarded and fetching must recommence from the correct point.

Interrupts are another source of complexity. Suppose an interrupt occurs and transfers control to an interrupt-handling routine. The worst-case execution time must then take into account the interrupt-handling time.

TWO-STAGE PIPELINE. In this section, we will show how to make timing estimates for a processor designed as a two-stage pipeline for some stretch, $I_1, I_2, \ldots, I_N$, of straight-line code. The first pipeline stage fetches instructions from the main memory and writes them into a prefetch buffer. The second stage handles everything else, including the operand read/write operations. Both the first and second stages will thus have occasion to access the memory, the first stage for fetching instructions and the second for loading/storing operands. They will thus have to coordinate their actions. We will assume that if the second stage needs to read one or more operands from main memory, there is a one-cycle delay in handshaking with the first stage. Similarly, if it needs to write some operands, there is a one-cycle handshaking delay. Also, the second stage will have nonpreemptive priority over the first stage for memory accesses; that is, if the second stage wishes to access the memory it will wait for any ongoing opcode fetches to finish before accessing the memory. A block diagram for the architecture is provided in Figure 2.7. In our discussion, we will assume that no cache memory is used, and that all the software and variables are memory-resident. Thus, there is no delay due to page faults. We will also ignore the effects of preemption or interrupts. Estimates of the delays caused by preemption and interrupts must be added to the estimates of the execution time. To further simplify our analysis, we will assume that if an instruction is executing that needs to access the memory (e.g., to load or store an operand), no instruction fetches will be begun during its execution. Also, the second (execute)

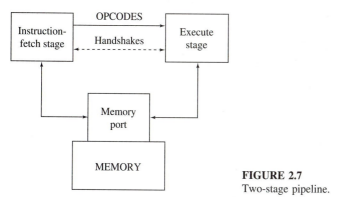

FIGURE 2.7
Two-stage pipeline.

stage is not itself pipelined; it can handle at most one instruction at any one time.

We begin with some notation.

b_i Portion of the I_i execution not overlapped with the execution of any previous instruction (excluding handshake delays); note that in the execution time of an instruction we include the fetch time.

e_i Second-stage execution time of I_i (i.e., excluding the instruction fetch time).

η_i Execution time of I_i excluding memory accesses.

f_i Number of bytes in the instruction buffer at the moment I_i completes execution.

g_i Number of bytes of opcode fetched during the time I_i is in the execute stage of the pipeline, assuming the buffer is of infinite size.

h_i Time spent in fetching the latest byte of the instruction-fetch operation if there is an instruction fetch ongoing at time τ_i (if no instruction fetch is in progress at τ_i, $h_i = 0$).

m Number of CPU cycles for a memory access (read or write).

N_{buff} Size of the instruction-fetch buffer in bytes.

v_i Size of instruction i opcode in bytes.

r_i Number of data memory reads required by I_i.

t_i Execution time of I_i not overlapped with execution of any previous instruction (including handshake delays).

τ_i Instant at which I_i completes.

w_i Number of data memory writes required by I_i.

An expression for t_i can be written by inspection as:

$$t_i = \begin{cases} b_i & \text{if } (r_i = 0) \wedge (w_i = 0) \\ b_i + 1 & \text{if } ((r_i \neq 0) \wedge (w_i = 0)) \vee ((r_i = 0) \wedge (w_i \neq 0)) \\ b_i + 2 & \text{if } (r_i > 0) \wedge (w_i > 0) \end{cases} \qquad (2.5)$$

To compute b_i, we need an expression for e_i and we need to consider the effects of the instruction I_i fetch and other memory effects. e_i is easily derived:

$$e_i = \eta_i + m(r_i + w_i) \tag{2.6}$$

To complete the b_i derivation, we must consider the following special cases:

Case b1. $v_i > f_{i-1}$. $(v_i - f_{i-1})$ bytes of the I_i opcode still need to be fetched at time τ_{i-1}, when I_{i-1} finishes executing. This will take a further $m(v_i - f_{i-1}) - h_{i-1}$ time.

Case b2. $v_i \leq f_{i-1}$. The entire I_i opcode has been fetched. There are two subcases:

Case b2.1. $(r_i + w_i = 0) \vee (h_{i-1} = 0)$. No time needs to be added for memory accesses.

Case b2.2. $(r_i + w_i > 0) \wedge (h_{i-1} > 0)$. I_i needs to read/write some operands. However, since $h_{i-1} > 0$, until $m - h_{i-1}$ cycles after I_i has started executing, the instruction-fetch unit is going to be accessing the memory. It is only after that time that any operand reads or writes can be started. In the worst case, this time must be added to the execution time.

We can thus write an expression for b_i as follows:

$$b_i = \begin{cases} e_i + m(v_i - f_{i-1}) - h_{i-1} & \text{if Case b1 applies} \\ e_i & \text{if Case b2.1 applies} \\ e_i + m - h_{i-1} & \text{if Case b2.2 applies} \end{cases} \tag{2.7}$$

In order to complete the derivation, we need expressions for f_i, and h_i. Let us start by writing an expression for the auxiliary variable, g_i, which is the number of bytes of opcode brought into the instruction buffer by the first stage when I_i is occupying the second stage of the pipeline. In making the computation for g_i, we disregard the possibility that the buffer is full and can take no more prefetches; this will be taken care of in a subsequent step. Once again, we consider a number of cases.

Case g1. $r_i + w_i = 0$. The execution of I_i will not interfere with any opcode fetches. There are the following subcases:

Case g1.1. $(v_i \leq f_{i-1}) \wedge (h_{i-1} > 0) \wedge (e_i < m - h_{i-1})$. All the opcode of I_i has been fetched by τ_{i-1}, but there is not enough time for the ongoing opcode fetch to finish by the time I_i finishes execution. Therefore, $g_i = 0$.

Case g1.2. $(v_i \leq f_{i-1}) \wedge (h_{i-1} > 0) \wedge (e_i \geq m - h_{i-1})$. All the opcode of I_i has been fetched by τ_{i-1}, and the opcode fetch that was ongoing when I_i started execution will have time to finish and will be followed by subsequent fetches. The number of these subsequent fetches is

$$\left\lfloor \frac{e_i - (m - h_{i-1})}{m} \right\rfloor$$

Therefore,

$$g_i = 1 + \left\lfloor \frac{e_i - (m - h_{i-1})}{m} \right\rfloor$$

Case g1.3. $(v_i > f_{i-1}) \vee (h_{i-1} = 0)$. Either some of the opcode of I_i has not been fetched by time τ_{i-1} or there is no ongoing opcode fetch at time τ_{i-1}. In either event, the number of bytes of opcode fetched during I_i execution is given by $g_i = \lfloor e_i/m \rfloor$.

Case g2. $r_i + w_i > 0$. I_i needs to access memory during its execution. Recall that the second stage of the pipeline has nonpreemptive priority over the first for memory accesses. There are the following subcases:

Case g2.1. $(v_i > f_{i-1}) \vee (h_{i-1} = 0)$. When the execution of I_i begins, there is no ongoing instruction fetch. Since $r_i + w_i > 0$, we will prevent the instruction-fetch unit from prefetching any instructions lest that interfere with the memory operations of the second stage as it executes I_i. Hence $g_i = 0$.

Case g2.2. $(v_i \leq f_{i-1}) \wedge (h_{i-1} > 0) \wedge (e_i \geq m - h_{i-1})$. The ongoing instruction fetch at τ_{i-1} will complete, but we will prevent any further prefetches by the first stage for the reason mentioned in Case g2.1. Hence, $g_i = 1$.

We now introduce another auxiliary variable, s_i. At τ_{i-1}, there are f_{i-1} bytes in the instruction buffer. s_i is obtained by adding f_{i-1} and the bytes brought in during the interval $[\tau_{i-1}, \tau_i]$, assuming that the buffer is of infinite size. We can therefore write (the reader is invited to prove this in the exercises)

$$s_i = \begin{cases} f_{i-1} + g_i & \text{if } v_i \leq f_{i-1} \\ v_i + g_i & \text{otherwise} \end{cases} \tag{2.8}$$

The equation for f_i is then:

$$f_i = \begin{cases} 0 & \text{if } i = 0 \\ \min\{s_i, N_{\text{buff}}\} - v_i & \text{if } i > 0 \end{cases} \tag{2.9}$$

We turn now to h_i. We will once again work through a number of cases.

Case h.1. $(r_i + w_i > 0)$. Recall that in such a case, we do not allow any new instruction fetches to start once any ongoing fetch at τ_i is done. No new instruction fetches are begun; hence $h_i = 0$.

Case h.2. $(r_i + w_i = 0)$. There are four subcases:

Case h.2.1. $(s_i \geq N_{\text{buff}})$. Since the buffer is full, no new instruction fetches can be started; hence, $h_i = 0$.

Case h.2.2. $(s_i < N_{\text{buff}}) \wedge ((h_{i-1} = 0) \vee (v_i > f_{i-1}))$. If $h_{i-1} = 0$, there is no ongoing instruction fetch at τ_{i-1}. If $(v_i > f_{i-1})$ also, there is no ongoing instruction fetch when I_i starts execution. This is because I_i begins execution the instant the last byte of its opcode is brought into the buffer. In both cases, g_i instruction fetches are completed during the execution of I_i. Hence, $h_i = e_i - mg_i$.

Case h.2.3. $(s_i < N_{\text{buff}}) \wedge (h_{i-1} > 0) \wedge (v_i \le f_{i-1}) \wedge (e_i < m - h_{i-1})$.
The ongoing instruction fetch at τ_{i-1} does not have time to complete
before I_i completes. Hence, $h_i = e_i + h_{i-1}$.

Case h.2.4. $(s_i < N_{\text{buff}}) \wedge (h_{i-1} > 0) \wedge (v_i \le f_{i-1}) \wedge (e_i \ge m - h_{i-1})$.
It takes $m - h_{i-1}$ cycles to finish the instruction fetch that is ongoing at
τ_{i-1}, and a further mg_i to finish the g_i fetches that complete during the
execution of I_i. The time left over is thus $h_i = e_i - (m - h_{i-1}) - mg_i$.

We now have all the ingredients required to compute t_i, and hence an estimate of the execution time.

Example 2.9. Consider the following five-instruction stretch of straight-line code:

Instruction	η_i	v_i	r_i	w_i
I_1	10	2	0	0
I_2	4	1	0	0
I_3	10	3	0	0
I_4	2	2	2	0
I_5	5	2	0	0

Let us assume that $m = 4$, (i.e., it takes four processor cycles to make a memory
access). Since $v_1 = 2$, the fetch stage has to read two bytes from the main memory
before I_1 can start executing. This takes a total of $2 \times 4 = 8$ cycles. Thus, I_1 starts
executing at time 8, and completes at time $\tau_1 = 8 + 10 = 18$. Since I_1 has no operand
reads or writes, there is no chance that there will be any operand accesses that are
held up while the fetch unit is accessing the memory. The fetch unit starts fetching
the opcodes for the following instructions at time 8. By time 12, it has brought in
the opcode for I_2, and by time 24 the opcode for I_3. I_2 completes execution at 22.
However, I_3 cannot start execution at this time because all of its opcode has not yet
been fetched; this happens at time 24. I_3 executes over the interval [24, 34]. I_4 starts
at 34. Since $r_4 > 0$, it needs to access the memory to read operands. This cannot
happen until the fetch stage completes bringing in the first byte of the I_5 opcode,
which is at time 36. Thus, $h_3 = 2$ and $t_4 = 2 + 2 + (2 \times 4) + 1 = 13$. I_4 thus
occupies the execute stage over the interval [34, 47]. During [36, 47], the fetch unit
is precluded from accessing the memory. Over [47, 51], the fetch unit brings in the
second byte of the I_5 opcode and I_5 can begin at that time. Figure 2.8 summarizes
this activity.

This study of a two-stage machine brings out the intricacy of any estimation of execution time. The machine under study is a particularly simple
one, far simpler than many of the microprocessors currently on the market.
There are only two stages to the processor pipeline and no more than one instruction can reside in the second stage at any one time. By contrast, modern
processors have multiple instructions in the execute stage at the same time,
and they can even complete out of program sequence. In our example, external interrupts are not accounted for, nor are problems associated with exceptions generated by the program (e.g., as a result of an arithmetic overflow).

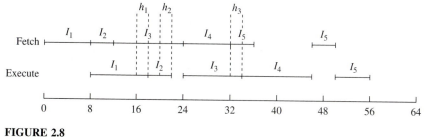

FIGURE 2.8
Two-stage example.

Only straight-line code is considered; no branches are taken into account. Despite these simplifications, the analysis is tedious and long. Essentially, one has to account for all possible cases that might affect the timing. This gets more difficult as the processor complexity increases and more cases must be considered.

2.3.3 Caches

Caches are meant to ameliorate the effects on execution of the wide disparity that exists between processor and main memory cycle times. However, they can also impair our ability to obtain good execution-time bounds. The time taken by an access depends on whether or not the word being accessed is in the cache. If it is, the access time is simply the cache access time; if it is not, it is the time to access the main memory, which is much larger.[5]

It is fairly difficult to predict whether a given access will result in a cache miss, since the cache contents are not easy to predict—they are a function of the size, organization, and replacement strategy of the cache, in addition to the sequence of accesses by the processor. Once a block is brought into the cache, it will remain there until it has to be removed to make room for another block. To determine accurately the presence or absence of a data block thus requires that we know the sequence of accesses. It is impossible in most cases to predict exactly what this sequence is going to be. Two of the main reasons are:

Conditional branches: These determine the actual execution path of the program. We don't know in advance which branches are going to be taken and we cannot explicitly follow through on every possible execution path, since these increase exponentially in number with the number of conditional branches.

Preemptions: When task *A* is preempted by task *B*, the blocks that were brought into the cache by task *A* may have to be removed to make room for *B*'s accesses. As a result, when *A* resumes execution it will encounter a flurry

---

[5] We are assuming that everything is in main memory and that page faults do not occur. If they do, this will cause even longer delays.

```
A(i) = 0, i = 1, ..., n. /*A(i) is the number of partitions
                           assigned to Tᵢ so far.*/
while (number_of_partitions_left ≠ 0) do
    i_max = {i |δ(i, A(i)) is maximized }.
    A(i_max) = A(i_max) + 1
    number_of_partitions_left = number_of_partitions_left - 1
end while
end
```

FIGURE 2.9
Allocation of partitions to tasks.

of cache misses. This can be avoided by giving each task its own portion of the cache so that during its lifetime, each task "owns" its portion and no other task is allowed access to it.

Of course, one can always obtain a worst-case execution time by assuming that every access will result in a cache miss, but such an estimate is likely to be very inaccurate. How to make reasonably accurate estimates where caches are concerned is a matter for research.

The Strategic Memory Allocation for Real-Time (SMART) cache was developed to get around this difficulty. A SMART cache is broken down into exclusive partitions and a shared area. When a critical task starts executing, it is assigned one or more exclusive partitions. It restricts its cache accesses to its partitions and to the shared area. Until that task has completed or aborted, it has exclusive rights over its assigned partitions. Even if it is preempted, no other task can overwrite the contents of its partitions.[6] Such a policy prevents a flurry of misses upon task resumption and permits more accurate performance estimates.

How many partitions should be assigned to each task? This is a discrete optimization problem; like most such problems it is NP-hard and requires suboptimal heuristics. One heuristic is as follows. Let $\epsilon_i(k)$ be the run time of task T_i if k partitions have been assigned to it. We will assume that we have some means of estimating $\epsilon_i(k)$. If f_i is the average frequency with which T_i is executed (f_i is the inverse of the period for periodic tasks and is the inverse of the average interinvocation interval for aperiodic tasks), define the weight $w_i(k) = f_i\epsilon(k)$. Define $\delta(i, k) = w_i(k) - w_i(k + 1)$. Given a set of tasks $T_1, \ldots, T_n$ assign the partitions one by one using the gradient descent algorithm in Figure 2.9. This is a greedy algorithm that allocates the partitions one by one.

---

[6]The shared area contents could be overwritten unless they are locked in the cache.

2.3.4 Virtual Memory

Virtual memory is a major source of execution-time uncertainty. That is why it is wise to avoid using virtual memory whenever possible. The time taken to handle page faults, for example, can very widely and obtaining a good bound on the page-fault rate is almost impossible.

2.4 SUGGESTIONS FOR FURTHER READING

A brief survey of performance measures for computer controllers, with many references to the technical literature, is provided in [10]. Capacity reliability is described in [6], and computation reliability and computation threshold in [2]. Performability is covered in [17], and a detailed example is worked out in [18]. Example 2.7 is based on [17]. Furchtgott [5] is a particularly detailed exposition of performability. Cost functions are covered in [8, 9], which contain some further examples of their calculation. See [20] for a derivation of hard deadlines and cost functions relating to an aircraft in the process of landing. A procedure for the computation of hard deadlines for linear time-invariant control systems is described in [18]. There is a vast literature on life-cycle costing; see, for example, [1].

Not much has been published on estimating task run times. Our discussion in Section 2.3.1 is based largely on [15, 17], and that in Section 2.3.2 on [21]. Some other interesting work related to Section 2.3.1 can be found in [14, 16]. Work on studying the impact of pipelined architectures on program run times is described in [3, 7, 11]. The effect of caches is also considered in [11].

EXERCISES

2.1. Select accomplishment levels to describe the performability of a controller for
  (a) a motor car
  (b) traffic lights
2.2. Define accomplishment levels for a nongracefully degrading system (e.g., a light-bulb) so that performability reduces to traditional reliability.
2.3. Suppose you are designing a collision-avoidance system for a car. The system monitors the distance between the car and the one in front of it, and slows the car down whenever it is too close. Write accomplishment levels for such a system.
2.4. There are two ways of implementing a time limit specified for executing a loop. The first is for the compiler to set a maximum number of iterations that may be carried out. The second is to maintain during execution a timer that determines if allowing another iteration would cause the limit to be exceeded. Discuss the advantages and disadvantages of each approach.
2.5. Pick some two-stage pipelined microprocessor for which you have access to the hardware manual. Write a twenty-instruction stretch of straight-line code and compute an estimate of how long it will take to execute.
2.6. Prove Equation (2.8).
2.7. Suppose you have a two-stage pipelined system with two memory modules. Instructions are stored in one memory module, and operands in the other. As a result,

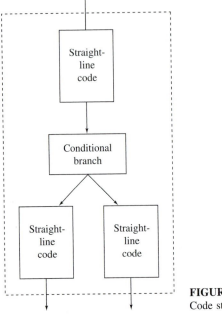

FIGURE E2.8
Code structure for Exercise 2.8.

the memory operations of the fetch stage will not affect those of the execute stage. Repeat the derivation in Section 2.3.2 for this case.

2.8. In Section 2.3.2, we focused on straight-line code. Repeat that derivation for the code structure shown in Figure E2.8. This structure has one entry point and two exit points, as shown. The fetch stage continues to fetch instructions in sequence, except when the execute stage decodes a conditional branch and determines whether or not it is taken. If the branch is not taken, instructions will continue to be executed in sequence. If the branch is taken, the instruction buffer is flushed and the fetch unit starts fetching at the target of the conditional branch. Make any reasonable assumptions you like.

REFERENCES

[1] Barasia, R. K., and T. D. Kiang: "Development of a Life-Cycle Management Cost Model," *Proc. IEEE Reliability and Maintainability Symp.*, pp. 254–259, IEEE, Los Alamitos, CA, 1978.

[2] Beaudry, M. D.: "Performance-Related Reliability Measures for Computing Systems," *IEEE Trans. Computers* C-27:501–509 1978.

[3] Choi, Y.-Y., I. Lee, and I. Kang: "Timing Analysis of Superscalar Processor Programs Using ACSR," *Proc. 11th Worshop on Real-Time Operating Systems and Software*, pp. 63–67, IEEE, Los Alamitos, CA, 1994.

[4] Ellert, F. J., and C. W. Merriam: "Synthesis of Feedback Controls Using Optimization Theory—An Example," *IEEE Trans. Automatic Control* AC-8:89–103, 1963.

[5] Furchtgott, D. G.: *Performability Models and Solutions*, PhD thesis, University of Michigan, 1984.

[6] Gay, F. A., and M. L. Ketelson: "Performance Evaluation for Gracefully Degrading Systems," *Proc. 7th IEEE Int'l Symp. on Fault-Tolerant Computing*, pp. 51–58, IEEE, Los Alamitos, CA, 1979.

[7] Harmon, M., T. P. Baker, and D. B. Whalley: "A Retargetable Technique for Predicting Execution Time," *Proc. IEEE Real-Time Systems Symp.*, pp. 68–77, IEEE, Los Alamitos, CA, 1992.

[8] Krishna, C. M.: *On the Design and Analysis of Real-Time Computers*, PhD thesis, University of Michigan, 1984.

[9] Krishna, C. M., and K. G. Shin: "Performance Measures for Multiprocessor Controllers," in *Performance '83* (A. K. Agrawala and S. K. Tripathi, eds.), pp. 229-250, North-Holland, Amsterdam, 1983.

[10] Krishna, C. M., and K. G. Shin: "Performance Measures for Control Computers," *IEEE Trans. Automatic Control* AC-32:467–473, 1987.

[11] Lim, S.-S., Y. H. Bae, G. T. Jang, B. D. Rhee, S. L. Min, C. Y. Park, H. Shin, K. Park, and C. S. Kim: "An Accurate Worst Case Timing Analysis Technique for RISC Processors," *Proc. IEEE Real-Time Systems Symp.*, pp. 97–108, IEEE, Los Alamitos, CA, 1994.

[12] Meyer, J. F.: "On Evaluating the Performability of Degradable Computing Systems," *IEEE Trans. Computers* C-29:720–731, 1980.

[13] Meyer, J. F., D. G. Furchtgott, and L. T. Wu: "Performability Evaluation of the SIFT Computer," *IEEE Trans. Computers* C-29:501–509, 1980.

[14] Mok, A. K.: "Evaluating Tight Execution Time Bounds of Programs by Annotations," *Proc. 6th IEEE Workshop on Real-Time Operating Systems and Software*, pp. 74–80, IEEE, Los Alamitos, CA, 1989.

[15] Park, C. Y., and A. C. Shaw: "Experiments with a Program Timing Tool Based on Source-Level Timing Schema," *IEEE Computer* 24:48–57, 1991.

[16] Puschner, P., and C. Koza: "Calculating the Maximum Execution Time of Real-Time Programs," *Journal of Real-Time Systems* 1:159–176, 1989.

[17] Shaw, A. C.: "Reasoning about Time in Higher-Level Language Software," *IEEE Trans. Software Engineering* 15:875–889, 1989.

[18] Shin, K. G., and H. Kim: "Derivation and Application of Hard Deadlines for Real-Time Control Systems," *IEEE Trans. System, Man, and Cybernetics* 22(6):1403–1413, 1992.

[19] Shin, K. G., and C. M. Krishna: "New Performance Measures for Design and Analysis of Real–Time Multiprocessors," *Journal of Computer Science and Engineering Systems* 1:179–192, 1986.

[20] Shin, K. G., C. M. Krishna, and Y.-H. Lee: "A Unified Method for Characterizing Real-Time Computer Controller and Its Application," *IEEE Trans. Automatic Control* AC-30:357–366, 1985.

[21] Woodbury, M. H., and K. G. Shin: "Performance Modeling and Measurement of Real-Time Multiprocessors with Time-Shared Buses," *IEEE Trans. Computers* 37:214–244, 1988.

[22] Zhang, N., A. Burns, and M. Nicholson: "Pipelined Processors and Worst-Case Execution Times," *Journal of Real-Time Systems* 5:319–343, 1993.

CHAPTER

3

TASK ASSIGNMENT
AND SCHEDULING

3.1 INTRODUCTION

The purpose of real-time computing is to execute, by the appropriate deadlines, its critical control tasks. In this chapter, we will look at techniques for allocating and scheduling tasks on processors to ensure that deadlines are met.

There is an enormous literature on scheduling: indeed, the field appears to have grown exponentially since the mid-1970s! We present here the subset of the results that relates to the meeting of deadlines.

The allocation/scheduling problem can be stated as follows. Given a set of tasks, task precedence constraints, resource requirements, task characteristics, and deadlines, we are asked to devise a feasible allocation/schedule on a given computer. Let us define some of these terms.

Formally speaking, a *task* consumes resources (e.g., processor time, memory, and input data), and puts out one or more results. Tasks may have *precedence constraints*, which specify if any task(s) needs to precede other tasks. If task T_i's output is needed as input by task T_j, then task T_j is constrained to be preceded by task T_i. The precedence constraints can be most conveniently represented by means of a *precedence graph*. We show an example of this in Figure 3.1. The arrows indicate which task has precedence over which other task. We denote the precedent-task set of task T by $\prec(T)$; that is, $\prec(T)$ indicates which tasks must be completed before T can begin.

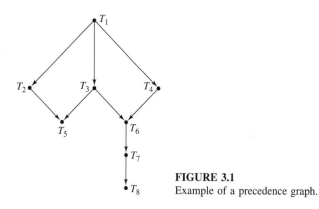

FIGURE 3.1
Example of a precedence graph.

Example 3.1. In Figure 3.1, we have

$$
\begin{aligned}
\prec (1) &= \emptyset \\
\prec (2) &= \{1\} \\
\prec (3) &= \{1\} \\
\prec (4) &= \{1\} \\
\prec (5) &= \{1, 2, 3\} \\
\prec (6) &= \{1, 3, 4\} \\
\prec (7) &= \{1, 3, 4, 6\} \\
\prec (8) &= \{1, 3, 4, 6, 7\}
\end{aligned}
\tag{3.1}
$$

We can also write $i \prec j$ to indicate that task T_i must precede task T_j. (We can also express this by $j \succ i$). Commonly, for economy of representation, we only list the immediate ancestors in the precedence set; for example, we can write $\prec (5) = \{2, 3\}$ since $\prec (2) = \{1\}$. The precedence operator is transitive. That is,

$$ i \prec j \quad \text{and} \quad j \prec k \quad \Rightarrow i \prec k $$

In some cases, $\succ$ and $\prec$ are used to denote which task has higher priority; that is, $i \succ j$ can mean that T_i has higher priority than T_j. The meaning of these symbols should be clear from context.

Each task has *resource requirements*. All tasks require some execution time on a processor. Also, a task may require a certain amount of memory or access to a bus. Sometimes, a resource must be *exclusively* held by a task (i.e., the task must have sole possession of it). In other cases, resources are nonexclusive. The same physical resource may be exclusive or nonexclusive depending on the operation to be performed on it. For instance, a memory object (or anything else to which writing is not atomic) that is being read is nonexclusive. However, while it is being written into, it must be held exclusively by the writing task.

The *release time* of a task is the time at which all the data that are required to begin executing the task are available, and the *deadline* is the time by which the task must complete its execution. The deadline may be hard or soft, depending on the nature of the corresponding task. The *relative deadline* of a task is the absolute deadline minus the release time. That is, if task T_i has a relative deadline

d_i and is released at time τ, it must be executed by time $\tau + d_i$. The *absolute deadline* is the time by which the task must be completed. In this example, the absolute deadline of T_i is $\tau + d_i$.

A task may be periodic, sporadic, or aperiodic. A task T_i is *periodic* if it is released periodically, say every P_i seconds. P_i is called the *period* of task T_i. The periodicity constraint requires the task to run exactly once every period; it does not require that the tasks be run exactly one period apart. Quite commonly, the period of a task is also its deadline. The task is *sporadic* if it is not periodic, but may be invoked at irregular intervals. Sporadic tasks are characterized by an upper bound on the rate at which they may be invoked. This is commonly specified by requiring that successive invocations of a sporadic task T_i be separated in time by at least $t(i)$ seconds. Sporadic tasks are sometimes also called aperiodic. However, some people define *aperiodic* tasks to be those tasks which are not periodic and which also have no upper bound on their invocation rate.

> **Example 3.2.** Consider a pressure vessel whose pressure is measured every 10 ms. If the pressure exceeds a critical value, an alarm is sounded. The task that measures the pressure is periodic, with a period of 10 ms. The task that turns on the alarm is sporadic. What is the maximum rate at which this task can be invoked?

A task assignment[1]/schedule is said to be *feasible* if all the tasks start after their release times and complete before their deadlines. We say that a set of tasks is *A*-feasible if an assignment/scheduling algorithm *A*, when run on that set of tasks, results in a feasible schedule. The bulk of the work in real-time scheduling deals with obtaining feasible schedules.

Given these task characteristics and the execution times and deadlines associated with the tasks, the tasks are allocated or assigned to the various processors and scheduled on them. The schedule can be formally defined as a function

$$S: \text{Set of processors} \times \text{Time} \rightarrow \text{Set of tasks} \qquad (3.2)$$

$S(i, t)$ is the task scheduled to be running on processor i at time t. Most of the time, we will depict schedules graphically.

A schedule may be precomputed (offline scheduling), or obtained dynamically (online scheduling). *Offline scheduling* involves scheduling in advance of the operation, with specifications of when the periodic tasks will be run and slots for the sporadic/aperiodic tasks in the event that they are invoked. In *online scheduling*, the tasks are scheduled as they arrive in the system. The algorithms used in online scheduling must be fast; an online scheduling algorithm that takes so long that it leaves insufficient time for tasks to meet their deadlines is clearly useless.

The relative priorities of tasks are a function of the nature of the tasks themselves and the current state of the controlled process. For example, a task that controls stability in an aircraft and that has to be run at a high frequency

---

[1]In this book, we will use the terms "task allocate" and "task assign" interchangeably.

can reasonably be assigned a higher priority than one that controls cabin pressure. Also, a mission can consist of different phases or modes and the priority of the same task can vary from one phase to another.

> **Example 3.3.** The flight of an aircraft can be broken down into phases such as takeoff, climb, cruise, descend, and land. In each phase, the task mix, task priorities, and task deadlines may be different.

There are algorithms that assume that the task priority does not change within a mode; these are called *static-priority* algorithms. By contrast, *dynamic-priority* algorithms assume that priority can change with time. The best known examples of static- and dynamic-priority algorithms are the rate-monotonic (RM) algorithm and the earliest deadline first (EDF) algorithm, respectively. We shall discuss each in considerable detail.

The schedule may be preemptive or nonpreemptive. A schedule is *preemptive* if tasks can be interrupted by other tasks (and then resumed). By contrast, once a task is begun in a *nonpreemptive* schedule, it must be run to completion or until it gets blocked over a resource. We shall mostly be concerned with preemptive schedules in this book—wherever possible, critical tasks must be allowed to interrupt less critical ones when it is necessary to meet deadlines.

Preemption allows us the flexibility of not committing the processor to run a task through to completion once we start executing it. Committing the processor in a nonpreemptive schedule can cause anomalies.

> **Example 3.4.** Consider a two-task system. Let the release times of tasks T_1 and T_2 be 1 and 2, respectively; the deadlines be 9 and 6; and the execution times be 3.25 and 2. Schedule S_1 in Figure 3.2 meets both deadlines. However, suppose we follow the perfectly sensible policy of not keeping the processor idle whenever there is a task waiting to be run; then, we will have schedule S_2.
>
> This results in task T_2 missing its deadline!

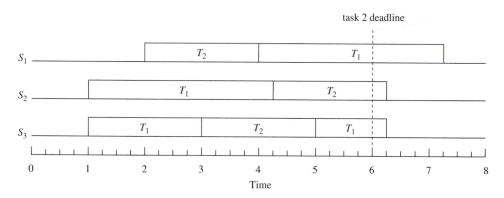

FIGURE 3.2
Preemptive and nonpreemptive schedules.

Notice that for schedule S_1 to have been implemented in the first place, we must have had some notion when T_1 arrived at time 1 that task T_2 would be on its way, and that its deadline would be too tight to allow task T_1 to complete ahead of it.

By contrast, S_3 is a preemptive schedule. When T_1 is released, it starts executing. When T_2 arrives, T_1 is preempted and run to completion, thus meeting its deadline. Then T_1 resumes from where it left off and also meets its deadline.

There is, however, a penalty associated with preemption. In order to allow a task to resume correctly, some housekeeping chores must be done by the system. The register values must be saved when a task is preempted and then restored when it resumes. Preemption is not always possible. For example, consider a disk system in the middle of writing a sector. It cannot simply abort its current operation—it must carry through to completion or the affected sector will not be consistent.

The vast majority of assignment/scheduling problems on systems with more than two processors are NP-complete. We must therefore make do with heuristics. Most heuristics are motivated by the fact that the uniprocessor scheduling (i.e., scheduling a set of tasks on a single processor) problem is usually tractable. The task of developing a multiprocessor schedule is therefore divided into two steps: first we assign tasks to processors, and second, we run a uniprocessor scheduling algorithm to schedule the tasks allocated to each processor. If one or more of the schedules turn out to be infeasible, then we must either return to the allocation step and change the allocation, or declare that a schedule cannot be found and stop. One example of this process is summarized in Figure 3.3. Many variations of this approach are possible; for example, one can check for schedulability after the allocation of each task.

3.1.1 How to Read This Chapter

This chapter is long and potentially intimidating. Many of the algorithms we cover have fairly involved proofs. For those of you interested only in checking if this chapter contains an algorithm that meets your immediate needs, and not interested in all the associated mathematical trappings, we summarize below the key features of the algorithms covered here. Simply go through the list, turn to the detailed algorithm description, and skip all the proofs. If, on the other hand, you are interested in the proof techniques used in scheduling theory, you will find many good examples here.

UNIPROCESSOR SCHEDULING ALGORITHMS.* As shown in Figure 3.3, uniprocessor scheduling is part of the process of developing a multiprocessor schedule. Our ability to obtain a feasible multiprocessor schedule is therefore linked to our ability to obtain feasible uniprocessor schedules. Most of this chapter deals with this problem.

Traditional rate-monotonic (RM): The task set consists of periodic, preemptible tasks whose deadlines equal the task period. A task set of n tasks is schedulable under RM if its total processor utilization is no greater than $n(2^{1/n}-1)$.

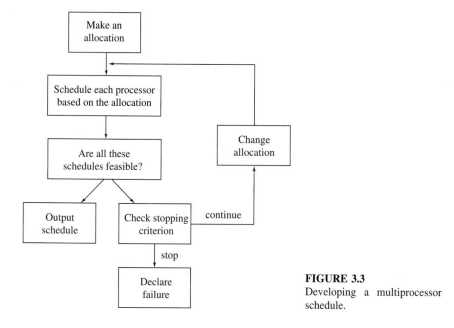

FIGURE 3.3
Developing a multiprocessor schedule.

Task priorities are static and inversely related to their periods. RM is an optimal static-priority uniprocessor scheduling algorithm and is very popular. Some results are also available for the case where a task deadline does not equal its period. See Section 3.2.1.

Rate-monotonic deferred server (DS): This is similar to the RM algorithm, except that it can handle both periodic (with deadlines equal to their periods) and aperiodic tasks. See Section 3.2.1 (in Sporadic Tasks).

Earliest deadline first (EDF): Tasks are preemptible and the task with the earliest deadline has the highest priority. EDF is an optimal uniprocessor algorithm. If a task set is not schedulable on a single processor by EDF, there is no other processor that can successfully schedule that task set. See Section 3.2.2.

Precedence and exclusion conditions: Both the RM and EDF algorithms assume that the tasks are independent and preemptible anytime. In Section 3.2.3, we present algorithms that take precedence conditions into account. Algorithms with exclusion conditions (i.e., certain tasks are not allowed to interrupt certain other tasks, irrespective of priority) are also presented.

Multiple task versions: In some cases, the system has primary and alternative versions of some tasks. These versions vary in their execution time and in the quality of output they provide. Primary versions are the full-fledged tasks, providing top-quality output. Alternative versions are bare-bones tasks, providing lower-quality (but still acceptable) output and taking much less time to execute. If the system has enough time, it will execute the primary; however, under conditions of overload, the alternative may be picked. In Section 3.2.4, an algorithm is provided to do this.

IRIS tasks: IRIS stands for increased reward with increased service. Many algorithms have the property that they can be stopped early and still provide useful output. The quality of the output is a monotonically nondecreasing function of the execution time. Iterative algorithms (e.g., algorithms that compute π or e) are one example of this. In Section 3.3, we provide algorithms suitable for scheduling such tasks.

MULTIPROCESSOR SCHEDULING. Algorithms dealing with task assignment to the processors of a multiprocessor are discussed in Section 3.4. The task assignment problem is NP-hard under any but the most simplifying assumptions. As a result, we must make do with heuristics.

Utilization balancing algorithm: This algorithm assigns tasks to processors one by one in such a way that at the end of each step, the utilizations of the various processors are as nearly balanced as possible. Tasks are assumed to be preemptible.

Next-fit algorithm: The next-fit algorithm is designed to work in conjuction with the rate-monotonic uniprocessor scheduling algorithm. It divides the set of tasks into various classes. A set of processors is exclusively assigned to each task class. Tasks are assumed to be preemptible.

Bin-packing algorithm: The bin-packing algorithm assigns tasks to processors under the constraint that the total processor utilization must not exceed a given threshold. The threshold is set in such a way that the uniprocessor scheduling algorithm is able to schedule the tasks assigned to each processor. Tasks are assumed to be preemptible.

Myopic offline scheduling algorithm: This algorithm can deal with nonpreemptible tasks. It builds up the schedule using a search process.

Focused addressing and bidding algorithm: In this algorithm, tasks are assumed to arrive at the individual processors. A processor that finds itself unable to meet the deadline or other constraints of all its tasks tries to offload some of its workload onto other processors. It does so by announcing which task(s) it would like to offload and waiting for the other processors to offer to take them up.

Buddy strategy: The buddy strategy takes roughly the same approach as the focused addressing algorithm. Processors are divided into three categories: underloaded, fully loaded, and overloaded. Overloaded processors ask the underloaded processors to offer to take over some of their load.

Assignment with precedence constraints: The last task assignment algorithm takes task precedence constraints into account. It does so using a trial-and-error process that tries to assign tasks that communicate heavily with one another to the same processor so that communication costs are minimized.

CRITICAL SECTIONS. Certain anomalous behavior can be exhibited as a result of critical sections. In particular, a lower-priority task can make a higher-priority task wait for it to finish, even if the two are not competing for access to the same critical section. In Section 3.2.1 (in Handling Critical Sections), we present algorithms to get around this problem and to provide a finite upper bound to the period during which a lower-priority task can block a higher-priority task.

MODE CHANGES. Frequently, task sets change during the operation of a real-time system. We have seen in Chapter 2 that a mission can have multiple phases, each phase characterized by a different set of tasks, or the same task set but with different priorities or arrival rates. In Section 3.5, we discuss the scheduling issues that arise when a mission phase changes. We look at how to delete or add tasks to the task list.

FAULT-TOLERANT SCHEDULNG. The final part of this chapter deals with the important problem of ensuring that deadlines will continue to be met despite the occurrence of faults. In Section 3.6, we describe an algorithm that schedules backups that are activated in the event of failure.

3.1.2   Notation

The notation used in this chapter will be as follows.

n	Number of tasks in the task set.
e_i	Execution time of task T_i.
P_i	Period of task T_i, if it is periodic.
I_i	kth period of (periodic) task T_i begins at time $I_i + (k-1)P_i$, where I_i is called the *phasing* of task T_i.
d_i	Relative deadline of task T_i (relative to release time).
D_i	Absolute deadline of task T_i
r_i	Release time of task T_i
$h_T(t)$	Sum of the execution times of task iterations in task set T that have their absolute deadlines no later than t.

Additional notation will be introduced as appropriate.

3.2   CLASSICAL UNIPROCESSOR SCHEDULING ALGORITHMS

In this section, we will consider two venerable algorithms used for scheduling independent tasks on a single processor, rate-monotonic (RM) and earliest deadline first (EDF). The goal of these algorithms is to meet all task deadlines. Following that, we will deal with precedence and exclusion constraints, and consider situations where multiple versions of software are available for the same task.

The following assumptions are made for both the RM and EDF algorithms.

A1. No task has any nonpreemptable section and the cost of preemption is negligible.

A2. Only processing requirements are significant; memory, I/O, and other resource requirements are negligible.

A3. All tasks are independent; there are no precedence constraints.

These assumptions greatly simplify the analyses of RM and EDF. Assumption **A1** indicates that we can preempt any task at any time and resume it later without penalty. As a result, the number of times that a task is preempted does not change the total workload of the processor. From **A2**, to check for feasibility we only have to ensure that enough processing capacity exists to execute the tasks by their deadlines; there are no memory or other constraints to complicate matters. The absence of precedence constraints, **A3**, means that task release times do not depend on the finishing times of other tasks.

Of course, there are also many systems for which assumptions **A1** to **A3** are not good approximations. Later in this chapter, we will see how to deal with some of these.

3.2.1   Rate-Monotonic Scheduling Algorithm

The rate-monotonic (RM) scheduling algorithm is one of the most widely studied and used in practice. It is a uniprocessor static-priority preemptive scheme. Except where it is otherwise stated, the following assumptions are made in addition to assumptions **A1** to **A3**.

A4. All tasks in the task set are periodic.

A5. The relative deadline of a task is equal to its period.

Assumption **A5** simplifies our analysis of RM greatly, since it ensures that there can be at most one iteration of any task alive at any time.

The priority of a task is inversely related to its period; if task T_i has a smaller period than task T_j, T_i has higher priority than T_j. Higher-priority tasks can preempt lower-priority tasks.

> **Example 3.5.** Figure 3.4 contains an example of this algorithm. There are three tasks, with $P_1 = 2$, $P_2 = 6$, $P_3 = 10$. The execution times are $e_1 = 0.5$, $e_2 = 2.0$, $e_3 = 1.75$, and $I_1 = 0$, $I_2 = 1$, $I_3 = 3$. Since $P_1 < P_2 < P_3$, task T_1 has highest priority. Every time it is released, it preempts whatever is running on the processor. Similarly, task T_3 cannot execute when either task T_1 or T_2 is unfinished.

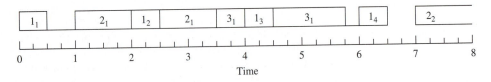

FIGURE 3.4
Example of the RM algorithm; K_j denotes the jth release (or iteration) of Task T_K.

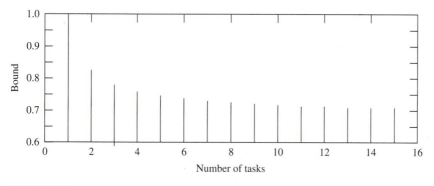

FIGURE 3.5
Utilization bound for the RM algorithm.

There is an easy schedulability test for this algorithm, as follows:

If the total utilization of the tasks is no greater than $n(2^{1/n} - 1)$, where n is the number of tasks to be scheduled, then the RM algorithm will schedule all the tasks to meet their respective deadlines. Note that this is a sufficient, but not necessary, condition. That is, there may be task sets with a utilization greater than $n(2^{1/n} - 1)$ that are schedulable by the RM algorithm.

The $n(2^{1/n} - 1)$ bound is plotted in Figure 3.5.

Let us now turn to determining the necessary and sufficient conditions for RM-schedulability. To gain some intuition into what these conditions are, let us determine them from first principles for the three-task example in Example 3.5.

Assume that the task phasings are all zero (i.e., the first iteration of each task is released at time zero). Observe the first iteration of each task. Let us start with task T_1. This is the highest-priority task, so it will never be delayed by any other task in the system. The moment T_1 is released, the processor will interrupt anything else it is doing and start processing it. As a result, the only condition that must be satisfied to ensure that T_1 can be feasibly scheduled is that $e_1 \leq P_1$. This is clearly a necessary, as well as a sufficient, condition.

Now, turn to task T_2. It will be executed successfully if its first iteration can find enough time over $[0, P_2]$. Suppose T_2 finishes at time t. The total number of iterations of task T_1 that have been released over $[0, t]$ is $\lceil t/P_1 \rceil$. In order for T_2 to finish at t, every one of the iterations of task T_1 released in $[0, t]$ must be completed, and in addition there must be e_2 time available to execute T_2. That is, we must satisfy the condition:

$$t = \left\lceil \frac{t}{P_1} \right\rceil e_1 + e_2$$

If we can find some $t \in [0, P_2]$ satisfying this condition, we are done.

Now comes the practical question of how we check that such a t exists. After all, every interval has an infinite number of points in it, so we can't very well check exhaustively for every possible t. The solution lies in the fact that $\lceil t/P_1 \rceil$ only changes at multiples of P_1, with jumps of e_1. So, if we show that there exists some integer k such that $kP_1 \geq ke_1 + e_2$ and $kP_1 \leq P_2$, we have met the necessary and sufficient conditions for T_2 to be schedulable under the RM algorithm. That is, we only need to check if $t \geq \lceil t/P_1 \rceil e_1 + e_2$ for some value of t that is a multiple of P_1, such that $t \leq P_2$. Since there is a finite number of multiples of P_1 that are less than or equal to P_2, we have a finite check.

Finally, consider task T_3. Once again, it is sufficient to show that its first iteration completes before P_3. If T_3 completes executing at t, then by an argument identical to that for T_2, we must have:

$$ t = \left\lceil \frac{t}{P_1} \right\rceil e_1 + \lceil \frac{t}{P_2} \rceil e_2 + e_3 $$

T_3 is schedulable iff there is some $t \in [0, P_3]$ such that the above condition is satisfied. But, the right-hand side (RHS) of the above equation has jumps only at multiples of P_1 and P_2. It is therefore sufficient to check if the inequality

$$ t \geq \left\lceil \frac{t}{P_1} \right\rceil e_1 + \left\lceil \frac{t}{P_2} \right\rceil e_2 + e_3 $$

is satisfied for some t that is a multiple of P_1 and/or P_2, such that $t \leq P_3$.

We are now ready to present the necessary and sufficient condition in general. We will need the following additional notation:

$$ W_i(t) = \sum_{j=1}^{i} e_j \lceil \frac{t}{P_j} \rceil $$

$$ L_i(t) = \frac{W_i(t)}{t} $$

$$ L_i = \min_{0 < t \leq P_i} L_i(t) $$

$$ L = \max\{L_i\} $$

$W_i(t)$ is the total amount of work carried by tasks $T_1, T_2, \ldots, T_i$, initiated in the interval $[0, t]$. If all tasks are released at time 0, then task T_i will complete under the RM algorithm at time t', such that $W_i(t') = t'$ (if such a t' exists).

The necessary and sufficient condition for schedulability is as follows.

Given a set of n periodic tasks (with $P_1 \leq P_2 < \ldots \leq P_n$). Task T_i can be feasibly scheduled using RM iff $L_i \leq 1$.

As in our previous example, the practical question of how to check for $W_i(t) \leq t$ is easily answered by examining the defining equation $W_i(t) = \sum_{j=1}^{i} e_j \lceil t/P_j \rceil$. We see that $W_i(t)$ is constant, except at a finite number of points when tasks are released. We only need to compute $W_i(t)$ at the times

$$ \tau_i = \{\ell P_j | j = 1, \cdots, i; \ell = 1, \cdots, \lfloor P_i/P_j \rfloor\} \tag{3.3} $$

Then, we have two RM-scheduling conditions:

RM1. If $\min_{t \in \tau_i} W_i(t) \leq$, task T_i is RM-schedulable.

RM2. If $\max_{i \in \{1,\ldots,n\}} \{\min_{t \in \tau_i} W_i(t)/t\} \leq 1$ for $i \in \{1,\ldots,n\}, t \in T_i$, then the entire set T is RM-schedulable.

Example 3.6. Consider the set of four tasks where

i	e_i	P_i	i	e_i	P_i
1	20	100	3	80	210
2	30	150	4	100	400

Then,

$$\tau_1 = \{100\}$$

$$\tau_2 = \{100, 150\}$$

$$\tau_3 = \{100, 150, 200, 210\}$$

$$\tau_4 = \{100, 150, 200, 210, 300, 400\}$$

Let us check the RM-schedulability of each task. Figure 3.6 contains plots of $W_i(t)$ for $i = 1, 2, 3, 4$. Task T_i is RM-schedulable iff any part of the plot of $W_i(t)$ falls on or below the $W_i(t) = t$ line.

In algebraic terms, we have:

- task T_1 is RM-schedulable iff $e_1 \leq 100$
- task T_2 is RM-schedulable iff

$$\begin{aligned} e_1 + e_2 &\leq 100 \qquad \text{OR} \\ 2e_1 + e_2 &\leq 150 \end{aligned} \tag{3.4}$$

- task T_3 is RM-schedulable iff

$$\begin{aligned} e_1 + e_2 + e_3 &\leq 100 \qquad \text{OR} \\ 2e_1 + e_2 + e_3 &\leq 150 \qquad \text{OR} \\ 2e_1 + 2e_2 + e_3 &\leq 200 \qquad \text{OR} \\ 3e_1 + 2e_2 + e_3 &\leq 210 \end{aligned} \tag{3.5}$$

- task T_4 is RM-schedulable iff

$$\begin{aligned} e_1 + e_2 + e_3 + e_4 &\leq 100 \qquad \text{OR} \\ 2e_1 + e_2 + e_3 + e_4 &\leq 150 \qquad \text{OR} \\ 2e_1 + 2e_2 + e_3 + e_4 &\leq 200 \qquad \text{OR} \\ 3e_1 + 2e_2 + e_3 + e_4 &\leq 210 \qquad \text{OR} \\ 3e_1 + 2e_2 + 2e_3 + e_4 &\leq 300 \qquad \text{OR} \\ 4e_1 + 3e_2 + 2e_3 + e_4 &\leq 400 \end{aligned} \tag{3.6}$$

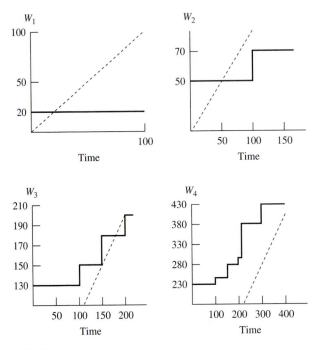

FIGURE 3.6
$W_i(t)$ for Example 3.6; the dotted line indicates the locus of $W_i(t) = t$.

From Figure 3.6 and the above equations, we can see that tasks T_1, T_2, and T_3 are RM-schedulable, but task T_4 is not.

SPORADIC TASKS. Thus far, we have only considered periodic tasks. Let us now introduce sporadic tasks. These are released irregularly, often in response to some event in the operating environment. While sporadic tasks do not have periods associated with them, there must be some maximum rate at which they can be released. That is, we must have some minimum interarrival time between the release of successive iterations of sporadic tasks. Otherwise, there is no limit to the amount of workload that sporadic tasks can add to the system and it will be impossible to guarantee that deadlines are met.

One way of dealing with sporadic tasks is to simply consider them as periodic tasks with a period equal to their minimum interarrival time. Two other approaches are outlined below.

Perhaps the simplest way to incorporate sporadic tasks is to define a fictitious periodic task of highest priority and of some chosen fictitious execution period. During the time that this task is scheduled to run on the processor, the processor is available to run any sporadic tasks that may be awaiting service. Outside this time, the processor attends to the periodic tasks.

Example 3.7. Figure 3.7 provides an illustration. We have here a fictitious highest-priority task with period of 10 and execution time of 2.5. This task occupies the

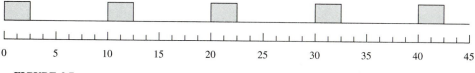

FIGURE 3.7
Incorporating sporadic tasks: method 1.

processor during the time shown by the shaded portion, which has been set aside to execute any pending sporadic tasks—every 10 time units, the processor can execute up to 2.5 units of sporadic tasks. If, during that time, there is no sporadic task awaiting service, the processor is idle. The processor cannot execute sporadic tasks outside the shaded intervals.

The deferred server (DS) approach is less wasteful. Whenever the processor is scheduled to run sporadic tasks and finds no such tasks awaiting service, it starts executing the other (periodic) tasks in order of priority. However, if a sporadic task arrives, it preempts the periodic task and can occupy a total time up to the time allotted for sporadic tasks.

Example 3.8. In Figure 3.8, the occupancy of the processor by sporadic tasks is indicated by shaded rectangles. 2.5 time units are allocated every 10-unit period for sporadic tasks. A sporadic task requiring 5 units arrives at time 5 and takes over the processor. At time 7.5, the processor has given the task its entire quota of 2.5 units over the current period, and so the sporadic task is preempted by some other task. At time 10, the next sporadic-task period begins and the remaining 2.5 units of service are delivered. The next sporadic task, with a total execution time requirement of 7.5 units arrives at time 27.5. It has available to it the 2.5 units from the current period of [20, 30] plus the 2.5 units from the next period of [30, 40]. It therefore occupies the processor over the interval [27.5, 32.5]. At that point, its quota of time on the processor (for the [30, 40] period) is exhausted and it relinquishes the processor. At time 40, a new sporadic-task period begins and the sporadic task receives its last 2.5 units of service, completing at 42.5.

Schedulability criteria can be derived for the DS algorithm in much the same way as for the basic RM algorithm. When the relative deadlines of all tasks equal their periods, and U_s is the processor utilization allocated to the sporadic tasks, we can show that it is possible to schedule periodic tasks if the total task utilization

FIGURE 3.8
Incorporating sporadic tasks: method 2 (deferred server).

(including the sporadic contribution) U satisfies the following bound:

$$U \leq \begin{cases} 1 - U_s & \text{if } U_s \leq 0.5 \\ U_s & \text{if } U_s \geq 0.5 \end{cases} \tag{3.7}$$

When $U_s \geq 0.5$, it is possible to construct a periodic task set of arbitrarily low (but positive) utilization that cannot be feasibly scheduled.

Example 3.9. Suppose $P_s = 6$ is the period of the deferred server and $P_1 = 6$ for periodic task T_1. Let the execution time reserved for the sporadic task be $e_s = 3$, that is, $U_s = 3/6 = 0.5$. Then, if the sporadic tasks occupy back-to-back time-slices of 3 each, an entire period of P_1 will pass with no time available for T_1.

Equation 3.7 is a sufficient, though not necessary, condition for schedulability: It is easy to construct feasible periodic task sets even when $U_s \geq 0.5$.

TRANSIENT OVERLOADS. One drawback of the RM algorithm is that task priorities are defined by their periods. Sometimes, we must change the task priorities to ensure that all critical tasks get completed. We motivate this using the following example.

Example 3.10. Suppose that we are given, in addition to the task periods P_i and worst-case execution times e_i for task T_i, average execution times a_i. Consider the four-task set with the following characteristics that we considered in Example 3.6.

i	e_i	a_i	P_i
1	20	10	100
2	30	25	150
3	80	40	210
4	100	20	400

Suppose that tasks T_1, T_2, and T_4 are critical, and that T_3 is noncritical. It is easy to check that if we run the RM algorithm on this task set, we cannot guarantee the schedulability of all four tasks if they each take their worst-case execution times. However, in the average case, they will all be RM-schedulable. The problem is how to arrange matters so that all the critical tasks meet their deadlines under the RM algorithm even in the worst case, while T_3 meets its deadline in many other cases.

The solution is to boost the priority of T_4 by altering its period. We will replace T_4 by task T_4' with the following parameters: $P_4' = P_4/2$, $e_4' = e_4/2$, $a_4' = a_4/2$. It is easy to check that tasks T_1, T_2, and T_4' are RM-schedulable even in the worst case. T_3 now has a lower priority than T_4'. Whenever the algorithm schedules T_4', we can run the code for T_4. Because of the way we obtained e_4', if $\{T_1, T_2, T_4'\}$ is an RM-schedulable set, there will be enough time to complete the execution of T_4.

An alternative to reducing the period of T_4 is to try to lengthen the period of T_3. This can be done only if the relative deadline of T_3 can be greater than its original period. In this case, we can replace T_3 by two tasks T_3' and T_3'', each with period 420 (i.e., 210×2), with worst-case execution times $e_3' = e_3'' = 80$ and average-case execution times $a_3' = a_3'' = 40$. The scheduler will have to phase T_3' and T_3'' so that they are released $P_3 = 210$ units apart. If the resultant task set $\{T_1, T_2, T_3', T_3'', T_4\}$ is RM-schedulable, we are done.

In general, if we lengthen the period by a factor of k, we will replace the original task by k tasks, each phased by the appropriate amount. If we reduce the period by a factor of k, we will replace the original task by one whose execution time is also reduced by a factor of k.

This procedure of period transformation ultimately results in two sets of tasks, C and NC, with the following properties:

- C contains all the critical tasks and possibly some noncritical tasks.
- NC contains only noncritical tasks.
- $P_{c,\max} \leq P_{n,\min}$, where $P_{c,\max}$ and $P_{n,\min}$ are the maximum and minimum periods of tasks in C and NC, respectively.
- C is RM-schedulable under worst-case task execution times.

The procedure is to first set C to be the set of critical tasks and NC the set of non-critical tasks. If $P_{c,\max} \leq P_{n,\min}$, we are done. If this is not the case, then we move those noncritical tasks whose periods are less than or equal to $P_{c,\max}$ into the set C. If the new set C is RM-schedulable under worst-case task execution times, we are done. If not, then we try to lengthen the periods of the noncritical tasks in C by as much as possible until C is RM-schedulable. If this is not possible, then we reduce the periods of the higher-priority critical tasks and move back into NC all noncritical tasks in C whose periods are larger than the largest period of any critical task in C. We continue this process until we arrive at C and NC with the above properties.

MATHEMATICAL UNDERPINNINGS.* Let us develop the properties of the RM algorithm. In particular, we are interested in what processor utilizations are possible and how to determine whether a given task set is feasible.

We begin with two definitions. Let $R_i(x)$ be the response time of task T_i if it is released at time x. x^* is said to be a *critical time instant* for task T_i if $R_i(x^*) \geq R_i(x) \; \forall x$. In other words, x^* is the worst time at which to release T_i, with respect to its response time. A *critical time zone* of task T_i is defined as the interval $[x^*, x^* + R_i(x^*)]$; that is, it is the interval between a critical time instant and when the task (initiated at that time) finishes.

Theorem 3.1. A critical time instant of any task occurs when that task is requested at the same time as all other higher-priority tasks.

Proof. Number the tasks in descending order of priority. The response time of a task is the execution time plus the interval over which the task was waiting to execute.

Let us begin with the case where there are only two tasks, T_1 and T_2. Define the time axis so that $I_2 = 0$. Task T_1 occupies the time intervals $[I_1, I_1 + e_1]$, $[I_1 +$

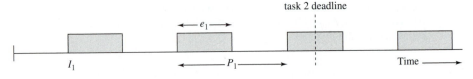

FIGURE 3.9
Theorem 3.1; the shaded portions indicate that the processor is occupied by task T_1.

$P_1, I_1 + P_1 + e_1], \ldots, [I_1 + nP_1, I_1 + nP_1 + e_1], \ldots$. The response time of task T_2 is given by

$$e_2 + n_{p2}(1)e_1$$

where $n_{pi}(j)$ is the number of times task T_i is preempted by task T_j. Task T_2 executes for I_1 before the first iteration of task T_1 arrives. After that, it executes for at most $P_1 - e_1$ between successive iterations of task T_1. Hence,

$$(n_{p2}(1) - 1)(P_1 - e_1) + I_1 < e_2 \leq n_{p2}(1)(P_1 - e_1) + I_1 \tag{3.8}$$

To maximize the response time of task T_2, we must maximize $n_{p2}(1)$, subject to the constraint in (3.8). The only variable is I_1; all the other parameters (P_1, e_1, e_2) are constants. From (3.8), it follows immediately that $n_{p2}(1)$ is maximized when $I_1 = 0$.

This is probably easier to see geometrically as in Figure 3.9. Task T_2 can only execute in the unshaded portions and will complete whenever these intervals have a total duration of e_2. Altering I_1 is tantamount to moving the train of shaded portions. From the diagram, it is apparent that the response time of T_2 is maximized when T_1 has zero phasing, i.e., $I_1 = 0$.

A similar argument holds for an arbitrary number of tasks.   **Q.E.D.**

A given set of tasks is said to be *RM-schedulable* if the RM algorithm produces a schedule that meets all the deadlines. It follows from Theorem 3.1 that a set of tasks is RM-schedulable for any values of $I_1, I_2, \ldots$, if it is RM-schedulable for $I_1 = I_2 = \cdots = 0$. Therefore, to check for RM-schedulability, we only need to check for the case where all task phasings are zero. Theorem 3.2 is what has made RM so popular.

Theorem 3.2. The RM algorithm is an optimal static-priority algorithm. That is, if any static-priority algorithm can produce a feasible schedule, so can RM.

Proof. We proceed by contradiction. Suppose there exists some task set and some other static-priority algorithm A such that A generates a feasible schedule, but RM does not.

Since A is a static-priority algorithm, it proceeds by assigning priorities to tasks and then scheduling on the basis of these priorities. Since A is different from RM and optimal (while RM, under the hypothesis, is not), there must be some task set T for which

- algorithm A allocates task priorities differently from algorithm RM, and
- algorithm A successfully schedules the tasks in T, while under RM one or more deadlines are missed.

In particular, there will be tasks T_i, T_j in the set T with the following properties:

1. Priority(T_i) = Priority$(T_j) + 1$ under algorithm A's priority assignment.
2. $P_i > P_j$, so that under RM T_i has a lower priority than T_j.

Denote by S_A the schedule that is produced by A. Now, consider the schedule, S', obtained by interchanging the priorities (as defined by algorithm A) of T_i and T_j, and keeping all the other priority assignments the same as in algorithm A. If all the task deadlines are met under S_A, all task deadlines will continue to be met under S'. (Can you work out why this should be the case?)

If this interchange leads to the same priority assignment as the RM algorithm, then this shows that T is RM-schedulable, thus contradicting our original hypothesis. If it is still different from the RM priority assignment, we can continue interchanging priorities as before and obtain a feasible schedule each time. This process stops when we get the same priority assignment as for RM and the proof is complete.   **Q.E.D.**

Let us now generate some conditions on the processor utilization possible under this algorithm. If there are n tasks, the processor utilization is given by

$$U = \sum_{i=1}^{n} \frac{e_i}{P_i} \tag{3.9}$$

A set of tasks is said to *fully utilize* the processor if

- the RM-schedule meets all deadlines, and
- the task set is no longer RM-schedulable if the execution time of any task is increased.

It is important to keep in mind that the utilization of a processor that is fully utilized, under the above definition, is not necessarily 1 over the entire interval $[0, \infty)$.

Example 3.11. A two-task set with $P_1 = 5$, $P_2 = 7$, $e_1 = 2$, $e_2 = 3$, and $I_1 = I_2 = 0$ fully utilizes the processor; see Figure 3.10. If either e_1 or e_2 is increased, a deadline is missed. The processor utilization is less than 1: It is $2/5 + 3/7 = 0.83$.

We will show that if the task set is such that the processor utilization is no greater than $n(2^{1/n} - 1)$, the task set is RM-schedulable. This will provide us with a simple check on RM-schedulability. Our proof will proceed by showing that the least upper bound of utilization for schedulability is $n(2^{1/n} - 1)$. Hence, if the utilization of any set of tasks is no greater than $n(2^{1/n} - 1)$, we will know

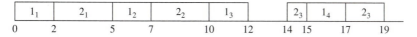

FIGURE 3.10
A task set that fully utilizes the processor.

that it is RM-schedulable. In what follows, assume the tasks are numbered so that $P_1 \leq P_2 \leq \ldots \leq P_n$. Let us begin with a task set consisting of only two tasks (i.e., $n = 2$).

Lemma 3.1. If there are two tasks, T_1, T_2, and

$$\frac{e_1}{P_1} + \frac{e_2}{P_2} \leq 2(\sqrt{2} - 1)$$

then the tasks are RM-schedulable.

Proof. We have assumed that $P_2 \geq P_1$, so that task T_2 has a lower priority than task T_1. During one period of task T_2, there are $\lceil P_2/P_1 \rceil$ releases of task T_1. Let us determine the maximum value of e_2 (as a function of e_1) so that the task set remains RM-schedulable. We have two cases.

Case 1. The processor is not executing task T_1 at time P_2.
Since task T_1 has preemptive priority over task T_2, Case 1 will only happen if every iteration of T_1 that was released in the interval $[0, P_2]$ has been completed by P_2. The last iteration of T_1 within $[0, P_2]$ is released at time $P_1 \lfloor P_2/P_1 \rfloor$. Hence, we must have

$$P_1 \left\lfloor \frac{P_2}{P_1} \right\rfloor + e_1 \leq P_2 \tag{3.10}$$

A total of $\lceil P_2/P_1 \rceil$ executions of task T_1 are completed during one period of T_2, and each consumes e_1 time. Since task T_2 must finish within its period, the maximum possible value of e_2 is

$$e_2 = P_2 - e_1 \left\lceil \frac{P_2}{P_1} \right\rceil \tag{3.11}$$

The processor utilization is then given by

$$\frac{e_1}{P_1} + \frac{e_2}{P_2} = \frac{e_1}{P_1} + 1 - \frac{e_1 \lceil P_2/P_1 \rceil}{P_2} \tag{3.12}$$

Since

$$\frac{1}{P_1} - \frac{\lceil P_2/P_1 \rceil}{P_2} \leq 0$$

the processor utilization is monotonically nonincreasing in e_1 whenever $P_1 \lfloor P_2/P_1 \rfloor + e_1 \leq P_2$.

Case 2. The processor is executing task T_1 at time P_2.
Case 2 occurs when

$$P_1 \left\lfloor \frac{P_2}{P_1} \right\rfloor + e_1 > P_2 \tag{3.13}$$

If this happens, then task T_2 must complete its execution by the time the last iteration of T_1 in $[0, P_2]$ is released. But this release happens, as we have noted above, at time $P_1 \lceil P_2/P_1 \rceil$. So, task T_2 must complete execution over the interval $[0, P_1 \lfloor P_2/P_1 \rfloor]$. Over this interval, however, T_1 occupies the processor for a total time of $\lfloor P_2/P_1 \rfloor e_1$. So, the total time available for T_2 is

$P_1 \lfloor P_2/P_1 \rfloor - \lfloor P_2/P_1 \rfloor e_1$. This means that the maximum possible value for e_2 is as given below:

$$e_2 = \left\lfloor \frac{P_2}{P_1} \right\rfloor \{P_1 - e_1\} \tag{3.14}$$

The corresponding processor utilization is

$$\frac{e_1}{P_1} + \frac{e_2}{P_2} = \frac{e_1}{P_1} + \left\lfloor \frac{P_2}{P_1} \right\rfloor \left\{ \frac{P_1}{P_2} - \frac{e_1}{P_2} \right\}$$

$$= \frac{P_1}{P_2} \left\lfloor \frac{P_2}{P_1} \right\rfloor + e_1 \left\{ \frac{1}{P_1} - \frac{\lfloor P_2/P_1 \rfloor}{P_2} \right\} \tag{3.15}$$

Since

$$\frac{1}{P_1} - \frac{\lfloor P_2/P_1 \rfloor}{P_2} \geq 0$$

we see that when $P_1 \lfloor P_2/P_1 \rfloor + e_1 > P_2$, the processor utilization is monotonically nondecreasing in e_1.

From Equations (3.12) and (3.15), we find that the minimum value that processor utilization can have if the task set fully utilizes the processor occurs when

$$P_1 \left\lfloor \frac{P_2}{P_1} \right\rfloor + e_1 = P_2 \tag{3.16}$$

Denote the integral part of P_2/P_1 by I and its fractional part by f. By definition, $0 \leq f < 1$. Then, $\lfloor P_2/P_1 \rfloor = I$, and

$$\left\lceil \frac{P_2}{P_1} \right\rceil = \begin{cases} I & \text{if } f = 0 \\ I+1 & \text{otherwise} \end{cases}$$

Using Equations (3.12), (3.16), and a little algebra, we can write an expression for the processor utilization when the processor is fully utilized by the task set:

$$U = 1 + \frac{P_2 - P_1 \lfloor P_2/P_1 \rfloor}{P_1} - \frac{P_2 - P_1 \lfloor P_2/P_1 \rfloor}{P_2} \left\lceil \frac{P_2}{P_1} \right\rceil$$

$$= 1 - \left\{ \left\lfloor \frac{P_2}{P_1} \right\rfloor + \left\lceil \frac{P_2}{P_1} \right\rceil - \frac{P_1}{P_2} \left\lfloor \frac{P_2}{P_1} \right\rfloor \left\lceil \frac{P_2}{P_1} \right\rceil - \frac{P_2}{P_1} \right\}$$

$$= \begin{cases} 1 & \text{if } f = 0 \\ \dfrac{I + f^2}{I + f} & \text{otherwise} \end{cases} \tag{3.17}$$

For $f > 0$, utilization is minimized when I is minimized. But $I \geq 1$ (since $P_2 \geq P_1$), so the minimal value of U is attained for $I = 1$. From elementary calculus, we have

$$\frac{d}{df} \left\{ \frac{I + f^2}{I + f} \right\} = \frac{2f}{1+f} - \frac{1 + f^2}{(1+f)^2} \tag{3.18}$$

Therefore, U is minimized when

$$\frac{2f}{1+f} - \frac{1 + f^2}{(1+f)^2} = 0 \Rightarrow f = \sqrt{2} - 1 \tag{3.19}$$

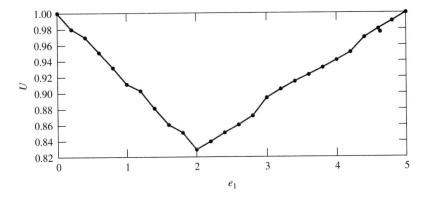

FIGURE 3.11
Processor utilization when the processor is fully utilized.

From this, we find the minimum value of U under full utilization to be $2(\sqrt{2} - 1)$. This is the least upper bound. **Q.E.D.**

Example 3.12. Consider a two-task set with $P_1 = 5$, and $P_2 = 7$. In Figure 3.11, we plot the utilization as a function of e_1 when the processor is fully utilized (e_2 is chosen for full utilization).

Let us now extend this to more than two tasks. We do so in two steps. First we will consider the case $P_n < 2P_1$. In this case, the longest period, P_n, contains only two releases of each higher-priority task; this will greatly simplify our analysis. We will show that the least upper bound for schedulability in this case is given by $n(2^{1/n} - 1)$. Then we will consider the $P_n \geq 2P_1$ case. For each set S of n tasks for which $P_n \geq 2P_1$, we will construct a set S' of n tasks for which $P_n' < 2P_1'$ (where P_i' is the period of the ith task in set S') with the property that if S fully utilizes the processor, so does S'. We will show that the utilization of the processor under S' is no greater than the utilization under S. As a result, the least upper bound of the utilization for the $P_n \geq 2P_1$ case cannot be less than that for the $P_n < 2P_1$ case. The overall least upper bound for schedulability is therefore $n(2^{1/n} - 1)$.

Lemma 3.2. Given n tasks in the task set S with execution times e_i for task T_i, if $e_i = P_{i+1} - P_i$ for $i = 1, \ldots, n - 1$, and $e_n = 2P_1 - P_n$, with $P_n < 2P_1$, then under the RM algorithm

- the task set fully utilizes the processor,
- there does not exist any other task set that also fully utilizes the processor and that has a lower processor utilization, and
- the processor utilization is at least $U = n(2^{(1/n)} - 1)$.

Proof. As before, assume that the tasks are numbered so that $P_1 \leq P_2 \leq \ldots \leq P_n$. Let U denote the processor utilization under this task set. The task set fully utilizes the processor.

We will show that the utilization is minimized when $e_1 = P_2 - P_1$ by checking out the cases when $e_1 > P_2 - P_1$ and $e_1 < P_2 - P_1$. A similar argument yields the best values for the execution time of the other tasks.

Consider the case where $e_1 > P_2 - P_1$, that is,

$$e_1 = P_2 - P_1 + \Delta \qquad \Delta > 0 \qquad (3.20)$$

Figure 3.12a illustrates this situation for the tasks T_1, T_2. The first release of task T_2 must complete before time P_1 (since the interval $[P_1, P_2]$ will be fully occupied by the second release of task T_1).

Now, define another task set S' with task execution times

$$e'_1 = e_1 - \Delta$$
$$e'_2 = e_2 + \Delta$$
$$e'_3 = e_3$$
$$\vdots$$
$$e'_n = e_n$$

Task set S' will also fully utilize the processor. The additional slack created in the interval $[0, P_1]$ by reducing the T_1 execution time is cancelled out by increasing the execution time of task T_2. See Figure 3.12a.

If U' denotes the processor utilization under task set S', we have

$$U - U' = \frac{\Delta}{P_1} - \frac{\Delta}{P_2} > 0 \qquad (3.21)$$

Now, suppose that instead of Equation (3.20), we have

$$e_1 = P_2 - P_1 - \Delta \qquad \Delta > 0 \qquad (3.22)$$

In such a case, to fully utilize the processor, tasks $T_2, T_3, \ldots$, must fill the intervals $[P_1, P_2]$ and $[P_1 + e_1, P_2]$.

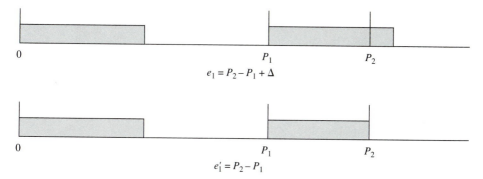

FIGURE 3.12a
Lemma 3.2; the shaded portion indicates when T_1 is executing.

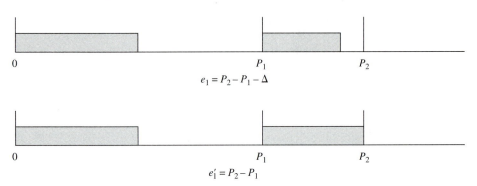

FIGURE 3.12b
Lemma 3.2; the shaded portion indicates when T_1 is executing.

Define another task set S'' with task execution times

$$e_1'' = e_1 + \Delta$$

$$e_2'' = e_2 - 2\Delta$$

$$e_3'' = e_3$$

$$\vdots$$

$$e_n'' = e_n$$

Task set S'' will also fully utilize the processor. Task T_1 will consume an extra Δ time units in the interval $[0, P_1]$, and an additional Δ time units in $[P_1, P_1 + e_1'']$. To make up for this, we reduce the execution time of task T_2 by 2Δ; otherwise T_2 cannot meet its deadline. See Figure 3.12b.

If U' denotes the processor utilization under task set S', we have

$$U - U' = -\frac{\Delta}{P_1} + \frac{(2\Delta)}{P_2} > 0 \qquad \text{(since } P_2 < 2P_1\text{)} \qquad (3.23)$$

From Equations (3.21) and (3.23), we have that if task set S minimizes the utilization factor,

$$e_1 = P_2 - P_1 \qquad (3.24)$$

Using an identical argument, we can show that $e_i = P_{i+1} - P_i$ for $i = 2, \ldots, n-1$. To ensure that the set fully utilizes the processor, we must also have $e_n = 2P_1 - P_n$. To see why, prepare a diagram showing the schedule that results when the execution times are as chosen here. You will see that the only place left for the first iteration of T_n in the schedule is the interval between when the first iteration of T_{n-1} finishes and the second iteration of T_n begins.

The processor utilization under task set S is given by

$$U = \frac{P_2 - P_1}{P_1} + \frac{P_3 - P_2}{P_2} + \cdots + \frac{P_n - P_{n-1}}{P_{n-1}} + \frac{2P_1 - P_n}{P_n}$$

$$= \frac{P_2}{P_1} + \frac{P_3}{P_2} + \cdots + \frac{P_n}{P_{n-1}} + \frac{2P_1}{P_n} - n \qquad (3.25)$$

To obtain the minimum possible U so that S completely utilizes the processor, we must therefore choose $P_1, P_2, \ldots, P_n$ to minimize

$$u = \frac{P_2}{P_1} + \frac{P_3}{P_2} + \cdots + \frac{P_n}{P_{n-1}} + \frac{2P_1}{P_n} \tag{3.26}$$

subject to the constraint that $P_n < 2P_1$.

Constrained minimization is quite easy, but unconstrained minimization is even simpler. Let us carry out the unconstrained minimization (i.e., by ignoring the constraint that $P_n < 2P_1$), and see if the result that we obtain satisfies the constraint $P_n < 2P_1$.

To find the unconstrained minimum of u, we must solve the equations

$$\frac{\partial u}{\partial P_1} = \frac{\partial u}{\partial P_2} = \cdots = \frac{\partial u}{\partial P_n} = 0 \tag{3.27}$$

This results in the following equations:

$$P_i = \frac{P_2^{(i-1)}}{P_1^{(i-2)}} \qquad \text{if } 3 \le i \le n \tag{3.28}$$

$$P_n^2 = 2P_1 P_{n-1} \tag{3.29}$$

These equations yield

$$P_i = 2^{(i-1)/n} P_1 \tag{3.30}$$

In particular, if we set $i = n$ in Equation (3.30), we have $P_n = 2^{(n-1)/n} P_1 \Rightarrow P_n < 2P_1$, which satisfies the constraint.

After a little algebra, the corresponding utilization can be shown to be equal to

$$U = n(2^{1/n} - 1) \tag{3.31}$$

Q.E.D.

In fact, we can do better than Lemma 3.2. We can prove the same result without the constraint that $P_n < 2P_1$.

Consider a task set S that satisfies all the conditions in the statement of Lemma 3.2, except the one that $P_n < 2P_1$. Then, there exist tasks T_i such that $P_n \ge 2P_i$. Let $Q \subset S$ denote the set of such tasks. Construct another task set S' by starting with T and

- replacing every task $T_i \in Q$ with a task T_i' that has $P_i' = \lfloor P_n/P_i \rfloor P_i$ and $e_i' = e_i$, and
- replacing task T_n with T_n', which has its execution time increased over that of T_n by the amount required to fully utilize the processor. Let Δ_i be the amount of the increase that compensates for the replacement of T_i by T_i'.

It is easy to see that $\Delta_i \leq (\lfloor P_n/P_i \rfloor - 1)e_i$. Therefore, if U' denotes the utilization of task set T', we have

$$U' = U + \sum_{i \in Q} \left\{ \frac{\Delta_i}{P_n} + \frac{e_i}{P_i'} - \frac{e_i}{P_i} \right\}$$

$$\leq U + \sum_{i \in Q} \left\{ \left(\frac{\lfloor P_n}{P_i \rfloor} - 1 \right) \frac{e_i}{P_n} + \frac{e_i}{P_i'} - \frac{e_i}{P_i} \right\}$$

$$= U + \sum_{i \in Q} \left\{ \left(\left\lfloor \frac{P_n}{P_i} \right\rfloor - 1 \right) e_i \left[\left(\frac{1}{P_n} \right) - \left(\frac{1}{P_i'} \right) \right] \right\} \qquad (3.32)$$

But, $P_n \geq P_i'$. We therefore have from Equation (3.32) that

$$U' \leq U \qquad (3.33)$$

So, task set S', which satisfies the condition that $P_n' < 2P_1'$ in Lemma 3.2, has a lower utilization than S, which has the condition $P_n \geq 2P_1$. However, we know from Lemma 3.2 that $U' \geq n(2^{1/n} - 1)$. It therefore follows that $U \geq n(2^{1/n} - 1)$ for any periodic task set S that fully utilizes the processor. Hence, we have proved the following theorem.

Theorem 3.3. Any set of n periodic tasks that fully utilizes the processor under RM must have a processor utilization of at least $n(2^{(1/n)} - 1)$.

The necessary and sufficient conditions for schedulability are proved below.

Theorem 3.4. Given a set of n periodic tasks (with $P_1 \leq P_2 < \ldots \leq P_n$), task T_i can be feasibly scheduled using RM iff $L_i \leq 1$.

Proof. If $L_i \leq 1$, then there exists $t \in [0, P_i]$, such that $W_i(t)/t \leq 1$, that is, $W_i(t) \leq t$. Since $I_i = 0$ for all $i = 1, \ldots, n$ (recall that we have shown that we only need to check the case $I_1 = \ldots = I_n = 0$), $W_i(t) \leq t$ implies that by time t, the computational needs of tasks T_1 to T_i have been met. As $t \leq P_i$ task T_i meets its deadline.
    Conversely, if $W_i(t) > t$ for all $t \in [0, P_i]$, there is insufficient time to execute task T_i before its deadline, P_i.   **Q.E.D.**

WHEN A TASK DEADLINE IS NOT EQUAL TO ITS PERIOD.* We have so far assumed that the relative deadline of a task is equal to its period. Let us relax this assumption. If we do so, the RM algorithm is no longer an optimum static-priority scheduling algorithm. Consider first the case where the relative deadline is less than the period. Then, a moment's reflection shows that the necessary and sufficient condition for task T_i to be RM-schedulable is

$$W_i(t) = t \qquad \text{for some } t \in [0, d_i] \qquad (3.34)$$

The case $d_i > P_i$ is much harder. Let us begin by considering again our result that the worst-case response time of a task occurs when the task phasings are all zero. When $d_i \leq P_i$, at most one initiation of the same task can be alive at any one time. As a result, to check for schedulability it is sufficient to set the phasings of all members of the task set to zero and to check that the first initiation of each task meets its deadline. That is, in fact, the origin of RM-scheduling conditions **RM1** and **RM2**. When $d_i > P_i$, however, it is possible for multiple initiations of the same task to be alive simultaneously, and we might have to check a number of initiations to obtain the worst-case response time. To clarify this, consider the Example 3.13.

Example 3.13. Consider a case where $n = 2$, $e_1 = 28$, $e_2 = 71$, $P_1 = 80$, and $P_2 = 110$. Set all task deadlines to infinity. The following table shows the response times of task T_2.

Initiation	Completion time	Response time
0	127	127
110	226	116
220	353	133
330	452	122
440	551	111
550	678	128
660	777	117
770	876	106

As we can see, the worst response time is not for the first initiation, but for the third. This indicates that it is not sufficient just to consider the first initiation of all the tasks.

We must do some additional work before we can write down the schedulability condition for the $d_i > P_i$ case. In this case, more than one iteration of a task can be alive at any one time. As before, we assume that T_i has priority over T_j iff $P_i < P_j$; indeed, we number the tasks in the ascending order of their periods (and thus in the descending order of their priorities).

Let $S_i = \{T_1, \ldots, T_i\}$. We define the *level-i busy period* as the interval $[a, b]$ such that

- $b > a$
- only tasks in S_i are run in $[a, b]$,
- the processor is busy throughout $[a, b]$, and
- the processor is not executing any task from S_i just prior to a or just after b.

Example 3.14. Define $S_i = \{T_1, \ldots, T_i\}$ for $i = 1, \ldots, 5$. In the schedule in Figure 3.13 shows the five busy-period levels.

Theorem 3.5. Task T_i experiences its greatest response time during a level-i busy period, initiated with phasings $I_1 = \ldots = I_i = 0$.

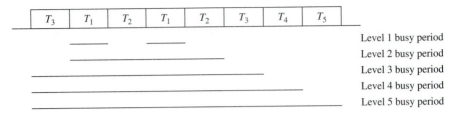

Level 1 busy period
Level 2 busy period
Level 3 busy period
Level 4 busy period
Level 5 busy period

FIGURE 3.13
Busy periods.

Proof. The proof is immediate for the highest-priority task, task T_1. So, consider tasks T_i, for $i > 1$ and, without loss of generality, assume that $I_1 = 0$. Suppose $[0, b)$ is a level-i busy period and $I_i > 0$. By the definition of busy period, only tasks of higher priority than T_i execute in the interval $[0, I_i)$. Decreasing I_i will not change the times at which these higher-priority tasks finish; all it will do is to increase the response time of T_i. Similarly, if $I_k > 0$ for some $k < i$, reducing I_k will either increase or leave unchanged the processing demands of T_k over the interval $[0, b)$. That is, reducing I_k will either increase or leave unchanged the finishing time of T_k. This completes the proof.   **Q.E.D.**

Thus, to determine RM-schedulability, we can continue to concentrate on the case where all phasings are zero. However, to ensure that task T_i meets its deadline, we must check that all its initiations in a level-i busy period beginning at time 0 meet their deadlines.

Let $t(k, i)$ be when the kth initiation (within the busy period) of task T_i completes execution. We leave for the reader to show that $t(k, i)$ is the minimum t for which the following expression holds:

$$t = \sum_{j=1}^{i-1} e_j \left\lceil \frac{t}{P_j} \right\rceil + k e_i \tag{3.35}$$

This kth initiation will meet its deadline if

$$t(k, i) < (k - 1) P_i + d_i \tag{3.36}$$

To what value of k should we check that the above condition holds to ensure that all iterations of T_i meet their deadline? We leave for the reader to show that it is sufficient to check that iterations 1 to ℓ_i meet their deadlines, where

$$\ell_i = \min\{m \,|\, m P_i > t(m, i)\} \tag{3.37}$$

Task T_i is thus RM-schedulable iff

$$t(k, i) < (k - 1) P_i + d_i, \qquad \forall k \le \ell_i \tag{3.38}$$

and the entire task set is RM-schedulable iff all the tasks in it are RM-schedulable.

Can we obtain a results similar to Theorem 3.3 for the case $d_i \ne P_i$? It is surprisingly difficult to do this and few results are known. We will state some of these without proof. Suppose we have a task set for which there exists a γ such that $d_i = \gamma P_i$, for all the tasks. Then it is possible to show the following result.

Theorem 3.6. Any set of n periodic tasks that fully utilizes the processor under RM must have a processor utilization of at least

$$
U = \begin{cases}
n\left(2^{1/n} - 1\right) & \text{if } \gamma = 1 \\[2ex]
\gamma(n-1)\left[\left(\dfrac{\gamma+1}{\gamma}\right)^{1/(n-1)} - 1\right] & \text{if } \gamma = 2, 3, \ldots \\[2ex]
\gamma & \text{if } 0 \le \gamma \le 0.5 \\[1ex]
\log_e(2\gamma) + 1 - \gamma & \text{if } 0.5 \le \gamma \le 1
\end{cases}
\tag{3.39}
$$

HANDLING CRITICAL SECTIONS. In our discussions so far, we have assumed that all tasks can be preempted at any point of their execution. However, sometimes tasks may need to access resources that cannot be shared. For example, a task may be writing to a block in memory. Until this is completed, no other task can access that block, either for reading or for writing. A task that is currently holding the unsharable resource is said to be in the *critical section* associated with the resource.

One way of ensuring exclusive access is to guard the critical sections with *binary semaphores*. These are like locks. When the semaphore is locked (e.g., by setting it to 1), it indicates that there is a task currently in the critical section. When a task seeks to enter a critical section, it checks if the corresponding semaphore is locked. If it is, the task is stopped and cannot proceed further until that semaphore is unlocked. If it is not, the task locks the semaphore and enters the critical section. When a task exits the critical section, it unlocks the corresponding semaphore. For convenience, we shall say that a critical section S is locked (unlocked) when we mean that the semaphore associated with S is locked (unlocked).

We will assume that critical sections are properly nested. That is, if we have sections S_1, S_2 on a single processor, the following sequence is allowed: Lock S_1. Lock S_2. Unlock S_2. Unlock S_1, while the following is not: Lock S_1. Lock S_2. Unlock S_1. Unlock S_2.

Everything in this section refers to tasks sharing a single processor. We assume that once a task starts, it continues until it (a) finishes, (b) is preempted by some higher-priority task, or (c) is blocked by some lower-priority task that holds the lock on a critical section that it needs. We do not, for example, consider a situation where a task suspends itself when executing I/O operations or when it encounters a page fault. The results of this section can easily be extended for this case, however (see Exercise 3.12).

It is possible for a lower-priority task T_L to block[2] a higher-priority task, T_H. This can happen when T_H needs to access a critical section that is currently

---

[2] When a lower-priority task is in the way of a higher-priority task, the former is said to *block* the latter.

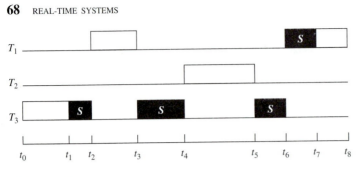

FIGURE 3.14
Priority inversion.

being accessed by T_L. Although T_H has higher priority than T_L, to ensure correct functioning, T_L must be allowed to complete its critical section access before T_H can access it.

Such blocking of a higher-priority task by a lower-priority task can have the unpleasant side effect of priority inversion. This is illustrated in Example 3.15.

Example 3.15. Consider tasks T_1, T_2, T_3, listed in descending order of priority, which share a processor. There is one critical section S that both T_1 and T_3 use. See Figure 3.14. T_3 begins execution at time t_0. At time t_1, it enters its critical section, S. T_1 is released at time t_2 and preempts T_3. It runs until t_3, when it tries to enter the critical section S. However, S is still locked by the suspended task T_3. So, T_1 is suspended and T_3 resumes execution. At time t_4, task T_2 is released. T_2 has higher priority than T_3, and so it preempts T_3. T_2 does not need S and runs to completion at t_5. After T_2 completes execution at t_5, T_3 resumes and exits critical section S at t_6. T_1 can now preempt T_3 and enter the critical section.

Notice that although T_2 is of lower priority than T_1, it was able to delay T_1 indirectly (by preempting T_3, which was blocking T_1). This phenomenon is known as *priority inversion*. Ideally, the system should have noted that T_1 was waiting for access, and so T_2 should not have been allowed to start executing at t_4.

The use of *priority inheritance* allows us to avoid the problem of priority inversion. Under this scheme, if a higher-priority task T_H is blocked by a lower-priority task T_L (because T_L is currently executing a critical section needed by T_H), the lower-priority task temporarily inherits the priority of T_H. When the blocking ceases, T_L resumes its original priority. The protocol is described in Figure 3.15. Example 3.16 shows how this prevents priority inversion from happening.

Example 3.16. Let us return to Example 3.15 to see how priority inheritance prevents priority inversion. At time t_3, when T_3 blocks T_1, T_3 inherits the higher priority of T_1. So, when T_2 is released at t_4, it cannot interrupt T_3. As a result, T_1 is not indirectly blocked by T_2.

1. The highest-priority task T is assigned the processor. T relinquishes the processor whenever it seeks to lock the semaphore guarding a critical section that is already locked by some other job.

2. If a task T_1 is blocked by T_2 (due to contention for a critical section) and $T_1 \succ T_2$, task T_2 inherits the priority of T_1 as long as it blocks T_1. When T_2 exits the critical section that caused the block, it reverts to the priority it had when it entered that section. The operations of priority inheritance and the resumption of previous priority are indivisible.

3. Priority inheritance is transitive. If T_3 blocks T_2, which blocks T_1 (with $T_1 \succ T_2 \succ T_3$), then T_3 inherits the priority of T_1 through T_2.

4. A task T_1 can preempt another task T_2 if T_1 is not blocked and if the current priority of T_1 is greater than that of the current priority of T_2.

FIGURE 3.15
The priority inheritance protocol.

Unfortunately, priority inheritance can lead to deadlock. This is illustrated by Example 3.17.

Example 3.17. Consider two tasks T_1 and T_2, which use two critical sections S_1 and S_2. These tasks require the critical sections in the following sequence:

T_1: Lock S_1. Lock S_2. Unlock S_2. Unlock S_1.
T_2: Lock S_2. Lock S_1. Unlock S_1. Unlock S_2.

Let $T_1 \succ T_2$, and suppose T_2 starts execution at t_0. At time t_1, it locks S_2. At time t_2, T_1 is initiated and it preempts T_2 owing to its higher priority. At time t_3, T_1 locks S_1. At time t_4, T_1 attempts to lock S_2, but is blocked because T_2 has not finished with it. T_2, which now inherits the priority of T_1, starts executing. However, when at time t_5 it tries to lock S_1, it cannot do so since T_1 has a lock on it. Both T_1 and T_2 are now *deadlocked*.

There is another drawback of priority inheritance. It is possible for the highest-priority task to be blocked once by every other task executing on the same processor. (The reader is invited in Exercise 3.8 to construct an example of this.)

To get around both problems, we define the priority ceiling protocol. The *priority ceiling* of a semaphore is the highest priority of any task that may lock it. Let $P(T)$ denote the priority of task T, and $P(S)$ the priority ceiling of the semaphore of critical section S.

Example 3.18. Consider a three-task system T_1, T_2, T_3, with $T_1 \succ T_2 \succ T_3$. There are four critical sections, and the following table indicates which tasks may lock which sections, and the resultant priority ceilings.

Critical section	Accessed by	Priority ceiling
S_1	T_1, T_2	$P(T_1)$
S_2	T_1, T_2, T_3	$P(T_1)$
S_3	T_3	$P(T_3)$
S_4	T_2, T_3	$P(T_2)$

The priority ceiling protocol is the same as the priority inheritance protocol, except that a task can also be blocked from entering a critical section if there exists any semaphore currently held by some other task whose priority ceiling is greater than or equal to the priority of T.

Example 3.19. Consider the tasks and critical sections mentioned in Example 3.18. Suppose that T_2 currently holds a lock on S_2, and task that T_1 is initiated. T_1 will be blocked from entering S_1 because its priority is not greater than the priority ceiling of S_2.

The priority ceiling protocol is specified in Figure 3.16. The key properties of the priority ceiling protocol are as follows:

P1. The priority ceiling protocol prevents deadlocks.

P2. Let B_i be the set of all critical sections that can cause the blocking of task T and $t(x)$ be the time taken for section x to be executed. Then, T will be blocked for at most $\max_{x \in B_i} t(x)$.

---

1. The highest-priority task, T, is assigned the processor. T relinquishes the processor (i.e., it is blocked) whenever it seeks to lock the semaphore guarding a critical section which is already locked by some other task Q (in which case it is said to be blocked by task Q), or when there exists a semaphore S' locked by some other task, whose priority ceiling is greater than or equal to the priority of T. In the latter case, let S^* be the semaphore with the highest priority among those locked by some other tasks. We say that T is blocked on S^*, and by the task currently holding the lock on S^*.

2. Suppose T blocks one or more tasks. Then, it inherits the priority of the highest-priority task that it is currently blocking. The operations of priority inheritance and resumption of previous priority are indivisible.

3. Priority inheritance is transitive.

4. A task T_1 can preempt another task T_2 if T_2 does not hold a critical section which T_1 currently needs, and if the current priority of T_1 is greater than that of the current priority of T_2.

FIGURE 3.16
The priority ceiling protocol.

Priority ceiling property **P2** allows us to conduct a schedulability analysis on systems using the priority ceiling protocol. Take, for example, the rate-monotonic scheduling algorithm that we discussed earlier in this section. We can revise Theorem 3.6 as follows (here we use T_i to denote both the task and its period—which one it represents is obvious from the context):

Theorem 3.7. Any set of n periodic processes that fully utilizes the processor under RM must have, for each $i \in \{1, \ldots, n\}$

$$\frac{e_1}{T_1} + \frac{e_2}{T_2} + \cdots + \frac{e_i}{T_i} + \frac{b_i}{T_i} \le i(2^{1/i} - 1)$$

where $b_i = \max_{x \in B_i} t(x)$.

Proof. The proof is left to the reader as an exercise.

As a result of Theorem 3.7, we know that task T_i can be scheduled under the RM algorithm to meet its deadline if

$$\frac{e_1}{T_1} + \frac{e_2}{T_2} + \cdots + \frac{e_i}{T_i} + \frac{b_i}{T_i} \le i(2^{1/i} - 1).$$

The necessary and sufficient conditions for RM-schedulability can be similarly written.

MATHEMATICAL UNDERPINNINGS OF THE PRIORITY CEILING ALGORITHM.* To prove that priority ceiling properties **P1** and **P2** hold, we will need the following series of results.

Lemma 3.3. Task T_1 can only be blocked by a lower-priority task T_2 if T_2 is in a critical section at the time that T_1 arrives.

Proof. If T_2 is not in a critical section when T_1 arrives, it will be preempted and will never regain the processor until after T_1 leaves.   **Q.E.D.**

Lemma 3.4. Task T_1 can only be blocked by a lower-priority task T_2 if the priority of T_1 is no greater than the greatest priority of all the semaphores currently locked by all lower-priority tasks.

Proof. This follows immediately from the definition of the priority ceiling protocol.   **Q.E.D.**

Lemma 3.5. Suppose that task T_2 is currently executing critical section S_2, and that it is preempted by a higher-priority task T_1 that then executes critical section S_1. It is impossible for T_2 to inherit a priority greater than or equal to that of T_1, until T_1 finishes execution.

Proof. T_1 can only execute S_1 if

$$P(T_1) > \text{ceil}(S_2) \tag{3.40}$$

T_2 can only inherit the priority of some task T if T is being blocked on S_2. But then,

$$\text{ceil}(S_2) \geq P(T) \tag{3.41}$$

It follows from Equations (3.40) and (3.41) that

$$P(T_1) > P(T) \tag{3.42}$$

Q.E.D.

Lemma 3.6. The priority ceiling protocol prevents transitive blocking.

Proof. Again, we prove the result by contradiction. Let the lemma be false. Then there must exist tasks T_1, T_2, T_3 such that $T_1 \succ T_2 \succ T_3$ and where T_3 blocks T_2, which blocks T_1. But this would mean that T_3 would inherit the priority of T_1. This contradicts Lemma 3.5.   **Q.E.D.**

We now have the means to prove property **P1**.

Theorem 3.8. The priority ceiling protocol prevents deadlocks.

Proof. Deadlock can only occur if we have a cycle of n tasks each blocking on the one in front of it; see the example in Figure 3.17. (We are assuming that a task never deadlocks with itself.) Since we have shown in Lemma 3.6 that transitive blocking is impossible, the largest cycle we can have consists of just two tasks (i.e., $n = 2$). Assume that T_2 is preempted by T_1 when T_2 is in a set of critical sections σ_2. Suppose that then T_1 enters some critical section S_1. This can only happen if no member $S_2 \in \sigma_2$ is ever required by T_1 itself (otherwise S_2 would have priority equal to that of T_1 and T_1 would not be allowed to enter any critical section as long as T_2 was holding S_2). Thus there is no possibility of a deadlock.   **Q.E.D.**

In the following, let $T_1 \succ T_2$, and $B_{1,2}$ be the set of critical sections of T_2 that can block T_1. Let $b_{1,2}$ be the critical section in $B_{1,2}$ that takes the longest time to execute.

Lemma 3.7. T_1 can be blocked by T_2 by at most $b_{1,2}$.

Proof. Since $T_1 \succ T_2$, T_1 can only be blocked by T_2 if T_2 is executing a critical section in $B_{1,2}$, deadlock is not possible (by Theorem 3.8). T_2 (which will inherit the priority of T_1) will exit that critical section within at most $b_{1,2}$ unless it is preempted by some task $T \succ T_1$. If such a preemption happens, T_1 will no longer be blocked by T_2. If no such preemption occurs, T_2 will exit T_2 within at most $b_{1,2}$ and not resume execution until T_1 has completed execution.   **Q.E.D.**

We are now ready to prove that property **P2** holds. To facilitate this, define β_i as the set of all critical sections used by tasks T_j such that $T_i \succ T_j$. Define b_i as the greatest execution time of any critical section in β_i.

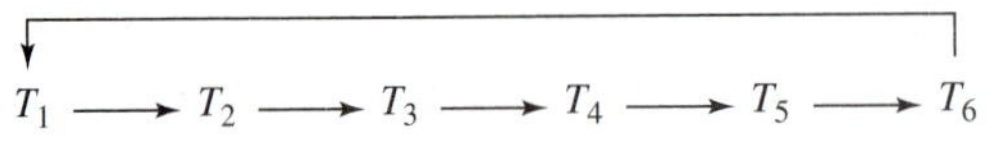

$T_1 \longrightarrow T_2 \longrightarrow T_3 \longrightarrow T_4 \longrightarrow T_5 \longrightarrow T_6$

FIGURE 3.17
Six-task deadlocked system; the arrows indicate a "waiting-for" relationship.

Theorem 3.9. Task T_i can be blocked by at most one lower-priority task, and for a duration of at most b_i.

Proof. We prove this result by contradiction. Suppose task T_i can be blocked by more than b_i. This can only happen if it is blocked by $n > 1$ distinct tasks (since we know from Lemma 3.7 that T_i can be blocked at most once by any one lower-priority task).

Suppose that T_i is blocked by T_1 and T_2. Assume, without loss of generality, that $T_1 \succ T_2$. Of course, $T_i \succ T_1$ and $T_i \succ T_2$. Suppose T_i is blocked by T_1 in S_1 and by T_2 in S_2. (If either or both of these tasks is in a nested set of semaphores, focus on the outermost one). Then, T_1 and T_2 must have been in S_1 and S_2, respectively, when T_i arrived. Furthermore, T_2 must have been in S_2 when T_1 arrived.

Since T_1 enters S_1 with T_2 in S_2, we must have

$$P(T_1) > \text{ceil}(S_2) \tag{3.43}$$

Since T_i is blocked by T_1 on S_1, we must have

$$P(T_i) \le \text{ceil}(S_1) \tag{3.44}$$

Similarly, since T_i is blocked by T_2 on S_2,

$$P(T_i) \le \text{ceil}(S_2) \tag{3.45}$$

But, this implies that

$$P(T_1) > P(T_i) \tag{3.46}$$

which is a contradiction. **Q.E.D.**

3.2.2 Preemptive Earliest Deadline First (EDF) Algorithm

A processor following the EDF algorithm always executes the task whose absolute deadline is the earliest. EDF is a *dynamic-priority* scheduling algorithm; the task priorities are not fixed but change depending on the closeness of their absolute deadline. EDF is also called the deadline-monotonic scheduling algorithm.

Example 3.20. Consider the following set of (aperiodic) task arrivals to a system.

Task	Arrival time	Execution time	Absolute deadline
T_1	0	10	30
T_2	4	3	10
T_3	5	10	25

When T_1 arrives, it is the only task waiting to run, and so starts executing immediately. T_2 arrives at time 4; since $d_2 < d_1$, it has higher priority than T_1 and preempts it. T_3 arrives at time 5; however, since $d_3 > d_2$, it has lower priority than T_2 and must wait for T_2 to finish. When T_2 finishes (at time 7), T_3 starts (since it has higher priority than T_1). T_3 runs until 15, at which point T_1 can resume and run to completion.

In our treatment of the EDF algorithm, we will make all the assumptions we made for the RM algorithm, except that the tasks do not have to be periodic.

EDF is an optimal uniprocessor scheduling algorithm. That is, if EDF cannot feasibly schedule a task set on a uniprocessor, there is no other scheduling algorithm that can.

If all the tasks are periodic and have relative deadlines equal to their periods, the test for task-set schedulability is particularly simple:

> If the total utilization of the task set is no greater than 1, the task set can be feasibly scheduled on a single processor by the EDF algorithm.

There is no simple schedulability test corresponding to the case where the relative deadlines do not all equal the periods; in such a case, we actually have to develop a schedule using the EDF algorithm to see if all deadlines are met over a given interval of time. The following is a schedulability test for EDF under this case.

Define $u = \sum_{i=1}^{n}(e_i/P_i)$, $d_{\max} = \max_{1 \leq i \leq n}\{d_i\}$ and $P = \text{lcm}(P_1, \ldots P_n)$. (Here "lcm" stands for least common multiple.) Define $h_T(t)$ to be the sum of the execution times of all tasks in set T whose absolute deadlines are less than t. A task set of n tasks is not EDF-feasible iff

- $u > 1$ or
- there exists

$$t < \min\left\{P + d_{\max}, \quad \frac{u}{1-u}\max_{1 \leq i \leq n}\{P_i - d_i\}\right\}$$

such that $h_T(t) > t$.

MATHEMATICAL UNDERPINNINGS.[*] As we said earlier, EDF is an optimal uniprocessor scheduling algorithm (i.e., if a set of tasks cannot be feasibly scheduled under EDF, there is no other uniprocessor algorithm that can feasibly schedule them).

Theorem 3.10. EDF is optimal for uniprocessors.

Proof. The proof is by contradiction. Assume that the theorem is not true and that there is some other algorithm Σ that is optimal. Then, there must exist some set of tasks S such that S is Σ-schedulable but not EDF-schedulable. Let us focus on this set S.

Suppose that t_2 is the earliest absolute deadline that is missed by the EDF algorithm. Define t_1 as the last instant, prior to t_2, at which EDF had the processor working on a task whose absolute deadline exceeded t_2. If no such instant exists, set $t_1 = 0$. Since only tasks with absolute deadlines $\leq t_2$ are scheduled by EDF in the interval $[t_1, t_2]$, any task executing in that interval must have been released at or after t_1. The reason is that at t_1, the processor was executing a task with an absolute deadline $> t_2$, which would only have been possible under EDF if there was no pending task at t_1 with an absolute deadline $\leq t_2$.

Define

$$A = \{T_i | T_i \text{ is released in } [t_1, t_2] \text{ and } D_i < t_2\}$$

$$B = \{T_i | T_i \text{ is released in } [t_1, t_2] \text{ and } D_i \geq t_2\}$$

By the definition of t_2, B is nonempty. Also by the definition of the t_2, all the deadlines of the tasks in A are met by both EDF and Σ. We have two cases.

Case 1. Under EDF, the processor is continuously busy over $[t_1, t_2]$.

Let $E^{\text{EDF}}(A)$, $E^{\text{EDF}}(B)$, $E^{\Sigma}(A)$, $E^{\Sigma}(B)$ be the execution time over $(t_1, t_2]$ allocated by EDF and Σ to the tasks in A and B, respectively. Then,

$$E^{\text{EDF}}(A) + E^{\text{EDF}}(B) = t_2 - t_1 \qquad (3.47)$$

Since all the deadlines of the tasks in A are met by both EDF and Σ,

$$E^{\text{EDF}}(A) = E^{\Sigma}(A) \qquad (3.48)$$

However, since at least one task in B misses its deadline under EDF, we must have

$$E^{\text{EDF}}(B) < E^{\Sigma}(B) \qquad (3.49)$$

Hence, in the interval $(t_1, t_2]$, under Σ, the processor is used for

$$E^{\Sigma}(A) + E^{\Sigma}(B) > E^{\text{EDF}}(A) + E^{\text{EDF}}(B) \quad \text{[from (3.48) and (3.49)]}$$

$$= t_2 - t_1 \qquad \text{[from (3.47)]} \qquad (3.50)$$

But that is plainly impossible, and we have a contradiction.

Case 2. Under EDF, the processor is idle over some part of $(t_1, t_2]$.

Let t_3 be the last instant in $(t_1, t_2]$ at which the processor is idle under the EDF discipline. Since EDF causes a deadline to be missed at t_2, $t_3 < t_2$.

The processor can only be idle at t_3 if there are no pending requests for execution, that is, if every task released prior to t_3 has been executed. The argument we made in Case 1 over the interval $(t_1, t_2]$ now applies over the interval $(t_3, t_2]$, and so here too we have a contradiction. This completes the proof. **Q.E.D.**

Let us now turn to periodic task sets. We will first consider the case where for every task the relative deadline equals the task period, and show that the necessary and sufficient condition for a task set to be schedulable is $\sum_{i=1}^{n} e_i / P_i \leq 1$. To begin with, as with the RM algorithm, it is sufficient to consider the case where all the task phasings are zero. We then proceed in two steps. First, we show that if a deadline is indeed missed under EDF, the processor will be continuously busy from time 0 to when it missed the deadline. This tells us the amount of work that the processor has completed up to that time. We can then use this information to show that if $\sum_{i=1}^{n} e_i/P_i \le 1$, all deadlines will indeed be satisfied. In what follows, we will assume that all task phasings are zero.

Lemma 3.8. If a deadline is missed for the first time at t_f, the processor is continuously busy throughout the interval $[0, t_f]$.

Proof. We proceed by contradiction. Suppose this lemma is not true and that the processor was idle at some time within the interval $[0, t_f]$ when all the task phasings are 0 (i.e., the first iteration of each task is released at time 0). Let t_1 be the last such time; that is, the processor was idle at t_1, but busy in the interval $(t_1, t_f]$.

If the processor was idle at t_1, it must be that all the tasks released prior to t_1 have been completed by t_1. Therefore, all tasks executing in the interval $(t_1, t_f]$ must have been released in that interval and no task released prior to t_1 will affect the scheduling in $(t_1, t_f]$ (since all such tasks have completed and left the system). Now, construct a new task phasing so that every task has one iteration released at t_1. (See Figure 3.18). Under this case, also, a deadline will be missed; in particular,

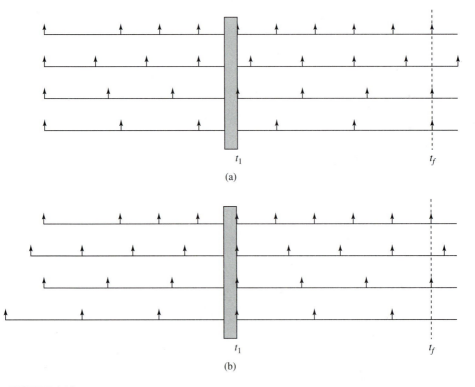

(a)

(b)

FIGURE 3.18
Lemma 3.8: (a) schedule with zero phasing; (b) schedule with new phasing. The processor is idle over the shaded portions.

it will be missed at time $t' \leq t_f$. Also, the processor cannot be idle at any time in $(t_1, t']$ under this new task phasing. (Why?)

Now, compare the situation under the new task phasing over the interval $(t_1, t_f]$ with the situation under the zero task phasing over the interval $(0, t_1]$. The load presented to the processor at time t_1 is the same under the new task phasing as it was at time 0 under the zero task phasing. But, we have argued that under the new phasing, the processor will be busy throughout $(t_1, t']$, and miss a deadline at t'. Therefore, under the zero task phasing the processor cannot have been idle before the deadline was missed. We therefore have a contradiction and the lemma is proved. **Q.E.D.**

Now, we are ready to prove Theorem 3.11, which contains the necessary and sufficient condition:

Theorem 3.11. Suppose we have a set of n periodic tasks, each of whose relative deadline equals its period. They can be feasibly scheduled by EDF iff

$$\sum_{i=1}^{n} (e_i/P_i) \leq 1$$

Proof. Proving that scheduling is impossible if $\sum_{i=1}^{n}(e_i/P_i) > 1$ is the easy part—we simply show that the processor utilization would have to exceed 1, which is impossible. Suppose that $\sum_{i=1}^{n}(e_i/P_i) > 1$. Let P be the least common multiple (lcm) of $\{P_1, \ldots, P_n\}$ and $\ell_i = P/P_i$. Then, over the interval $[kP, (k+1)P]$, $k = 0, 1, \ldots$, the processor will receive requests for a total of

$$\sum_{i=1}^{n} \ell_i e_i = P \left\{ \sum_{i=1}^{n} \frac{e_i}{P_i} \right\} > P \qquad (3.51)$$

units of work. Requests for processor time thus arrive at a higher rate than they can be met and the unfinished work will pile up without limit as time goes on. Hence, the task set cannot be feasibly scheduled if $\sum_{i=1}^{n}(e_i/P_i) > 1$.

Next we must prove that if $\sum_{i=1}^{n}(e_i/P_i) \leq 1$, EDF will indeed schedule successfully. This is a little harder and we proceed by contradiction. Suppose that this theorem is not true and that there exists some task set S of n tasks that are not EDF-schedulable, despite $\sum_{i=1}^{n}(e_i/P_i) \leq 1$. Let t_f be the earliest time at which a deadline is missed. Since the set of tasks is finite, such an earliest time does exist and $t_f > 0$. Let S_f denote the set of tasks in S with an absolute deadline equal to t_f.

From Lemma 3.8, we know that the processor must be busy throughout the interval $[0, t_f]$. There are now two cases to consider:

Case 1. None of the tasks executed in $[0, t_f]$ have absolute deadlines beyond t_f. The number of iterations of task T_i that have to be completed in $[0, t_f]$ is $\lfloor t_f/P_i \rfloor$, since all other iterations have absolute deadlines expiring after t_f. But the processor is busy throughout the interval $[0, t_f]$. Hence, it must be that the tasks whose absolute deadlines were less than t_f imposed a demand of an execution time of more than t_f on the processor. In other words, we must have:

$$\left\lfloor \frac{t_f}{P_1} \right\rfloor e_1 + \left\lfloor \frac{t_f}{P_2} \right\rfloor e_2 + \cdots + \left\lfloor \frac{t_f}{P_n} \right\rfloor e_n > t_f$$

$$\Rightarrow \left(\frac{t_f}{P_1} \right) e_1 + \left(\frac{t_f}{P_2} \right) e_2 + \cdots + \left(\frac{t_f}{P_n} \right) e_n > t_f$$

$$\Rightarrow \sum_{i=1}^{n} \frac{e_i}{P_i} > 1 \tag{3.52}$$

which contradicts the assumption that $\sum_{i=1}^{n} (e_i/P_i) \leq 1$.

Case 2. Some tasks executed in the interval $[0, t_f]$ have absolute deadlines beyond t_f. We handle this much as we handled Lemma 3.8. Let τ be the last time before t_f that a task with absolute deadline greater than t_f was executed. Since we are using the EDF algorithm, if such a task was being executed at τ, there must be, at time τ, no tasks awaiting service that have absolute deadlines expiring at or before t_f. Thus, all the tasks that are executed in the interval $[\tau, t_f]$ must be released in that interval. But since a deadline was missed, we must have that the total demand upon the processor during that interval was greater than the length of that interval. In other words, we must have:

$$\left\lfloor \frac{(t_f - \tau)}{P_1} \right\rfloor e_1 + \left\lfloor \frac{(t_f - \tau)}{P_2} \right\rfloor e_2 + \cdots + \left\lfloor \frac{(t_f - \tau)}{P_n} \right\rfloor e_n > t_f - \tau$$

$$\Rightarrow \left[\frac{(t_f - \tau)}{P_1} \right] e_1 + \left[\frac{(t_f - \tau)}{P_2} \right] e_2 + \cdots + \left[\frac{(t_f - \tau)}{P_n} \right] e_n > t_f - \tau$$

$$\Rightarrow \sum_{i=1}^{n} \frac{e_i}{P_i} > 1 \tag{3.53}$$

which is a contradiction.

This completes the proof.   **Q.E.D.**

Theorem 3.11 allows us to quickly check the feasibility of any allocation when the relative task deadlines equal their periods. Unfortunately, there is no efficient way to check feasibility if the relative deadlines do not all equal their periods or if there are sporadic tasks. In order to verify schedulability, we have to actually schedule the task set using EDF and then check if all the deadlines have been satisfied. Since we can't check schedulability for an infinite number of cases, we must obtain a *finiteness* result, which says that if deadlines are ever missed the time of the earliest missed deadline will have a known upper bound. Then we only need to check feasibility up to that point.

Just as with the RM algorithm, it is easy to show that the worst-case execution time of a task occurs when all the task phasings are zero. So, if we verify schedulability for this case, it will hold for all task phasings.

For the finiteness result, we define $u = \sum_{i=1}^{n}(e_i/P_i)$, $d_{\max} = \max_{1 \le i \le n}\{d_i\}$ and $P = \text{lcm}(P_1, \ldots P_n)$. Define $h_T(t)$ to be the sum of the execution times of all the tasks in set T whose absolute deadlines are less than or equal to t.

Theorem 3.12. A task set of n tasks is not EDF-feasible iff

- $u > 1$ or
- there exists

$$t < \min \left\{ P + d_{\max}, \ \frac{u}{1-u} \max_{1 \le i \le n} \{P_i - d_i\} \right\}$$

such that $h_T(t) > t$.

Under this theorem, we only need to check for feasibility up to some finite time. We can build the proof of Theorem 3.12 using the following series of lemmas.

Lemma 3.9. A given set T of periodic tasks is not EDF-schedulable iff there exists some time t such that $h_T(t) > t$.

Proof. This has been left to the reader.

Lemma 3.10. Given a set T of n periodic tasks, if $u \le 1$,

$$h_T(t + P) > t + P \Rightarrow h_T(t) > t \qquad \text{for all } t \ge d_{\max}$$

Proof

$$
\begin{aligned}
h_T(t) + P &= \sum_{i=1}^{n} e_i \left(\left\lfloor \frac{t - d_i}{P_i} \right\rfloor + 1 \right) + P \\
&\ge \sum_{i=1}^{n} e_i \left(\left\lfloor \frac{t - d_i}{P_i} \right\rfloor + 1 \right) + P \sum_{i=1}^{n} \frac{e_i}{P_i} \\
&= \sum_{i=1}^{n} e_i \left(\left\lfloor \frac{t - d_i + P}{P_i} \right\rfloor + 1 \right) \qquad \text{since } P \text{ is a multiple of } P_i \\
&= h_T(t + P)
\end{aligned}
$$

Hence,

$$h_T(t + P) > t + P \Rightarrow h_T(t) > t \qquad\qquad (3.54)$$

Q.E.D.

Lemma 3.11. If task set T is not EDF-feasible and $u \le 1$, then there exists $t < P + d_{\max}$ such that $h_T(t) > t$.

Proof. Follows immediately from Lemma 3.10. **Q.E.D.**

Lemma 3.12. Suppose T is not feasible and $u \leq 1$. Then $h_T(t) > t$ implies

$$t < d_{\max} \quad \text{or} \quad t < \max_{1 \leq i \leq n}\{P_i - d_i\}\frac{u}{1 - u}$$

Proof. Suppose that $t > d_{\max}$. We have

$$h_T(t) \leq \sum_{i=1}^{n} e_i \frac{t - d_i + P_i}{P_i}$$

$$= t\sum_{i=1}^{n} \frac{e_i}{P_i} + \sum_{i=1}^{n} \frac{P_i - d_i}{P_i}$$

$$\leq \sum_{i=1}^{n}\left[\frac{e_i}{P_i}\left(t + \max_{1 \leq i \leq n}\{P_i - d_i\}\right)\right] \quad (3.55)$$

If $h_T(t) > t$, we will have from (3.55),

$$t < \sum_{i=1}^{n} \frac{e_i}{P_i}\left(t + \max_{1 \leq i \leq n}\{P_i - d_i\}\right)$$

$$\Rightarrow t < \max_{1 \leq i \leq n}\{P_i - d_i\}\frac{u}{1 - u} \quad (3.56)$$

Q.E.D.

3.2.3 Allowing for Precedence and Exclusion Conditions*

We have assumed in the above sections that tasks are independent and are always preemptible by other tasks. We will now relax both these assumptions and present several scheduling heuristics.

Consider a set of tasks with a precedence graph, which are released at time 0. A deadline is specified for each task. It is assumed that the deadlines are chosen so that even if a task completes at its deadline, there will be enough time to execute its children in the task graph by their deadlines. If all the tasks that form a task graph are assigned to the same processor, then we can use the algorithm in Figure 3.19.

Example 3.21. Consider the task graph shown in Figure 3.20a, where the task execution times and deadlines are as follows:

Task T_i	e_i	d_i	Task T_i	e_i	D_i
1	3	6	2	3	7
3	2	20	4	5	21
5	6	27	6	6	28

Tasks are numbered so that $D_1 \leq D_2 \leq \ldots \leq D_n$.
1. Schedule task T_n in the interval $[D_n - e_n, D_n]$.
2. while `all the tasks have not been scheduled` do
   Let A be the set of as-yet-unscheduled tasks all of whose successors,
   if any, have been scheduled.
   Schedule task $T_k, k = \max\{m | m \in A\}$ as late as possible.
   end do
3. Move the tasks forward to the extent possible, keeping
   their order of execution as specified in step 2.

FIGURE 3.19
Algorithm PREC1.

The schedule as generated upon the completion of step 2 is shown in Figure 3.20b, and after moving the tasks forward in step 3 is shown in Figure 3.20c.

An interesting variation on the standard problem is scheduling with AND/OR constraints. In the standard problem, all the precedents of a task must be completed before that task can begin. In the AND/OR system, there are two types of tasks, AND tasks and OR tasks. AND tasks cannot commence computing before all their precedents have completed. OR tasks can commence after any one of their precedents has completed.

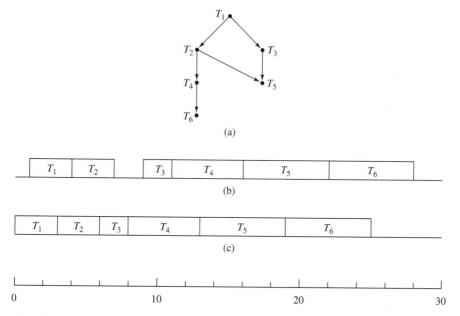

FIGURE 3.20
Example of algorithm PREC1: (a) task graph; (b) schedule after step 2 applies; (c) schedule after step 3 applies.

while A = set of all OR tasks is nonempty do:
    Choose task $T_i \in A$ none of whose precedents is an OR task.
    Find k such that $L(k) \leq L(j)$ for all $j \in \mathbf{P}_i$.
    In G, remove all edges terminating in T_i, except for the one from T_k.
    Relabel T_i as an AND task.
end do

FIGURE 3.21
Algorithm MINPATH.

Before presenting the scheduling heuristic for this problem, we first introduce some notation. Let $\mathbf{P}_i$ denote the set of all the immediate predecessors of task T_i according to the precedence graph, G. That is, if $T_k \in \mathbf{P}_i$, there is an edge from node T_k to node T_i in G. Define

$$L(i) = \begin{cases} e_i & \text{if } T_i \text{ has no precedents} \\ e_i + \max\{L(k)|T_k \in \mathbf{P}_i\} & \text{otherwise} \end{cases} \qquad (3.57)$$

The minimum path algorithm, MINPATH, shown in Figure 3.21, reduces the AND/OR problem to the standard problem (consisting only of AND tasks) by suitably pruning the precedence graph. Scheduling can then be completed by using, for example, PREC1 or some other algorithm.

> **Example 3.22.** Consider a set of eight tasks with execution times 5, 6, 8, 1, 2, 4, 1, 2, respectively. Tasks T_6, T_7, T_8 are OR tasks. The precedence graph and the graph as pruned by MINPATH are shown in Figure 3.22.

Let us now consider a more powerful and complex heuristic to handle precedence conditions. This algorithm enumerates the schedules that are possible under preemption or precedence limitations until we arrive at a feasible schedule. In the worst case, we might have to enumerate every possible schedule before finding a feasible schedule. However, simulation experiments have indicated that most of the time this algorithm finds a feasible schedule (assuming one exists) well before it has enumerated all the possible schedules.

Our task model is as follows. We have a set of tasks, $T = \{T_1, T_2, \ldots, T_n\}$. For each task T_i we are given the worst-case execution time e_i, the deadline d_i, and the release time r_i. In addition, we are given the following relations between every pair of tasks:

- T_i PRECEDES T_j is TRUE if T_i is in the precedence set of T_j, that is, if T_j needs the output of T_i and we cannot start executing T_j until T_i has finished executing.
- T_i EXCLUDES T_j is TRUE if T_i is not allowed to preempt T_j.
- T_i PREEMPTS T_j is TRUE if, when T_i is ready to run and T_j is currently running, T_j is always preempted by T_i.

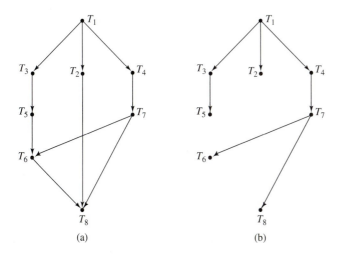

FIGURE 3.22
Task graph transformation by MINPATH: (a) original graph; (b) pruned graph. The node numbers are the task numbers.

Initially, we start with a set of PRECEDES and EXCLUDES relations as given by the set of tasks to be scheduled. The PREEMPT relation is initially empty. Clearly, some relations between a given pair of tasks are inconsistent with some other relations. For example, we cannot have both (T_i PRECEDES T_j) and (T_j PRECEDES T_i). We cannot have both (T_i PRECEDES T_j) and (T_j PREEMPTS T_i). The reader is invited to generate a few more examples of inconsistent relations.

A task is said to be *eligible* to run if it has been released and if all its precedent tasks have completed execution. We also define the *modified release time* of each task as follows.

$$r_i' = \begin{cases} r_i & \text{if no task PRECEDES } T_i \\ \max\{r_i, r_j' + e_j | T_j \text{PRECEDES} T_i\} & \text{otherwise} \end{cases} \tag{3.58}$$

Example 3.23. Figure 3.23 shows the task graph for a four-task set, where the execution and modified release times are:

Task	e_i	r_i	r_i'
0	5	0	0
1	4	1	5
2	9	10	10
3	3	11	19

This algorithm proceeds by first generating a valid initial schedule. If this solution meets all deadlines, we are done. If not, then we try to modify the schedule in order to minimize the extent to which deadlines are missed.

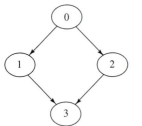

FIGURE 3.23
Example of modified release times.

A task T_i is said to be eligible to run at time t if the following properties are satisfied:

- all tasks T_j such that T_j PRECEDES T_i have completed by time t,
- T_i has not yet been completed by time t, and
- there is no as-yet-unfinished task T_k that was started before t, and such that T_k EXCLUDES T_i.

A schedule is said to be *valid* if it satisfies the following properties:

V1. The processor is not idle if there are one or more tasks that are ready to run.
V2. Exclusion, precedence, and preemption constraints are all satisfied throughout the schedule.

Within the context of these constraints, the EDF algorithm is used. If two tasks are both eligible to run (under the constraints) and have identical deadlines, the tie is broken on the basis of which one has the greater execution time. That is, an eligible task T_j will not run if there is a task T_i that is as yet unfinished but eligible to run, such that:

- T_i PREEMPTS T_j,
- $[d_i < d_j]$ and $\neg$ $[T_j$ PREEMPTS $T_i]$,[3] and
- $[d_i = d_j]$ and $\neg$ $[T_j$ PREEMPTS $T_i]$ and $e_i > e_j$.

Example 3.24. It is important to realize that validity property **V1** may not be optimal when there are tasks that cannot be preempted. To see this, consider the task set $T = \{T_1, T_2\}$, such that T_2 EXCLUDES T_1 and T_1 EXCLUDES T_2. Suppose $D_1 = 10, D_2 = 20, r_1 = 1, r_2 = 0, e_1 = 5$, and $e_2 = 10$. Assume that there are no precedence constraints. Then, when T_2 arrives at time 0, it starts executing. T_1 arrives at time 1, but cannot preempt T_2; it has to wait until T_2 finishes at time 5. By then, it is too late: T_1 simply does not have enough time to finish executing before its deadline. By contrast, if the processor is kept idle over the interval $[0, 1]$, it can execute first T_1 and then T_2, and meet the deadlines of both tasks. See Figure 3.24.

---

[3] $\neg$ stands for logical NOT.

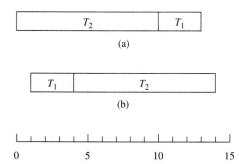

FIGURE 3.24
Example of a scheduling anomaly: (a) an infeasible schedule; (b) a reordered, and feasible, schedule.

The algorithm for generating a valid initial schedule is outlined in Figure 3.25. $f(i)$ is defined as the finishing time of task T_i in the schedule.

Example 3.25. Consider a four-task system with the following parameters:

	T_1	T_2	T_3	T_4
r_i	1	0	14	13
e_i	1	10	2	3
D_i	5	30	18	25

Suppose no precedence conditions exist, and that the only EXCLUDE relation is T_2 EXCLUDES T_1. Then, the valid initial schedule will be generated as follows. Task T_2 is released at time 0, and is scheduled to start running at that point. The next point to be examined is time 1 T_1 arrives and is prevented from preempting T_2 due to the EXCLUDES relation. The third point to be examined is time 10, when T_2 finishes. At this time, task T_1 is started and runs until 11. The processor is then idle until 13, when it starts executing T_4. T_3 arrives at 14 and, because it has an earlier deadline, it

---

$t = 0$
while (there are still unfinished tasks) *do*
    if $(\exists i : t = r'_i \vee t = f(i))$ *then*
        select for execution the highest-priority eligible task with the minimum
            deadline.
        If more than one eligible task has the same minimum deadline,
        break ties according to their execution times, giving priority
        to the one with the greatest execution time.
    end if
    $t = t + 1$
end while

FIGURE 3.25
Algorithm for generating a valid initial schedule.

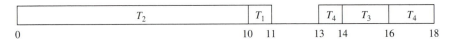

FIGURE 3.26
Valid initial schedule example.

preempts T_4 and executes to completion at time 16. T_4 then resumes and completes at 18. As currently scheduled, T_1 misses its deadline because it must wait for T_2 to finish. See Figure 3.26. A processor busy period is a time interval during which the processor is continuously busy. In the above example, the processor busy periods for the valid initial schedule are [0, 11] and [13, 18].

Our next step is to check if any tasks have missed their deadlines. If none of them has done so, we are done. If some deadlines have been missed, then we try to rectify this situation by reordering the tasks in the schedule. In this example, we can obviously make the processor idle until time 1, and then start executing T_1. T_2 can start executing after T_1 has finished.

Note that it is only useful to reorder the tasks in the same busy period as the one that missed its deadline. It is no use tinkering with the order of T_3, T_4 to try to affect T_1, T_2; these tasks arrive after both T_1 and T_2 have finished executing.

Denote by $Z(i)$ the set containing the tasks that are in the same busy period as T_i, the tasks that are scheduled before T_i, and T_i itself. We can obtain $Z(i)$ recursively as follows ($s(i)$ is the start time of T_i in the schedule):

- $T_i \in Z(i)$
- $T_k \in Z(i)$ if $\exists T_\ell \in Z(i)$ such that

$$\big([f(k) = s(\ell)] \wedge [\exists \ell' \in Z(i) : r'_{\ell'} < f(k)]\big) \vee [s(\ell) < f(k) < f(i)]$$

Example 3.26. In the valid initial schedule in Figure 3.26, $Z(1) = \{1, 2\}$, $Z(2) = \{2\}$, $Z(3) = \{3, 4\}$, and $Z(4) = \{4\}$.

Note that $f(i)$ is also the earliest possible time by which all the tasks in $Z(i)$ will finish execution.

Define the *lateness* of task T_i as $L(i) = f(i) - D_i$. If a task has a positive lateness in a schedule, it has missed its deadline according to that schedule. The lateness of a schedule is the maximum task lateness.

We now introduce two sets, $G_1(i)$ and $G_2(i)$. $G_1(i)$ is a set of tasks that cannot be preempted by T_i (because of EXCLUDES relations), but that, if moved in the schedule to execute after T_i, may reduce the maximum lateness of the system. $G_2(i)$ is a set of tasks that, if preempted by T_i, may reduce the maximum lateness. We obtain $G_1(i)$ by listing all tasks T_m satisfying all of the following properties:

- $T_m \in Z(i)$,
- $D_i < D_m$,

- $\neg(T_m$ PREEMPTS $T_i)$,
- $\neg(T_m$ PRECEDES $T_i)$, and
- T_m EXCLUDES T_i.

$G_2(i)$ is obtained by listing all tasks T_m satisfying all of the following properties:

- $T_m \in Z(i)$,
- $D_i < D_m$,
- $\neg(T_m$ EXCLUDES $T_i)$,
- $\neg(T_m$ PRECEDES $T_i)$,
- $\neg(T_m$ PREEMPTS $T_i)$, and
- There is no third task T_ℓ scheduled to run between T_i T_m, such that $(T_m$ PRECEDES $T_\ell) \vee (T_m$ PREEMPTS $T_\ell)$.

Let us now compute a lower bound on the lateness of a valid initial schedule. Define set $K(i)$ as follows. $T_k \in K(i)$ iff each of the following is true:

- $T_k \in Z(i)$,
- $k \neq i$,
- $D_i < D_k$,
- $\neg(T_k$ PRECEDES $T_i)$,
- $\neg(T_k$ PREEMPTS $T_i)$.

If T_i is a task with the maximum lateness of any task in the system and $K(i) = \emptyset$, then we cannot improve the lateness of T_i by moving other tasks—doing so will cause lateness in one or more of the moved tasks that is at least equal to the current lateness of T_i. If $K(i) \neq \emptyset$, then we can improve on the maximum lateness by moving a task in $K(i)$. We will see examples of this shortly.

A lower bound on the lateness can be determined as follows. Suppose we have a busy period of the processor occupying the interval $[a, b]$. Note that we can never adjust the tasks to move the right endpoint of this interval back; all that we can do is to either leave it as it is (which is what will happen if we simply reorder the tasks within the busy period, without leaving any gaps), or move it further to the right (which will happen if we move a task in such a way that gaps are formed). For instance, consider the busy period $[0,11]$ that was formed in Example 3.25. If we make the processor idle until the arrival of T_1, we are creating a gap of 1 unit in the left end of the interval $[0,11]$ and moving the right endpoint of the busy period to 12.

Define the function $GAP(k, i)$ as follows.

$$GAP(k, i) = \begin{cases} 0 & \text{if } \neg(T_k \text{ EXCLUDES } T_i) \\ \max\{0, -s(k) + \min\{r'_\ell \mid [\ell \in Z(i)] \\ \qquad \wedge [k \neq \ell] \\ \qquad \wedge [s(k) < s(\ell) \leq s(i)] \\ \qquad \wedge [\neg(T_k \text{PRECEDES } T_\ell)]\}\} & \text{otherwise} \end{cases} \tag{3.59}$$

$GAP(k, i)$ is the gap that would be left in the busy period if we moved T_k out to the right of T_i.

Define the function $LB(i)$ as follows.

$$LB(i) = \begin{cases} f(i) - D_i & \text{if } K(i) = \emptyset \\ f(i) + \min_{k \in K(i)}\{GAP(k, i) - D_k\} & \text{otherwise} \end{cases} \tag{3.60}$$

If $K(i) = \emptyset$, then there are no tasks that can be moved to reduce the maximum lateness of the schedule. As a result, the lateness of task T_i remains $f(i) - D_i$. If $K(i) \neq \emptyset$, then the right endpoint of $Z(i)$ moves right by $GAP(k, i)$, (i.e., it is now $f(i) + GAP(k, i)$). The lower bound of the lateness with respect to the busy period up to and including T_i is thus given by $f(i) + \min_{k \in K(i)} \{GAP(k, i) - D_k\}$.

Now, define:

$$LB_1(i) = \min\{LB(i), f(i) - D_i\} \tag{3.61}$$

$$LB_2(i) = r'_i + e_i - D_i \tag{3.62}$$

$LB_1(i)$ provides a lower bound on the lateness of the schedule under the constraints of the PREEMPT, EXCLUDE, and PRECEDE relations. $LB_2(i)$ is a lower bound defined by the task parameters and cannot be reduced. $r'_i + e_i$ is the earliest that we can execute task T_i, by definition.

It follows that a lower bound of the lateness of the schedule is given by

$$\mathcal{L} = \max\{LB_1(i), LB_2(i)\} \tag{3.63}$$

The schedule is obtained by first running the algorithm in Figure 3.25 to obtain a valid initial schedule. If this schedule either is feasible or achieves the lower bound on the lateness in the root node schedule, we are done. If not, some modifications need to be made to this schedule (i.e., some tasks have to be moved around in it), in order to reduce the lateness. Treat the valid initial schedule as the root node.

We identify a task T_j with the maximum lateness and strive to reduce it. Recall that $G_1(j)$ consists of all the tasks in the schedule that, if scheduled to run after T_j, can reduce the lateness of T_j. There are $\|G_1(j)\|$ such tasks.[4] Associate

---

[4] $\|A\|$ means the number of elements in set A.

a child node with each such task; there will thus be $\|G_1(j)\|$ such nodes. In the child node that corresponds to T_k being run after T_j to reduce the lateness, we can force this to happen by adding the relation T_j PRECEDES T_k.

Recall also that $G_2(j)$ consists of tasks that, if preempted by T_j, may reduce the maximum lateness; so we want to make T_j preempt such tasks where possible. We generate $\|G_2(j)\|$ additional child nodes to the root node, with one child node corresponding to each element in $G_2(j)$. Consider $T_k \in G_2(j)$. If we have some other task T_ℓ sandwiched between T_k and T_j in the schedule and if T_k is prohibited from preempting T_ℓ, we want to interchange T_ℓ and T_k by adding the relation T_ℓ PRECEDES T_k. If we have tasks T_q such that $\neg(T_k$ EXCLUDES and $T_q)$, and T_q executes between T_k and T_j, add the relation T_q PREEMPTS T_k and T_j PREEMPTS T_k.

We proceed by developing the node (i.e., the schedule) that has the minimum lateness. The scheduling algorithm is shown in Figure 3.27, and Examples 3.27 and 3.28 illustrate how it works.

Example 3.27. Consider a two-task system whose parameters are:

	T_1	T_2
r_i	0	5
D_i	30	15
e_i	10	10

Note: T_1 EXCLUDES T_2.

The valid initial schedule is:

T_1	T_2

0   10   20

Task T_2 misses its deadline and its lateness is $20-15 = 5$. $K(2) = \{1\}$. $GAP(1, 2) = 10$. The lower bound of the lateness is therefore

$$\min_{k \in K(2)} \{f(2) + GAP(1, 2) - D_k\} = 0$$

We develop this node further. $G_1(2) = \{1\}$, so we add the relation T_2 PRECEDES T_1. When the scheduling algorithm is run under this condition, we have the schedule shown below, which meets all the deadlines.

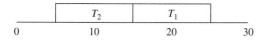

0   10   20   30

The algorithm puts out this schedule and stops.

1. Run the algorithm in Figure 3.25 to obtain a valid initial schedule. Compute the lower bound of the lateness of this schedule. If a feasible schedule results or the lateness equals the lower bound, output the schedule and stop. Otherwise, let the task with the maximum lateness be T_j. Define ml as the lateness of this schedule. Go to the next step.

2. Treat the valid initial schedule obtained above as the root node of a graph generated as follows. Find sets $G_1(j)$ and $G_2(j)$ with respect to the root node and create $\|G_1(j)\| + \|G_2(j)\|$ child nodes. For each node that corresponds to some task $T_k \in G_1(j)$, introduce a new relation T_j PRECEDES T_k.

   For each node corresponding to some task $T_k \in G_2(j)$, do the following.

   a. For all tasks T_ℓ with the properties that T_k EXCLUDES T_ℓ and T_ℓ executes between the execution of T_k and T_j, introduce a new relation T_ℓ PRECEDES T_k.

   b. For all tasks T_q with the properties that the relation T_k EXCLUDES T_q does NOT hold and T_q executes between T_j and T_k, introduce the new relations T_q PREEMPTS T_k and T_j PREEMPTS T_k.

   A child node also inherits all relations of its parent node.

   Recompute a valid initial schedule for each of the child nodes.

3. If steps 4 and 5 have been completed for all the child nodes, close the parent node and go to step 5. Otherwise, pick the child node T_n that has minimum lateness under the valid initial schedule and go to step 4.

4. Set $ml \leftarrow \min\{ml, \text{lateness(child node } n)\}$. If ml is no greater than the least lower bound of the lateness of all the open nodes, we have achieved the best schedule possible—output the schedule and stop. Otherwise, this node can never be developed into a solution better than the currently achieved ml; close this node and go to step 3.

5. Pick from among all the open nodes the one with the least lower bound for the lateness. If more than one open node has the least lower bound, pick the one with the smallest lateness. Define this node as the root node and go to step 2.

FIGURE 3.27
Scheduling algorithm.

Example 3.28. Consider now a four-task system whose parameters are:

	T_1	T_2	T_3	T_4
r_i	0	25	40	80
e_i	50	20	20	20
D_i	148	145	125	100

Note: T_1 EXCLUDES T_4.

The valid initial schedule at the root node is:

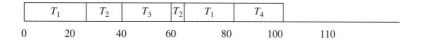

T_4 misses its deadline and the lateness of the schedule is 5. Let us calculate the lower bound of the lateness under the constraints specified here. We have the following:

$$K(4) = \{1, 2, 3\} \tag{3.64}$$

$$GAP(1, 4) = -s(1) + \min\{r'(2), r'(3)\}$$

$$= 25 \tag{3.65}$$

$$GAP(2, 4) = 0 \quad (\text{because } \neg(T_2 \text{ EXCLUDES } T_4)) \tag{3.66}$$

$$GAP(3, 4) = 0 \quad (\text{because } \neg(T_3 \text{ EXCLUDES } T_4)) \tag{3.67}$$

$$LB(4) = f(4) + \min_{k \in K(4)} \{GAP(k, i) - D_k\}$$

$$= 105 + \min\{25 - 148, 0 - 145, 0 - 125\}$$

$$= 105 - 145 = -40 \tag{3.68}$$

$$LB_1(4) = \min\{-40, 5\} = -40 \tag{3.69}$$

$$LB_2(4) = 80 + 20 - 100 = 0 \tag{3.70}$$

$$\mathcal{L}(4) = \max\{LB_1(4), LB_2(4)\} = 0 \tag{3.71}$$

Since $\mathcal{L}(4)$ is less than the lateness of the schedule, there could be room for improvement. We write out $G_1(4)$ and $G_2(4)$:

$$G_1(4) = \{1\} \tag{3.72}$$

$$G_2(4) = \{2, 3\} \tag{3.73}$$

We now create three child nodes of the root node. The first of these represents an additional constraint we shall place with respect to T_1 (connected with $G_1(4) = \{1\}$). This additional constraint is T_4 PRECEDES T_1. The schedule that results is:

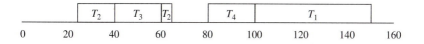

The lateness of this schedule is 2, which is equal to the lower bound of the lateness (in particular, it is equal to $LB_2(1)$). This lower bound is worse than that of the root node. No further improvement is possible along this path and we close this node.

Let us now turn to the second child node of the root. This corresponds to T_2 (since $2 \in G_2(4)$). We add the relations: T_1 PREEMPTS T_2, T_3 PREEMPTS T_2, and

T_4 PREEMPTS T_2. With these added relations, we run the scheduling algorithm in Figure 3.25 to obtain the following schedule:

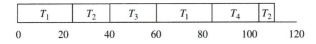

The lateness of this schedule is 5 (T_4 again misses its deadline by 5 units; all the other tasks meet their deadlines). This node is not closed because, as before, we can make the following calculations:

$$K(4) = \{1, 2, 3\} \tag{3.74}$$

$$GAP(1, 4) = -s(1) + \min\{r'(2), r'(3)\}$$

$$= 25 \tag{3.75}$$

$$GAP(2, 4) = 0 \qquad (\text{because } \neg(T_2 \text{ EXCLUDES } T_4)) \tag{3.76}$$

$$GAP(3, 4) = 0 \qquad (\text{because } \neg(T_3 \text{ EXCLUDES } T_4)) \tag{3.77}$$

$$LB(4) = f(4) + \min_{k \in K(4)} \{GAP(k, i) - D_k\}$$

$$= 105 + \min\{25 - 148, 0 - 145, 0 - 125\}$$

$$= 105 - 145 = -40 \tag{3.78}$$

$$LB_1(4) = \min\{-40, 5\} = -40 \tag{3.79}$$

$$LB_2(4) = 80 + 20 - 100 = 0 \tag{3.80}$$

$$\mathcal{L}(4) = \max\{LB_1(4), LB_2(4)\} = 0 \tag{3.81}$$

Let us, however, turn to the third child node. This corresponds to using $3 \in G_2(4)$. We add the relations T_1 PREEMPTS T_3, T_2 PREEMPTS T_3, and T_4 PREEMPTS T_3. Under these additional relations, the algorithm in Figure 3.25 returns the following schedule:

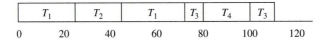

This is feasible, and so the algorithm puts out this schedule and stops.

There is an interesting multiprocessor extension of this algorithm. See Section 3.7 for a pointer to the literature.

3.2.4 Using Primary and Alternative Tasks

Throughout this chapter, we have assumed that there must always be sufficient time for the critical tasks to execute. In order to ensure that critical tasks will complete before their deadline, we carry out a scheduling that assumes that each critical task will run to its worst-case time. Quite often, the worst-case execution time of such tasks is much greater than the average-case execution time. This results in much more time being scheduled for the tasks than is really needed. One way of retaining a high utilization of the hardware is to reclaim for less critical functions the time left unused when the critical tasks do not need all their scheduled time.

In this section, we shall consider a second approach to the problem. Suppose that for each critical task, we have two versions, a primary and an alternative. Completing either the primary or alternative version successfully results in the critical task being executed. However, the alternative is a "bare-bones" version that provides service that is just acceptable, while the primary may be capable of providing better-quality service. The alternative version has a much smaller worst-case execution time than the primary. Since only one of these versions has to execute in time to ensure acceptable service, we can avoid having to preallocate the primary for its worst-case time.[5]

Example 3.29. To illustrate, let us consider the very simple example of a one-task set, consisting of a primary and an alternative. The relative deadline is equal to the task period. The parameters are shown in the following table:

	Primary	Alternative
Worst-case run time	20	5
Average run time	7	4
Period	15	15

If only the primary version were available, this task set would be impossible to schedule; there simply wouldn't be time to complete executing the primary if it ran to its worst-case time. However, since we now have an alterative, we can set up the schedule shown in Figure 3.28. We allow 10 time units for the primary version to run in each period of 15 units; we call this the *run-time limit* of the primary version. Much of the time (since the average run time is only 7) the primary version will have completed by that time, and we can reclaim the time beyond the completion time for other activities. However, if the primary runs for more than 10, we abort it and start up the alternative task. While it does not provide results that are as good as

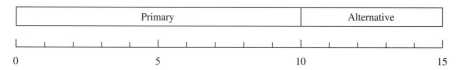

FIGURE 3.28
Example of using primary and alternative versions.

---

[5]In Section 3.3, this concept will be taken one step further.

the primary does, the alternative at least is guaranteed to generate acceptable output within a worst-case execution time of 5. Thus, we are assured of at least one of the two versions executing by the deadline (given that there are no failures, of course).

Assume that the set of tasks is periodic, and that the periods are in the set $\{P_m, 2P_m, 2^2 P_m, \ldots, 2^i P_m\}$. Clearly, P_m is the smallest period of any task in the set. A task is said to be of *level-i* if its period is $2^i P_m$, $i = 0, 1, 2, \ldots$. Assume that r is the highest level (i.e., there is no task whose period exceeds $2^r P_m$). With each primary version π_i of task T_i, associate a run-time limit ℓ_i. If the primary runs beyond this run-time limit, we will abort it and turn to the corresponding alternative version.

We now present two uniprocessor scheduling algorithms, one for generating the initial schedule and another for reclaiming unused time from the initial schedule.

The initial schedule is generated as follows. First, we schedule all level-0 tasks over an interval P_m, ensuring that all alternative versions of such tasks are scheduled, and then schedule the maximum number of primary versions that will fit in the remaining time. The alternative version of a task is never scheduled to run before its primary. Call this schedule S_0.

Next, concatenate two S_0 schedules to form one schedule of length $2P_m$. Schedule all level-1 tasks in the following manner. First, schedule the alternative versions. If there is insufficient space in the schedule to fit all the alternatives, drop some of the primary versions of the level-0 tasks, as necessary. If primary versions have to be dropped, drop the ones that have the longest run-time limits (the idea is to drop as few of them as possible). Once all the level-1 alternatives have been scheduled, see if any of the level-1 primaries can be scheduled in the space available. If they fit, do so. Primaries are checked for inclusion in ascending order of their run-time limits. Then, check to see if any as-yet-unscheduled level-1 primaries have a lower run-time than any primary already scheduled. If so, drop the already-scheduled primary with the longest run-time limit and replace it with the level-1 primary. When this has been done, concatenate two copies of the resultant schedule together to form a schedule of length $2^2 P_m$. Schedule level-2 tasks in the same way—drop level-1 or level-0 primaries as necessary to schedule level-2 alternatives, dropping the ones with the longest run-time limit first. Continue in this way until all tasks have at least their alternative versions scheduled to run in each task period.

Example 3.30. Consider the following task set of five tasks. Denote by $\alpha(i)$ the worst-case run time of the alternative version of T_i, and by $\ell(i)$ the run-time limit of the corresponding primary version.

	T_1	T_2	T_3	T_4	T_5
$\ell(i)$	10	10	15	10	5
$\alpha(i)$	3	2	1	7	4
$P(i)$	20	20	20	40	40

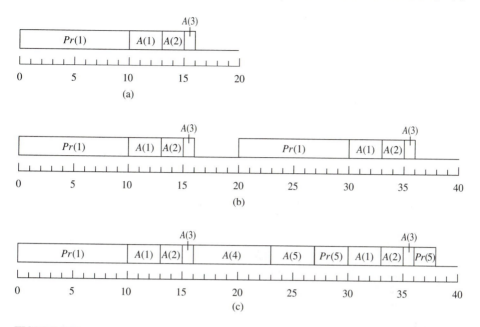

FIGURE 3.29
Example of primary and alternative-version scheduling: (a) schedule S_0; (b) two copies of schedule S_0 concatenated; (c) incorporating level-1 tasks. $Pr(i)$ = primary of T_i; $A(i)$ = alternative of T_i.

The level-0 tasks are T_1, T_2, T_3, and the level-1 tasks are T_4, T_5. Generate schedule S_0. After scheduling the three alternative versions, we have only 15 time units left. We pick a primary with the least run-time limit (of task T_1) and schedule it. The alternative versions are scheduled to run after this primary. See Figure 3.29a.

Next, we concatenate two copies of S_0 (see Figure 3.29b). Our first order of business is to ensure that the alternative versions of T_4 and T_5 are scheduled. This requires a total of 11 time units. We do not have 11 units free in this schedule, so we drop one of the iterations of the T_1 primary version (say the second one), and add the alternatives of T_4 and T_5. We also have enough space to add $Pr(5)$—it is executed in two parts over the intervals [27, 30] and [36, 38]. See Figure 3.29c. Here the algorithm ends.

How do we choose the run-time limit of the primary? The simplest option is to set it equal to the worst-case execution time. However, this might result in only a small number of primaries being scheduled. Another option is to pick a time sufficiently large so that with some large probability, the primary can be expected to complete within the run-time limit.

Example 3.31. Suppose the probability density function of the execution time of a primary is as shown in Figure 3.30. The density function has a long "tail." However, most of the probability is concentrated in the interval $[0, t_1]$. Hence, we might choose to set the run-time limit at t_1 rather than at the worst-case execution time.

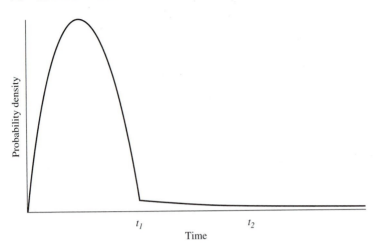

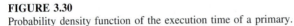

FIGURE 3.30
Probability density function of the execution time of a primary.

If a primary version completes successfully, we do not need its corresponding alternative for that period. This time can then be reclaimed. Such reclamation can result in time becoming available for other primaries, which were not part of the original schedule, to be executed. The algorithm for doing this is a simple modification of the above and is left to the reader as an exercise.

3.3 UNIPROCESSOR SCHEDULING OF IRIS TASKS

Thus far in this chapter, we have assumed that to obtain an acceptable output a task has to be run to completion. Put another way, if the task is not run to completion, we get zero reward from it (i.e., it may as well not have been run). However, there is a large number of tasks for which this is not true. These are iterative algorithms. The longer they run, the higher the quality of their output (up to some maximum run time).

> **Example 3.32.** Figure 3.31 contains an algorithm for computing the value of π. The more times step 2 is executed, the more accurate P is as an approximation of π (subject, of course, to limitations due to finite numerical precision).
>
> The difference between the calculated value and the actual value of π (the "error") as a function of the iteration number is provided in Table 3.1. The error is greatest for the first iteration; it diminishes rapidly after that.

Search algorithms for finding the minimum of some complicated function are also examples of iterative tasks. The longer we search the parameter space, the greater is the chance that we will obtain the optimum value or something close to it.

1. Set $A = \sqrt{2}$, $B = \sqrt[4]{2}$, $P = 2 + \sqrt{2}$.

Repeat step 2 as many times as necessary.

2. Compute

$$A := \frac{\sqrt{A} + 1/\sqrt{A}}{2}$$

$$P := P\left(\frac{A+1}{B+1}\right)$$

$$B := \frac{B\sqrt{A} + 1/\sqrt{A}}{B+1}$$

B is an approximation of π.

FIGURE 3.31
Algorithm for calculating π.

TABLE 3.1
Errors in calculating π

Iteration	Error
1	0.0010141003518293623280764403399
2	0.00000000073762509920351088518841
3	0.00000000000000000000183130608478

Example 3.33. Chess-playing algorithms evaluate the goodness of moves by looking ahead several moves. The more time they have, the further they can look and the more accurate will be the evaluation.

Tasks of this type are known as *increased reward with increased service* (IRIS) tasks. The reward function associated with an IRIS task increases with the amount of service given to it. Typically, the reward function is of the form

$$R(x) = \begin{cases} 0 & \text{if } x < m \\ r(x) & \text{if } m \le x \le o + m \\ r(o+m) & \text{if } x > o + m \end{cases} \tag{3.82}$$

where $r(x)$ is monotonically nondecreasing in x. The reward is 0 up to some time m; if the task is not executed up to that point, it produces no useful output. Tasks with this reward function can be regarded as having a mandatory and an optional component. The *mandatory* portion (with execution time m) must be completed by the deadline if the task is critical; the *optional* portion is done if time permits. The optional portion requires a total of o time to complete. In each case, the execution of a task must be stopped by its deadline d.

The scheduling task can be described as the following optimization problem:

Schedule the tasks so that the reward is maximized, subject to the requirement that the mandatory portions of all the tasks are completed.

It can be shown that this optimization problem is NP-complete when there is no restriction on the release times, deadlines, and reward functions. However, for some special cases, we do have scheduling algorithms. We now turn to these. In what follows, m_i and o_i denote the execution time of the mandatory and optional parts, respectively, of T_i.

3.3.1   Identical Linear Reward Functions

For task T_i, the reward function is given by

$$R_i(x) = \begin{cases} 0 & \text{if } x \leq m_i \\ x - m_i & \text{if } m_i \leq x \leq o_i + m_i \\ o_i & \text{if } x > m_i + o_i \end{cases} \tag{3.83}$$

That is, the reward from executing a unit of optional work is one unit. A schedule is said to be optimal if the reward is maximized subject to all tasks completing at least their mandatory portions by the task deadline.

Theorem 3.13. The EDF algorithm is optimal if the mandatory parts of all tasks are 0.

Proof. If the mandatory portions are zero, then we can execute as little of any task as we please. It is easy to see that the reward is maximized if the processor is kept busy for as much time as possible. But this is exactly what the EDF algorithm does; if the processor is idle at some time t, this is because (a) all the previously released tasks have either completed or their deadlines have expired by time t, and (b) no other tasks have been released.   **Q.E.D.**

We can use this result to develop an optimal scheduling algorithm for the case when the mandatory portions are not all zero. The tasks $T_1, \ldots, T_n$ have mandatory portions $M_1, \ldots, M_n$ and optional portions $O_1, \ldots, O_n$. Define

$$\mathbf{M} = \{M_1, \ldots, M_n\}$$

$$\mathbf{O} = \{O_1, \ldots, O_n\}$$

$$\mathbf{T} = \{T_1, \ldots, T_n\}$$

The optimal algorithm, IRIS1, is shown in Figure 3.32. Although it looks a little forbidding, the idea behind it is quite simple. First, since we receive one unit of reward for each unit of the optional portion completed for any task, the highest reward, subject to the constraint that all the mandatory portions are completed, is obtained when the processor carries out as much execution as possible.

1. Run the EDF algorithm on the task set **T** to generate a schedule S_t.
   If this is feasible,
   >An optimal schedule has been found: STOP.

   Else,
   >go to step 2.

   end if

2. Run the EDF algorithm on the task set **M**, to generate a schedule S_m.
   If this set is not feasible,
   >**T** cannot be feasibly scheduled: STOP.

   Else,
   >Define a_i as the ith instant in S_m when either the scheduled task changes, or the processor becomes idle, $i = 1, 2, \ldots$.
   >>Let k be the total number of these instants.
   >
   >Define a_0 as when the first task begins executing in S_m.
   >Define $\tau(j)$ as the task that executes in S_m in $[a_j, a_{j+1}]$,
   >Define $L_t(j)$ and $L_m(j)$ as the total execution time given to
   >>task $\tau(j)$ in $S_t(j)$ and $S_m(j)$ respectively, after time a_j.
   >
   >Go to step 3.

   end if

3. $j = k - 1$
   do while $(0 \le j \le k - 1)$
   >if $(L_m(j) > L_t(j))$ then
   >>Modify S_t by
   >>>(a) assigning $L_m(j) - L_t(j)$ of processor time in $[a_j, a_{j+1}]$
   >>>to $\tau(j)$, and
   >>>(b) reducing the processor time assigned to other tasks in
   >>>$[a_j, a_{j+1}]$ by $L_m(j) - L_t(j)$.
   >>
   >>Update $L_t(1), \ldots, L_t(j)$ appropriately.
   >
   >end if
   >$j = j - 1$

   end do
end

FIGURE 3.32
Algorithm IRIS1.

We begin by running the EDF algorithm for the total run time of each task. Call the resulting schedule S_t. S_t maximizes the total processor busy time. If S_t is a feasible schedule, we are clearly done—we have given each task as much time as it needs to finish executing both its mandatory and optional portions, and have still met each task deadline. Suppose we do not obtain a feasible schedule; that is, some task cannot be given its full execution time and still meet its deadline.

In this case, we run the EDF algorithm on the mandatory portions of each task to yield schedule S_m. If this results in an infeasible schedule, then we must stop since we can't execute even the mandatory portions of each task. Suppose that S_m is feasible. Then we adjust S_t to ensure that each task receives at least its mandatory portion of service.

Example 3.34. Consider the set of four tasks with parameters shown in the following table.

Task number	m_i	o_i	r_i	D_i
1	1	4	0	10
2	1	2	1	12
3	3	3	1	15
4	6	2	2	19

In step 1 of the IRIS1 algorithm, we run the EDF algorithm with task execution times 5, 3, 6, and 8, respectively (for tasks 1 to 4), to produce S_{t0} in Figure 3.33. It is impossible to meet the deadline of task 4. Hence, we go to step 2.

Running the EDF algorithm on the task set **M** produces the feasible schedule S_m shown in Figure 3.33. All the deadlines are met, so we can proceed to step 3. We have $a_0 = 0, a_1 = 1, a_2 = 2, a_3 = 5, a_4 = 11$. Also, $k = 4$.

Now we move to step 3 of the algorithm. Let us start with a_3. We have task T_4 scheduled in S_m over the interval $[a_3, a_4]$ and given 6 units of time. In schedule S_{t0}, T_4 is given only 5 units of time. Hence, we modify S_{t0} by adding $6 - 5 = 1$ unit of time to T_4 in the interval $[a_3, a_4)$ and taking away 1 unit from the task originally scheduled at a_3 in S_{t0}, namely T_2. This results in task T_4 being scheduled for a total of 6 units beyond a_3. The resulting schedule is S_{t1}. Let us now move to the interval $[a_2, a_3)$. T_3 is scheduled beyond that time in S_m, for a total of 3 units. In S_{t1}, T_3 has been scheduled for a total of 6 units beyond a_2. Therefore, no modifications are needed; T_3 has enough time to meet its mandatory portion. Next, we consider $[a_1, a_2)$. T_2 is scheduled for that interval in S_m. Let us consider the time given to T_2 beyond a_1 in S_{t1}. It is 2 units, which is greater than the mandatory requirement, so

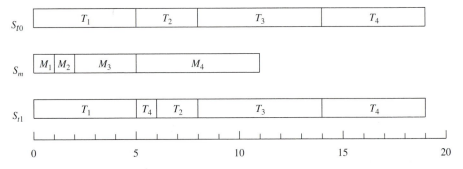

FIGURE 3.33
Schedules produced by algorithm IRIS1 for Example 3.34.

no modifications are needed. Finally, consider $[a_0, a_1)$. T_1 is given 1 unit in schedule S_m. In S_{t1}, T_1 is scheduled for 5 units, which exceeds the time given in S_m. So, no modifications are needed, and the optimal schedule is S_{t1}.

Theorem 3.14. For IRIS tasks with reward functions of the type being considered in this section, algorithm IRIS1 is optimal.

Proof. We leave the formal proof to the reader. Here, we will merely sketch the ideas behind the proof. If a feasible schedule is generated in step 1, then each task has been run to completion and we are done. If not, then from Theorem 3.13, we know that the EDF algorithm is optimal when none of the tasks has any mandatory portion; in that case, the schedule we would obtain would be S_t in step 1. But, the transformations that we do in step 3 do not change the total time for which the processor runs; it only ensures that all the mandatory portions are completed. This completes the proof sketch. **Q.E.D.**

3.3.2 Nonidentical Linear Reward Functions

The reward function for task T_i is given by

$$R_i(x) = \begin{cases} 0 & \text{if } x \leq m_i \\ w_i(x - m_i) & \text{if } m_i \leq x \leq m_i + o_i \\ w_i o_i & \text{if } x > m_i + o_i \end{cases} \qquad (3.84)$$

Each task has a weight w_i associated with it. Assume that the tasks are numbered in nonincreasing order of weights, $w_1 \geq w_2 \geq \ldots \geq w_n$. The procedure for optimally scheduling such tasks is obvious: Always run the available task with the greatest weight, subject to the need to execute the mandatory portions of all the tasks by their respective deadlines. This is done by algorithm IRIS2, which is shown in Figure 3.34.

The idea behind the IRIS2 algorithm is the following. As with IRIS1, we check to see if we can feasibly schedule all the mandatory portions. If not, we stop right away. If we succeed, we proceed by running IRIS1 with a mandatory task set equal to the mandatory portions of the tasks, and the set of optional portions equal only to optional portion of task T_1 (the optional portions of the other tasks are considered not to exist). IRIS1 is executed. It provides as much time as possible to T_1, consistent with the need to meet the mandatory portions of all the tasks.

We now take this schedule and label as mandatory the part of the optional portion of T_1 that was scheduled by IRIS1. Next, we run the IRIS1 algorithm with this revised mandatory portion and the optional portion of T_2, and continue in this way for the remaining tasks.

Theorem 3.15. If the reward functions are as defined in this section, algorithm IRIS2 is optimal.

Proof. Once again, we will leave the formal proof as an exercise and merely provide a brief sketch. We know from Theorem 3.14 that O'_n is the maximum amount of

1. Set $\mathbf{M}'$ to be the set of mandatory portions of all the tasks, and $\mathbf{O}' = \emptyset$. Run the EDF algorithm, and let S_m be the resulting schedule.

2. If S_m is not feasible,
>   the task set $\mathbf{T}$ is not schedulable: STOP.
> else
>> $i = 1$
>>   do while $(1 \le i \le n)$
>>>   Set $\mathbf{O}' = \mathbf{O}' \cup \{O_i\}$, and use IRIS1 to find an optimal schedule
>>>   Define O'_i to be the part of O_i scheduled by IRIS1.
>>>   Set $\mathbf{M}' = \mathbf{M}' \cup \{O'_i\}$
>>> $i = i + 1$
>>   end do
> end if
end

FIGURE 3.34
Algorithm IRIS2. (After Shih, Liu, and Kung [24].)

service that can be given to O_n (which is the task with the greatest weight) if all the mandatory tasks are to meet their deadlines. Similarly, we have that O'_{n-1} is the maximum amount of service that can be given to O_{n-1}, subject to the constraint that all mandatory tasks must meet their deadlines and that as much of O_n as possible should be executed. In general, for $i < n$, we have that O'_i is the maximum amount of service that can be given to O_i, subject to the constraint that all mandatory tasks must meet their deadlines and that as much of $O_{i+1}, \ldots, O_n$ as possible should be executed. The result follows from this observation.   **Q.E.D.**

3.3.3   0/1 Reward Functions

We assume here that for any task i the reward function is given by

$$R_i(x) = \begin{cases} 0 & \text{if } x < m_i + o_i \\ 1 & \text{if } x \ge m_i + o_i \end{cases} \tag{3.85}$$

That is, we get no reward for executing the optional portion partially. If we run the optional portion to completion, we obtain one unit of reward; otherwise we get nothing.

The optimal strategy would therefore be to complete as many optional portions as possible, subject to the constraint that the deadlines of all the mandatory portions must be met. Unfortunately, when the execution times are arbitrary, the problem of obtaining an optimal schedule can be shown to be NP-complete.

Finding an efficient optimal scheduling algorithm under the 0/1 case is therefore a hopeless task. We must therefore make do with heuristics. One rather obvious heuristic is shown in Figure 3.35. The IRIS3 algorithm is based on the following reasoning. Since we get the same reward for completing the optional

1. Run the EDF algorithm on the set **M** of mandatory tasks.
   If **M** is not EDF-schedulable, then
   > Task set **T** cannot be feasibly scheduled: STOP.

   else
   > Go to step 2.

   end if

2. **O** is the set of optional portions.
   Assign $w_i = 1/o_i$ for $i = 1, \ldots, n$.
   Renumber the tasks so that their weights are in a non-ascending sequence, i.e.,
   $w_1 \geq w_2 \geq \ldots \geq w_n$.

3. Run algorithm IRIS2 on a task set composed of
   > the mandatory set **M** and optional set **O** to obtain schedule S_o.

4. If all the optional tasks in **O** are executed to completion in S_o,
   > Return S_o and STOP.

   else
   > Let $i_{\min}$ be the smallest index i such that
   >> o_i is not run to completion in S_o.
   >
   > Redefine $\mathbf{O} = \mathbf{O} - \{o_{i_{\min}}\}$.
   > Go to step 3.

   end if

end

FIGURE 3.35
Algorithm IRIS3: a simple heuristic for the 0/1 case.

---

portion of any task, it is best to run the tasks with the shorter optional portions. Therefore, we assign weights according to the inverse of the duration of the optional portions and run IRIS2. If an optional part is not run to completion in the resulting schedule, we remove its optional portion from consideration and rerun IRIS2. We continue in this manner until each optional portion has been either scheduled to completion or dropped altogether.

3.3.4 Identical Concave Reward Functions (No Mandatory Portions)

In this section, we consider tasks with identical release times and with mandatory portions of zero. We assume that the reward function of T_i is given by

$$R_i(x) = \begin{cases} f(x) & \text{if } 0 \leq x < o_i \\ f(o_i) & \text{if } x \geq o_i \end{cases} \tag{3.86}$$

where the function f is one-to-one and concave. Recall that a function $f(x)$ is concave iff for all x_1, x_2, and $0 \le \alpha \le 1$,

$$f(\alpha x_1 + [1 - \alpha]x_2) \ge \alpha f(x_1) + (1 - \alpha) f(x_2) \tag{3.87}$$

Geometrically, this condition can be expressed by saying that, for any two points on a concave curve, the straight line joining them must never be above the curve. An example of a concave function is $1 - e^{-x}$.

We will also assume that the functions $f(x)$ are differentiable, and define $g(x) = df(x)/dx$. We will assume that the inverse function g^{-1} of g exists for all $i = 1, \ldots, n$. This will happen if the functions g are monotonically decreasing and we assume that they are. The tasks are numbered in nondecreasing order of their absolute deadlines (i.e., $D_1 \le D_2 \le \ldots \le D_n$). For notational convenience, define $D_0 = 0$.

Since f is a concave function, we have nonincreasing marginal returns, and so the optimum is obtained by balancing the execution times as much as possible. If all the deadlines are equal (i.e., if $D_1 = \ldots = D_n = \delta$), then the algorithm is trivial—just allocate to each task a total of δ/n of execution time before its deadline. If the deadlines are not all equal, the algorithm is a little more complicated. We will leave to the reader the problem of writing out this algorithm, IRIS4, formally. Here is an informal description.

The basic idea behind this algorithm is to equalize, as much as possible, the execution times of the tasks. The algorithm starts at the latest deadline and works backwards. In the interval $[D_{n-1}, D_n]$, only task T_n can be executed and it is allocated up to $a_n = \max\{D_n - D_{n-1}, e_i\}$ units of time in that interval. Next, we move to the interval $[D_{n-2}, D_{n-1}]$; over this interval, tasks T_{n-1} and T_n can be executed. In this interval, we also allocate time to T_{n-1} and T_n so that, in the interval $[D_{n-2}, D_n]$, the execution time these tasks receive is equalized as much as possible (subject to the obvious constraints). We then go on to the interval $[D_{n-3}, D_{n-2}]$, over which tasks T_{n-2}, T_{n-1}, T_n are available, and so on until the beginning.

Example 3.35. We have a five-task aperiodic system with deadlines $D_1 = 2$, $D_2 = 6$, $D_3 = 8$, $D_4 = 10$, and $D_5 = 20$; each task has an execution time of 8.

Let us begin with the interval $(10, 20]$. Only task T_5 can be scheduled in that interval, and we can give to it its entire execution time of 8. So, the allocation of execution times so far is:

T_1	T_2	T_3	T_4	T_5
0	0	0	0	8

Next, move to the interval $(8, 10]$. Tasks T_4, T_5 can be scheduled in that interval, but we have already given a full execution-time to T_5, so we don't consider that task here. We devote this entire interval to T_4. The execution time allocations are now:

T_1	T_2	T_3	T_4	T_5
0	0	0	2	8

Now, consider $(6, 8]$. T_3, T_4, T_5 are eligible to run in that interval. As before, we don't have to consider T_5. We give the 2 units to T_3 so that it is equalized with T_4. (This is the best possible balancing of the execution times.) The execution-time allocations are now:

T_1	T_2	T_3	T_4	T_5
0	0	2	2	8

Move on to $(2, 6]$. T_2, T_3, T_4, T_5 are eligible to run in this interval. Give 2 units to T_2 so that T_2, T_3, T_4 are each allocated 2 units. This leaves 2 units which we can allocate equally to each of these tasks over that interval. The execution-time allocations are now:

T_1	T_2	T_3	T_4	T_5
0	2.66	2.66	2.66	8

Finally, consider $(0, 2]$. Here, we must clearly allocate 2 units to T_1, and the final allocations are:

T_1	T_2	T_3	T_4	T_5
2	2.66	2.66	2.66	8

It is easy to check that the execution times have been balanced as much as possible, under deadline and execution time constraints. The schedule is shown in Figure 3.36.

Theorem 3.16. Algorithm IRIS4 is optimal under the conditions listed in Section 3.3.4.

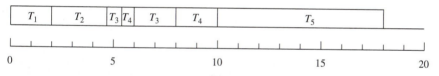

FIGURE 3.36
Example of the IRIS4 algorithm.

Proof. This has been left as an exercise for the reader.   **Q.E.D.**

3.3.5   Nonidentical Concave Reward Functions*

As in the previous section, we consider tasks with identical release times and with mandatory portions of zero. There are n tasks in all. We assume that for any task T_i the reward function is given by

$$R_i(x) = \begin{cases} f_i(x) & \text{if } 0 \le x < o_i \\ f_i(o_i) & \text{if } x \ge o_i \end{cases} \tag{3.88}$$

where the functions f_i are one-to-one and concave.

Let $x_{ij}(S)$ denote the service that task T_i receives in the interval $[D_{j-1}, D_j]$ under schedule S.[6] The total amount of service that task T_i receives is given by $s_S(i) = \sum_{j=1}^{i} x_{ij}(S)$.[7] The optimization problem therefore reduces to maximizing

$$P = \sum_{i=1}^{n} f_i(s(i)) \tag{3.89}$$

subject to the constraints that

$$\sum_{i=1}^{n} x_{ij} = D_j - D_{j-1} \qquad 1 \le j \le n \tag{3.90}$$

$$x_{ij} \ge 0 \qquad\qquad 1 \le j \le i \le n \tag{3.91}$$

This is a standard constrained-maximization problem, which can be solved using Lagrange multipliers.[8] The solution to this optimization problem can be obtained by solving the following set of equations, where μ_j and v_{ij} are Lagrange multipliers.

$$-g_i(s(i)) + \mu_j + v_{ij} = 0 \qquad 1 \le j \le i \le n \tag{3.92}$$

$$\sum_{i=j}^{n} x_{ij} - (D_j - D_{j-1}) = 0 \qquad j = 1, \ldots, n \tag{3.93}$$

$$x_{ij} \ge 0, \quad v_{ij}x_{ij} = 0, \quad v_{ij} \le 0 \qquad 1 \le j \le i \le n \tag{3.94}$$

---

[6] In this discussion, we will frequently omit S where this is convenient and write simply x_{ij}, where S can be understood from the context.

[7] As with x_{ij}, we will drop the S from $s_S(i)$, where this can be done without confusion.

[8] Readers unaware of this approach should consult any book on mathematical optimization, such as D. G. Luenberger, *Introduction to Linear and Nonlinear Programming*, Reading, MA: Addison-Wesley, 1973. If you haven't heard of Lagrange multipliers before, simply consider them to be constants and assume (3.92) to (3.94) to be true.

If $x_{ij} = 0$, from (3.94), $v_{ij} \leq 0$, and so from Equation (3.92),

$$g_i(s(i)) \leq \mu_j \qquad 1 \leq j \leq i \leq n \tag{3.95}$$

If $x_{ij} > 0$, we have $v_{ij} = 0$, and so from Equation (3.92),

$$g_i(s(i)) = \mu_j \qquad 1 \leq j \leq i \leq n \tag{3.96}$$

Let $s^*(i)$ and x_{ij}^* denote values for $s(i)$ and x_{ij} $(i, j = 1, \cdots, n)$ that satisfy Equations (3.92) to (3.94). Then an examination of these equations yields the following conclusions.

Lemma 3.13. For any i, j, if there is some k $(1 \leq k \leq i, j \leq n)$ such that $x_{ik}^* > 0$ and $x_{jk}^* > 0$, then

$$g_i(s^*(i)) = g_j(s^*(j)) \tag{3.97}$$

Proof. This follows immediately from Equation (3.96). **Q.E.D.**

Proof. An alternative proof that argues from first principles is as follows. Suppose that the lemma is false, and that we have some i, j such that $g_i(s^*(i)) \neq g_j(s^*(j))$ for optimal schedule S^*. Consider the case $g_i(s^*(i)) < g_j(s^*(j))$. Since $x_{ik}^*, x_{jk}^* > 0$ and the g_i are continuous functions, there exists some $\delta > 0$ such that

- $\delta \leq \min\{x_{ik}^*, x_{jk}^*\}$, and
- $g_i(s^*(i) - \delta) < g_j(s^*(j) + \delta)$.

Construct another schedule S' that is identical to S^* except that task T_i receives δ less service and task T_j receives δ more service. It is clearly possible to do this without any deadlines being missed. Denote the rewards under S^* and S' by $R(S^*)$ and $R(S')$, respectively. Then,

$$\begin{aligned} R(S') - R(S^*) &= f_i(s^*(i) - \delta) - f_i(s^*(i)) + f_j(s^*(j) + \delta) - f_j(s^*(j)) \\ &\geq -\delta \left(\max_{x \in [s^*(i) - \delta, s^*(i)]} g_i(x) \right) + \delta \left(\min_{x \in [s^*(j), s^*(j) + \delta]} g_j(x) \right) \\ &= -g_i(s^*(i) - \delta)\delta + g_j(s^*(j) + \delta)\delta \\ &> 0 \end{aligned} \tag{3.98}$$

A similar result holds for the case where $g_i(s^*(i)) > g_j(s^*(j))$.

The total reward for S' will be thus greater than that for S^*, contradicting the optimality of S^*. **Q.E.D.**

Lemma 3.14. For any $i, j \in \{1, \ldots, n\}$, if there is some k $(1 \leq k \leq i, j \leq n)$ such that $x_{ik}^* > 0$ and $x_{jk}^* = 0$, then

$$g_i(s^*(i)) \geq g_j(s^*(j)) \tag{3.99}$$

Proof. This follows immediately from Equations (3.95) and (3.96). **Q.E.D.**

Lemma 3.15. If $s^*(j) = 0$ for any $j \in \{1, \ldots, n\}$, then for all $i \in \{1, \ldots j - 1\}$,

$$g_i(s^*(i)) \geq g_j(0) \tag{3.100}$$

Proof. $s^*(j) = 0$ means that $x_{jk}^* = 0$ for all k. This, together with Lemma 3.14, proves the result.   **Q.E.D.**

Lemma 3.16. If there is some task T_k such that $x_{ki}^* > 0$ and $x_{kj}^* > 0$, then

$$\mu_i = \mu_j \qquad \text{for all } 1 \leq i, j \leq k \leq n \tag{3.101}$$

Proof. The proof is an immediate consequence of Equation (3.96).   **Q.E.D.**

Lemma 3.17. $\mu_i \geq \mu_{i+1}$ for $1 \leq i < n$.

Proof. We prove this by contradiction. Suppose that this lemma is false, and there exists some i such that $\mu_i < \mu_{i+1}$. Then, from Lemma 3.16, we know that there is some task T_m such that $x_{m,i+1}^* > 0$ but $x_{m,i}^* = 0$. But, $x_{m,i}^* = 0$ implies from Equation (3.95) that $g_m(s^*(m)) \leq \mu_i$, and $x_{m,i+1}^* > 0$ implies from Equation (3.96) that $g_m(s^*(m)) = \mu_{i+1}$. That is, $\mu_i \geq \mu_{i+1}$, a contradiction.   **Q.E.D.**

Lemma 3.18. There exists an optimal schedule S under which for all i such that $s_S(i) > 0$,

$$g_i(s_S(i)) \geq g_j(s_S(j)) \qquad \text{for all } 1 \leq i < j \leq n \tag{3.102}$$

Proof. We prove this result by construction. That is, we show that any optimal schedule can be transformed into another optimal schedule for which Equation (3.102) holds.

Suppose we are given an optimal schedule U and wish to transform it to another schedule Y for which Equation (3.102) holds. Take tasks T_i and T_j, with $i < j$ such that $s_U(i), s_U(j) > 0$. Define $v = \max\{k | x_{ik}(U) > 0\}$ and $w = \max\{k | x_{jk}(U) > 0\}$. In words this means that tasks T_i and T_j do not, under U, receive any service after time D_{v+1} and D_{w+1}, respectively. There are three cases.

Case 1. $v = w$. From Lemma 3.13, we know that $g_i(s_U(i)) = g_j(s_U(j))$. Define $x_{ik}(Y) = x_{ik}(U)$ and $x_{jk}(Y) = x_{jk}(U)$ for all $k \in \{1, \ldots, n\}$.

Case 2. $v < w$. From Equation (3.96) and Lemma 3.17, we have $g_i(s_U(i)) \geq g_j(s_U(j))$. Define $x_{ik}(Y) = x_{ik}(U)$ and $x_{jk}(Y) = x_{jk}(U)$, for all $k \in \{1, \ldots, n\}$.

Case 3. $v > w$. By shifting the execution of the tasks in time (while keeping the total time allocated to each task the same in both schedules U and Y), we can reduce Case 3 to either Case 1 or Case 2. In particular, in Schedule Y we have:

$$x_{iv}(Y) = x_{iv}(U) - \min(x_{iv}(U), x_{jw}(U))$$

$$x_{jv}(Y) = x_{jv}(U) + \min(x_{iv}(U), x_{jw}(U))$$

$$x_{iw}(Y) = x_{iw}(U) + \min(x_{iv}(U), x_{jw}(U))$$

$$x_{jw}(Y) = x_{jw}(U) - \min(x_{iv}(U), x_{jw}(U))$$

We are shifting some of the T_i execution from $(D_{v-1}, D_v]$ to $(D_{w-1}, D_w]$, and some of the T_j execution from $(D_{w-1}, D_2]$ to $(D_{v-1}, D_v]$.

If $x_{iv}(Y) > 0$, then we have

$$\max\{k | x_{ik}(Y) > 0\} = \max\{k | x_{jk}(Y) > 0\} = v$$

and Case 1 can now be applied. On the other hand, if $x_{iv}(Y) = 0$, then

$$\max\{k | x_{ik}(Y) > 0\} < \max\{k | x_{jk}(Y) > 0\} = v$$

and Case 2 can be applied to tasks T_i and T_j.

Thus, by repeatedly applying this construction procedure to every pair of tasks T_i, T_j for which $s_U(i) > 0$, $s_U(j) > 0$, we obtain the schedule Y.   **Q.E.D.**

Assuming that the tasks are all released at time 0 and have deadlines $D_1 \leq D_2 \leq \ldots \leq D_n$, we can define n scheduling problems, $q_1, q_2, \ldots, q_n$, where q_i is the following problem (for notational convenience, assume $D_0 = 0$):

Assuming that tasks $T_i, \ldots, T_n$ all arrive at time D_{i-1}, schedule them in the interval $[D_{i-1}, D_n]$ so that the reward is maximized.

The overall scheduling problem is therefore q_1. Solving q_n is trivial; as only task n can be scheduled in the interval $(D_{n-1}, D_n]$. We will show now how to solve q_i as a function of the solution of q_{i+1}.

Theorem 3.17. Let an optimal solution of q_{i+1} involve allocating service time $s^*_{i+1}(j)$ to task T_j ($i + 1 \leq j \leq n$). Let K be the set of tasks that receives a nonzero allocation of service time in the interval $[D_{i-1}, D_i]$ in the optimal solution to q_i. Then, an optimal solution to q_i satisfies the equation

$$\sum_{k \in K} g_k^{-1}(\mu^{(i)}) = \sum_{k \in K} s^*_{i+1}(k) + D_i - D_{i-1} \tag{3.103}$$

where $\mu^{(i)} = \mu_k^{(i)}$ for all $k \in K$.

Proof. The server does not idle while there are tasks waiting for service. Consequently,

$$\sum_{k \in K} \left(s^*_i(k) - s^*_{i+1}(k) \right) = D_i - D_{i-1}$$

$$\Rightarrow \sum_{k \in K} s^*_i(k) = \sum_{k \in K} s^*_{i+1}(k) + D_i - D_{i-1} \tag{3.104}$$

But from Lemmas 3.13 and 3.14 we know that all tasks served in the interval $(D_{i-1}, D_i]$ have the same marginal reward rate, and that other tasks in q_i have lower marginal reward rates. That is, there exists some $\mu^{(i)}$ such that $g_k(s^*_i(k)) = \mu^{(i)}$ for all $k \in K$. Thus, we have from Equation (3.104),

$$\sum_{k \in K} g_k^{-1}\left(\mu^{(i)}\right) = \sum_{k \in K} s^*_{i+1}(k) + D_i - D_{i-1} \tag{3.105}$$

   Q.E.D.

We now hold all the keys to an optimal scheduling algorithm. As mentioned earlier, the solution of q_n is trivial and we will work backwards through $q_{n-1}, \ldots, q_1$. Suppose we have solved problem q_{i+1}. In the solution of q_i, we consider the set of tasks $T_i = \{T_i, \ldots, T_n\}$. For notational convenience, define

- $s^*_{i+1}(j) = 0$ for all $j \leq i$, and
- $\pi(j) = \{x | g_x(s^*_{i+1}(x))$ is the jth largest of the set

$$\{g_x(s^*_{i+1}(i)), \ldots, g_x(s^*_{i+1}(n))\}\}.$$

From the foregoing results, we know that tasks $T_{\pi(1)}, \ldots, T_{\pi(y)}$ will be served in $(D_{i-1}, D_i]$ if it is possible to find some $\hat{\mu} \geq 0$ such that

$$\sum_{j=1}^{y} g^{-1}_{\pi(j)}(\hat{\mu}) = D_i - D_{i-1} + \sum_{j=1}^{y} s^*_{i+1}(j) \tag{3.106}$$

This leaves us with the problem of obtaining y and $\hat{\mu}$. The brute-force way of doing this is to try every value of i from 1 to y, where Equation (3.106) no longer allows $\hat{\mu} > 0$. The clever(er) way of doing this is to observe that if task k is served in $(D_i, D_{i+1}]$, then $s^*_i(k) > s^*_{i+1}(k)$. In any event, for all tasks T_j such that $D_j > D_i$ we must have $s^*_i(j) \geq s^*_{i+1}(j)$, since only such tasks can be served beyond D_i. The complete algorithm is shown in Figure 3.37. Concave reward functions are probably the most realistic since they exhibit the property of nonincreasing marginal returns. The greatest gains in the accuracy of most numerical iterative algorithms, for example, come in the first few moments of execution.

---

1. $L = \emptyset$, $x_i = 0$, $i = 1, \ldots, n$. $D_0 = 0$. $m = n$.
2. while $(m > 0)$ do

        Insert task T_m into L.

        Define $\pi(i) = \{\alpha | g_\alpha(x_\alpha)$ is the ith largest among $g_\ell(x_\ell), \ell \in L\}$.

        Use binary search to find ℓ such that

$$\sum_{i=1}^{\ell+1} \left[g^{-1}_{\pi(i)}(g_{\ell+1}(x_{\ell+1}) - x_{\pi(i)} \right] > D_m - D_{m-1} \geq \sum_{i=1}^{\ell} \left[g^{-1}_{\pi(i)}(g_\ell(x_\ell)) - x_{\pi(i)} \right]$$

        Solve for μ in the equation

$$\sum_{i=1}^{\ell} g^{-1}_{\pi(i)}(\mu) = \sum_{i=1}^{\ell} x_{\pi(i)} + D_m - D_{m-1}$$

        We have $x_{\pi(i)} = g^{-1}_{\pi(i)}(\mu)$, $i = 1, \ldots \ell$.

        $m = m - 1$

    end while

end

FIGURE 3.37
Algorithm IRIS5.

3.4 TASK ASSIGNMENT

The optimal assignment of tasks to processors is, in almost all practical cases, an NP-complete problem. We must therefore make do with heuristics. These heuristics cannot guarantee that an allocation will be found that permits all tasks to be feasibly scheduled. All that we can hope to do is to allocate the tasks, check their feasibility, and, if the allocation is not feasible, modify the allocation to try to render its schedules feasible.

Heuristics typically allocate according to some simple criterion and hope that feasibility will follow as a side effect of that criterion. For example, if we keep the utilization below $n(2^{1/n} - 1)$ for all processors in a system running periodic tasks whose deadlines equal the respective periods, we know that the resulting task allocation is RM-feasible.

When checking an allocation for feasibility, we must account for communication costs. For example, suppose that $T_1 \prec T_2$. Task T_2 cannot start before receiving the task T_1 output. That is, if f_i denotes the completion time of task T_i and c_{ij} is the time to communicate from T_i to T_j,

$$r_2 \geq f_1 + c_{12} \tag{3.107}$$

If tasks T_1 and T_2 are allocated to the same processor, then $c_{12} = 0$. If they are allocated to separate processors, c_{12} is positive and must be taken into account while checking for feasibility.

Example 3.36. Consider the situation discussed above where $\prec (2) = \{1\}$. Then, if $D_2 < f_1 + c_{12} + e_2$, the allocation is not feasible.

Sometimes an allocation algorithm uses communication costs as part of its allocation criterion.

3.4.1 Utilization-Balancing Algorithm

This algorithm attempts to balance processor utilization, and proceeds by allocating the tasks one by one and selecting the least utilized processor. The algorithm is shown in Figure 3.38.

This algorithm takes into account the possibility that we might wish to run multiple copies of the same task simultaneously for fault-tolerance. In particular, it assigns r_i copies of task T_i to separate processors. Let u_i^* and u_i^B denote the utilizations of processor p_i under an optimal algorithm that minimizes the sum of the squares of the processor utilizations and under the best-fit algorithm, respectively. If $r_1 = \ldots = r_n = r$, and there are p processors in all, it is possible to show that

$$\frac{\sum_{i=1}^{p} \left(u_i^B\right)^2}{\sum_{i=1}^{p} \left(u_i^*\right)^2} \leq \frac{9}{8} \frac{p}{p - r + 1} \tag{3.108}$$

If $p \gg r$, this ratio tends to 1.125, which is agreeably small.

1. For each task T_i, do

Allocate one copy of the task to each of the r_i least utilized processors.

Update the processor allocation to account for the allocation of task T_i.

end do

end

(where r_i is the redundancy, i.e., the number of copies of task i that must be scheduled.)

FIGURE 3.38
Utilization-balancing algorithm.

3.4.2   A Next-Fit Algorithm for RM Scheduling

There is a utilization-based allocation heuristic that is meant specifically to be used in conjunction with the rate-monotonic scheduling algorithm. The task set has the properties that we assumed in Section 3.2.1 on RM scheduling (i.e., independence, preemptibility, and periodicity). The multiprocessor is assumed to consist of identical processors and tasks are assumed to require no resources other than processor time. Define $M > 3$ classes as follows, where M is picked by the user. Task T_i is in class $j < M$ if

$$2^{1/(j+1)} - 1 < e_i/P_i \leq 2^{1/j} - 1 \tag{3.109}$$

and in class M otherwise. Corresponding to each task class is a set of processors that is only allocated the tasks of that class.

We allocate tasks one by one to the appropriate processor class until all the tasks have been scheduled, adding processors to classes if that is needed for RM-schedulability. Example 3.37 clarifies this process.

Example 3.37. Suppose we have $M = 4$ classes. Then the following table lists the utilization bounds corresponding to each class.

Class	Bound
C_1	(0.41,1]
C_2	(0.26,0.41]
C_3	(0.19,0.26]
C_4	(0.00,0.19]

Consider the following periodic task set.

	T_1	T_2	T_3	T_4	T_5	T_6	T_7	T_8	T_9	T_{10}	T_{11}
e_i	5	7	3	1	10	16	1	3	9	17	21
P_i	10	21	22	24	30	40	50	55	70	90	95
$u(i)$	0.50	0.33	0.14	0.04	0.33	0.40	0.02	0.05	0.13	0.19	0.22
Class	C_1	C_2	C_4	C_4	C_2	C_2	C_4	C_4	C_4	C_4	C_3

Note: $u(i) = e_i / P_i$

Since we have at least one task in each of the four classes, let us begin by earmarking one processor for each class. In particular, let processor p_i be reserved for tasks in class C_i, $1 \le i \le 4$. T_1 is assigned to p_1, T_2 to p_2, and T_3 to p_4. $T_4 \in C_4$, and since $\{T_3, T_4\}$ is RM-schedulable on the same processor, we assign T_4 also to p_4. $T_5 \in C_2$, and since $\{T_2, T_5\}$ is RM-schedulable on the same processor, we assign T_5 also to p_2. $T_6 \in C_2$. However, $\{T_2, T_5, T_6\}$ is not RM-schedulable on the same processor, so we assign an additional processor p_5 to C_2 tasks and assign T_6 to p_5. $T_7 \in C_4$ and $\{T_3, T_4, T_7\}$ is RM-schedulable on the same processor, so we assign it to p_4. We proceed similarly for T_8, T_9, T_{10}. Finally, assign T_{11} to p_3. The assignments are summarized below.

Processor	Tasks
p_1	T_1
p_2	T_2, T_5
p_3	T_{11}
p_4	$T_3, T_4, T_7, T_8, T_9, T_{10}$
p_5	T_6

With this assignment, we can run the RM scheduling algorithm on each processor.

It is possible to show that this approach uses no more than N times the minimum possible number of processors, where

$$N = \begin{cases} 1.911 & \text{if there is no task with utilization in } (\sqrt{2} - 1, 0.5] \\ 2.340 & \text{otherwise} \end{cases} \quad (3.110)$$

3.4.3 A Bin-Packing Assignment Algorithm for EDF

Suppose we have a set of periodic independent preemptible tasks to be assigned to a multiprocessor consisting of identical processors. The task deadlines equal their periods. Other than processor time, tasks require no other resources.

We know that so long as the sum of the utilizations of the tasks assigned to a processor is no greater than 1, the task set is EDF-schedulable on that processor. So, the problem reduces to making task assignments with the property that the sum of the utilizations of the tasks assigned to a processor does not exceed 1.

```
Initialize i to 1. Set U(j) = 0, for all j.
while i ≤ n_T do
        Let j = min{k|U(k) + u(i) ≤ 1}.
        Assign the ith task in L to p_j.
        i ← i + 1.
end while
```

FIGURE 3.39
First-fit decreasing algorithm.

We would like to minimize the number of processors needed. This is the famous bin-packing problem and many algorithms exist for solving it.

The algorithm we present here is the first fit decreasing algorithm. Suppose there are n_T tasks to be assigned. Prepare a sorted list L of the tasks so that their utilizations (i.e., $u(i) = e_i/P_i$) are in nonincreasing order. Figure 3.39 shows the algorithm.

Example 3.38. Consider the following task set:

	T_1	T_2	T_3	T_4	T_5	T_6	T_7	T_8	T_9	T_{10}	T_{11}
e_i	5	7	3	1	10	16	1	3	9	17	21
P_i	10	21	22	24	30	40	50	55	70	90	95
$u(i)$	0.50	0.33	0.14	0.04	0.33	0.40	0.02	0.05	0.13	0.19	0.22

Note: $u(i) = e_i/P_i$

The ordered list is $L = (T_1, T_6, T_2, T_5, T_{11}, T_{10}, T_3, T_9, T_8, T_4, T_7)$. The assignment process is summarized in the following table. The vector $\mathbf{U} = (U_1, U_2, U_3, \ldots)$ contains the total utilizations of processor p_i in U_i.

Step	Task T_i	$u(i)$	Assigned to	Post-assignment U vector
1	T_1	0.50	p_1	(0.50)
2	T_6	0.40	p_1	(0.90)
3	T_2	0.33	p_2	(0.90,0.33)
4	T_5	0.33	p_2	(0.90,0.66)
5	T_{11}	0.22	p_2	(0.90,0.88)
6	T_{10}	0.18	p_3	(0.90,0.88,0.18)
7	T_3	0.14	p_3	(0.90,0.88,0.32)
8	T_9	0.13	p_3	(0.90,0.88,0.45)
9	T_8	0.06	p_1	(0.96,0.88,0.45)
10	T_4	0.04	p_1	(1.00,0.88,0.45)
11	T_7	0.02	p_2	(1.00,0.90,0.45)

It is possible to show that when the number of processors required is large, the ratio

$$\frac{\text{Number of processors used by the first-fit decreasing algorithm}}{\text{Number of processors used by optimal algorithm}}$$

approaches $11/9 = 1.22$, when a large task set is used. In fact, this limit is approached quickly, so that 1.22 is a good measure even for relatively small systems.

3.4.4 A Myopic Offline Scheduling (MOS) Algorithm

Thus far, we have assumed that tasks can be preempted. The *myopic offline scheduling* (MOS) heuristic is an assignment/scheduling algorithm meant for non-preemptive tasks. This algorithm takes account not only of processing needs but also of any requirements that tasks may have for additional resources. For instance, a task may need to have exclusive access to a block of memory or may need to have control over a printer. MOS is an offline algorithm in that we are given in advance the entire set of tasks, their arrival times, execution times, and deadlines.

MOS proceeds by building up a schedule tree. Each node in this tree represents an assignment and scheduling of a subset of the tasks. The root of the schedule tree is an empty schedule. Each child of a node consists of the schedule of its parent node, extended by one task. A leaf of this tree consists of a schedule (feasible or infeasible) of the entire task set.

The schedule tree for an n_T-task system consists of $n_T + 1$ levels (including the root). Level i of the tree (counting the root as being of level 0) consists of nodes representing schedules including exactly i of the tasks.

Generating the complete tree is tantamount to an exhaustive enumeration of all possible allocations. For any but the smallest systems, it is therefore not practical to generate the complete tree; instead, we try to get to a feasible schedule as quickly as we can.

The algorithm can be informally described as follows. We start at the root node, which is an empty schedule; that is, it corresponds to no task having been scheduled. We then proceed to build the tree from that point by developing nodes. A node n is developed as follows. Given a node n, we try to extend the schedule represented by that node by one more task. That is, we pick up one of the as-yet-unscheduled tasks and try to add it to the schedule represented by node n. The augmented schedule is a child node of n.

There are two questions that must be answered. First, which task do we pick for extending an incomplete schedule? Second, when do we decide that a node is not worth developing further and turn to another node?

1. The task that we chose to extend an incomplete schedule is one that minimizes a heuristic function H. H may be any of the following functions:
  - task execution time,

- deadline,
- earliest start time (i.e., earliest time at which the resources for that task will become available after it has been released),
- laxity,[9] or
- weighted sum of any of the above.

For instance, if $H(i) = D_i$, then the next task to be chosen for scheduling will be the as-yet-unscheduled task with the earliest deadline.

2. We only develop a node if it is strongly feasible. A node is *strongly feasible* if a feasible schedule can be generated by extending the current partial schedule with any one of the as-yet-unscheduled tasks. If a node is not strongly feasible, it means that none of its descendants that are leaves can represent a feasible schedule. If we encounter a node that is not strongly feasible, we backtrack. That is, we mark that node as hopeless, and then go back to its parent, resuming the schedule-building from that point.

One difficulty with the MOS algorithm is that, if the number of tasks is very large, it can take a long time to check if a node is strongly feasible. In particular, at level i, we will need to check feasibility of extending the schedule by each of the $n_T - i$ as-yet-unscheduled tasks. As a result, the number of comparisons needed to generate one root-to-leaf path is

$$n_T + (n_T - 1) + (n_T - 2) + \cdots + 0 = \frac{n_T(n_T + 1)}{2}$$

To reduce the number of comparisons, we can replace the strong feasibility check at each node by means of a myopic procedure as follows. For each nonleaf level-i node n, this procedure picks the first $\min\{k, n_T - i\}$ as-yet-unscheduled tasks and checks to see if the schedule represented by n can be feasibly extended by each of these tasks. (The parameter k is used by the algorithm to limit the scope of the search.) If not, we mark the node as hopeless and backtrack as before. Otherwise, we develop children for that node.

Example 3.39. We have a five-task set to be scheduled on a two-processor system. The tasks are nonpreemptive. The parameters of these tasks are as follows:

	T_1	T_2	T_3	T_4	T_5
r_i	0	10	0	15	0
e_i	15	5	16	9	10
D_i	15	20	18	25	50

---

[9]The laxity of task T_i is given by $D_i - e_i$. It is the latest time at which T_i may be started and be guaranteed to meet its deadline.

There are no other resource requirements. Suppose we use $H(i) = r_i$. We set $k = 5$ for the myopic procedure. The tree generated by the algorithm is shown in Figure 3.40.

The root node is the empty schedule. There are three tasks with release times of 0; we pick T_1 first. A level-1 node is generated, that contains a schedule for T_1. This node is strongly feasible—any of the other tasks can be feasibly scheduled given the position that T_1 occupies in the schedule.

Next, we pick T_3 and schedule it to form a level-2 node. This, too, is strongly feasible. Then, we generate a level-3 node, which involves augmenting the previous schedule with T_5. Unfortunately, this is not strongly feasible; in particular, it would be impossible to augment this schedule with T_2. So, we backtrack to the level-2 (i.e., the parent) node. We pick T_2 rather than T_5 (the next task in order of release time) and schedule it. This results in a strongly feasible schedule.

Next, we form a level-5 node by adding T_5 to the schedule. This is not strongly feasible—T_4 cannot be added to it. So, we abandon this node, return to the parent (level-4) node, and generate a schedule by adding T_4. This is strongly feasible, and its child, formed by adding the final task to it, is a leaf node that represents a feasible scheduling of all the tasks.

The reader should run the algorithm on this set of tasks with $H(i) = D_i$ and see if it runs any faster for that function.

The running time of the algorithm depends on k and H. No definitive statements can be made about how to choose these quantities. Let us examine k. This bounds the number of tasks that the algorithm considers in determining the strong feasibility of a node. If k is too small, it is possible for us to declare a node to be strongly feasible and develop it further, only to find that none of its descendants is strongly feasible. If k is too large, we will spend a great deal of time (especially in the levels of the tree close to the root) checking the strong feasibility of nodes. In general, the tighter the constraints, the greater must be the value of k. In other words, if the task laxities are low or if many tasks use resources in addition to the processor, k must be large. It has been suggested, from extensive simulations, that $k \approx 13$ is the largest value ever required.

As far as H is concerned, a weighted sum of the deadline and earliest start time is perhaps the most promising function. Recall that the earliest start time of a task is the earliest time after the task has been released that all the nonprocessor resources needed by that task become available.

3.4.5 Focused Addressing and Bidding (FAB) Algorithm

The focused addressing and bidding (FAB) algorithm is simple enough to be an online procedure and is used for task sets consisting of both critical and noncritical real-time tasks. Critical tasks must have sufficient time reserved for them so that they continue to execute successfully, even if they need their worst-case execution times. The noncritical tasks are either processed or not, depending on the system's ability to do so.

The underlying system model is as follows. The noncritical tasks arrive at individual processors in the multiprocessor system. If a noncritical task arrives at

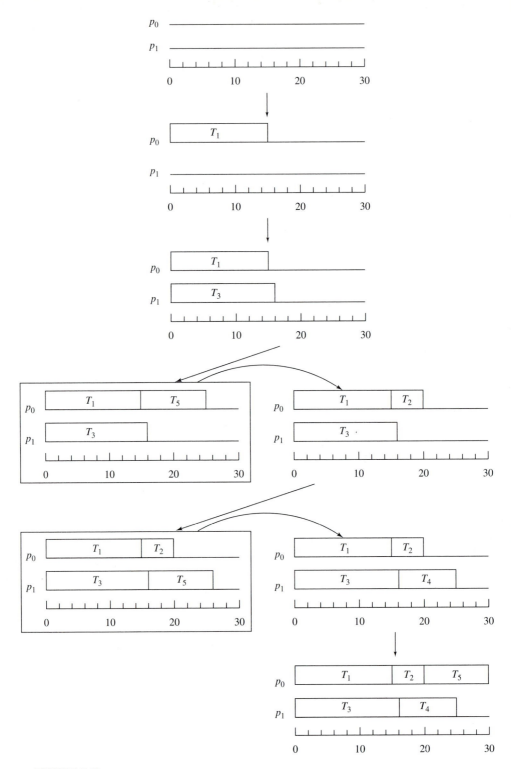

FIGURE 3.40
Example of the MOS algorithm; boxed nodes are not strongly feasible.

processor p_i, that processor checks to see if it expects to have the resources and time to execute it by the specified deadline[10] without missing any of the deadlines of the critical tasks or of the previously guaranteed noncritical tasks. If it does, p_i guarantees the successful execution of that task, adds that task to its list of tasks to be executed, and reserves time on its schedule to execute that task. Since this is a noncritical task, the guarantee can be based on the expected run time of the task rather than on the worst-case run time. In other words, we can accept that some noncritical tasks might turn out to be not executable in a timely fashion because their actual run times turn out to be much greater than anticipated.

The FAB algorithm is used when p_i determines that it does not have the resources or time to execute the task. In that case, it tries to ship that task out to some other processor in the system.

The problem of load-sharing by moving tasks from one processor to another has long been studied in general-purpose distributed systems. Many solutions have been suggested. Perhaps the simplest is a random-threshold algorithm. In this algorithm, a processor that finds its load exceeding a threshold simply sends an incoming task out to another processor, chosen at random. Another algorithm has lightly loaded processors touting for business by announcing they are lightly loaded and are willing to process excess tasks from other processors. We shall see a variant of this (adapted for real-time purposes) when we study the buddy algorithm.

The FAB algorithm is as follows. Each processor maintains a status table that indicates which tasks it has already committed to run. These include the set of critical tasks (which were preassigned statically), and any additional noncritical tasks that it may have accepted. In addition, it maintains a table of the surplus computational capacity at every other processor in the system. The time axis is divided into *windows*, which are intervals of fixed duration, and each processor regularly sends to its colleagues the fraction of the next window that is currently free (i.e., is not already spoken for by tasks). Since the system is distributed, this information may never be completely up to date.

When shopping for a processor on which to offload a task, an overloaded processor checks its surplus information and selects a processor (called the *focused processor*) p_s that it believes to be the most likely to be able to successfully execute that task by its deadline. It ships the task out to that processor. However, as we pointed out, the surplus information may have been out of date and it is possible that the selected processor will not have the free time to execute the task. As insurance against this, and in parallel with sending out the task to the focused processor p_s, the originating processor decides whether to send out requests for bids (RFB) to other lightly loaded processors. The RFB contains the vital statistics of the task (its expected execution time, any other resource requirements, its deadline, etc.), and asks any processor that can successfully execute the task to send a bid to the focused processor p_s stating how quickly it can process the task.

---

[10]Recall that in a real-time system, the resource and execution-time requirements of all the tasks are known in advance.

An RFB is only sent out if the sending processor estimates that there will be enough time for timely responses to it. In other words, it computes the sum of the estimated time taken by the RFB to reach its destinations, the estimated time taken by the destinations to respond with a bid, and the estimated time taken to transmit the bid to the focused processor. Call this sum t_{bid}. It also computes the latest time at which the focused processor can offload the task onto a bidder without the task deadline being missed; this time is given by the expression

$t_{offload} =$

task deadline $-$ (current time $+$ time to move the task $+$ task-execution time)

If $t_{bid} \leq t_{offload}$, then an RFB is sent out.

When processor p_t receives an RFB, it checks to see if it can meet the task requirements and still execute its already-scheduled tasks successfully. First, it estimates when the new task will arrive and how long it will take to be either guaranteed or rejected. This time is given by

$t_{arr} =$ Current time $+$ time for bid to be received by p_s

$+$ time taken by p_s to make a decision

$+$ time taken to transfer the task

$+$ time taken by p_t to either guarantee or reject the task

Next, it figures out the surplus computational time $t_{surplus}$ that it currently has between t_{arr} and the task deadline D. This is done by first estimating the computational time already spoken for in the interval $[t_{arr}, D]$:

$t_{comp} =$ time allotted to critical tasks in $[t_{arr}, D]$

$+$ time needed in $[t_{arr}, D]$ to run already-accepted noncritical tasks

$+$ fraction of recently accepted bids

$\times$ time needed in $[t_{arr}, D]$ to honor pending bids

$t_{surplus} =$ $D -$ current time $- t_{comp}$

The degree to which the bid is aggressive or conservative can vary with the nature of the time estimates. If the task worst-case run times are used, the bids will be very conservative indeed. If average-case values are used instead, the bids will be less conservative.

If $t_{surplus} <$ task execution time, then no bid is sent out. If $t_{surplus} \geq$ task execution time, p_t sends out a bid to p_s. The bid contains t_{arr}, $t_{surplus}$, and an estimate of how long a task transferred to p_t will have to wait before it is either guaranteed or rejected.

All bids are sent to the focused processor p_s. If p_s is unable to process the task successfully, it can review the bids it gets back to see which other processor is most likely to be able to do so, and transfer the task to that processor. p_s

waits for a certain minimum number of bids to arrive or until a specified time has expired since receiving the task, whichever is sooner. It then evaluates each bid. For each bidding node p_i, p_s computes the estimated arrival time $\eta(i)$ of the task at that node. Denote by $t_{surplus}(i)$ and $t_{arr}(i)$ the $t_{surplus}$ and t_{arr} values contained in the bid received from p_i. Then, p_s computes the following quantity for each bid:

$$t_{est}(i) = t_{surplus}(i)\frac{D - \eta(i)}{D - t_{arr}(i)} \tag{3.111}$$

Suppose $t_{est}(j)$ is the maximum such value. Then, if p_s cannot itself guarantee the task, it ships the task out to p_j.

The cardinal rule in bidding is that no new noncritical task can be allowed to cause any critical task or previously guaranteed noncritical task to miss its (guaranteed) deadline. Assessing the schedulability of a newly arrived task or responding to an RFB takes time, and can be indulged in only if doing so does not cause any guaranteed deadlines to be missed. There are two ways of determining this. The first is to introduce into the schedule a periodic task to check for schedulability; every t seconds, this task will assess the schedulability of tasks that have arrived over the last period. The second is to set a flag that indicates if the processor has the time to check the schedulability of a new task and still meet all guaranteed deadlines. If the flag is set when a new task arrives, the executing task is preempted and the processor deals with this new task. If the flag is reset, the processor is not interrupted and the new task must wait until the processor has time to handle it. A similar flag can be used to decide if there is enough time to respond to an RFB.

An issue worth discussing is how aggressive the bid should be. In many instances, worst-case task execution times are much greater than average-case times. Also, not all bids sent out by a processor are accepted. If the bidding is done too conservatively, by assuming that already-scheduled tasks will take their worst-case times and that all the bids will be successful, processors that could otherwise have successfully run the task in question may not bid. If the bidding is done too aggressively, then the probability is high that it will not be possible to honor the bid (should it be accepted). If an accepted bid cannot be honored, then a task, which might have been able to execute successfully on some other processor may miss its deadline. The designer must decide how to resolve this trade-off between aggressive and conservative bidding by finding a happy medium between them. One possible solution is for the system to adapt its bidding strategy based on experience. That is, if a processor has been unable to honor many recent bids, that processor is being too aggressive and can be made more conservative in its subsequent bidding. If, on the other hand, a processor has a lot of idle time despite declining to bid on tasks (which in hindsight it could have processed successfully), it is being too conservative and should become more aggressive.

3.4.6 The Buddy Strategy

The buddy strategy attacks the same type of problem as the FAB algorithm. Soft real-time tasks arrive at the various processors of a multiprocessor and, if an individual processor finds itself overloaded, it tries to offload some tasks onto less lightly loaded processors. The buddy strategy differs from the FAB algorithm in the manner in which the target processors are found.

Briefly, each processor has three thresholds of loading: under (T_U), full (T_F), and over (T_V). The loading is determined by the number of jobs awaiting service in the processor's queue. If the queue length is Q, the processor is said to be in:

state U	(underloaded)	if $Q \leq T_U$
state F	(fully loaded)	if $T_F < Q \leq T_V$
state V	(overloaded)	if $Q > T_V$

A processor is judged to be in a position to execute tasks transferred from other processors if it is in state U. If it is in state V, it looks for other processors on which to offload some tasks. A processor in state F will neither accept tasks from other processors nor offload tasks onto other processors.

When a processor makes a transition out of or into state U, it broadcasts an announcement to this effect. This broadcast is not sent to all the processors; rather, its distribution is limited to a subset of the processors. This is called the processor's *buddy set*. Each processor is aware of whether any members of its buddy sets is in state U. If it is overloaded, it chooses an underloaded member (if any) in its buddy set on which to offload a task.

There are three issues worth discussing at this point. First, consider how the buddy set is to be chosen. If it is too large, the state-change broadcast will heavily load the interconnection network. If it is too small, the communication costs will be low, but the overloaded processors will be less successful in finding an underloaded processor in their buddy sets. Clearly, this applies only to multihop networks. If the interconnection network is a bus, for example, every broadcast will be seen by every processor and there is no saving in restricting delivery to a subset. If, on the other hand, a multihop network is used and the buddy set of a processor is restricted to the processors that are "close" to it (in terms of the number of hops between them), there will be a substantial saving of network bandwidth. The size of the buddy set will therefore depend on the nature of the interconnection network.

The second issue is a little more subtle. Suppose a node is in the buddy set of many overloaded processors, and that it delivers a state-change message to them, saying it is now underloaded. This can result in each of the overloaded processors simultaneously and independently dumping load on it, thus overloading that processor. To reduce the probability of this happening, we construct an ordered list of preferred processors. First we list the processors that are one hop away from the processor, then those which are two hops away, and so on. An overloaded processor searches its list in sequence, looking for underloaded processors, and sends a load to the first underloaded processor on its list. If the lists of the various processors are ordered differently, the probability of a node being simultaneously dumped on is reduced.

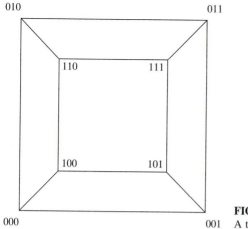

010   011

110   111

100   101

FIGURE 3.41

000   001   A three-dimensional hypercube network.

Example 3.40. Suppose the network is a three-dimensional hypercube. See Figure 3.41. Each processor in this system is connected to three other processors. Suppose the buddy set of each processor has been defined to be its immediate neighbors. Under the standard hypercube labeling, each node label will differ from its neighbors' labels in exactly one bit. Order the buddy list of each processor according to which bit is different. For example, if we give highest priority to processors differing in the LSB, then to the middle bit, and then to the MSB, the priority list of each of the processors is as shown in Table 3.2. For example, node 000 is in the buddy set of 001, 010, 100. It is the first priority node for node 001 (i.e., if node 001 is overloaded, it will check if node 000 is underloaded first. It is the second priority node for node 010 and the third priority node for node 100. Both nodes 001 and 010 will only simultaneously dump load on node 000 if (a) they are both overloaded, and (b) node 011 is not in state U. This is clearly an event that is much less probable than if 000 were the first on the list of all three of its neighbors.

For large buddy sets, if the priority lists are staggered properly, it is extremely unlikely that more than a small fraction of the processors in a buddy set will simultaneously dump a load on a given processor. Some simulation experiments indicate that buddy-set sizes of 10 to 15 are best, even for very large

TABLE 3.2
Example of priority list

Node	Priority list		
000	001	010	100
001	000	011	101
010	011	000	110
011	010	001	111
100	101	110	000
101	100	111	001
110	111	100	010

systems. Keeping the size of buddy sets constant and independent of the system size results in the state-update traffic per processor being constant and not a function of the system size.

The third issue of importance is the choice of the thresholds T_U, T_F, and T_V. In general, the greater the value of T_V, the smaller the rate at which tasks are transferred from one node to another. From simulation experiments, it appears that setting $T_U = 1$, $T_F = 2$, and $T_V = 3$ produces good results for a wide range of system parameters. Of course, which thresholds are best for a given system depends on the particular characteristics of that system, including the size of the buddy set, the prevailing load, and the bandwidth and topology of the interconnection network.

There is, at present, no general model of how well the buddy algorithm performs. An approximate model has been derived under the simplifying assumption that all tasks take one unit time to execute. The reader is referred to Section 3.7 for references in the technical literature.

3.4.7 Assignment with Precedence Conditions

In this section, we present a simple algorithm that assigns and schedules tasks with precedence conditions and additional resource constraints. The basic idea behind the algorithm is to reduce communication costs by assigning (if possible) to the same processor tasks that heavily communicate with one another.

The underlying task model is as follows. Each task may be composed of one or more subtasks. The release time of each task and the worst-case execution time of each subtask are given. The subtask communication pattern is represented by a task graph: that implicitly defines the precedence conditions (i.e., which subtask feeds output to which other subtask). We are also given the volume of communication between subtasks. It is assumed that if subtask s_1 sends output to s_2, this is done at the end of the s_1 execution, and must arrive before s_2 can begin executing.

Associated with each subtask is a latest finishing time (LFT). The LFT of a subtask s_i is computed as follows. Suppose that n_i is the number of paths in the task graph emanating from s_i. Let $\{v_{k,1}^\ell, v_{k,2}^\ell, \ldots, v_{k,m_\ell}^\ell\}$ be the nodes on the ℓth such path. Let η_ℓ be the sum of the execution times of the subtasks represented by the nodes on that path, and D_{v_{k,m_ℓ}^ℓ} be the deadline of the last node on this path. We have:

$$\text{LFT}(n_i) = D_{v_{k,m_\ell}^\ell} - \eta_\ell \tag{3.112}$$

Example 3.41. Consider the task graph shown in Figure 3.42. The execution times are as follows:

Subtask	Execution time
s_0	4
s_1	10
s_2	15
s_3	4
s_4	4

The labels within the circles are the subtask subscripts and the arc labels denote the volume of communication between the tasks. Suppose the overall deadline for this task (i.e., the deadline of subtask s_4) is 30. The LFT for s_4 is clearly 30, and for s_1, s_2, s_3 is $30 - e_4 = 26$. The LFT for s_0 is $30 - e_4 - \max\{e_1, e_2, e_3\} = 30 - 4 - 15 = 11$. Note two things from this. First, we are not accounting for any communication time here. Second, we are assuming that s_1, s_2, s_3 are run in parallel. If they were run in tandem (say, on the same processor), the LFT of s_0 would be $30 - (e_1 + e_2 + e_3 + e_4)$. If a subtask does not finish by its LFT, we are sure to miss a deadline, especially if the subtasks consume their worst-case execution times. However, meeting the LFT does not always guarantee that deadlines will all be met.

The algorithm is a trial-and-error process. We start with the set of subtasks and assign them to the processors one by one, in the order of their LFT values. If two subtasks have the same LFT value, the tie is broken by giving priority to the subtask with the greatest number of successor subtasks.

We check for feasibility with each assignment—if one assignment is not feasible, we try another, and so on. If no assignment works for this particular subtask, we backtrack and try changing the assignment of the previously assigned subtask and continue from there.

Subtasks that communicate with each other a lot are assigned to the same processor if this allows for feasible scheduling. A threshold policy is followed for this. If e_i and e_j are the execution times of subtasks s_i and s_j, respectively, and c_{ij} is the volume of communication between them, we try assigning s_i and s_j to the same processor if

$$\frac{e_i + e_j}{c_{ij}} < k_c$$

where k_c is a given parameter (to be discussed below). The idea behind this is to balance the benefits of assigning subtasks to the same processor (the communication cost is zero) against the potential benefits of assigning them to different processors (evening out the load and in some cases reducing the subtask finishing times by letting them run in parallel). The assignment is done in part by checking each pair of communicating subtasks to see if they must be assigned to the same processor.

Example 3.42. Consider again the task graph shown in Figure 3.42. Suppose $k_c = 3$. Then, $\{s_1, s_4\}$, $\{s_2, s_4\}$, and $\{s_3, s_4\}$ must all be placed on the same processor. (The

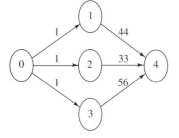

FIGURE 3.42
Task graph for calculating the latest finishing time.

side effect of this is that s_1, s_2, s_3 must be on the same processor, even though there is no communication between them.)

k_c is a tunable parameter. If k_c is 0, then intersubtask communication will simply not be taken into account when we do the assignment. If k_c is very high, then, most of the time, we will be forced to assign tasks to the same processor. This may result in the schedule becoming infeasible. In that case, we will be forced to reduce k_c adaptively to relax this constraint.

The algorithm can be informally described as follows:

1. Start with the set of tasks that need to be assigned and scheduled. Choose a value for k_c and determine, based on this value, which tasks need to be on the same processor.

2. Start assigning and scheduling the subtasks in order of precedence. If a particular allocation is infeasible, reallocate if possible. If feasibility is impossible to achieve because of the tasks that need to be assigned to the same processor, reduce k_c suitably and go to the previous step. Stop when either the tasks have been successfully assigned and scheduled, or when the algorithm has tried more than a certain number of iterations. In the former case, output the completed schedule; in the latter, declare failure.

Example 3.43. Let us now illustrate this algorithm with an example consisting of one task with eight subtasks, as specified in the table below, with task graph shown in Figure 3.43.

Subtask	Execution time	Deadline	LFT
s_0	4	–	7
s_1	10	–	24
s_2	15	22	22
s_3	4	–	26
s_4	18	–	42
s_5	3	–	42
s_6	6	–	32
s_7	3	45	45
s_8	8	40	40

The output to the "outside world" is provided by s_2, s_7, s_8, and so these are the only subtasks whose deadlines are specified. Table 3.3 shows, for each communicating pair of tasks, the ratio between the total execution time and communication volume. If, for example, we set $k_c = 1.5$, we would have to have the following pairs assigned to the same processor: $\{s_0, s_1\}$, $\{s_0, s_2\}$, $\{s_0, s_3\}$, $\{s_5, s_7\}$, $\{s_3, s_6\}$, and $\{s_6, s_8\}$. This implies that the following tasks must all be assigned to the same processor: $s_0, s_1, s_2, s_3, s_6, s_8$.

Suppose we have a system consisting of two processors, p_0 and p_1, on which we seek to assign these tasks. The following is a list of the steps of this algorithm. We start with $k_c = 1.5$ and assume that the interconnection network is a single bus used by a two-processor system.

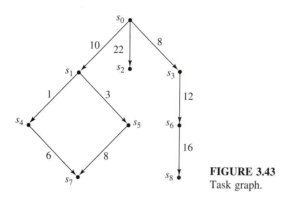

FIGURE 3.43
Task graph.

1. Assign s_0 to processor p_0 over the interval $[0, 4]$ (assuming time 0 is when this task is released).

2. Assign s_1 to processor p_0 and schedule it over $[4, 14]$. (No communication costs are incurred because s_1 is on the same processor as s_0).

3. Assign s_2 to processor p_0. It is immediately clear that we cannot schedule both s_1 and s_2 so that they complete before their respective LFT values. Therefore, we need to change k_c. Let us reduce it to $k_c = 1.0$. Now, the following pairs must be assigned to the same processor: $\{s_0, s_2\}$, $\{s_5, s_7\}$, $\{s_3, s_6\}$, and $\{s_6, s_8\}$.

4. Now, assign s_1 to p_1, and schedule it over $[14, 24]$. Also schedule the network path between p_0 and p_1 for $[4, 14]$ (for the communication between s_0 and s_1).

5. Assign s_2 to p_0 and schedule it over $[4, 19]$.

6. Assign s_3 to p_0 and schedule it over $[19, 23]$.

7. Assign s_4 to p_0 and schedule it over $[23, 41]$.

8. Assign s_5 to p_0. This is infeasible, as we can check easily. Backtrack to the previous step.

9. Reassign s_4 to p_1 and schedule it over $[24, 42]$.

10. Reassign s_5 to p_0 and schedule it over $[27, 30]$.

11. Assign s_6 to p_0 and schedule it over $[23, 29]$. Move s_5 to $[29, 32]$.

TABLE 3.3
Execution time to communication volume ratio.

Pair s_i, s_j	$e_i + e_j$	c_{ij}	$(e_i + e_j)/c_{ij}$
s_0, s_1	14	10	1.40
s_0, s_2	19	22	0.86
s_0, s_3	8	8	1.00
s_1, s_4	28	14	2.00
s_1, s_5	13	3	4.33
s_4, s_7	21	6	3.50
s_5, s_7	6	8	0.75⁻
s_3, s_6	10	12	0.83
s_6, s_8	14	16	0.88

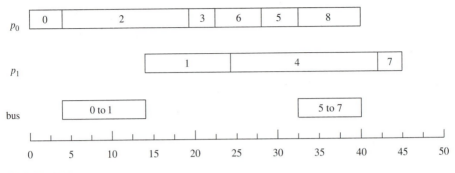

FIGURE 3.44
Example of the task assignment and scheduling algorithm.

12. The assignment of s_7 to p_0 is infeasible, so assign s_7 to p_1 and schedule it over [42,45].

13. Assign s_8 to p_0 and schedule it over [32, 40].

The schedule is shown in Figure 3.44. Note that we are scheduling each task in the task set. If the task set is periodic, then we only need to consider the tasks released during the least common multiple of the task periods.

3.5   MODE CHANGES

The workload of a real-time computer can change over time, as the mission phase changes or as processor failures dictate. Tasks may be added or deleted from the schedule, or may have their period or execution time changed. In this section, we look at how such mode changes can be accommodated under the rate-monotonic scheduling algorithm. Our objective is to allow the system to incorporate some new tasks (or delete some current ones) and still meet all the hard deadlines.

When critical sections are not involved, mode changes are quite simple to implement. Deleting a task (assuming its output is not needed by any other task) clearly does not adversely affect the schedulability of the other tasks. That is, if a task set $S = \{T_1, \ldots, T_n\}$ is RM-schedulable, $S - \{T_i\}$ is also RM-schedulable. This brings up the question of when the time allocated to the deleted task(s) can be reclaimed for use by other tasks. In order for schedulability to continue to be met, the time can only be reclaimed after the end of the period of the last iteration of the deleted task. That is, suppose we are deleting task T in Figure 3.45. T completes execution for the last time at t_0. However, its current period runs until t_1, and its deletion does not take effect until that time. This ensures that the schedulability rules we derived for the RM algorithm continue to hold throughout the mode-change process.

Adding a task is just as simple. We need only to check that it meets the RM-schedulability conditions outlined earlier in this chapter.

Example 3.44. Consider a system that is currently executing task set $\{T_1, T_2, T_3\}$ with $P_1 = 5, P_2 = 8, P_3 = 13$, and $e_1 = 1, e_2 = 3, e_3 = 4$. This task set is

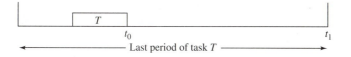

FIGURE 3.45
Mode changing: task T is not deleted until t_1.

RM-schedulable since

$$e_1 \leq P_1$$

$$2e_1 + e_2 \leq P_1$$

$$3e_1 + 2e_2 + e_3 \leq P_3$$

Assume that all these tasks have zero phasings. Suppose that at time 30 we wish to replace task T_3 by T_4, with parameters $P_4 = 14, e_4 = 5$. First, we check if the set $\{T_1, T_2, T_4\}$ is RM-schedulable. It is, because of the following inequalities:

$$e_1 \leq P_1$$

$$e_1 + e_2 \leq P_1$$

$$3e_1 + 2e_2 + e_4 \leq P_4$$

When can we add task T_4? Under the RM algorithm, T_3 has run part of its third iteration at time 30. As a result, we cannot replace T_3 by T_4 until the end of the current T_3 period, that is, until 39. At that time, T_4 may be inducted into the task set.

If the priority ceiling protocol is used to handle the accesses to exclusive resources, the priority ceilings of the semaphores are lowered or raised as appropriate when the underlying tasks that give rise to these priorities are deleted or added. Recall that the priority ceiling of a critical section is the maximum of the priorities of all tasks that can access it.

The rule for deleting tasks is the same as when no critical sections are involved. A task may be added if the following two conditions are satisfied:

- the resultant task set is RM-schedulable, and
- when adding the task will result in the increase of the priority ceilings of any of the semaphores, those ceilings are raised before the task is added.

If the priority ceiling of a semaphore needs to be changed, the rules are:

- If the semaphore is unlocked, the ceiling is changed immediately in an indivisible action.
- If the ceiling is to be raised and the semaphore is locked, we wait until it is unlocked before raising it.
- If, as a result of some tasks being deleted, the priority celings decrease, this occurs at the time of deletion.

Example 3.45. Suppose that we have three semaphores, S_1, S_2, S_3, and four tasks T_1, T_2, T_3, T_4 in the overall task set. (As usual, we assume $T_1 \succ T_2 \succ T_3 \succ T_4$.) The following chart indicates which task may lock the semaphores:

Semaphore	Tasks
S_1	T_1, T_3
S_2	T_2, T_3, T_4
S_3	T_1, T_3, T_4

Suppose now that we wish to delete task T_2 from the task set. At the moment that T_2 is deleted, the priority ceiling of S_2 will drop from the priority of T_2 to that of T_3.

Assume that S_1 is currently locked and we wish to add task T_0 to the task set (with $T_0 \succ T_1$). Then, the priority ceilings of S_1 and S_3 will need to be raised to the priority of T_0. This may not be done, however, until the lock on S_1 is released. At that moment, the ceiling of S_1 is raised. Note that until this happens, we cannot add T_0 to the task set.

The mode change protocol has the same properties as the priority ceiling protocol. In particular, under the mode change protocol, there is no deadlock, nor can a task be blocked for more than the duration of a single outermost critical section. The proofs are similar to those derived earlier for the priority ceiling protocol, and are omitted.

3.6 FAULT-TOLERANT SCHEDULING

The advantage of static scheduling is that more time can be spent in developing a better schedule. However, static schedules must have the ability to respond to hardware failures. They do this by having a sufficient reserve capacity and a sufficiently fast failure-response mechanism to continue to meet critical-task deadlines despite a certain number of failures.

The approach to fault-tolerant scheduling that we consider here uses additional *ghost* copies of tasks, which are embedded into the schedule and activated whenever a processor carrying one of their corresponding primary or previously-activated ghost copies fails. These ghost copies need not be identical to the primary copies; they may be alternative versions that take less time to run and provide results of poorer but still acceptable quality than the primaries.

We will assume a set of periodic critical tasks. Multiple copies of each version of a task are assumed to be executed in parallel, with voting or some other error-masking mechanisms (see Chapter 7 for a detailed discussion of such mechanisms.) When a processor fails, there are two types of tasks affected by that failure. The first type is the task that is running at the time of failure, and the second type comprises those that were to have been run by that processor in the future. The use of forward-error recovery is assumed to be sufficient to compensate for the loss of the first type of task. The fault-tolerant scheduling algorithm we describe here is meant to compensate for the second type by finding substitute processors to run those copies.

We assume the existence of a nonfault-tolerant algorithm for allocation and scheduling. This algorithm will be called as a subroutine by the fault-tolerant scheduling procedure that we will describe. We assume that the allocation/scheduling procedure consists of an assignment part Π_a and an EDF scheduling part Π_s.

We are now in a position to define our problem more precisely. Suppose the system is meant to run $n_c(i)$ copies of each version (or iteration) of task T_i, and is supposed to tolerate up to n_{sust} processor failures. The fault-tolerant schedule must ensure that, after some time for reacting to the failure(s), the system can still execute $n_c(i)$ copies of each version of task i, despite the failure of up to n_{sust} processors. These processor failures may occur in any order.

The output of our fault-tolerant scheduling algorithm will be a ghost schedule, plus one or more primary schedules for each processor. If one or more of the ghosts is to be run, the processor runs the ghosts at the times specified by the ghost schedule and shifts the primary copies to make room for the ghosts. Example 3.45 illustrates this.

> **Example 3.46.** Figure 3.46 shows an example of a pair of ghost and primary schedules, together with the schedule that the processor actually executes if the ghost is activated. Of course, this pair of ghost and primary schedules is only feasible if, despite the ghost being activated, all the deadlines are met.

A ghost schedule and a primary schedule are said to form a *feasible pair* if all deadlines continue to be met even if the primary tasks are shifted right by the time needed to execute the ghosts. Ghosts may overlap in the ghost schedule of a processor. If two ghosts overlap, only one of them can be activated. For example, in Figure 3.47, we cannot activate both g_1 and g_2 or both g_2 and g_3. We can, however, activate both g_1 and g_3. There are two conditions that ghosts must satisfy.

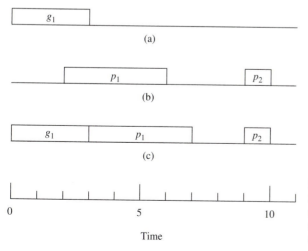

(a)

(b)

(c)

Time

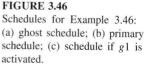

FIGURE 3.46
Schedules for Example 3.46:
(a) ghost schedule; (b) primary schedule; (c) schedule if $g1$ is activated.

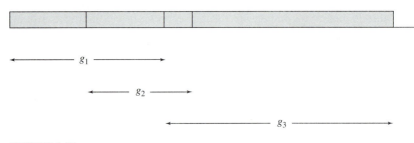

FIGURE 3.47
Overlapping ghosts.

C1. Each version must have ghost copies scheduled on n_{sust} distinct processors. Two or more copies (primary or ghost) of the same version must not be scheduled on the same processor.

C2. Ghosts are *conditionally transparent*. That is, they must satisfy the following two properties:

    a. Two ghost copies may overlap in the schedule of a processor if no other processor carries a copy (either primary or ghost) of both tasks.

    b. Primary copies may overlap the ghosts in the schedule only if there is sufficient slack time in the schedule to continue to meet the deadlines of all the primary and activated ghost copies on that processor.

> **Theorem 3.18.** Conditions **C1** and **C2** are necessary and sufficient conditions for up to n_{sust} processor failures to be tolerated.

Proof

    Necessity of C1. Suppose some version had ghost copies allocated to n processors $\pi_1, \ldots, \pi_n$. The failure of the processors $\pi_1, \ldots, \pi_n$, together with the failure of any processor carrying a primary copy of this task, would make the system no longer capable of running the required number of copies. Thus, if $n < n_{sust}$, the system cannot tolerate n_{sust} processor failures.

    Necessity of C2a. Consider ghost copies g_1 and g_2 of the ith versions of tasks I and T, which overlap in the ghost schedule of some processor p_1. Suppose there exists some other processor p_2 that is allocated primary copies of both of these versions. There is a total of n_{sust} ghost copies of each version. If n_{sust} processors (other than p_1), carrying either the ghost or primary version, fail, then since we cannot activate both g_1 and g_2 in the schedule of p_1, we cannot maintain the required number of active copies.

    Necessity of C2b. This is obvious.

    Sufficiency of C1 and C2. This part is similar to the proof of the necessity of **C1** and **C2**, and is left as an exercise for the reader.   **Q.E.D.**

Theorem 3.18 provides the conditions that the fault-tolerant scheduling algorithm must follow in producing the ghost and primary schedules.

    Perhaps the simplest fault-tolerant scheduling algorithm is FA1, shown in Figure 3.48. Under algorithm FA1, the primary copies will always execute in the positions specified in schedule S, regardless of whether any ghosts happen to be

1. Run Π_a to obtain a candidate allocation of copies to processors. Denote by π_i and θ_i the primary and ghost copies allocated to processor p_i, $i = 1, \ldots, n_p$.
2. Run $\Pi_s^*(\pi_i \cup \theta_i, i)$. If the resultant schedule is found to be infeasible the allocation as produced by Π_a is infeasible; return control to Π_a in step 1. Otherwise, record the position of the ghost copies (as put out by Π_s^*) in ghost schedule G_i, and the position of the primary copies in schedule S.

FIGURE 3.48
Algorithm FA1.

1. Run Π_a to obtain a candidate allocation of copies to processors. Denote by π_i and θ_i the primary and ghost copies allocated to processor p_i, $i = 1, \ldots, n_p$. For each processor, p_i, do steps 2 and 3.
2. Run $\Pi_s^*(\pi_i \cup \theta_i, i)$. If the resultant schedule is found to be infeasible, the allocation as produced by Π_a is infeasible; return control to Π_a in step 1. Otherwise, record the position of the ghost copies (as put out by Π_s^*) in ghost schedule G_i. Assign static priorities to the primary tasks in the order in which they finish executing, i.e., if primary π_i completes before π_j in the schedule generated in this step, π_i will have higher priority than π_j.
3. Generate primary schedule S_i by running Π_{s2} on π_i, with the priorities assigned in step 2.

FIGURE 3.49
Algorithm FA2.

activated, since the ghost and primary schedules do not overlap. The drawback of FA1 is that the primary tasks are needlessly delayed when the ghosts do not have to be executed. While all the tasks will meet their deadlines, it is frequently best to complete execution of the tasks early to provide slack time to recover from transient failures (see Chapter 7). Such a needless delay does not occur in Algorithm FA2, shown in Figure 3.49. We use an additional scheduling algorithm Π_{s2}, which is a static-priority preemptive scheduler. That is, given a set of tasks, each with its own unique static priority, Π_{s2} will schedule them by assigning the processor to execute the highest-priority task that has been released but is not yet completed.

Theorem 3.19. The ghost schedule G_i and the primary schedule S_i form a feasible pair.

Proof. The primary tasks will complete no later than the time specified in $\Pi_s^*(\pi_i \cup \theta_i, i)$, even if all the space allocated to ghosts in G_i is, in fact, occupied by them.
Q.E.D.

Example 3.47. Consider the case where a processor p has been allocated ghosts g_4, g_5, g_6, and primaries π_1, π_2, π_3. The release times, execution times, and deadlines are as follows:

	π_1	π_2	π_3	g_4	g_5	g_6
Release time	2	5	3	0	0	9
Execution time	4	2	2	2	2	3
Deadline	6	8	15	5	6	12

Suppose that there exists some processor q to which the primary copies of g_4 and g_5 have both been allocated. Then, we cannot overlap g_4 and g_5 in the ghost schedule of processor p. As a result, the ghost schedule will be as shown in Figure 3.50. It is easy to check that under these constraints, the allocation of $\pi_1, \pi_2, \pi_3, g_4, g_5, g_6$ to p is infeasible—π_2 will miss its deadline if all the ghosts are activated.

However, suppose that we have some other allocation that also allocates $\pi_1, \pi_2, \pi_3, g_4, g_5, g_6$ to p. Under this new allocation, there is no other processor to which primary or ghost copies of both g_4 and g_5 have been allocated. As a result, we can overlap g_4 and g_5 in the ghost schedule, producing the ghost schedule shown in Figure 3.51. Under these constraints, a feasible schedule can be constructed for p; see Figure 3.52.

FIGURE 3.50
Ghost schedule of p if g_4 and g_5 cannot overlap.

FIGURE 3.51
Ghost schedule of p if g_4 and g_5 can overlap.

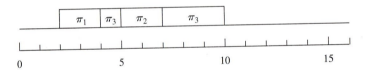

FIGURE 3.52
Feasible primary schedule of p if g_4 and g_5 can overlap.

3.7 SUGGESTIONS FOR FURTHER READING

A good, if slightly dated, introduction to the theory of scheduling is provided in [5, 6]. The RM and EDF scheduling algorithms are considered in detail in Liu and Layland [16]. The necessary and sufficient conditions for RM-schedulability are published in [13]. The case where deadlines do not equal the task periods for the RM algorithm is found in [12]. The deferred server algorithm is presented in [14]. Some practical issues relating to the RM algorithm are discussed in [23]. See [11] for additional discussions of the EDF algorithm.

Determining EDF-schedulability for sporadic tasks is presented in [3]. The MINPATH algorithm is described in [4]. The algorithm for taking precedence and exclusion constraints into account appears in [27].

The source for the primary/alternative task scheduling algorithm is [14]. IRIS tasks are studied in [8, 17, 18]. The algorithm for computing the value of π is from [19].

The next-fit algorithm for assigning RM-schedulable tasks is published in [7]. The utilization-balancing algorithm is taken from [2]. The bin-packing assignment algorithm for EDF is based on [9] and is well described in [5]. The MOS heuristic is presented in [20].

The priority ceiling protocol is introduced in [22]. A refinement of this protocol is presented in [1].

Focused addressing and bidding are discussed in [21]. The buddy strategy for assigning tasks to processors is reported in [25].

The primary/ghost algorithm for fault-tolerant scheduling was described in [8].

EXERCISES

3.1. Construct a set of periodic tasks (with release times, execution times, and periods), which can be scheduled feasibly by the EDF algorithm, but not by the RM algorithm.

3.2. Describe situations in which a task should not be preempted.

3.3. In the proof of Theorem 3.1, we considered only a two-task system. Generalize the proof to n tasks for $n > 2$.

3.4. We have been assuming in this chapter that preemption incurs no overhead. Let us now relax that assumption. Consider a two-task system where each preemption has an overhead of x. Given e_1, e_2, P_1, P_2, obtain the maximum value of x for which the task set is RM-schedulable.

3.5. This question relates to transient overloads. Consider a set of five tasks with the following characteristics.

i	e_i	a_i	P_i
1	30	5	100
2	10	5	130
3	20	15	140
4	80	10	140
5	10	10	200

Tasks T_1, T_3, T_5 are critical, but T_2, T_4 are not. Carry out a period transformation for this task set to ensure that the critical tasks always meet their deadlines.

3.6. Prove that $t(k, i)$ is the minimum t for which Equation (3.35) holds.

3.7. Prove Lemma 3.9. (Hint: This is very similar to the proof of Theorem 3.11.)

3.8. Assuming that the priority inheritance algorithm is followed, construct an example where there are N tasks, and the highest-priority task is blocked once by every one of the other $N - 1$ tasks.

3.9. Prove Theorem 3.7.

3.10. Write the time-reclamation algorithm mentioned in Section 3.2.4.

3.11. Redefine L_i so that Theorem 3.4 continues to hold when the priority ceiling algorithm is used.

3.12. Suppose a task can suspend itself. Show that if a task T_i suspends itself n times, it can be blocked by at most $n + 1$ (not necessarily distinct) members of B_i.

3.13. Prove Theorem 3.14.

3.14. Prove Theorem 3.15.

3.15. Prove Theorem 3.16.

3.16. Find the computational complexity of IRIS5.

3.17. From Equation (3.96), it follows that if the solution of problem q_i results in tasks in some set A receiving any service during an interval $(d_{i-1}, d_i]$ their reward functions must all have equal derivatives for problems $q_{i-1}, \ldots q_1$ as well. We can therefore group all tasks in A together during the solution of $q_{i-1}, \ldots q_1$. Modify IRIS5 to take advantage of this fact. Find the computational complexity of your modified algorithm.

REFERENCES

[1] Baker, T. P.: "A Stack-Based Resource Allocation Policy for Realtime Processes," *Proc. IEEE Real-Time Systems Symp.*, pp. 191–200, IEEE, Los Alamitos, CA, 1990.

[2] Bannister, J. A., and K. S. Trivedi: "Task Allocation in Fault-Tolerant Distributed Systems," *Acta Informatica* 20:261–281, 1983.

[3] Baruah, S. K., A. K. Mok, and L. E. Rosier: "Preemptively Scheduling Hard-Real-Time Sporadic Tasks on One Processor," *Proc. IEEE Real-Time Systems Symp.*, pp. 182–190, IEEE, Los Alamitos, CA, 1990.

[4] Bettati, R. D., Gillies, C. C. Han, K. J. Lin, C. L. Liu, J. W. S. Liu, and W. K. Shih: "Recent Results in Real-Time Scheduling," in *Foundations of Real-Time Computing: Scheduling and Resource Management* (A. van Tilborg and G. Koob, eds.), Kluwer Academic, Boston, pp. 91–128, 1991.

[5] Coffman, E. G.: *Computer and Job-Shop Scheduling Theory,* Wiley, New York, 1976.

[6] Conway, R. W., W. L. Maxwell, and L. W. Miller: *Theory of Scheduling,* Addison-Wesley, Reading, MA, 1967.

[7] Davari, S., and S. K. Dhall: "An On Line Algorithm for Real-Time Tasks Allocation," *Proc. IEEE Real-Time Systems Symp.*, pp. 194–200, IEEE, Los Alamitos, CA, 1986.

[8] Dey, J. K., J. F. Kurose, D. F. Towsley, C. M. Krishna, and M. Girkar: "Efficient On-Line Processor Scheduling for a Class of IRIS Real-Time Tasks," *SIGMETRICS 1993*, pp. 217–228, ACM, New York, 1993.

[9] Johnson, D. S.: *Near-Optimal Bin-Packing Algorithms*, PhD thesis, Massachusetts Institute of Technology, 1974.

[10] Krishna, C. M., and K. G. Shin: "On Scheduling Tasks with a Quick Recovery from Failure," *IEEE Trans. on Computers* C-35:448–455, 1986.

[11] Kurose, J. F., D. F. Towsley, and C. M. Krishna: "Design and Analysis of Processor Scheduling Policies for Real-Time Systems," in *Foundations of Real-Time Computing: Scheduling and Resource Management* (A. van Tilborg and G. Koob, eds.), Kluwer, Boston, pp. 63–90, 1991.

[12] Lehoczky, J. P.: "Fixed Priority Scheduling of Periodic Task Sets with Arbitrary Deadlines," *Proc. IEEE Real-Time Systems Symp.*, pp. 201–210, IEEE, Los Alamitos, CA, 1990.

[13] Lehoczky, J. P., L. Sha, and Y. Ding: "The Rate Monotonic Algorithm: Exact Characterization and Average-Case Behavior," *Proc. IEEE Real-Time Systems Symp.*, pp. 166–171, IEEE, Los Alamitos, CA, 1989.

[14] Lehoczky, J. P., L. Sha, and J. K. Strosnider: "Enhanced Aperiodic Responsiveness in Hard Real-Time Environments," *Proc. IEEE Real-Time Systems Symp.*, pp. 261–270, IEEE, Los Alamitos, CA, 1987.

[15] Liestman, A. L., and R. H. Campbell: "A Fault-Tolerant Scheduling Problem," *IEEE Trans. Software Engineering* SE-12:1089–1095, 1986.

[16] Liu, C. L., and J. W. Layland: "Scheduling Algorithms for Multiprogramming in a Hard-Real-Time Environment," *Journal of the ACM*, 20(1):46–61, 1973.

[17] Liu, J. W. S., K. J. Lin, W.-K. Shih, A. C. Yu, J. Y. Chung, and W. Zhao: "Imprecise Computations," *Proc. IEEE* 82:83–94, 1994.

[18] Liu, J. W. S., W.-K. Shih, K.-J. Lin, R. Bettati, and J.-Y. Chung: "Algorithms for Scheduling Imprecise Computations," in *Foundations of Real-Time Computing: Scheduling and Resource Management* (A. van Tilborg and G. Koob, eds.), Kluwer, Boston, pp. 203–250, 1991.

[19] Press, W. H., S. A. Teukolsky, W. T. Vetterling, and B. P. Flannery: *Numerical Recipes in FORTRAN*, Cambridge University Press, Cambridge, 1992.

[20] Ramamritham, K. J., A. Stankovic, and P.-F. Shiah: "Efficient Scheduling Algorithms for Real-Time Multiprocessor Systems," *IEEE Trans. on Parallel and Distributed Systems*, 1:184–194, 1990.

[21] Ramamritham, K. J., A. Stankovic, and W. Zhao: "Distributed Scheduling of Tasks with Deadlines and Resource Requirements," *IEEE Trans. Computers* 38:1110–1123, 1989.

[22] Sha, L., R. Rajkumar, and J. P. Lehoczky: "Priority Inheritance Protocols: An Approach to Real-Time Synchronization," *IEEE Trans. on Computers*, 39:1175–1185, 1990.

[23] Sha, L., R. Rajkumar, and S. S. Sathaye: "Generalized Rate-Monotonic Scheduling Theory: A Framework for Developing Real-Time Systems," *Proc. IEEE*, 82:68–82, 1994.

[24] Shih, W. K., J. W. S. Liu, and J. Y. Chung: "Algorithms for Scheduling Tasks to Minimize Total Error," *SIAM Journal of Computing* 20:537–552, 1991.

[25] Shin, K. G., and Y.-C. Chang: "Load Sharing in Distributed Real-Time Systems with State-Change Broadcasts," *IEEE Trans. Computers* 38:1124–1142, 1989.

[26] Xu, J.: "Multiprocessor Scheduling of Processes with Release Times, Deadlines, Precedence, and Exclusion Relations," *IEEE Trans. Software Engineering* 19:139–154, 1993.

[27] Xu, J., and D. L. Parnas: "Scheduling Processes with Release Times, Deadlines, Precedence, and Exclusion Properties," *IEEE Trans. Software Engineering* 16:360–369, 1990.

CHAPTER
4

PROGRAMMING LANGUAGES AND TOOLS

4.1 INTRODUCTION

Programming languages are the medium in which computer programs are written. We know from experience with natural languages that a language shapes not only how we express an idea but also the very idea itself. In ways that we do not fully understand, language acts, in part, as a framework for ideas. The same is true of programming languages. A good programming language enables the programmer to state, with a low probability of error, his directions to the computer. It also forces the programmer into the discipline of formatting his thoughts according to the computer language framework; this can increase clarity of thought and consequently improve the quality of the resulting software.

In this chapter, we consider the features that characterize a good real-time programming language. We assume that all our readers have considerable experience with general-purpose computer languages, such as FORTRAN, C, or PASCAL, and are familiar with such basic software engineering concepts as structured programming. While almost everything we say is also applicable to general-purpose computing, we will focus on the issues that arise in real-time programming. In most cases, our examples will be from Ada. While Ada has its detractors, it is the official programming language of the U.S. Department of Defense, which is the largest purchaser of real-time software in the world. It has therefore become the de facto standard language for real-time computing. Ada9X is a new, currently emerging, version of Ada.

We should emphasize that this chapter is not meant as a programming manual for Ada or any other language. The Further Readings section contains a list of references for the aspiring real-time programmer.

4.2 DESIRED LANGUAGE CHARACTERISTICS

Many of the desired characteristics of a real-time language are similar to those of general-purpose languages. Languages must be readable, must have constructs that enhance comprehensibility, be portable across different hardware platforms, be modular, and lend themselves to being debugged and compiled separately. However, real-time applications place additional demands on the programmer in two ways. First, they require that deadlines be met. The programmer must therefore be allowed to specify priorities and run-time requirements. There must be some means for the programmer to specify absolute time intervals, and for the system to enforce timing constraints. Second, real-time computers often interact with devices (such as sensors or actuators) of widely varying cycle times. A good real-time language therefore makes it possible to write device interfaces effectively.

As we have stressed repeatedly throughout this book, real-time systems must be highly reliable. In most systems, the software is much more complex than the hardware. As a result, the probability of a software-design fault is usually higher than the probability of a hardware-design fault. Programming languages must reduce the probability of error by catching as many careless or typing errors as possible. The chief means of doing this is through data typing, that is, making it necessary for the programmer to specify the properties of each of the variables used in the program. The system can then indicate (preferably at compile time) if those properties are being violated. Another way is to render programs as readable as possible. Readability is important for two reasons. First, it makes the debugging process easier. Second, it makes possible the maintenance of the program even if the original developers are no longer available.

The traditional approach to ensuring readability is to use comments; programmers are encouraged to freely use comments throughout the program. Additionally, they can choose variable names that are suitably evocative. For example, the variable `student name` is much easier on human readers than `sn`. To aid in this, a good programming language will place few, if any, restrictions on the length of variable names. Several languages, such as Ada, allow the use of the underscore (_), and others the period (.), in order to improve readability. In other languages, the programmer may mix upper- and lower-case letters (e.g., `StudentName`) to achieve the same effect. In addition to the program and the comments, there are flowcharts and other descriptions of the program structure. However, ideally we would like to have the program itself structured in such a way that it is largely self-explanatory. Indeed, for many well-written programs, the code is its own best documentation.

The program must be laid out (structured) so as to aid comprehensibility. "Pretty-printing" features, which indent the source code appropriately (to indicate nesting), are important. In most languages, indentation is solely to help the human programmer—the number of spaces by which a line is indented is irrelevant to the computer. An exception to this is occam2, where indentation is syntactically important. For example, consider the following code:

```
INT a, b:
SEQ
    a: = a PLUS b
    b: = b MINUS a
```

The SEQ instruction says that the instructions that lie within its scope must be executed sequentially. The scope of the SEQ instruction is defined by the indentation of the following lines; they are all aligned on the Q in SEQ. Note that we do not have a semicolon ending each instruction; different instructions must be on separate lines. Nor do we have an end that specifies when the SEQ scope ends; that is determined by the indentation of the instructions.

A good language is as portable as possible. For example, a programmer should have the option of specifying the minimum acceptable precision of each variable, and this precision should be guaranteed, irrespective of the host machine on which the program is run. Portability also requires a certain discipline in the production of compilers—all compilers for that language must be functionally the same. This is not the case for many general-purpose languages, as any programmer knows who has tried to "port" a program written and debugged on one machine to another.

Portability is difficult to ensure unless there is a central authority that ensures that compilers written by different vendors are truly equivalent. The difficulty is often compounded by ambiguities in language specification, as different compiler writers may interpret these ambiguities differently. There are two ways to avoid this problem. The first is to ensure that specifications are written formally with no ambiguities. In such a case, care should be taken to ensure that the compiler writers can understand the formalisms used in the specification; the more abstruse the formalism, the greater is the probability of misinterpreting the specification. The second approach is to have a committee to whom compiler writers can turn when they detect an ambiguity in the specification. There is such a committee for Ada, which has handled hundreds of enquiries.

Language complexity is another factor that potentially limits portability. If we insist that every feature in every implementation of the language must exist in every other implementation, one of two things can happen. The first is that the language may be spare and austere, with few features. The second is that, to accommodate the disparate needs of a wide variety of users, the language may be overloaded with features that every compiler is forced to support. Ada has tried to avoid both problems. It defines a core set of features and several annexes. Each compiler for Ada9x must support the core features, but the annexes are optional. If an annex is supported, then all of it must be supported—the compiler writer cannot pick and choose bits and pieces from it. This allows one to specify the capabilities of the compiler by simply listing the set of annexes that it supports.

There is, however, a limit to how portable a real-time program can be. Each real-time program is meant for a particular application and a particular set of devices. Insofar as the program is tailored to these particular aspects, it is machine-dependent, and cannot be "ported" to run on a system with a different set of devices. The best that we can do is to ensure that there is a sharp distinction between the machine-dependent and machine-independent parts of the program.

Real-time programs have to deal with a large variety of I/O devices. While traditional languages need to consider interfacing only to such devices as printers, tape, and disk drives, real-time systems acquire their input from and deliver their output to many different kinds of sensors and actuators. The traditional way of dealing with this is to write the part of the software that interfaces with such devices in machine code. This is clearly not a good practice, since it lowers the programming efficiency and increases the probability of error. It should be possible to write such code in a good real-time programming language. To be able to do this, the programmer should be able to specify absolute addresses. For example, in a memory-mapped architecture, the output register of some sensor might have the address 1990FA. The language should allow the programmer to specify that address. In some cases, it may be essential to write some of the code in assembly language. The programming language must make it easy to embed such inserts in the program.

A good real-time language must give the programmer flexibility as to the scheduling of processors and other resources. The programmer must be able to specify when a particular task is to be run and have control over the scheduling of all resources. None of the well-known languages (i.e., C, PASCAL, FORTRAN) has this capability. Many real-time systems have cyclic executives (i.e., the tasks are periodically executed) with time slots for each task. The programmer must manually fit the tasks into these time slots so as to meet all hard deadlines. Since the duration of these slots cannot be changed by the programmer, it is sometimes necessary to contort the code to make it fit in the slot. This contortion can lead to poorly structured code, which is difficult to understand and maintain.

Example 4.1. Suppose we have a cyclic executive with a cycle time of 100 ms, and a task with a period of 340 ms. Since 340 is not a multiple of 100, ensuring that the task runs at the appropriate frequency is not an easy job for the programmer.

Another important feature is that programs must lend themselves to analysis for schedulability. In other words, given a real-time program, we must be able to analyze it to determine if it meets all the task deadlines. To do this, we must avoid features (in both the hardware and the software) that make it impossible to derive accurate and tight execution-time bounds. Many features of present-day languages do not lend themselves to timing analysis. For example, if variable-sized arrays are allowed, the time taken to allocate and deallocate memory will also be variable. The time taken to execute while loops is also not easy to predict. This is because a while loop executes until some logical termination condition is satisfied. To determine a bound on how many iterations it can take before this condition is guaranteed to be satisfied, we must do a detailed and difficult analysis of the termination condition. In many cases, this is practically impossible. (By contrast, a `for` loop with static loop bounds, which specifies in advance the maximum number of iterations, can be easily analyzed for schedulability.) Recursion is also difficult to bound in its execution time. Some researchers have therefore suggested that such features be removed from real-time languages, or at least that programmers writing real-time code be instructed not to use them. The problem of estimating worst-case execution times is covered in Chapter 2.

It goes without saying that a real-time system must have an accurate clock. At the hardware level, this calls for stable quartz clocks and fault-tolerant synchronization methods (see Chapter 9). At the language level, this translates into the need for being able to precisely specify delays. For example, the programmer should have the ability to ask the processor to wait for a specified amount of time. The granularity of the clock must be sufficiently fine for all practical purposes; for example, the Ada9X real-time annex specifies a granularity no coarser than 1 μs.

In this context, it is worth mentioning that there is a problem that arises when one tries to link the clock time to the time told by clocks in everyday life. The former must always be a monotonically increasing function of time. However, the latter is sometimes adjusted to account for the slowing-down of Earth's rotation. This adjustment can result in everyday clock time being occasionally frozen for a few fractions of a second. Everyday clocks are also adjusted whenever time zones are crossed. It is therefore best to keep the real-time and everyday clocks separate.

The language must support features (such as `if-then-else` clauses) that improve comprehensibility and modularity. Modularity is, in fact, essential. The code for a moderately large real-time system can be tens or hundreds of thousands of lines long, and is likely to be written by teams of programmers. The overall program is decomposed into portions or modules. Interface specifications are written for each module; that is, we specify the inputs and outputs of each module, and its function. This is a critical part of the enterprise, and an error in specifying the interface or the function of a single module can have expensive ripple effects that affect other modules. This part of the work is therefore usually undertaken by experienced personnel and is checked rigorously.

Once the specifications have been written, the code for each module can written concurrently by different programmers. The language must support such features as *information hiding*, where what happens inside a module is invisible outside the scope of that module (except as may be expressed through the interface). For example, one module may not access variables that are declared as private to another module.

It must be possible to compile and debug modules separately. Debugging and testing typically take much more time than writing the code in the first place. A program that is broken down cleanly into interacting modules is much easier to debug than one that is chaotically structured. Separate compilation also saves time. Many real-time programs take hours or days of CPU time to compile. If we need to compile the entire program every time a small change is made in some obscure module somewhere, this greatly increases software development costs and lowers productivity.

4.3 DATA TYPING

When a programmer defines a variable as belonging to a particular data type, he is defining certain properties that the variable must satisfy. For instance, if a variable x is defined as Boolean, the programmer means x to have only two values (1 and 0, or TRUE and FALSE), and an assignment statement x:=5; is clearly illegal. Data types are used by programmers for two main purposes: (a) to guard against programming errors, and (b) to specify the desired degree of numerical precision.

An example of a language in which data types do not provide much security from programming errors is FORTRAN. Consider the example in Figure 4.1. The programmer meant to construct a DO-loop. Unfortunately, he typed a period instead of a comma in the DO-loop statement. Due to this error, a FORTRAN compiler reads the intended DO statement as the perfectly legal assignment statement[1] do100i = 1.50, which leads to an error in processing the loop. An unmanned NASA space probe to Venus was lost due to an error of this kind.

In FORTRAN, in the absence of an explicit programmer declaration, a variable type is inferred from the variable name.[2] The default is that any variable that begins with a letter in the sequence a to h and o to z is treated as a floating-point, single-precision real number; while any variable beginning with one of the letters k, l, m, n is treated as an integer. Thus, if the programmer does not explicitly declare otherwise, the variable a400 is a single-precision real number, while nasdf is an integer. Also, FORTRAN does implicit type conversion. For instance, suppose that a is a real variable and i an integer. The assignment statement a = i results in the value of i being stored as a real quantity in a. Conversely, the

```
        do 100 i = 1, 50
          j = j + i
        100 continue
```

```
        do 100 i = 1.50
          j=j+i
        100 continue
```

(a)   (b)

FIGURE 4.1
A cautionary example from FORTRAN: (a) what the programmer meant; (b) what the programmer typed.

---

[1] FORTRAN compilers ignore spaces, so that to the compiler there is no difference between
      do 100 i   and   do100i

[2] FORTRAN does allow the programmer to require that all variables be declared explicitly using the implicit none command, but that is a detail that we shall not consider here.

statement i = a results in the integer portion of the real variable a being stored as the value of variable i.

A somewhat stronger set of data typing rules is needed to provide some security from errors. In a strongly-typed language,

- each variable must be explicitly declared as belonging to a particular data type;
- each data type has, associated with it, a set of values and a set of operations that can be performed on those values;
- implicit type conversions using assignment statements are not allowed; and
- explicit type conversions are possible.

In a strongly-typed language, the mistake made in Figure 4.1 would have been caught by the compiler, since the programmer would not have declared do100i as a variable. Also, the assignment statement i = a would be illegal; if the programmer had intended the integer part of a to be stored in i, he would have explicitly converted the type on the RHS (right-hand side) of the assignment statement to be consistent with the LHS (left-hand side), for example, i = integer(a).

To enable strong typing to provide adequate security, most modern languages allow the programmer to construct idiosyncratic data types. For instance, consider the following declarations written in Ada:

```
type PRESSURE is new float;
type TEMPERATURE is new float;
p1, p2, p3: PRESSURE;
t1, t2: TEMPERATURE;
```

The programmer has constructed two data types: pressure and temperature. As we have said, it is important that all assignment statements follow *type equivalence* (i.e., the name of the data type on the LHS of an assignment statement should be the same as that of the data type on the RHS). Under such conditions, an attempt to mix variables of the types temperature and pressure without explicit type conversion, for example, is illegal. For instance, p1 = t1; should cause the compiler to flag an error, despite both variables being stored as real numbers.

Types such as pressure and temperature are known as *derived types*. A derived type inherits all the components and operations (e.g., addition, subtraction, etc.) of its "parent" type.

It is also useful to allow variable ranges to be defined. For example, if we are representing the altitude of a conventional aircraft, it is safe to assume that any variable representing its altitude in feet must be no greater than 100,000. We can specify this range while specifying the altitude data type as follows:

```
type ALTITUDE is new float range 0..100000;
```

It is sometimes useful to have different variables of the same type, but with different ranges. We can define *subtypes* to accommodate this need. For example:

```
type TIME is new float range 0..23.59;
```

```
subtype MORNING is TIME range 0..11.59;
subtype AFTERNOON is TIME range 12.01..18.59;
```

Unlike derived types, two subtypes of the same type can be mixed in assignment statements without any explicit type conversions. For example, morning := afternoon−1.5; would be perfectly legal. The sole purpose of a subtype is to specify a different range of possible values.

In addition to the standard types, modern languages also allow *enumeration* types. In such types, the set of values that the type allows is specified in sequence. For example,

```
type day is (mon, tue, wed, thur, fri, sat, sun);
```

Let us now turn to the issue of numerical precision. C specifies different types such as float (single precision), double (double precision), and long double (extended double precision). However, the actual precision that is delivered (i.e., the actual number of bits used in the number representation) can vary from one implementation to another. In some implementations, long double and double may provide exactly the same precision; in others, long double may provide more precision.[3] This means that to determine whether the computations will be sufficiently precise, the programmer must know the target machine.

To get away from this requirement, we can let the programmer explicitly specify the precision. For example,

```
type prec1 is digits 8  range -1e20..1e20;
type prec2 is digits 12 range -1e20..1e20;
```

defines prec1 and prec2 as having at least 8 and 12 significant decimal digits of precision, respectively. This lower limit on the precision will remain unaffected by the machine on which the program runs; the burden of ensuring that adequate precision is delivered is now shifted to the compiler. As before, explicit type conversions are required if numbers of different precision are mixed in the same statement. For example, if we have the types prec1 and prec2 as defined above, we might have:

```
p11,p12: prec1;
p21,p22: prec2;
begin
    p11:= p11+p12+prec1(p21)+prec1(p22);
end;
```

Another important type is *fixed-point* type, where the programmer specifies the accuracy constraint followed by an optional range constraint. For example,

```
type A1 is delta 0.001 range 0.000..0.999;
```

---

[3]The authors have even come across an implementation where long double offers less precision than double!

The system will implement this type by allocating variables of this type a sufficient number of significant bits to achieve this level of precision.

The same notion of types can be applied to arrays. For example,

```
type SMALLINT is integer range 0..20;
type a1 is array(1..30) of SMALLINT;
```

defines an array type `a1` with 30 index values. Each element of `a1` must take an integer value in the range 0 to 20. It is possible to define an array type or an array with variable index range whose value is not known in advance:

```
type X is array(integer range <>) of integer;
A: X(1..MAX);
```

One can have multidimensional arrays following the same approach.

A *record* is a data type that allows the grouping of different data types, and is especially useful in databases. For example, associated with each student's name (represented by a character string 40 characters in length), we might have her current grade-point average:

```
type STRING is array(<>) of character;
type nametype is STRING(40);
type gpatype is float range 0.0..4.0;
type student is
    record
        NAME: nametype;
        GPA: gpatype;
    end record;
```

The dot notation can be used to access individual fields of a record. For example, `student.name` denotes the NAME field of the record `student`.

However, new components may not be added. For example, if we define the type `student1` as a type derived from the type `student`, we cannot add another component, say `social_security_number`. This limitation is removed in Ada9X by the introduction of the tagged data type; that is, we could define type `student1` as derived from `student` but with the additional component:

```
type student1 is new student with
    record
        social_security_number: integer;
    end record;
```

One of the most useful aspects of tagged types is that if we need to extend a data type to augment the program in some way, we can do so by defining a new derived type with that extension, and augment the program without having to modify the whole system and recompile it.

Data types (and other objects) have *attributes* associated with them. For example, in a specific machine, the type `integer` may be able only to represent the range of values $-32768, \ldots, 32767$; Ada allows the programmer to access the attributes of data types:

X'First   If x is a scalar type (e.g., integer), it denotes the lower bound of the x range. If x is an array it denotes the lower bound of the first index range.

X'Last   Similar to X'First, except that it denotes the upper bound.

X'Delta   When x is of the fixed-point subtype, this denotes the delta which specifies the accuracy of x.

X'Small   If x is a real subtype, this returns the smallest nonzero number of that subtype.

4.4 CONTROL STRUCTURES

Most languages implicitly assume a sequential execution of instructions, unless otherwise specified. Decision structures providing if-then-else, for, and do while clauses are especially useful in producing correct readable code.

     Anyone who has programmed in C or PASCAL will be familiar with these structures, so we here simply provide a few examples drawn from Ada. The following is an example of an if-then-else construct, and is self-explanatory.

     Example 4.2

```
if y<0 then
        x := 4;
elseif d=0 then
        x := 6;
else
        q := 5;
end if
```

The following is an example of a for-do loop:

     Example 4.3

```
for i in 0..10 loop
      d(i) := i*j;
end loop;
```

and this is an example of a while loop:

     Example 4.4

```
while x < p loop
      x := x + i;
end loop;
```

In Ada, the difference between the for and while loops is that in the former the number of iterations is fixed in advance, while in the latter there is a test that must be checked for completion after each iteration. This difference is crucial in determining whether a reasonably accurate estimate of the worst-case program run time can be made. A `for` loop runs for a certain fixed number of iterations. A `while` loop runs for as long as is necessary for the termination condition to be satisfied; deciding how long this will be is often impossible.

We must also have the ability to abort a loop. This can be done using a **goto** or **exit** command. Consider the following example from FORTRAN:

```
      do 1 i = 1, 100
          x = x + i
          if (x .gt. 900.) go to 2
1         continue
2         continue
```

and from Ada:

```
      loop
          get (a);
          sum:=sum + a;
          if sum < 0 then
                  exit;
          end if;
      end loop;
```

The **exit** command immediately terminates the enclosing loop and transfers control to the end of the enclosing loop, while the **goto** command allows a transfer to anywhere the programmer chooses. Many people believe that **goto** has too much flexibility for the programmer's own good and should be abolished, or at least used very sparingly.

Some languages, such as Ada, also have `case` statements. Suppose x is an integer type taking the values 1 and 2. Then, consider the following fragment of code:

```
case x is
    when 1 => y:=x;
    when 2 => y:=0;
end case
```

In the above example, if $x = 1$ we execute `y:=x`; if $x = 2$ we execute `y:=0;`. Note that every possible value of the conditioned variable must be taken account of (e.g., if we had omitted the **when** 1 line, the compiler would have indicated an error). To make life easier, we can sometimes use the term **others** to capture all the cases not otherwise listed. For instance, if `i` is an integer type taking values in the range $-100, \ldots, 100$, the construct

```
case i is
    when -5 => y:=x;
    when others => y:=0;
end case
```

executes `y:=x;` if i=−5, and executes `y:=0;` if i takes any other value.

4.5 FACILITATING HIERARCHICAL DECOMPOSITION

The software for complex systems can run to hundreds of thousands of lines of code. No one person can understand the detailed workings of all of this code, much less develop it all alone. Programming must be a team effort.

Our main weapon against complexity in software, as in daily life, is abstraction. Knowledge is, after all, a hierarchy of abstractions, or frames of reference, that sift out the irrelevant. For example, when we buy a watch, we are interested in its ability to keep time accurately. The display and the controls form the interface between the watch and the outside world, and we are in effect imposing a specification on the interface when we require the watch to lose or gain no more than a minute every month. We do not think about the internal structure of the watch or the mechanical or electronic parts of which it is made. So far as we are concerned, the watch is a black box with a set of interfaces.

The frame of reference of a watch designer is very different. He is concerned with its low-level design. If it is an electronic watch, he is concerned with the stability of the quartz crystal and the design of the circuitry. For him, the quartz crystal is a black box with certain properties. He is not interested, for example, in the quantum-mechanical equations that give rise to its structure.

In this section, we consider four aids to decomposition: blocks, procedures, functions, and packages. You will undoubtedly be familiar with the first three, and so we will pass over them relatively quickly. The concept of packages is, however, fairly new, and we will cover that in some depth.

4.5.1 Blocks

A block consists of two parts: a specification, which defines the variables used within the block, and a body, which contains the statements to be executed. A block may be placed anywhere in a program that a statement is written.

The main purpose of a block is information hiding. A variable declared within a block is accessible only within that block and nowhere outside. When a block is exited, the storage allocated for all such variables is released. Also, if a variable is redefined within a block (i.e., if it is defined within the block after being declared outside), its redefinition ceases to have any impact at the block boundary. For example, consider the following piece of pseudocode:

```
var i, x: integer;
begin
    x:=0;
    for i in 0..100 loop
        block
            var i: integer;
        begin
            for i in 1..5 loop
                x := x + i;
            end loop;
```

> **end;**
> **end loop;**
>   . . .

The variables i and x are defined outside, while variable i is redefined within the block. The value of i cycles through 1 to 5 every time the block is executed. When the block is exited, however, the value of i reverts to what it was before the block was entered. In other words, the variable i inside the block is a different variable from the variable i outside the block.

4.5.2 Procedures and Functions

The disadvantage of blocks is that they have to be explicitly repeated every time they are needed. In contrast, a procedure or function can be written out once and called whenever it is needed. This allows economy and permits a hierarchical decomposition of programs. The entire program can be broken down into a set of procedures and functions, each of which may itself call other procedures and functions. For example, consider the following function, written in pseudocode, which finds the maximum of two integers.

```
function MAXIMUM(A, B: integer) return integer is
    begin
        if A>B then
            return A;
        else
            return B;
        end if;
    end MAXIMUM;
```

Given this, we could write anywhere in the program from which this function was visible,

```
D := C + MAXIMUM(A,B);
```

and the function would be understood. As with blocks, the local variables used inside a procedure or function are invisible to the outside world.

Because of these properties, procedures and functions are extremely important programming tools.

4.6 PACKAGES

Packages take the concept of procedures and functions one step further. A package consists of a package *specification*, which is the interface to the outside world, in the package declaration, together with a package body. The declaration portion consists of variable-type specifications, and a (possibly empty) set of functions that operate on these variables. The package *body*, which is optional, consists of the executable statements associated with the functions. Nothing in the package body is accessible to any code outside the package. Figure 4.2 illustrates this.

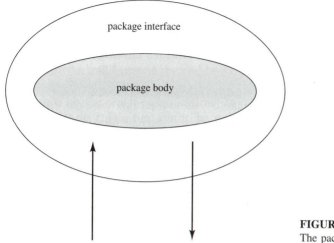

FIGURE 4.2
The package is a black box.

There are several benefits from using packages:

Packages can be written, debugged, and compiled independently of one another. All a programmer has to know about a package being developed by someone else is its specification. This improves efficiency on large projects involving teams of programmers.

Packages can be placed in a library and made accessible to everyone who has access to that library. Thus, the same package, once written, can be used by more than one programmer for more than one project. Taking this to its logical extreme, it is possible to conceive of a universally available library, to which programmers from many corporations from all over the world contribute. Anybody wishing to put together a program can go through a catalog of available packages and integrate these into their own software. This allows us to amortize the cost of developing software over a large number of users. Experience has shown, however, that this type of immediate reuse rarely occurs in practice; usually, some changes to the body or the specification are needed.

Packages promise improved security. Since nothing inside a package body is accessible to any code outside it, no programming error outside the body can affect the correctness of the code within the body, and vice versa.[4] The package construct allows the designer to restrict the operations that can be carried out on variables defined in the package header, thus further reducing the chances of programmer error.

Packages make software maintenance more efficient. So long as the package interface is not altered, the package body can be modified as desired, without

---

[4]The exception is that if "correct" code calls a subprogram in a package that is incorrectly implemented and does not meet its specification, the calling code is technically no longer correct.

affecting any other module. For example, if a package computes Bessel functions and an improved algorithm for calculating Bessel functions is discovered, we can implement this improvement in the package body without having to disturb anything outside the package.

The following fragment of code, written in Ada, is a package for carrying out the basic arithmetic functions in complex algebra. We begin with the declaration part, which specifies the COMPLEX data type and the four functions that operate on this type.

```
package COMPLEX_ALGEBRA is
      type COMPLEX is
            record
                  REAL_PART, IMAGINARY_PART: float;
            end record;
      function ADD(A,B: COMPLEX) return COMPLEX;
      function SUBTRACT(A,B: COMPLEX) return COMPLEX;
      function MULTIPLY(A,B: COMPLEX) return COMPLEX;
      function DIVIDE(A,B: COMPLEX) return COMPLEX;
end COMPLEX_ALGEBRA;
```

The package body is separate, and is shown below.

```
package body COMPLEX_ALGEBRA is
      with ROOTS; use ROOTS;
      with TRIGONOMETRY; use TRIGONOMETRY;
      function ADD(A,B: COMPLEX) return COMPLEX is
      begin
            return ( (A.REAL_PART+B.REAL_PART),
                  (A.IMAGINARY_PART+B.IMAGINARY_PART));
      end ADD;
      function SUBTRACT(A,B: COMPLEX) return COMPLEX is
      begin
            return ( (A.REAL_PART-B.REAL_PART),
                  (A.IMAGINARY_PART-B.IMAGINARY_PART));
      end SUBTRACT;
      function MULTIPLY(A,B: COMPLEX) return COMPLEX is
      begin
            return ( (A.REAL_PART*B.REAL_PART -
                  A.IMAGINARY_PART* B.IMAGINARY_PART),
                  (A.IMAGINARY_PART*B.REAL_PART +
                  A.REAL_PART*B.IMAGINARY_PART) );
      end MULTIPLY;
      function DIVIDE(A,B: COMPLEX) return COMPLEX is
            MAGNITUDE_A, MAGNITUDE_B, MAGNITUDE_DIV,
                  ANGLE_A, ANGLE_B, ANGLE_DIV: float;
```

```
begin
      MAGNITUDE_A := MAGNITUDE(A);
      MAGNITUDE_B := MAGNITUDE(B);
      ANGLE_A := ANGLE(A);
      ANGLE_B := ANGLE(B);
      MAGNITUDE_DIV := MAGNITUDE_A / MAGNITUDE_B;
      ANGLE_DIV := ANGLE_A - ANGLE_B;
      return ( (MAGNITUDE_DIV*COS(ANGLE_DIV) ),
            (MAGNITUDE_DIV*SIN(ANGLE_DIV) ) );
  end DIVIDE;
  function MAGNITUDE(A: COMPLEX) return float is
  begin
      return( SQUARE_ROOT(A.REAL_PART**2 +
          A.IMAGINARY_PART**2) );
  end MAGNITUDE;
  function ANGLE(A: COMPLEX) return float is
  begin
      return ( ARCTAN(A.IMAGINARY_PART/A.REAL_PART) );
  end
end COMPLEX_ALGEBRA;
```

This package can now be included in a library of Ada routines. Anybody who uses it can use the COMPLEX type and the associated functions ADD, SUBTRACT, and MULTIPLY, but will not have access to what happens in the private portion of the package. For example, we can say

```
with COMPLEX_ALGEBRA;
procedure ABCD is
      use COMPLEX_ALGEBRA;
      A: COMPLEX:= (1,2);
      B: COMPLEX:= (3,4);
      C: COMPLEX;
begin
      A:= ADD(A,B);
      C:= MULTIPLY(A,B);
end;
```

The **with** COMPLEX_ALGEBRA command informs the compiler that the COMPLEX_AL-GEBRA package is to be retrieved from the library. The **use** COMPLEX_ALGEBRA comand says to make everything in the declaration of that package visible to procedure ABCD. Notice that the package COMPLEX_ALGEBRA contains two functions MAGNITUDE and ANGLE that are not visible to the outside world; any attempt to use either function from anywhere other than the body of package COMPLEX_ALGEBRA will result in an error. Also, note that the package is not self-contained—it uses results from two other packages assumed to be in the library: ROOTS (which contains the SQUARE_ROOT function) and TRIGONOMETRY (which contains the SIN and COS functions).

Notice that we have so far come across two kinds of variables. One, which is defined in the package declaration, is visible to the outside world and can be manipulated outside. For example, the structure of the COMPLEX data type as a record with two fields, each of type float, is known to the outside; if we declare X to be COMPLEX, we can access and manipulate its real and imaginary parts X.REAL_PART and X.IMAGINARY_PART, respectively. The second kind of variable is defined within the package body and is therefore invisible outside the package (e.g., MAGNITUDE_A).

It is convenient to create two additional kinds of variables, which fall somewhere between the two kinds mentioned above. These are the private and limited private kinds.

In the following example, the ACCOUNT type is *private*.

```
package BANK_ACCOUNT is
      type ACCOUNT is private;
      type MONEY is delta 0.01;
      function DEPOSIT(AMOUNT: MONEY, PERSON: ACCOUNT)
              return ACCOUNT;
      function WITHDRAW(AMOUNT: MONEY, PERSON: ACCOUNT)
              return ACCOUNT;
      function MAKE_ACCOUNT(ID: integer; STATUS: MONEY;
              ACCOUNT: out ACCOUNT);
private
      type ACCOUNT is
           record
                ACCOUNT_NUMBER: integer;
                ACCOUNT_STATUS: MONEY;
           end record;
end BANK_ACCOUNT;
```

The outside world cannot directly access (or indeed know about) the structure of the type ACCOUNT. For example, the assignment statement

```
x:= ACCOUNT_TYPE.ACCOUNT_NUMBER;
```

would be illegal outside the package body. This does not mean, however, that there is no way to set the fields of ACCOUNT_TYPE; if that were the case, private variables would be worthless. We must provide a function (MAKE_ACCOUNT in our example) within the package body (recall that ACCOUNT_TYPE is fully visible in the body) to enable us to do that. In fact, the limitations on private types are more severe than not knowing their exact structure. The only operations that can be carried out (outside the package) on a private type are the functions and procedures defined in the package, and the assignment and equality check.

The *limited private* kind of variable has even more restrictions placed on its use outside the package body. It can only be used as arguments to the functions and procedures defined in the package. That is, unless the assignment and equality check are defined in the package, it is impossible to do those functions on the limited private data type.

4.7   RUN-TIME ERROR (EXCEPTION) HANDLING

There are two kinds of errors. Compile-time errors are detected by the compiler; run-time errors escape the compiler and occur during execution of the software.

When a program written in a language such as FORTRAN or C encounters a run-time error, it usually crashes after leaving some more or less cryptic error message. While this approach is fine for general-purpose applications, it is unacceptable for real-time systems. For example, the stability-control program of an aircraft should not simply tell the pilot "FLOATING POINT EXCEPTION AT 011FF," and crash. Real-time languages must have the ability to respond to a run-time error in a more graceful way, perhaps by switching to a temporarily degraded mode of operation that ensures the continued safety of the controlled process.

Mechanisms for exception handling in general must have the following rather obvious properties.

- They must be simple to use without making the software difficult to read.
- They should have low run-time overheads.
- The programmer should have the freedom to specify the recovery actions in response to various kinds of run-time error.

Ada handles run-time errors by raising *exceptions*. An exception causes control to be transferred to an *exception handler*, which is a program for suitably handling that exception. Every exception condition has a unique name. There are five exception conditions that are predefined, and the programmer is able to define additional conditions. The predefined conditions are:

- CONSTRAINT_ERROR: Asserted whenever a variable value goes outside its prescribed bounds, if any.
- NUMERIC_ERROR: Asserted to indicate an inability to maintain the required levels of precision (usually due to an attempt to divide by zero).
- STORAGE_ERROR: Asserted when the program runs out of memory space.
- PROGRAM_ERROR: Asserted whenever an exception occurs that is not captured by any of the other conditions.
- TASKING_ERROR: Asserted in connection with errors that arise due to the incorrect use of the tasking mechanism.

The programmer has to explicitly state the response to an exception.

Example 4.5

```
declare
        type gpa is delta 0.01 range 0.00..4.00;
```

```
begin
      gpa := calc_gpa(student);
exception
      when CONSTRAINT_ERROR => put ("gpa is in error: it is
                                          out of range");
end;
```

The block executes normally, except when it encounters an error. If a gpa outside the range 0 to 4 is returned by `calc_gpa`, it will immediately transfer control to the exception-handling portion and print out the warning message.

Example 4.6

```
declare
      x,y,z: float;
begin
      get(x); get(y);
      z := x/y;
exception
      when NUMERIC_ERROR =>
              put("Numeric Error: Possibly an attempt to di-
                  vide by zero");
              return 0;
end
```

If `y` happens to be zero, the NUMERIC_ERROR exception is raised and control is immediately transferred to the exception-handling portion. This prints out a warning message, and returns a value 0 to the caller of the subprogram enclosing this block. Note that this is in contrast to programs written in most traditional programming languages, which would notify the user of a divide-by-zero attempt and then simply crash. Another difference is that the programmer does not have to explicitly check for the occurrence of the NUMERIC_ERROR—the system does this automatically.

It is possible for the programmer to define additional exception conditions. The name of the exception is defined much as a variable type is declared. The programmer must then explicitly raise the exception where it is warranted. For example, consider a system which controls the temperature of a boiler. Procedure READ_TEMPERATURE returns the boiler temperature. There is a thermostat arrangement to keep the temperature between 400 and 450 degrees. If the temperature goes outside this range, there has been a failure and the operator must be notified by the system's printing an appropriate message.

```
declare
      TEMPERATURE: float;
      TOO_HOT, TOO_COLD: exception;
begin
      loop
            READ_TEMPERATURE(TEMPERATURE);
```

```
            if TEMPERATURE < 400
                  raise TOO_COLD;
            elseif TEMPERATURE > 450
                  raise TOO_HOT;
            end if;
      end loop;
      exception
            when TOO_COLD =>
                  put("Warning: Too cold");
            when TOO_HOT =>
                  put("Warning: Too hot");
end;
```

The control remains within the loop until an exception is raised. Then it is transferred to the exception-handling routine, which prints out the appropriate warning message and exits the block. An exception handler may be attached to a block, procedure, function, or task body.

What happens if an exception is raised in a block, procedure, or function, but there is no handling routine within that unit? In Ada, the normal execution of the unit ceases and the exception keeps propagating until it finds an exception handler. If the exception occurs in a block, control is transferred to a point just after the end of the block; if it occurs in a procedure or function, control is transferred to a point just after where that procedure was called.

> **Example 4.7.** As an example, consider three procedures, A, B, and C. Procedure A calls B, which in turn calls C. Suppose an exception is raised in C, which does not have a handler for the exception. The execution of C is then terminated, and control—with the exception—is propagated back to B. Suppose that B does have a handler for this exception; then, B executes that code and returns control to A at the point just after where it was called by A. Figure 4.3 illustrates this.

> **Example 4.8.** A second example is shown in Figure 4.4. Procedure A calls procedure B, which contains a block C. As before, there is an exception raised in C for which there is no handler within C. Control passes to B, which deals with the exception and returns control to A.

There is a troublesome issue associated with the propagation of exceptions. Suppose that EXCEPTION_1 and EXCEPTION_2 are the only exceptions declared in B, but that C has two declared exceptions TOO_HIGH and TOO_LOW, with no exception-handling routine. If B calls C and the exception TOO_HIGH is raised in C, control is returned to B. B knows that an exception has been raised. However, procedure B has no way of recognising TOO_HIGH, since it was not declared in B. In fact, it has no way to determine whether it is TOO_HIGH or TOO_LOW that has been raised. We say that the exception has become *anonymous* in B. We can use a catchall clause when others to handle anonymous exceptions. The handler in the when others case is something that is executed for all exceptions that do not

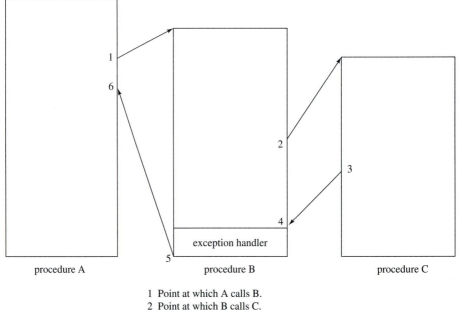

1 Point at which A calls B.
2 Point at which B calls C.
3 Point at which exception is raised in C.
  (C has no exception handler; control transfers to B.)
4 Exception-handler code starts here.
5 End of exception-handling routine.
6 Point in A following point 1 (when B was called by A).

FIGURE 4.3
Transfers of control upon an exception; three procedures.

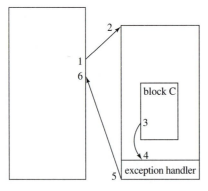

1 Point at which A calls B.
2 Starting point of B.
3 Exception is raised here.
  (C has no exception handler; control transfers to B.)
4 Exception handler of B begins here.
5 Exception handler of B ends here.
6 Point in A immediately after point 1.

FIGURE 4.4
Transfers of control upon an exception; two procedures and a block.

have a specific handler declared. Thus, for example, the exception-handling part of B might look like the following:

```
exception
      when EXCEPTION_1 =>
             -- code for handling this exception.
      when EXCEPTION_2 =>
             -- code for handling this exception.
      when others =>
             put("Exception: I don't know which");
end;
```

The when others clause is also useful when there is common handling for a large set of exceptions; it saves the programmer having to type out each exception separately in the handler routine.

When an exception-handling routine is entered, the exception condition is reset. We can, if we like, issue a command raise, which has the effect of reasserting the exception. This will occur even if the exception is anonymous. For example, consider the exception-handling routine of B that we just wrote out. If the when others case was executed because exception TOO_LOW originally raised, the raise command will have the effect of raising TOO_LOW, even though that exception is anonymous in B.

4.8 OVERLOADING AND GENERICS

It is possible for the same variable name to represent different variables of differing types. Take, for instance, the enumerations:

```
type SCIENTIST is (GALILEO, NEWTON, EUCLID);
type SPACECRAFT is (VIKING, PIONEER, SOYUZ, SPUTNIK, GALILEO);
```

There are two variables named GALILEO; one is of the type SCIENTIST, and the other of the type SPACECRAFT. Every time GALILEO occurs in the program, the compiler will need to determine either from the context or by an indication from the programmer whether this is of type SCIENTIST or SPACECRAFT. The variable GALILEO is said to be *overloaded*.

Functions and procedures can be overloaded, too. If we stop to think about it, there are several functions that operate on not just one, but several, data types. The simplest examples of all are the basic arithmetic functions +, −, ∗, /. For instance, the operator + will add two numbers, whether they are of type float or integer. Strictly speaking, there is not just one + function, but several; one for each data type. The compiler determines, from the types of the input data, which of these is to be used.

There can be programmer-defined overloaded functions, too. For instance, one may write routines to produce a sorted list of N numbers. One routine may deal with integers, another with floats, and so on, and all can have the same name. All these routines will be identical, except for the type of the data that they operate on. The compiler figures out, from the type of the argument, which routine is to be called.

The inconvenience of the programmer-defined overloaded function is that the one has to repeat the code for each version. For example, we would need to have one routine for sorting integers, another for floats, and so on. To avoid this, Ada uses the concept of *generics*, which takes the concept of overloading one step further. To illustrate this, consider the example provided below, which returns the smaller of two numbers.

Example 4.9

```
generic
      type NUMBER is (<>);
function SMALLER (X,Y: NUMBER) return NUMBER is

      -- end of the generic specification; the body follows.
function SMALLER (X,Y: NUMBER) return NUMBER;
begin
      if (X>Y) then
            return Y;
      else
            return X;
      end if;
end SMALLER;
```

The above is just a template, which must be suitably instantiated before the function SMALLER can be used. Suppose we want a function SMALL that would work on integers or floating-point numbers. Then, we introduce the following statements into the declaration portion of the appropriate code:

```
function SMALL is new SMALLER (integer);
function SMALL is new SMALLER (float);
```

4.9 MULTITASKING

Traditional programming languages, such as FORTRAN, C, and COBOL, assume a single thread of control. Instructions are assumed to be executed sequentially. Even when the underlying hardware is such that some overlapped processing takes place (as is the case with pipelined machines), to the programmer it usually appears as if one instruction is completed before another begins execution. Since real-time computers are usually parallel processors, it is important that a real-time programming language have the ability to handle concurrency.

Example 4.10. Let us consider a simple example. Suppose we want to run three tasks, X, Y, and Z, concurrently. These tasks do not communicate with one another in any way. The following program in Ada does the trick.

```
procedure ABC is
        task X;
        task body X is
                -- task body
        end X;

        task Y;
        task body Y is
                -- task body
        end Y;

        task Z;
        task body Z is
                -- task body
        end Z;

begin
        --procedure body consisting of at least a null statement
end ABC;
```

The three tasks are defined in the declaration portion of procedure ABC. When the system executes the begin of ABC, all three tasks plus whatever is in the procedure body are concurrently initiated. The procedure will complete once all the tasks have completed.

Example 4.10 is simple, since there was no communication between the concurrent tasks. Suppose that we want the structure shown in Figure 4.5.

Example 4.11. We want to concurrently run simultaneously three processes, A, B, and C. Partway through its execution, process A is to provide output in the form of a

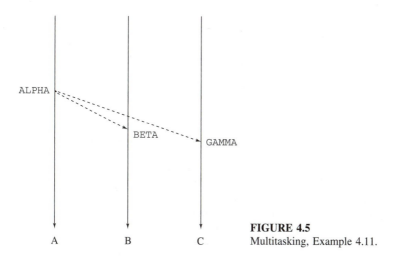

FIGURE 4.5
Multitasking, Example 4.11.

real variable X that will be used by B and C at points BETA and GAMMA, respectively. Let us see how to program this in Ada.

```
procedure CONCURRENT
        task A;
        task body A is
                --declarations, program up to point ALPHA
                B.BETA(X)
                C.GAMMA(X)
                --program after point ALPHA
        end A;

        task B is
                entry BETA (X:float);
        end B;
        task body B is
                --program up to point BETA
                accept BETA(X:float);
                --program after point BETA
        end B;

        task C is
                entry GAMMA(X:float);
        end C;
        task body C is
                --program up to point GAMMA
                accept GAMMA(X:float);
                --program after point GAMMA
        end C;


    begin
    end CONCURRENT;
```

When the begin statement of CONCURRENT is executed, tasks A, B, and C are begun concurrently. Tasks A, B, and C have rendezvous points ALPHA, BETA, and GAMMA, respectively. The tasks will execute concurrently until their respective rendezvous points are reached. Suppose, for the purposes of illustration, that task A gets to point ALPHA first, then task B gets to point BETA, and then C gets to point GAMMA. Task A will suspend execution after reaching point ALPHA until task B gets to point BETA. At that time, it will communicate to task B the variable X. Task B will then accept that input and go its way; at this time, the instruction B.BETA(X) has been executed. Then task A will wait until task C gets to its point GAMMA, and then communicate X to C. Following this, A and C are free to go their own ways.

What if C gets to point GAMMA before B gets to point BETA? The way we have written the program, it has to wait until A has executed its C.GAMMA(X) instruction. However, this does not happen until after A executes the B.BETA(X) instruction, and so C will wait until after B has reached point BETA.

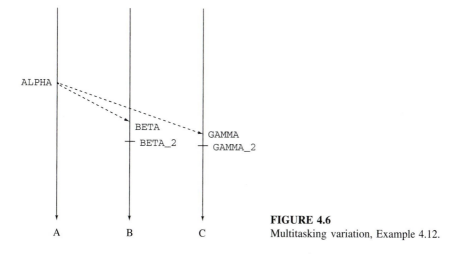

FIGURE 4.6
Multitasking variation, Example 4.12.

It is important to note that when a task suspends execution, the processor is then free to run some other tasks. This improves the utilization of the processing resources. Let us consider a variation on Example 4.11.

Example 4.12. Suppose we have the requirement that A not proceed beyond point ALPHA unless B has executed up to point BETA_2 and C has executed up to point GAMMA_2; see Figure 4.6. The code for this is shown below. Task A waits until the portion of code between the accept . . . do and the corresponding end statements have been executed.

```
procedure CONCURRENT
    task A;
    task body A is
        --declarations, program up to point ALPHA
        B.BETA(X)
        C.GAMMA(X)
        --program after point ALPHA
    end A;

    task B is
        entry BETA (X:float);
    end B;
    task body B is
        --program up to point BETA
        accept BETA(X:float) do
            -- program between BETA and BETA_2
        end BETA;    --program after point BETA_2
    end B;
    task C is
        entry GAMMA(X:float);
    end C;
```

```
task body C is
      --program up to point GAMMA
      accept GAMMA(X:float) do
            -- program between GAMMA and GAMMA_2
      end GAMMA;
      --program after point GAMMA_2
end C;


begin
end CONCURRENT;
```

Example 4.13. Here is another example. There is a server S that serves tasks from either of two queues, A and B.

```
task S is
      entry A_TASK(X,Y: float)
      entry B_TASK(X,Y: float)
end S;
task body S is
begin
      loop
            select
                  accept A_TASK(X,Y: float);
                  -- code for what to do for this task
            or
                  accept B_TASK(X,Y:float);
                        -- code for what to do for this task
            or
                  terminate;
            end select;
      end loop;
end S;
```

Task S consists of an infinite loop—meaning the server is always working or available for work. Whenever it completes a task, it checks whether there is anything waiting in queue A or B. If there is, it executes the head-of-the-line task from one of the queues. If only one queue is nonempty, then the task will be taken from that queue. If both are nonempty, then the `select` statement will pick one queue at random and serve the head-of-the-line task from that queue. The `terminate` command allows this task (which has an infinite loop) to terminate whenever the scope that contains it terminates. Tasks can be added to queues A and B simply by making the calls `S.A_TASK(X,Y);` and `S.B_TASK(X,Y);`, respectively.

It is possible to put guards on the `select` statements. The *guards* will allow an action to be selected only if a condition is satisfied. For example, if we want queue A to be served only when some variable Z was positive, we write:

```
task S is
      entry A_TASK(X,Y: float)
      entry B_TASK(X,Y: float)
end S;
task body S is
begin
      loop
            select
                  when Z > 0 =>
                  accept A_TASK(X,Y: float) do
                        -- code for what to do for this task
                  end A_TASK;
            or
                  accept B_TASK(X,Y:float) do
                        -- code for what to do for this task
                  end B_TASK;
            end select;
      end loop;
end S;
```

If all the alternatives of a select statement have guards on them, then the logical condition associated with at least one of the guards must be TRUE; if not the system will raise a PROGRAM_ERROR.

Tasks can be used to ensure the exclusive control of resources. Consider the following code, which implements a classic semaphore-type resource lock to manage concurrent access to a resource that cannot be shared:

```
task RESOURCE_CONTROL is
      entry CAPTURE;
      entry RELEASE;
end RESOURCE_CONTROL;

task body RESOURCE_CONTROL is
      FREE: Boolean := TRUE ;
      begin
            loop
                  select
                        when FREE =>
                              accept CAPTURE do
                                    FREE => FALSE;
                              end CAPTURE;
                  or
                              accept RELEASE do
                                    FREE => TRUE;
                  or
                              terminate;
                  end select;
```

```
            end loop;
    end RESOURCE_CONTROL;
```

This is an infinite loop. If there are no tasks waiting to either CAPTURE or RELEASE the resource, the terminate statement is used to end that iteration of the loop. To capture the resource, a task must make the call RESOURCE_CONTROL.CAPTURE. To release, the command RESOURCE_CONTROL.RELEASE is used.

So far, we have said nothing about time. We can use the delay command in Ada to specify a delay of a given number of seconds before action is taken. The delay until command specifies a delay until the clock has reached a specific point, for example, delay until 300 says to delay until the clock has reached 300.

Example 4.14. Consider the case of an alertness button, used to ensure that the operator is awake. The operator must press the button at least once every 90 seconds. If he goes to sleep and does not press the button as specified, an alarm goes off. Here is the task that generates the alarm.

```
    task ALARM is
        entry AWAKE;
    end ALARM ;

    task body ALARM is
    begin
        loop
            select
                accept AWAKE;
            or
                delay 90.0;
                SOUND_ALARM;
            end select;
        end loop;
    end ALARM;
```

Suppose the AWAKE button is pressed at time 0; we assume that pressing the button causes the AWAKE entry of task ALARM to be called. At time 0, the task ALARM will accept the AWAKE call. In the next iteration of the loop, suppose the AWAKE signal is not asserted. Control will therefore pass to the delay statement, where it will remain for 90 seconds. If, during this interval, the button is pressed, the AWAKE signal will be accepted. If not, then the procedure SOUND_ALARM is executed.

It is a drawback of Ada that when we specify a delay of 90 seconds, all that can be guaranteed is a delay of at least 90 seconds. In Example 4.14, if the 90-second timer expires without the button having been pushed and all processors are busy executing something else, the SOUND_ALARM action will not happen right away; it will happen only when there is a processor available to execute it. To avoid this problem, we can make SOUND_ALARM a very high priority task, so that lower-priority tasks will be preempted by it.

Let us now turn to the issue of task priority. So far, when we have spoken of concurrency, we have implicitly assumed that there are sufficient processors to ensure real concurrency. If there are not, the system will be forced to time-share processors. Programming languages should always have a way of expressing the relative priority of tasks to guide the system in this time-sharing.

Example 4.15. For example, suppose we have three concurrent tasks A, B, and C, with A having priority over B and B over C. The following is how we would code it in Ada. A *pragma* is an instruction to the compiler; users can define them as appropriate. The pragma PRIORITY is defined to define a static priority level.

```
procedure PRIORITY is
        task A;
        task body A is
             pragma PRIORITY(3);
        begin
             -- task body
        end A;

        task B;
        task body B is
             pragma PRIORITY(2);
        begin
             -- task body
        end B;

        task C;
        task body C is
             pragma PRIORITY(1);
        begin                  -- task body
        end C;

begin
        --procedure body, if any
end ABC;
```

The priority of a rendezvous between processes A and B is max(priority(A), priority(B)). This allows for priority inheritance (see Chapter 3).

In the Ada9X real-time annex, the actual number of priorities supported by any system is implementation-dependent; however, every system is required to support at least 31 distinct priority classes. The range of priorities, specified by the integer subtype SYSTEM.ANY_PRIORITY, is divided into two nonoverlapping subranges, specified by the subtypes SYSTEM.PRIORITY and SYSTEM.INTERRUPT_PRIORITY, respectively. Tasks that need to be of sufficiently high priority to block one or more interrupts must be in the SYSTEM.INTERRUPT_PRIORITY range. The following conditions must be satisfied:

```
SYSTEM.ANY_PRIORITY'FIRST = SYSTEM.PRIORITY'FIRST
SYSTEM.INTERRUPT_PRIORITY'FIRST = SYSTEM.PRIORITY'LAST + 1
```

```
SYSTEM.ANY_PRIORITY'LAST = SYSTEM.INTERRUPT_PRIORITY'LAST
SYSTEM.PRIORITY'LAST - SYSTEM.PRIORITY'FIRST ≥ 30
```

The intrinsic priority of a task (also called its base priority) can be specified in two ways. The first is by default. The default priority is just the average of the SYSTEM.PRIORITY range, that is,

$$\frac{\text{SYSTEM.PRIORITY'FIRST} + \text{SYSTEM.PRIORITY'LAST}}{2}.$$

The second way is to use either pragma PRIORITY(x) or pragma INTERRUPT_PRI-ORITY(y), where x,y are expressions (or numbers) whose value is the task priority, and which are in the SYSTEM.PRIORITY and SYSTEM.INTERRUPT_PRIORITY ranges, respectively.

4.10   LOW-LEVEL PROGRAMMING

General-purpose computers have a fairly standard set of I/O devices. They are usually limited to tape drives, disk systems, printers, terminals, and so on. To enable the system to interact with such devices, special-purpose drivers usually come as part of the operating system.

Real-time systems, on the other hand, have no standard I/O devices—the devices are determined by the application. For example, the I/O devices of an aircraft-control system are very different from those of a chemical plant. The devices can vary in their speeds and in the volume of data that they can input/output.

The traditional approach to writing device drivers is to use assembly language. However, as anyone who has written programs in assembly language will tell you, it is a slow and painful task, which all too often produces code that is difficult to understand and maintain. It should ideally be possible to write device drivers in high-level programming languages. This is all the more important for real-time systems since the cost of producing such code has to be spread over the sale of a smaller number of units than for general-purpose systems.

In this discussion, we will assume a memory-mapped I/O. That is, device registers are part of the system address space and can be accessed by specifying their addresses; thus to make I/O possible, we need to be able to specify the addresses of the various devices and access them. For example, consider the following Ada code for reading a temperature sensor.

```
task TEMP_READER is
    entry START(TEMP: out INTEGER);
    entry DONE;
    for DONE use at 8#1046#;
end TEMP_READER;

task body TEMP_READER is
    B: OFFON;
    TEMP_BUFFER: INTEGER range 0..1024;
    for TEMP_BUFFER use at 8#11306#;
```

```
      for B use at 8#156# range 0..0;
begin
      loop
          accept START(TEMP: out INTEGER);
              B := ON;
              accept DONE;
              TEMP:= TEMP_BUFFER;
          end START;
      end loop;
end TEMP_READER;
```

Here, OFFON is an enumerated data type with the values (OFF, ON). We assume we have previously defined this type as being a 0 if it is OFF, and 1 if it is ON. Ada allows one to do this by saying:

```
for OFFON'SIZE use 1; -- specifies size of OFFON type to be 1 bit
for OFFON use (OFF=>0, ON=>1); -- specifies OFF is 0 and ON is 1
```

We define two accept points, START and DONE. DONE is an interrupt whose vector address is 8#1046# (which means 1046 octal).[5] There is a TEMP_BUFFER that is written into by the temperature sensor (with the temperature), whose address is 8#11306#. That is, reading the address location 8#11306# will result in reading the TEMP_BUFFER. The sensor is initiated by setting one of its lines high; this line is the zeroth bit of the contents of address 8#156#. When this control line is raised, the sensor starts measuring the temperature. When it completes, it places the temperature in its TEMP_BUFFER. It also resets the control line and interrupts the calling task. The calling task initiates a temperature reading by saying READ_TEMP.START(TEMP);, and then reading the temperature from variable TEMP.

You will have noted that this type of code is not portable—we are specifying the absolute addresses of the device registers. However, this is only to be expected. When we are trying to control individual devices, we have to deal with such low-level details. Because assembly language programming is such a slow business, expressing this level of detail in a high-level language has the potential to greatly increase programmer productivity.

4.11 TASK SCHEDULING

We have seen two scheduling mechanisms so far, first-in–first-out (FIFO) and static priority (using pragma PRIORITY()). As we know from Chapter 3, real-time systems need much more sophisticated scheduling algorithms, such as earliest deadline first and rate-monotonic scheduling. Unfortunately, none of the established programming languages supports such scheduling constructs, and some run-time support is often necessary.

---

[5]In general, by a#b# we mean b expressed in base-a.

As an example of what developments are likely in the near future, let us look at the Ada9X language specifications. The real-time annex of Ada9X offers some assistance to the programmer in (among other things) task dispatching, entry queueing, and a ceiling priority policy for a new type—protected. Let us consider each of them in turn.

4.11.1 Task Dispatching Policy

The default dispatching policy is as follows. Each task has a base and an active priority associated with it. The base priority is designated either by the programmer or by default. It can be changed by a call to the DYNAMIC_PRIORITIES package (which will be discussed later). The active priority of a task is the maximum of the base priority and of any active priorities that are inherited. For example, during a rendezvous, if task A accepts an entry call from task B, A inherits the active priority of B. Thus, the active priority of A would be

max(base priority of A, active priority of B)

Note that the active priority of a task can reduce, as well as increase, with time; if the condition that caused the inheritance of the active priority ceases to hold, the inheritance ceases also.

Each processor has a set of ready queues associated with it. There is one queue for each priority class. When a task becomes ready for execution, it is placed at the tail of the queue associated with its active priority. If, while a task is in a ready queue, its active priority changes, the task is moved to the tail of the queue corresponding to its new active priority. If the base priority of a task is changed, the task moves to the tail of the queue for its active priority. This happens whether or not the active priority changes, and whether or not the task is currently executing. When the running task is suspended (e.g., waiting for a rendezvous) or completes, the task at the head of the highest priority nonempty queue is chosen for execution. Note that we do not necessarily have physical queues corresponding to the ready queues. These are conceptual and compiler writers may implement them any way they like.

A task is allowed to be on the ready queue of more than one processor. Such a task will be executed by the first processor that finds all its higher-priority ready queues empty. When a task begins execution on one processor, it is removed from all the ready queues it belongs to.

Task preemption is allowed; that is, a task with higher priority can preempt a lower-priority task. The preempted task will return to the head of the ready queue corresponding to its current active priority.

In addition to this default policy, the compiler may support other dispatching policies through a pragma (recall that in Ada a pragma is an instruction to the compiler). The format for specifying which policy is to be used is as follows:

```
pragma TASK_DISPATCHING_POLICY (policy_name [,
            compilation_unit_name]);
```

4.11.2 Entry Queueing Policy

The entry queueing policy specifies the order in which entry calls are served. It allows the programmer to specify, for example, how the system should choose from among several available alternatives for a selective wait statement.

Associated with each entry point in a task are one or more queues. Ada has just one queue associated with each entry point. Entry calls are served in FIFO order, regardless of the priority of the calling task. This can be a severe constraint on the programmer.[6] The real-time annex of Ada9X makes the programmer's life a little easier by specifying an alternative queueing policy, PRIORITY_QUEUEING. This allows multiple queues, one per priority class, associated with each entry point; entry calls are served in the order of the active priority of the calling task. If the active priority of a calling task changes while the call is in a queue, the call is not moved to a new queue unless the base priority of the calling task is updated. If this happens, the task is moved to the tail of the queue representing its new active priority.

If more than one alternative of a selective wait statement is open, we choose the alternative that has the highest-priority queued call waiting for it. If there are more than one alternative with equal priority calls waiting for them, the alternative that appears first in textual order is chosen.

The programmer is by no means limited to using the facilities of the PRIOR-ITY_QUEUEING package. Compiler writers are allowed to define additional packages that control the access to entry points in tasks. The default queueing policy is FIFO. In addition, there is a priority-queueing policy.

4.11.3 Protected Data Types

Ada9X defines protected operations, which are exported by objects of the protected data type. A task executing a protected operation (including functions, procedures, and entries) is protected against abortion and against the concurrent execution of other conflicting operations on the same object. Protected objects have semantics similar to those of monitors.

Every protected object has a ceiling priority, which is an upper bound on the active priority that a task may have when it makes protected operations on that protected object. If a task has a higher active priority than the ceiling priority when it attempts to make these protected operations, an exception is raised. A task executing a protected operation inherits the ceiling of the protected object and is protected against being preempted by any task with a priority lower than the ceiling of the protected object.

Protected data types help maintain data consistency efficiently in a memory-sharing system. If some portion of shared memory is to be accessed, the compiler can execute protected operations to read that portion from memory, carry out

---

[6]This problem can be circumvented by using tricks, such as multiple entry points—one to each priority class—or entry families. We shall not discuss these here.

whatever manipulations are called for by the program, and then complete the access to the protected object by writing back the modifications to the memory.

4.12   TIMING SPECIFICATIONS

A good real-time language should make it easy to specify timing requirements. Unfortunately, none of the established languages does this.[7] It is likely, however, that the next-generation languages will have means to do this.

Ideally, we would like to be able to do the following:

1. Specify that the duration between two events is no longer than a specified maximum and no shorter than a specified minimum.
2. Specify the maximum run time that we are willing to allocate to a particular task. If this time is exceeded, an exception is generated. This results in an asynchronous transfer of control.
3. Specify the absolute time at which a given task is to begin execution.
4. Specify that a particular task begins *n* seconds after some other task has completed.
5. Specify how soon a message is to be received after it is sent.
6. Specify how soon after receipt a message must be processed by the receiving task.
7. Specify the periodic scheduling of a task.
8. Specify for each loop the maximum time allowed for processing that loop.
9. Specify upper bounds on the size of any dynamic data structures, thus specifying a bound on the time required to pass them between procedures, or to allocate and deallocate storage.

If the system is unable to meet one or more of these requirements, it must raise an exception. The programmer can write exception handlers for these. For instance, if a task misses its deadline, perhaps the system must switch to a backup task to meet the minimal requirements. If we have an imprecise computation (see Chapter 3), we should have the ability to terminate it prematurely and still use the result. In Ada-9X notation, this would be done as follows:

```
select
    delay until 100;
then abort
    -- abortable part of the imprecise computation
end select;
```

---

[7]PEARL has sophisticated timing-requirement primitives, but the language is meant largely for uniprocessors. It appears to be hard to use it for distributed applications. There are experimental languages, such as Real-Time Euclid, which have some of these features. We touch upon Euclid later in this chapter.

A good example of time-keeping is the REAL_TIME package in the Ada9X real-time annex. Time can be read by calling the function CLOCK; this returns an integer of type TIME. If CLOCK returns a value i, that corresponds to time in the interval [E+i*TIME_SMALL, E+(i+1)*TIME_SMALL). TIME_SMALL is no greater than 1 μs. E is the time origin and is implementation-determined. It could be some calendar epoch (e.g., 00:00 UTC on January 1, 1990) or whenever the system is booted up. The range of time values must be sufficient to uniquely represent time between the system start-up and at least 50 years after that event.

The clock ticks about once every AVG_TICK seconds, where AVG_TICK is implementation-defined under the constraint that AVG_TICK must be no greater than 1 ms. If the clock is to be regularly synchronized with respect to some external timing reference, information about the frequency of such synchronization and the external timing reference should be included in the documentation.

4.13 SOME EXPERIMENTAL LANGUAGES

In this section, we look at two experimental languages. We will look at the distinctive features of these languages, rather than covering the languages themselves in detail. The value of these languages is not in programming them—most experimental languages never make it out of the university research laboratory. Rather, the value is in becoming sensitive to how various issues in real-time programming are recognised and addressed by contemporary researchers.

4.13.1 Flex

Flex is an experimental language developed at the University of Illinois. It has two distinct characteristics: it has a powerful array of constraint specifications, and it has the ability to select, from among multiple algorithms, the best one.

Flex is a derivative of C++. The Flex compiler consists of a preprocessor that puts out C++ code, which can then be compiled by a C++ compiler. The purpose behind the development of Flex is to try to turn a general-purpose language into a real-time language by the addition of suitable primitives.

CONSTRAINT SPECIFICATIONS. In Flex, time and resource constraints are expressed through the constraint block. Such a construct has the following structure:

```
[label:] (constraint; constraint; constraint; ...)
[↝ { Exception-handling routine } ] {
    Block of code
}
```

The first element is the label that the block is named. The second is a set of constraints that must be satisfied when the block of code is being executed. The third is an optional exception-handling routine, which is invoked whenever any of these constraints is violated. The fourth is the block of code itself. The following time attributes are defined:

A.start   Start time of block A
A.finish   Finish time of block A
A.duration   Execution time of block A
A.interval   Interval between the start time of two successive executions of A

For example, A: (start $\geq a$; finish $< b$; altitude $\geq c$) means that block A cannot be started before time a, that it must be completed by time b, and that the variable altitude must be at least c throughout the execution. If the block is not completed by time b or altitude becomes less than c, it is terminated and the optional exception-handling routine is invoked.

It is possible to link one block's time attributes to another. For example, if we want block A to start when block B starts and finish when B finishes, we write the following code:

```
A:(finish ≥ B'.finish) {
    A':(start ≥ B.start) {
        code for block A
    }
}

B:(finish ≥ A'.finish){
    B':(start ≥ A.start) {
        code for block B
    }
}
```

If we want block A to start after B has finished, we write the following code:

```
A:(start ≥ B.finish) {
    code for module A
}

B:(1) {
    code for module B
}
```

The (1) as a condition for B indicates a condition that is always true. That is, there is no constraint on B.

The system automatically records when execution of a block starts, and when it finishes.

CHOOSING FROM MULTIPLE ALTERNATIVES. Given a task, there can be multiple algorithms available to carry out that task. Some algorithms are best used when the available time is short or when there are memory or other resource constraints; others are best used when the constraints are not quite so tight. Flex allows the user to specify a number of algorithms from which the system can choose the best one to use at a given time. The user can specify, by means of a pragma, what the objective function is. For example, the objective function might be to minimize execution time or to maximize the accuracy of the output.

The programmer does not necessarily have to supply the system with the run time or with other attributes of the program; there is a tool to estimate this. For example, the programmer might specify only that the execution time of a program is a linear function of the problem size (i.e., that it is of the form $An + B$ where A and B are constants). The system can carry out experiments on the program and determine the values of A and B by using standard statistical techniques. Of course, this kind of thing is not advisable during actual operations! Rather, this is done ahead of time, during software development, and the system is informed about the performance characteristics of each alternative. During run time, it picks the best alternative on the basis of these inputs.

IMPRECISE COMPUTATION. To run imprecise computations in Flex, the programmer can simply specify that the computation must terminate by some specified time. This time may be static and known at compile time, or it may be dynamic and a function of the start or finish time of some other tasks. If the computation runs to completion by the specified time, then well and good. Otherwise, it is prematurely stopped at the deadline and its results put out for use. If the imprecise computation consists of a mandatory portion and one or more optional portions, then its results will only be of use if there is enough time to complete at least the mandatory portion.

4.13.2 Euclid

Euclid is an experimental language developed at the University of Toronto. It has the features of strong type checking and the ability to declare variables at specified memory addresses, which are necessary as security against errors and for handling I/O devices, respectively. It also has extensive user-defined exception-handling facilities. These are features not unique to Euclid (we have seen something similar in Ada). What is particularly noteworthy about Euclid is that it is specifically designed to allow for reasonably accurate estimates of worst-case program run times. Such estimates make it possible to determine the schedulability of the real-time workload, that is, to find out if the real-time tasks of the workload can all meet their hard deadlines.

To facilitate such estimates, many programming features are disallowed in Euclid. In particular, dynamic data structures are not allowed. The reason for this is that the time taken to allocate memory is a function of the size of the data structure and, if the latter is not known at compile time, neither is the former. However, there is a partial escape from this requirement. Each system implementation allows a maximal size for each data structure (e.g., arrays, strings, etc.). The programmer can specify that a data structure has the maximal size. This is especially useful when passing parameters to a process, when we do not know at compile time exactly what the size of the passed data structure is going to be. At run time, the actual size of the data structure is known and the required space (which can be no greater than the maximal size) can be allocated.

Other features that are disallowed are recursion and `while` loops. Disallowing recursion does not really limit the scope of the programmer—everything that can be done using recursion can also be done iteratively. `while` loops are disallowed because it is difficult or impossible to predict in advance how many iterations are needed before the termination condition is satisfied. In place of `while` loops, the programmer can use either time-bounded loops or `for` loops. Time-bounded loops specify that the loop must not run for longer than a specified amount of time; `for` loops explicitly specify an upper bound on the number of iterations (they are an upper bound since we can exit a loop before this number has been executed).

The syntax of the process declaration in Euclid shows how much timing control the programmer is given in this language.

```
process id: activation information
    [list of items imported into this process]
    [precondition that must be true upon each activation
        of this process.]
    [postcondition that must be true upon the end of each
        process execution]
    [exception handler]
        [process code]
    end id
```

The activation information is used to determine when to run the process. The syntax for the activation information is as follows.

atEvent [condition] [frame information]
periodic [frame information] **first activation** [time or event]

The **atEvent** condition specifies that the process is to be run for the first time when the specified condition is satisfied. The frame information specifies the interval between successive initiations of the process. The **periodic** command is similar.

4.14 PROGRAMMING ENVIRONMENTS

The development of software for real-time systems is a very difficult business. The programs that control even moderately complex systems tend to be tens of thousands of lines long. It is estimated that the proposed NASA space station will require over a million lines of code.

The production of such code requires huge teams of programmers and other staff. The code generated by each programmer has to be tested individually, integrated into the whole, and tested again in the context of the whole system. Maintenance is another important issue. A large piece of software will undergo many changes over its lifetime. There are two reasons for this. First, as the software goes into operation, programming faults will be uncovered that must be fixed. Second, we often need to upgrade the software to increase or modify its capabilities in response to changing needs. The complexity of writing, debugging, and maintaining hundreds of thousands of lines of code has led to the cost of software increasingly dominating the overall system cost.

Programming environments can be regarded as a set of tools that enhance the efficiency and reliability of software production. Why do we need them? Let us look at the difference between one person writing a small program and a team of programmers.

Consider Project A. You are writing a small program, of a few hundred lines or so, all by yourself to solve a problem you understand well. What are the challenges? First, the problem is well understood, and so the probability of making a mistake by not knowing what you are trying to accomplish is low. Second, you can, if you are fairly experienced, let the program grow organically, without a prior decision having to be made on how to structure it. That is, as you code, you can define and write modules on the fly. Third, you are writing the entire program, so you will be familiar with the insides of each of its modules. You know which module calls which other module. If, while debugging the code, you find that a module needs to be fixed or changed, you know which other modules it will affect and how. Fourth, if after a few months you need to alter the software to solve a slightly different problem, you can use the comments that you have liberally sprinkled throughout the program to recall the logic behind it, and alter it.

Now suppose you are writing Project B, a slightly larger program of a few thousand lines. You have recruited a reasonably intelligent programmer to help you with it. How does this project differ from Project A? For one thing, you will have to explain the problem precisely to your colleague. You will both have to agree in advance to a division of labor in the writing of it, by deciding how to break up the code into modules and how these modules will interact with each other. So, the code must be structured into modules and the modules must be defined before you can begin to write the code. In particular, you will need to predefine the input and output interfaces of all the modules in advance. Once this has been done, you and your colleague can embark upon the task of writing the code.

As you write the code, suppose you find that one or more of the module specifications is incomplete or wrong. You cannot simply fix it by yourself and continue. You must inform your colleague and decide on how to modify the specifications so that as few as possible of the other modules that have already been written have to be rewritten. Just one critical mistake in specifying one of the modules can result in most of the software having to be rewritten.

How do you test the code? You will want to compile and test each module separately, not wait for the entire code to be ready before debugging begins. This might cause difficulties if that module calls other modules. You will want some means of testing the module even though the called modules are not yet available.

How do you maintain the code? Suppose that three years from now, you have to fix some faults that have been uncovered in a module written by your colleague. If your colleague has since moved on to greener pastures, you will have to fix it yourself. How do you understand the logic behind her code? Obviously there must be extensive documentation to help you to do this.

We can see the increase in complexity that results in going from a small program to a larger one of a few thousand lines. This complexity further increases if you are responsible for producing a piece of software that is a million lines long. This is not a job for one or two people, but for a whole army of programmers. The enterprise becomes extremely complex.

For this project, first of all, you have a greater need for an effective and unambiguous means of specifying the software. In Project A, you could change the specifications all by yourself. In Project B, it took a meeting between you and your colleague to review them; when you had to change the specifications of the module that your colleague was responsible for, you could both sit down together and discuss the changes. You cannot do this very easily with a thousand programmers, who may be in a dozen different locations; indeed, the number of possible programmer interactions increases as the square of the number of programmers. The more complex the software, the greater the possibility that either (a) the specification contains an error or (b) the specification is misunderstood, and the greater the cost of fixing the problems that result when either (a) or (b) happens. Second, you have an increased need for some way of testing the various software modules independently of one another. Third, you need to have a whole database of documentation. This database must indicate the author of each module, the logical structure of the code, and everything else that is necessary to understand the code.

Fourth, there must be some support for program maintenance. Suppose a fault has been found in a module, and a programmer is asked to fix it. This programmer is probably not the author of the code, and so will rely on the documentation to help him understand it. The programmer must formally check out the module he is to work on, much as one checks out a library book. When the code is changed, it creates a new version of the software, which is integrated back into the software after full testing.

Fifth, there must be security. The project involves hundreds of people in varying roles. Access must be controlled based on these roles. For example, a person who prepares the documentation must be given read, but not write, access to the source code. If a portion of the source code includes classified information, it must be possible to protect that portion from being read by people with insufficient clearance.

It is the job of a programming support environment (PSE) to provide these facilities. A good PSE is as important to software development as a good programming language. This was understood by the sponsors of Ada. While the language was being developed, they also developed a PSE for it. The final specification document is called Stoneman. Let us consider the Stoneman specifications.

Stoneman suggests a layered approach to building a PSE; see Figure 4.7. At the base are the hardware and the kernel. Surrounding this are three layers, consisting of a kernel Ada programming support environment (KAPSE), a minimal Ada programming support environment (MAPSE), and an Ada programming support environment (APSE). A KAPSE uses the tools of the kernel; a MAPSE

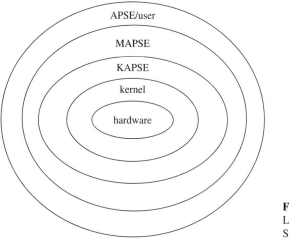

FIGURE 4.7
Layered PSE suggested by the
Stoneman document.

does not normally deal directly with the kernel but uses the tools provided by the KAPSE; and an APSE or the user usually deals with the tools provided by the MAPSE and is unconcerned with the KAPSE.

The logic behind these layers is to maximize portability by making the support environment as independent of the underlying hardware and kernel as possible. A PSE is itself a very complex piece of software, and we cannot afford to write a whole new PSE for each machine type. The solution is to segregate all the kernel-dependent activities in the KAPSE; the KAPSE is then tailored to the machine on which it runs. The layers above it, however, can be portable. The KAPSE is, in this sense, analogous to a compiler. Most programmers do not have to worry about the details of the underlying machine; the compiler takes care of the machine-dependent details.[8] A KAPSE might, in some cases, have a mechanism by which it can be bypassed and the kernel functions accessed directly. To ensure portability, there is a standard KAPSE interface, called the common APSE interface set (CAIS).

The MAPSE can now be built atop the KAPSE, using the KAPSE interface. Since the KAPSE layer hides the machine-level details, it becomes possible to have an identical MAPSE running on different machines. The MAPSE provides the user with a set of tools for program development. The MAPSE toolset includes a text editor, a pretty printer (which formats the program by indenting lines to help the programmer better understand its structure), a command language interpreter (which is similar to the job-control language that most readers are familiar with), a compiler, linker, loader, a tool for generating cross-references between the modules, a symbolic debugger, and a file manager. Further tools can be added in the APSE layer that interfaces with the MAPSE.

---

[8]There are a few exceptions, such as precision, that can depend on the machine word length, but we do not discuss these here.

A good programming environment should also have online assistance. To improve its usefulness, the online help facility may be organized hierarchically. A good help facility should provide the required format for instructions, as well as tutorial explanations for all the commands. It should also provide detailed explanations for all the error and diagnostic messages that are produced by the tools or the command language interpreter. Another useful facility is statistical profiling, which tells the user the frequency with which a given instruction occurs in the code, or how often a given routine is invoked.

The environment should facilitate testing. In particular, it should allow the use of stubs for modules that are not yet available. A *stub* is a placeholder for a module whose specification is available, but whose body is unavailable. For example, suppose module A has been written and is being tested. Module A calls module B, which is not yet available. The environment should allow us to replace B with a stub for purposes of testing A. In addition, the test management part of the environment should keep a record of test results and of the percentage of tests in a given test suite that have been completed.

Central to the APSE is the database, which can include objects such as the source code, documentation, specifications, and a chart that indicates the control flow of the code. The objects might be organized hierarchically, much as files are organized into hierarchical directories, with different individuals being allowed different forms of access to them. An object can be specified on the basis of its position in the hierarchy, much as we can specify a file in a hierarchical directory system.

An object will have attributes associated with it; perhaps the most useful are the history, categorization, and access attributes. The history attribute records when an object was created and its author(s). The categorization attribute tells us what kind of object this is. For example, we may choose to categorize objects into classes such as "source code," or "documentation." We can also specify whether the object is a file, a device, or something else. The access attribute specifies who has what kind of access to the object. We have already seen that for security and other reasons, not everyone who has access to the database should have unlimited access to every object in it. A user may have different levels of access to different objects. This is analogous to the read-write-execute access with which anyone who has worked on any modern operating system is familiar.

The database can have different versions of an object. These are best explained by means of an example. Suppose we have an object A. It is to be changed in response to either a reported bug or a modification in the specification. The programmer to whom the task is assigned can check out the object, modify it suitably, and then check it back in again. Checking in the object will not cause the old object to be deleted from the database, rather it will create a new version of A, distinguished from its predecessor(s) by its version number. Occasionally, a designer needs to work, not on the most recently-created version, but on an older one. The system must keep track of the lineage of each version. Figure 4.8 shows an example. In the figure, A.4 is the most recent version, but the designer wishes to backtrack to version A.2 and create modifications there to produce versions A.2.1 and A.2.2. Note that there will now be two "latest" versions of A: A.4 and

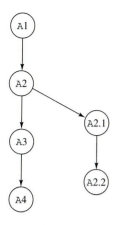

FIGURE 4.8
Keeping track of the version lineage of an object.

A.2.2. The user may decide to merge the modifications in both of them to form a new version A.5. In such a case, the system must keep track of the fact that A.5 is descended from both A.4 and A.2.2.

Such operations are particularly useful when a new compiler version becomes available. Typically, managers specify a transition period over which both the old and new releases of the compiler are used. This is facilitated by keeping track of the lineage of versions. One line of versions can deal with the old compiler and another with the new one.

It should also be possible to define configurations or sets of objects, and to handle these as single entities. That is, we assign version numbers to the configurations, and check them out and in the same way as we can with objects. In such cases, the system must maintain full documentation on the lineage of the configuration.

The database should have a mechanism to express the relationship between objects. This can be done primarily through the hierarchical structuring of the database. However, there can also be relationships that cannot be well described by such a structure, and there must be a mechanism for expressing such relationships.

The database provides dependency information. That is, it can tell the user which module depends on which other module. This is useful for three reasons. First, it allows the user to understand the relationship between the modules. Second, it allows the database to answer impact-of-change queries. That is, the user can ask the database what would be the effect of changing one particular object in the system. Third, it allows for consistency checking. When an object is modified, it may be necessary for all the units that depend on that object to be recompiled before being executed.

4.15 RUN-TIME SUPPORT

The key tools of the run-time support are the compiler, the linker, the debugger, and the kernel.

4.15.1 Compiler

The compiler translates the source code into machine language. It goes without saying that a good compiler will have an excellent diagnostic capability, which is used to improve the efficiency of the debugging process. The compiler should also list, on demand, the machine instructions of the compiled unit; this is useful in making timing estimates. A good compiler used in real-time applications should have hooks, which are used to report statistical information about the program when it is running; for example, how often the various functions, blocks, or other procedures are entered, and the amount of time taken to execute them.

Compilers often carry out optimizations to reduce the execution time. It should be possible to give directives on how this optimization is to be done. This is done in Ada by using pragmas.

4.15.2 Linker

Before the machine code from the compiler can be executed, it must be linked with any library or other routines that the program may be using. This is the task of the linker. It links together the parts (which may be separately compiled units of the program, or library routines) that make up the program. It determines which unit is the main part (when the program begins to run, control will be transferred to this part) and allocates storage space for the instructions and data. It also generates a list showing how the various units are linked together.

4.15.3 Debugger

A good debugger is vital to efficient program development. The debugger typically offers the following facilities.

- It allows program execution to be suspended and then resumed on the programmer's command. It makes variable values visible to the programmer. It allows the variable values to be changed by the programmer before execution is resumed.
- It allows the insertion of breakpoints into the program. When a program encounters a breakpoint, it suspends execution so that the programmer can inspect the variable values at that point. Sometimes, breakpoints are conditional. For example, the programmer may say "Stop the program if $x < 0$ at this point." If hardware support is not provided, this feature slows execution considerably.
- It allows the programmer to execute the program step by step. The programmer can then inspect variable values following every source-code instruction.

4.15.4 Kernel

The kernel is responsible for managing the resources of the system. It includes routines for allocating and scheduling the tasks, managing the memory, running the algorithm for interprocessor communication, handling processor failures, and carrying out input and output operations. Features of the kernel are treated in much more detail in other chapters.

4.16 SUGGESTIONS FOR FURTHER READING

For a general introduction to real-time programming languages, see the book by Young [10]. A somewhat more recent—and advanced—survey is provided by Burns and Wellings [4]. There are many books on Ada; see, for example, [1, 6, 11]. Burns, Lister, and Wellings [3] is an excellent overview of Ada tasking. The Cambridge University Press has put out a set of books in "The Ada Companion Series," which considers various special topics in Ada. Ada9X is described in [2, 9]. Additional documentation can also be obtained by anonymous ftp from `sw-eng.falls-church.va.us`. APSE is described in [5]. Flex is described by Kenny and Lin [7], while Kligerman and Stoyenko [8] provides a good overview of the Euclid language.

EXERCISES

4.1. The following code in Flex ostensibly ensures that blocks A and B start and finish at the same time. What is wrong with it?

```
A:(start ≥ B.start) {
      code for module A
}

B:(start ≥ A.start) {
      code for module B
}
```

4.2. Write Ada code to find the smallest and largest value of the `integer` data type on your machine.

4.3. What is printed out by the following stretch of Ada code?

```
BLOCK_A:
declare
      A: integer := 250;
      begin
      put (A);
      BLOCK_B:
            declare
                  A: integer := 900;
                  begin
                      put (A);
                  end BLOCK_A;
            put (A);
      end BLOCK_B;
```

4.4. Suppose we want to be able to add integer vectors by means of the + instruction. That is, if A, B, C are integer vectors, we want to be able to sum the corresponding terms of A and B and assign the result to the corresponding element in C by issuing the instruction C:=A+B;. Write code in Ada to enable this.

4.5. Provide a practical example of where Ada's limited private data type is useful.

4.6. Write Ada code that samples a ground-proximity sensor every 50 ms and sounds a warning if the altitude is less than 300 feet.

4.7. Write Ada code to control a water pump that must be turned on when the water level in an overhead tank falls below level ℓ_1 and must be turned off when the water level rises above level ℓ_2. Assume you have a sensor that samples the water level every 100 ms.

4.8. Write Ada code that maintains a FCFS queue feeding four processors. As processors become free, they are assigned jobs from the queue in FCFS fashion.

4.9. You are asked to add a total of 300 numbers. Write Ada code to do this using four processes. Each of three of the processes adds up 100 of the numbers and they then pass on the results to the fourth process, which adds up these partial sums.

4.10. In general, would you prefer a real-time language to use static or dynamic binding?

4.11. In what ways is Ada a better language for real-time software than the general-purpose programming language with which you are most familiar?

4.12. Use Ada tasks to implement binary and counting semaphores. Discuss the possible overhead of your implementations, as well as priority inversion issues.

REFERENCES

[1] Barnes, J. G. P.: *Programming in Ada Plus an Overview of Ada 9X*, Addison-Wesley, Reading, MA, 1994.

[2] Pazy, Offer, and T. P. Baker: "The Real-Time Systems Annex of the proposed Ada 9X standard," in *Ada Yearbook 1994* (C. Loftus, ed.), IOS Press, Burke, VA, 1994.

[3] Burns, A., A. M. Lister, and A. J. Wellings: *A Review of Ada Tasking*, Springer-Verlag, Berlin, 1987.

[4] Burns, A., and A. Wellings: *Real-Time Systems and Their Programming Languages*, Addison-Wesley, Wokingham, U.K., 1990.

[5] Freedman, R. S.: *Programming with APSE Software Tools*, Petrocelli Books, Princeton, NJ, 1985.

[6] Gilpin, G.: *Ada: A Guided Tour and Tutorial*, Prentice-Hall, New York, 1986.

[7] Kenny, K. B., and K.-J. Lin: "Building Flexible Real-Time Systems Using the Flex Language," *IEEE Computer* 24(5):70–78, 1991.

[8] Kligerman, E., and A. D. Stoyenko: "Real-Time Euclid: A Language for Reliable Real-Time Systems," *IEEE Trans. Software Engineering* SE-12(9):941–949, 1986.

[9] Stoyenko, A. D., and T. P. Baker: "Real-Time Schedulability-Analyzable Mechanisms in Ada9X," *Proc. IEEE* 82:95–107, 1994.

[10] Young, S. J.: *Real-Time Languages: Design and Development*, Ellis Horwood, Chichester, U.K., 1982.

[11] Young, S. J.: *An Introduction to Ada*, Ellis Horwood, Chichester, U.K., 1984.

CHAPTER
5

REAL-TIME
DATABASES

5.1 INTRODUCTION

Databases are a structured and convenient way to manage the sharing of large quantities of data among multiple tasks. In many cases, interaction between tasks can be defined in terms of read and write operations by those tasks on the database.

Real-time databases occur in many important applications. The most obvious are the databases in airline reservation, banking, and stock market systems. In airline reservation and banking systems, the response time needs to be kept low in order not to annoy customers. In stock market systems, the slow execution of orders can be very expensive in volatile markets. However, both are soft real-time systems, in the sense that there is no precise deadline after which catastrophe is inevitable.[1]

There are many hard real-time database applications, as well. For example, an early-warning system needs to correlate incoming radar images with a database of threats, and determine whether an alarm should be sounded and the interceptors scrambled.

---

[1] Of course, catastrophe is a relative term. To a trader, the excessively slow execution of orders might indeed mean "catastrophe," as she defines it.

5.2 BASIC DEFINITIONS

A *transaction* is a sequence of read and write operations. If τ is a set of transactions, a *history* over τ is an interleaving of the reads and writes in the transactions in τ. If transaction I reads from, or writes into, datum x, we denote that operation by $R_I(x)$ and $W_I(x)$, respectively. A transaction is said to be a *query* if it consists only of read operations, and an *update* otherwise.

Transactions may be aborted for a variety of reasons, for example, deadlock or a floating-point overflow. Hence, all updates executed by a transaction must initially be regarded as tentative. If the transaction must subsequently be aborted, such updates will have to be undone. Only after the transaction has passed its *commit* point (i.e., when we are certain that it will be completed successfully) is the update permanent. Commit is a point of no return: once a transaction has committed, we are certain that its updates will never be undone.

In conventional databases, transactions must satisfy the following properties.

Atomicity: The end result of running transactions must be the same as when each transaction is an atomic action. An action is said to be *atomic* if it is either done completely or not at all. Thus, if a transaction specifies several steps, the end result must be as if either all or none of these steps are carried out.

Consistency: The transaction transforms the database from one consistent state to another. A *consistent state* is one that results from the execution of some given sequence of transactions.

Isolation: The actions of a transaction are not visible to any other transactions until and unless that transaction has committed.

Durability: The actions of a transaction on a database (upon commitment) are permanent.

Collectively, these are called the ACID properties.

A given history S is *serial* if only one transaction is active in the system at any one time. For example, suppose that S has transactions T_1, T_2, T_3, and they execute in the following sequence. T_1 starts at time 0 and completes at time 5; T_2 starts at time 10 and ends at 29, and T_3 starts at 40 and finishes at 55.

A history S is said to be *final-state serializable* or to maintain *final-state serialization consistency* if the net effect of the operations is as if the transactions were executed in some serial order. The actual serial order is not specified; there just has to exist some serial order that satisfies this requirement.

Example 5.1. The history $R_1(x)W_1(x)R_2(x)W_2(x)R_1(y)R_2(y)$ is finite-state serializable; the net effect is as if we first executed transaction T_1 to completion, and then began transaction T_2. By contrast, the history $R_1(x)R_2(x)W_1(x)W_2(x)$ is not serializable. If we run transaction T_1 first and then transaction T_2, T_2 will read the value of x written by T_1; and if we reverse this order, T_1 will read the value of x as updated by T_2.

Two operations *conflict* with one another if they relate to the same data item and at least one of them is a write. If operations θ_1 and θ_2 conflict with each other, and θ_1 is executed earlier than θ_2 in history S, we denote this by $\theta_1 <_S \theta_2$.

5.3 REAL-TIME VS. GENERAL-PURPOSE DATABASES

Real-time databases have to deal with many of the same issues as general-purpose databases, in addition to the timing issues that lie at the heart of any real-time system. These make themselves felt in two ways. First, queries to the database have deadlines associated with them. Depending on the application, these deadlines may be either hard or soft. In some cases, there is some value to a response after the deadline has passed; in others there is not. Secondly, the data returned in response to a query must have both absolute consistency and relative consistency.

5.3.1 Absolute vs. Relative Consistency

Absolute consistency is accuracy; that is, data about the operating environment must be consistent with the environment. If, for example, we interrogate a database to find the current temperature or pressure in a chemical reactor vessel, we want the returned data to be close to the current temperature or pressure. *Relative consistency* means that, for multiple data, the data must have been collected reasonably close to one another.

> **Example 5.2.** If we want to obtain a composite picture of the pressure and the temperature of a boiler, the temperature and pressure measurements should be taken within a short time of each other. Suppose the temperature and pressure as a function of time are as shown in Table 5.1.
>
> If our database query returns values of 100 for the temperature (measured at time 100) and 100 for the pressure (measured at time 300), the composite temperature-pressure picture is inconsistent.

We can express the absolute and relative consistency requirements more formally as follows. Associate with each datum a consistency interval, over which it is absolutely consistent. Associate with each pair of data (x, y) a compatibility or relative consistency interval $c(x, y)$ of duration $t_c(x, y)$. Denote by t_x, t_y the timestamps on data (x, y). Define v_x, v_y so that x is absolutely consistent over the interval $[t_x, t_x + v_x]$, and y is absolutely consistent over the interval $[t_y, t_y + v_y]$. The pair (x, y) is only consistent at time t if $|t_x - t_y| \leq t_c(x, y)$, and if both x and y are absolutely consistent at that time (i.e., $t - t_x \leq v_x$ and $t - t_y \leq v_y$). v_x, v_y and $c(x, y)$ could vary with time.

> **Example 5.3.** Consider Figure 5.1. The absolute consistency intervals of x and y are shown as shaded bars. The timestamps of x and y are 0 and 1.75, respectively.

TABLE 5.1
Boiler temperatures and pressures

Time	Temperature	Pressure
100	100	360
200	300	720
300	700	100

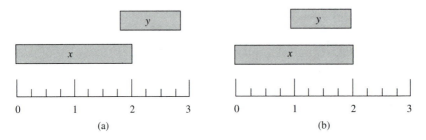

FIGURE 5.1
Example of (a) absolute consistency and (b) absolute and relative consistency.

Assume that $t_c(x, y) = 1.5$. In Figure 5.1(a), x and y have absolute consistency in the intervals $A_x = [0.00, 2.00]$ and $A_y = [1.75, 2.75]$, respectively. Even though over the interval $A_x \cap A_y = [1.75, 2.00]$, they are both absolutely consistent, the pair (x, y) is not relatively consistent anywhere, since the timestamps of x and y differ by more than $t_c(x, y)$. In Figure 5.1(b), x and y are absolutely consistent over $A_x = [0.00, 2.00]$ and $A_y = [1.00, 2.00]$, and the pair (x, y) is relatively consistent over the interval $R_{x,y} = [1.00, 1.50]$. Relative consistency is defined with respect to a set of data; absolute consistency is defined with respect to an individual datum.

The timestamp associated with the pair (x, y) is usually taken to be the earlier of the timestamps of x and y. However, this rule can be modified depending on circumstances. For instance, suppose that x is the mass of an asteroid and y is its position. Since the masses of asteroids do not change (unless they suffer a collision in space), the pair (x, y) should be timestamped with the timestamp of y, not with that of x.

Both absolute and relative consistency requirements are functions of the application to which the data are put. For instance, in our example of the boiler, if we are making decisions on whether to open a safety valve or not, we must do so on the basis of recently collected information, and so the absolute consistency interval of the pressure data will be fairly small. On the other hand, if we are querying the database to obtain a historical listing of the pressure data for analysis, the consistency interval is unlimited.

It is possible to derive some data variables from others. For example, let $w = f(u, v)$ be a function of data variables u, v; and $z = g(x, y)$ be another function of data variables x, y. The timestamp to be associated with the pair w, z, as well as their absolute and relative consistency intervals, must be determined from the absolute and relative consistency intervals of u, v, x, y and the functions f and g.

As with hard deadlines, the absolute and relative consistency intervals of a real-time database associated with a controlled process depends on the state of the controlled process. For example, the absolute consistency interval of the altitude data of an aircraft will be less during takeoff and landing than during cruise.

The consistency intervals of a data variable determine how often they must be measured. Data variables that are used in computations must be absolutely consistent, and relatively consistent with respect to any other data variable with which it may be used.

5.3.2 Need for Response-Time Predictability

Since tasks in real-time systems have deadlines associated with them, it is important that transaction response times be predictable. There are many factors that make it difficult to predict the response times of transactions.

- The requirement to meet the ACID properties can entail significant overhead that is difficult to predict. Transactions may be aborted one or more times before they are finally completed. Transaction aborts may be needed to avoid deadlock or to ensure serialization consistency. The direct effect of an abortion is to delay the affected transaction. There is also a side effect on other transactions, in that the processor has wasted time that could have been spent more usefully on other transactions.

- Databases are often much too large to entirely fit in the main memory,[2] and must therefore rely on disk systems. Page faults can occur if the desired record is not in main memory. The overhead imposed by page faults can vary a good deal; it depends greatly on the position of the read/write head with respect to the data.

- Transaction accesses (reads/writes) may be data-dependent. For example, if we have a transaction that is supposed to deduct a certain amount from a bank balance, it will have one set of accesses if the balance is large enough and another if it is not.

- Transactions may suffer a delay because they are waiting to access a datum that is currently locked by another transaction.

If a database is used in a hard real-time system, we must make worst-case assumptions to guarantee that critical hard deadlines will continue to be met. If the response-time variance is very large, however, such worst-case assumptions may require the system to be grotesquely overdesigned.

In some cases, it might be advantageous to preanalyze transactions in order to estimate the time and other resources that they will need. In preanalysis, we carry out what amounts to a partial dry run of the transaction to evaluate its processor, data, and other needs. Once the dry run is completed, if the system finds it has the resources to complete the transaction by the deadline, it guarantees its completion. This assumes, of course, that the dependencies in the final run are going to be the same as in the dry run.

During this dry run, the transaction is not allowed to alter the state of the database—no writes are permitted. Also, it is assumed that there are no conflicts with other transactions. All the data required by the transaction are brought into the main memory by the time the dry run ends. As a result, at the end of the dry run, we have no disk accesses to worry about (assuming that there have been no updates to those pages by other transactions since the pages were read in).

---

[2]Exceptions to this rule, called main memory databases, are discussed in Section 5.4.

We know how long the transaction will take to run in the absence of conflicts with other transactions. With this information, we try to schedule the transaction, keeping in mind the resource allocations already made to the previously guaranteed transactions. If we can schedule the transaction to meet its deadline, we guarantee it; otherwise we abort it. Since the transaction has not written into the database during this phase, there is no need for any recovery procedure to restore the database. Once the transaction is guaranteed, it will complete by the deadline (barring system failures). Therefore, no aborts need be done because of failure to meet deadlines.

In the event that some of the data that have been brought into the main memory have been subsequently written into by an already-guaranteed transaction, we must repeat the prefetch phase.

Whether a designer wishes to use this approach or not depends on whether she is willing to pay the overhead of the prefetch phase. We discuss this further in Section 5.9.

5.3.3   Relaxing the ACID Properties

As we have seen before, real-time applications are far more specific than general-purpose applications. As a result, it is possible to determine from the application what services should be provided by the database. Leaving out unnecessary capabilities can, in many cases, dramatically reduce overhead. In some applications, it may not be necessary to ensure that all the ACID properties are met. For example, in a database that is embedded in a machine-tool control system, the current tool position is not regarded as durable data and is discarded after it becomes outdated. In such an application, data durability is not worth maintaining if new measurements are frequently collected.

In some cases, it might be possible to sacrifice serialization consistency. Serialization consistency is a very strong constraint, and maintaining it can prevent certain transactions from executing concurrently. Moreover, in some applications, a violation of serialization consistency is acceptable. The following example is based on work by Garcia-Molina [6].

> **Example 5.4.** Consider an airline reservation database. When a reservation is made, the number of seats sold in each flight in the itinerary must be increased by one. For example, if a flight from Hartford (HFD) to Detroit (DTW) involves changing planes in Chicago (ORD), the reservation R(HFD,DTW) would consist of the following two steps:
>
> **Step 1:** Reserve a seat on a flight from Hartford to Chicago.
> If over 100 seats are sold, assign 5 flight attendants to the flight; otherwise assign 3 attendants.
>
> **Step 2:** Reserve a seat on a flight from Chicago to Detroit.
> If over 100 seats are sold, allocate 5 flight attendants to the flight; otherwise assign 3 attendants.
>
> Similarly, the cancellation of the reservation C(HFD,DTW) entails releasing one seat from each of these flights:

Step 1: Release a seat on a flight from Hartford to Chicago.
If the number of reservations drops below 85, assign only 3 flight attendants to this flight.

Step 2: Release a seat on a flight from Chicago to Detroit.
If the number of reservations drops below 85, assign only 3 flight attendants to this flight.

Note that we reduce the number of flight attendants only if the reservations drop below 85 (and not 100, which is when the number was increased from 3 to 5); this hysteresis is meant to prevent the assigned number from oscillating rapidly if the number of reservations oscillates around 100.

Serialization consistency would be violated if the reservation and cancellation transactions were interleaved. Suppose, for example, we have sold 99 seats on both the HFD→ORD and the ORD→DTW flights, and 3 flight attendants are currently allocated to each flight. Suppose now that one reservation and one cancellation request are received. To retain serialization consistency, we first have to execute one transaction and then the other; we cannot interleave them. If we execute the reservation first and then the cancellation, the final state is that there are 99 reservations on both flights, but 5 flight attendants are assigned to each of them. If we reverse the order of execution, we have 99 reservations on both flights and 3 flight attendants are assigned to each of them. On the other hand, if we interleave the transactions so that the order of execution is as follows:

Step 1 of R(HFD,DTW),

Step 1 of C(HFD,DTW),

Step 2 of C(HFD,DTW),

Step 2 of R(HFD,DTW),

then we still end up with 99 reservations on both flights. However, we allocate 5 flight attendants to the HFD→ORD flight, and 3 to the ORD→DTW flight. This violates serialization consistency, since there is no serial order in which the transactions can be executed that results in such a situation. If this inconsistency does not matter to the airline, then such a sacrifice of serialization consistency (in exchange for concurrent processing) may be worth it.

If we are willing to relax serialization consistency, we must provide some means for recovery when one of the interleaved transactions is aborted. See the reference mentioned in Section 5.12 for a discussion on this.

5.4 MAIN MEMORY DATABASES

Since disk accesses are extremely slow, one way of improving the response time of database operations is to have the entire database resident in main memory and use disks only for backups and storing logs.

Such an approach is not widely practiced in general-purpose databases. For one thing, most databases are too large. However, if the real-time database is sufficiently small, this approach becomes practical. As technology improvements drive down the costs of main memory and drive up their densities, main memory databases might well become more commonplace in real-time applications.

Many problems associated with disk storage become less pressing when main memory databases are used; examples are the problem of how to prioritize and schedule disk accesses, and how to position data on the disks so that access time is minimized. When disk accesses are done away with, transaction response times can be expected to improve significantly. The lower the response time, the lower the probability of lock contention (since transactions will be in the system for a smaller duration). Accordingly, it might be possible to increase the locking granularity. A *lock granule* is a database object that is under the purview of a single lock. Put another way, each lock has a domain of data elements; setting that lock amounts to locking all the elements within its domain, called the *granule*. If the locking granularity is very fine (i.e., the individual granules are small), there will be more locks to be maintained, and this adds to the overhead. However, if the granularity is very coarse (i.e., the individual granules are very large), the probability is higher that multiple active transactions will want access to the same granule, and will contend for the lock. If transactions take less time to finish, we can expect the lock contention to decrease. To summarize, contention will increase both with the granule size and the transaction duration. If the transaction duration can be reduced, we may be able to increase the granule size without adversely affecting the concurrency that the system can support.

Some people have suggested that we could, in uniprocessor systems, force purely sequential processing by such databases and do away with the need for concurrency control. This has the merit of not imposing concurrency-control overhead, of automatically ensuring serialization consistency, and of reducing the number of context switches because of transaction blocking. This may have the advantage of reducing the overall cache miss rate. Whenever context is switched, with a process being replaced by another and then being brought back into execution again after some other process has used the processor in the intervening period, the process finds that most of its contents in the cache have been displaced by the intervening computation. This results in a period during which the cache miss rate is very high. Of course, doing away with concurrency is not good when transactions vary a great deal in length. If a short transaction has the misfortune to have a long transaction in front of it, its response time can be much greater than if concurrency is allowed.

Stable main memory can be used to write in the log when a transaction commits. Clearly, the entire log is too large to be held in main memory. Instead, we can initially write in the log into stable main memory (which acts as a buffer), and have a dedicated processor copy it onto disk. This can happen either transaction by transaction or in batch mode. In the former case, every time a transaction commits, its log is written to disk. In the latter, the system waits until a certain volume has accumulated in the buffer, and then copies the entire batch over to the disk system. This obviates the need for a transaction to wait for disk accesses during its commit operation.

Main memory databases can be organized differently from disk-based systems. Following pointers in main memory is much cheaper than following them on disks. For this reason, it is possible to conserve memory if a datum occurs more than once in the database (e.g., is a member of several tuples in a relational database). We can simply store one copy of the item, and have pointers to it. Using pointers also makes the task of executing relational operations, such as joins, simpler.

The indexing scheme can also be different for main memory databases. The conventional indexing schemes in disk-based systems are the B-tree and the B$^+$-tree. Since the index is stored on disk in blocks, it must be shallow; three levels is as high as an index usually gets. By contrast, since deeper trees are much less expensive to traverse in main memory than on disk, we can have trees of many more levels for main memory databases. A variation of the B-tree, called the T-tree, has been proposed for such systems. The T-tree is a binary tree, with multiple elements per node. Each node has the structure shown in Figure 5.2.

However, main memory databases suffer from the drawback that durability becomes harder to maintain. Frequent backups are necessary to disk or tape. However, since

$$\frac{\text{Disk or tape access time}}{\text{Main memory access time}} \gg \frac{\text{Tape access time}}{\text{Disk access time}}$$

we can expect that backups will be relatively more expensive (relative to transaction-processing time) in main memory databases than in disk-based databases. This is unfortunate, since we will have to make backups more frequently. Disks are passive data-storage devices, which will hold data unless they are physically damaged in some way (e.g., by the disk head crashing onto the disk surface). A system crash does not usually affect the integrity of the disk system. This is not true for main memory; main memory usually has to be restored after a system crash.

Disk systems are also more gracefully degradable than main memory. When a single disk unit fails, the data on the other units are not affected. If a main memory board fails, however, the machine must be powered down and the entire main memory restored.

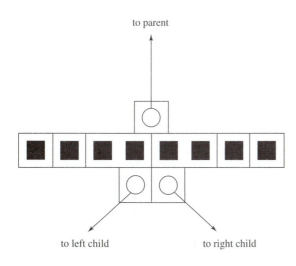

FIGURE 5.2
Structure of a T-tree node; shaded areas indicate data.

Once a failure occurs, the database must be restored using the checkpointed data, together with the log of all the operations that occurred after the checkpoint was taken. One way to speed up recovery is to first load such blocks of data as are required by pending transactions. In any case, the disk-to-memory bandwidth should be maximized by using arrays of disks that can be accessed in parallel. There are many ways in which this can be done. For example, we can have each data word (including error-control bits) spread over multiple disks. The spread should be such that the load to each disk is approximately balanced.

5.5 TRANSACTION PRIORITIES

Transactions are granted access to the processors based on their priorities. These priorities are designed to ensure that some system measure of performance is optimized. The most obvious performance measure is the fraction of transactions that do not meet their deadline. This implicitly assumes that all transactions have equal value to the system. If this is not true, then some means must be found to incorporate the value of the transaction in the priority assigned to it. For example, we may weight the fraction of deadline-missing transactions by the values of those transactions.

In general, the problem of optimally scheduling transactions is computationally intractable. We must therefore content ourselves with heuristics. One approach is to use the EDF algorithm, covered in Chapter 3. Depending on the application, we may either have to discard transactions that have missed their deadline or continue to serve all transactions (whether or not they are late). In the latter case, we can classify transactions into two categories, those that have missed their deadlines (or are sure to do so) and those that have not. The latter category can be scheduled using the EDF algorithm, while the former can be kept in background and executed whenever there are no transactions that haven't missed their deadlines awaiting service.

EDF works very well unless the workload is very heavy. In that case, matters may be improved by introducing some congestion control. Congestion control generally takes the form of refusing to admit additional transactions (or taking some other similar action) when the load exceeds a certain level. Without congestion control, almost all the transactions in a heavily-loaded system have long response times; with congestion control, at least some of the transactions have acceptable response times.

The adaptive earliest deadline (AED) algorithm combines congestion control with the EDF algorithm. It works as follows. When a transaction arrives, the system randomly inserts it in a list of pending transactions. If its assigned position in the list is in $1, \ldots, H$ (where H is a parameter), the transaction is assigned to a group called HIT, while the remaining ones are assigned to a group called MISS. Our objective is to try to meet all the deadlines of the HIT group, and—if any time is left over—to serve the transactions in the MISS group. Transactions within the HIT group are prioritized according to the EDF algorithm. Transactions within the MISS group are served if no pending transactions exist in the HIT group, and in the order of their positions in the list. Of course, this can only be done when there are no dependencies among the transactions, and the ordering among them is irrelevant.

When a transaction is completed, it is removed from the list. Once a transaction is assigned to a group, it stays there. In other words, transactions assigned to HIT do not get pushed into MISS just because several new transactions have arrived that are randomly inserted in the list ahead of them. Similarly, just because transaction departures move a transaction assigned to MISS into one of the first H places on the list does not mean that it will be reassigned as a HIT task.

H is the control parameter for this system. If $H = \infty$, the scheme degenerates into EDF; if $H = 0$, we have a random service scheme. H can be set adaptively according to the following algorithm. The system maintains data on the following parameters:

$$\text{Success(HIT)} = \frac{\text{Number of transactions in HIT class that meet their deadlines}}{\text{Total number of transactions in the HIT class}} \tag{5.1}$$

$$\text{Success(ALL)} = \frac{\text{Total number of transactions that meet their deadlines}}{\text{Total number of transactions}} \tag{5.2}$$

These quantities are measured repeatedly. When the system starts a measurement, it marks the next N_H HIT transactions that arrive and the next N_A transactions (of either class) that arrive. It then observes over time what fraction of these marked transactions meet their deadlines. Once all of these marked transactions have either completed execution or have missed their deadlines, the Success parameters are computed, and a new measurement cycle begins.

The quantities N_H and N_A must be set by the designer. If they are too large, the system will take a long time to complete a measurement. Also, some of the statistics it gathers will be outdated. If N_H and N_A are too small, the measurement will not be reliable, since it will depend on only a small number of data points.

In response to each of the measurements, the system keeps increasing H in steps of 5% until Success(ALL) is less than 0.95. When Success(ALL) drops below 0.95, H is corrected. More formally, the following steps are followed in response to a new computation of the Success parameters (N_trans is the total number of transactions currently in the system).

1. $H = \text{Success(HIT)} * H * 1.05$
2. If $\text{Success(ALL)} < 0.95$, then
   $H = \min\{H, \text{Success(ALL)} * N\_trans * 1.25\}$

This algorithm ensures that when the load is low enough, almost all the transactions can be placed in the HIT class. When the load increases to the point where Success(ALL) is less than 0.95 (i.e., more than 5% of the transactions miss their deadlines), H is revised downward. The factor of 1.25 was chosen intuitively, and experimental results indicate that this algorithm gives better results than the straightforward EDF algorithm.

The AED algorithm implicitly assumes that the transactions all have the same value to the system. Suppose this is not true; that is, some transactions have higher values than others. This must be taken into account while scheduling them to ensure that priority is given to the higher-value transactions. The AED algorithm can be modified by dividing the transactions into priority classes. The classes are defined dynamically, based on the transaction values. If x is the average value of the transactions in class C, then class C contains transactions whose priority values fall in the range $[x/SF, x * SF]$ where SF is a spread factor, defined by the user. Thus, as transactions arrive and depart, the range of values covered by each class will change. If a class has no transactions in it, it is deleted.

When a transaction arrives, we check to see if it falls within any of the existing classes. If it does, we assign it to that class and recompute the upper and lower bounds. If it does not, we create a new class.

The transactions in each class are assigned to HIT and MISS groups, according to the procedure described above for the AED algorithm. That is, once a transaction has been assigned to a value class, we randomly insert it in the list of pending transactions and decide if it falls within the HIT or MISS groups for that value class. We compute for each of the classes a control parameter H_i, which is analogous to H in the AED algorithm. The priority scheme is as follows:

1. Transactions in a higher-value class (whether assigned to the HIT or MISS group inside that class) always have priority over transactions in a lower-value group.
2. If transactions A, B both belong to the HIT group of the same value class, the one with the earlier deadline is given priority.
3. If A belongs to the HIT and B to the MISS group of the same value class, A has priority over B.
4. If both A and B belong to the MISS group of the same value class,
    a. and the value of A is greater than the value of B, then A has priority.
    b. and they both have the same value, the tie is broken on the basis of their relative positions in the list of pending transactions.

These algorithms suffer from one drawback—they discriminate against long transactions. In particular, a short transaction that arrives just before its deadline will be given priority over a long transaction that arrives much before its deadline. As a result, experiments have shown that long transactions suffer considerably greater deadline-miss rates than shorter transactions under both the ED and the AED algorithms.

The adaptive earliest virtual deadline (AEVD) algorithm, an extension of AED, seeks to correct for this bias. The only difference between AEVD and AED is the way in which transactions in the HIT class are prioritized. In the AED algorithm, this is done in the inverse order of the transaction deadlines. In the AEVD algorithm, we replace the absolute deadline by a virtual deadline, and prioritize transactions in the inverse order of their virtual deadlines.

Virtual deadlines are computed as follows. Assume that we can estimate the run time of an arriving transaction T; let it be C_T (we discuss how to get rid of this assumption in a moment). Let the maximum and minimum transaction run times over all transactions in the system be C_{max} and C_{min}. Then, define a pace factor associated with transaction T as follows:

$$PF_T = \alpha + (1 - \alpha) \times \left(\frac{C_{max} - C_T}{C_{max} - C_{min}} \right)^2 \tag{5.3}$$

where α is a control parameter such that $0 \le \alpha \le 1$. If d_T is the absolute deadline of T, then its virtual deadline at time t is given by

$$V_T(t) = (d_T - t) \times PF_T + t \tag{5.4}$$

The value of α determines the extent to which we improve the lot of the longer transactions. Increasing the pace factor of a transaction increases its virtual deadline and thus lowers its priority. The longest transaction, whose execution time is C_{max}, has pace factor α, and the shortest, whose execution time is C_{min}, has pace factor 1.

Figure 5.3 illustrates how the pace factor depends on α and the transaction execution time C_T. A small value of α produces the greatest spread between the pace factors for the shortest and longest transactions. This spread decreases monotonically to zero as α rises to 1.

The system can adaptively set the value of α. It measures the miss rates of the transactions as a function of their execution times and then uses linear regression (least-mean-square error) to fit these data in a straight line. If the slope of this line is positive, then longer transactions are suffering (on the average) a higher miss rate than shorter transactions, and so α must be decreased (unless it is already at 0). If the slope is negative, then α must be increased. If the slope is zero, we have an ideal situation where there is no discrimination on the basis of execution time.

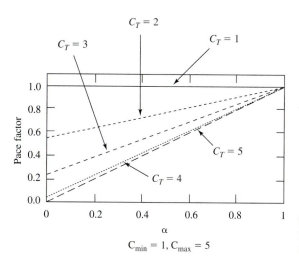

FIGURE 5.3
Pace factors for the AEVD algorithm.

We have assumed so far that we know the values C_{min}, C_{max}, and C_T. If we don't, then we can take C_{min} and C_{max} to be the shortest and longest transaction seen by the system over some window of time. If we have no information about the value of C_T, we can assume a linear correlation between the execution time and the deadline, and assume that C_T is proportional to the difference between its absolute deadline and its time of arrival.

5.6 TRANSACTION ABORTS

There are two kinds of transaction abortions, *termination* and *nontermination*. A transaction that suffers a termination abort is not restarted after being aborted. This can happen for several reasons. For example, the user may decide to cancel the transaction, there may be an arithmetical error (e.g., an attempt to divide by zero), or the transaction may have been delayed for so long that its value has declined to zero.

In contrast, when a transaction suffers a nontermination abort, it is restarted. Such an abortion may occur because of data conflicts with another higher-priority transaction, or because of deadlock. It is quite possible, however, for a transaction to suffer so many nontermination abortions that its value declines to zero; then it is subject to a termination.

5.7 CONCURRENCY CONTROL ISSUES

The problem of concurrency control is to allow transactions to execute in parallel while ensuring that the net effect of their execution on the database is as if they had been executed in some serial order.

There are two basic approaches to concurrency control, pessimistic and optimistic. In the *pessimistic* approach, we first ensure that the transaction will not violate serialization consistency before letting it execute. In the *optimistic* approach, we first carry out the transaction execution, and only then check to see if the execution of that transaction has violated serialization consistency. In this section, we examine one example each of pessimistic and optimistic concurrency control.

5.7.1 Pessimistic Concurrency Control

The most commonly used approach (in centralized databases) is *two-phase locking*. The procedure requires that the transaction lock and unlock in two distinct phases. In the locking phase, it acquires the read and write locks it needs. In the unlocking phase, it releases the locks. The unlocking phase must follow (and not overlap) the locking phase. Thus, the transaction must have obtained all the locks it will need before it releases any locks. This process has the potential to deadlock. For example, suppose both transactions A and B need to exclusively lock data items X and Y. If the execution proceeds in such a way that A obtains the lock on X and B the lock on Y, then A will not be able to complete since it cannot get the lock on Y. Similarly, B will wait for A to release the lock on X, but it never will since A is waiting for the lock on Y to be released (which can only happen after B has got the lock for X). This difficulty can be resolved by running deadlock detection algorithms, which can then abort one of the transactions and let the other complete in peace. When we abort a transaction, we lose all the computation it has done so far. Since we would prefer to waste as little processsing as possible, when two transactions deadlock, it is best to keep the older transaction and abort the newer transaction. This can be achieved by timestamping transactions.

Let us consider how two-phase locking can be modified for use in real-time systems. From a real-time systems perspective, unmodified two-phase locking has the disadvantage of priority inversion (i.e., of forcing higher-priority transactions to wait while lower-priority transactions complete their work). Priority inversion is covered in detail in Chapter 3. Recall that there are two consequences of a higher-priority task, H waiting for a lower-priority task, L due to data conflicts. First and most obviously, H is blocked from execution by L. Second, if we have a task M of higher priority than L but lower than H, which does not have any data conflicts with L, M can preempt L and cause further delays to H (which is awaiting the completion of L).

To obviate this problem, L can be made to inherit the priority of H. Such an approach, which works well in general real-time applications, is not as useful in real-time databases. The problem is that database tasks tend to require much more time to complete than do other real-time tasks. So, it may not be practical to make a higher-priority task wait while the lower-priority task completes execution.

The simple solution to this problem is to abort the lower-priority transaction. However, this is wasteful, since all the work done by it up to that point is thrown away. A more sophisticated approach is to weigh the consequences of aborting the lower-priority transaction against those of making the higher-priority transaction wait. If we know how close the lower-priority transaction is to finishing, we can use the following (informal) threshold-based algorithm. If the lower-priority task is sufficiently close to completion (sufficiently defined by the threshold), we let it inherit the priority of the higher-priority task and make the higher-priority task wait until it finishes. If not, the lower-priority task is aborted, and the higher-priority task can start right away. Thus, the time for which the higher-priority task is blocked is bounded by the threshold.

An obvious extension of the algorithm is to make the threshold a function of the difference in priority levels between the higher-priority and lower-priority transactions. In general, the greater this difference, the smaller the value of the threshold. Thus, if we have a transaction A, which is only slightly more important than the executing transaction B, we allow A to be blocked for a long time. By contrast, if A is of much higher priority, then the threshold will be set so that it is blocked for no more than a short time.

The question of how to choose the threshold immediately arises. There are no hard and fast rules for this: it depends on the nature of the transactions (i.e., their run times, the CPU loading, etc.). One approach is to use an adaptive learning procedure and let the system modify the threshold until it reaches a good value.

TABLE 5.2
Locking rules for a general multiversion database system

Locks already set	Requested lock		
	Read	**Write**	**Certify**
Read	Granted	Granted	Blocked
Write	Granted	Granted	Granted
Certify	Blocked	Granted	Blocked

Another approach is to use multiple versions of data. In the multiversion scheme, in addition to the traditional read and write locks, there are certify locks. When a transaction writes a data item, it does not lock the database copy of it; rather, it writes into its own private copy. Thus, a transaction can obtain a write lock without interfering with any other transaction. That is, write locks on a granule will not be exclusive in this implementation. When the transaction has completed execution, it copies all of its writes over to the database. This operation is called *certification*, and the transaction must receive a certify lock on the data item(s) being certified before this stage can go ahead. When the certify stage is reached, the transaction is committed.

Transactions are limited to reading the latest certified version of data. This constraint ensures that cascading aborts are avoided. For example, suppose transaction B reads an uncertified version written by transaction A, and produces a result read by C, which in turn produces a result read by D, and so on. If transaction A is aborted, then all its writes have to be undone. This means that the data that B read is illegal, and B must be aborted. Similarly, since C depended on B, C also must abort, and so on.

Table 5.2 shows under what conditions read, write, and certify locks are granted for some data item on which there is already a lock by another transaction. When a read lock is requested, it is granted if there is already a read or write lock upon it. Read locks are always nonexclusive, anyway, and write locks are to private versions only. However, if another transaction currently has a certify lock on the data item, the read request is blocked; we must wait until the certified data are available. A write lock request is always granted since this amounts only to allowing a transaction to write into its own private space. A certify lock is blocked if there is either a pending read or a certify lock on that item, since certify locks grant permission to write into the database. It is granted if there is a write lock for reasons mentioned above.

Such conventional multiversion schemes suffer from the priority inversion problem. For example, if a higher-priority transaction tries to obtain a certify lock on some data item that is currently read-locked by a lower-priority transaction, it must then wait for the lower-priority task to commit or abort before it can commit. Similarly, if the higher-priority task has been granted a write lock on a data item, and then a lower-priority task requests a read lock on the same item, this request will be granted and, when the higher-priority task tries to finish

TABLE 5.3
Locking rules to deal with priority inversion problems

Locks already set by lower-priority transaction	Lock requested by a higher-priority transaction		
	Read	**Write**	**Certify**
Read	Granted	L-Aborted	Cannot occur
Write	Granted	Granted	Granted
Certify	Conversion	Granted	Conversion

Locks already set by higher-priority transaction	Lock requested by higher-priority transaction		
	Read	**Write**	**Certify**
Read	Granted	Granted	Blocked
Write	Blocked	Granted	Blocked
Certify	Blocked	Granted	Blocked

Note: L-Aborted = Lower-priority transaction is aborted.
Conversion = Lower-priority transaction lock converted to Write.

its work by obtaining a certify lock on the data item and then copying it to the database, it is blocked until the lower-priority task has either committed or aborted.

These problems can be handled by modifying the locking rules suitably. The new rules are shown in Table 5.3. For example, when a lower-priority transaction holds a certify lock on a granule and a higher-priority transaction requests a write lock, the request is granted (and the lower-priority transaction is aborted).

It should be fairly easy for the reader to work out why these locking rules avoid the priority inversion problem. These rules, however, are probably too stringent in that they may cause the lower-priority transaction to abort in a large number of cases. We can modify them to reduce the number of such abortions, while still not delaying higher-priority transactions too long. The modified rules are shown in Table 5.4. The main differences are that when the lower-priority task has a certify lock on a data item, the higher-priority task is made to wait for a read lock on that item, and when a lower-priority task requests a certify lock on an item that is write-locked by a higher-priority task, the request is granted. The idea is not to hold up the lower-priority task if it is close to finishing.

There have been some simulation studies of multiversion systems that indicate that they outperform single-version systems, especially at high loads. However, no analytical models exist for these algorithms. Of course, multiple versions consume more memory.

5.7.2 Optimistic Concurrency Control

Under optimistic concurrency control, the execution of each transaction consists of three phases, a read phase, a validation phase, and (if necessary) a write phase,

TABLE 5.4
Modified locking rules to reduce abortions

Locks already set by lower-priority transaction	Lock requested by a higher-priority transaction		
	Read	**Write**	**Certify**
Read	Granted	Granted	L-Aborted
Write	G/B	Granted	Granted
Certify	Blocked	Granted	Conversion

Locks already set by higher-priority transaction	Lock requested by a lower-priority transaction		
	Read	**Write**	**Certify**
Read	Granted	Granted	Blocked
Write	Blocked	Granted	G/B
Certify	Blocked	Granted	Blocked

Note: G/B = Either granted or blocked, depending on implementation.
L-Aborted = Lower-priority transaction aborted.

in that order. During the read phase, the transaction reads the data it needs, and writes only into its own private address space. During the validation phase, the system checks to see if any of the writes has potentially violated serialization consistency. For every transaction A whose timestamp antedates that of transaction T, serialization consistency is not violated due to T if the following conditions hold.

- A has completed its write phase before T starts its read phase.
- The read set[3] of A is distinct from the write set of T, and A has finished its write phase before T starts its write phase.
- The write set of A is distinct from both the read and write sets of T.

If these conditions are not satisfied, T must be aborted. Since a transaction confines its writes to its own private space until it is validated, such an abortion requires no cleaning up of the database itself and can be done with little recovery overhead. Of course, aborting a transaction leads to the loss of all the work that was done on that transaction.

It should now be clear as to why this approach is called optimistic. A transaction carries out its execution optimistically expecting that all the serialization consistency conditions will be satisfied. Only after it completes does it check to see if they actually are. Obviously, this approach will work well only when such optimism is justified.

---

[3] The *read* and *write sets* of a transaction are the set of data items it reads and writes, respectively.

Clearly, the longer a transaction, the greater the probability that it will be aborted before it reaches its commit point. To quantify this, let us set up a simple mathematical model. Consider a transaction consisting of an initialization step, followed by N data-access steps, taking a total processing time proportional to $N+1$. Assume that each of the data-access steps is an exclusive access to one of D data items, chosen randomly. Suppose there are, on average, u items updated per unit time per committing transaction in the system. Let the state of a transaction be the number of data items it has accessed so far.

If the current state of a transaction is m (i.e., m distinct data items have been accessed so far), the transaction will be aborted if any of the m data items are updated by committing transactions. Hence, the probability that it is aborted by some committing transaction before it makes another access is approximately mu/D. The probability that it is not aborted when in state m is thus $1 - (mu/D)$, and the probability that it is not aborted at any time during the first m steps is approximately $(1 - u/D)(1 - 2u/D) \cdots (1 - mu/D)$. So, the probability that this transaction is aborted before it completes is approximately

$$A(N) \approx 1 - \left(1 - \frac{u}{D}\right)\left(1 - \frac{2u}{D}\right) \cdots \left(1 - \frac{Nu}{D}\right)$$

$$\approx \frac{N(N+1)u}{2D} \tag{5.5}$$

Thus, the probability of a transaction being aborted is roughly proportional to the square of its length and to the system load (as expressed by u). This system therefore discriminates heavily against long transactions, and this discrimination gets worse as the system load increases.

One variation of the basic optimistic algorithm is the broadcast commit algorithm. When a transaction commits, it tells all the transactions that it conflicts with so that they abort (and then possibly restart). Another modification to the optimistic algorithm introduces priorities. When a transaction T is about to commit, any lower-priority transactions that conflict with it are aborted. Also, the system checks to see if any higher-priority transactions currently in the system conflicts with T. Call this conflict set H. If H is nonempty, one of the following actions is taken.

- *The sacrifice policy*: T is aborted (it can be restarted).
- *The wait policy*: T is put into a wait state until the tasks in H commit. If they do, T is aborted (and can be restarted).
- *The wait-X policy*: T commits unless more than $X\%$ of the transactions that conflict with it are of higher priority (i.e., belong to H). Of course, this means that all the transactions it conflicts with are aborted. If more than $X\%$ are of higher priority, it waits for them to commit.

The sacrifice policy is potentially wasteful. The problem is that there is no guarantee that the higher-priority transaction (which causes the abort) will itself commit. If all the transactions in H abort, then T has been aborted for nothing.

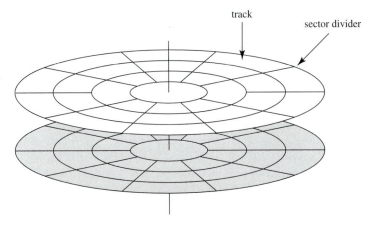

FIGURE 5.4
Disk organization.

The wait policy does away with this problem. Also, since the conflict relation is not symmetric (i.e., just because T conflicts with a transaction $B \in H$, does not necessarily imply that B conflicts with T), it may well be that no transactions in H conflict with T, and T can commit after all transactions in H have done so. Waiting does, however, have its own drawbacks. First, if the transaction commits after waiting, it aborts all of the lower-priority transactions that conflict with it. This can cause some of them to miss their deadlines. Secondly, the longer the time that the transaction is alive in the system, the greater tends to be the number of transactions with which it will be in conflict.

The wait-X policy tries to compromise between the sacrifice and wait policies. If X is set to 0, it degenerates to the sacrifice policy; if it is set to 100, it becomes the wait policy.

Experimental results indicate that the sacrifice policy performs the worst of the three. Since aborted transactions are usually restarted, this approach increases the system workload. The wait policy performs well when there is little data contention. Experimental results indicate that the wait-50 policy (i.e., wait-X with $X = 50$) gives perhaps the best results, in terms of a low deadline miss rate, over a wide parameter range. If X is increased to above 50, performance under heavy loading improves a little but that under normal loading degrades. The opposite is the case when X is decreased.

5.8   DISK SCHEDULING ALGORITHMS

In most cases, databases are too large to be held in main memory in their entirety. In such systems, many transactions result in disk accesses.

The organization of a disk system is shown in Figure 5.4. Disks are stacked and the data are stored in concentric rings, called *tracks*. Each track is divided into several *sectors* (the dividing lines extend radially from the center in Figure 5.4). When a command goes out to a disk to access a sector, the arm moves to float over the appropriate track, and waits for the desired sector to rotate under it. At that time, it is ready to start the access (provided that a channel to the CPU is free; however, we shall not pursue that issue here). Until recently, disks rotated at around 3600 rpm, taking about 16.67 ms to complete a rotation. Newer models rotate at between 5400 and 7900 rpm.

The time it takes to complete an access is given by

$$t_a = t_w + t_p + t_t$$

where

t_w Time spent in queue, if any.

t_p Time to position the arm over the track, and for the correct sector to rotate under it.

t_t Time to transfer the desired block of data.

t_p is on the order of several milliseconds, which is an eternity to systems whose CPU clock time is less than 50 ns. Also, the variance of t_p can be considerable. As a result, disk-based database systems are generally unsuitable for hard real-time systems. Our discussions will therefore focus on their use in soft real-time applications.

The disparity between CPU and disk speeds is likely to get worse with time. CPU speeds rapidly increase year by year. Processor speeds approximately double every year. Disk access time, however, halves about once every ten years, and disk transfer rates double about once every three years. We must therefore concentrate on managing disk access in such a way as to improve overall performance, in terms of reducing the number of missed deadlines.

If the database is I/O bound, much of the time is spent trying to access the disk system. t_w is the time spent waiting for higher-priority accesses to complete. Deciding on the priority of each access so as to ensure good performance is a difficult problem. Traditional real-time algorithms, such as the EDF algorithm, do not work well in this case because they do not take into account the time taken by the arm movements.

Example 5.5. Consider the access requests listed in Table 5.5. Suppose it takes $5 + 3\sqrt{k}$ time units for the arm to travel k tracks ($k > 0$). Assume that it takes 5 units in each case for the appropriate sector to rotate under the arm (this is actually a variable quantity, depending on the rotational phase of the disk, but we assume

TABLE 5.5
Example of access requests

Number	Track	Sector	Deadline	EDF service starts
1	1	10	1	0
2	441	5	20	73
3	4	7	40	146
4	441	2	60	218

it to be constant here for illustrative purposes) and for the access to be completed. Suppose the arm is in position above track 1 to begin with. The service start times for the EDF policy are shown in Table 5.5.

If we serve this list of requests in order of increasing deadlines, the disk arm will first position itself above track 1, then move to track 441, then move to track 4 and then move back to track 441. This involves considerable arm movement and drives up the access time. On the other hand, if we serve requests in the order $1 \rightarrow 3 \rightarrow 2 \rightarrow 4$, a great deal of arm movement can be avoided and the access start times will be 0, 88, 15, and 93, respectively, for accesses 1, 2, 3, and 4.

Reducing the total arm movement does not, however, guarantee minimizing the number of transaction deadlines missed. As an exercise, the reader can construct an example where the EDF algorithm works better than this procedure.

There has not been much research on how to schedule requests to disk so that the number of transactions that meet their deadlines is maximized. Let us look at some of the policies that have been studied. The first three have been introduced for nonreal-time applications and are not deadline-sensitive.

The simplest strategy of all is the first-come-first-served (FCFS) algorithm. A queue of requests is maintained, and they are served in the order in which they arrive. It is easy to see that such a policy, which takes no account of deadlines or arm movements, will work poorly when the queue of requests is fairly long.

The next strategy is called the elevator or scan policy. In this policy, the arm moves in one direction, serving requests along that direction as it goes. When no further scan requests remain, it reverses direction and serves accesses along the reverse direction. It keeps oscillating like this to serve the requests.

Example 5.6. In Figure 5.5, the arm visits successively tracks 3, 4, 5, and 9 on the journey in one direction. At that point, it reverses direction, since there are no requests pending for any higher track numbers. Then it serves access requests for tracks 2, 1, and 1.

There is a variation of the elevator algorithm in which the arm only scans in one direction. When it comes to the end, it goes back without serving any tracks on its return jouney, and resumes service from the beginning. If such an algorithm

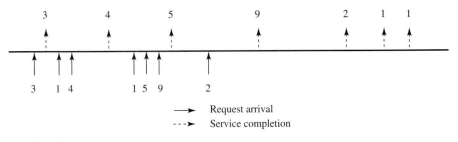

FIGURE 5.5
Example of the elevator algorithm.

is used to serve the requests in Figure 5.5, the tracks would be visited in the sequence 3,4,5,9,1,1,2.

The shortest seek time policy serves the request that is closest to the current arm position. It is a greedy policy with the objective of minimal arm movement between successive requests.

The elevator algorithm has been modified for use in real-time systems. One approach is to classify requests into priority classes, according to their deadlines or other characteristics. At the end of each service, if there are requests of higher priority than the one just served, the arm goes to the highest-priority request pending. If there is more than one such highest-priority request, it goes to the nearest one and starts executing the elevator algorithm from that point. If, on the other hand, there are no requests of higher priority, it simply continues with the elevator algorithm. If the only request(s) pending are of lower priority than the one that has just been served, it picks the highest-priority request pending (with ties broken in favor of the one requiring the least arm movement) and starts the elevator algorithm from that point. The question now is how to define the priority levels. Some preliminary work indicates that having a small number of priority levels (say, three), is best; however, nobody knows how to choose them for optimum performance.

Another variation is as follows. Check each request to see if it is feasible, (i.e., if the system estimates that it can meet it). Pick the feasible access request with the earliest deadline and move the arm in that direction, stopping along the way to serve all the requests pending that lie in between.

Yet another policy considers both the deadline for each request and the time taken to move the arm to serve it. It keeps a queue in which the requests pending are stored in ascending order of deadline. The algorithm considers the first q elements in the queue, where q is called the *window size*. Limiting consideration to these reduces the computational complexity of the algorithm. We order each request by its position in the queue, and the ith element in it is given weight w_i. The weights satisfy the inequality $w_i \leq w_j$ if $i > j$. If δ_i is the distance the arm has to move from its current position to serve request ρ_i, then the priority of request ρ_i is given by $p_i = 1/w_i \delta_i$. Service is given to the highest-priority request. The question here is how to choose w_i, the weights. The creators of this algorithm propose using $w_i = \beta^{i-1}$, where $\beta \geq 1$ is a suitably chosen constant (their simulations indicate that $\beta = 2$ is appropriate), and recommend selecting a window size of three or four. Not much is known about which values of β are best or if some other way of selecting weights might be better.

The above policy takes only the order of deadlines into account. A simple extension of this yields the final policy we will describe here. Let d_i denote the deadline associated with request r_i. Pick a constant α such that $0 \leq \alpha \leq 1$, and serve the request that has the minimum value of the function $f(d_i, \delta_i) = \alpha\delta_i + (1 - \alpha)d_i$. α is a design parameter. If it is small, it increases the influence of the deadline; if it is large, it increases the influence of the arm movement in selecting the next request to be served. The authors of this policy have found that choosing α in the range 0.7 to 0.8 is likely to give good results.

5.9 A TWO-PHASE APPROACH TO IMPROVE PREDICTABILITY

Two of the principal causes of uncertainty in estimating the execution time of a real-time transaction are data-dependent I/O and serialization consistency. Data-dependent I/O causes uncertainty because we do not know in advance where the required data will be on disk or indeed how many pointers will have to be followed to determine which data are required. The need to maintain serialization consistency causes uncertainty because a transaction can be blocked by another, or because a transaction can be aborted.

One way of dealing with these problems is to use a two-phase approach. In the first phase, we carry out the operations that get rid of much of the uncertainty. In the second phase, we do the rest of the work. We will discuss here the skeleton and the optimistic approaches.

In the skeleton algorithm, the system determines in the first phase which data items are required and completes all the required disk accesses to bring the desired items into the main memory. This may require some processing; for example, we could have branches, and in that case the branch conditions have to be evaluated. (Variables whose values determine the branch conditions are called the *determinant variables*.) Transactions cannot be blocked in the first phase. All other computational activity associated with the transaction is deferred to the second phase.

At the end of the first phase, all data items that the transaction will need are in main memory. We know the resources needed by the transaction. Unless these data items are concurrently changed by some other transaction, predicting the remaining execution time of the transaction is not difficult, and by passing on the list of resource requirements to the scheduler, we cause the rest of the transaction (phase two) to be scheduled. Phase two consists of carrying out the prescribed computations.

In the optimistic algorithm, the first phase consists of bringing in the required data from disk to the main memory (as in the skeleton algorithm) and carrying out all the computations associated with the transaction. Locks are ignored in this phase. At the end of this phase there is a validation step, where the system determines if serialization consistency has been satisfied by the transaction operations. If it has, the transaction commits and phase two is not required. If the activity in phase one cannot be validated, the situation is the same as at the end of phase one of the skeleton algorithm—the required data have been moved into main memory and we know what resources are required to complete executing the transaction. In that event, we then execute phase two. Phase two of the transaction execution (identical to phase two of the skeleton case) is scheduled so as to satisfy serialization consistency. Note that we do not need to execute phase two more than once; since the system knows the resource requirements and potential data conflicts, it can schedule the transaction so that phase two need not be aborted due to such conflicts. The worst that can happen is that we will have to throw away the computations carried out during phase one. This is another way of saying that under the optimistic approach, no transaction will be aborted more than once.

As in Section 5.7.2, the system carries out all the computations without first checking for serialization consistency. It is only after completing them that it checks for consistency. This optimistic approach will only perform well if the probability of violating consistency is sufficiently small.

In our discussion so far, we have assumed that the execution path as derived during the first phase is exactly the path required in the second phase. This is called the assumption of *access invariance*. If any of the following happens, the two-phase approach can break down.

A1. The sequence of access instructions changes from phase one to phase two.

A2. Exception **A1** does not happen, but the parameter values are different.

A3. Neither exception **A1** nor **A2** happens, but the set of data items accessed with a given lookup value has changed from phase one to phase two.

Exception **A1** happens if some other transaction has concurrently changed the value of some variable that is used in a conditional branch test. There are three ways to avoid this. First, we can place a lock on all the items that can be updated by transactions already executing in the system, blocking the transactions that need them for evaluating conditional branch tests. Second, we can abort the transaction if we detect a difference in the branch-variable value from one phase to the other. Third, we can cover all the paths of a conditional branch in phase one, that is, bring into memory everything needed by any execution path. **A2** can be handled in a way similar to **A1**.

Exception **A3** can occur if certain rows are added or deleted between phase one and phase two.

> **Example 5.7.** Consider, for example, a bond market database, where bonds are added and deleted from the offerings list. Buyers decide, based on their degree of risk aversion and their desire for return, what mix of bonds to purchase. Suppose we have a bond selection transaction to do this, and that after phase one of the transaction, certain new offerings of bonds are added. Then, phase two will have to consider the new offerings as well. This will entail accesses not predicted in phase one.

The simplest way to deal with **A3** is to forbid the insertion of new data (in the tables being accessed by a yet-to-be-completed transaction) when any transaction is between phases one and two. A transaction that completes phase one can simply lock the data it needs, preventing any changes from altering its phase two execution. Depending on the application, this may or may not be acceptable to the user. Another way is to force the transaction to access in phase two only those data that were available during phase one. To return to Example 5.7 concerning the bond market, the transaction will consider exactly those bonds in phase two that it did in phase one; it will ignore any additions or deletions. This approach has the obvious drawback of using outdated data, which may not be acceptable for the application in question. (The reader should be able to construct easily a few examples where using outdated information is not acceptable.) Such examples occur in supplier-consumer situations such as the stock or bond market, where supplier transactions represent the offering of stocks or bonds and consumer transactions represent the buying of stocks or bonds. In such a case, we can make the database system alternate between two modes. In the first mode, we only allow supplier transactions; in the second mode we only allow consumer transactions.

An interesting question is how to schedule these transaction phases. It is not a good idea to alternate between a mode in which only phase one of the transactions is executed and a mode in which phase two is executed. The reason for this is that phase one is usually rich in I/O operations and much poorer in CPU utilization, while the opposite is the case for phase two. The ideal solution would probably be a dynamic resource-allocation approach, in which we adaptively allocate resources based on the deadlines of the various transactions and the state of the system. This is a topic worthy of future research.

Let us now carry out a simple performance evaluation of this approach. We use the following notation.

C_{Sk}	CPU time to execute phase one of the skeleton algorithm.
C_{Op}	CPU time to execute phase one of the optimistic algorithm.
C_{comp}	CPU time to execute computations not carried out in phase one of the skeleton algorithm.
C_2	CPU time to run phase two (the same for both skeleton and optimistic algorithms, and includes commit time).
C_{Sys1}	CPU time for phase-one system service (e.g., OS services, disk accesses, thread switching, etc.; this is common to both skeletal and optimistic algorithms).
C_{Sys2}	CPU time for phase-two system service, other than commitment (includes scheduling and thread-switching times).
C_{Valid}	CPU time for phase-one optimistic algorithm validation (not a commit).
C_{commit}	Time for commitment of a transaction.
C_{Det}	Time for calculating all the determinant variables.
P_{fail}	Probability that optimistic phase one will end in failure.

We can write the following equations by inspection:

$$C_{Sk} = C_{Det} + C_{Sys1} \tag{5.6}$$

$$C_{Op} = C_{Det} + C_{Sys1} + C_{comp} + C_{valid} \tag{5.7}$$

$$C_2 = C_{comp} + C_{Sys2} + C_{commit} \tag{5.8}$$

If the first phase of the optimistic algorithm ends in failure, the second phase will have to be executed; otherwise the first phase can be followed immediately by a transaction commit. The time to complete the optimistic algorithm is thus given by

$$t_{Op} = \begin{cases} C_{Op} + C_{commit} & \text{with probability } 1 - P_{fail} \\ C_{Op} + C_2 & \text{with probability } P_{fail} \end{cases} \quad (5.9)$$

The time to complete the skeletal algorithm is

$$t_{Sk} = C_{Sk} + C_2 \quad (5.10)$$

We therefore have:

$$t_{Op} - t_{Sk} = \begin{cases} C_{valid} - C_{Sys2} & \text{with probability } 1 - P_{fail} \\ C_{valid} + C_{comp} & \text{with probability } P_{fail} \end{cases} \quad (5.11)$$

Whether we prefer the skeletal algorithm over the optimistic algorithm will depend on C_{valid} and P_{fail}; if one or both of these quantites are large, the skeletal algorithm will be preferred.

The two-phase approach has several performance advantages. It cuts down on the number of transaction abortions and arrives as early as it can at a point where it is possible to predict the remaining (worst-case) run time of transactions. Once this happens, we can use scheduling algorithms to determine exactly when to run the remainder of the transactions to completion, and to reduce the chances of data contention.

The skeletal algorithm has the important feature that its phase-one run time is usually small. For this small price, it generates the information needed to estimate how long the remainder of the transaction will take. When the load is very heavy, and we need to decide early whether to abort some transactions to provide an acceptable service to the others, this is especially useful.

Note that no transaction can be aborted more than once. This is a sharp departure from traditional concurrency control approaches, where there is no limit to the number of times a transaction can be aborted. Very little work is duplicated in phases one and two (i.e., very little overlap exists between what is done in phase one and what is done in phase two). An exception is when the validation step fails in phase one of the optimistic approach (but this is treated as a transaction abort).

5.10   MAINTAINING SERIALIZATION CONSISTENCY

The set of transactions must maintain serialization consistency. That is, even though transactions may be run concurrently, the end result must be as if they were executed in sequential order. There are two ways of maintaining serialization consistency, without and with the alteration of serialization order.

5.10.1   Serialization Consistency without Alteration of Serialization Order

In this strategy for maintaining serialization consistency, the system assigns a particular order to the transactions and aborts any that do not maintain serialization consistency as defined by that order. The serialization order can be defined based on any of the following parameters.

Start time: If transaction A has an earlier start time than transaction B, then it must occur before B in the serialization order.

Completion time: If transaction A has an earlier completion time than transaction B, then A precedes B in the serialization order. This is the approach followed by the classical optimistic concurrency control algorithm.

Item access order: If transaction A conflicts with B on some data item x, then whichever one, A or B, that accesses x first will come first in the serialization order. Any inconsistencies must be dealt with by aborting transactions suitably. Serialization order is transitive. That is, if A precedes B, and B precedes C, then the data items must be accessed in such a way that A precedes C.

5.10.2   Serialization Consistency with Alteration of Serialization Order

In some cases, it is possible to reduce the number of transaction abortions by suitably adjusting serialization order. For example, consider the sequence of operations $S = R_A(x)R_A(y)R_A(z)R_B(x)R_A(u)W_A(x)W_B(v)$, where $R_\alpha(r)$, $W_\alpha(r)$, C_α mean that transaction α is reading r and writing r, respectively. In this section, we adapt the optimistic concurrency protocol to handle the dynamic assignment of serialization order.

If we serialize by start order, then B is deemed to follow A. This causes B to be aborted, since it has read the wrong value of x (i.e., it should have read the value of x that was written by A). A similar characterization applies to serialization by completion order. However, an examination of this sequence shows that if we have B preceding A in the order, the sequence is serializable and so neither transaction is aborted.

Some improvement in performance can therefore be obtained by having a flexible way of assigning serialization order. This can be done by assigning timestamps to committing transactions in such a way that if the timestamp of transaction A, $t(A)$ precedes that of transaction B, $t(B)$, then the database state is the same as it would be if A were run before B in a sequential processing system.

The procedure for assigning such timestamps is fairly straightforward. The timestamps assigned to committed transactions cannot be changed—by definition, the action of committing a transaction cannot be undone. In order to validate a transaction successfully, we must assign it a timestamp that does not violate any of the constraints imposed by the transactions that have already committed. Let us now examine these constraints.

Let us maintain in connection with each data granule a list of its read and write timestamps. The read and write timestamps of a data granule are the latest timestamps of committed transactions that have read and updated it, respectively. When a transaction T that reads x commits, the read timestamp of x is set to the maximum of its current read timestamp and the timestamp of transaction T. If T updates x, then the following rule is applied.

- If the current write timestamp of x is less than the timestamp assigned to T, the update is written into the database, and the write timestamp of x is made equal to the timestamp of T.

- If, on the other hand, the current write timestamp of x is greater than the timestamp of T, the update is not written into the database.

The system maintains a historical list of all the read and write timestamps of each data granule.

Example 5.8. Suppose transaction T is assigned a timestamp of 25 when it commits (how this assignment is done is explained below). Let its read set be x_1, x_2, x_3 and its write set be x_3, x_4. Suppose the read and write timestamps of these variables (prior to adjusting for the commitment of T) are as follows:

	Variable			
	x_1	x_2	x_3	x_4
Read timestamp	4	4	40	2
Write timestamp	1	2	3	60

When T commits, these timestamps are changed to the following:

	Variable			
	x_1	x_2	x_3	x_4
Read timestamp	25	25	40	2
Write timestamp	1	2	25	60

x_3 is updated in the database, but x_4 is not (since the database already has a version written by a transaction with timestamp 60).

Let us now turn to how to assign timestamps to transactions so that serialization consistency is maintained. The general rule is the following. We start by trying to timestamp the transaction with the current time (i.e., the time told by the real-time clock) or by the time at which it was released, and check to see if consistency is maintained. If it is, the transaction can be committed with that timestamp. If not, we must try to adjust the timestamp so that serialization consistency is not violated. To understand how to do this, we must first understand how the assignment of a timestamp can violate consistency.

Example 5.9. Consider first a variable x that is read (but not updated) by transaction T. Figure 5.6 indicates when x was updated and the write timestamps associated with each of its updates. We should emphasize that the numbers below the solid

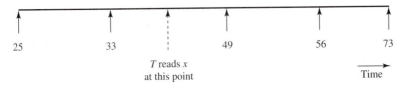

FIGURE 5.6
Updates of variable x: the numbers below the arrows indicate the write timestamps associated with each update of x; the positions of the arrows denote when, in real-time, the updates were written into the database.

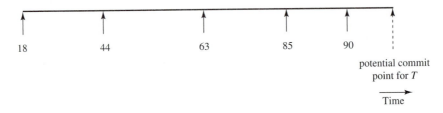

FIGURE 5.7
Reads of variable y: the numbers below the arrows indicate the read timestamps associated with each read of y; the positions of the arrows denote when, in real-time, the reads were carried out.

arrows are not necessarily when the updates were written into the database; they are the timestamps associated with the committed transactions that caused these updates. T reads x between updates timestamped at 33 and 49. What constraints does this impose on the timestamp $\tau(T)$ that we can assign to T?

If $\tau(T) < 33$, the fact that T reads an update timestamped 33 violates serialization consistency, because it appears to violate causality. (That is, T cannot possibly have seen the updates of a transaction that—in the serialization—is supposed to be run after T finishes). Similarly, $\tau(T) > 49$ is also not allowed; if it were, then T would be reading an overwritten value of x. If we assign $\tau(T) \in (33, 49)$, this will meet consistency constraints. (Why do we not want to assign $\tau(T) = 33$ or $\tau(T) = 49$?)

Consider next a variable y that is updated by transaction T. Figure 5.7 indicates when y is read and the read timestamps associated with each read. The update made by T will not have been seen by any of the transactions that already read y (since T has not committed yet). So, we must have $\tau(T) > 90$.

We therefore have the conflicting requirements that $33 < \tau(T) < 39$ and $\tau(T) > 90$. Consequently, there is no way to assign timestamps to T to maintain serialization consistency. T must therefore be aborted.

In contrast, suppose the reads of y are as shown in Figure 5.8. The latest committed transaction that read y is timestamped 45. Setting $\tau(T) > 45$ will therefore meet the consistency requirements. Thus, constraints due to x and y will both be met if we set $45 < \tau(T) < 49$, and serial consistency can be preserved.

We can now write out more formally the rules for assigning timestamps to a transaction, T.

1. List the set of variables that the transaction read.

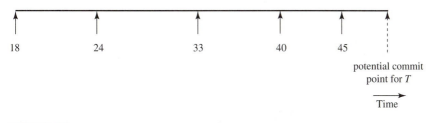

FIGURE 5.8
Reads of variable y, second case: the numbers below the arrows indicate the read timestamps associated with each read of y; the positions of the arrows denote when, in real-time, the reads were carried out.

2. Determine the validity intervals of these data (i.e., the range of timestamps over which these data are valid). For example, in Figure 5.6, the value of x as read by T has a validity interval of $(33, 49)$.

3. Take the intersection of all these validity intervals. If this intersection is empty, then abort T. If the intersection time is nonempty, let it be $I_T = (\ell_T, u_T)$.

4. Now list all the variables that T has updated.

5. Let $\max_T$ be the maximum read timestamp of all of these variables. If $\max_T \geq u_T$, then abort T. Otherwise, choose a timestamp in the interval $(\max_T, u_T)$, and commit T.

This approach considers only the transaction that is being validated in the context of the transactions that have already been committed. We can go one step further by considering the relative priority of active transactions. This approach is not purely optimistic concurrency control, in the sense that we do not always wait for the transaction to reach the validation stage before deciding to abort it.

As before, we assume that database updates are not written into the database until the transaction commits. All the writes by active transactions are to locations in private memory that can then be copied over to the database upon commitment.

The basic principle is to allow high-priority transactions to complete before low-priority ones. Consider two active transactions, A and B, with A having higher priority than B. Suppose that variable x is in the read set of A and in the write set of B. Unless B is committed and in the process of writing its updates into the database, we will maintain the serialization order in which A precedes B. If B is already committed, we can hold up A's reading of x until this copying has finished. Otherwise, consider a variable y that is in the write set of A and in the read set of B. In this case, we must maintain the order in which A precedes B by delaying B's reading of y until A has committed and written its update of y into the database. If B has already read y before we know of A's need to write into it, we simply abort B. This approach can help higher-priority transactions avoid being blocked by lower-priority ones.

5.11   DATABASES FOR HARD REAL-TIME SYSTEMS

The approaches we have considered so far are meant to improve the fraction of tasks that meet their deadlines. However, we need to go further if we are to integrate databases in hard real-time systems, where, in some cases, the missing of even a single deadline is unacceptable.

No conventional databases exist that can meet the requirements of hard real-time systems. All the real-time databases of which we are aware have an average transaction time of more than 100 ms. This is an average time, and many individual transactions suffer far longer response times. Part of the problem is that designers have traditionally used the client-server approach. That is, the entity requesting the service is regarded as a client. This request is passed along to the machines (servers) on which the requisite data are stored. Communication between client and server is usually by means of remote procedure calls (RPCs). The drawback of this is that RPCs are extremely time-consuming. They typically vary from 1 to 20 ms. Indeed, in many applications, the time to execute the actual transaction instructions is only a few microseconds, while the communications overhead runs to several milliseconds. While several researchers have tried to tune systems to allow high-speed RPCs, this is not easy; it is best to avoid RPCs as much as possible. The client-server approach can also cause a serial bottleneck at the server. If multiple transactions seek to use the same object, and thus the same server, their requests will be serialized.

In this section, we describe an experimental hard real-time database system that departs from the client-server model, MDARTS, and use it as a vehicle to demonstrate how hard real-time databases may be constructed.

MDARTS stands for multiprocessor database architecture for real-time systems. It is meant primarily for control applications, such as controlling machine tools or robots. MDARTS is a library of C++ data-management classes, and is an object-oriented system. The real-time constraints of the applications are specified in the object declarations. These include two string parameters, a unique object identifier and a set of semantic and timing constraints. The timing constraint is a bound on the execution time plus the blocking time for operations on that object. Since the same object can support multiple operations (e.g., an array can support the operation "return the minimum of the array" and "return the first element of the array," among others), MDARTS allows a timing constraint to be associated with each operation.

Each of the data-management classes has a certain performance characteristic and certain capabilities. Based on these and other constraints, MDARTS can choose a data-management class that is best suited to the needs of that object. For example, if it is specified that a particular object will only be updated by one task, the system might choose a database class that is best for single-writer control. That is, since the system knows that there is a single writer, concurrent updates are impossible. As a result, the system need not use in connection with this class any of the the locking machinery associated with managing concurrency. This can save considerable overhead and make it easier to meet hard deadlines.

```
/* Declaration of Point object in sensor task */
      Array<Point> position_sensors ("position_sensors",
             "exclusive_update; size = 6; write (element)<= 50 μsec" CREATE);
/* sensor task updates the data:  */
      position_sensors [6] = Point(1.2,0.866,3.4);


/*Declaration of Point object in control task:*/
      ReadOnlyArray<Point> position_sensors("position_sensors",
             "read(element) <= 80μsec");
/*Control task reads the data:*/
      int i = position_sensors("size")-1;
      Point end_effector_position =position_sensors[i];
```

FIGURE 5.9
MDARTS programming interface.

Figure 5.9 contains an example of the programming interface. There is a structure called Point, which contains the current position of a robot arm. Sensors update the robot arm position. This datum is read by the task whose function is to control the arm position. Note that Point is defined in the sensor task as an array, and in the control task as a read-only array. This ensures that the control task can never update Point. If, due to a programming error, the programmer has the control task update Point, it will conflict with the declaration and will be flagged by the compiler. With this approach, it is not necessary to check for access permissions in real time; the checks can be done during compilation and object initialization.

When the application declares an object, the system sends the relevant information (e.g., object name, type, contract string) to a shared data manager (SDM) server. Associated with each class is an *exemplar*, which is an instance of that class. The SDM then searches through its library of exemplars for one that meets the application constraints. If no such exemplar is available, the SDM reports failure. If such an exemplar is found, the SDM clones it to create a new object of that type, allocates shared memory as appropriate, sets all the associated pointers, and returns the object type and shared memory information.

Shared memory can be encapsulated using the object-oriented approach. Figure 5.10 shows an example. The figure shows an SDM and three application tasks—factory monitor, sensor, and control—which share a common object on a shared-memory multiprocessor. The sensor task has exclusive updating rights on that location; the other tasks can only read from that data. The boxes in each task are local objects with internal pointers to the shared memory containing the common data structure.

MDARTS does not use the standard relational database model. Instead, each object provides context and identity for its data. Conventional databases require

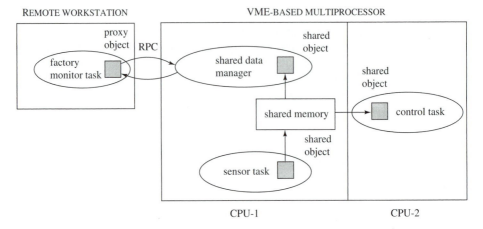

FIGURE 5.10
Shared memory access.

that indexes be searched to locate data. Instead, MDARTS objects use direct memory pointers to their data. Critical sections are guarded by spinlock queues in multiprocessors and the locking is managed by the system, not by the applications. A task that is waiting for a lock or is executing its critical section is not preempted; this helps bound priority inversion.

By doing away with many of the structures in conventional databases, it is possible to reduce many transaction times to less than 100 μs. MDARTS can be queried to obtain guaranteed transaction times; it can guarantee in advance if individual transaction deadlines can be met. This allows the system to take alternative emergency actions in the event that some critical transaction cannot be guaranteed to meet its deadline.

To know if a transaction can meet its deadline, it is necessary to bound the transaction run time as well as the time for which it can be blocked by other transactions. This is difficult to do in conventional systems, which permit the execution of an unlimited number of operations within each transaction, with the transaction controlling its scope and duration. The role of the system is to police the concurrently running transactions to ensure that they do not violate consistency and any other properties that need to be maintained. The duration for which locks are held is under the control of the transactions. As a result, the system cannot estimate the time for which this transaction will block others (which may have a resource conflict with it). To avoid this problem, MDARTS does not allow transactions to contain multiple database operations. Instead, a transaction executes the code within a database object. As we shall see, it is possible to make calibration runs to estimate the execution time of such objects. Of course, if a transaction uses the interconnection network, we must use a communications protocol that allows network delays to be bounded.

MDARTS can reserve resources for transactions in advance to ensure that hard deadlines are met. This keeps guarantees valid, even if temporary overloads happen.

MDARTS has an interesting way of checking for execution time requirements. There is a function called `calibrate()` which runs a set of experiments on the database operations to determine how long each operation takes. The calibration run consists of two components. First, the operation is run without taking concurrency constraints into account. Next, the maximum blocking time (i.e., the time spent waiting to enter critical sections) is computed. The total time estimate is the sum of the execution time and the blocking time.

The blocking time is computed as follows. Suppose an operation on an object consists of N_c critical sections, the maximum critical section time is T_c, and N_{cpu} the total number of processors running tasks that share that object. Then, the time spent waiting to access a critical section is upper-bounded by $Q + T_c N_{cpu}$, where Q is queueing overhead. The total blocking time is therefore upper-bounded by $N_c(Q + T_c N_{cpu})$.

Clearly, the execution time required for an operation will depend on the hardware used. One way of dealing with this is to make several calibration runs, one on each type of hardware. Another is to define speedup factors, based on an analysis of the hardware. That is, we might be able to say that a processor of type A is twice as fast as a processor of type B. These factors can be used to scale the calibration run for each processor type.

Let us now consider another approach to hard real-time systems. Thus far, we have assumed that real-time transactions have deadlines associated with them. We have seen in Chapter 2 how such deadlines are calculated in control systems from the dynamics of the controlled process. An alternative to associating each transaction with a deadline is to place a limit on how long the application can be allowed to be in certain dangerous states, and to schedule the transactions appropriately. For example, if we notice the pressure in a reactor vessel above a certain threshold, the specifications may require that one or more actions be taken to bring the pressure back to safe limits. The temperature might be lowered, a pressure valve opened, or some other action taken. This may require the running of not just one but several transactions. In conventional real-time databases, each of these transactions has a deadline associated with it. However, this is artificial. As far as the application is concerned, all we care about is that the pressure is brought back to safe limits within a certain time; that is, we don't care how long each individual transaction takes, so long as the overall effect is to limit the time that the system spends in an unsafe state. In general terms, deadlines need not be associated with transactions but with the time allowed to bring a system out of an unsafe state. When the controller is built around a database, there are three kinds of transactions.

External-input transactions: These are transactions that record external events in the database. Such transactions are usually write-only. For example, in an aircraft application, a transaction may update the current altitude.

Internal transactions: The purpose of this type of transaction is to run application tasks to help control the process. Internal transactions may be nested. That is, it is possible for a transaction to call another transaction, which itself calls yet another transaction, etc.

External-output transactions: These are transactions by which the computer system specifies the action to be taken. For example, a rudder setting would be an external-output transaction. External-input transactions may be periodic (e.g., a temperature sensor that reports the temperature every second) or sporadic (e.g., a ground-proximity sensor that provides an output only when the altitude is less than a given amount).

External-output transactions report the output generated by internal transactions, and can be scheduled immediately after them. Internal transactions can be scheduled, not with respect to individual deadlines but in such a manner as to bring the controlled process into a desired state within an overall deadline. Which transactions are actually scheduled to be run depends on the deadline, the transaction run times, and the current and desired states of the controlled process.

5.12 SUGGESTIONS FOR FURTHER READING

Two good introductions to real-time database systems are the papers by Ramamritham [20] and Yu et al. [22]. Serialization consistency is discussed at length in Papadimitriou [19]. The possibility of relaxing the serialization consistency constraint is suggested in Garcia-Molina [5]. Disk-scheduling algorithms are described by Chen et al. in [3]. Our description of optimistic concurrency control methods includes Franaszek et al. [4] and Haritsa et al. [7]. The AED algorithm and use of the HIT/MISS lists are introduced in [8], and the AEVD algorithm in [18]. Our discussion of concurrency control is based on the framework described in [22]. Priority inheritance is discussed by Huang et al. [10], and the use of multiple versions in real-time databases by Kim and Srivastava [11]. Lin and Son [15] discusses issues connected with dynamically adjusting serialization order, while Yu et al. [21] discuss timestamping for concurrency control. The idea of making a dry run of a transaction to obtain its resource requirements is explored in O'Neil et al. [17]. Main memory databases are surveyed in [6], and their index structures discussed in [14]. The MDARTS system for hard real-time systems is fully described in Lortz [16]. Cases where individual transactions need not have deadlines, but instead groups of transactions (for a particular task) are assigned an overall deadline based on application requirements is explored in [12].

EXERCISES

5.1. Which of the following sequences is serializable?
   (a) $S_a = R_1(x)R_2(x)W_1(x)R_3(x)R_4(x)W_3(x)$.
   (b) $S_b = R_1(x)W_1(x)R_2(x)W_2(x)W_3(x)W_4(x)R_5(x)$.
   (c) $S_c = R_1(x)W_1(x)W_2(x)R_2(x)$.
5.2. Suppose we have periodic processes π_1 and π_2, which measure pressure and temperature, respectively. The absolute validity interval of both these parameters is 100 ms. The relative validity interval of a temperature-pressure pair is 50 ms. What

is the maximum period of π_1 and π_2 that ensures that we always have a valid temperature-pressure pair reading?

5.3. Sometimes, a transaction that would have been aborted under the two-phase locking scheme can commit successfully under the optimistic scheme. Why is this?

5.4. Explain why EDF does not work well in heavily-loaded real-time database systems and why the AED algorithm can improve the success rate. Will AED perform better than EDF for non-database real-time applications?

5.5. We showed that when each granule has an equal probability of being accessed, the probability of a transaction being aborted is roughly proportional to the square of its length and to the system load. Suppose the database has two categories of granules. The probability that an access to a new granule is to Category 1 is $2/D$, while the probability that it is to Category 2 is $1/D$, where D is the size of the database. Find the probability that a transaction of N accesses is aborted before it commits. Assume that $D \gg N$, where N is the number of accesses by a transaction.

5.6. Construct an example of scheduling disk accesses for which the EDF policy meets all the deadlines but the elevator policy does not.

5.7. Construct an example of scheduling disk accesses for which EDF fails but the elevator policy does not.

5.8. In Chapter 3, we showed that EDF is an optimal uniprocessor scheduling algorithm. Why is EDF not always optimal for disk-access scheduling?

5.9. Generate an example of an application where it is permissible to relax the ACID properties of a real-time database.

5.10. Suppose a transaction T has a timestamp of 100. Its read set is x_1, x_2, and its write set is x_3, x_4, x_5. The read timestamps of these variables (prior to adjustment for the commitment of T) are 5, 10, 15, 16, 18; and the write timestamps are 90, 500, 600, 300, 5, respectively. Write out the read and write timestamps following the commitment of T.

5.11. For Example 5.9, construct a history for variables x and y that results in the allowed timestamp of T, $\tau(T)$, being in the range $[34, 37]$.

5.12. In deriving Equation (5.5), we assumed that a transaction is equally likely to update any granule. Suppose, instead, that each granule can be assigned to either set H or to set C, where a granule in H is twice as likely to be accessed as a granule in C. Obtain an expression for $A(N)$ in this case.

REFERENCES

[1] Abbott, R. K., and H. Garcia-Molina: "Scheduling Real-Time Transactions: A Performance Evaluation," *ACM Trans. Database Systems* 17(3):513–560, 1992.

[2] Chen, M.-I., and K.-J. Lin: "Dynamic Priority Ceilings: A Concurrency Control Protocol for Real-Time Systems," *Real-Time Systems* 2(4):325–346, 1990.

[3] Chen, S., J. A. Stankovic, J. F. Kurose, and D. F. Towsley: "Performance Evaluation of Two New Disk Scheduling Algorithms for Real-Time Systems," *Real-Time Systems* 3(3):307–336, 1991.

[4] Franaszek, P. A., J. T. Robinson, and A. Thomasian: "Concurrency Control for High Contention Environments," *ACM Trans. Database Systems* 17(2):304–345, 1992.

[5] Garcia-Molina, H.: "Using Semantic Knowledge for Transaction Processing in a Distributed Database," *ACM Trans. Database Systems* 8:186–213, 1983.

[6] Garcia-Molina, H., and K. Salem: "Main Memory Database Systems: An Overview," *IEEE Trans. Knowledge and Data Engineering* 4(6):509–516, 1992.

[7] Haritsa, J. R., M. J. Carey, and M. Livny: "Dynamic Real-Time Optimistic Concurrency Control," *Proc. IEEE Real-Time Systems Symp.*, pp. 94–103, IEEE, Los Alamitos, CA, 1990.

[8] Haritsa, J. R., M. Livny, and M. J. Carey: "Earliest Deadine Scheduling for Real-Time Database Systems," *Proc. IEEE Real-Time Systems Symp.*, pp. 232–242, IEEE, Los Alamitos, CA, 1991.

[9] Huang, J., J. A. Stankovic, D. Towsley, and K. Ramamritham: "Experimental Evaluation of Real-Time Transaction Processing," *Proc. IEEE Real-Time Systems Symp.*, pp. 144–153, IEEE, Los Alamitos, CA, 1989.

[10] Huang, J., J. A. Stankovic, D. Towsley, and K. Ramamritham: "On Using Priority Inheritance in Real-Time Databases," *Proc. IEEE Real-Time Systems Symp.*, pp. 210–221, IEEE, Los Alamitos, CA, 1991.

[11] Kim, W., and J. Srivastava: "Enhancing Real-Time DBMS Performance with Multiversion Data and Priority Based Disk Scheduling," *Proc. IEEE Real-Time Systems Symp.*, pp. 222–231, IEEE, Los Alamitos, CA, 1991.

[12] Korth, H. F., N. Soparkar, and A. Silberschatz: "Triggered Real-Time Databases with Consistency Constraints," *Proc. 16th Conference on Very Large Data Bases*, pp. 95–116, Morgan-Kaufmann, Palo Alto, CA, 1990.

[13] Kung, H. T., and J. T. Robinson: "On Optimistic Methods for Concurrency Control," *ACM Trans. Database Systems* 6(2):213–226, 1981.

[14] Lehman, T. J., and M. J. Carey: "A Study of Index Structures for Main Memory Database Management Systems," *Proc. 12th Conference on Very Large Data Bases*, pp. 294–303, Morgan-Kaufmann, Palo Alto, CA, 1986.

[15] Lin, Y., and S. H. Son: "Concurrency Control in Real-Time Databases by Dynamic Adjustment of Serialization Order," *Proc. IEEE Real-Time Symp.*, pp. 104–112, IEEE, Los Alamitos, CA, 1990.

[16] Lortz, V. B.: An Object-Oriented Real-Time Database System for Multiprocessors, CSE-TR-210-94, Dept. of Electrical Engineering and Computer Science, University of Michigan, 1994.

[17] O'Neil, P. E., K. Ramamritham, and C. Pu: A Two-Phase Approach to Predictable Scheduling Real-Time Transactions, technical report 92-35, Computer Science Department, University of Massachusetts, 1992.

[18] Pang, H., M. Livny, and M. J. Carey: "Transaction Scheduling in Multiclass Real-Time Database Systems," *Proc. IEEE Real-Time Systems Symp.*, pp. 23–34, IEEE, Los Alamitos, CA, 1992.

[19] Papadimitriou, C.: *The Theory of Database Concurrency Control,* Computer Science Press, Rockville, MD, 1986.

[20] Ramamritham, K.: "Real-Time Databases," *Distributed and Parallel Databases* 1:199–226, 1993.

[21] Yu, P. S., H.-U. Heiss, and D. M. Dias: "Modeling and Analysis of a Time-Stamp History Based Certification Protocol for Concurrency Control," *IEEE Trans. Knowledge and Data Engineering* 3(4):525–537, 1991.

[22] Yu, P. S., K.-L. Wu, K.-J. Lin, and S. H. Son: "On Real-Time Databases: Concurrency Control and Scheduling," *Proc. IEEE* 82(1):140–157, 1994.

CHAPTER

6

REAL-TIME COMMUNICATION

6.1 INTRODUCTION

Effective communication between the various devices of a real-time system is vital to its correct functioning. In embedded systems, data flows from the sensors and control panels to the central cluster of processors, between processors in the central cluster, and from processors to the actuators and output displays. The communication overhead adds to the computer response time. Hard real-time systems must therefore use communication protocols that allow the communication overhead to be bounded.

In soft real-time systems, such as multimedia or videoconferencing, where voice and image data are being transmitted, the need to deliver messages in a timely fashion is equally obvious; excessive delays in message delivery can significantly degrade the quality of service provided. However, in such applications, the occasional failure to meet message-delivery deadlines is not fatal.

The goals of communication protocols in real-time systems are somewhat different from those in traditional nonreal-time data-communication systems. In traditional systems, the key performance measure is system throughput, that is, how much data can be transferred over the network in one unit time from source to destination. In real-time systems, the key measure is the probability of delivering a message by a certain deadline. Note that a lost message has an infinite delivery time, so that this measure captures both the speed with which messages are delivered and the probability of losing messages. Message delay is caused by the following overheads.

- Formatting and/or packetizing the message.
- Queueing the message, as it waits for access to the communication medium.
- Sending the message from the source to the destination.
- Deformatting the message.

Real-time traffic can typically be categorized into multiple message classes, with each class being characterized by its deadline, arrival pattern, and priority. In hard real-time systems, such as embedded applications, the deadline of the traffic is related to the deadline of the task to which that communication belongs. In multimedia-type applications, the deadline is related directly to the application.

Priority is based on the importance of that message class to the application. If there is an overload of traffic, message priority can be used to determine which messages are dropped to ensure that the more important traffic is delivered in a timely fashion.

Most real-time sources generate traffic that fall into one of the following two categories.

Constant rate: Fixed-size packets are generated at periodic intervals. Many sensors produce such traffic. Constant rate traffic is the easiest to handle since it is smooth and not bursty. The smoother the traffic, the smaller the number of buffers that must be provided at each node.

Variable rate: This may take the form of fixed-size packets being generated at irregular intervals or of variable-size packets being generated at regular intervals. Bursty traffic makes greater demands on buffer space. Voice and video traffic typically exhibit variable rates. For example, voice sources can consist of *talkspurts* (a burst of packets, followed by a period of silence). See Figure 6.1. Video packets are an example of variable-sized packets being generated at regular intervals.

As mentioned earlier, traffic characteristics may change as packets flow through multiple hops in a network. At these intermediate nodes, the various traffic classes compete for bandwidth on the node's output link, and thus interfere with one another. Consider, for example, a high-priority bursty traffic class (Class 1) competing with a lower-priority constant-rate traffic class (Class 2) at some node n. See Figure 6.2. Since Class 1 has priority at node n, it will cause Class 2 to pile

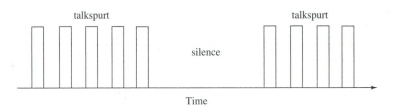

FIGURE 6.1
Voice traffic.

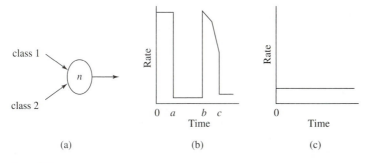

(a)   (b)   (c)

FIGURE 6.2
(a) Two competing classes at a node; (b) Class 1 (high-priority, bursty); (c) Class 2 (lower-priority, constant).

up at that node over the intervals $[0, a]$ and $[b, c]$. As a result of this, the output of Class 2 from this node will also become bursty.

6.1.1 Communications Media

While most of this chapter will be devoted to studying communications protocols, it is useful to be aware of the underlying physical communications medium. Each medium has a distinct set of properties. Let us consider the three most important media.

ELECTRICAL MEDIUM. This is the medium with which readers will be most familiar. Electrical media are manifested as a twisted pair of wires or as coaxial cable. Coaxial cable has a copper conductor at its core, surrounded by some insulation, surrounded by an outer conductor, and finally surrounded by a plastic coating. Twisted wires have bandwidths of several kHz, while broadband coaxial cable bandwidth can be as high as 450 MHz.

    Devices can be connected to coaxial cables either by breaking the cable and inserting a T-junction (illustrated in Figure 6.3) or by using a vampire tap. A vampire tap is constructed by drilling through the outer layers of the cable to its core and connecting the core to the device via a conductor.

OPTICAL FIBERS. In a system with an optical medium, the electrical signals from the nodes are converted to light pulses by means of laser diodes. These diodes can be operated at up to 10 Gbps (technological improvements keep increasing

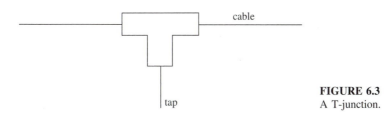

FIGURE 6.3
A T-junction.

this bound). The optical pulses thus generated are then launched on the fiber medium. The receiver then converts them back to electrical signals by means of photodiodes at the receiver.

As a light pulse travels down a fiber, two things happen to it. First, the pulse amplitude decreases, that is, the signal is *attenuated*. Second, the pulse width tends to increase with the distance travelled, a phenomenon called *dispersion*. Dispersion is linked to the nature of the optical fiber as well as the range of frequencies that are transmitted (physical transmitters cannot transmit pure sine waves). Thus, the size of a network is linked to the power that is needed at the transmitter end and to the maximum frequency that can be supported.

Optical fiber has two main advantages over electrical media. First, the raw bandwidth of a typical fiber can be as high as several hundred GHz. Second, optical signals are immune to the effects of electromagnetic interference.

One disadvantage with optical fiber is that it is difficult to passively tap them without a significant signal loss. Optical amplifiers to restore signal levels are expensive, and so taps are impractical unless the system is very small. There are two network structures that work well with optical fiber, point-to-point networks and the passive star.

In *point-to-point networks*, there are no taps, but there are optical-to-electric and electric-to-optical converters at each interface. See Figure 6.4. The first stage of the interface converts optical signals into electrical ones. The node then checks

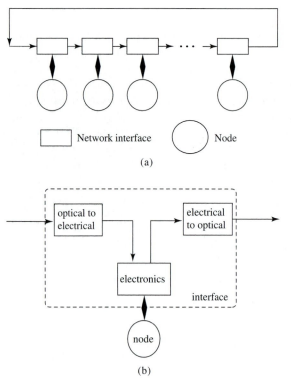

(a)

(b)

FIGURE 6.4
Optical point-to-point network: (a) example structure; (b) interface detail.

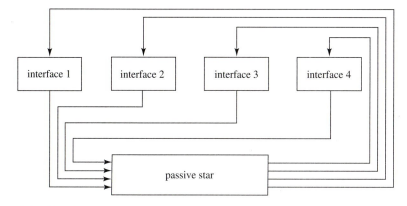

FIGURE 6.5
Star-configured architecture.

to see if the message was addressed to it or to someone downstream on the network. If the former, it accepts the message. If the latter, it retransmits the message by using the second stage of the interface, which converts the electrical signal from the node to light.

The passive star arrangement is as shown in Figure 6.5. Each interface delivers its optical output to a glass cylinder, the *passive star*, which delivers at its output the sum of all the signals at the input. This output energy is divided among the fibers that go out of the cylinder. Thus, every interface receives the input for all the interfaces in the system, and simply picks the ones addressed to it. For this arrangement to work, the output from the passive star must have sufficient energy to be detected by each of the interfaces even after being divided among them. This requires sensitive receivers or powerful transmitters, or both.

The fiber bandwidth is, as we have explained above, of the order of hundreds of GHz. This is well above the speed of the electronics at the interface. This mismatch requires us to either run the fiber at the speed of the interface electronics, which would waste most of the fiber bandwidth, or use *wavelength-division multiplexing* (WDM) to divide the fiber channel into several virtual channels, each of sufficiently low bandwidth to match the interface-electronics bandwidth. The details of how this is done is out of the scope of this book. (Section 6.4 contains sources about WDM.) All that we need to know here is that the single physical channel is divided into multiple virtual channels, each with its own interface. Figure 6.6 shows how such a fiber is connected to the node interface receiver. Its light signal is split into a number of channels, each of which carries a fraction of the input signal. Each such channel has an interface attached to it, with an optical detector tuned to the wavelength of a virtual channel. The interface component associated with each channel provides its node with an electrical signal corresponding to the corresponding virtual channel. The transmission of messages follows the same lines; the optical output from each channel is summed at the fiber input.

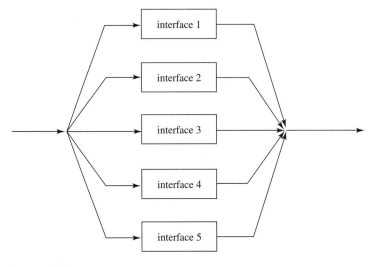

FIGURE 6.6
Interfacing to a WDM network.

The design of tunable lasers and receivers is currently the focus of much research. The challenge is to produce devices that can be tuned at high speed to enable a transmitter or receiver to hop through a wide range of the frequency spectrum; however, this area is outside the scope of this book.

WIRELESS. There has recently been mounting interest in wireless communication (using microwave radio) between computers. The advantage of such a medium is that it does not require wired contact between communicating nodes. As a result, ad hoc networks can be rapidly set up and reconfigured. However, the potential for interference is much greater than for either electrical or optical media. The distance over which a radio link can be maintained depends on the transmitter power, receiver sensitivity, noise levels, type of error-control coding used, and any attenuating barriers (e.g., walls, partitions, equipment, filing cabinets) between the transmitter and the receiver. At the time of writing, wireless bandwidths are around a few megabits/second (Mb/s). This is expected to increase with time. Very little work on real-time protocols specifically geared toward wireless links has been done; the protocols described in this chapter are geared towards electrical and optical media.

6.2 NETWORK TOPOLOGIES

The network topology for a computer or a distributed system must be carefully chosen since it affects the system response time and reliability. The following features are important.

Diameter: This is the maximum distance (number of hops) between any two nodes in the system, as a function of the number of nodes. Ideally, the diameter should increase only slowly as a function of the number of nodes. In a completely connected network, where each node has a dedicated link to every other node, the diameter is one, regardless of the number of nodes; at the other extreme, in a linear array (where the nodes are connected as a one-dimensional string), the diameter is the number of nodes minus one.

Node degree: This is the number of edges adjacent to each node, and determines the number of I/O ports per node and the number of links in the system. The greater this number is, the greater the cost. In some networks (such as the mesh or the linear array) the node degree is independent of the number of nodes: this is convenient since adding nodes to a network does not then require the architecture of each node to change.

Fault-tolerance: This measures the extent to which the network can withstand the failure of individual links and nodes while still remaining functional. The *node (link) connectivity* is the minimum number of nodes (links) that must fail before the network is disconnected. The *node (link) diameter stability* is the minimum number of nodes (links) that must fail before the network diameter is increased. There is no single measure that adequately captures the fault-tolerant capability of a network.

Network topologies can be broadly classified into point-to-point and shared (or broadcast) categories. In a *point-to-point* topology, nodes are connected by dedicated links. If a node wishes to send a message to a destination that is not its neighbor, that message must be forwarded by intermediate nodes. In a *shared* (or *broadcast*) topology, the nodes all have access to the communications channel and only one node can transmit at any time over a channel.

> **Example 6.1.** Figure 6.7 shows examples of point-to-point and shared networks. In the point-to-point network, there is no edge connecting nodes 1 and 3. A message going from node 1 to node 3 must thus pass through either node 2 or node 4. That is, it must take two hops from input to output. In contrast, if the shared network is used, a node can communicate with any other node in one hop.

Buses and rings are the most popular topologies. Figure 6.8 shows examples of them. In a bus network, the ends are terminated by matching impedances to sharply attenuate reflections. The interfaces can either consist of taps or of forwarding points.

A ring network is a set of network interfaces connected in a ring by point-to-point links. Bits arriving at the input end of an interface are copied into a buffer. They can then be processed (if necessary) and transmitted at the output end of the interface.

> **Example 6.2.** Node 1 wishes to send a message to node 5 through nodes 2, 3, and 4. It transmits its message, with a header to specify the destination, to node 2. The node-2 interface receives the message and checks the message destination. Realizing that it is for node 5, it transmits the message, unaltered, to the node-3 interface. This in turn forwards it to node 4, which forwards it to node 5. Node 5 reads in the

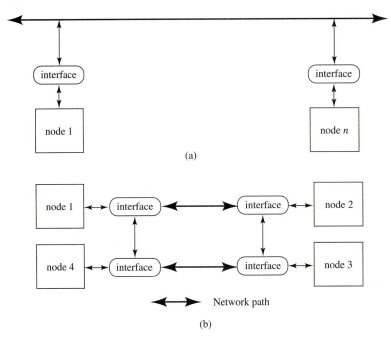

FIGURE 6.7
(a) Shared network and (b) point-to-point network.

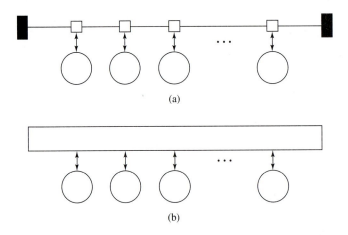

FIGURE 6.8
(a) A single-bus system and (b) a ring system.

message and passes it along to the next node. Ultimately, the message comes back to node 1, which removes it from the ring.

Other popular topologies are illustrated in Figures 6.9 and 6.10. The hyper-cube (see Figure 6.10) is defined as follows. There are 2^n nodes in an n-dimen-

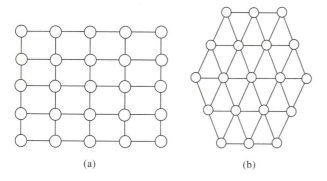

FIGURE 6.9
Mesh networks: (a) rectangular mesh; (b) hexagonal mesh.

sional hypercube. Label the nodes in binary from 0 to $2^n - 1$, and connect by a line those nodes whose labels differ in exactly one bit position. An n-dimensional hypercube is built by taking two $(n - 1)$-dimensional hypercubes and connecting like nodes.

Another popular topology is the multistage network. This is built out of switchboxes, typically 2×2 switchboxes. Four possible configurations of an individual switch are shown in Figure 6.11. An 8-input, 8-output network built out of such switches is shown in Figure 6.12.

Many structures can support either a point-to-point or a shared topology. Consider the single-bus system in Figure 6.8, which uses forwarding interfaces. If each interface, upon receiving a message at one end, copies it out on the other regardless of its destination, the network behaves as a broadcast topology. On the

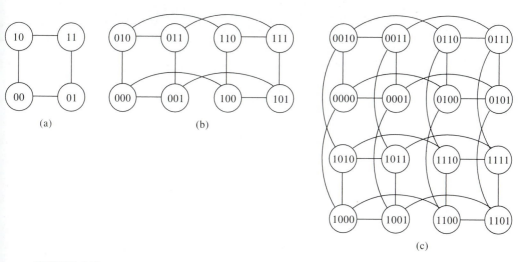

FIGURE 6.10
Hypercube networks: (a) two-dimensional; (b) three-dimensional; (c) four-dimensional.

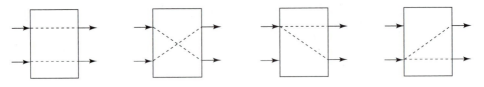

FIGURE 6.11
Four configurations of a 2×2 switch.

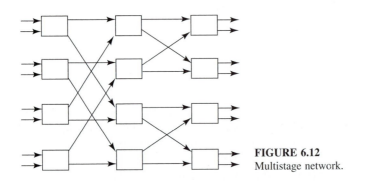

FIGURE 6.12
Multistage network.

other hand, if the interface checks the destination and only forwards the message if the path to the destination lies through it, the network behaves as a point-to-point topology.

It is sometimes important to distinguish between the physical and virtual topologies. The *physical* topology is the structure determined by the physical connections. On this base, we can sometimes build many different virtual topologies. This is illustrated in Example 6.3.

> **Example 6.3.** We have an optical network using a passive star as its physical topology and using wavelength-division multiplexing. Each node has three receivers and three transmitters. We want this to support a three-dimensional hypercube as a virtual network. This is done by assigning wavelengths to the receivers and transmitters so that each node has a unique wavelength on which it communicates with its neighbor in the hypercube. The wavelength allocations are shown in Table 6.1. Thus, for example, node 000 has its transmitters tuned to wavelengths λ_1, λ_2, and λ_3; and its receivers tuned to λ_4, λ_7, and λ_{13}.

6.2.1 Sending Messages

Three common ways of sending messages are: packet switching, circuit switching, and wormhole routing.

PACKET SWITCHING. The message is broken down into *packets*, which are messages of a standard or variable length. Packets have *headers*, which specify their source, destination, and any other information that may be required. They are then sent to their destination by the routing and flow-control algorithm.

TABLE 6.1
Wavelength allocations for embedding a hypercube in a passive star

From	To	Wavelength	From	To	Wavelength
000	001	λ_1	100	000	λ_{13}
000	010	λ_2	100	101	λ_{14}
000	100	λ_3	100	110	λ_{15}
001	000	λ_4	101	001	λ_{16}
001	011	λ_5	101	100	λ_{17}
001	101	λ_6	101	111	λ_{18}
010	000	λ_7	110	010	λ_{19}
010	011	λ_8	110	100	λ_{20}
010	110	λ_9	110	111	λ_{21}
011	001	λ_{10}	111	011	λ_{22}
011	010	λ_{11}	111	101	λ_{23}
011	111	λ_{12}	111	110	λ_{24}

Example 6.4. The network is a two-dimensional hypercube shown in Figure 6.10. Node 00 is sending a packet to node 11. There are two possible paths: $00 \rightarrow 01 \rightarrow 11$, and $00 \rightarrow 10 \rightarrow 11$. Suppose the first of these is chosen. Node 00 sends the packet to node 01, which notes its destination from the packet header, and forwards the packet to that node.

CIRCUIT SWITCHING. A circuit is set up between the source and the destination for such time as is required to send the message. The entire circuit is then meant exclusively for this message; any other messages that require all, or part, of this path must wait for the transmission to be completed. In other words, circuit-switching involves setting up a dedicated path from source to destination for the duration of the message transfer.

Example 6.5. In the multistage network shown in Figure 6.13, if we wish to send a message from S to D, the switches are set as shown by the heavy line and the circuit is held until the message has been delivered.

WORMHOLE ROUTING. Wormhole routing is a way of pipelining packet transmission in a multihop network. Each packet is broken down into a train of flits,

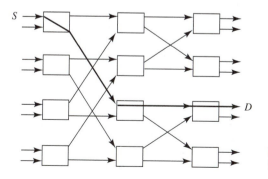

FIGURE 6.13
Setting up a circuit.

each about one or two bytes long. The sender transmits one flit per unit time, and the flits are forwarded from node to node until they reach their destination. Over time, a train of flits, in contiguous nodes, forms and makes its way to its destination.

Example 6.6. The network is a three-dimensional hypercube, as shown in Figure 6.10. A message is to be sent from node 000 to node 111. Node 000 breaks up its packet into flits, and sends them to node 001 at the rate of one flit per cycle. Node 001 forwards the flits it receives to node 011, which forwards them to 111. If the packet consists of six flits, the activity is as follows.

Time	000 →001	001 →011	011 →111
0	Flit 0	–	–
1	Flit 1	Flit 0	–
2	Flit 2	Flit 1	Flit 0
3	Flit 3	Flit 2	Flit 1
4	Flit 4	Flit 3	Flit 2
5	Flit 5	Flit 4	Flit 3
6	–	Flit 5	Flit 4
7	–	–	Flit 5

The final flit is received at the destination at time 7.

Only the header flit in a train has the destination information; each node simply forwards the next flit to the same node that it sent the previous flit to in the train. It is therefore impossible to interleave one train of flits with another; successive flits in the same train must be in either the same or adjacent nodes. Wormhole routing requires less buffer space in the forwarding nodes, since nodes deal with flits rather than packets.

If we are not careful, multiple trains of flits can cause deadlock. Figure 6.14 shows an example. Train α is prevented from turning at node m since that would

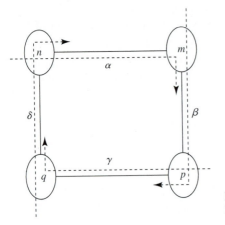

FIGURE 6.14
Deadlock in wormhole routing.

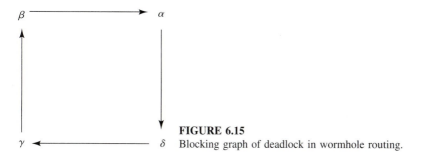

FIGURE 6.15
Blocking graph of deadlock in wormhole routing.

cause it to be interspersed with train β. Similarly, β is prevented from turning at node p due to train γ; γ is prevented from turning at node q due to train δ; δ is prevented from turning at n due to α. The situation is illustrated graphically in Figure 6.15, where an arrow from node α to node δ indicates that train α is stopping δ. The graph is cyclic, indicating a deadlock.

6.2.2   Network Architecture Issues[1]

HIGH-LEVEL ARCHITECTURAL ISSUES. At the highest level, a distributed system comprises a set of nodes communicating through an interconnection network. Each node may itself be a multiprocessor comprising application, system, and network processors; a shared memory segment; and I/O interfaces. Although the application processor may be an off-the-shelf product, the system and network processors usually have to be custom-designed because they provide the specialized support necessary for real-time applications. The memory subsystem may also be specially designed to provide fast and reliable communication between the processors at a node. For example, the memory subsystem may support a mailbox facility to support efficient interprocessor communication within a node of a distributed system.

The nodes of the system must be interconnected by a suitable network. In the past, for small systems, the network was a custom-designed broadcast bus with redundancy to meet the fault-tolerance requirements. More recently, however, architects have turned to either a high-speed token ring or a point-to-point network with a carefully-chosen topology. For example, the Spring system at the University of Massachusetts uses a high-speed optical interconnect called Scramnet, whereas the HARTS project at The University of Michigan uses a point-to-point interconnection network called the C-wrapped hexagonal mesh topology.

Irrespective of the exact topology, the network architecture should support scalability, ease of implementation, and reliability. It should also have support for efficient one-to-one, as well as one-to-many, communications. For instance,

[1] Section 6.2.2 is based on K. G. Shin and P. Ramanathan, "Real-Time Computing: A New Discipline of Computer Science and Engineering," *Proceedings of the IEEE*, Vol. 82, No. 1, 1994. © IEEE. Used with permission.

the C-wrapped hexagonal mesh topology used in HARTS has a $\theta(1)$ algorithm for computing all the shortest paths between any two nodes in the system. The information about all the shortest paths can also be easily encoded using just three integers and included as part of each message so that the intermediate nodes need not do much computation. The routing algorithm can fully exploit advanced switching techniques like wormhole routing, in which packets do not always have to be buffered at intermediate nodes before being forwarded to the next node in the route. Broadcasting can also be done fairly efficiently and in a fault-tolerant manner using the multiple disjoint paths between any two nodes in the system. Such capabilities are very important because reliable and timely exchange of information is crucial to the distributed execution of any real-time application.

LOW-LEVEL ARCHITECTURAL ISSUES. Low-level architectural issues involve packet processing, routing, and error/flow control. In a distributed real-time system, there are additional issues related to the support for meeting deadlines, time management, and housekeeping. Since the support of these low-level issues impedes the execution of application tasks, nodes in a distributed real-time system usually have a custom-designed processor for handling these chores. In the description below, this special processor is referred to as the network processor (NP).

The main function of the NP is to execute operations necessary to deliver a message from a source task to its intended recipient(s). In particular, when an application task wants to transmit a message, it provides the NP with information about the intended recipient(s) and the location of the message data, and then relies on the NP to ensure that the information reaches the recipients in a reliable and timely fashion.

The NP must establish connections between the source and destination nodes. It must also handle end-to-end error detection and message retransmission. As far as routing is concerned, the NP may select primary and alternative routes, allocate bandwidths necessary to guarantee timely delivery, packetize the information into data blocks and segments, and reassemble packets at the destination node. In point-to-point interconnections, the NP must support and choose an appropriate switching method such as wormhole routing, store-and-forward, or circuit switching. In token rings, the NP must select suitable protocol parameters to guarantee the deadlines of all messages. The NP must also perform framing, synchronization, and packet sequencing.

The NP must implement buffer management policies that maximize the utilization of buffer space, but guarantee the availability of buffers to the highest priority messages. Similarly, if noncritical messages hold other resources that are needed by more critical ones, NP must provide a means for preemption of such resources for use by the critical messages.

The NP may also have to monitor the state of the network in terms of the traffic load and link failures. The traffic load affects the ability of the NP to send real-time messages to other processors, while link failures affect system reliability. It may also keep track of the processing load of its host (or hosts), and use the information for load balancing/sharing and task migration operations.

I/O ARCHITECTURE. Little work has been done on network architectures for the I/O subsystem. Clearly, a real-time computer can process data no faster than it acquires it from sensors and operators. The nature of I/O devices in a real-time environment, consisting as it does of sensors and actuators, is quite different from the magnetic disks and tapes that are the I/O devices commonly encountered in general-purpose systems.

To improve I/O, multiple I/O devices need to be distributed and managed by relatively simple and reliable controllers. Moreover, to improve both accessibility (reliability) and performance, there must be multiple access paths (called *multi-accessibility* or *multi-ownership*) to these I/O devices.

One possible way to provide multi-accessibility, used in HARTS, is to cluster the I/O devices together and assign a controller to manage access to the devices in each cluster. The controller has a set of full-duplex links to certain nodes of the distributed system. In order to limit the number of links in each controller while providing multi-accessibility, a controller is connected to three nodes in the system as shown in the Fig. 6.16. Since each controller can be accessed by three nodes, different management protocols are proposed for handling the I/O requests. In a static scheme, one node is assigned the primary responsibility of managing the controller with the proviso that the other nodes can take over control if the primary node becomes faulty. In a dynamic scheme, all three nodes connected to a controller manage the controller using a more complicated protocol.

An alternative approach for connecting the I/O controllers to the nodes of the system is to connect an I/O controller to just one node. However, the placement of the I/O controllers must be done in such a way that a node is at most one hop away from a node with an I/O controller connected to it. To achieve fault-tolerance,

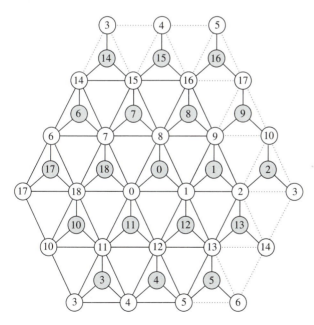

FIGURE 6.16
I/O controller placement.

TABLE 6.2
List of protocols

Protocol	Deadline guarantees?	Network
VTCSMA	No	Broadcast
Window	No	Broadcast
Timed token	Yes	Ring
IEEE 802.5	Yes	Ring
Stop-and-go	Yes	Point-to-point
Polled bus	No	Bus
Hierarchical round-robin	Yes	Point-to-point
Deadline-based	No	Point-to-point

schemes for the placement of I/O controllers have also been proposed in which a node is at most one hop away from j nodes with I/O controllers, where j is a design parameter.

Although the above solutions have made some headway in dealing with the I/O architectural issue, there is a lot of work that needs to be done in designing communication networks that can perform the levels of I/O needed for real-time systems.

6.3 PROTOCOLS

In the following sections, we describe protocols suitable for real-time systems. In Table 6.2, we provide a directory of these protocols. Some of these offer deadline guarantees; that is, they guarantee that messages will be delivered before their assigned deadlines. Others do not, but are "best-effort" algorithms, suitable only for soft real-time systems.

6.3.1 Contention-Based Protocols

These are distributed protocols that assume a broadcast medium. Nodes monitor the channel and transmit only when they detect that it is idle. If multiple nodes start transmitting at about the same time, there is a collision of packets and the transmissions have to be aborted and then retried.

> **Example 6.7.** Consider the bus network shown in Figure 6.17 Let τ_{ij} denote the propagation delay between nodes i and j. Node m is transmitting from t_1 to t_2. Nodes n and q see the end of this transmission, which is followed by silence on the bus, at times $t_2 + \tau_{mn}$ and $t_2 + \tau_{mq}$, respectively. Suppose node n has some packet awaiting transmission. It starts transmitting at time $t_2 + \tau_{mn} + \epsilon$, where ϵ is some positive number. This transmission does not reach q until $t_q = t_2 + t_{mn} + \epsilon + \tau_{nq}$. Suppose a packet arrives at node q at time t_y, where $t_y \in (t_2 + \tau_{mn}, t_2 + \tau_{mn} + \epsilon + \tau_{nq})$. Since q has not heard the node-n tranmission yet, it transmits the packet starting at $t_y + \epsilon$. The two messages collide; and upon detecting the collision, nodes n and q cease transmission, and each back off for a random time before trying again.

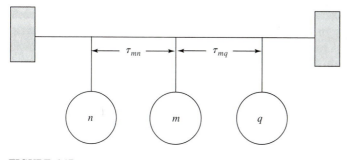

FIGURE 6.17
Bus network.

VIRTUAL-TIME CARRIER-SENSED MULTIPLE ACCESS (VTCSMA). The VTC-SMA protocol has been designed for single-channel broadcast networks and for the bus and ring topologies.

In carrier-sensed multiple access (CSMA) protocols, all the nodes can monitor the communication channel. Suppose a node has something to transmit. If it observes that the channel is busy, it will refrain from interfering with the ongoing transmission. When it senses that the channel is free, the node will transmit its message. Since there is no coordination between the nodes, this can result in a collision resulting from multiple nodes attempting to transmit simultaneously. When a collision occurs, the transmitting nodes, which monitor the channel continually, abort their transmission and retransmit after waiting for a time. There are various types of CSMA, each with its own formula for computing the retransmission epoch. CSMA is an efficient communication scheme when the end-to-end transmission delay is much less than the average time to transmit a packet and when the load is not very high.

CSMA is a truly *distributed* algorithm, with each node deciding when it will transmit. It may seem a hopeless task to implement a priority algorithm, where one node with a lower-priority packet is supposed to defer to another with a higher-priority packet, using CSMA. This is not so, however. While there is no explicit coordination between the nodes, the nodes do see a consistent time if their clocks are synchronized, and they observe the same channel (slight differences can exist due to transmission delays). This common information can be exploited to obtain quite effective priority communications algorithms, including a priority based on deadlines.

Suppose that a node has a set of packets to transmit. How is it to determine when to transmit them on the channel? The information it has is

- the state of the channel,

- the priorities of the packets waiting in its transmission buffer to be transmitted over the network, and

- the time according to the synchronized clock.

The node does not have any idea of the priorities of any packets that may be awaiting transmission at the other nodes. Simply using the state of the channel and the priorities of its packets is not sufficient; the time information must also be used. The key to the VTCSMA algorithm that we present below is that if the priority of the packet can be computed as a function of the current time, as well as of some other parameters, it may be possible to use the time information to implicitly arrive at some global ordering of priorities. For example, we can strive to serve packets according to their deadlines, arrival times, and laxities. The way this is done will become apparent when we describe the algorithm.

The VTCSMA algorithm uses two clocks at each node. One is the real clock (RC), which tells the "real time," and is synchronized with the clocks at the other nodes. The second is the virtual clock (VC), which behaves as follows. When the channel is busy, the VC freezes; when the channel becomes free, the VC is reset (according to a formula that we will present) and then runs at the rate $\eta > 1$. That is, the VC runs faster than the RC when the channel is free, and not at all when it is busy.

> **Example 6.8.** Figure 6.18 illustrates the operation of the VC for $\eta = 2$. The abscissa denotes the real time and the ordinate the virtual time. From real time 0 to $t1$, the channel is busy, and so the virtual time remains frozen at $t1'$. At real time $t1$, the channel becomes idle, and the VC is set equal to the RC and starts running at a rate of 2. At real time $t2$, the channel becomes busy again, and so the virtual time freezes at $t2'$. At real time $t3$, when the channel is idle, it is initialized and starts running again at rate 2. And so on.

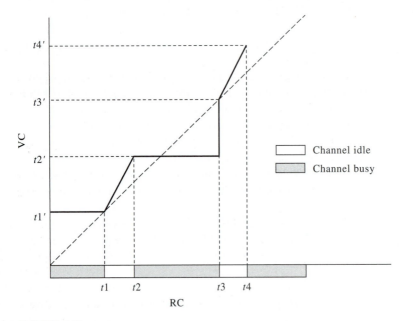

FIGURE 6.18
Operation of the virtual clock.

Since the real clocks are assumed to be synchronized and the virtual times are regularly reset with respect to the real times, the virtual times told at the various nodes are the same, plus or minus some small skew. This is the common information that is used to impose a global priority on the packets to be transmitted. Each node computes a virtual time to start transmission VSX(M), for every packet M awaiting transmission at that node. When the virtual time is greater than or equal to VSX(M), packet M becomes eligible for transmission. We leave to the reader the easy task of figuring out which packet is transmitted by a node that has multiple packets eligible for transmission at any one time. If a collision occurs, the VSX of that packet is modified suitably. The formula used for computing VSX depends on the type of VTCSMA that is used, and is described below.

Figure 6.19 is a flowchart that specifies the algorithm. How is the VC initialized when the channel becomes free, and the VSX(M) modified when there is a collision involving packet M? There are many ways of doing this, and each approach results in a different variation of VTCSMA. First, we need some notation.

τ Propagation time from one end of the network to the other.

A_M Arrival time of message (or packet) M.

T_M Time required to transmit message M.

D_M Deadline by which message M must be delivered to its destination.

L_M Latest time by which the message must be sent to be able to meet the deadline. That is, $L_M = D_M - T_M - \tau$.

$\Lambda_M(t)$ Maximum amount of time that message M can be delayed at time t before missing its deadline. That is, $\Lambda_M(t) = D_M - T_M - \tau - t$.

We will list four variations of VTCSMA, with suffixes A, T, L, and D, respectively. When packet M arrives, we have:

$$\text{VSX}(M) = \begin{cases} A_M & \text{for VTCSMA-A} \\ T_M & \text{for VTCSMA-T} \\ L_M & \text{for VTCSMA-L} \\ D_M & \text{for VTCSMA-D} \end{cases} \tag{6.1}$$

When a collision occurs, each node involved in the collision either retransmits M immediately, with probability p, or (with probability $1 - p$), the node modifies VSX(M) to be a random number drawn from the following interval I:

$$I = \begin{cases} (\text{current VC}, L_M) & \text{for VTCSMA-A} \\ (0, T_M) & \text{for VTCSMA-T} \\ (\text{current RC}, L_M) & \text{for VTCSMA-L} \\ (\text{current RC}, D_M) & \text{for VTCSMA-D} \end{cases} \tag{6.2}$$

When the channel switches state from busy to idle, the VC is initialized as follows:

$$VC = \begin{cases} \text{no change} & \text{for VTCSMA-A} \\ 0 & \text{for VTCSMA-T} \\ \text{RC} & \text{for VTCSMA-L and VTCSMA-D} \end{cases} \tag{6.3}$$

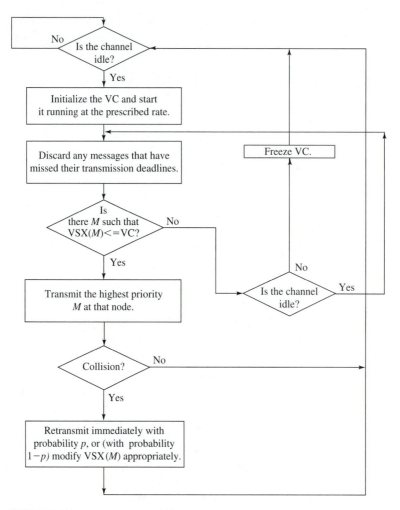

FIGURE 6.19
Flowchart of the VTCSMA algorithm.

It is easy to show that VTCSMA-A, VTCSMA-T, VTCSMA-D, and VTCSMA-L implement the earliest-arrival-first, the minimum-transmission-time-first, the earliest-deadline, and the minimum-laxity priority algorithms, respectively. The VC is consistent (plus or minus a small skew) for all the nodes, and the transmission is based on the relationship between VC and VSX(M) for each packet M.

Example 6.9. As an example of how these algorithms work, consider the VTCSMA-L algorithm. Let $\eta = 2$ (i.e., the VC runs twice as fast as the RC when the channel is idle). Let us assume that the transmission time for each packet is $T_M = 15$, and that the propagation time is $\tau = 1$. Suppose the packets arrive according to the following table:

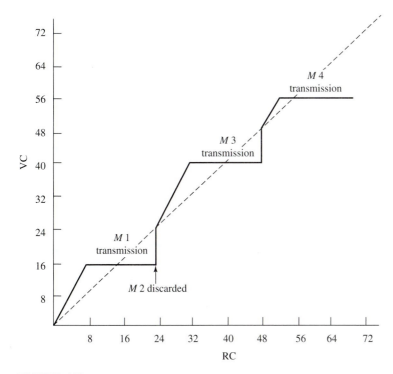

FIGURE 6.20
VC-RC trajectory for Example 6.9: $\eta = 2$.

Node	M	RC at arrival	D_M	L_M
1	1	0	32	16
2	2	10	36	20
3	3	20	56	40
4	4	20	72	56

Figure 6.20 summarizes what happens. M1 starts transmission at RC = 8 (when VC = L_1) and completes at RC = 8 + 16 = 24. This is too late for M2 to start transmitting, and so it is discarded. The VC is initialized at 24 and is restarted. When it reaches $L_3 = 40$, 1M3 starts transmitting. And so on.

Note that despite there being sufficient time to transmit all four packets successfully, M2 had to be discarded. This is because the channel was needlessly idle from RC = 0 to RC = 8. This happened because η was not sufficiently large.

Let us see what happens if we make $\eta = 4$. Figure 6.21 tells the story—all four packets get successfully transmitted.

Does this mean that the larger the value of η, the better the performance of the system? Not necessarily. Consider the following example. Once again, the algorithm is VTCSMA-L.

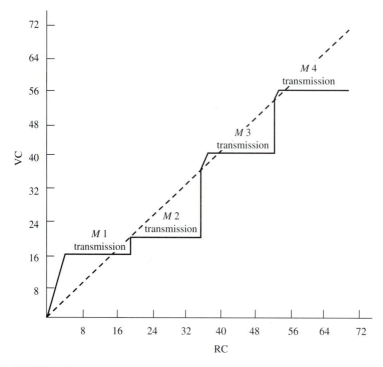

FIGURE 6.21
VC-RC trajectory for Example 6.9: $\eta = 4$.

Example 6.10. Let the parameters be as in the following table.

Node	M	RC at arrival	D_M	L_M
1	1	6	22	6
2	2	6	40	24

Let the other parameters be as in Example 6.9. We encourage the reader to draw the VC-RC trajectory for the cases $\eta = 2$ and $\eta = 4$. For $\eta = 2$, both packets are successfully transmitted; for $\eta = 4$, M1 and M2 collide and, as a result, M1 has to be discarded since there is not time enough after the collision is resolved to successfully transmit it.

The reader will have noticed that in Example 6.9, the channel is needlessly idle for some time even when it has a packet awaiting transmission. This is to accomodate later arrivals with tighter deadline requirements, as in Example 6.11.

Example 6.11. The following table lists some packet arrivals. Let $\eta = 2$ and the other parameters be as in Example 6.9.

Node	M	RC at arrival	D_M	L_M
1	1	0	40	24
2	2	5	24	8

The reader can easily check that keeping the channel idle over the interval [0, 5], despite M1 awaiting transmission, has enabled M2, which arrived at RC = 5 but had an earlier deadline, to be transmitted successfully.

Thus far, we have assumed clock skew to be negligible. No systematic study of the effects of clock skew have been carried out, but its effects are easy to demonstrate.

Example 6.12. Consider again VTCSMA-L, and the following arrival pattern.

Node	M	Actual RC at arrival	D_M	L_M
1	1	8	32	16
2	2	9	36	20

Let the clocks be skewed with respect to the actual real time as follows.

Node	RC at node
1	Actual RC − 1
2	Actual RC + 1

We leave it to the reader to show that for $\eta = 2$, this will cause nodes 1 and 2 to transmit their respective packets on the network at the same time, causing a collision and also ensuring that M1 cannot be successfully transmitted.

Clock skew is not always deleterious. To see this, the reader should consider the packet arrival times in Example 6.9, and develop a set of skews for which all four packets are successfully transmitted for $\eta = 2$.

Performance of the VTCSMA algorithm. No analytical model exists to calculate the fraction of packets that miss their deadline under the VTCSMA algorithm. However, simulation studies have been carried out by Zhao and Ramamritham [22], and the following conclusions can be drawn from them.

1. VTCSMA protocols have a better loss rate (i.e., rate at which deadlines are missed), in general, than the CSMA protocols.
2. The best performance in terms of fraction of loss rate is obtained by the VTCSMA-D algorithm.

3. The performance is a function of the value of η; however, as long as the transmission delays are not too great and the network is not overloaded, the range of η values over which each protocol performs close to its best is large.

WINDOW PROTOCOL. Like the VTCSMA protocol, the window protocol is based on collision sensing. Again, it cannot be guaranteed that messages will be transmitted in time to meet their deadlines. This protocol is therefore only suitable for soft real-time systems.

As with VTCSMA, the system consists of a set of nodes connected on a bus. Each node continuously monitors the bus to receive any messages that may be addressed to it. Since all activity on the bus is equally visible to all the nodes, we can assume that each node knows when a transmission has succeeded and when multiple simultaneous transmissions collide, even if the transmissions in question neither originate from, nor are destined for, that node. Events on the bus thus become a mechanism for synchronizing the actions of the nodes.

The protocol owes its name to the window maintained at each node. The window is a time interval, and the windows of all the nodes are identical. When the latest-time-to-transmit (LTTT) of a packet falls within this window and the channel is idle, the packet is eligible to be transmitted. If more than one packet is eligible for transmission at a node, one of them is picked based on some criterion (e.g., LTTT).

We assume that the clock skews are fairly small (i.e., the nodes are tightly synchronized). The time axis is broken down into *slots*, where each slot is an interval of time equal to the end-to-end network propagation time. A node may begin transmitting a packet only at the beginning of a time slot.

Figures 6.22 to 6.25 describe the window algorithm. We use the following notation:

δ	Predefined integer constant.
t	Present time.
$LTTT_M$	LTTT associated with message M.
Random(a,b)	Random number, distributed uniformly between a and b.
T_M	Number of slots needed to transmit message M.

The algorithm maintains a stack in each node to record the window history. Each stack entry is a two-tuple (u,i). The u field reflects the upper bound of a window in which a collision occurred, and the i field is zero unless the node has a message involved in the collision; in such an event, i contains the ID of that message. We can informally describe the protocol as follows. Central to the algorithm is the window, which is a duration of time (in integral multiples of slots). Each node in the system has exactly the same window. The initial window size is δ. The window is modified based on events occurring on the bus. Since the bus is continually monitored by all the nodes, all the nodes can maintain, by means of a distributed algorithm, an identical copy of the window.

If a node has a packet to transmit, it checks if there is an ongoing transmission on the bus. If there is, it waits until that transmission ceases; this can be

```
Initialization:
    up := t + δ;
    empty the stack;
    If one or more messages have LTTT in the interval [t,up), transmit
        the one with minimum LTTT.

At the beginning of each slot:
    Find out if there is any message with (LTTT < t),
        and drop it, since it has missed its deadline.
    Discard any stack contents whose u field is less than t;
    If the channel is busy due to a collision, then
        abort any ongoing transmission by this node;
    else if the channel is idle following a collision
        contract_window_and_send(up, t);
    else if the channel is occupied by a message transmission
        continue the transmission, if any;
    else if the channel is idle after a successful transmission, then
        pop_and_send(up, t);
    else if the channel continues idle, then
        expand_window_and_send(up, t);
    end if;
end;
```

FIGURE 6.22
Window protocol. (W. Zhao, et al., "A Window Protocol for Transmission of Time-Constrained Messages," *IEEE Trans. Computers*, Vol. 39, No. 9, 1990. ©IEEE 1990. Reprinted with permission.)

detected by noting that the bus has been idle for at least one slot. The node then transmits its message on the channel at the beginning of the next slot provided that the LTTT of that message is within the current window. If more than one node starts transmitting in the same slot, the packets collide. This collision is detected, and both transmissions are aborted. The nodes now cause the window to contract, and then only those messages that have LTTTs within the contracted window are transmitted. If there is only one such message, the transmission is successful. If there is more than one message, there is another collision and the window contracts again.

If the contraction of the window is followed by silence on the bus, it means that none of the packets has an LTTT within the current window. The window must then either be expanded or translated to the right.

If there is a collision despite the window's shrinking to one slot, it means that there are multiple packets with the same LTTT. Then, each node

- with probability p, retransmits its message in the next slot (p is a design parameter set by the user or designer), or

```
Procedure contract_window_and_send(up, t);
BEGIN
    if (up > t) then
        if (up > t+1) then
            if this node was involved in the collision then
                i = identifier of its message that collided;
            else
                i = 0;
            end if;
            push (up,i) onto the stack;
            up = t + ⌈ (up - t)/2 ⌉;
            send out the message if its LTTT is in [t,up);
        else
            if (this node was involved in the collision) then
                if (Random(0,1) > P)
                    retransmit message that collided;
                else
                    if (t is the latest time to transmit
                        the message to meet its deadline) then
                        discard the message that collided;
                    else
                        LTTT_M = Random(t+2, D_M-T_M);
                            /*M is the collided message*
                    end if;
                end if;
            end if;
        end if;
    else
        pop_and_send(up,t);
    end if;
END;
```

FIGURE 6.23
Procedure contract_window_and_send. (W. Zhao, et al., "A Window Protocol for Transmission of Time-Constrained Messages," *IEEE Trans. Computers*, Vol. 39, No. 9, 1990. © IEEE 1990. Reprinted with permission.)

- with probability $(1 - p)$, it does not retransmit in the next slot, but reassigns to the message a new randomly-generated LTTT (which will still enable the message deadline to be met). If this is not possible (i.e., the message must be transmitted in this slot or it will miss its deadline), the message is discarded.

At the end of this operation, the window is also modified suitably.

Correctly managing the window size is central to the success of this algorithm. If the size is very small, the likelihood increases that the channel will be

```
Procedure pop_and_send(up, t);
BEGIN
    if the stack is non-empty, then
        Pop the stack and set (up = u field of popped item)
    else
        up = max(up, t) + δ;
    end if;
    transmit the message with smallest LTTT
        if its LTTT is in [t,up);
END
```

FIGURE 6.24

Procedure pop_and_send. (W. Zhao, et al., "A Window Protocol for Transmission of Time-Constrained Messages," *IEEE Trans. Computers*, Vol. 39, No. 9, 1990. ©IEEE 1990. Reprinted with permission.)

```
Procedure expand_window_and_send(up, t);

BEGIN
    if the stack is empty, then
        up = t + δ;
        Send out message, if any, with minimum LTTT which is in [t,up);
    else
        u_top = the u field of the top item in the stack;
        i_top = the i field of the top item in the stack;
        if (up < u_top - 1 ) then
            up = ⌈ (up + u_top)/2 ⌉;
            Send out message, if any, with minimum LTTT which is in [t,up);
        else /* there is a tie between the LTTT of two messages*/
            if there is a message M in the queue with
            identifier equal to i_top, then
            if Random(0,1) > P
                transmit M;
            else
                set LTTT_M = Random(t + 2, D_M - τ_M);
            end if;
        end if;
        Pop the stack and set up = u field of popped item.
    END;
```

FIGURE 6.25

Procedure expand_window_and_send. (W. Zhao, et al., "A Window Protocol for Transmission of Time-Constrained Messages," *IEEE Trans. Computers*, Vol. 39, No. 9, 1990. ©IEEE 1990. Reprinted with permission.)

idle even though nodes have packets to transmit. If it is too large, the likelihood of collisions increases.

> **Example 6.13.** Let us consider the performance of this algorithm for a system consisting of three nodes, N_1, N_2, and N_3. We use $\delta = 20$, and assume each message takes one slot to transmit. Assume that, when the algorithm starts, nodes N_1, N_2, N_3 each has one packet awaiting transmission with LTTT values 19, 19, and 3, respectively. The identifier of each of these packets is 1. No other packets arrive over the first dozen slots.
>
> At the beginning of slot 0, the window is set by each node to [0,20). Since each node has a packet in this window, they all attempt to transmit. There is a collision and it is detected by the end of the slot. In slot 1, the channel is idle after a collision. At the beginning of slot 2, each node contracts its window to [2,11). The three nodes each push (20,1) into their respective stacks. Only N_3 has a packet whose LTTT falls within this new window, and it transmits successfully. This transmission is completed by the end of slot 2, and the channel is idle following a successful transmission during slot 3.
>
> At the beginning of slot 4, the nodes run the pop_and_send algorithm. The value of up is changed from 11 back to 20. The window is now [4,20). Nodes N_1 and N_2 both attempt to transmit and then collide. The channel is idle following another collision during slot 5.
>
> At the beginning of slot 6, the nodes run the contract_window_and_send algorithm. The previous value of up is pushed into the stack, and the new value is calculated as $6 + \lceil (20-6)/2 \rceil = 13$. Neither N_1 nor N_2 can transmit in this window, and so the channel continues to be idle during slot 6. At the beginning of slot 7, the nodes run the expand_window_and_send algorithm. Since up $= 13 < 20 - 1$, the value of up is reset to $\lceil (13 + 20)/2 \rceil = 17$. The window is now [7,17); N_1 and N_2 still cannot transmit.
>
> At the beginning of slot 8, the nodes run the expand_window_and_send algorithm again. The value of up is now changed to $\lceil (17 + 20)/2 \rceil = 19$. Once again, since the window is [8,19), no transmission takes place (note that the window is open at the right, i.e., the LTTT of 19 is not covered by it).
>
> At the beginning of slot 9, the nodes run the expand_window_and_send algorithm again. However, since up $= 20 - 1$, we now detect a tie in LTTT values. Suppose N_1 goes ahead and transmits during this interval while N_2 resets its LTTT to 16. The channel is idle following a successful transmission during slot 10. At the beginning of slot 11, the pop_and_send algorithm is run by each node. This results in N_2 transmitting successfully.
>
> Now, suppose that δ is 10 instead of 20. In such a case, the initial window is [0,10), and N_3 is successful in transmitting during slot 0. The reader is invited to list what happens following this slot in this case.

Performance of the window algorithm. No analytical model of the window algorithm has yet been published. However, some simulation studies were carried out for a Poisson message arrival process, and the following conclusions can be drawn from them:[2]

---

[2] Keep in mind that these conclusions may or may not be valid for non-Poisson processes.

- The window algorithm was compared to an idealized centralized algorithm, which featured a central controller, with instantaneous knowledge of the state of each node (e.g., the contents of each buffer, etc.). Centralization does away with the collisions, since the central controller decides which node is to transmit at any one time. However, since the overheads associated with the collection of the status information and with the dissemination of the control instructions are assumed to be zero, this centralized algorithm is not realizable in practice. The simulation studies indicate that the window protocol performs close to that of the centralized algorithm.

- It appears that the window protocol is relatively insensitive to the value of δ.

- As with other collision-detection protocols, this protocol exhibits a deadline anomaly: If the deadlines of some messages are relaxed, this can actually worsen system performance.

DISCUSSION. Contention protocols are best when the traffic is light, and the ratio

$$\frac{\text{End-to-end transmission delay}}{\text{Time to transmit a bit}}$$

is low. If the traffic is heavy, then the probability of collisions (and thus the number of aborted transmissions) increases, and bandwidth is wasted. If the delay-to-bit-transmission-time ratio is high, a large number of bits may have been transmitted by the time a collision is detected. A packet affected by a collision has to be retransmitted in its entirety, and so any bits transmitted before a collision is detected waste the network bandwidth.

6.3.2   Token-based Protocols

A *token* is a grant of permission to a node to transmit its packets on the network. When the token-holding node completes its transmission, it surrenders the token to another node. A node is only permitted to transmit on the network if it currently holds the token.

> **Example 6.14.** Token protocols are typically run on buses or rings. An example of a typical ring structure is shown in Figure 6.26. It consists of two rings, with one carrying traffic clockwise and the other counterclockwise. When everything is operational, we have two independent rings operating. If a link on the ring fails, we can reconfigure what is left into a single ring; see Figure 6.27. Similarly, there is the capability to bypass a failed or powered-down node.
>
> Each ring has a token circulating in the appropriate direction. When a node receives the token, it is allowed to start transmitting its messages. It puts them out on the ring. Every other node's network interface receives and then retransmits the packet. When the packet returns to the sender, this node then removes as much of it from the ring as it can. Any remaining fragments of the packet are removed by whichever node currently has the token.
>
> The reason that a node cannot always remove its entire packet from the ring is that it is not until after it has read the source address field that it knows that it was the sender of the packet. By that time, it may have retransmitted the earlier

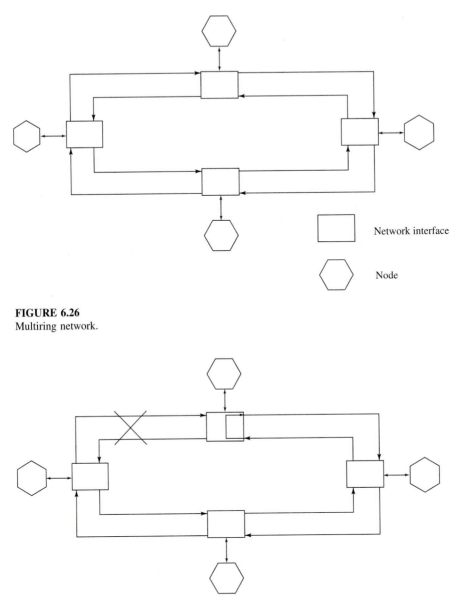

FIGURE 6.26
Multiring network.

FIGURE 6.27
Dealing with failure in a multiring network.

bits of the packet—this constitutes the remaining fragment that is then removed by the current token-holding node. A token-holding node removes from the ring all the packets that it receives. Thus, if the sender of a packet is still holding the token when one of its packets returns to it, it will remove that packet entirely.

Token algorithms incur the following overheads:

Medium propagation delay: It takes a certain time for a message to propagate from one node to the next.

Token transmission time: Sending out the token takes some time. Since the token is usually much smaller than a frame that contains information, this overhead is typically very small.

Token capture delay: There is usually some time lag between when a node captures the token and when it begins transmitting.

Network interface latency: At each network interface, the input is retransmitted to the output (except for packets that are removed from the ring). The network interface latency is the time between when a bit is received by the network interface and when it is retransmitted.

Token-based protocols are better suited to optical networks than collision-sensing because the ratio of the end-to-end delay time to the time taken in putting out a packet on the ring is large in such networks.

TIMED-TOKEN PROTOCOL. The timed-token protocol is a simple mechanism by which each node is guaranteed timely access to the network. It distinguishes between two basic classes of traffic, synchronous and asynchronous. *Synchronous traffic* is the real-time traffic; the protocol guarantees that each node can send out up to a certain amount of synchronous traffic every T time units. *Asynchronous traffic* is nonreal-time traffic that takes up any bandwidth left unused by the synchronous traffic. It can itself consist of multiple priority classes, but we shall not concern ourselves with that here. We will concentrate solely on the way this protocol handles the synchronous traffic.

The key control parameter of this protocol is the target token-rotation time, TTRT. The protocol attempts to ensure that the cycle time of the token (i.e., the time for the token to make a complete circuit around the nodes of the network) is no more than the TTRT. This is not always possible. However, as we see below, it is possible to guarantee that, barring network failures, the token cycle time is no more than twice the target time ($2 \times$ TTRT). Every time the token visits it, a node is allowed to transmit up to a preassigned quota of synchronous traffic. Thus, if it is necessary to ensure that each node can send out some synchronous traffic once every T units, we can set the TTRT $= T/2$. TTRT can thus be set by interaction between the nodes. Each node indicates the maximum acceptable interval between two successive visits by the token to that node. The minimum of these times is halved, and set as the TTRT, so that the constraints of all the nodes are met. We will return to the choice of the TTRT below.

The total volume of synchronous traffic that can be transmitted during any cycle is easy to calculate. Denote by B the bandwidth of the network in bits per unit time, and by Θ the control overhead per cycle. Then, the time available to carry packets per cycle is given by

$$t_p = \text{TTRT} - \Theta$$

and the total number of bits of traffic that the network can support during a cycle is given by Bt_p. Each node i is allocated a fraction of this quantity, f_i, that it can transmit during any cycle. That is, it is allocated a quota of $f_i t_p B$ bits of synchronous traffic that it may transmit during any one cycle.

We now have the background to describe the timed-token protocol. When the system begins operating, no data packets are transmitted during the first cycle. Instead, the nodes spend the first cycle determining the value of the TTRT. They do this by broadcasting the value they want (recall that if a node wishes to be able to broadcast at least once every T time units, it needs TTRT $= T/2$), and picking the smallest value requested. During the second cycle of the token, only synchronous traffic is transmitted. The steady-state portion of the algorithm after the end of the second cycle is shown in Figure 6.28. When the token arrives, the node checks to see if the cycle time (i.e., the duration between the current time and the previous arrival time of the token at that node) is greater than the TTRT. If it is, the token is said to be *late*; it transmits only its synchronous traffic (up to the prescribed maximum) and passes on the token to the next node. If it is not (i.e., the token is *early*), it transmits not only the synchronous traffic, but also a certain amount of asynchronous traffic, if it has any awaiting transmission.

How does each node decide how much of its asynchronous traffic to transmit per cycle? There are many ways to do this. The standard way is to allow a packet of asynchronous traffic to begin transmitting so long as the token is not late. That is, if the token was last released by a node n at time t, it will not be allowed to start

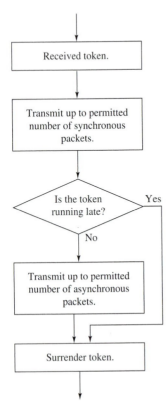

FIGURE 6.28
Flowchart of the timed-token protocol after the second cycle.

transmitting an asynchronous packet if the current time is later than $t +$ TTRT. Note that under this approach, it is possible to have *asynchronous overrun*; that is, it is possible to start transmitting an asynchronous packet just before $t +$ TTRT so that the token is late when the packet is completed. Asynchronous overrun can be regarded as another component of the overhead.

Asynchronous overrun can be easily avoided by not starting an asynchronous packet unless we can ensure that the duration between when the token is given up by this node during the current cycle and when it was given up during the last cycle is no greater than the TTRT. This ensures that the target token-rotation time is not exceeded due to the asynchronous traffic. It is possible to show, although we will not provide the proof here, that the average token-cycle time is no greater than the TTRT.

Protocol analysis. The timed-token protocol is attractive to real-time engineers because it guarantees that the token-cycle time is bounded.

> **Theorem 6.1.** In the absence of failures, the maximum cycle time of the token is no greater than twice the TTRT.

> **Proof.** For ease of exposition, we ignore the impact of the overhead in this proof; incorporating the overhead into the result is quite simple, and is left as an exercise.
>
> Denote by (a, b) the ath visit of the token to node b. That is, it is the visit to node b of the token in the ath cycle. Let $t(a, b)$ denote the time when the token completes its ath visit to node b. The ath token-cycle time, $C(a, b)$ as seen by node b, $C(a, b)$, is defined as $C(a, b) = t(a, b) - t(a - 1, b)$. That is, it is the interval between when the token left node b during its ath visit and when it left node b during its $(a - 1)$st visit. Figure 6.29 illustrates this.
>
> Let $S(x, y)$ and $A(x, y)$ denote the volume of the synchronous and asynchronous traffic, respectively, transmitted during (x, y). Consider visit (a, b) of the token. We now consider three cases.
>
> > **Case 1.** The token has been early or on time throughout the entire cycle preceding visit (a, b). That is, it has not been late during any of the visits

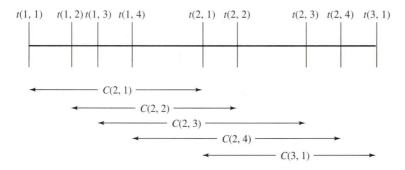

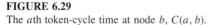

FIGURE 6.29
The ath token-cycle time at node b, $C(a, b)$.

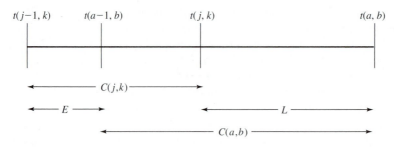

FIGURE 6.30
Case 3: when the token is early for part of the cycle.

$(a - 1, b + 1), \cdots, (a - 1, b - 1), (a, b).$[3] In such a case, there is nothing to prove. The cycle time has, by definition, been less than the TTRT throughout that cycle.

Case 2. The token has been late throughout the entire cycle preceding visit (a, b). In such a case, none of the nodes during this sequence of visits has been allowed to transmit asynchronous traffic; each has transmitted only its quota of synchronous traffic. Since we are ignoring overhead, this means that

$$C(a, b) = \sum_{x,y=a-1,b+1}^{a,b} S(x, y)$$

$$\leq \text{TTRT} \sum_{x,y=a-1,b+1}^{a,b} f_i$$

$$\leq \text{TTRT}$$

indicating that there cannot be two consecutive cycles of duration greater than the TTRT.

Case 3. The token has been early for part of the cycle preceding (a, b). Let (j, k) be the visit preceding (a, b) for which the token was early. See Figure 6.30. Since the token was early at $t(j, k)$, by definition,

$$C(j, k) \leq \text{TTRT}$$

The token is late over the entire interval L, and so only synchronous traffic is broadcast during that time. From Figure 6.30, we have:

$$C(a, b) = C(j, k) - E + L$$

$$\leq \text{TTRT} - E + \sum_{x,y=j,k}^{a,b} S(x, y)$$

$$\leq \text{TTRT} + \sum_{x,y=j,k}^{a,b} S(x, y)$$

---

[3]All additions are modulo the ring, i.e., if $b = N$, $(a - 1, b + 1)$ is really $(a, 1)$, where $N =$ number of nodes.

$$\leq \text{TTRT} + \text{TTRT}$$

$$= 2\text{TTRT}$$

This completes the proof. **Q.E.D.**

Theorem 6.2, which we state without proof, generalizes Theorem 6.1.

Theorem 6.2. The total duration of ℓ consecutive cycles of the token is upper-bounded by $(\ell + 1)\text{TTRT}$, for $\ell = 1, 2, \ldots$.

Corollary 6.1. It follows from Theorem 6.2 that over any interval of duration τ, node n_i will be able to transmit at least

$$\left\lfloor \frac{\tau}{\text{TTRT}} - 1 \right\rfloor f_i t_p B$$

bits.

What impact does the choice of TTRT have on the available bandwidth? The overhead Θ is essentially a constant per cycle, regardless of the volume of data transmitted.[4] So, if the cycle time is the TTRT, the useful time available per cycle is $\text{TTRT} - \Theta$, which means that the utilization of the ring is upper-bounded by

$$\Psi = \frac{\text{TTRT} - \Theta}{\text{TTRT}}$$

We therefore have a tradeoff between the upper bound of the delay, which we have shown to be $2 \times \text{TTRT}$, and the throughput, which is $\Psi \times B$ (the channel bandwidth).

Supporting periodic message loads. The timed-token protocol is well suited to supporting periodic message loads. Suppose that over every period P_i, node n_i has to transmit c_i bits of real-time traffic. Since the token-rotation time is upper-bounded by 2TTRT, the following constraint must be satisfied

$$\text{TTRT} \leq \frac{P_i}{2} \qquad (6.4)$$

to guarantee that node n_i will have a chance to transmit at least once every P_i seconds, for all i.

Having fixed the TTRT, our next step is to allocate the synchronous quota. From Corollary 6.1, we immediately have:

$$\left\lfloor \frac{P_i}{\text{TTRT}} - 1 \right\rfloor f_i t_p B \geq c_i \qquad (6.5)$$

as the condition necessary to guarantee that node n_i has a sufficient synchronous quota. Equation (6.5) can be solved for f_i. Equations (6.4) and (6.5) are necessary

---

[4] We assume that asynchronous overrun is prevented from occurring.

and sufficient conditions for node n_i to be able to transmit c_i bits of real-time traffic every P_i seconds.

Who sets the value of f_i? The simple approach is for some central authority to set it to satisfy the necessary and sufficient conditions. However, if c_i changes rapidly with time, this may impose an unacceptable overhead on the system. In such a case, we would like to give each node n_i the freedom to pick its own f_i. The following theorem, stated without proof, provides the answer.

> **Theorem 6.3.** If the system consists of nodes $n_1, \ldots, n_m$, let each node n_i pick the minimum f_i so that the constraint in Equation (6.5) is satisfied for $i = 1, \ldots m$. Let
>
> $$\text{TTRT} = \min\left\{\frac{P_1}{2}, \frac{P_2}{2}, \ldots, \frac{P_m}{2}\right\} \qquad (6.6)$$
>
> Then, so long as
>
> $$\sum_{i=1}^{m} \frac{c_i}{P_i} \leq \frac{1 - \Theta/\text{TTRT}}{3} \qquad (6.7)$$
>
> every node n_i will be able to transmit c_i bits of synchronous traffic every P_i seconds.

Fault-tolerance. Since a token loss can bring the entire network to a halt, fault-detection and recovery are important in token-based protocols. We have already proved that, under normal operation, the token cannot be late at any station for two consecutive cycles—this is an indication of failure. Ring recovery involves the nodes again negotiating the value of the TTRT; each node i announces TTRT(i), the value of the token-rotation time that it desires, and transmission is restarted with the node that has requested the smallest value. In the event that more than one node has requested the smallest value, the tie is broken by selecting from among them the node with the smallest index. This policy is easy to implement. When a node starts ring recovery, it continuously sends out *claim-token* packets, which contain the value of TTRT requested by that node. When a node receives a claim-token packet, it follows the procedure depicted in Figure 6.31. It is easy to see that only one node will receive its own claim-token packet back; this is the node that will reinitiate transmission. If there is a physical break in the ring or some similar malfunction, no node will receive its claim-token packet back.

Note that every node i should receive either the claim-token packet back or a normal packet within TTRT(i) after it transmitted the claim-token packet. If this does not happen, that is an indication of either another loss of the token, or a loss of the message, or a physical malfunction. To identify physical malfunctions, beacon packets are used, as shown in Figure 6.32. If there is a break in the ring, the only node that will keep transmitting is the station immediately downstream from the break. The system software that controls the ring must then decide how to reconfigure it, by switching in backup links if necessary and available, to restore functioning.

If the deadlines are so short that the delays associated with such recovery techniques are unacceptable, we can use forward error masking. Instead of one physical fiber, we use N and give each processor one physically distinct interface connecting it to each of the fibers. Then we transmit N copies of everything.

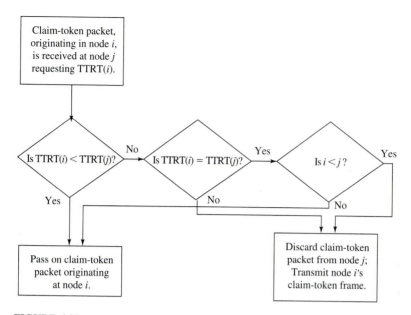

FIGURE 6.31
Handling the claim-token packet.

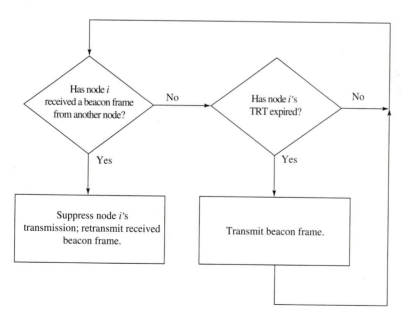

FIGURE 6.32
Beacon packet transmission.

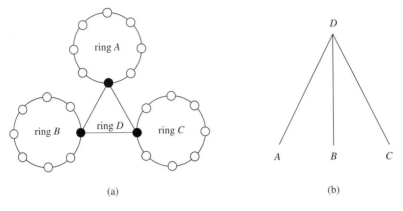

FIGURE 6.33
A two-level structure of rings: (a) ring structure; (b) ring hierarchy.

Use of the timed-token protocol in hierarchical networks. The timed-token protocol can also be used in hierarchical networks, where the nodes are connected in rings and the rings are connected to other rings to form additional levels.

> **Example 6.15.** Figure 6.33 shows a two-level ring structure. Figure 6.33b shows the hierarchy of the four rings. The black nodes in Figure 6.33a are the interconnecting elements, which are responsible for forwarding packets between rings. There is one token circulating through all four rings. A message that originates in ring A and is destined for a node in ring C is sent to the interconnecting element of A, then travels on ring D to the interconnecting element of C, and finally travels on ring C to its destination.

As mentioned earlier in Section 6.1.1, it is frequently necessary to use multiplexing techniques to divide the fiber channel into virtual subchannels in order to better utilize the very large raw fiber bandwidth. It is possible to use the timed-token protocol in such multichannel systems, with one token circulating along each channel.

IEEE 802.5 TOKEN-RING PROTOCOL. In this section, we look at how the RM algorithm (see Chapter 3) can be implemented on the standard IEEE 802.5 token-ring protocol.

Some 802.5 basics. The token and data packet[5] formats are shown in Figure 6.34. The starting and ending delimiters indicate the start and end of the token or data frame. The frame control field indicates that it is a data frame, and the frame status indicates whether or not the destination is present, powered up, and the message has been received successfully. In particular, if FS $= 00$, it means that

---

[5]The term *frame* is used synonymously with *packet* in this discussion.

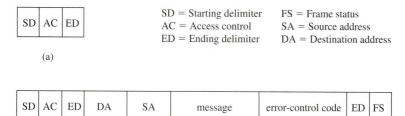

SD = Starting delimiter   FS = Frame status
AC = Access control   SA = Source address
ED = Ending delimiter   DA = Destination address

(a)

| SD | AC | ED | DA | SA | message | error-control code | ED | FS |

(b)

FIGURE 6.34
(a) Token format; (b) data packet format.

the destination node was not available (e.g., it was not powered up or was faulty). If FS = 10, the frame could not copied at the destination, although the destination was available. If FS = 11, the frame was successfully received by its destination. The FS field is checked by the sender when the data frame comes back to it. The sender removes the data frame from the ring when it returns after making one round trip of the ring.

Of particular interest to us is the priority arbitration scheme in this protocol. The access control field contains three bits for the current and reserved priorities. Suppose the highest-priority message at node n_i has priority p_i. When a data frame or token goes by, n_i checks the reserved priority (or reservation) bits. If these indicate a priority greater than or equal to p_i, it does nothing; there is another node wishing to use the network with a message of higher or equal priority. If the reserved priority bits indicate a priority of less than p_i, n_i writes priority p_i onto the reservation field. When the current data transmission has been completed, the sender issues a token with the priority level indicated by the reservation bits.

> **Example 6.16.** Consider a five-node ring, with the highest priorities of the packets awaiting service at the nodes being 2, 4, 1, 6, and 8, at n_1, n_2, n_3, n_4 and n_5, respectively. (The lower the priority index, the greater the priority). The ring is currently serving node n_1. n_1 writes priority 2 in the reservation bits of its data frame and sends it out. n_2 does not change it, since its highest-priority message has lower priority than that. However, node n_3 has a higher priority message, and so writes its priority onto the reservation field. Nodes n_4 and n_5 have lower priority packets, and so they do not update the reservation field.
>
> When the packet returns to node n_1, the node generates a token of priority 1 and sends it out. This token cannot be captured by either n_1 or n_2, since they have lower priority. It is seized by n_3, which then starts transmitting its data packet.

A node that increases the priority of the reservation field is also responsible for reducing it to its prior value. Otherwise, the token priority would never decrease! A node may hold the token for at most a preset token-holding time (the default is 10 ms). Of course, the same node may seize the token multiple times in succession if its message priority equals or exceeds the value written into the reservation field.

A key parameter of the ring is the *walk time* W_T, which is the time it takes a token to make a complete circuit of the ring. It can be shown that the walk time in an n-node system is given by

$$W_T = (n-1)D_B + L + T_{\text{prop}} \tag{6.8}$$

where

n	Number of nodes in the ring.
D_B	Station delay; delay caused by each node.
L	Buffer latency.
T_{prop}	Message propagation time round the ring.

Schedulability analysis. We make the assumption that the traffic consists of a periodic load whose deadline is upper-bounded by the period. Scheduling packets for transmission is different from scheduling tasks in the following respects.

- A packet transmission cannot be preempted and then resumed without penalty; if a packet transmission is interrupted, it has to be retransmitted all over again.
- Overhead is incurred in transmitting a message. It is not just the message bits that are transmitted, but also a header (consisting of the SD, AC, ED, and destination and source fields) and a trailer associated with each packet.
- Since the system is distributed, decisions as to which packet has the highest priority may be made on the basis of outdated information.

Example 6.17. Consider the token ring shown in Figure 6.35. Node n_1 has traffic generated at periods of 5, 6, and 10, respectively; n_2 periods of 5, 9, and 11, n_3 periods of 4 and 6, and n_4 of period 10. Table 6.3 shows the priorities of the packets[6] awaiting transmission on each node along with their arrival time.

Consider what happens when the token flows past the four nodes at times 6, 7, 9, and 10, respectively. At time 6, node n_1 writes the priority of its most important packet on the reservation field. At time 7, n_2's highest priority is the same, so it does not overwrite the reservation field. At time 9, when the token goes past it,

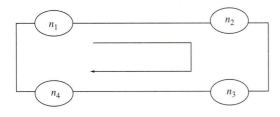

FIGURE 6.35
Token ring for Example 6.17.

---

[6]The lower the priority number, the higher the priority.

TABLE 6.3
Packet priorities and
arrival times

Node	(Period, arrival time)
n_1	(5, 5), (6, 6), (10, 10)
n_2	(5, 5), (9, 9), (11, 11)
n_3	(5, 5), (4, 10)
n_4	(10, 10)

n_3's highest priority is also the same, and so again the token reservation bits are not changed. The reservation bits are also unchanged by n_4. Suppose the token returns to n_1 at time 12. The reservation bits allow transmission of a packet with period 5. Since n_1 has a packet of this period, it is allowed to transmit. At this time, though, it is not n_1 but n_3 that has the highest-priority packet (of period 4). However, n_3 will not have a chance to update the reservation bits until the next transit of the token, and so the decision to allow n_1 to transmit is based on outdated information.

We can now write the necessary and sufficient conditions for the set of tasks to be schedulable. Let d_i be the deadline associated with task T_i; we assume $d_i \le P_i$. b_i is the maximum time for which a T_i packet can be blocked.

Theorem 6.4. The task set $T_1, T_2, \ldots, T_n$ is schedulable iff for all $i = 1, \ldots, n$, there is some t, $0 < t \le d_i$ such that

$$\sum_{j=1}^{i} e_j \left\lceil \frac{t}{P_j} \right\rceil + \text{System overhead} + b_i \le t \qquad (6.9)$$

Proof. This is virtually identical to the corresponding result for uniprocessor scheduling in Section 3.2.1 (in Handling Critical Sections) and therefore the proof is omitted.

The necessary and sufficient conditions for schedulability require us to know e_j, P_j, b_j, and the system overhead. Of these, P_j is defined by the application, and the system overhead is defined by the system. This leaves e_j and b_j.

e_j is the execution time associated with sending a message of T_j. It has three components.

1. The time it takes to capture the token when the node has the highest-priority message. Even when a correct reservation has been made and blocking by a lower-priority packet does not occur, this can be as large as W_T per packet. For example, the node that currently owns the token may have the highest priority message to transmit next, but it still needs to send the token through all the other nodes before it can send out the next packet.

2. The time it takes to transmit the message. Suppose we are given that T_j transmits a message of up to m_j bits every P_j seconds. Let m_{enc} be the number of bits in the encapsulation part of each packet (i.e., the portion of the packet that is

not the message bits). Then, each packet can carry up to $m_{\text{payload}} = P_{\max} - m_{\text{enc}}$ message bits. To transmit m_j bits of message thus requires $\lceil m_j/m_{\text{payload}} \rceil$ packets. The total number of bits transmitted for a total of m_j message bits is thus $m_j + \lceil m_j/m_{\text{payload}} \rceil m_{\text{enc}}$ bits. If the ring can transmit at the rate of b bits a second, this takes a total of

$$\tau_{\text{trans}} = \frac{m_j + \lceil m_j/m_{\text{payload}} \rceil m_{\text{enc}}}{b} \tag{6.10}$$

seconds.

3. The time it takes to transmit the token when the packet transmission is over. This is given by τ_{token}, which is a system parameter.

Denote by τ_{SA} the time taken for the sending node to receive the SA part of the packet back on the ring. Now, consider two cases.

Case 1. The message fits within one packet. If $m_j + m_{\text{enc}} \geq W_T + \tau_{\text{SA}}$, the transmitting node will have received back the header of its own packet before it finishes transmitting the packet, and recognized it as its own. Hence, the moment that packet transmission ceases, a new token can be issued. For this case, we therefore have $e_j = W_T + \tau_{\text{trans}} + \tau_{\text{token}}$. If, on the other hand, $m_j + m_{\text{enc}} < W_T + \tau_{\text{SA}}$, then the transmitting node will have to wait until it gets the SA field of its own packet. For this case, $e_j = 2W_T + \tau_{\text{SA}} + \tau_{\text{token}}$. We can therefore write:

$$e_j = \begin{cases} W_T + \tau_{\text{trans}} + \tau_{\text{token}} & \text{if } m_j + m_{\text{enc}} \geq W_T + \tau_{\text{SA}} \\ 2W_T + \tau_{\text{SA}} + \tau_{\text{token}} & \text{otherwise} \end{cases} \tag{6.11}$$

Case 2. The message fits within multiple packets. The reasoning is the same as for Case 1, except that we have to account for multiple waits for the token. The packets will each be of size $P_{\max}$, except possibly the last one, which may be smaller. Let us make the approximation that all the packets are of size $P_{\max}$. Following exactly the reasoning in Case 1, we can write:

$$e_j \approx \begin{cases} m_j + \lceil m_j/m_{\text{payload}} \rceil (\tau_{\text{trans}} + W_T + \tau_{\text{token}}) & \text{if } W_T + \tau_{\text{SA}} \leq P_{\max} \\ \lceil m_j/m_{\text{payload}} \rceil (2W_T + \tau_{\text{SA}} + \tau_{\text{token}}) & \text{otherwise} \end{cases} \tag{6.12}$$

Deriving b_j, the maximum time for which a T_j packet can be blocked, is somewhat simpler. The worst-case blocking occurs if a higher-priority packet arrives just after the reservation bits associated with the a lower-priority transmission have gone past it, and there is another lower-priority packet that has been successful in setting its reservation bits. We saw an illustration of this in Example 6.17. In such a case, the higher-priority packet will have to wait until after both the ongoing and the following transmission have completed. From this, and using reasoning similar to that of the derivation for e_j, it is possible to show that

$$b_j \leq \begin{cases} 2(P_{\max} + \tau_{\text{token}}) + W_T & \text{if } W_T + \tau_{\text{SA}} \leq P_{\max} \\ 2(W_T + \tau_{\text{SA}} + \tau_{\text{token}}) + W_T & \text{otherwise} \end{cases} \tag{6.13}$$

Some implementation issues. In our derivation, we have assumed that there are enough reservation bits to express the full range of priority levels. The 802.5

standard specifies three priority bits; that is, it can support up to eight priority levels. If the number of task priority classes is greater than eight, the only recourse is to map multiple task-priority classes into the same ring-priority levels. This can cause additional blocking.

> **Example 6.18.** Suppose we have a total of 16 task priority classes. Since we only have eight priority levels in the ring, we can group priority classes $(2i - 1)$ and $2i$ into ring-priority level i. Thus, priority classes 1 and 2 will be grouped into ring-priority level 1; classes 3 and 4 into ring-priority level 2, and so on. As the ring gives the same priority to both classes 3 and 4, and this may cause a class-3 packet to be blocked by a class-4 packet.

If possible, the implementation should therefore be modified to allow additional priority levels to be supported. In retrospect, it is unfortunate that the 802.5 standard specifies only three bits for priority. Allocating just a few additional bits would have made the protocol much more useful for real-time systems.

Another issue is P_{max}, the maximum packet size. If this is very small, the overhead associated with the encapsulating bits will be dominant. If it is very large, this can increase packet blocking. P_{max} must be chosen carefully, based on the designer's knowledge of the application.

6.3.3   Stop-and-Go Multihop Protocol

The stop-and-go protocol is another technique to meet hard deadlines on packet-delivery times. Unlike the previous algorithms, it is a multihop packet delivery algorithm (i.e., there is not necessarily a direct link between source and destination).

The algorithm meets hard deadlines by assigning fractions of the available bandwidth on each channel to several traffic classes in such a way that the time it takes to traverse each of the hops from source to destination is bounded. The upper bound to the overall packet-delivery time is then simply the sum of the upper bounds of each hop. The algorithm also bounds the demand for buffer space.

The concept of the frame is central to this algorithm. A *frame* is defined as an interval of time. Frames are associated with network links and are not synchronized across links. There can be multiple frame types, each defined as a different interval of time. We can visualize the generation of a virtual `frame-begin` signal at the input end of each link at appropriate times. This signal travels down the link and defines the beginning of the frame at each point at which it arrives. That is, the frame-beginning time varies from point to point along the link. An instance of a frame of type f_i ends when the next instance of f_i begins.

Each frame type is associated with a traffic class. When a packet associated with frame type f_i, called a type-i packet, arrives at an intermediate node n en route to its destination, it is held by node n at least until the beginning of the next instance of its frame f_i, and is transmitted during that frame. As long as we can suitably bound the number of packets associated with each frame type, we can

FIGURE 6.36
A two-hop path.

ensure that there will be time enough in each frame for every packet associated with that frame type to be transmitted during it.

> **Example 6.19.** Consider a type-1 packet, that is, one associated with frame type f_1, which must travel from node n_1 to node n_3 through node n_2. See Figure 6.36. There are two hops to the path taken by the packet. Let the propagation time over the link $\ell_{12} = n_1 \rightarrow n_2$ and $\ell_{23} = n_2 \rightarrow n_3$ be τ_{12} and τ_{23}, respectively. Figure 6.37 shows frames of type f_1 at the beginning and end of ℓ_{12} and ℓ_{23}, respectively.

In what follows, we will assume, without loss of generality, that $f_1 > f_2 > \cdots > f_{N_f}$, where there are N_f frame types.

THE PROTOCOL. The stop-and-go protocol is a distributed algorithm; each node works independently without central control. A type-i packet that arrives at node n_j, and must be retransmitted by that node, becomes eligible for transmission only on the beginning of the following f_i frame. All nodes eligible for transmission are served in nonpreemptive priority order, with the type-i packet having priority over all type-k packets for $k < i$. The node is idle (i.e., does not transmit) only when there are no packets left to transmit.

> **Example 6.20.** Consider a node n with one incoming and one outgoing link. There are two traffic types. Figure 6.38 shows the arrival of several packets, when they become eligible for transmission, and when they are actually transmitted. Class-1 frames at the outgoing link begin at epochs α, β, γ, δ, and class-2 frames at epochs

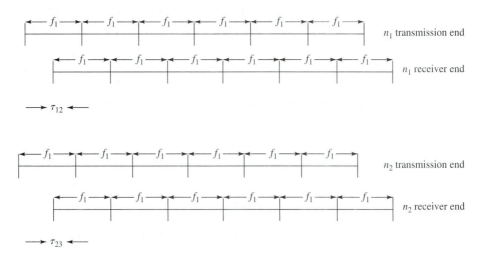

FIGURE 6.37
Frames at edges ℓ_{12} and ℓ_{23}.

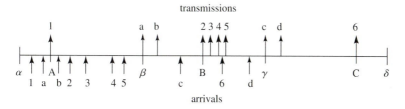

FIGURE 6.38
A two-class system.

A, B, C. There are six class-1 arrivals, labeled 1, 2, 3, 4, 5, 6, and four class-2 arrivals, labeled a, b, c, d.

PERFORMANCE. If the network loading is kept below a certain limit, a type-m packet will be transmitted within f_m time units of being marked eligible for transmission. This places an upper bound on the delay suffered by a packet at each node in the system.

More precisely, let C_ℓ^i denote the total load on link ℓ due to class-i packets, with C_ℓ denoting the total capacity of the link. Let Γ denote the maximum packet size. Then, if the following inequalities are satisfied

$$\sum_{i=j}^{N} C_\ell^i \left(1 + \left\lceil \frac{f_j}{f_i} \right\rceil \right) \frac{f_i}{f_j} - C_\ell^j \leq \begin{cases} C_\ell - \dfrac{\Gamma}{f_j} & \text{if } j = 2, \ldots, N \\ C_\ell & \text{if } j = 1 \end{cases} \tag{6.14}$$

then every type-m packet will be transmitted within f_m time units of becoming eligible. Furthermore, the buffer required per link ℓ for traffic of type i is bounded:

$$B_\ell^i < 3C_\ell^i \cdot f_i \tag{6.15}$$

For a pointer to the (somewhat lengthy) proof of this fact, we refer the reader to Section 6.4.

This algorithm therefore offers a means to meet hard deadlines on packet-delivery times by bounding the delay at each node. The time taken by a class-i packet to become eligible is at most f_i, and since it is transmitted within f_i of becoming eligible, it is not delayed by more than $2f_i$ at any node. Adding to this the message-propagation and packet-processing delays yields the upper bound on the packet-delivery delay.

Given messages of varying deadlines, the designer must provide enough link capacity, and determine what the frame sizes should be in order to meet the deadline requirements. Some of the related design issues are explored in the Exercises.

6.3.4 The Polled Bus Protocol

The polled bus protocol assumes a bus network with a bus-busy line. When a processor broadcasts on the bus, it also maintains this line high. When it finishes broadcasting, this line is reset. This can be done very easily if the line executes a *wired-OR operation*; by this we mean that if two signals a and b are put out on the line simultaneously, the resultant signal is $a.OR.b$.

All the processors are assumed to be tightly synchronized. The time axis is divided into slots. Each slot is of duration equal to the end-to-end propagation time of the bus.

When a processor has something to transmit on the bus, it checks the bus-busy line to see if it is busy. If it is, it waits until the transmission ceases. If it is not, it monitors the bus for one slot. If, during that slot, no other processor makes a request, the processor starts transmitting a poll number on the bus. This poll number is directly proportional to the priority of the message, as will become apparent in a moment.

The poll number is transmitted slowly, one bit per slot. After transmitting its bit, the processor monitors the bus to see if the signal on the bus is the same as its own output. If it is not, it means that there is a higher-priority processor asking for access, and this processor drops out of contention and stops transmitting its poll number. If, on the other hand, the bus signal is the same as the bit it transmitted at the beginning of the slot, the processor proceeds during the next slot to broadcast the next bit of the poll number. This process continues until it either sends out its entire poll number successfully (in which case, it has mastery of the bus and can start its transmission), or until it has to drop out of contention because it has detected a processor with a higher-priority message.

Let us examine this protocol. If one processor has already started transmitting its poll number no other processor can intervene, no matter what the relative priorities of their messages. If multiple processors transmit their poll numbers simultaneously, only one of them will not have dropped out by the end of the poll phase. For example, suppose there are two processors competing for the bus, with poll numbers $A = a_1 \cdots a_n$ and $B = b_1 \cdots b_n$, respectively. Since we have said that no two poll numbers can be identical (we will see later how this can be ensured), either $A > B$ or $A < B$. Suppose, without loss of generality, that $B > A$. In that case, there must be some i, $1 \le i \le n$ such that

- $a_j = b_j$ for all $1 \le j < i$ (this, obviously, only applies if $i > 1$), and
- $a_i < b_i$ (i.e., $a_i = 0, b_i = 1$).

Let B_k denote the bus output during slot k. Since the bus implements a wired-OR operation, we have

- $B_j = (a_j O R b_j) = a_j = b_j$ for all $1 \le j < i$, and
- $B_i = (a_i O R b_i) = b_i \ne a_i$.

Thus, at the end of the ith slot, the processor with poll number A will drop out of contention.

Example 6.21. Suppose $A = 01110011$, $B = 01110100$. Figure 6.39 shows what happens.

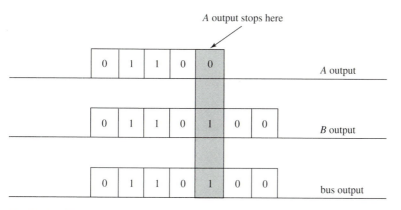

FIGURE 6.39
Poll numbers and contention resolution, Example 6.21.

If the slot duration (i.e., the end-to-end bus propagation time) is s and the poll number has p bits, then the polling procedure takes sp units of time. The value of p depends on what kind of priority scheme we are implementing. Suppose that we have a straightforward priority scheme, where each message has one of K priorities. To ensure that the poll number transmitted by each process is unique, we must append to this priority the id of the processor. If there are n_{proc} processors, then $p = \log_2 K + \log_2 n_{\mathrm{proc}}$.

Suppose, instead, that we have to implement a deadline-driven scheme. The poll number will now consist of two fields, a field containing the negative of the deadline (in 2's complement), followed by a field containing the processor id. The size of the deadline field will depend on the maximum possible deadline that is allowed (relative to some suitably-defined origin).

This approach is very versatile. Suppose, for example, that we want to implement a combined deadline-driven and priority scheme. If two messages have the same deadline, then the tie is broken on the basis of their priorities. If they have both the same deadline and the same priority level, the tie is broken based on the processor id. In such a case, we will have three fields in the poll number: one for the 2's complement of the deadline, a second for the priority, and a third for the processor id. Note that it is essential to have the processor id, since only that ensures that each processor transmits a unique poll number.

Because of the polling overhead, this algorithm is efficient only on systems with small end-to-end propagation time.

6.3.5 Hierarchical Round-Robin Protocol

This protocol guarantees that each traffic class i can transmit up to m_i packets every T_i time units, for prespecified m_i and T_i. As with the stop-and-go protocol, we can bound the delay encountered by a packet at each intermediate node. Multiplying this by the number of hops between the sender and the destination gives an upper bound for the total network delay.

All traffic is classified into n classes, for a suitable n. Associated with each traffic class i is a three-tuple (n_i, b_i, Φ_i), where Φ_i is the frame associated with class i. Assume, without loss of generality, that $\Phi_1 < \Phi_2 < \cdots < \Phi_n$. The time unit is the time taken to transmit a single packet. The maximum number of class-i packets that may be transmitted during any given frame is n_i, of which each source j can be allocated a certain maximum number $\alpha_i(j)$. If this number has been transmitted, or there are no class-i packets left for transmission, then the server goes on to serve class-$(i + 1)$ packets, if any, and so on, for a maximum of b_i packets during that class-i frame. There is no prespecified order in which the packets must be served, so long as each class receives its allotted service per frame. Also, this protocol is non-work-conserving, which is to say that it is possible for the transmitter to be idle even though there are packets awaiting transmission. This happens when these packets have exhausted their quota under the current frame and must wait for the next frame.

Example 6.22. Consider a system of three classes, with the following allocations:

i	n_i	b_i	Φ_i
1	3	3	6
2	3	1	10
3	1	0	20

Source	Class	Allocation
s_1	1	3
s_2	1	1
s_3	2	2
s_4	3	1

Figure 6.40 shows the schedule that results. In each frame Φ_1 of duration 6, class-1 traffic takes up three slots and the rest are reserved for classes 2 and 3. Similarly, in each frame Φ_2 of duration 10, class-2 traffic takes up three slots, with one being reserved for class 3.

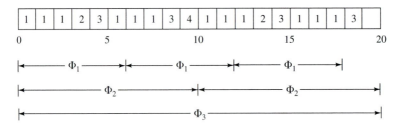

FIGURE 6.40
Schedule for hierarchical round-robin scheduling.

It is straightforward to compute the maximum delay at each hop, as well as the buffer requirements. If α_i packets are allocated to a source per frame, the buffer requirement for that source will be upper-bounded by $2\alpha_i$. The worst case will occur when α_i packets arrive at the end of one frame and another α_i at the beginning of the next. The delay at a node for class-i traffic will be upper-bounded by $2\Phi_i$. The worst-case delay occurs when a packet arrives just after the quota for its class has been exhausted, and it must wait for its next frame. It follows that messages that must be delivered quickly must have frames that are particularly short.

6.3.6 Deadline-Based Protocols

A deadline-based protocol on a point-to-point network consists of each node transmitting the packet with the earliest deadline. There are two variations on this, preemptive and nonpreemptive. In preemptive protocols, if a node receives a packet with a deadline earlier than the one it is currently transmitting, it aborts the current transmission, and starts transmitting the new arrival immediately thereafter. In nonpreemptive protocols, no interruption is allowed. It is also possible to define a continuum of protocols between these extremes, where an ongoing transmission is aborted as a function of the deadlines of the packets, and the fraction of the currently transmitted packet that has already been sent out.

The simplest version of this protocol runs on such networks as unidirectional rings, which have a unique path from any source to any destination. Here we focus on multihop systems, and present the earliest-due-date-deadline (EDD-D) protocol. This is designed with local-area networks in mind, rather than multiprocessor/distributed system interconnects, but it can be used in either setting.

When sender s wishes to be assured of real-time communication with destination d, EDD-D sets up an $s \to d$ channel that has enough capacity to meet the real-time requirements. EDD-D recognises three kinds of traffic.

Guaranteed traffic: The system must ensure that every packet in such traffic arrives by its deadline.

Statistical real-time traffic: No more than a certain percentage of these packets of any stream may miss their deadline.

Nonreal-time traffic: These packets are not deadline-sensitive and may only be sent over a link when neither of the first two classes requires it.

Associated with these traffic categories are deadline, statistical, and nonreal-time channels, respectively.

The traffic between any source-destination pair i is characterized as follows.

$x_{\min,i}$	The minimum interarrival time between successive packets.
x_{av}	The minimum of the average packet interarrival time, over some interval of duration I for a given number I.
$s_{\max}$	The maximum packet size.
$t_{\max,i}$	The maximum service time at each node for the packets.

For guaranteed traffic, we specify the packet-delivery deadline; for statistical real-time traffic, both the packet-delivery deadline and the acceptable percentage of packets that can miss that deadline.

The protocol reserves bandwidth for source-destination pairs, one by one. When source s wishes to have deadline channel i set up to destination d, the system sets up a path from s to d. If the path is of length n, up to $nt_{\max,i}$ time can be consumed in the process of storing and forwarding each packet. If the packet deadline is D_i, the available slack is $\sigma_i = D_i - nt_{\max,i}$. This slack is divided equally among all the nodes; that is, each node along the way has its own local deadline and has to forward the packet within $\delta_i = (t_{\max,i} + \sigma_i)/n$ time of receiving it.

If node s wishes a statistical real-time channel i set up to node d, the acceptable deadline-missing probability, $\pi_{\mathrm{miss},i}$ is divided among the n nodes on the $s \rightarrow d$ path. The slack time is also divided among the nodes in the same manner as for guaranteed traffic. Each node m along the $s \rightarrow d$ path must not miss this deadline with more than probability $\pi_{\mathrm{miss},i,m}$, where $\sum_m \pi_{\mathrm{miss},i,m} \leq \pi_{\mathrm{miss},i}$. We deal below with how to pick $\pi_{\mathrm{miss},i,m}$.

NODE CONSTRAINTS. All the nodes on channel i are chosen to satisfy some constraints. The following constraints are with respect to node m. We denote by D_m and S_m the set of deadline and statistical channels passing through m, respectively. We define $C_m = D_m \cup S_m$.

Deterministic constraint. The node must have enough processing capacity to deal with all the traffic that is passing through it. If C_m is the set of channels passing through node m, we must have

$$\sum_{j \in D_m} t_{\max,j}/x_{\min,j} \leq 1 \tag{6.16}$$

If this bound is not satisfied, the node will not be able to cope with all the guaranteed packets it has to deal with. Of course, this constraint is vacuous if $D_m = \emptyset$, (i.e., if node m is not carrying any guaranteed traffic).

Statistical constraint. The statistical constraint applies to nodes that are carrying statistical real-time traffic. It ensures that the fraction of packets that miss their deadline is below the specified limit. To compute this, we must calculate the probability of deadline overflow.

The probability that channel i is active (i.e., carrying packets) at a random epoch in an interval of duration I is given by

$$p_i = x_{\min,i}/x_{\mathrm{av},i} \tag{6.17}$$

The probability that at any time, channels in set $S \subset C_m$ are simultaneously active is[7]

$$\Pi(S) = \prod_{i \in S} p_i \prod_{i \in C_m - S} (1 - p_i) \tag{6.18}$$

Define an *overflow combination* as a set of channels $\Phi_m \subseteq C_m$ such that

$$\sum_{j \in \Phi_m} t_{\max, j} / x_{\min, j} > 1 \tag{6.19}$$

If channels in Φ_m are active for sufficiently long, they will overwhelm node m, and render it incapable of meeting deadlines. The probability that this happens is given by $\Pi(\Phi_m)$. If Θ_m is the set of all overflow combinations for node m, then the probability that node m will suffer deadline overflow is given by

$$P_{\text{do}, m} = \sum_{X \in \Theta_m} \Pi(X) \tag{6.20}$$

The statistical constraint is satisfied if

$$P_{\text{do}, m} \leq \pi_{\text{miss}, i, m} \tag{6.21}$$

The statistical constraint is not sufficient to ensure that the statistical traffic will perform as specified. We require a further constraint.

Scheduler saturation constraint. Scheduler saturation occurs whenever it is mathematically impossible to meet deadline constraints. For example, if a node receives two packets at times 1 and 2, respectively, each of which has a deadline of 10 and requires 9 time units to be forwarded, it is impossible to meet both deadlines. The scheduler saturation constraint is meant to check for this possibility.

Let us divide the deadline and statistical channels passing through node m into two sets as follows:

$$A = \left\{ i \middle| \delta_i < \sum_{j=1}^{\|C_m\|} t_{\max, j} \right\} \tag{6.22}$$

$$B = C_m - A \tag{6.23}$$

Without loss of generality, number the channels in set A as $1, \ldots, \|A\|$, and the channels in set B as $\|A\| + 1, \ldots, \|C_m\|$. Then, we have the scheduler saturation constraint to be

$$\delta_i \geq \sum_{j=1}^{i} t_{\max, j} + \max_{j \in C_m} t_j \tag{6.24}$$

It is not difficult to show that if Equation (6.24) is satisfied, scheduler saturation will not occur. This is left for the reader as an exercise.

---

[7]We assume that these channels are statistically independent.

Buffer space constraint. How much buffer space must be available at a node to ensure that no guaranteed or statistical packets are dropped because of insufficient space? If we assume that a packet is dropped the moment it violates its deadline, each packet of connection i will stay in node m for no more than δ_i. The maximum space needed by channel-i packets at node m will thus be

$$\beta(i, m) = s_{\max, i} \lceil \delta_i / x_{\min, i} \rceil \qquad (6.25)$$

Assume that the nonreal-time packets are dropped to make room for guaranteed or statistical packets wherever necessary. The total buffer space needed at node m is thus equal to

$$B(m) = \sum_{i \in C_m} \beta(i, m). \qquad (6.26)$$

Constraint application. All nodes must satisfy the buffer constraint if no buffer overflow is to be tolerated for the real-time traffic. A node carrying guaranteed traffic must satisfy the deterministic and scheduler saturation constraints, and a node carrying statistical traffic must satisfy the statistical and scheduler saturation constraints.

As we have said earlier, when s asks to establish a channel to d, the system picks a path from s to d such that each node on that path satisfies the appropriate constraints. If the channel being established is statistical, the nodes must be picked so that $\sum_m \pi_{\text{miss}, i, m} \leq \pi_{\text{miss}, i}$. (Alternatively, we may set $\pi_{\text{miss}, i, m} = \pi_{\text{miss}, i} / n$.) The process of establishing the channel consists mainly of trial and error. When there are multiple paths from s to d, we try them one by one until we can find a path that meets all constraints.

Each node has three queues, one each for deadline, statistical and nonreal-time traffic. The packets in the first two queues are stored in increasing order of deadline. The packets in the deadline queue may have their deadlines transformed as follows. If we have two packets whose LTTT (to meet their respective deadlines) would cause them to overlap, we move the deadline of one of them forward so that this does not happen.

> **Example 6.23.** Two packets with LTTTs of 30 and 34, respectively, have arrived. It takes five time units to transmit each of them. If we begin each packet at its LTTT, they collide. Hence, we adjust the LTTT of the first packet from 30 to $34 - 5 = 29$.

The packet to be transmitted is picked as follows. The deadline of the head-of-the-line (HOL) packet in the statistical queue is compared with the LTTT of the HOL packet in the deadline queue. If the former is no sooner than the latter, the guaranteed packet is transmitted; otherwise the statistical packet is chosen. If both the deadline and statistical queues are empty, the nonreal-time traffic is served.

It may be possible to provide better service to the nonreal-time queue by allowing its packets to be served when that can be done without any deadline or statistical packet missing its deadline.

DELAY JITTER. Let us now turn to the issue of jitter. Delay jitter is variance in the delay. In many applications, such as multimedia, the early arrival of a packet is almost as bad as a late arrival. In addition to the deadline, we can have a jitter bound for each channel. That is, we can require that packets transmitted on channel i have a source-to-destination delay in the range $[D_i - J_i, D_i]$. A guaranteed channel ensures that each packet satisfies this range; a statistical channel ensures that the probability of packet-delivery times being outside this range is below $\pi_{\text{miss}, i}$.

The EDD–D algorithm can easily be modified to bound the jitter. In addition to the LTTT, each node has an earliest-time-to-transmit. The details are left for the reader as an exercise.

6.3.7 Fault-Tolerant Routing

When there is more than one path from a source to a destination, there is the option of flooding. This is a concept borrowed from packet-radio networks. Multiple copies of the packet are transmitted, each copy along a different path, (i.e., through different sets of intermediate nodes). This guards against a single packet being delayed beyond its deadline by other packets using part of the same path. It also protects against failures that cause some paths to be broken.

The question now is how many copies to send out. The more copies of a message we send out, the greater the probability that it will reach its destination before its deadline. We might, therefore, want to send out many copies of those messages with tight deadlines. However, if we send out too many copies of such messages, other time-critical messages with later deadlines may find it impossible to reach their destinations on time, although multiple copies of the tight-deadline messages are delivered on time. Given that, on a point-to-point network, each node has only local information about the traffic, it is impossible to compute the optimal number of messages to be sent out. It is tempting to conjecture that the function for the optimal number of copies has the form shown in Figure 6.41. Packets with very tight deadlines are unlikely to encounter higher-priority packets on their way, and packets with very loose deadlines are unlikely to require multiple copies in order to meet their deadlines. The number of copies of such messages can thus be kept small. However, a proof of this, and of other characteristics of this protocol, awaits further research.

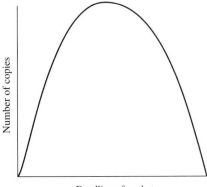

FIGURE 6.41
Possible function for the optimal number of copies.

6.4 SUGGESTIONS FOR FURTHER READING

Tannenbaum [19] is an excellent introduction to computer networks in general. The VTCSMA algorithm was invented by Molle and Kleinrock [15] for general-purpose systems, and modified for real-time traffic by Zhao and Ramamritham [22]. This reference also has detailed simulation studies of the performance of the algorithm. The window protocol is introduced by Zhao, Stankovic, and Ramamritham [23].

The timed-token protocol is described by Grow [8] and Ulm [20]. The bounds on the token-rotation time are due to Sevcik and Johnson [18] and Agrawal, Cheng, and Zhao [1]. A good description of its fault-tolerance measures is provided in Johnson [11]. The October 1989 issue of *IEEE Communications* is an excellent tutorial introduction to optical networks. Particularly noteworthy, from our point of view, are Henry [10], which is a description of optical networks, Lee and Zah [14], which describes tunable optical transmitters (lasers), and Kobrinski and Cheung [13], which is an excellent source for tunable optical receivers. See also [9] for an introduction to optical systems.

Implementing the RM algorithm atop the IEEE 802.5 protocol has been discussed by Sathaye and Strosnider [17].

Golestani [7] is the source for the discussion of the stop-and-go protocol; it contains the proof of the delay and buffer upper bounds.

The hierarchical round-robin protocol is due to Kalmanek et al. [12], and the EDD-D protocol to Ferrari and Verma [4]. A discussion of the buffer space requirements of the EDD-D protocol is provided in [5], and the modification of it to bound jitter can be found in [21].

The concept of flooding was first described in connection with packet-radio networks. See, for example, Gitman, et al. [6]. Ramanathan and Shin [16] suggested its use for real-time systems, and presented an approximate mathematical model for its analysis.

The protocols presented here are not by any means the only ones that have been studied for real-time systems. For example, Choi and Krishna [2] describe a token-based algorithm that allows a very large number of traffic classes, with time-varying priority, to share the same network. This is particularly useful when the volume of real-time traffic that a node must transmit can vary widely from cycle to cycle. Another interesting protocol is weighted fair queueing, described in [3].

EXERCISES

6.1. Consider the packet arrival times in Example 6.9 and develop a set of clock skews for which all four packets are successfully transmitted for $\eta = 2$.

6.2. We always set $\eta > 1$ in the VTCSMA algorithm. What would happen if $\eta < 1$?

6.3. Given a five-node system, assume that the packet transmission time is 1 and the end-to-end network delay is 4. This means that to meet its deadline of d, a packet must start its transmission no later than $d - 5$. Use the VTCSMA-D algorithm to do the following.

    (a) Construct a situation (i.e., arrival times and deadlines) in which all packets are transmitted successfully if $\eta = 10$, but some packets miss their deadlines if $\eta = 4$.

    (b) Construct another situation in which all packets are transmitted successfully if $\eta = 4$, but where some packets miss their deadlines if $\eta = 10$.

6.4. Assuming that the clock skews are zero, show that the VTCSMA-A, VTCSMA-T, VTCSMA-D, and VTCSMA-L implement the earliest-arrival-first, the minimum-transmission-time-first, the earliest-deadline-first, and the minimum-laxity priority algorithms, respectively.

6.5. Suppose that $\delta = 10$ in the window protocol, run on a network with four nodes. The following table shows, for each slot, the LTTT of the packet (if any) that arrived during that slot. Assume that each packet takes 2 slots to transmit. Determine when each packet is transmitted.

Slot	N_1	N_2	N_3	N_4
0	4	11		33
1			4	14
2	19	19	19	9

6.6. When two messages collide in the window protocol, due to having identical LTTT values, what would happen if the random number generators associated with the respective nodes generated the same sequence of random numbers?

6.7. Prove that if no two messages have identical LTTT values, the window protocol provides service in ascending order of LTTT. Assume clock skews to be zero.

6.8. In the window protocol, what factors should you take into account when determining the default window size δ?

6.9. Consider the use of the timed-token protocol in the following situation. We have five nodes in the system. The real-time requirement is that node n_i be able to put out up to b_i bits over each period of duration P_i, where b_i and P_i are as given in the following table:

Node	b_i	P_i
n_1	1K	10,000
n_2	4K	50,000
n_3	16K	90,000
n_4	16K	90,000

The overhead is negligible, and the system bandwidth is 1 K/unit time. (That is, it takes one unit time to transmit 1 KB of data). Choose an appropriate TTRT and obtain suitable values of f_i.

6.10. Prove Theorem 6.2.

6.11. Assuming Theorem 6.2, prove Corollary 6.1.

6.12. Show that if Equation (6.24) is satisfied, scheduler saturation will not occur.

6.13. Devise a distributed algorithm to set up a statistical or deadline channel in the EDD–D algorithm.

6.14. In the EDD–D algorithm, we distribute the slack evenly among all the nodes in the channel.

(a) This approach has the advantage of simplicity. What are the disadvantages?

(b) Construct an example where the uneven distribution of slack renders a channel feasible (i.e., able to meet source-to-destination delay constraints) and an even distribution renders it infeasible.

(c) Modify the channel setup procedure in Exercise 6.13 to allow for the uneven distribution of slack.

(d) Modify the EDD–D algorithm to bound jitter.

6.15. In the 802.5 protocol, derive an expression for the ring utilization for the cases $W_T + \tau_{SA} \leq P_{max}$, and $W_T + \tau_{SA} > P_{max}$.

REFERENCES

[1] Agrawal, G., B. Chen, and W. Zhao: "Local Synchronous Capacity Allocation Schemes for Guaranteeing Message Deadlines with the Timed Token Protocol," *INFOCOM '93*, pp. 186–193, IEEE, Piscataway, NJ, 1993.

[2] Choi, M., and C. M. Krishna: "An Adaptive Algorithm to Ensure Differential Service in a Token-Ring Network," *IEEE Trans. Computers* 39(1):19–33, 1990.

[3] Demers, A., S. Keshav, and S. Shenker: "Analysis and Simulation of a Fair Queueing Algorithm," *SIGCOMM Symp. on Communications Architectures and Protocols*, pp. 1–12, ACM, New York, 1989.

[4] Ferrari, D., and D. C. Verma: "A Scheme for Real-Time Channel Establishment in Wide-Area Networks," *IEEE Journal on Selected Areas in Communications* 8:368–379, 1990.

[5] Ferrari, D., and D. C. Verma: Buffer Space Allocation for Real-Time Channel in a Packet Switching Network, unpublished paper, 1990.

[6] Gitman, I., R. M. Van Slyke, and H. Frank: "Routing in Packet-Switching Broadcast Networks," *IEEE Trans. Communications* COM-24(8):926–930, 1976.

[7] Golestani, S. J.: "A Framing Strategy for Congestion Management," *IEEE Journal on Selected Areas in Communications* 9:1064–1077, 1991.

[8] Grow, R. M.: "A Timed-Token Protocol for Local Area Networks," *Electro '82: Token Access Protocols*, Paper 17/3, 1982.

[9] Henry, P. S.: "Lightwave Primer," *IEEE Journal of Quantum Electronics* QE-21(12):1862–1879, 1985.

[10] Henry, P. S.: "High-Capacity Lightwave Local Area Networks," *IEEE Communications* 27(10):20–26, 1989.

[11] Johnson, M. J.: "Reliability Mechanisms of the FDDI High Bandwidth Token Ring Protocol," *Proc. 10th Conference on Local Computer Networks*, pp. 124–133, IEEE, Piscataway, NJ, 1985.

[12] Kalmanek, C. R., H. Kanakia, and S. Keshav: "Rate Controlled Servers for Very High Speed Networks," *Proc. GLOBECOM*, pp. 12–20, IEEE, Piscataway, NJ, 1990.

[13] Kobrinski, H., and K.-W. Cheung: "Wavelength-Tunable Optical Filters: Applications and Technologies," *IEEE Communications* 27(10):53–63, 1989.

[14] Lee, T. P., and C.-E. Zah: "Wavelength-Tunable and Single-Frequency Semiconductor Lasers for Photonics Communications Networks," *IEEE Communications* 27(10):42–52, 1989.

[15] Molle, M. L., and L. Kleinrock: "Virtual Time CSMA: Why Two Clocks are Better than One," *IEEE Trans. Communications* COM-33(9):919–933, 1985.

[16] Ramanathan, P., and K. G. Shin: "A Multiple Copy Approach for Delivering Messages under Deadline Constraints," *Digest of Papers, IEEE Fault-Tolerant Computing Symp.*, pp. 300–307, IEEE, Piscataway, NJ, 1991.

[17] Sathaye, S. S., and J. K. Strosnider: "Conventional and Early Token Release Scheduling Models for the IEEE 802.5 Token Ring," *Real-Time Systems* 7:5–32, 1994.

[18] Sevcik, K. C., and M. J. Johnson: "Cycle Time Properties of the FDDI Token Ring Protocol," *IEEE Trans. Software Engineering* SE-13(3):376–385, 1987.

[19] Tannenbaum, A. S.: *Computer Networks*, Prentice-Hall, Englewood Cliffs, NJ, 1991.

[20] Ulm, J. N.: "A Timed Token Ring Local Area Network and its Performance Characteristics," *Proc. 7th Conference on Local Computer Networks*, pp. 50–56, IEEE, Piscataway, NJ, 1982.

[21] Verma, D. C., H. Zhang, and D. Ferrari: "Delay Jitter Control for Real-Time Communication in a Packet-Switched Network," *Proc. Tricomm '91*, pp. 35–43, IEEE, Piscataway, NJ, 1991.

[22] Zhao, W., and K. Ramamritham: "Virtual Time CSMA Protocols for Hard Real-Time Communication," *IEEE Trans. Software Engineering* SE-13(8):938–952, 1987.

[23] Zhao, W., J. A. Stankovic, and K. Ramamritham: "A Window Protocol for Transmission of Time-Constrained Messages," *IEEE Trans. Computers* 39(9):1186–1203, 1990.

CHAPTER
7

FAULT-TOLERANCE
TECHNIQUES

7.1 INTRODUCTION

The failure rates of real-time computers must be extraordinarily small. Indeed, they must be smaller than the failure rates of the components from which they are built. Such computers must therefore be *fault-tolerant*, that is, be able to continue operating despite the failure of a limited subset of their hardware or software. They must also be *gracefully degradable*; that is, as the size of the faulty set increases, the system must not suddenly collapse but continue executing part of its workload. Figure 7.1 shows how a properly designed fault-tolerant system behaves as the failures increase in number and scope. Initially, the performance is kept from degrading despite a limited number of failures. This is done by such tactics as switching in spares and using up slack computational capacity. As the extent of the failures increases, performance starts to degrade. The system runs out of slack capacity, and the operating system must begin shedding computational load. The less critical tasks are shed, and the system is still able to carry out the critical core of tasks that are vital to the survival of the controlled process. Finally, when the extent of the failures is so great that the computer can no longer meet even these critical computational requirements, we have system failure, which

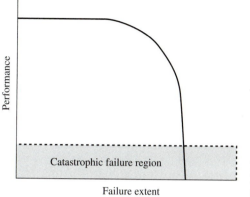

Performance

Catastrophic failure region

Failure extent

FIGURE 7.1
Performance degradation of a fault-tolerant system.

may have catastrophic consequences for the application. The goal of the system designer is to ensure that the probability of system failure is acceptably small.

The first step in making a system robust is to reduce the number of faults that the system will encounter. This means reducing the number of design and manufacturing faults, and reducing its vulnerability to disturbances in the operating environment.

Reducing the incidence of design faults requires careful specification and design, followed by extensive design reviews. The system must be built of high-grade components to reduce the probability of manufacturing defects. For example, each VLSI chip from which it is built must be tested carefully to reduce the probability of using a bad component. Extensive system-wide testing must also be conducted before the system is released for use. Indeed, the system must be *designed for testability*, i.e., it should be designed to facilitate thorough testing. Testing is not a trivial process. Most systems are so complex, with so many inputs and operating conditions, that it is impossible to test the system under every condition and every combination of inputs. We can never be sure that a complex system leaves the factory with no faults in it; all that can be done is to minimize the probability of faults. Designing for testability is an entire subject in its own right, and we do not cover it here.

Making the system robust against interference from the operating environment requires shielding and the use of appropriate (i.e., radiation-hardened) components. In such applications, using the latest integrated-circuit technology is not necessarily a good idea. The more mature the technology, the more likely it is to produce robust circuits.

But no matter how robustly the system is designed, it is likely that there will always be faults in it, either at the time it is released or later while it is in use. The system must thus be able to tolerate a certain number of failures and still function.

Since real-time systems must meet deadlines, there must be both a short-term and a long-term response to failure. The short-term response consists of quickly correcting for a failure to allow immediate deadlines to be met. The long-term response consists of locating the failure, determining the best response to it, and initiating a recovery and reconfiguration procedure.

In this chapter, we will survey techniques for fault-tolerance applied at the system level. There is also a large body of research in fault-tolerance at the circuit level, which is outside the scope of our discussion. Such fault-tolerance is used to make individual components or chips more reliable (using self-checking circuits, interstitial redundancy, complementary logic, etc.), but is more within the province of the designer of integrated circuits than of the system designer. In addition, we will not cover fault-tolerant synchronization here; that topic is so important that we have an entire chapter devoted to it (see Chapter 9).

7.1.1   Definitions

A *hardware fault* is some physical defect that can cause a component to malfunction. A broken wire or the output of a logic gate that is perpetually stuck at some logic value (0 or 1) are hardware faults.

A *software fault* is a "bug" that can cause the program to fail for a given set of inputs.

An *error* is a manifestation of a fault. For example, a broken wire will cause an error if the system tries to propagate a signal through it. A program that has a fault that induces incorrect outputs for some set I of inputs will generate errors if that set of inputs is applied.

The *fault latency* is the duration between the onset of a fault and its manifestation as an error. This duration can be considerable. Since the faults themselves are invisible to the outside world, only showing themselves when they cause errors, such latency can, as we shall see, impact the reliability of the overall system. As an example of fault latency consider an AND gate that has one of its inputs (say, input line 2) stuck at 0. That is, the gate behaves as if the input on that wire were 0, regardless of what the actual input happens to be. Figure 7.2 illustrates the concept of fault latency.

The *error latency* is the duration between when an error is produced and when it is either recognized as an error or causes the failure of the system. Like fault latencies, error latencies can have a considerable impact on the overall system reliability.

Error recovery is the process by which the system attempts to recover from the effects of an error. There are two forms of error recovery; forward and backward. In *forward error recovery*, the error is masked without any computations having to be redone. In *backward error recovery*, the system is rolled back to a moment in time before the error is believed to have occurred (this roll back involves the restoration of system state to the state at that moment), and the computation is carried out again. Backward error recovery uses time redundancy, since it consumes additional time to mask the effects of failure. We shall encounter examples of both forward and backward recovery in this chapter.

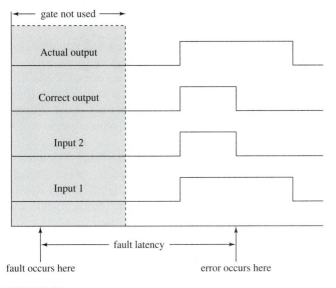

FIGURE 7.2
Fault latency.

7.2 WHAT CAUSES FAILURES?

There are three causes of failure: errors in the specification or design, defects in the components, and environmental effects.

Mistakes in the specification and design are very difficult to guard against. Many hardware failures and all software failures occur due to such mistakes. Specification can be regarded as a mapping from the real world into an artificial specification space. The real-world requirements are expressed in formal or informal terms that can be understood by the computer designer. The person who writes the specification must thoroughly understand the application and the environment in which that application will operate. The specification is, strictly speaking, the only link in the design process between the real world of the application and the more cloistered world of the computer designer. If the specification is wrong, everything that proceeds from it—the design and implementation—is likely to be unsatisfactory. A specification must be unambiguous; that is, it must not admit to more than one interpretation. It must be complete, not requiring additions to define a whole system. And yet, it should not be so restrictive that it unduly takes away the designer's initiative. There is no mechanical way of writing a specification, although it is possible to develop languages in which specifications can be conveniently written. Specification is intrinsically an art, which, because it provides an interface with the undefinable real world, is itself incapable of being completely mechanized.

It is very difficult to ensure that the specification is completely right. Common sense checks can be made. Specifications can be reviewed by persons unconnected with writing them to increase the chances of mistakes being caught. Detailed "defenses" of a specification can be carried out, where each line of the specification is defended before a committee playing devil's advocate. "Be careful" is the best advice we can give to a specification writer.

By contrast, the design that is developed from a formal specification can, theoretically, be checked formally. Indeed, any design is just one realization of the specification and, theoretically speaking, can therefore be formally checked against it. Reality is, alas, quite different. Formal techniques are too primitive to be of much value in large-scale systems. However, the large number of researchers working in this area makes it possible that the situation could change in the medium-term future.

The second cause of faults is defects in components. Hardware components can develop defects. These may arise from manufacturing defects, or from defects caused by the wear and tear of use. For example, a MOSFET may fail due to electromigration, which is the drifting away over time of metal atoms towards the cathode.

The third cause of faults is the operating environment. Devices can be subjected to a whole array of stresses, depending on the application. Poor ventilation or excessively high ambient temperatures can melt components or otherwise damage them.[1] If the computer is in a missile, it can undergo high g-forces and vibrational stress.

Sometimes, especially in aerospace or robotics applications, there can be considerable electromagnetic or elementary-particle (such as α-particle) radiation, which can cause spurious changes in the state of flip-flops. For example, there is an area between 600 and 6000 nautical miles above the South Atlantic, called the South Atlantic Anomaly, that is especially rich in elementary particles. Some spacecraft are exposed to as much as 10^5 rads[2] per hour. In silicon dioxide, ionizing radiation produces about 7.6×10^{12} electron-hole pairs per rad per cubic centimeter. This charge can cause devices to change state.

A rough idea of how the reliability of a component can be affected by some of these factors can be obtained by considering the following expression for failure rate, which was developed by the U.S. Department of Defense [21]:

$$\lambda = \pi_L \pi_Q (C_1 \pi_T \pi_V + C_2 \pi_E) \tag{7.1}$$

where:

π_L	Represents the fabrication process (1 if mature technology; 10 otherwise).
π_Q	Represents the testing process to discard devices that have manufacturing defects (ranges between 0.25 and 20).
C_1, C_2	Complexity factors expressed as a function of the number of transistors in the device and the number of pins

---

[1] In general, the hotter a component, the higher its failure rate.

[2] A *rad* is a unit of radiation, that measures how much energy is absorbed per unit of mass. It stands for radiation absorbed dose. Each rad corresponds to the absorption of 100 ergs per gram.

π_T Represents the effects of temperature and is a function of the type of device (ranges between 0.1 and 1000).

π_V Represents the voltage stress for CMOS devices (1 if the device is not CMOS; ranges from 1 to 10 if it is CMOS).

π_E Represents other stresses in the operating environment (ranges between 0.38 and 220).

A glance at the range of these parameters shows how potent the impact of the operating environment is. Voltage (for CMOS) and temperature stresses are multiplicative, and their product ranges across four orders of magnitude. A component used in a benign environment can be up to 10,000 times more reliable than the same component used in a harsh environment. While the actual numbers mentioned above are likely to change with advances in technology, the importance that Equation (7.1) ascribes to the operating environment is unlikely to change in the near future.

7.3 FAULT TYPES

Faults are classified according to their temporal behavior and output behavior. A fault is said to be *active* when it is physically capable of generating errors and to be *benign* when it is not.

7.3.1 Temporal Behavior Classification

There are three fault types: permanent, intermittent, and transient. A *permanent* fault does not die away with time, but remains until it is repaired or the affected unit is replaced. An *intermittent* fault cycles between the fault-active and fault-benign states. A *transient* fault dies away after some time. See Figure 7.3 and the table below.

Fault type	Condition
Permanent	$a(t) > 0, \ b(t) = c(t) = d(t) = 0$
Transient	$a(t) > 0, \ b(t) = 0, \ c(t) > 0, \ d(t) = 0$
Intermittent	$a(t) > 0, \ b(t) > 0, \ c(t) = 0, \ d(t) > 0$

In the figure, $a(t)$ and $b(t)$ are the rates at which the fault switches states, and t is the age of the fault.

Intermittent faults can be caused, for example, by loose wires. Transient faults can be caused by environmental effects. For instance, if there is a burst of electromagnetic radiation and the memory is not properly shielded, the contents of the memory can be altered without the memory chips themselves suffering any structural damage. When the memory is rewritten, the fault will go away. Experiments suggest that the vast majority of hardware faults are transient, and that only a minority are permanent. Transient failures are hard to catch, since

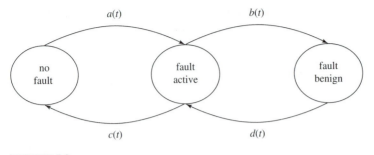

FIGURE 7.3
State diagram of the fault classes.

quite often by the time the system has recognized that such a failure has occurred it has disappeared, leaving behind no permanent defect that can be located.

It is likely that as devices become faster, their vulnerability to environmental effects that lead to transient failure will increase. This is because the principal way of making a device run faster is to make it smaller, so that signal propagation times, as well as the volume of charge required to switch a flip-flop from one state to the other, is reduced. It therefore becomes more likely that a charged particle passing through a device or electromagnetic induction will cause a spurious change in the device state. This problem is especially serious in real-time systems that operate in hazardous environments that are replete with such radiation, such as space.

7.3.2 Output Behavior Classification

A fault is also characterized by the nature of the errors that it generates. There are two categories of output behavior, nonmalicious and malicious.

To understand the difference, consider a unit A, which is providing output to units $B_1, \ldots, B_n$. If A has a nonmalicious fault, any errors it generates will be interpreted in a consistent way by all of the units B_i. For example, if A has an output line that is stuck at logic 0, this is a nonmalicious fault because all the units that receive input from this line will read the line as producing a logic 0.

It is possible, however, for A to fail in such a way that the B_i see nonidentical values of output for the same physical signal. For example, let an output line of A float rather than be stuck at 0. Now, logic circuits are designed to interpret a certain range of voltages (say $[0_\ell, 0_h]$) as corresponding to a logical 0 and another range (say $[1_\ell, 1_h]$) as corresponding to a logical 1. So long as the output voltage maintained by that faulty output line is in one of these ranges it will be interpreted consistently by all the B_i. However, if the voltage is outside these ranges (e.g., between the values that would cause it to be interpreted as a 0 or as a 1), consistency breaks down; it is then possible for the same voltage signal to be interpreted as representing a different logic value by different receivers (see Figure 7.4).

Failures corresponding to an inconsistent output are much harder to neutralize than the nonmalicious type. Indeed, we may think of them—somewhat whimsically—as the output of some malicious intelligence that has captured the device and is putting forth errors in such a way as to cause maximum disruption to

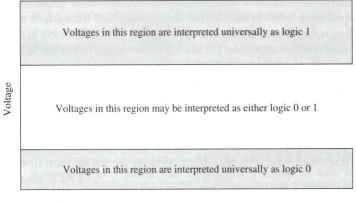

Voltages in this region are interpreted universally as logic 1

Voltage

Voltages in this region may be interpreted as either logic 0 or 1

Voltages in this region are interpreted universally as logic 0

FIGURE 7.4
Interpretation of voltages as logic values.

the functioning of the system. Such failures are known as *malicious* or *Byzantine* failures. In short, a malicious fault is one that is assumed to behave arbitrarily.

In this context the terms fail-safe and fail-stop can be defined. A unit is said to be *fail-stop* if it responds to up to a certain maximum number of failures by simply stopping, rather than putting out incorrect output. Fail-stop units typically consist of multiple processors running the same tasks and comparing results. Faults are detected by comparing outputs; if the outputs are different, the whole unit turns itself off. A simple example is a system with two processors, each running the same tasks on the same inputs and comparing its output to that of the other processor. If either processor detects a discrepancy between these outputs, it has the ability to turn off the interface to the network, thus isolating itself from the rest of the system.

A system is said to be *fail-safe* if its failure mode is biased so that the application process does not suffer catastrophe upon failure. The classic example of a fail-safe system is a traffic-light controller. If, when it fails, it sets all the lights to green, catastrophe ensues. On the other hand, if it is designed so that a failure of the controller results in the lights all turning to red or to flashing yellow, it is fail-safe. Some applications may not admit of a fail-safe mode.

7.3.3 Independence and Correlation

Component failures may be independent of one another or correlated. A failure is said to be *independent* if it does not directly or indirectly cause another failure. Failures are said to be *correlated* if they are related in some way; for example, they may be triggered by the same cause or one of them might cause the others to occur. Failures can be correlated due to a physical or electrical coupling of units, or because the same external event (e.g., a lightning strike) affects both units. Correlated failures are far more difficult to deal with than independent failures, and means must be found to avoid them, if at all possible. Designers should consider shielding the electronics so that the probability of a transient upset due to the environment is reduced. They may also want to ensure that the sources of power for the processors are disparate. Sometimes, the hardware is physically separated, so that the probability of multiple processors being affected by the same environmental event is reduced; for example, the processors of an aircraft-control computer might be distributed among multiple instrument bays.

7.4   FAULT DETECTION

There are two ways to determine that a processor is malfunctioning; online and offline.

Online detection goes on in parallel with normal system operation. One way of doing this is to check for any behavior that is inconsistent with correct operation. The following actions are indicative of a faulty processor.

- Branching to an invalid destination.
- Fetching an opcode from a location containing data.
- Writing into a portion of memory to which the process has no write access.
- Fetching an illegal opcode.
- Inactive for more than a prescribed period.

A monitor (called a *watchdog processor*) is associated with each processor, looking for signs that the processor is faulty. The watchdog processor watches the data and address lines, as shown in Figure 7.5. A second approach is to have multiple processors, which are supposed to put out the same result, and compare the results. A discrepancy indicates the existence of a fault.

Offline detection consists of running diagnostic tests. When a processor is running such a test, it obviously cannot be executing the applications software. Diagnostic tests can be scheduled just like ordinary tasks. The greater the failure rate, the greater must be the frequency with which these tests are run.

7.5   FAULT AND ERROR CONTAINMENT

When a fault or error occurs in one part of the system, it can, if unchecked, spread through the system like an infectious disease. A fault in one part of the system

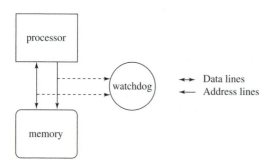

→← Data lines
←— Address lines

FIGURE 7.5
Online detection using a watchdog processor.

might, for example, cause large voltage swings in another; a fault-free processor can put out erroneous results as a result of using erroneous input from a faulty unit. Faults and errors must therefore be prevented from spreading through the system. This is called *containment*. The concept is an old one, and has been widely used in other fields. For example, ships have long been divided into separate watertight compartments, so that damage to a small number of the compartments does not sink the ship. Similarly, persons suffering from highly infectious diseases, like the plague or tuberculosis, have traditionally been placed in hospital isolation wards.

The system is divided into *fault-* and *error-containment zones* (FCZ and ECZ, respectively). An FCZ is a subset of the system that operates correctly despite arbitrary logical or electrical faults outside the subset. That is, the failure of some part of the computer outside an FCZ cannot cause any element inside that FCZ to fail. Hardware inside an FCZ must be isolated from hardware outside it. The isolation should be sufficiently robust to withstand either a short-circuit or the application of the maximum voltage imposed on the lines connecting an FCZ to the outside world. Each FCZ should have an independent power supply and its own clocks. Of course, these clocks can be synchronized with the clocks in other FCZs provided that a malfunction in these outside clocks will not cause those inside the FCZ to fail. Typically, an FCZ consists of a whole computer (including processors, memory, input/output, and control interfaces).

The function of an ECZ is to prevent errors from propagating across zone boundaries. This is typically achieved by voting redundant outputs, as we shall see in the next section.

7.6 REDUNDANCY

Fault-tolerance consists of using and properly managing redundancy. In other words, if the system is to be kept running despite the failure of some of its parts, it must have spare capacity to begin with. There are four types of redundancy, and we shall consider each in some detail:

Hardware redundancy: The system is provided with far more hardware than it would need if all the components were perfectly reliable, typically, between two and three times as much.

Software redundancy: The system is provided with different software versions of tasks, preferably written independently by different teams of programmers, so that when one version of a task fails under certain inputs, another version can be used.

Time redundancy: The task schedule has some slack in it, so that some tasks can be rerun if necessary and still meet critical deadines.

Information redundancy: The data are coded in such a way that a certain number of bit errors can be detected and/or corrected.

Using redundancy to enhance reliability is not new, as the following quotation from an article by D. Lardner in the *Edinburgh Review* of 1824 shows.

The most certain and effectual check upon errors which arise in the process of computation is to cause the same computations to be made by separate and independent computers;[3] and this check is rendered still more decisive if their computations are carried out by different methods.

7.6.1   Hardware Redundancy

Hardware redundancy is the use of additional hardware to compensate for failures. It can be used in two ways. The first is its use for fault detection, correction, and masking. Multiple hardware units may be assigned to do the same task in parallel and their results compared. If one or more of these units is faulty, we can expect this to show up as a disagreement in the results. This is fault detection. If only a minority of the units are faulty, and a majority of the units produce the same output, we can use this majority result and thus mask the effects of failure. If more than a minority of the units disagree, at least we have detected the failure and can use other methods, such as repeating the computation on other processors, to correct for the fault(s). Correction and masking are short-term measures. They neutralize the effects of the observed failure.

The second—and long-term—use of hardware redundancy is to replace the malfunctioning units. It is possible for systems to be designed so that spares can be switched in to replace any faulty units.

These two ways complement each other. The extent to which they are employed depends on the nature of the application. If the computer is used aboard an unmanned deep-space probe that must function unattended and unrepairable for more than a decade, it must include sufficient spare modules for that duration, and ways to automatially switch them in. If, on the other hand, it is used in a chemical-plant application, where the computer is accessible to repair, we are primarily interested in providing short-term measures to respond to failure, since the malfunctioning module can be manually replaced soon after the malfunction is detected.

Redundancy is expensive. Duplicating or triplicating hardware is a luxury that is only justified in the most critical applications. Traditionally, such use has been largely confined to aerospace applications. As computers are increasingly present in more cost-sensitive applications, such as automobiles, only the most critical functions can be allocated such high levels of redundancy. In aerospace and other applications, redundancy is more often limited by how much power consumption, heat dissipation, or volume can be accommodated.

There is an infinity of ways to structure hardware redundancy, and it would be an instructive exercise for the reader to conjure up a few. Below is a description of some popular structures for hardware redundancy, each of which forms an error-containment zone. First, however, we turn to the important issue of voting and consensus.

---

[3]Back in 1824, "computers" meant "people who compute."

VOTING AND CONSENSUS. Recall that one way of using redundancy is to have multiple units execute the same task and compare their outputs. If at least three units are involved, this comparison can choose the majority value (a process called *voting*), and thus mask the effects of some failures. If two units are used, the comparison can detect (but not correct) an error.

The designer must decide whether exact or approximate agreement is expected between functioning units. For example, if one processor produces an output of 1.400984 and another 1.400978, are the two to be considered in agreement or not? They are certainly not in *exact* agreement, by which is meant bit-by-bit equality. However, they are close. How close should the values be to be regarded as practically the same? One approach with approximate agreement is to accept the median value (if $N \geq 3$) as the true one. This does not, however, solve the problem of whether to treat a different output as a fault or not. If there are three units A, B, C, and both A and B produce the value x while C produces the value $x \pm \alpha$, for what values of α is C to be considered as faulty?

This problem does not arise if all the processors are exactly the same model, receive exactly the same external interrupts at the same time, and are running the same software to the same input. Under such conditions, they should produce the same output if they are functioning properly. However, to provide resistance to design faults, we sometimes use diverse processor types with different software. Roundoff errors can cause divergence in the less significant bits of the output. If the designer sets the value of α too high, the probability increases that C is faulty without being treated as such by the system. On the other hand, if α is too low, there is the chance of a false alarm, with a functional C being wrongly treated as faulty. There is thus a trade-off here, but its resolution depends so much on the numerical properties of the algorithms being executed and on the nature of the hardware, that very little general guidance can be given.

Approximate agreement may be used in cases where sensors are measuring the physical environment. Consider, for example, temperature sensors placed in a boiler. Even if they are highly accurate, it is impractical to expect them to produce exactly the same temperature reading. For one thing, they will be mounted slightly apart, and the temperature at one point may be slightly different from the temperature at another. Second, they will always have certain tolerances. To get a good output, the voter must then take the median; this ensures that if the faulty units are in a minority, the chosen output is either the output of a functioning sensor or the output of a failed sensor whose value is sandwiched between the values of good sensors. Either way, the output is acceptable. The question of how to distribute the output of a sensor to processors so that they see consistent values is important, and we will return to it later in this chapter.

We now introduce three types of voters, which can function in cases where approximate agreement is required: the formalized majority voter, the generalized $k-$plurality voter, and the generalized median voter. We will require in each case a distance metric, which measures how far apart the outputs from redundant units are. Let $d(x_1, x_2)$ denote the distance between outputs x_1 and x_2. If x_1, x_2 are real numbers, we may simply define $d(x_1, x_2) = |x_1 - x_2|$. If they are vectors of real numbers, other suitable metrics (e.g., Cartesian distance) may be chosen. In

TABLE 7.1
Comparison of voter types

Case	Majority voter	k-plurality voter	Median voter
All outputs correct and SE	Correct	Correct	Correct
Majority correct and SE	Correct	Correct	Correct
k correct and SE	No output	Correct	Possibly correct
All outputs correct but none SE	No output	No output	Correct
All outputs incorrect and none SE	No output	No output	Incorrect
Majority incorrect and SE	Incorrect	Incorrect	Incorrect

Note: SE = Sufficiently equal
Adapted from Larczak, Caglayan, and Eckhardt [14].

each case, assume that there are N outputs to be voted on, and that N is an odd number. Table 7.1 contains a comparison of these voters for various cases.

Formalized majority voter. The formalized majority voter works as follows. From an analysis of the software, suppose that it is reasonable to assume that if $d(x_1, x_2) \leq \epsilon$, x_1 and x_2 are sufficiently equal for all practical purposes.[4] Note that "sufficiently equal" does not satisfy the transitivity relation of a true equality. That is, if x_1 is sufficiently equal to x_2 and x_2 is sufficiently equal to x_3, this does not necessarily imply that x_1 is sufficiently equal to x_3.

Then, the voter constructs a set of classes, $P_1, \ldots, P_n$ such that

- $x, y \in P_i$ iff $d(x, y) \leq \epsilon$, and
- P_i is maximal; that is, if $z \notin P_i$, then there exists some $w \in P_i$ such that $d(w, z) > \epsilon$.

The classes may share some elements. Take the largest P_i thus generated. If it has more than $\lceil N/2 \rceil$ elements in it, any of its elements can be chosen as the output of the voter.

> **Example 7.1.** Let $\epsilon = 0.001$ for some five-unit system. Let the five outputs be 1.0000, 1.0010, 0.9990, 1.0005, and 0.9970. The classes will be $P_1 = \{1.0000, 1.0010, 1.0005\}$, $P_2 = \{1.0000, 0.9990\}$, and $P_3 = \{0.9970\}$. Note that 1.0000 is in both P_1 and P_2. P_1 is the largest class, and has $3 > \lceil N/2 \rceil$ elements. Any element in P_1 can be picked as the output of the voter.

Generalized k-plurality voter. The *generalized k-plurality voter* works along the same lines as the generalized majority voter, except that it simply chooses any output from the largest partition P_i, so long as P_i contains at least k elements (k is selected by the system designer).

---

[4]Note that by setting $\epsilon = 0$, sufficiently equal becomes truly equal. Thus, sufficient equality is a weaker condition than true equality.

Generalized median voter. The *generalized median voter* works by selecting the middle value (since N is assumed to be odd, such a middle value always exists). The middle value is selected by successively throwing away outlying values until only the middle value is left. The algorithm is as follows. Let the outputs being voted on be the set $S = \{x_1, \ldots, x_N\}$.

1. Compute $d_{ij} = d(x_i, x_j)$ for all $x_i, x_j \in S$ for $i \neq j$.
2. Let $d_{k\ell}$ be the maximum such d_{ij}. (Break any ties arbitrarily.) Define $S = S - \{x_k, x_\ell\}$. If S contains only one element, that is the output of the voter; else, go back to Step 1.

STATIC PAIRING. One of the simplest schemes of all is to hardwire processors in pairs, and to discard the entire pair when one of the processors fails. Figure 7.6 illustrates a system that uses this approach. The pair runs identical software using identical inputs, and compares the output of each task. If the outputs are identical, the pair is functional. If either processor in the pair detects nonidentical outputs, that is an indication that at least one of the processors in the pair is faulty. The processor that detects this discrepancy switches off the interface to the rest of the system, thus isolating this pair. This approach will work well so long as the interface does not fail, and both processors do not fail identically and around the same time. The second is an acceptable assumption; the first is not necessarily acceptable. To get around the interface being a critical point of failure, we can introduce an interface monitor (see Figure 7.7). This checks to ensure that the interface correctly transmits/receives messages, and switches it off whenever the interface is seen to be faulty. Likewise, the interface can check the output of the monitor, and turn itself off if it detects a fault in the monitor. This will work correctly unless both the monitor and the interface fail at the same time.

The probability of the pair being allowed to continue functioning despite failure is the probability that either both processors will fail in exactly the same way and produce exactly the same wrong result, or both the monitor and the interface will fail simultaneously. The actual expressions for this depend on the design of these components; however, the probability is usually sufficiently low that it can be assumed to be zero. On the other hand, the probability that the pair will be available for use is—if the simultaneous failures mentioned above are

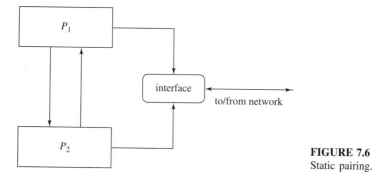

FIGURE 7.6
Static pairing.

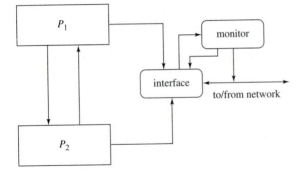

FIGURE 7.7
Use of a monitor.

regarded as a second-order effect—the probability that there is no failure in any of the four components: the two processors, the monitor, and the interface.

Just because a fault has caused a static pair to be taken offline does not mean that the pair will never again be used. As mentioned above, the majority of failures tend to be transient, and if the pair has suffered a transient failure, it can be reinitialized and brought back on line after the failure has died. Checking to see if a previously faulty pair has recovered can be done by running test programs.

An analogy of this type of redundancy at the circuit level is the self-checking circuit. The simplest example of a self-checking circuit is the two-rail checker. Here, logic is duplicated into two modules and the output of the duplicates are compared. A fault that generates an error in one module will cause a discrepancy in the outputs that can be detected.

N-MODULAR REDUNDANCY. N-modular redundancy (NMR) is a scheme for forward error recovery. It works by using N processors instead of one, and voting on their output. N is usually odd. Figure 7.8 illustrates this scheme for $N = 3$. One of two approaches is possible. In design (a), there are N voters and the entire cluster produces N outputs. In design (b), there is just one voter.

To sustain up to m failed units, the NMR system requires $(2m + 1)$ units in all. The most popular is the *triplex*, which consists of a total of 3 units and can can mask the effects of up to one failure.

Usually, the NMR clusters are designed to allow the purging of malfunctioning units. That is, when a failure is detected, the failed unit is checked to see

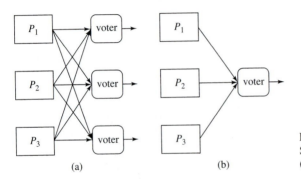

(a) (b)

FIGURE 7.8
Structure of an NMR cluster: (a) N voters, (b) single voter.

whether or not the failure is transient. If it is not, it must be electrically isolated from the rest of the cluster, and a replacement unit is switched in. The faster the unit is replaced, the more reliable the cluster.

For example, consider a triplex. If a processor fails, that failure will be detected the next time there is a vote. Suppose the system determines that the failure is not transient. (This can be done by waiting for some time and then checking to see if the fault has gone away. If it has not, it is labeled a permanent fault. The actual waiting time depends on how long we expect the transient failures to be.) This processor is then isolated so that the cluster becomes, for the time being, only a duplex. During this time, if another processor fails, it will be possible to detect but impossible to mask it. A spare processor (assuming one is available) will be inducted into the cluster. Before it can start executing, it must first be *aligned*; that is, its memory must be made consistent with that of the other members of the cluster, and its clock synchronized with theirs. Once this is completed, the cluster has been restored to health.

Purging can be done either by hardware or by the operating system. Self-purging consists of a monitor at each unit comparing its output against the voted output. If there is a difference, the monitor disconnects the unit from the system. The monitor (see Figure 7.9) can be described as a finite-state machine with two states, connect and isolate. There are two signals: *diff*, which is set to 1 whenever the module output disagrees with the voter output, and *reconnect*, which is a command from the system to reconnect the module (after it has been tested by the system diagnostic circuitry and found to be no longer faulty). The reconnect signal is very important because most faults are transient; permanently disconnecting a processor if it undergoes failure therefore wastes hardware and increases the probability of running out of functioning processors.

Another way to remove faulty units is through sift-out redundancy. Figure 7.10 shows the structure of a sift-out cluster of N processors. The comparator produces a total of $\binom{N}{2}$ outputs, one output for each pair of processors; if the pair disagrees, the corresponding output line is, say, a 1, while it is 0 if the pair produces a coincident output. The detector is a circuit that disconnects a module that disagrees with the majority. It recognizes this by analyzing the controller outputs. As with self-purging redundancy, a disconnected module can be reconnected on system command. Finally, the collector, which is a simple OR/AND circuit, produces output by sifting out the processors that have been disconnected by the

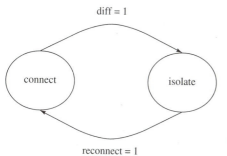

FIGURE 7.9
Monitor as a finite-state machine with two states.

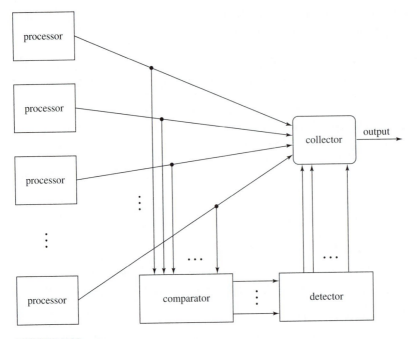

FIGURE 7.10
Sift-out redundancy.

detector. The circuitry for the detector, collector, and comparator are very simple and left to the reader.

A cluster of $N = 2m + 1$ processors is sufficient to guard against up to m failures if the processor failures are not malicious. If they are malicious, a more so-phisticated mechanism must be used. To see why, consider three sensors connected as in in Figure 7.11. Suppose that sensor 1 in Figure 7.11 is maliciously faulty, and sensors 2 and 3 are good (and provide identical inputs to the three voters). Let the values reported by the sensors to the various voters be as in Table 7.2. The median value put out by the voters will be 14, 15, and 16, respectively, due to the inconsistent outputs of faulty sensor 1. We will show later in this chapter that for the system to be proof against up to m malicious failures, we require $N \geq 3m + 1$ processors.

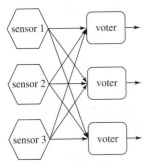

FIGURE 7.11
Voting on sensor values.

TABLE 7.2
The effects of malicious failure

Sensor number	Output to		
	Voter 1	Voter 2	Voter 3
1	11	15	35
2	14	14	14
3	16	16	16

Whether one voter or N are used depends on the application. Most applications require a single output. For example, if some valve is to be set to a particular position, what is needed is one output signal to that valve. On the other hand, some applications are specifically designed to take multiple outputs from the computer. For example, a control surface in an aircraft may be driven by the total force generated by N actuators, each obtaining input from a separate voter. The system can be designed so that even if a minority of the actuators outputs are wrong (either because they receive incorrect inputs or the actuators themselves are faulty), the remainder have sufficient force to be able to set the control surface correctly.

A cluster with just one voter is clearly vulnerable to the failure of that one voter; fortunately the voter circuitry is so much simpler than that of the processor that voters can be expected to fail much less often than processors. Clusters with N voters are sometimes called *restoring organs*, because they produce N correct results so long as a majority of the processors (and all voters) are nonfaulty.

A voter should not wait until all the inputs have been received. (If it did that, a failed processor that never produces an output would cause the voter to wait indefinitely, and thus cause deadlines to be missed). If enough coincident signals are received to make up a majority of the number in the cluster, that is sufficient. This approach is especially useful when hardware diversity is used. To avoid the effects of hardware design faults, the N processors in the cluster are not always identical, but might be different (diverse) models; the hope is that a design fault that causes a particular make of processor to fail on a given set of inputs will not be present in the others. Since the diverse processors have different speeds and perhaps different instruction sets, they can be expected to complete execution of the same task at different times. Waiting for only a majority of coincident signals means not having to wait for the laggards. We have two options regarding processors that have not completed execution before a majority of their functioning colleagues. The first is to terminate their execution, since a correct output has been calculated already. The second is to let them run to completion and check their results against the consensus to detect any faults in these lagging processors.

If a voter waits until all functioning processors have produced output, it must be provided with a *watchdog timer*. This is a device that indicates when it has waited long enough. When the timer goes off, any processors that have not yet delivered output are labeled faulty. The setting of the watchdog timer depends on the run times of the cluster workload.

The designer has to decide at what level NMR is to be applied. An NMR cluster is an error-containment zone, in that errors that are generated within it are masked (so long as a majority of the units are functioning) and never leak into the rest of the system. Intuitively, it should be clear that the smaller the error-containment zone, the better the reliability. However, there are problems with an excessive use of the NMR concept. The most obvious is that it is expensive. The second is that voting takes time and having a very large number of voters between input and output can add an appreciable delay to the entire system. For example, it is possible to migrate the concept all the way to the gate level and have N gates replicating in parallel what one gate would do otherwise. This approach is very expensive, however, and the authors are not aware of anyone using such an approach.

NMR is used in practice at the board or module level. The architecture, speed, and reliability of the system are determined substantially by the level at which the redundancy is used. Let us consider a few alternatives to illustrate redundancy at the module level.

The simplest—and the most common—scheme is to allocate each processor its own private memory, and to treat the processor-memory combination as an integral unit, that is, a module. When the processor finishes a task, its output is applied to a voter, along with those of its colleagues in the cluster.

An alternative to this is to treat each processor and each memory as a separate module. There are several choices, of which we consider three here. Suppose we have a system of three processors and three memory modules. Figure 7.12 illustrates three ways to arrange them, depending on when votes are taken. Keep in mind that the three processors are running the same workload since they are part of a single triplex cluster. In Figure 7.12a, the memory modules are arranged so that a read operation by a processor is replicated and goes to all three modules. The output of these memories is voted on, and the processor receives the result of the read. However, if a processor wishes to write, it may do so into one of the memory modules without affecting the others. In Figure 7.12b, the reverse is the case. To write into a memory module, a vote of the corresponding write operations of the three processors is carried out, while a read can be done on just one processor. Finally, in Figure 7.12c, both reads and writes are voted on.

There are advantages and disadvantages to each of these schemes. Every time there is a vote, there is the opportunity to mask out an error. For example, memories sometimes undergo transient failure due to charged particles passing through them and changing 0s to 1s or vice versa. A vote-before-read means that up to one such failure can be masked. Similarly, if a processor undergoes failure, that can be masked with respect to the memory by a vote-before-write policy. However, voting is expensive. Not only is there a delay caused by the voting process itself (i.e., propagation time through the voter), but the voter can only commence computation after a majority of the voter inputs are available. Thus, this scheme will result in complications unless the processors are identical and produce outputs or read requests at very nearly the same time. Even then, there will be an excessive demand on memory bandwidth in the vote-before-read case. In this case, each memory module will see the sum total of all the read requests generated by all the processors. One way of getting around this is to vote on

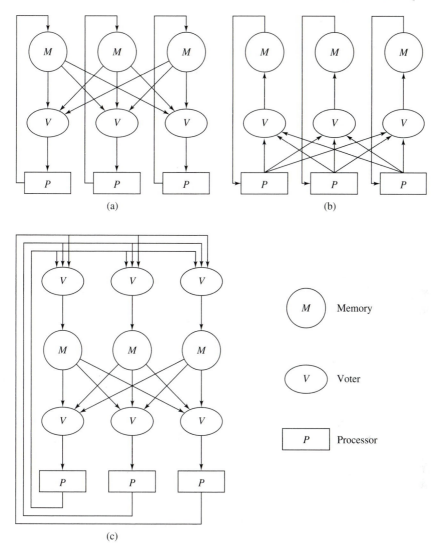

FIGURE 7.12
Some NMR design alternatives: (a) vote before read; (b) vote before write; (c) vote after read and write.

the read requests themselves and, instead of receiving a read request from each processor, amalgamate coincident read requests for the same location into one.

Yet another alternative is to chop up the task into portions and vote on the output of each portion. This is equivalent to cascading NMR clusters, as shown in Figure 7.13. Each of the stages in this cascade acts as a fault-containment unit. Deciding how the task should be divided is a trade-off. If it is divided into many portions, there will be many votes and resistance to failure will be high. The price for this is that the voting overhead will be high.

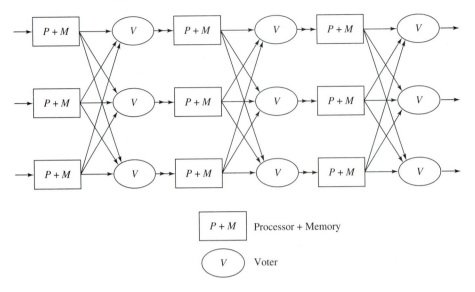

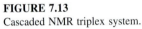

FIGURE 7.13
Cascaded NMR triplex system.

7.6.2 Software Redundancy

Unlike hardware fault-tolerance, software fault-tolerance is a new and emerging field, and the state of the art is primitive.

As every programmer knows, it is practically impossible to write any large piece of software without introducing faults in it. Software faults are quite unlike hardware faults, however. Software never wears out, so that faults are never spontaneously generated during system operation. Software faults can be regarded instead as faults in design. As systems become more complex, the ratio of software to hardware failures keeps increasing. Anecdotal evidence suggests that the software failure rate of modern systems is many times that of the hardware failure rate.

To provide reliability in the face of software faults, we must use redundancy. However, simply replicating the same software N times will not work; all N copies will fail for the same inputs. Instead, the N versions of the software must be diverse so that the probability that they fail on the same input is acceptably small. Such diversity in software can be introduced by having independent teams of programmers, with no contact between the teams, generating software for the same task. However, even then, there can be common-mode failures (i.e., multiple versions failing on the same input). For example, if the teams all work off the same specification, they may interpret an ambiguity in the specification in the same (incorrect) way. If they use similar numerical algorithms, the system is vulnerable to inputs for which these algorithms exhibit numerical instabilities. In every experiment that we are aware of, common-mode software failures have been significant. There is also the issue of cost. Single-version software is already more expensive than the hardware in most large systems; demanding N versions of software for even small N can be very expensive.

The designer needs answers to the following questions.

- What is the minimum number of versions required to ensure acceptable levels of software reliability?
- What procedures should be established to minimize common-mode failures among the various independently generated versions?
- How should the software be tested?

There are, as yet, no good answers to these questions. We do not have good models of software reliability (i.e., given a program, how do we determine how many faults it has?). Software reliability models are much less reliable than their hardware counterparts since hardware failure occurs due to physical reasons, which can be modeled fairly well, while software failure occurs due to a design fault. Design faults, both hardware and software, are difficult to model since the processes that give rise to them are poorly understood.[5] Clearly, the number of faults is likely to be a function of the size of the software, its complexity, the skills of the programming team, the programming language used, the clarity and correctness of the specifications, and so on. All of these parameters, with the exception of program size, are difficult to measure—or even to define—precisely. Indeed, as we shall see in Chapter 8, on reliability evaluation, an argument can be made that it is impractical to model the reliability of real-time software.

The number of software versions will depend on the extent of the common-mode failures. How to measure this in an acceptably short time is another unsolved (and perhaps unsolvable) problem. The testing of the multiple versions of the software can be done back-to-back. That is, since these versions must produce approximately, the same output for the same input (approximately, since the versions may generate different roundoff and other numerical errors), any mismatch in outputs for the same input indicates an error. Of course, this will not catch those faults that are common to all the versions.

There are two approaches to handling multiple versions. *N-version programming* involves running all *N* versions in parallel and voting on the output. In contrast, the *recovery-block* approach involves running only one version at any one time. The output of this version is put through an *acceptance test*, which checks to see if it is in an acceptable range. If it is, the output is passed as correct. If it is not, another version is executed, with its output being checked by the acceptance test, and so on. Figure 7.14 illustrates these approaches.

N-**VERSION PROGRAMMING.** *N*-version programming owes whatever reliability it can provide to the diversity of the software. Such a system will fail whenever

---

[5]However, since the hardware is typically many times simpler than the software for most systems, the number of hardware design faults tends to be small, while there is usually a large number of software design faults. Thus, the problem of design faults is much more pressing in software than in hardware.

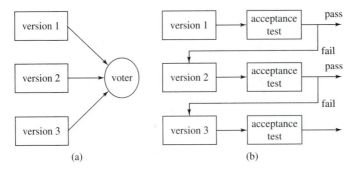

FIGURE 7.14
Software fault-tolerant structures: (a) N-version programming; (b) recovery-block approach.

a majority of the versions fails on some input, and so the probability of common-mode failures must be minimized. To ensure this, we pick teams of programmers who never communicate with one another, and who work to develop independent versions of the required software.

Let us consider a few factors that affect the diversity of the multiple versions. The first factor is the requirements specification. Errors and ambiguities in the specification are a major factor in limiting diversity. A mistake in the specification that causes a wrong output to be delivered in response to a given set of inputs will be translated into software versions that jointly fail on that set. If there is an ambiguity, programmers can be expected to interpret the specifications in a way that reflects their biases. Multiple teams of programmers may have similar biases, as a result of their professional training or other cultural factors. Such similarity translates into the possibility of common-mode failures.

One response to this is to write the specifications in very formal terms and subject them to a rigorous process of checking. However, being very formal in a specification can render the specification difficult to understand. If a programmer, who most likely has at most a baccalaureate degree in computer science, comes across a specification written in some strange formalism that he cannot understand fully, what is he to do? Typically, he will either try to get the specifications translated into natural language or base his understanding of what is required on some examples provided with the specifications. Both approaches are fraught with possibilities for error. The former vitiates the formality of the specification and may introduce errors from the translation; the latter may not cover all possible cases. So, it is not sufficient for the specifications to be thoroughly checked and written out formally; they must also be lucid. It is not easy to be formal and lucid at the same time.

A second factor affecting the diversity of multiple software versions is the programming language. The nature of the language affects the programming style greatly. A program written in FORTRAN is structured very differently from one in C. It is not unlikely that two programmers working independently with the same set of specifications in the same language will come up with similar software. One example will suffice to drive home this point. When they were developing the Unix^{TM} system, Thompson and Ritchie of the Bell Telephone Laboratories parceled out the jobs of developing the various subroutines and procedures between themselves. Once, as a result of a mistake, both were assigned the same procedure to write. When they compared these two independently written versions of the same procedure, they were identical, line by line! Writing programs in the same language increases the probability of common-mode failures. If the same compiler is used, that adds yet another possible source of common-mode failures.

A third factor is the numerical algorithms that are used. Algorithms implemented to a finite precision can behave quite differently for certain sets of inputs than do theoretical algorithms, which assume infinite precision. If the teams are implementing the same algorithm, they will duplicate the same numerical instabilities.

A fourth factor is the nature of the tools that are being used. If the same tools (e.g., static and dynamic analyzers, expert systems to aid debugging, etc.) are being used, the probability of common-mode failure might increase.

A fifth factor is the training and quality of the programmers, and the management structure. If the programmers have identical or similar educational backgrounds, they can be expected to make similar mistakes. If they have a low level of skill, this can translate not only into an increased incidence of errors but also into more common-mode failures due to similar incorrect interpretations of what is required. If they have a great deal of experience with similar projects, they may well carry over in their minds some aspects of the specifications of those other projects. The management style can also affect the quality of the code. Some mangement aproaches insist that the programmers who develop the code not be the ones to test it, and indeed that the authors of the code not be allowed to directly contact the testing team. Other management approaches allow the programmers to work together in informal structures, where tasks are not well-defined and tests are carried out informally.

There does not yet exist any reliable way of quantifying diversity, except to subject the programs to testing and checking whether they fail on common inputs. This is, however, an area of continuing research. For example, the ESPRIT software project supported by the European Union is developing a diversity assessment technique based on fuzzy logic.

There is very little available data on the incidence of common-mode failures in multiple versions. The major difficulty in arranging large-scale experiments is cost; software is labor-intensive. A small number of experiments have been carried out. However, they have all been done in the academic environment, and it is open to debate as to how representative the results are of software developed under industrial conditions. Let us consider one such experiment, carried out at the University of Virginia (UVA) and the University of California at Irvine (UCI) by Knight and Leveson [10].

The application was a simple antimissile system. The software was meant to receive radar input and judge whether the signals indicated any incoming missiles. The specifications were written in English and pseudocode. The programmers were a mix of undergraduate and graduate students with varying levels of computer experience. The software was written in Pascal. The compilers used at the two

TABLE 7.3
Correlated failures between UCI and UVA versions

UCI versions	UVA versions								
	1	2	3	4	5	6	7	8	9
10	0	0	0	0	0	0	0	0	0
11	0	0	58	0	0	2	1	58	0
13	0	0	1	0	0	0	71	1	0
14	0	0	28	0	0	3	71	26	0
15	0	0	0	0	0	0	0	0	0
16	0	0	0	0	0	1	0	0	0
17	2	0	95	0	0	0	1	29	0
18	0	0	2	0	0	1	0	0	0
19	0	0	1	0	0	0	0	1	0
20	0	0	325	0	0	3	2	323	0
21	0	0	0	0	0	0	0	0	0
22	0	0	52	0	0	15	0	36	2
23	0	0	72	0	0	0	0	71	0
24	0	0	0	0	0	0	0	0	0
25	0	0	94	0	0	0	1	94	0
26	0	0	115	0	0	5	0	110	0
27	0	0	0	0	0	0	0	0	0

Note: From J. Knight and N. Leveson, "An Experimental Evaluation of Independence in Multiversion Programming," *IEEE Trans. Software Engineering,* Vol. SE-12, No. 1, January 1986. © IEEE 1986. Reprinted with permission.

universities were different, although all the programmers at the same university used the same compiler. Contact among the teams (27 in all) was discouraged, and questions about the specifications were to be submitted and answered by electronic mail. This allowed a record to be kept of all interactions. Any specification errors that were uncovered were announced to all the programmers, also by electronic mail.

In all, 27 versions were written. They were then tested to indicate their reliability. To do this, the versions were tested against each other for the same input sets, and against a program written to the same specifications as part of an earlier NASA experiment. This last program had been extensively tested and was believed to be highly reliable. The only errors that would escape notice would be those that caused identical errors in all 28 versions (the 27 student-written versions plus the NASA version). Table 7.3 indicates the extent of the correlated failures between the versions written at UVA and UCI. For example, there were 323 instances where versions 8 and 20 failed on the same input.

RECOVERY-BLOCK APPROACH. As in *N*-version programming, multiple versions are used in the recovery-block approach. There is a primary version and one or more alternatives. Unlike *N*-version programming, however, only one version is run at any one time. This is a backward error-recovery scheme.

We have seen a schematic diagram of the recovery-block approach in Figure 7.14. The primary software is run in the first instance. Its output is passed through an acceptance test, which is supposed to indicate whether the output is acceptable or not. This is the weakest point in the entire design, for the acceptance test has no prior way of knowing what the correct output should be (if it did, there would be no need to run the primary). It makes "sanity" checks; these consist of making sure that the output is within a certain acceptable range or that the output does not change at more than the allowed maximum rate. For example, if the task is one of calculating the position of a ship, any output that claims that the ship is 10,000 miles away from where it was computed to be a few milliseconds before is clearly wrong. These ranges and rates are functions of the application and must be specified by the designer.

An alternative version need not always use the same inputs as the primary; it may use other approaches to carry out the computation.[6] As we know, much of the load in real-time systems consists of the same tasks being repeatedly executed. If the ith iteration has failed to produce an acceptable output, or has not terminated within a prespecified time, the alternative is invoked. If this also fails, there may be yet another version that can be invoked. The system can keep trying until one of the following happens: one of the versions passes the acceptance test, the system runs out of versions, or the deadline is missed. Let us now turn to an example of how acceptance tests are determined.

> **Example 7.2.** Ships compute their position by timing inputs from the Global Positioning System, which consists of a constellation of satellites in Earth's orbit. We know the position of the ship a few milliseconds (or seconds) ago as a result of a prior iteration of the position-calculation algorithm. We also know the ship's speed and its heading. Based on this, we can clearly estimate the current position by dead reckoning within some range. To pass the acceptance test, the output of a version must be within this range.

Setting acceptance tests places the designer in the following dilemma. If the allowed ranges are set too strictly, the acceptance tests will generate a lot of false alarms (by labeling as bad output that which happens to be correct). If they are set too loosely, the probability is high that incorrect outputs will be accepted as good. Setting acceptance tests is an art, and the state of that art is very unsatisfactory at the moment.

When the acceptance test fails one version and invokes another, all global state changes made by the failed version must be reversed. This can be done using a recovery cache, and is further discussed in Section 7.6.3.

There is, of course, a time overhead incurred by using recovery blocks. This overhead occurs when the primary has failed, and consists of reversing the global state changes and running one or more alternatives.

---

[6]Indeed, on the theory that increased complexity gives rise to an increased probability of faults, we may want the alternative modules to be simpler than the primary so that they are less prone to producing errors. We may have to pay for this by allowing the alternatives to produce outputs of lower quality (e.g., outputs that are not as accurate, but are still acceptable) than the primary.

7.6.3 Time Redundancy—Implementing Backward Error Recovery

Backward error recovery can take multiple forms. The simplest is *retry*, where the failed instruction is repeated. Other options include rolling the affected computation back to a previous checkpoint and continuing from there, or restarting the computation all the way from its beginning.

Critical to a succesful implementation of backward error recovery is the restoration of the state of the affected processor or system to what it was before the error occurred.[7] By doing so, we are, in effect, wiping out all traces of the faulty program or process. Corrective action, such as assigning another processor to carry on with the execution beyond this point or retrying on the same processor with the corrected state information, can then be taken.

RECOVERY POINTS. One way of implementing backward error recovery is to store the process state at prespecified moments in time. Such snapshots are called *checkpoints*. Figure 7.15 provides a simple example. There are three checkpoints, taken at *recovery points* $R1$, $R2$, $R3$; these are points to which we want to be able to roll back the process. If an error is identified, state restoration is done by simply reading the last checkpoint before the error is known to have occurred.

If we don't know exactly when the error occurred, we might have to roll back all the way to the earliest checkpoint that we have. In Figure 7.16, for example, an error in a processor occurs between checkpoints c_3 and c_4, and is detected after c_8.

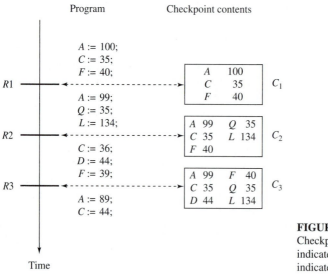

FIGURE 7.15

Checkpointing a program (Ri indicate recovery points; c_i indicate checkpoints).

---

[7]By *state* we mean all the information that enables us to restart the process from that point on. Typically, it includes the values of all the registers and the working set in memory.

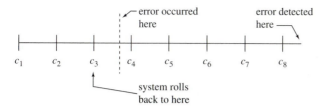

FIGURE 7.16
Checkpoints and rolling back the process (c_i indicate checkpoints).

If we know at that time that the error occurred between c_3 and c_4, the proper action is to roll the processor back to the checkpoint immediately preceding the onset of the error, that is, to c_3. This presupposes two things; first, that we have enough memory available to keep checkpoints c_3 to c_8 and, second, that we know when the error occurred. Most often, neither condition is satisfied. Due to limitations of memory, typically only the last one or two checkpoints are kept. Also, there is no way to know when the error occurred unless we have some information—from the nature of the error, from any acceptance tests that have been passed, or by some other means—to guide us. When we do not know when the error occurred, we can roll back to the oldest checkpoint that is stored and hope that the error did not occur prior to that time. Otherwise, we have to roll all the way back to the starting point of the computation; that is, we will have to restart the computation.

The designer must decide when checkpoints are to be taken by balancing the cost against the benefits. The cost is in terms of the amount of memory required to store the state (this depends on the system) and in terms of the time it takes to store the checkpoints. The benefit in having many checkpoints taken at short intervals is that the extent of the rollback is limited. Sometimes there are places in the code that are natural points for checkpointing. For example, if we have an acceptance test of certain outputs, we can checkpoint just after these outputs have been produced and have passed the acceptance test. Another way is to use redundancy and voting to check that the output is correct before the state is saved to form the checkpoint. This way, we have some confidence in the quality of the checkpoint.

Since each time we checkpoint we must make a copy of the entire process state, checkpointing is expensive in memory and time. This is potentially wasteful because unnecessary copies of the same variable value may be made. This expense can be reduced by taking incremental checkpoints. The idea is to only record a variable value when it is going to be changed. If this is done, however, we cannot simply discard old checkpoints, since some of the information they contain may still be relevant.

One mechanism for checkpointing incrementally is the recovery cache.[8] Figure 7.17 illustrates how this works. Associated with each recovery point is a

---

[8]The term "cache" as used here is unfortunate, because it has nothing to do with the standard computer-architecture meaning of cache. The word was apparently chosen to convey its original dictionary meaning of a safe place (to put the recovery information).

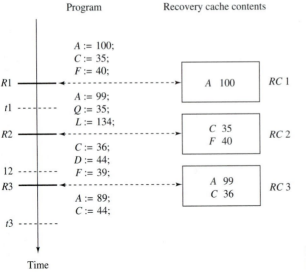

Program   Recovery cache contents

FIGURE 7.17

Time   Recovery caches.

recovery cache. The recovery cache contains the value, at the associated recovery point, of the variables that are changed before the next recovery point. For example, the only variable that is changed between $R1$ and $R2$ is A, and so the recovery cache for $R1$ only contains the old value of A.

Let us consider how the recovery cache contents can be used to restore the state to the recovery points. For example, consider that a failure is detected at $t2$, and the system decides to roll back to $R1$. To restore the state to what it was at $R1$ (with values 100 in A, 35 in C, and 40 in F; the values of Q, L, D are irrelevant since they are not defined at $R1$), we set C to 35 and F to 40 from RC 2. Then, we use RC 1 to set A to 100.

Suppose instead that the failure was detected at $t1$, and the system decides to roll back to $R1$. RC 1 is used to set A to 100. Nothing need be done to C and F since they still have the same values as they did at $R1$.

It is clear that the recovery cache saves memory. Does it necessarily also save time? We do save time in not having to save as many things as in the standard checkpointing scheme. However, whenever the program changes a variable value, it has to check if this is the first change in that variable since the last recovery point. If it is, the old variable value (i.e., the one current at the last recovery point) needs to be saved in the appropriate recovery cache. This check can be done in two ways. First, the system can check the recovery cache to see if a value has been saved for that variable—if it has been, nothing needs to be done; if not, we need to save it. This takes a great deal of time, involving an additional read (or two, depending on the memory access system) for each variable update. The second way is to associate a flag with each variable, which is set whenever that variable has been saved in the current recovery cache; note that these flags will all have to be reset every time a recovery point is encountered.

Discarding a recovery point when using recovery caches is also more complicated than in checkpointing.[9] Discarding a checkpoint only requires us to throw away its contents. We cannot always do that when using recovery caches since each recovery block may contain unique information. For example, suppose we decide at $t3$ to get rid of recovery point $R2$, keeping $R1$ and $R3$. Before discarding RC 2, we will have to store the values of 35 for C and 40 for F in RC 1. On the other hand, if we decide to get rid of $R1$ (i.e., the oldest extant recovery cache) RC 1 can simply be deleted.

Thus far, we have assumed that each process is independent, not working in cooperation with any other process. If this is not the case and the processes interact, things become more complex. Consider what happens in Figure 7.18. There are two processes $P1$ and $P2$, which communicate as shown. An error is discovered after $t1$, which forces $P1$ to roll back to its previous recovery point. However, to undo the process, the effects of the message from $P1$ to $P2$ must also be undone. The only way to do this is to roll back $P2$ to its previous checkpoint, which in this example happens to be the beginning. If $P2$ is to be rolled back, everything it did must be undone. This includes its message to $P1$ at time $t0$. But this causes everything done by $P1$ after $t0$ to be undone, and $P1$ must roll back to the checkpoint immediately preceding $t0$, which in this example happens to be the beginning of the execution. So, both $P1$ and $P2$ are rolled back to the beginning. This is an example of how rollbacks can propagate and is called the *domino effect*.

The domino effect can be countered by insisting that all the processes have their recovery points or checkpoints at the same time. The proof of this is left as an exercise for the reader.

AUDIT TRAILS. A second way of enabling backward error recovery is through audit trails. These are especially popular in databases. An *audit trail* consists of a record of all the actions that have been taken by the system, together with a time-stamp indicating when each action was taken. Backward recovery to some time t is effected by undoing actions taken after time t and then restarting from that point.

IRRECOVERABLE ACTIONS. We have hitherto assumed that all actions are reversible. This is the basis of backward error recovery. However, some actions are not reversible since they are out of the control of the computer system. Two examples will suffice. Suppose a process has had something printed on a line printer.

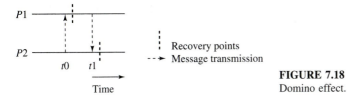

FIGURE 7.18
Domino effect.

---

[9]We have to regularly discard recovery points, otherwise we will run out of memory.

The computer has no way of unprinting it. (While it may be possible to print a correction message, the computer has no way of ensuring that the correction has been put out in time for the outside world to cancel any actions taken as a result of the printout.) Or consider an antiballistic missile system that, on the mistaken belief that it is under missile attack, launches an antimissile missile. Even if it later discovers the error, it will be impossible for the computer to unlaunch the missile.

7.6.4 Information Redundancy

In this section, we consider the use of coding to detect or correct errors. There has been a tremendous amount of research in coding in recent years, in both computing and communication networks. Since the coding used in real-time systems is no different from that used in general-purpose computers, we provide only a brief and partial survey.

The basic idea of information redundancy is to provide more information than is strictly necessary and to use that extra information to check for errors. We use coding all the time ourselves, while correcting for typographical errors. For example, if we encounter the word "startegic," we will most likely unconsciously correct it to "strategic." This was possible because (a) there is no such word as "startegic," and (b) "strategic" is the closest word that we can think of to "startegic." If, on the other hand, there is a misprint "taut" instead of "taught," we are able to discover the error only by reading the context, since "taut" is as much a word as "taught."

The conditions (a) and (b) are at the basis of all coding theory. All computer words are strings of 0s and 1s. Coding ensures that not all strings of 0s and 1s are legal (i.e., are valid). An illegal combination of bits indicates an error. Sometimes there is an unambiguous "nearest" valid word that the impermissible combination can be read as, thus correcting the error. Here "nearest" is computed by defining the distance between two words as the number of bit positions by which they differ. This is called the *Hamming distance*, H_d. The greater the Hamming distance between valid combinations (code words), the more errors can be corrected or detected. In general, a code can correct up to c bit errors and detect up to d additional bit errors iff $2c + d + 1 \leq H_d$. We will omit the proof for this.

When assessing a coding scheme, we want to know how many extra bits it adds to the words, and how many bit errors it can detect or correct. We are also interested in how much work it takes to encode and decode.

A code may be separable or nonseparable. In a *separable* code, the coded word consists of the original (uncoded) word, concatenated with a number of code bits. The process of decoding to get the original word back is thus limited to stripping away the code bits. A *nonseparable* code does not have this property of separability and is more complex to decode.

DUPLICATION. The simplest code of all is duplication. Each word is duplicated. An error in a bit position is detected by the discrepancy between the bit and its duplicate. Note that it is not possible to correct any errors. If a discrepancy is detected, we have no way to know whether it is the bit or the duplicate that is in error. While this code is simple, it requires 100% redundancy; that is, the coded word is twice the length of the uncoded word.

PARITY CODING. Another simple and widely used code is parity. Parity coding, or variations of it, is widely used in memory chips. It consists of adding an extra bit (called the parity bit) to each word to ensure that the number of 1s in it is always even (even parity) or odd (odd parity). For example, if even parity is being used, the word 001101 has its parity bit set to 1 so that the word is now 0011011. It is possible to detect all one-bit errors using this code. For instance, if through some faults, the word is recorded as 0011010, we know by counting the 1s that there is an error in that word. However, we can't correct that error, since violation of parity may have been caused by any of the bits being wrong. Also, we cannot always detect errors if two or more bits are wrong. For instance, if the word 0011011 is recorded as 0000011, the parity rule is satisfied and the errors will not be detected. Parity is widely used because of its simplicity and the small overhead it imposes.

The basic parity rule can be varied to provide additional protection against errors. Instead of having just one parity bit per word, we can subdivide the word into portions and associate a parity bit with each portion. Another interesting variation is interlaced parity, which has the ability to correct some bit errors, rather than just detect them. Here again, the word is divided into portions and a parity bit is associated with each portion. However, in interlaced parity, the portions are not disjoint but overlap. Table 7.4 provides an example for the case where there are eight bits, $w_7 \cdots w_0$, in the uncoded word and the parity bits are associated to the code as follows.

- P_0 covers bits w_0, w_2, w_3, w_6, w_7, P_0.
- P_1 covers bits w_0, w_1, w_3, w_5, w_6, P_1.
- P_2 covers bits w_0, w_1, w_2, w_4, w_5, w_7, P_2.
- P_3 covers bits w_0, w_1, w_2, w_3, w_4, P_3.

The idea is for a unique combination of parity bits to be in error for any single bit error. Whenever that combination occurs, we can use the table to determine which bit is in error. How many bits do we need for this scheme? If there are n bits of the uncoded word (called the *information bits*) and c parity bits, we must have the ability to distinguish between errors in $n + c$ positions. We must also be able to determine that there is no single-bit error. This makes a total of $n + c + 1$ cases to distinguish. So, choose c such that $n + c + 1 \leq 2^c$.

The same principle can be extended to obtain a code that will correct multiple-bit errors. The details are left to be worked out in the exercises.

CHECKSUM CODES. The checksum code is used when blocks of data are being transferred. Suppose that we are transferring a certain number of n-bit words. The sender computes the *checksum*, by adding together these words, and transmits it along with the words. The receiver computes the checksum of the words that it

TABLE 7.4
**Example of overlapping parity
with eight information bits**

	Leads to error in parity bit			
Bit error	P_3	P_2	P_1	P_0
w_0	×	×	×	×
w_1	×	×	×	
w_2	×	×		×
w_3	×		×	×
w_4	×	×		
w_5		×	×	
w_6			×	×
w_7		×		×
P_0				×
P_1			×	
P_2		×		
P_3	×			

receives, and compares it with the checksum obtained by the sender. If the two sums do not match, an error is detected. A checksum code can detect, but not correct, errors.

There are variations on the checksum, depending on how the addition is carried out. If the addition is modulo-2^n (with the overflow out of the nth bit being ignored), it is called the *single-precision checksum*. If it is modulo-2^{2n} (with the overflow out of the $2n$th bit being ignored), it is called a *double-precision checksum*. The *Honeywell checksum* works by concatenating two words to form words of $2n$-bit length, and then carries out a modulo-2^{2n} addition on these to form the $2n$-bit checksum. Figure 7.19 illustrates the various checksum codes for $n = 4$. The double-precision checksum captures some errors that are lost by its single-precision counterpart, for obvious reasons. The Honeywell checksum is useful in detecting errors that occur consistently in the same bit position; this will affect at least two bit positions of the checksum.

CYCLIC CODES. In a cyclic code any cyclic shift of a valid code word will produce another valid code word. Cyclic coding can be implemented with shift registers and exclusive-OR gates.

```
1011        1011
0101        0101
1110        1110      10110101
1111        1111      11101111

1101     00101101     10100100
 (a)        (b)         (c)
```

FIGURE 7.19
Three types of checksum on 1011, 0101, 1110, and 1111: (a) Single-precision; (b) Double-precision; (c) Honeywell.

Fundamental to cyclic coding is the interpretation of bits as the coefficients of a polynomial. This is not as unnatural as it might seem at first; a moment's reflection shows that all the numbers that we encounter are really coefficients of polynomials that represent their value. For example, consider the number 1101. Its value, if the number is in binary, is the polynomial $(1 \cdot 2^0) + (0 \cdot 2^1) + (1 \cdot 2^2) + (1 \cdot 2^3)$. If the number is in radix-r, its value is the polynomial $(1 \cdot r^0) + (0 \cdot r^1) + (1 \cdot r^2) + (1 \cdot r^3)$. When we multiply two numbers, we are really multiplying the underlying polynomials. The polynomial $G(X) = a_0 + a_1 X + \cdots + a_n X^n$ represents the word $a_n \ldots a_1 a_0$. The polynomial $1 + X + X^5$ represents the word 100011 (the 0-coefficient's terms are traditionally dropped from the polynomial representation). A polynomial of order n represents an $(n + 1)$-bit number.

Cyclic coding is carried out by multiplying the word to be coded by a polynomial, called the *generator* polynomial. All additions in this process are modulo-2. Multiplication by X^n essentially means shifting by n places. To see this, suppose we multiply the polynomial $1 + X + X^5$ (representing the word 100011) by X^2 (representing the word 100). The product is $X^2 + X^3 + X^7$, which represents the word 10001100—the original number 100011 has been shifted two places.

Let us consider more complex multiplication. Multiply the word to be coded, $1 + X + X^5$ (representing the number 100011), by the generator polynomial $1 + X + X^2$ (representing 101). We have $1 + (1 + 1)X + (1 + 1)X^2 + 1X^3 + 0X^4 + 1X^5 + 1X^6 + 1X^7$. Doing the additions modulo-2 (which means putting them through exclusive-OR gates) results in $1 + 0X + 0X^2 + 1X^3 + 0X^4 + 1X^5 = 1 + X^3 + X^5 + X^6 + X^7$, representing 11101001. The coded value corresponding to 100011 is therefore 11101001. The circuit in Figure 7.20 will carry out this coding operation. To begin, all flip-flops have their value set to 0. The flip-flops represent multiplication.

The coding circuit can be written down by inspection of the generator polynomial. Let us return to Figure 7.20; note that the input is fed in serially, bit by bit. When we ask for the multiplication (with modulo-2 addition) by $1 + X + X^2$, we are, in effect saying, "add, modulo-2, the present input bit to the previous one (representing X) to the input before that one (representing X^2)." The circuit follows immediately from that: The flip-flop produces the required delay, and the exclusive-OR gate carries out the modulo-2 addition.

To decode the codeword, we need to reverse the coding process by dividing by the generator polynomial. This turns out to be easy if we keep in mind that division just means having a multiplier in the feedback loop. Let the initial word to be coded be the polynomial $W(X)$, and the generator polynomial be

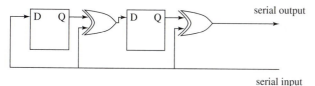

serial output

serial input

FIGURE 7.20
Coding with the generator polynomial $1 + X + X^2$.

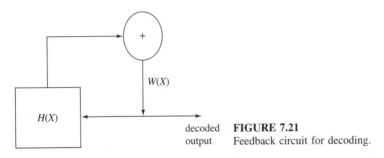

decoded   **FIGURE 7.21**
output   Feedback circuit for decoding.

$G(X) = g_0 + g_1 X + \cdots + g_n X^n$. Then, the coded value is $C(X) = W(X)G(X)$. Now, division by $G(X)$ should yield a quotient and no remainder. If a remainder does occur, that is an indication of an error.

This division process is implemented as follows. Let $H(X) = G(X) - 1$ (keep in mind that addition and subtraction are done modulo-2). That is, $H(X) = \bar{g}_0 + g_1 X + \cdots + g_n X^n$. We have

$$C(X) + H(X)W(X) = W(X)\{g_0 + \bar{g}_0 + (g_1 + g_1)X + \cdots + (g_n + g_n)X^n\}$$

$$= W(X) \quad \text{(since } g_0 + \bar{g}_0 = 1; \, g_i + g_i = 0 \text{ in mod-2)}$$

So, to recover the original codeword, the division process adds $H(X)W(X)$ to the codeword $C(X)$. We can do this by means of the feedback circuit shown in Figure 7.21. For example, if $G(X) = 1 + X + X^2$, we have the circuit in Figure 7.22. If, due to some errors, $C(X)$ is no longer a multiple of the generator polynomial, the codeword is invalid and a nonzero remainder occurs when it is divided by the generator. The remainder is the values held by the flip-flops after the decoding (i.e., the division) is completed, and so, if these hold nonzero values after decoding, it is an indication of error.

ARITHMETIC CODES. An arithmetic code has the property that given arithmetic operations on a valid codeword will produce another valid codeword. For example, if $C(a)$ and $C(b)$ are the codewords of a and b, respectively, and $A()$ is an arithmetic operation covered by the code, then $A(C(a), C(b)) = C(A(a, b))$. This is very useful for checking the correctness of the arithmetic operation.

The simplest arithmetic code that covers the addition and subtraction operations is the *AN* code, where a number is encoded by multiplying it by some constant. Table 7.5 shows some examples corresponding to the multiplier 5.

codeword

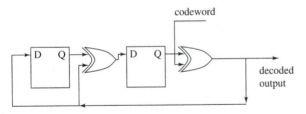

decoded   **FIGURE 7.22**
output   Feedback circuit for decoding
             with $G(X) = 1 + X + X^2$.

TABLE 7.5
AN code (multiplier = 5)

Number	Encoding
000	000000
001	000101
010	001010
011	001111
100	010100
101	011001
110	011110
111	100101

USE OF INFORMATION REDUNDANCY. The most frequent use of coding is to detect and/or correct errors in information transmission and memory. Error-correcting codes used in memory are used during memory *scrubbing*; periodically, each memory location is accessed and checked for integrity. If an error is detected, the system corrects it using the error-correcting property of the code, and writes it back. This prevents the accumulation of errors due to transient faults.

7.7 DATA DIVERSITY

Data diversity is an approach that can be used in association with any of the redundancy techniques considered above. The idea behind it is as follows. Sometimes, hardware or software may fail for certain inputs, but not for other inputs that are very close to them. So, instead of applying the same input data to the redundant processors, we apply slightly different input data to them. Thus we have in some cases another line of defense against failure. This approach will only work if the sensitivity of the output is either very small with respect to small changes in the input or if perturbing the output can be corrected analytically. Let us look at each case separately.

Case 1. If the output changes very little as a result of changing the input slightly, then we can perturb the input and carry out approximate voting on the results to obtain an approximate, but still acceptable, output. For example, instead of applying the same input x to all members of an NMR cluster, we apply $x, f_1(x), \ldots, f_N(x)$. Let $P(y)$ be the output of the program when the input is y. Then, the functions f_i must be chosen in such a way that $P(x) \approx P(f_i(x))$.

Case 2. The second case is when perturbing the input causes a change in the output that can be forecast analytically. This change can then be corrected. That is, suppose we can obtain a function $Q(x, y) = P(x) - P(y)$ for x, y sufficiently close to each other. Then, $P(x) = P(f_i(x)) - Q(f_i(x), x)$.

Figure 7.23 illustrates these two cases with voting.

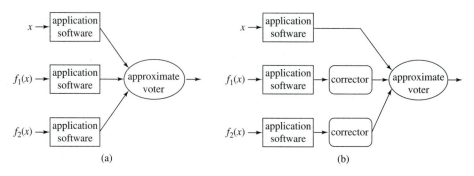

FIGURE 7.23
Data diversity with voting: (a) relative insensitivity of output to small changes in input; (b) adding a correction function.

Data diversity can also be used with recovery blocks. Instead of running alternative software when the primary fails the acceptance test, the primary can be reinvoked with slightly different data.

7.8 REVERSAL CHECKS

If there is a simple relationship between the inputs and outputs of a system, it may then be possible to calculate the inputs given the outputs. This can then be compared with the actual inputs as a check. For example, consider a task that finds the square root of a number. To see if the process is correct, we can square the output and check it against the original input. Or let the task consist of writing a block onto disk. The reverse operation consists of reading this block from the disk after writing and comparing it to the input to make sure that the two are the same. Reversal is a powerful method, but its applicability is limited to tasks where it is relatively easy to carry out the reverse computation.

7.9 MALICIOUS OR BYZANTINE FAILURES*

Whenever a failure can cause a unit to behave arbitrarily, malicious or Byzantine failure is said to happen. We have already seen an example of malicious failures in Section 7.3.2, where a sensor sends out conflicting information to different processors.

For correct operation, it is often the case that copies of the same data as seen by various processors must be consistent (i.e., the same). When communication is limited to two-party messages, the faulty units must be fewer than a third of the total number of units if consistency is to be guaranteed. This may come as a surprise to those who, conditioned by the simple majority voting covered in earlier sections, may believe intuitively that a system can maintain consistency so long as only a minority of units are faulty.

Figure 7.24 illustrates a situation where consistency is important. Data originating from a sensor are to be distributed among the processors shown. If the

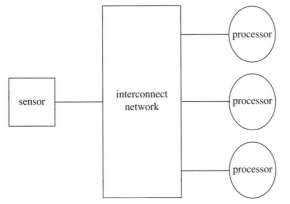

FIGURE 7.24
Distribution of sensor information.

sensor is nonfaulty, we would like all the functioning processors to read the sensor output consistently (i.e., for all the processors to see the same data value). If the sensor is faulty, we would like the processors also to agree on some input from the sensor (which may be a default value if they realize that the sensor is faulty).

Let us begin with what has become the canonical introductory example for the field of Byzantine failures, by showing that three units are insufficient to maintain consistency in the face of one malicious failure.

Example 7.3. Consider an army of the Empire of Byzantium (the genesis of the term "Byzantine" for such faults) engaged in besieging a city. The army consists of two divisions, each with its own divisional commander, L1 and L2. There is a supreme commander of the assault, G, and L1 and L2 function as his lieutenants. The three are physically separated and can only communicate by means of oral two-party messages, conveyed by messenger. At most one of the three commanders can be a traitor. The messengers are assumed to be loyal. *Interactive consistency* will be maintained if the following two conditions are satisfied.

IC1. All loyal lieutenants obey the same order.
IC2. If G is loyal, then every loyal lieutenant obeys the order he sends.

Both conditions will obviously be satisfied if everyone is loyal. Let us consider what happens if (a) G is a traitor, and (b) if one of L1 and L2 is a traitor. In each case, we will show that the traitor can force the consistency conditions to be violated. We assume that G, L1, and L2 have synchronized their watches, and that G must give an order ("attack" or "retreat") by a certain time.

Suppose G is a traitor, while L1 and L2 are loyal to the Empire. Let him send conflicting orders to L1 and L2, telling L1 to attack and L2 to retreat. If L1 and L2 do not communicate, neither knows of the conflict and, being loyal, each obeys his orders. Since these orders are conflicting, consistency condition **IC1** is violated.

Suppose L1 and L2 communicate with each other by sending to each other the order they received from G. L1 tells L2 that G told him to attack, while L2 tells L1 that G told him to retreat. Now consider what L2 should do. Should he believe

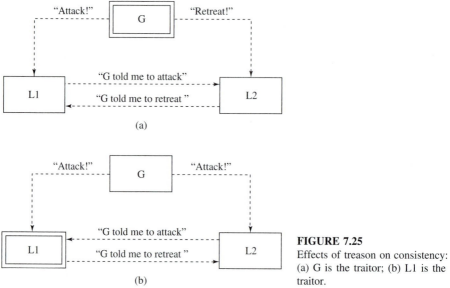

FIGURE 7.25
Effects of treason on consistency: (a) G is the traitor; (b) L1 is the traitor.

L1 or G? One of them is clearly a traitor since there is a conflict. If L1 is telling the truth, then he is accurately conveying to L2 the fact that G has sent conflicting orders and is therefore a traitor. If L1 is a traitor, he is lying to L2 about the order he received from G. So, in the absence of any further information, L2 cannot decide whether G is loyal. There is no way for him to act so that the consistency conditions are satisfied.

Now, consider the case where G is loyal, but L1 is a traitor. When L1 lies to L2, he constructs, from L2's point of view, a similar conflict. L2 knows that either L1 or G is a traitor, but he does not know which. Figure 7.25 summarizes this. Note that even if L1 and L2 each refer this discrepancy back to G, G can do nothing about it. If G is a traitor, he will then send L1 and L2 each a message confirming his original orders and telling L1 that L2 must be the traitor, and vice versa. If G is loyal, he will reiterate his prior messages to L1 and L2. Either way, L2 will see exactly the same set of messages, regardless of whether G or L1 is the traitor. This proves that it is impossible to guarantee satisfying the consistency conditions **IC1** and **IC2** with three generals and one traitor.

Let us now consider the case where the Byzantine army has three divisions, each with its own commander. These are lieutenants L1, L2, L3 of the commanding general G. Suppose once more that at most one of them can possibly be a traitor. Let us consider the case where G is the traitor and L1, L2, and L3 are loyal officers, trying to maintain the consistency conditions **IC1** and **IC2**. Suppose G sends out inconsistent orders: "attack" to L1 and L2, and "retreat" to L3. As before, the messages are two-party oral messages, conveyed by loyal messengers. To describe what ensues, we need some notation. Let $X1.X2.X3...Xn(a)$ denote the event that $Xn-1$ tells Xn that $Xn-2$ told $Xn-1$ that ... that $X1$ told $X2$ the value a. For example, $G.L1.L2.L3(attack)$ means that L2 told L3 that L1 told L2 that G told L1 to attack. Consider the messages that can be sent back and forth after G gives his inconsistent orders:

Messages		
Received by L1	**Received by L2**	**Received by L3**
G.L1 (attack)	G.L2 (attack)	G.L3 (retreat)
G.L2.L1 (attack)	G.L1.L2 (attack)	G.L2.L3 (attack)
G.L3.L1 (retreat)	G.L3.L2 (retreat)	G.L1.L3 (attack)

Simply by taking a majority vote on these messages, L1, L2, and L3 can behave consistently (they attack), satisfying **IC1** and **IC2**. In addition, L3 knows G is a traitor since there is at most one traitor, and so L1 and L2 cannot both be traitors (he knows that he himself is loyal). However, L3 has no way of convincing the others of this based on two-party messages (since as far as the others are concerned, L3 could be a traitor himself!).

Consider what happens if L1 is the traitor, and G, L2, and L3 are loyal. As before, the lieutenants compare notes about what they heard from G. Note that L1 can behave arbitrarily, by lying about what he heard from the others. However, despite this, the consistency conditions will continue to be satisfied: every message that does not pass through L1 will be the same. There are enough of such messages to override anything that L1 might do. Consider the messages that flow after G gives his orders. In the following table, m_1 and m_2 refer to the messages emanating from L1: each of these can be either "attack" or "retreat."

Messages		
Received by L1	**Received by L2**	**Received by L3**
G.L1 (attack)	G.L2 (attack)	G.L3 (attack)
G.L2.L1 (attack)	G.L1.L2 (m_1)	G.L2.L3 (attack)
G.L3.L1 (attack)	G.L3.L2 (attack)	G.L1.L3 (m_2)

L2 thus receives the following messages: attack, attack, m_1. L3 receives these messages: attack, attack, m_2. Taking a majority vote results in both L2 and L3 attacking, as required, irrespective of what m_1 and m_2 may be.

Traitors are difficult to handle because they can lie about the messages that were received. Suppose, instead, that *message authentication* is possible. For example, each sender can affix an unforgeable signature to a message. Any lieutenant who passes on the order he got to a colleague must do so by copying the message he got, with the signature on that message, and then adding his own signature. Any attempt to alter the message or the signature can be detected by anyone. As a result, nobody can lie without being found out, and so it will be impossible for a traitor to cause the consistency conditions to break down.

Example 7.4. Let us return to the case in Figure 7.25. Consider what happens when G is a traitor. He sends out signed messages to L1 and L2, saying "attack" and "retreat" respectively. L1 sends L2 a copy of the message he received from G, including G's signature, and vice versa. L1 knows that L2 cannot be lying, since he sees G's signature on the order to retreat and so knows that G did send out contradictory orders, and that G is therefore the traitor. Similarly, L2 also knows that G is the traitor. In such a case, both L1 and L2 can take some default action and the conditions of consistency will be satisfied. The case where L1 is a traitor is similar.

We can now state, without proof, the key result concerning malicious failures.

Theorem 7.1. If messages cannot be authenticated, then to sustain the consistency conditions **IC1** and **IC2** in the face of up to m traitorous generals requires a total of at least $3m + 1$ generals.

The field of Byzantine generals algorithms has become something of a cottage industry, with many new and improved (in terms of speed and memory requirements) algorithms appearing regularly in the literature. Here, we provide what is perhaps the simplest such algorithm.

BYZANTINE ALGORITHM. The algorithm Byz(m) is recursive and is a function of m, which is the specified maximum number of traitors that must be sustained. In the following, when we say that x sends a message to y, we assume either that such a message is received by y, or that y (upon a time-out after receiving no such message) assumes that x transmitted a default value (say "retreat").

Algorithm Byz(0):

1. The commander sends his order to every lieutenant.
2. The lieutenant uses the order he receives from the commander, or the default (say "retreat") if he receives no order.

Algorithm Byz(x):

1. The commander sends his order to every lieutenant. Let v_i be the order he sends to lieutenant Li.
2. For each i, lieutenant Li acts as the commander in a Byz($x-1$) algorithm, and sends out the order v_i to each of the $n-2$ other lieutenants. That is, the $n-2$ other lieutenants try to obtain consensus on lieutenant Li's order, for every i.
3. For each i, and $j \neq i$, let $w_{i,j}$ be the order that lieutenant Li received from Lj in step 2 (using the Byz($x-1$) algorithm), or the default (say "retreat") if he received no such order. Lieutenant Li follows the order majority$\{v_i, w_{i,j}, j \neq i\}$.

This is the same algorithm used in the four-general example considered earlier.

Example 7.5. Consider Byz(2) run on a seven-general system. In the first round, the commander sends his order to each of his generals. In the second round, each of these generals distributes to his colleagues the value he received from the commander using the Byz(1) algorithm. Once this has been concluded, each general can calculate the order that he is to follow.

Let us now prove that this algorithm satisfies the interactive consistency conditions.

Theorem 7.2. If there are at most m traitors and a total of $N \geq 3m + 1$ generals in all, algorithm Byz(m) guarantees interactive consistency.

Proof. We work by induction on m. If $m = 0$ (i.e., there are no traitors), then the algorithm obviously works. This forms the induction basis.

Assume that the algorithm satisfies conditions **IC1** and **IC2** for up to $m - 1$ traitors. There are two cases:

Case 1. *The supreme commander is loyal:* We must show that **IC2** is satisfied, that is, that all the loyal lieutenants follow their commander's order. Since the commander is loyal, all the lieutenants receive the same order, say v. Each loyal lieutenant then acts as the commander for a Byz($m - 1$) algorithm (step 2 of the Byz(m) algorithm for $m \geq 1$). There are at least $2m$ loyal lieutenants.

Case 1.1. $m = 1$: In such a case, every loyal lieutenant simply sends out the order he received to every other lieutenant.

Case 1.2. $m > 1$: If $N \geq 3m + 1$, $N - 1 > 3(m - 1) + 1$; so by the induction hypothesis, in step 2 of Byz($m - 1$) each loyal lieutenant agrees on the order v, sent out by every other loyal lieutenant. Now, since the commander is loyal, the majority vote in step 3 of Byz(m) results in the order v being carried out by each loyal lieutenant.

Case 2. *The supreme commander is a traitor:* Since the commander is one of the up to m traitors up to $m - 1$ of the lieutenants can be traitors, and the others must be loyal. There are at least $3m$ lieutenants, of whom up to $m - 1$ are traitors. $3m - 1 > 3(m - 1) + 1$. Hence by the induction hypothesis, we conclude that each invocation, by a loyal lieutenant, of Byz($m - 1$) in step 2 of Byz(m) satisfies the interactive consistency conditions. Consequently, each loyal lieutenant sees the same vector of values sent by every other lieutenant in step 2 of Byz(m). They therefore carry out the same order, and the theorem is proved.   **Q.E.D.**

The analogy between the Byzantine Empire and the world of computing should be apparent. Traitorous generals are analogous to processors that have suffered malicious (or Byzantine) failure, and loyal generals are analogous to functioning processors. Orders are analogous to some variable value on which consistency is to be obtained. Let us now consider the relevance of all this to real-time computing.

The Byzantine generals algorithm is important whenever we have a single sensor sending out variable values to processors in a redundant cluster that then vote on the result, using the schemes considered earlier in this chapter. (The analogy here is sensor = supreme commander; processor = lieutenant). For majority voting schemes to work, the inputs to the processors should be consistent. If the sensor can suffer Byzantine failure, then a Byzantine generals algorithm is required to obtain consistent values for the processors.

The Byzantine generals algorithm will also work with kinds of voting other than majority voting (in step 3). The details of this are left as an exercise.

Note that throughout we have assumed that the participants in this algorithm are expecting a message. This assumes either a synchronized clock or a watchdog timer, before whose expiry a message is expected. This is necessary; otherwise a traitor could cause everyone to wait forever by simply not providing any output.

A problem similar to the one we have considered arises when we try to synchronize clocks in the face of some failures. This is a problem of great importance in real-time computing, and is covered in Chapter 9.

7.10   INTEGRATED FAILURE HANDLING

When an error is detected, the system must respond swiftly to deal with it. In the short term, the error might be masked by voting. In the long term, the system will have to locate the failure that gave rise to the error and decide what to do with the failed unit. Three options are usually available: retry, disconnect, and replace.

Instruction retry simply consists of retrying the failed instruction, in the hope that the failure was caused by a transient fault, which has since gone away. To be able to do this, we need to be able to detect the error very quickly. If the error is detected after several further instructions have been executed, the question of which instruction caused the error is not easy to answer. To catch such errors, we need fast detection using *signal-level detection* mechanisms. Such mechanisms include error-detection codes, duplicated circuits with matchers, and so on. These mechanisms are distinct from *function-level detection* mechanisms, which operate at the function or module level, and take much more time to catch an error.

If instruction retry is impractical, it might be useful to wait for some time and then run a diagnostic on the affected processor. If the failure is a result of a transient fault that has since vanished, the processor will now pass this test. If, after a long time, the processor still exhibits faulty behavior, we can designate it as a permanent failure. How long we wait for the failure to go away before declaring the failure permanent depends on the lifetime of transient faults. Designers use their past experience, or use collected data on transient-fault durations to answer this question. Alternatively, the system might gather data on its own transients and dynamically adjust this waiting time.

If we decide that the processor has suffered permanent failure, it must be disconnected from the rest of the system. This can be done by preventing it from communicating on the network or by ignoring its output. If a processor is disconnected, we must find new processors to run the tasks that it was allocated. In Chapter 3, we discuss a fault-tolerant task assignment and scheduling algorithm that allows this to be done fairly quickly.

Replace is another way of responding to permanent failure. If spare processors exist, they can be switched in to take the place of the failed unit. All the duties previously performed by the failed processor will now be transferred to the replacement. The replacement processor must have its memory updated suitably to allow it to undertake these computations, and must have its clock synchronized with the rest of the system.

There are several issues to take into account when deciding which recovery action to follow. Four of these are:

Timing information: The overall aim is to meet the hard deadlines of the critical tasks. This is the ultimate test of success or failure, and everything is subordinated to the need to maximize the probability of meeting such deadlines. Timing information includes the worst-case requirements of the current workload, together with the requirements of any interrupt-issued tasks that may be released. It will also include any impending mode changes that can cause a change in the workload.

Recovery time: This is connected with the probability of meeting hard deadlines. Different recovery mechanisms take different amounts of time, and this therefore affects the choice of mechanism.

Probability of the recovery action succeeding: There is often a trade-off between low overhead and the probability of success. Instruction retry has perhaps the lowest overhead of all. However, if the failure is a transient one of long duration, or a permanent fault, it will not succeed. At the other end of the spectrum, the entire system (or a subsystem of it) can be reconfigured to isolate the failure. This has a high probability of success, but takes a long time. A recovery action that fails is worse than no recovery action at all, because it consumes precious time. On the other hand, a recovery action that could have succeeded with little overhead, but which was overlooked in favor of another higher-overhead action represents a waste of time that can affect reliability and performance.

State transition rates: The rate at which failures occur will play a role in determining what recovery action to take. If, for example, there is a reasonable probability that a second failure will occur while the first is still being dealt with, this will cause us to place an increased premium on short recovery actions.

In order to determine a response to failure, the system must be aware of the time taken by the various error-detection and failure-handling mechanisms. Unfortunately, very little is known about these times in practice. This is an area that requires extensive and systematic experimental research.

7.11 SUGGESTIONS FOR FURTHER READING

There are several well-known books on fault-tolerant computing. Among these are Anderson and Lee [1], Johnson [7], and Siewiorek and Swarz [20]. Most of the topics covered in this chapter are treated in greater detail in one or more of these books.

A full discussion of the failure rates of solid-state components and the factors that determine them is presented in [21]. The hostile environment that spacecraft operate in is described in detail in [9].

Some concepts related to fail-stop processors are presented in [18]. The concept of sift-out redundancy is introduced by deSouza and Mathur [5]. For a good discussion on voting schemes, see [14]. For papers on the placement of checkpoints in real-time systems, see [13, 19]. The issue of fault-containment is well discussed by Lala et al. [12]. Self-checking and fail-safe circuits are described in [6].

The Byzantine generals algorithm is introduced in Pease, Shostak, and Lamport in [15], and named as such in [13].

The recovery-block approach to software fault-tolerance is introduced in Randell [17]. For a detailed discussion of N-version programming, see [2, 3, 8, 10].

A good reference for coding theory for fault-tolerance and testing is [4]. There are also several good books on coding. The reader may consult [16] for a thorough—if slightly dated—coverage.

EXERCISES

7.1. Draw the logic diagram of a three-input majority voter voting on eight-bit inputs, assuming that exact agreement is required. The voter has five outputs: $\theta_1, \theta_2, w_1, w_2, w_3$. When at least two of the three inputs agree, θ_1 carries the majority value. θ_2 indicates whether or not at least two inputs agree. If a majority exists and input i does not agree with the majority, line w_i is set to 1; it is 0 otherwise.

7.2. Design the logic of an approximate voter, with the same inputs and outputs as in Exercise 1. Two inputs are said to agree if their values in the six most significant bits are identical. The majority value is here defined as the median value.

7.3. A block diagram of the sift-out redundancy system is shown in Figure 7.10. Draw the detailed logic diagram of such a system for eight-bit processor outputs (each processor has eight output lines). Assume there are four processors in all.

7.4. Write a subroutine that implements the formalized majority voter. This subroutine accepts as input ϵ, the number of inputs n_i, and a vector of length n_i containing the inputs to be voted on. The output will be the majority output if it exists. If no majority can be found, the subroutine will return with a variable NOMAJ set to 1; otherwise this variable value will be 0.

7.5. Suppose you are asked to design a fault-tolerant system that uses memory scrubbing to get rid of transient errors. The only fault-tolerance scheme used for the memory is an error-correcting code that can correct up to two bit errors per word. Failure occurs if more than two bit errors occur in a word. Suppose the coded word is 32 bits long, and that memory cells have a probability p of being corrupted in each clock cycle. Assume that these transient cell failures are independent of one another. Calculate the probability of a word suffering failure if the period between consecutive memory scrubs is P clock cycles.

7.6. What factors govern the optimal placement of checkpoints? Assume that the purpose is to minimize the probability of missing task deadlines.

7.7. Prove that the domino effect can be prevented by ensuring that the recovery points of all the parallel processes are taken at identical times.

7.8. Consider a Byzantine generals algorithm being run with a total of seven generals, with two of the lieutenants being traitors and the remaining officers being loyal. The traitors always convey the message "retreat" no matter what message they receive from their commander. Write out the sequence of messages that results, and show that the interactive consistency conditions are satisfied.

7.9. Consider a Byzantine generals algorithm being run with a total of five generals. The commanding general and one of her lieutenants are traitors; the remaining three lieutenants are loyal. Write out a sequence of messages they would send out to ensure that two of the loyal lieutenants attack and the third retreats.

7.10. In Theorem 7.1, we said that the existence of some algorithm whereby the Phoenecian generals achieve agreement for $N \leq 3m$ implies that such an algorithm, when run with three generals, will be able to successfully deal with up to one traitor. Prove that this is true.

7.11. Prove that if the commander produces a numerical value on which agreement is required, the Byzantine generals algorithm will also work with a voting scheme that picks the median value, rather than majority voting, in step 3.

7.12. Which of the following codes are separable: parity, checksum, cyclic? Explain your answer.

7.13. Design an interlaced parity scheme where the uncoded word has 16 bits and can correct up to two bit errors.

7.14. The following is the entire set of code words in some scheme.

A   1000001000
B   1111110000
C   1111110100

What is the Hamming distance for this code? Between which two words does it occur? If the word 0000000000 is received, which codeword does it map to?

7.15. Draw a circuit for coding with the generator polynomial $1 + X + X^4$. If the serial input is the byte 11110011, what is the output of this generator?

REFERENCES

[1] Anderson, T., and P. A. Lee: *Fault Tolerance, Principles and Practice,* Prentice-Hall, Englewood Cliffs, NJ, 1981.

[2] Avizienis, A., and L. Chen: "On the Implementation of N-Version Programming for Fault-Tolerance During Execution," *Proc. IEEE COMPSAC,* pp. 149–155, IEEE, Los Alamitos, CA, 1977.

[3] Avizienis, A., and J. P. J. Kelly: "Fault-Tolerance by Design Diversity," *IEEE Computer* 17:67–80, 1984.

[4] Bose, B., and J. Metzner: "Coding Theory for Fault-Tolerant Systems," in *Fault-Tolerant Computing* (D. K. Pradhan, ed.), pp. 265–335, Prentice Hall, Englewood Cliffs, NJ, 1986.

[5] de Sousa, P. T., and F. P. Mathur: "Sift-out Modular Redundancy," *IEEE Trans. Computers* C-27:624–627, 1978.

[6] Diaz, M., P. Azema, and J. M. Ayache: "Unified Design of Self-Checking and Fail-Safe Combinational Circuits and Sequential Machines," *IEEE Trans. Computers* C-28:276–281, 1978.

[7] Johnson, B.: *Design and Analysis of Fault Tolerant Digital Systems,* Addison-Wesley, Reading, MA, 1989.

[8] Kelly, J. P. J., and S. Murphy: "Dependable Distributed Software," in *Readings in Real-Time Systems* (Y.-H. Lee and C. M. Krishna, eds.), pp. 146–173, IEEE Computer Society Press, Cupertino, CA, 1993.

[9] Kerns, S. E., and K. F. Galloway, (eds.): Special Section on Space Radiation Effects, *Proc. IEEE* 76, 1988.

[10] Knight, J., and N. Leveson: "An Experimental Evaluation of Independence in Multiversion Programming," *IEEE Trans. Software Engineering* SE-12:96–109, 1986.

[11] Krishna, C. M., Y.-H. Lee, and K. G. Shin: "Optimization Criteria for Checkpoint Placement," *Communications of the ACM* 27:1008–1012, 1984.

[12] Lala, J. H., R. E. Harper, and L. S. Alger: "A Design Approach for Ultrareliable Real-Time Systems," *IEEE Computer* 24:12–24, 1991.

[13] Lamport, L., R. Shostak, and M. Pease: "The Byzantine Generals Algorithm," *ACM Trans. Programming Languages and Systems* 4:382–401, 1982.

[14] Lorczak, P. R., A. K. Caglayan, D. E. Eckhardt: "A Theoretical Investigation of Generalized Voters for Redundant Systems," *Proc. Fault-Tolerant Computing Symp.*, pp. 444–451, IEEE, Los Alamitos, CA, 1989.

[15] Pease, M., R. Shostak, and L. Lamport: "Reaching Agreement in the Presence of Faults," *Journal of the ACM* 25:228–234, 1980.

[16] Peterson, W. W., and E. J. Weldon, Jr.: *Error-Correcting Codes*, MIT Press, Cambridge, MA, 1972.

[17] Randell, B.: "System Structure for Software Fault-Tolerance," *IEEE Trans. Software Engineering* SE-1:220–232, 1975.

[18] Schlichting, R. D., and F. B. Schneider: "Fail-Stop Processors: An Approach to Designing Fault-Tolerant Computing Systems," *ACM Trans. Computing Systems* 1:222–238, 1983.

[19] Shin, K. G., T.-H. Lin, and Y.-H. Lee: "Optimal Checkpointing of Real-Time Tasks," *IEEE Trans. Computers* C-36:1328–1341, 1987.

[20] Siewiorek, D. P., and R. Swarz: *Reliable Computer Systems: Design and Evaluation,* Digital Press, Burlington, MA, 1992.

[21] U.S. Department of Defense, *Military Standardization Handbook: Reliability Prediction of Electronic Equipment*, MIL-HDBK-217E, Washington, D.C., 1986.

CHAPTER
8

RELIABILITY
EVALUATION
TECHNIQUES

8.1 INTRODUCTION

Computers used in life-critical applications must be so reliable that they cannot be validated by experiment alone. For example, suppose we have a system that is supposed to fail, on the average, once every 10^{10} hours. To validate this by experiment, we run this system and record the time between failures. Now, 10^{10} hours is over a million years, so we can expect to observe about one system-wide failure per system every million years or so. A million years is somewhat greater than the product cycle of most computer companies, and so the purely experimental approach is impractical in such a case.

To get around this difficulty, we use mathematical models of reliability. We construct a mathematical model of the real-time computer, and solve it. By doing this, we are adding one possible source of error—the assumptions of the mathematical model. If these are not correct, neither will be the results of our model. It is with this reservation in mind that we introduce reliability evaluation techniques. The correctness of the assumptions is a necessary condition of the correctness of the predictions of the model.

In this chapter, we discuss hardware- and software-reliability models. This discussion is inevitably mathematical, and is aimed at readers who are familiar with probability theory. The Appendix contains a brief refresher on the more common mathematical modeling techniques.

8.2   OBTAINING PARAMETER VALUES

The first step in developing a model is to decide what the input parameters should be. A model should always be based on parameters that can either be accurately measured or estimated with confidence.

8.2.1   Obtaining Device-Failure Rates

There are two ways to obtain device-failure rates, collecting field data and life-cycle testing in the laboratory. The former is more realistic, since it represents the failure rate when the devices are being used in their normal operating conditions. The latter is the only choice when the devices are new and field data do not exist.

In the laboratory, devices can be subjected to "accelerated testing." That is, to reduce the time it takes to gather the data, we can stress the devices so that their failure rate is increased by some factor. If we can estimate this acceleration factor, the failure rate under normal operating conditions can be derived by calculations based on these accelerated data.

The most common accelerant is temperature. As we explained in Chapter 7, the higher the temperature, the greater the failure rate. The acceleration factor is given by the following equation

$$R(T) = Ae^{-E_a/kT} \tag{8.1}$$

where:

A	Represents a constant.
E_a	Represents the activation energy and depends largely on the logic family used.
k	Represents the Boltzmann constant ($0.8625 \times 10^{-4} eV/\text{K}$).
T	Represents the temperature (in degrees kelvin).

At a temperature of T_1, the device failure rate can be expected to be

$$\frac{R(T_1)}{R(T_2)} = e^{-(E_a/k)(1/T_1 - 1/T_2)} \tag{8.2}$$

times the failure rate at a temperature of T_2. Figure 8.1 shows, for example, the testing of MOS devices. For such devices, $E_a \approx 0.7eV$. From the figure, we can see that testing for an hour at 100^oC is equivalent to testing for almost 250 hours at 25^oC.

Such testing acceleration must be used with caution, however. Device failure can also occur due to mechanical and electrical stresses, and there is no established formula for accelerated testing that takes these factors into account.

8.2.2   Measuring Error-Propagation Time

To measure how quickly an error can propagate, we use fault injection. This is best done on a prototype. Special-purpose hardware is used to simulate a fault on

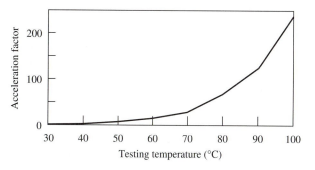

FIGURE 8.1
Acceleration factor with respect to operation at 25°C.

a selected line. The status of the related lines is monitored using logic analyzers to determine how far and how quickly the error propagates. If a prototype is not available, a software simulation can be substituted.

The flow of errors can be expressed via a directed graph. For example, consider Figure 8.2, which shows what happens to an error that originates at A and propagates to B and C. This error spawns an error in the output of these processors, and the output of C causes an error in the output of D. Finally, module E receives erroneous input from B and D, and puts out an erroneous result.

Such a graph, along with the time taken by each module to output the error(s) in response to an erroneous input, can be used to compute the error-propagation time from the output of A to the output of E. The time taken by a module to output an error in response to an erroneous output is a function of the module software and the task schedule. Figure 8.3 illustrates this. The task schedules for processors A and B are shown; tasks Ai and Bi are run on A and B respectively. The $A1$ output is erroneous and is used by task $B2$. The time for the propagation of the error from the $A1$ output to the $B2$ output depends on when $B2$ completes execution.

Due to variations in execution and message propagation times, the error-propagation time is a random variable, and must be characterized by a probability distribution function (PDF).

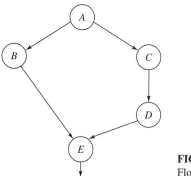

FIGURE 8.2
Flow of an error.

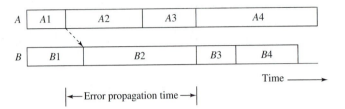

FIGURE 8.3
Error-propagation time ($A1$ output to $B2$ output).

8.2.3 Choosing the Best Distribution*

Suppose we are given a set of observed random variables $Y = \{y_1, \ldots, y_N\}$ and two probability distribution functions F and G. Which of these distribution functions best fits the observations? For example, the random variables could be the times between successive failure of a component, or between successive arrivals of a job to a system, or between the onset of an error and its propagation to some predefined point.

We shall provide two approaches. The first approach to determining which model best fits the data is as follows. Consider a positive-valued random variable that has an underlying probability distribution function $H(x)$, for $x > 0$. Assume for convenience that $H(x)$ is differentiable (i.e., an associated probability density function (pdf) exists[1]) and has pdf $h(x)$. This means that the probability that the random variable has value in $[0, x]$ is given by $H(x)$. Suppose we have observed a collection of N random variables, $Y = \{y_1, y_2, \ldots, y_N\}$, which follow this distribution. Then, by the central limit theorem of probability theory,

$$\lim_{N \to \infty} \frac{\text{Number of random variables in } Y \text{ with value in } [0, x]}{\text{Total number of random variables in } Y \text{ (i.e., } N)} = H(x) \quad (8.3)$$

Now, define $z_i = H(y_i)$. What is the distribution of the set of variables $Z = \{z_1, \ldots, z_N\}$? We have

$$\text{Prob}\{z_i \le \alpha\} = \text{Prob}\{H(y_i) \le \alpha\}$$

$$= \int_{\beta=0}^{\infty} \text{Prob}\{H(y_i) \le \alpha | y_i \in [\beta, \beta + d\beta]\} h(\beta) d\beta$$

$$= \int_{\beta=0}^{H(\beta)=\alpha} \text{Prob}\{H(y_i) \le \alpha | y_i \in [\beta, \beta + d\beta]\} h(\beta) d\beta$$

$$= \int_{\beta=0}^{H(\beta)=\alpha} h(\beta) d\beta$$

$$= \alpha \quad (8.4)$$

---

[1] An equivalent derivation exists for the case where no pdf exists.

Thus, the variables z_i are uniformly distributed in the interval $[0, 1]$. This is the key to the procedure for determining the best-fitting model.

Suppose, now, that the true distribution of these random variables, $H(x)$, is unknown, and we are trying to determine whether it is the distribution $G_{\mathbf{P(G)}}(x)$ or $F_{\mathbf{P(F)}}(x)$, where $\mathbf{P(G)}$ and $\mathbf{P(F)}$ are parameters of the distribution G and F, respectively. For example, if G is the exponential distribution, the parameter is μ, the reciprocal of the mean. If G is a Weibull distribution, the parameters are the intensity λ and the sharpness α. For every set of parameter values, we have a different PDF. Our first job is to obtain the parameters of the distributions F and G for that these distributions best fit the observed random variables. Let the values of the parameters that offer the best fit be $\mathbf{P^*(F)}$ and $\mathbf{P^*(G)}$, respectively.

To see whether F or G best fits the observed data $\{y_i\}$, we define the sequences $\phi_i = F_{\mathbf{P^*(F)}}(y_i)$ and $\gamma_i = G_{\mathbf{P^*(G)}}(y_i)$. Whichever sequence, $\{\phi_i\}$, or $\{\gamma_i\}$, that is closer to being uniformly distributed in the range $[0, 1]$ is the better fit to the observed data. We can use statistical hypothesis testing to determine which offers a better fit to the uniform distribution (thus reducing this method to a variant of hypothesis testing). Alternatively—and this is an attractive feature of this approach—it may be possible to make a judgement based on a visual inspection of a plot of ϕ_i and γ_i.

The second way is to compute what is called the prequential likelihood. Let $f_{\mathbf{P^*(F)}}$ and $g_{\mathbf{P^*(G)}}$ be the density functions associated with $F_{\mathbf{P^*(F)}}$ and $G_{\mathbf{P^*(G)}}$, respectively. It can be shown that if the prequential likelihood ratio (PLR) satisfies

$$\lim_{n \to \infty} \mathrm{PLR}(n) = \lim_{n \to \infty} \frac{\prod_{i=1}^{n} f_{\mathbf{P^*(F)}}(y_i)}{\prod_{i=1}^{n} g_{\mathbf{P^*(G)}}(y_i)} = \infty \tag{8.5}$$

we choose $F_{\mathbf{P^*(F)}}$ over $G_{\mathbf{P^*(G)}}$.

8.3 RELIABILITY MODELS FOR HARDWARE REDUNDANCY

The most difficult problem in reliability modeling is to keep the complexity of the models sufficiently small. This is not much of a problem when the various parameters of the model are exponentially distributed; however, to accurately model with parameters that observe other distributions usually results in an unacceptable complexity for all but the smallest systems. Current techniques to reduce the complexity of such models consist largely of state aggregation, in which multiple states are grouped together and treated as a single state; and decomposition, in which the overall model is broken down into submodels, each submodel is solved, and allowance is made for the interaction of the various submodels. These techniques are approximations only, but approximations mandated by the underlying difficulty of the problem.

In order to model the reliability of a system, we must express the reliability of each of its components, and take into account the impact of the failure of each component on the functioning of the overall system.

The reliability of components is usually specified through a probability distribution function of the lifetime of that component.[2] For example, if failures occur as a Poisson process with rate λ, the lifetime distribution is given by $F_\ell(t) = 1 - \exp(-\lambda t)$. If failures occur as a Weibull process with a shape parameter α and scale parameter λ, the lifetime distribution is $F_\ell(t) = 1 - \exp(-[\lambda t]^\alpha)$. We will denote by $f_\ell(t)$ the associated density function (we will assume here that $F_\ell(t)$ is differentiable).

The *hazard rate* $h(t)$ of a component with age t is defined as the rate of failure at time t, given that it has not failed up to time t. We can use Bayes's law to express the hazard rate as a function of the lifetime distribution function.

$$h(t)dt = \text{Prob}\{\text{System fails in } [t, t + dt] \mid \text{System has not failed up to } t\}$$

$$= \frac{\text{Prob}\{\text{System fails in } [t, t + dt] \cap \text{System has not failed up to } t\}}{\text{Prob}\{\text{System has not failed up to } t\}}$$

$$= \frac{f_\ell(t)dt}{1 - F_\ell(t)}$$

$$\Rightarrow h(t) = \frac{f_\ell(t)}{1 - F_\ell(t)} \tag{8.6}$$

If the failure process is Poisson with rate λ (i.e., if the lifetime distribution is exponentially distributed with mean $1/\lambda$), then the hazard rate is

$$h(t) = \frac{\lambda e^{-\lambda t}}{e^{-\lambda t}}$$

$$= \lambda \tag{8.7}$$

The hazard rate is thus independent of the age of the component if the failure process is Poisson. Hence, to analyze the reliability of systems built out of such components, we do not need to know their age. This simplifies modeling tremendously.

If the failure process is Weibull with shape and scale parameters α and λ, respectively, the hazard rate is given by

$$h(t) = \alpha\lambda(\lambda t)^{\alpha - 1} \tag{8.8}$$

If $0 < \alpha < 1$, then $h(t)$ decreases with time. This means that the failure rate of a component drops as it ages. Components with decreasing hazard rates are said to have the *used-better-than-new* property. If $\alpha = 1$, the failure process is Poisson. If $\alpha > 1$, $h(t)$ increases with time; that is, the failure rate increases with age, and such components have the *new-better-than-used* property.

Many real-life components have a hazard rate shaped according to the *bathtub curve*, shown in Figure 8.4. In the beginning the hazard rate is quite high, and then it begins to drop. This is known as the infant-mortality phase, where

---

[2]Once a component fails, its life is over. Unless otherwise stated, we do not assume any repair.

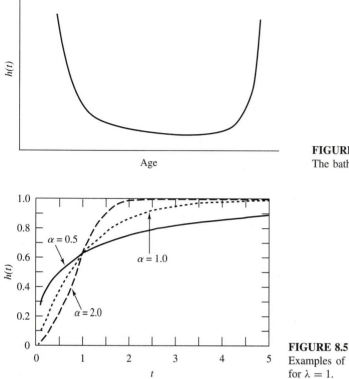

FIGURE 8.4
The bathtub curve.

FIGURE 8.5
Examples of lifetime distributions, for $\lambda = 1$.

components with manufacturing defects are weeded out. The rate then becomes approximately constant, before aging effects set in and cause the hazard rate to rise with age. Note that Figure 8.4 is not drawn to scale. Typically, the interval of constant hazard rate is much longer than either the infant-mortality or aging regions.

Define $\ell(t) = \int_0^t h(x)dx$. Then, the probability that the component will fail some time in the interval $[0, t]$, which is the PDF of the component lifetime, is given by $1 - e^{-\ell(t)}$. Figure 8.5 provides some numerical illustrations of the lifetime distribution associated with the Weibull distribution, $h(t) = \alpha\lambda(\lambda t)^{\alpha-1}$.

The impact of the failure of individual components on the reliability of the overall system depends on the structure of the system. The *coverage* with respect to a given component failure is the probability that the system will successfully recover from that failure.

Let us now turn to presenting a series of models, of varying complexity and scope, for systems using hardware redundancy.

8.3.1 Permanent Faults Only

SERIES-PARALLEL SYSTEMS. Let us begin with systems represented in series-parallel form. A set of components is connected in *series* if the failure of any of

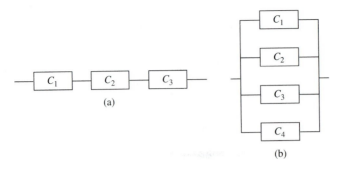

FIGURE 8.6
(a) Series connection and (b) parallel connection.

them will result in system failure. A *parallel* connection of components requires all the components to fail before the system fails. Figure 8.6 contains the structural representation of each of these forms. In Figure 8.6a, the system fails if any of the components C_1, C_2, or C_3 fails, while in Figure 8.6b, it fails only if all of the components C_1, C_2, C_3, and C_4 fail. Let $R(C_i)$ denote the reliability, over a given interval $[0, t]$, of component C_i. That is, $R(C_i)$ denotes the probability that the component does not fail in the interval $[0, t]$. Then, if the component failures are independent, the reliability over that interval of a series connection of n components is given by $\prod_{i=1}^{n} R(C_i)$, and that of a parallel connection is $1 - \prod_{i=1}^{n}[1 - R(C_i)]$. Systems can be built out of both series and parallel forms. An example of such a mixed system is provided in Figure 8.7. The reliability of such a system can be written recursively.

> **Example 8.1.** The system in Figure 8.7 is a series connection of modules M_1, C_1, C_2, and M_{10}. C_1 is itself a parallel connection of two modules, C_{1a} and C_{1b}, which are themselves serial connections of two modules each. Similarly, C_2 is a parallel connection of four modules. We can therefore write
>
> $$R(C_1) = 1 - [1 - R(C_{1a})][1 - R(C_{1b})]$$
> $$= 1 - [1 - R(M_2)R(M_4)][1 - R(M_3)R(M_5)] \tag{8.9}$$
> $$R(C_2) = 1 - [1 - R(M_6)][1 - R(M_7)][1 - R(M_8)][1 - R(M_9)] \tag{8.10}$$
>
> The reliability of the system is given by:
>
> $$R(\text{System}) = R(M_1)R(C_1)R(C_2)R(M_{10}) \tag{8.11}$$

NMR CLUSTERS. Consider an N-modular-redundant cluster. For the moment, let us assume that the fault latency is zero (i.e., faults start generating errors immediately when they arrive) and that faulty processors are immediately identified and disconnected from the system. As a result, the system will always consist of good processors only, and will continue to function until it has fewer than two functional processors. Assume also that the voters are perfectly reliable (this condition is trivial to remove and is dealt with later). The failures are all independent

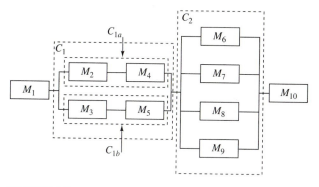

FIGURE 8.7
Composite series-parallel system.

and they are all permanent. There is no repair. Let the failure process be Poisson, with rate λ. We present two equivalent models for this system, one combinatorial and the other based on Markov chains.

Combinatorial model. The system will fail only if there are fewer than two functional processors left in the system. Since there is no repair and all the failures are assumed to be permanent, the failure probability can be found by counting (hence the term combinatorial) all the various ways in which fewer than two processors are left and weighting each by its probability of occurrence. The probability that an individual processor suffers failure some time in an interval of duration t is given by $F_\ell(t) = 1 - \exp(-\lambda t)$. The probability of system failure over this interval is given by

$$\text{Prob\{System failure in } [0, t]\} = \sum_{i=0}^{1} \text{Prob\{Exactly } i \text{ processors functional at } t\}$$

(8.12)

This is, of course, a Bernoulli process, and the probability that there are only i processors functional is given by

$$\binom{N}{i} F_\ell^{N-i}(t)(1 - F_\ell(t))^i$$

(8.13)

We therefore have, after some minor algebra,

$$\text{Prob\{System failure in } [0, t]\} = N F_\ell^{N-1}(t) - (N - 1) F_\ell^N(t)$$

(8.14)

Markov chain model. Markov chain models, while more complex than combinatorial models for such simple cases, are the solution method of choice when the systems are more complex. The system can be modeled as a Markov chain as shown in Figure 8.8, where the states represent the number of functional processors. Since failed units are removed immediately from the system, and there is no repair, we have a "pure-death process." This chain is identical to one discussed

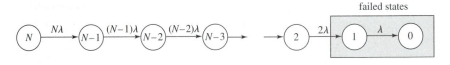

failed states

FIGURE 8.8
Markov chain for an NMR system.

in the Appendix. There it is shown that the probability $\pi_i(t)$ of the system being in state i at time t (given that it started in state N at time 0) is given by

$$\pi_i(t) = \sum_{j=0}^{N-i} A(i, j)e^{-(i+j)\mu t} \tag{8.15}$$

where

$$A(i, j) = (-1)^j \frac{N!}{i!j!(N - i - j)!} \tag{8.16}$$

The probability that the system has failed by time t is given by the probability that it is in either state 0 or 1, that is,

$$\text{Prob}\{\text{System failure}\} = \sum_{i=0}^{1} \pi_i(t) \tag{8.17}$$

In fact, there is no need, for our purposes, to distinguish between states 0 and 1. Indeed, we could have defined states 0 and 1 as one failed state, and computed the probability of ever entering that state up to time t.

Voter reliability. There are two typical designs for voter reliability, one in which there is exactly one voter providing output for the cluster, and the second in which there are N voters, one per processor. We focus on the first design, and leave the second as an exercise.

Let $F_{V,N}(t)$ be the PDF of the voter lifetime when it has to arbitrate among N inputs. This is a function of N, since the voter complexity is a function of N and lifetime tends to decrease as complexity increases. The system will fail whenever fewer than two processors are functioning or the voter fails. Assuming the two events are independent, the PDF of the system lifetime is thus given by

$$\Phi_N(t) = F_{V,N}(t)\{NF_\ell^{N-1}(t) - (N - 1)F_\ell^N(t)\} \tag{8.18}$$

This equation raises the possibility that because the voter becomes less reliable as the cluster size increases, an increase in the cluster size can actually decrease the reliability of the cluster. In particular, we have, after some algebra,

$$\Phi_N(t) < \Phi_{N+1}(t) \Rightarrow \frac{F_{V,N}(t)}{F_{V,N+1}(t)} < \frac{(N + 1)F_\ell(t) - NF_\ell^2(t)}{N - (N - 1)F_\ell(t)} \tag{8.19}$$

To make this more concrete, consider the following example of Poisson failures.

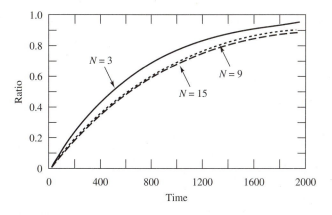

FIGURE 8.9
Critical ratio of voter reliabilities for an N-processor system.

Example 8.2. Let $F_\ell(t) = 1 - e^{-\mu t}$. Then, if

$$\phi_{\text{ratio}}(N) = \frac{F_{V,N}(t)}{F_{V,N+1}(t)} < \frac{(N+1)F_\ell(t) - NF_\ell^2(t)}{N - (N-1)F_\ell(t)} \qquad (8.20)$$

adding another processor to a cluster of N processors decreases reliability. Let us examine this expression. At $t = 0$, it is 0; that is, the ratio $F_{V,N}(t)/F_{V,N+1}(t)$ simply does not matter. As $t \to \infty$, this ratio approaches 1. Figure 8.9 plots the critical ratio for which the reliability of the N-processor system is the same as that of the $(N+1)$-processor system. If the actual ratio is greater than in the figure, an $(N+1)$-processor system exhibits a higher reliability. If it is lower, an $(N + 1)$-processor system exhibits a lower reliability than the corresponding N-processor system.

Notice that the ratio is a function of time; as $t \to \infty$, the allowance that we can make for the additional failure rate of the voter keeps reducing. The voter reliability thus is an increasingly limiting factor as time increases. That is, if we have an application with long periods during which the system cannot be repaired, the reliability of the single voter can limit the size of the cluster, and thus the overall reliability. The longer the system must go before it can be repaired, the greater the impact of the voter reliability. Deep-space unmanned vehicles that cannot be repaired and that must function usefully over long time periods should not use single voters for critical applications.

Example 8.2 assumes that processor failures follow a homogeneous Poisson process (i.e., that the hazard rate is constant). Let us now relax that condition. In particular, let the processor permanent-failure rate be a function $\lambda(t)$ of the processor age. Such a failure process is called a *nonhomogeneous Poisson* process.

In general, systems that fail according to time-varying rates are more difficult to solve since we have to keep track of the age of each processor. However, in the special case where all the processors are of the same age and where there is no repair, the problem is almost as simple as the constant failure-rate case. Let us construct a combinatorial model for this. Assume the age of each processor in the system when it begins operating is a. The probability $S(t)$ that an individual processor has a lifetime $\geq t$ is

$$S(t) = S(t - \Delta t) - S(t - \Delta t)\lambda(t + a)\Delta t + o([\Delta t]^2)$$

$$\Rightarrow \frac{dS(t)}{dt} = -S(t)\lambda(t + a)$$

$$\Rightarrow S(t) = e^{-\int_0^t \lambda(x+a)dx} \tag{8.21}$$

Hence, the probability that a processor has a lifetime $\leq t$ is given by $F_\ell(t) = 1 - S(t)$. Since all the processors have the same age, the probability that at time t there are i out of N processors functional can be computed by substituting this value of $F_\ell(t)$ in Equation (8.13), and the probability of system failure can be computed.

This calculation is simple because we have assumed that all the processors in the system have the same age. Now let us relax this by replacing it with the assumption that the age of a processor when the system begins service is a random variable with density $\alpha(t)$, and that the ages of the processors are independent of one another. Then the above derivation holds, except that the expression for $F_\ell(t)$ becomes

$$F_\ell(t) = 1 - \int_{a=0}^{\infty} e^{-\int_0^t \lambda(x+a)dx} \alpha(a)da \tag{8.22}$$

The fact that we are immediately uncovering faults and disconnecting the faulty processors contributes greatly to the reliability of the system. To see this, let us consider the case where the faulty processors are not disconnected, but are allowed to continue to participate in the functioning of the system. Such a system is only guaranteed to function correctly so long as a majority of the processors are functioning. If $N = 2m + 1$ is the total number of processors in the cluster, we have

$$\text{Prob}\{\text{System failure in } [0, t]\} = \sum_{i=0}^{m} \text{Prob}\{\text{Exactly } i \text{ processors functional at } t\}$$

$$= \sum_{i=0}^{m} \binom{N}{i} F_\ell^{N-i}(t)(1 - F_\ell(t))^i \tag{8.23}$$

A comparison of Equations (8.12) and (8.23) shows the substantial increase in the failure probability that results when faulty units are not purged promptly.

Example 8.3. In Figure 8.10, we consider the case when $F_\ell(t) = 1 - e^{-\mu t}$. The voter reliability is ignored. For purposes of comparison, we also provide a plot of the failure probability of a single-processor system (a *simplex*). Notice how, as time goes on, the failure probability of the system without purging actually becomes greater than that of the simplex. This happens when the failure probability of the simplex exceeds 0.5. When the system must go for long periods without repair, faulty components must therefore be purged. Even purging faulty components will not be better than using a simplex if the time period is so long that the failure probability of the purging system is about 0.85.

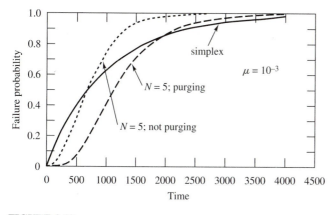

FIGURE 8.10
Comparison of the effects of purging, not purging, and using a simplex.

8.3.2 Fault Latency*

We have so far assumed that the fault latency time is zero (i.e., that a fault starts generating errors the moment it occurs). This is usually not the case. It is not until the fault is exercised that the fault generates an error. For example, if a wire is broken, it is not until some signal is meant to propagate down that wire that the fault manifests itself. Faults that have not yet manifested themselves are called *latent faults*.

The problem with latent faults is that because they do not generate errors, they are invisible to the system. When a unit is detected as faulty, it can be isolated from the system. If detection is not immediate, it is possible for units with latent faults to accumulate in the system. This can compromise the reliability of the system, as we show below.

Consider a system that configures its processors into multiple *triads* or *triplexes*, that is, into NMR clusters with $N = 3$. When a processor in a triad is found to be faulty, it is removed from active duty and a spare is electronically switched in to take its place. Faults are detected as a by-product of the voting process. Voting takes place every τ time units, and any faulty processor detected by the voting process is immediately replaced by a spare. For simplicity, assume that only permanent failure occurs and that processors fail independently of one another according to a Poisson process with rate λ. We have two cases depending on whether or not the fault-latency time is exponentially distributed.

EXPONENTIALLY-DISTRIBUTED FAULT-LATENCY. Let the fault-latency time be exponentially distributed with mean $1/\mu$. Assuming an infinite supply of spares, what is the reliability of the triad? Since the number of spares is unlimited, the triad will never fail because it runs out of replacement hardware. It will only fail if at least two processors start generating errors within the same intervoting interval. Figure 8.11 illustrates one such sequence of events.

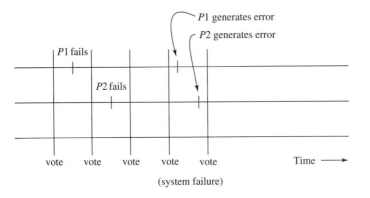

FIGURE 8.11
A sequence of events resulting in triad failure.

Determining the reliability of such a system is more complicated than for the systems we encountered earlier, and so we must take it in steps. A triad will fail if at least two of its processors start generating errors during the same intervote interval (as shown in Figure 8.11). We must therefore focus on the state of the system at each voting instant.

Our plan of attack is the following. Let us construct a Markov chain that captures the state of the system at each voting instant. Our chain will give us the state of the system at a voting instant as a function of the state at the previous voting instant. It will be a discrete-time chain. To use the jargon of mathematical modeling, this is a "semi-Markov chain embedded at voting epochs." Let us define the state of the system by a two-tuple (x, y) where x is the number of nonfaulty processors in the triad and y is the number of processors in the triad that have a latent fault (i.e., one that is faulty but that has not yet generated an error). Since the total number of processors in the triad is 3, the number of processors in the triad that have generated errors is given by $3 - x - y$. The probability that the triad will fail can then be expressed as a function of the states as

$$\text{Prob\{Failure\}} = \text{Prob\{System state} \in \{(0, 0), (0, 1), (1, 0)\}\} \qquad (8.24)$$

To obtain these probabilities, we require the state-transition probabilities for the chain; that is, we require the probability $p_{(x1,y1),(x2,y2)}$ of the state being (x_2, y_2) at the ith vote, given that it was (x_1, y_1) at the $(i - 1)$st vote. To get these state-transition probabilities, we must understand what can occur between two successive voting instants. Just after a vote, if there are two or more processors that have generated an error, the triad fails, and there is no transition out of the triad-failure state. If exactly one processor has generated an error, that error is detected at the vote, the affected processor is configured out of the system and a fresh (assumed nonfaulty) processor is inducted into the triad. If no processor has generated an error, no reconfiguration action is taken. We assume that this reconfiguration action takes negligible time to complete. Following this step, the triad runs its applications programs until the next vote, when the above process is repeated.

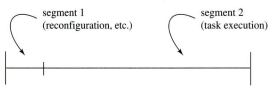

segment 1
(reconfiguration, etc.)

segment 2
(task execution)

FIGURE 8.12
Partitioning of the intervote interval.

The intervote interval can be divided into a first segment of negligible duration, during which any reconfiguration is carried out, and a second segment of length τ, which is when the application programs are run. Figure 8.12 illustrates this. The state of the system at the end of the first segment is the same state as at the beginning of the second. We will obtain the state-transition probability over an intervote interval by obtaining the state-transition probabilities over each of these segments.

If the system state at the vote is (x_1, y_1), then the state just after the reconfiguration, if any, is given by:

$$
\begin{array}{ll}
(x_1, y_1) & \text{if } x_1 + y_1 = 3 \\
(x_1 + 1, y_1) & \text{if } x_1 + y_1 = 2 \\
\text{FAIL} & \text{if } x_1 + y_1 \le 1
\end{array}
\tag{8.25}
$$

The justification is simple. If $x_1 + y_1 = 3$, there are no processors in the triad that have generated errors, and so no faults can be detected and the state at the end of the reconfiguration period is the same as at the beginning. (No failures take place during the reconfiguration period itself, since it is assumed to be of negligible duration.) If $x_1 + y_1 = 2$, exactly one of the three processors in the triad has generated an error over the preceding intervote interval, and this processor is identified and replaced by a nonfaulty spare. If $x_1 + y_1 \le 1$, two or more of the three processors have generated an error over the previous intervote interval, and the system fails (since a majority of the triad has produced erroneous results). At the end of the first segment, the state of the system is either FAIL or (x, y) such that $x + y = 3$. The state-transition matrix for this segment P_1 is given in Table 8.1.

TABLE 8.1
State-transition matrix for P_1

	(3,0)	(2,1)	(1,2)	(0,3)	(2,0)	(1,1)	(0,2)	(1,0)	(0,1)	(0,0)	FAIL
(3,0)	1	0	0	0	0	0	0	0	0	0	0
(2,1)	0	1	0	0	0	0	0	0	0	0	0
(1,2)	0	0	1	0	0	0	0	0	0	0	0
(0,3)	0	0	0	1	0	0	0	0	0	0	0
(2,0)	1	0	0	0	0	0	0	0	0	0	0
(1,1)	0	1	0	0	0	0	0	0	0	0	0
(0,2)	0	0	1	0	0	0	0	0	0	0	0
(1,0)	0	0	0	0	0	0	0	0	0	0	1
(0,1)	0	0	0	0	0	0	0	0	0	0	1
(0,0)	0	0	0	0	0	0	0	0	0	0	1

Note that, at the end of the first segment, the system can be in one of just five states: $(3, 0)$, $(2, 1)$, $(1, 2)$, $(0, 3)$, and FAIL. Given the state of the system at the end of the reconfiguration segment, we now have to compute the state probabilities at the next voting instant. This is not something that can be determined by inspection. In fact, to model the failure and error process over the second segment, we will require a continuous-time Markov chain. (We did not require such a chain for the first segment because it was of negligible duration.) Figure 8.13 shows the chains for when the second segment starts in a non-FAIL state. Figures 8.13b, c, and d are really subsets of Figure 8.13a, as is obvious from inspection. These are simple transient Markov chains, and we can write by inspection differential equations for the state probabilities. Let $\pi_{x,y}(t)$ denote the probability of being in state (x, y) at time t. Then, the differential equations for the chains in Figure 8.13 are

$$\frac{d\pi_{3,0}(t)}{dt} = -3\lambda\pi_{3,0}(t) \tag{8.26}$$

$$\frac{d\pi_{2,1}(t)}{dt} = 3\lambda\pi_{3,0}(t) - (2\lambda + \mu)\pi_{2,1}(t) \tag{8.27}$$

$$\frac{d\pi_{1,2}(t)}{dt} = 2\lambda\pi_{2,1}(t) - (\lambda + 2\mu)\pi_{1,2}(t) \tag{8.28}$$

$$\frac{d\pi_{0,3}(t)}{dt} = \lambda\pi_{1,2}(t) - 3\mu\pi_{0,3}(t) \tag{8.29}$$

$$\frac{d\pi_{2,0}(t)}{dt} = \mu\pi_{2,1}(t) - 2\lambda\mu_{2,0}(t) \tag{8.30}$$

$$\frac{d\pi_{1,1}(t)}{dt} = 2\mu\pi_{1,2}(t) + 2\lambda\pi_{2,0}(t) - (\lambda + \mu)\pi_{1,1}(t) \tag{8.31}$$

$$\frac{d\pi_{0,2}(t)}{dt} = 3\mu\pi_{0,3}(t) + \lambda\pi_{1,1}(t) - 2\mu\pi_{0,2}(t) \tag{8.32}$$

$$\frac{d\pi_{1,0}(t)}{dt} = \mu\pi_{1,1}(t) - \lambda\pi_{1,0}(t) \tag{8.33}$$

$$\frac{d\pi_{0,1}(t)}{dt} = 2\mu\pi_{0,2}(t) + \lambda\pi_{1,0}(t) - \mu\pi_{0,1}(t) \tag{8.34}$$

$$\frac{d\pi_{0,0}(t)}{dt} = \mu\pi_{0,1}(t) \tag{8.35}$$

These equations can be solved numerically. However, they are also simple enough that we can derive analytical expressions for them. This is because of the structure of this set of differential equations. We can solve the first of these equations directly; the solution of the first equation is an input to the second, and we can solve for $\pi_{2,1}(t)$ from that. This solution is an input to the third equation, and we can solve for $\pi_{1,2}(t)$; and so on. We will leave the details to the industrious reader.

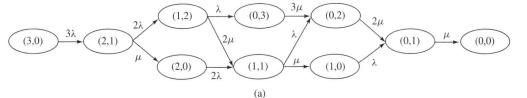

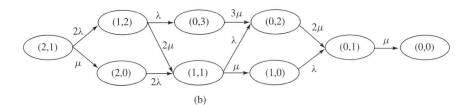

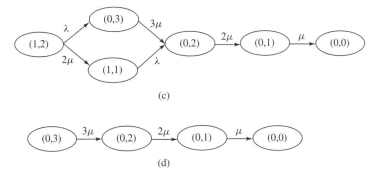

(d)

FIGURE 8.13
Modeling failure and error processes over the second segment: (a) initial state (3,0); (b) initial state (2,1); (c) initial state (1,2); (d) initial state (0,3).

The state-transition probability matrix for the second segment P_2 is then as in Table 8.2.

We are now in a position to write the state-transition probabilities over the entire intervote interval, that is, over the two segments combined. Denote by $p^{(i)}_{(a,b),(c,d)}$ $(i = 1, 2)$ the entry in the state-transition matrix P_i specifying the state-transition probability from (a, b) to (c, d). In matrix notation, the matrix of these probabilities is

$$P = P_1 \times P_2 \tag{8.36}$$

We are now done. If the system starts in some initial state at time 0, and runs for k intervote intervals, the vector of state-probabilities at the end of that run will be given by

$$\mathbf{X_f} = P^k \mathbf{X_0} \tag{8.37}$$

where $\mathbf{X_0}$ is the state-probability vector representing the initial state.

TABLE 8.2
State-transition matrix for P_2

	(3,0)	(2,1)	(1,2)	(0,3)	(2,0)
(3,0)	$\pi_{3,0}(\tau\|3,0)$	$\pi_{2,1}(\tau\|3,0)$	$\pi_{1,2}(\tau\|3,0)$	$\pi_{0,3}(\tau\|3,0)$	$\pi_{2,0}(\tau\|3,0)$
(2,1)	$\pi_{3,0}(\tau\|2,1)$	$\pi_{2,1}(\tau\|2,1)$	$\pi_{1,2}(\tau\|2,1)$	$\pi_{0,3}(\tau\|2,1)$	$\pi_{2,0}(\tau\|2,1)$
(1,2)	$\pi_{3,0}(\tau\|1,2)$	$\pi_{2,1}(\tau\|1,2)$	$\pi_{1,2}(\tau\|1,2)$	$\pi_{0,3}(\tau\|1,2)$	$\pi_{1,2}(\tau\|1,2)$
(0,3)	$\pi_{3,0}(\tau\|0,3)$	$\pi_{2,1}(\tau\|0,3)$	$\pi_{1,2}(\tau\|0,3)$	$\pi_{0,3}(\tau\|0,3)$	$\pi_{1,2}(\tau\|0,3)$
(2,0)	$\pi_{3,0}(\tau\|2,0)$	$\pi_{2,1}(\tau\|2,0)$	$\pi_{1,2}(\tau\|2,0)$	$\pi_{0,3}(\tau\|2,0)$	$\pi_{1,2}(\tau\|2,0)$
(1,1)	$\pi_{3,0}(\tau\|1,1)$	$\pi_{2,1}(\tau\|1,1)$	$\pi_{1,2}(\tau\|1,1)$	$\pi_{0,3}(\tau\|1,1)$	$\pi_{1,2}(\tau\|1,1)$
(0,2)	$\pi_{3,0}(\tau\|0,2)$	$\pi_{2,1}(\tau\|0,2)$	$\pi_{1,2}(\tau\|0,2)$	$\pi_{0,3}(\tau\|0,2)$	$\pi_{1,2}(\tau\|0,2)$
(1,0)	$\pi_{3,0}(\tau\|1,0)$	$\pi_{2,1}(\tau\|1,0)$	$\pi_{1,2}(\tau\|1,0)$	$\pi_{0,3}(\tau\|1,0)$	$\pi_{1,2}(\tau\|1,0)$
(0,1)	$\pi_{3,0}(\tau\|0,1)$	$\pi_{2,1}(\tau\|0,1)$	$\pi_{1,2}(\tau\|0,1)$	$\pi_{0,3}(\tau\|0,1)$	$\pi_{1,2}(\tau\|0,1)$
(0,0)	$\pi_{3,0}(\tau\|0,0)$	$\pi_{2,1}(\tau\|0,0)$	$\pi_{1,2}(\tau\|0,0)$	$\pi_{0,3}(\tau\|0,0)$	$\pi_{1,2}(\tau\|0,0)$
FAIL	0	0	0	0	0

	(1,1)	(0,2)	(1,0)	(0,1)	(0,0)	FAIL
(3,0)	$\pi_{1,1}(\tau\|3,)$	$\pi_{0,2}(\tau\|3,0)$	$\pi_{1,0}(\tau\|3,0)$	$\pi_{0,1}(\tau\|3,0)$	$\pi_{0,0}(\tau\|3,0)$	0
(2,1)	$\pi_{1,1}(\tau\|2,1)$	$\pi_{0,2}(\tau\|2,1)$	$\pi_{1,0}(\tau\|2,1)$	$\pi_{0,1}(\tau\|2,1)$	$\pi_{0,0}(\tau\|2,1)$	0
(1,2)	$\pi_{1,1}(\tau\|1,2)$	$\pi_{0,2}(\tau\|1,2)$	$\pi_{1,0}(\tau\|1,2)$	$\pi_{0,1}(\tau\|1,2)$	$\pi_{0,0}(\tau\|1,2)$	0
(0,3)	$\pi_{1,1}(\tau\|0,3)$	$\pi_{0,2}(\tau\|0,3)$	$\pi_{1,0}(\tau\|0,3)$	$\pi_{0,1}(\tau\|0,3)$	$\pi_{0,0}(\tau\|0,3)$	0
(2,0)	$\pi_{1,1}(\tau\|2,0)$	$\pi_{0,2}(\tau\|2,0)$	$\pi_{1,0}(\tau\|2,0)$	$\pi_{0,1}(\tau\|2,0)$	$\pi_{0,0}(\tau\|2,0)$	0
(1,1)	$\pi_{1,1}(\tau\|1,1)$	$\pi_{0,2}(\tau\|1,1)$	$\pi_{1,0}(\tau\|1,1)$	$\pi_{0,1}(\tau\|1,1)$	$\pi_{0,0}(\tau\|1,1)$	0
(0,2)	$\pi_{1,1}(\tau\|0,2)$	$\pi_{0,2}(\tau\|0,2)$	$\pi_{1,0}(\tau\|0,2)$	$\pi_{0,1}(\tau\|0,2)$	$\pi_{0,0}(\tau\|0,2)$	0
(1,0)	$\pi_{1,1}(\tau\|1,0)$	$\pi_{0,2}(\tau\|1,0)$	$\pi_{1,0}(\tau\|0,3)$	$\pi_{0,1}(\tau\|1,0)$	$\pi_{0,0}(\tau\|1,0)$	0
(0,1)	$\pi_{1,1}(\tau\|0,1)$	$\pi_{0,2}(\tau\|0,1)$	$\pi_{1,0}(\tau\|0,1)$	$\pi_{0,1}(\tau\|0,1)$	$\pi_{0,0}(\tau\|0,1)$	0
(0,0)	$\pi_{1,1}(\tau\|0,0)$	$\pi_{0,2}(\tau\|0,0)$	$\pi_{1,0}(\tau\|0,0)$	$\pi_{0,1}(\tau\|0,0)$	$\pi_{0,0}(\tau\|0,0)$	0
FAIL	0	0	0	0	0	1

A MORE GENERAL MODEL. In the model we just studied, we assumed that the failure process was Poisson and that the fault latencies were exponentially distributed. The advantage of this assumption is that the state descriptions are very simple. We do not need to know how long the system has been in a particular state to compute its transition rate out of that state; all that we need to know is how many failures have taken place and, of these, how many have generated errors (thus making them visible to the outside world).

We now consider how to handle fault latencies that are not exponentially distributed. We continue to assume that processor failures occur as independent Poisson processes, with (constant) rate λ. To keep the model tractable, we resort to an approximation. In reality, triad failure occurs when two processors start generating errors in the same intervote interval. Here we will assume that the triad will fail if and only if after a processor fails, a second processor fails before the first has generated any errors. After solving this model, we will recognize that this is not necessarily a conservative approximation. Since we are modeling reliability, we would like to err on the side of safety. Simple modifications to our approximate model will ensure that the approximation becomes conservative.

Let the density function of the fault-latency time be $f_L(t)$. Processor failures in a fully functional triad occur at a rate of 3λ. Given that a failure has occurred, what is the probability of a second failure happening before the first has generated an error? This can be computed as follows. Define time 0 as when the first failure occurred. Let the time when this failure first generates an error be in the interval $[t, t + dt]$. Triad failure will occur if there is a second processor failure by time t. The probability of this is given by $1 - \exp\{-2\lambda t\}$. The probability that the failure first generates an error in $[t, t + dt]$ is given by $f_L(t)dt$. Therefore the probability of a second failure occurring before the first has generated an error is

$$\int_{t=0}^{\infty} \{1 - \exp\{-2\lambda t\}\} f_L(t)dt = 1 - \int_{t=0}^{\infty} \exp\{-2\lambda t\} f_L(t)dt = 1 - \mathcal{F}_L^*(2\lambda)$$

(8.38)

where $\mathcal{F}_L^*$ is the Laplace transform of $f_L(t)$.

Since the first processor failure occurs at a rate of 3λ and $\mathcal{F}^*(2\lambda)$ is the approximate probability that this results in a triad failure, the rate of triad failure is approximately

$$3\lambda \left[1 - \mathcal{F}_L^*(2\lambda) \right]$$

(8.39)

Having derived this approximation, we ask if it is conservative. Since we are modeling the reliability of life-critical systems, we would prefer to have *conservative* approximations, that is, approximations that overestimate the failure probability. There are two sources of inaccuracy in the above analysis. First, we have assumed that triad failure will only occur if a second processor failure occurs before the first failure has generated an error. Second, we have implicitly assumed that when the first processor failure occurs, triad failure ensues immediately with probability $1 - \mathcal{F}_L^*(2\lambda)$.

Our first assumption does not cover all the possible events that can cause triad failure and is therefore not conservative. This is because we do not take into account the fact that errors are not caught immediately when they occur; it takes until the next vote to do so. Take, for example, the situation illustrated in Figure 8.14. A triad failure results despite the second processor failure occurring only after the first has generated errors. Fortunately, this is easy to correct. Let us

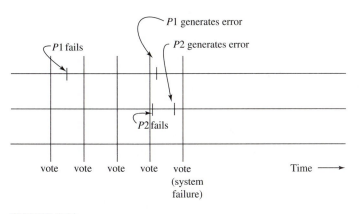

FIGURE 8.14
Regarding the first assumption.

assume that triad failure occurs whenever the second processor failure occurs at time t and the first processor failure starts generating errors by time $\max\{0, t - \tau\}$, where (as you recall) τ is the length of the interval between successive votes. This is a conservative approximation. We leave to the reader the derivation of the triad failure rate under this assumption.

Our second assumption is conservative. In reality, the system fails only when at least two processors in the triad have generated errors, not when the second processor suffers failure. Thus, if the first fault is isolated before the second processor starts generating errors, the triad will not fail.

8.3.3 Introduction of Transient Faults

Recall that the above computation assumes that all faults are permanent. This is unrealistic. Let us now remove this assumption. Let a and b be the permanent and transient failure rates, respectively, of each processor. Failures are assumed to occur as a Poisson process. Intermittent failures are ignored in this model. We assume that all the failures are independent of one another, and that faults manifest themselves immediately (i.e., the fault latency is zero). Processors that are taken offline due to a fault being detected are tested continuously to see if their fault is transient, and if it is, whether it has died away. If this is the case, the processor is inducted back into the cluster. Let the time between when a processor suffers transient failure and when it is brought back on line be exponentially distributed with mean $1/e$. We will ignore the time it takes to reintegrate it into the system; this can be taken into account by assuming it to be part of the decay time. What is the probability $p_{\text{FAIL}}(t)$ that such a system will fail by time t, given that it was in perfect working order at time 0? Here we assume that system failure occurs when there are fewer than two operational processors.

Once again, we use a Markov chain. However, unlike in the previous case where processors could only be in one of two states, permanently failed and good, in this model they can be in one of three states: permanently failed, currently offline due to transient failure, and good. Since the total number of processors is fixed at N, we need two state variables to denote the state of the system. Let us denote the state by (s_1, s_2) where s_1 and s_2 denote, respectively, the number of functional processors and the number of processors currently undergoing transient failure. The number of processors that have failed permanently is $N - s_1 - s_2$. The Markov chain for this model is shown in Figure 8.15. To avoid clutter, the individual arcs in the chain are not labeled with the associated transition rates; rather, the inset figures provide the transition rates out of each state (and by implication into each state). While it may look complicated, generating this chain is quite simple. Let us consider transitions out of state i, j. In this state, we have i functional processors and j processors that are currently suffering transient failure. The rest of the processors, numbering $N - i - j$, have suffered permanent failure. Of course, the system does not know whether a failed processor is suffering a transient or a permanent failure. It will keep trying to run tests on all the failed processors, and if a previously failed processor recovers, it will pass the test.

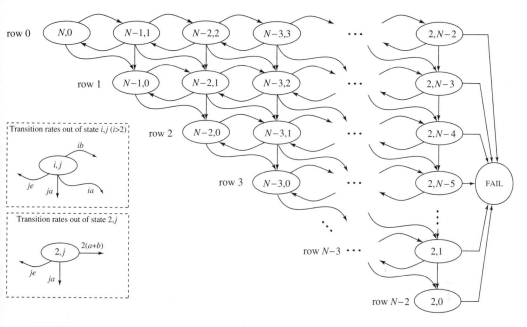

FIGURE 8.15
Markov chain for a system with transient and permanent failures.

The i functional processors may suffer either permanent or transient failure. The permanent failure rate per processor is a, so the overall rate due to permanent failure out of state i, j (and into state $i - 1, j$) is ia. Similarly, the overall rate due to transient failure out of state i, j (and into state $i-1, j+1$) is ib. Even processors that are currently suffering transient failures are not immune to permanent failures; this explains the transition from state i, j to $i, j - 1$ with a rate of ja. Transient faults die away in an exponentially distributed duration of mean $1/e$, and so the rate out of state i, j to $i + 1, j - 1$ is given by je. When only two processors are functional, the failure of any one of these spells failure for the whole system, which explains the transition to the FAIL state. Notice that FAIL is an *absorbing* state—once the system is in this state, there is no way out. Because we are modeling the onset of failure, we wish to compute the probability that the system will ever enter the FAIL state over any given interval $[0, t]$.

It only remains for us to write the differential equations connected with this process. This can be done by inspection of the Markov chain. Let $\pi_{i,j}(t)$ denote the probability of being in state i, j at time t for $i, j \geq 0$ and $i + j \leq N$. If $i < 0$, $j < 0$, or $i + j > N$, define $\pi_{i,j}(t) = 0$. The differential equations are

$$\frac{d\pi_{i,j}(t)}{dt} = -\{i(a + b) + j(a + e)\} \pi_{i,j}(t) + (i + 1)a\pi_{i+1,j}(t)$$

$$+(j + 1)a\pi_{i,j+1}(t) + (i + 1)b\pi_{i+1,j-1}(t)$$

$$+(j + 1)e\pi_{i-1,j+1}(t) \qquad\qquad i > 2$$

$$\tag{8.40}$$

$$\frac{d\pi_{2,j}(t)}{dt} = -\{2(a+b) + j(a+e)\}\,\pi_{2,j}(t) + 3b\pi_{3,j-1}(t)$$

$$+(j+1)a\pi_{2,j+1}(t) + 3a\pi_{3,j}(t) \tag{8.41}$$

where the initial condition reflects the fact that we start the system in state $N, 0$ (i.e., $\pi_{N,0}(0) = 1$). These equations can now be solved numerically.

8.3.4   The Use of State Aggregation*

In most instances, $e \gg \max\{a, b\}$; that is, transient faults die away much more quickly than either permanent or transient faults are generated. Also, as we have pointed out before, it is usually true that $b \gg a$. Let us assume here that $b \gg Na$. In such a case, we can obtain a good approximation to the system failure probability by using state aggregation.

Notice first that we have drawn the Markov chain in Figure 8.15 so that each row corresponds to a certain fixed number of processors that have not suffered permanent failure. For example, row 0 contains all the states where none of the processors has failed permanently. If we aggregate all the states in each row into a *metastate*, we obtain Figure 8.16 as an approximation of Figure 8.15. The system is in metastate i if exactly $N - i$ processors have suffered permanent failure.

The transition rates $f(i)$ to the failure state from each functional state i are computed as follows. The transition rate to the failure state from state $2, N-2-j$ in Figure 8.15 is $2(a + b)$. Hence the transition rate to the failure state of the corresponding aggregated state in Figure 8.16 is equal to $2(a + b)$ multiplied by the fraction of time the system spends in state $2, N - 2 - j$ when it is in that row

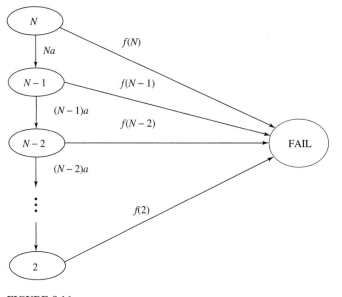

FIGURE 8.16
Aggregated state model.

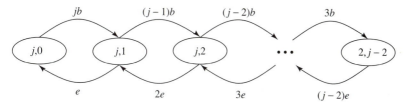

FIGURE 8.17
Computing $\pi_{2,j}$ for the aggregated state model.

of the chain. Since the transient failure rates are much greater than the permanent failure rates, it follows that we can obtain a good approximation of this fraction by solving for the steady-state probability of the chain given in Figure 8.17.

8.4 SOFTWARE-ERROR MODELS

Software-error models predict the rate at which software faults will produce errors and are meant to determine when to stop debugging, by providing some guidance on the reliability of the software at each stage of debugging. As we shall see later in this section, the usefulness of software-error models in ultrareliable computer systems is extremely limited.

In this section, we outline some of the better-known error models. There is no universally accepted software-error model, since software (and hardware-design) faults arise from causes much more complex (and thus much more difficult to model) than do hardware faults. Which model is best depends on the failure data. This is another way of saying that the failure data in software do not seem to follow a given law, but vary widely. What follows is a sampling of some of the more prominent models. In each case, the model is expressed in terms of unknown parameters, which must be determined for each piece of software by observing the error rate and using statistical methods. Perhaps the best strategy for the user to follow is to select the model that seems to best fit the observed fault data. That is, suppose the user has so far found a faults, and that the time between the discovery of the ith and $(i + 1)$th faults (measured in terms of program-execution time) is given by t_i for $i = 0, \ldots, a - 1$. She then determines which of the models best fit such data, and uses them to estimate the error-generation rate (and thus the reliability) of the software at the present moment.

The models express the error rate as a function of the number of faults in the software. As the software is debugged and the number of faults changes, so does the error rate. The simplest models (e.g., Jelinski-Moranda) assume that the error rate is directly proportional to the number of faults; as the software is debugged and faults are removed, the error rate falls appropriately. More complex models take into account the fact that the error-generation rate depends not only on the number of faults but on where these faults are placed in the program. Some faults are in parts of the program that are frequently executed—these will have a high error-generation rate—while others that are in parts that are rarely executed will have a low rate. The higher the error-generation rate of a fault, the more likely it is to be caught. Thus, it is likely that the faults that are removed earliest during debugging are those that have the highest rates, while those undetected have low rates. Indeed, it is possible for software to have a substantial number of faults and to produce no errors for long stretches of time. It is such faults that are especially troubling to the designer of high-reliability equipment, since there is no guarantee that such faults will not be exercised at inconvenient moments and cause system failure.

Jelinski-Moranda model: This is the earliest and perhaps the most widely used model. It models the error-generation rate as proportional to the number of faults in the software. That is, $\lambda(i) = Ji$, where $\lambda(i)$ is the failure rate of software with i faults, and J is the unknown parameter. If the software is run for t time units, the probability that no errors are generated, given that the software has N_0 faults, is $P_0 = 1 - \exp(-\lambda(N_0)t)$. The obvious drawback of this model is that the failure rate is assumed to be proportional to the number of faults remaining in the system. This assumption is untrue for the reasons that we have already discussed.

Goel-Okumoto model: This model assumes that the occurrence of errors is a nonhomogeneous Poisson process (NHPP) with rate $\lambda(t) = abe^{-bt}$, where a and b are the unknown parameters. This captures the idea that some faults are easy to detect and others difficult. If no error has occurred for a long time, it is reasonable to assume that any faults that do exist in the software are those that are exercised very infrequently.

Littlewood model: This model assumes that each fault i can generate errors according to a Poisson process with rate Φ_i. Since the Φ_i can vary, the model allows us the flexibility of assigning different error-generation rates to the various faults. If F is the set of faults in a piece of software, the failure rate is given by $\lambda_i = \sum_{i \in F} \Phi_i$. The N and Φ_i are unknown to begin with, and they are estimated by a maximum-likelihood approach based on the observed intervals between successive failures of the software. Initially, they are assumed to be independent identically distributed random variables following the gamma distribution. The probability density function of this distribution is

$$\gamma(x, \alpha, \beta) = \frac{x^{\alpha-1}e^{-\beta x}\beta^{\alpha}}{\Gamma(\alpha)} \tag{8.42}$$

where α and β are parameters with $\alpha > -1$ and $\beta > 0$, and

$$\Gamma(n) = \begin{cases} (n-1)\Gamma(n-1) & \text{if } n > 1 \\ \int_0^{\infty} e^{-x}x^{n-1}dx & \text{otherwise} \end{cases} \tag{8.43}$$

If i faults have been uncovered out of the N that the software has initially (of course, N is unknown also), Bayesian methods are used to obtain the value of error-generation rate for each of the remaining $N - i$ faults. Let $\omega(\phi)$ denote the pdf of this rate.

$$\omega(\phi|\text{Fault not caught in } (0,\tau)) = \omega(\phi|\text{Fault did not cause failure in } (0,\tau))$$
$$= \gamma(\phi, \alpha, (\beta + \tau)\phi) \tag{8.44}$$

The details of this derivation are left as an exercise. Recall that the overall failure rate is the sum of the rates due to each of the remaining faults. It is a useful property of the gamma distribution that the sum of k gamma-distributed random variables with pdf $\gamma(x, \alpha, \beta)$ is also a gamma-distributed random variable with pdf $\gamma(x, k\alpha, \beta)$. Hence, the overall pdf of the interval between the uncovering of the ith and $(i + 1)$th faults is given by $\gamma(x, (N - i)\alpha, \beta)$. From this pdf, the error-generation rate can be shown to be

$$\lambda_i(t) = \frac{(N - i)\alpha}{\beta + \tau + t} \tag{8.45}$$

Littlewood-Verall model: This model assumes that the time between failures has the density function

$$p(t_i) = \lambda_i e^{-\lambda_i t} \tag{8.46}$$

when there are i faults in the software. The unknown parameter λ_i is itself not a constant, but a random variable with the gamma density

$$p(\lambda_i) = \frac{[\psi(i)]^\alpha \lambda_i^{\alpha-1} e^{-\psi(i)\lambda_i}}{\Gamma(\alpha)} \tag{8.47}$$

The function $\psi(i)$ determines how the rate changes with the number of faults i. It is possible to show that if $\psi(i)$ is an increasing function of i, λ_i is stochastically greater than λ_j for $i > j$; that is

$$\text{Prob}\{\lambda_i > x\} > \text{Prob}\{\lambda_j > x\} \quad \forall \, x > 0 \tag{8.48}$$

The values of $\psi(i)$ and α are chosen by the user based on the observed data.

As we mentioned above, it is impossible to say in advance which model is best for any given program, and it is only by trial and error that we can choose one. Different models can give wildly different predictions. As an example, Table 8.3 contains some experimentally observed intervals between successive failures that are fitted against the Jelinski-Moranda and the Littlewood-Verall models. Figure 8.18 shows the median time between consecutive ith and $(i + 1)$th failures as predicted by these models as a function of i (i.e., after having observed the times between failure of the first i failures). As we can see, the models differ considerably from each other—they can't possibly both be right. Two conclusions can be drawn from this observation. First, it is useless to expect such failure models to provide any assurance that a given piece of software is highly reliable. Second, insofar as we wish to use such models to provide guidance regarding when to stop debugging, we need some mechanism to see which model is likely to provide the best predictions.

TABLE 8.3
Execution time between successive failures

3	30	113	81	115	9	2	91	112	15
138	50	77	24	108	88	670	120	26	114
325	55	242	68	422	180	10	1146	600	15
36	4	0	8	227	65	176	58	457	300
97	263	452	255	197	193	6	79	816	1351
148	21	233	134	357	193	236	31	369	748
0	232	330	365	1222	543	10	16	529	379
44	129	810	290	300	529	281	160	828	1011
445	296	1755	1064	1783	860	983	707	33	868
724	2323	2930	1461	843	12	261	1800	865	1435
30	143	108	0	3110	1247	943	700	875	245
729	1897	447	386	446	122	990	948	1082	22
75	482	5509	100	10	1071	371	790	6150	3321
1045	648	5485	1160	1864	4116				

Note: Read from left to right. (From A. A. Abdel-Ghaly et al., "Evaluation of Competing Software Reliability Predictions," *IEEE Trans. Software Engineering*, Vol. SE-12, No. 9, September 1986. © IEEE 1986. Reprinted with permission.)

Let us turn to this last issue of deciding which model is best based on some failure data. We are given the times between the occurrence of error; let t_i denote the time between the occurrence of the ith and $(i - 1)$th error. We have two candidate software error models, say A and B, that are under consideration.[3]

With each error comes debugging to remove the associated fault. It is always possible that the act of debugging itself adds one or more faults to the system. The debugger wishes to use software models to predict the current reliability of the software and when the next error is likely to occur. To do this, he must decide which model, A or B, is likely to be the better model for this particular piece of software, and use that model to make the desired predictions.

Consider the situation when i errors have been caught. At this point, $t_0, \ldots, t_{i-1}$ are known. Based on these data, the designer uses statistical techniques to obtain the parameters of the A and B models. These are parameters for which the respective models provide the best fit with the observed data. Let these parameters be $a_1^*, \ldots, a_k^*$ and $b_1^*, \ldots, b_\ell^*$ for the A and B models, respectively, and denote by A_i^* and B_i^* these models under these parameter sets. After this, we can use the techniques mentioned in Section 8.2.3 to determine which model to use. However, this approach is not practical for ultrareliable software, as we see below.

---

[3]We assume only two models under consideration for simplicity of exposition: extending it to more than two is elementary.

8.4.1   The Limited Usefulness of Software-Error Models

We have seen that there are many software-error models. The user must decide which model best fits the software being developed. This, though, runs into the problems illustrated in Figure 8.18; it is hard to extrapolate with confidence the results obtained from a limited testing of the software.

Even if we know which model to use, reducing the failure rate to acceptable levels is often impractical if we debug by running the software and fixing any errors that manifest themselves.

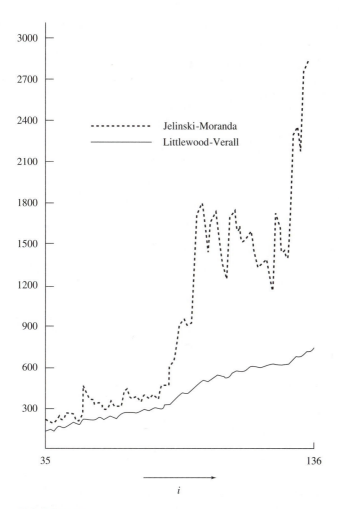

FIGURE 8.18
Median plots for Jelinski-Moranda and Littlewood-Verall models using Table 8.3 data. (From A. A. Abdel-Ghaly et al., "Evaluation of Competing Software Reliability Predictions," *IEEE Trans. Software Engineering*, Vol. SE-12, No. 9, September 1986. © IEEE 1986. Reprinted with permission.)

Example 8.4. We are given that a piece of software is accurately modeled by Goel-Okumoto model; that is, the failure rate per execution is given by $\lambda(t) = ab \exp(-bt)$, where a and b are constants. We debug for some time, and by collecting data on the way that the failure rate changes with the debugging time, we find that $a = 10^4$, and $b = 10^{-4}$. Suppose our goal is a failure rate of 10^{-9} per hour, and we are given that the software will be run 10,000 times an hour. This translates to a failure rate per iteration of 10^{-13}. We therefore have to debug by running the program t_d times, where

$$0.1e^{-0.1t_d} = 10^{-13}$$

$$\Rightarrow t_d = 2.993 \times 10^5 \tag{8.49}$$

For programs of even moderate size, this is impractical.

The problem gets worse if we are trying to model N-version programming. If the different versions of an N-version program (NVP) fail independently, modeling NVP reliability is identical to modeling NMR reliability.

This brings up the question of whether the independence assumption is justified. We have already seen, in Chapter 7, that the independence assumption is questionable. Here, we ask the more fundamental question of whether it is possible to test versions for independence.

Suppose we are testing the hypothesis that versions V_1 and V_2 are independent by applying inputs to each and observing the frequency with which both versions fail for the same input. If $p_i(x)$ is the probability that version V_i fails for input x, and $p_{ij}(x)$ is the probability that both i and j fail for input x, then V_1 and V_2 are independent iff

$$p_{12}(x) = p_1(x)p_2(x) \qquad \forall x \tag{8.50}$$

If $p_i(x)$ (for $i = 1, 2$) is small, then $p_1(x)p_2(x)$ will be even smaller. We therefore require an inordinately long time to check whether Equation (8.50) holds. Experimentally determining that two versions fail independently is therefore usually impractical for ultrareliable software.

Once we lose the independence assumption, modeling software reliability becomes impractical; it is very hard to determine the correlation between two failures. Hardware-reliability models are practical because of the following:

- Individual components fail at a rate that can be experimentally estimated with a fair degree of confidence.
- Design faults are a small minority of all the faults.
- The assumption that units fail independently of one another is justified based on practical considerations (e.g., individual processors have independent power supplies, fault-containment regions are used, etc.).

But in software, design faults are the only faults in existence and it is impossible to be confident from practical considerations that these are independent in different versions.

The bottom line of this discussion is that software-reliability modeling is often of only limited usefulness for writing ultrareliable software. Indeed, writing such software is an extremely difficult task for which no established fool-proof techniques exist.

8.5   TAKING TIME INTO ACCOUNT[4]

So far in this chapter, we have not shown how to take the hard deadlines and checkpoints into account. In this section, we provide a model to do this.

Let us analyze the following system. There is a real-time computer, which is running a repetitive workload. The tasks are run once every frame of T seconds. The system will fail if it does not execute a critical workload of t_{crit} per frame. Checkpoints are placed at intervals τ. The interval between two checkpoints constitutes a *miniframe*. N-modular redundancy is used and, before writing into a checkpoint, a vote is taken. The probability of writing incorrect information into a checkpoint is thus very small, and will be ignored. There is sufficient coding used in the memories that the probability of the checkpoint being corrupted is also negligible. The checkpoint is stored in static RAM, which is heavily shielded to make it immune to the vagaries of the operating environment. The time for encoding, decoding, and storing checkpoint data is included in the checkpointing overhead. When a failure is detected that requires rollback, the task is rolled back to the previous checkpoint. The checkpoints are synchronized, and so there is no possibility of a domino effect.

Three types of failure are considered in this model: permanent (this category includes intermittent faults), independent transient, and correlated transient. *Correlated transient failures* are suffered whenever the system is subjected to massive interference from the operating environment, which causes all the processors in each redundant cluster to fail.

The reliability of the system is the probability that it will, over every frame of its mission, deliver at least t_{crit} seconds of computation. This translates to $n_{\text{crit}} = \lceil t_{\text{crit}}/\tau \rceil$ miniframes. The work consists of constructing a Markov chain that depicts the reliability of the system over a single frame. This is then used to compute the reliability over the entire mission.

In our analysis, we assume that the interarrival times between the onset of successive transient failures are independent random variables. Processors are assumed to undergo permanent failure according to a Poisson process, with rate λ_p. To simplify the analysis, and as a pessimistic approximation, we assume that correlated transient failure results in all the processors suffering transient failure.

Let the state of the system be the number of processors that have failed. Let there be n_{proc} functioning processors in the system at the beginning. To ensure survival, at least x of these must correctly finish their workload for each frame

---

[4]Section 8.5 is based on C. M. Krishna and A. D. Singh, "Reliability of Checkpointed Real-Time Systems Using Time Redundancy," IEEE Trans. Reliability, Vol. 42, 1993, pp. 427–435. © IEEE 1993. Used with permission.

of the mission. As explained earlier, we can take x as either the majority of the n_{proc} or as 2, depending on whether we have a majority vote or are satisfied with two coincident (or close) outputs.

The discrete-time Markov chain that plots the state transitions over the duration of a frame is as follows. States $0, 1, \ldots, n_{\text{proc}} - x$ correspond to the nonfailed states; the others are the failed states. Since there is no repair and failure to compute the critical workload during even a single frame is sufficient to cause failure, the failed state is absorbing (i.e., there are no transitions out of it). It is therefore sufficient to group all the failed states together into one state, FAIL.

To analyze this chain, we require its probability transition matrix. Let $p(i, j)$ denote the probability that the state of the system is j at the end of a frame, given that it was i at the beginning of it. Since there is no repair, $p(i, j) = 0 \; \forall i < j$. As we have pointed out before, $p(\text{FAIL}, \text{FAIL}) = 1$. The other transition probabilities require more work.

Let n_{crit} be the size of the critical workload, expressed in miniframes. Denote by $\pi_c(m|n)$ and $\pi_i(m|n)$ the probability that m out of n miniframes are disrupted by a correlated failure and individual failure, respectively.

Denote by $\text{Prob}[NT(i|j)]$ the probability that if there are j functioning processors in a frame, and there are no hardware failures, exactly i of these processors do not manage to complete their critical workloads. Define $n_{\text{slack}} = n_{\text{min}\,i} - n_{\text{crit}}$, and denote by $\phi(n_{\text{slack}}, \xi, n_{\text{min}\,i})$ the term $\sum_{\eta=0}^{n_{\text{slack}} - \xi} \pi_i(n_{\text{slack}} - \xi - \eta | n_{\text{min}\,i} - \xi)$. Then, $\phi(n_{\text{slack}}, \xi, n_{\text{min}\,i})$ is the probability that out of $n_{\text{min}\,i} - \xi$ miniframes, a processor does not suffer a loss of more than $n_{\text{slack}} - \xi$ miniframes due to individual transient failure. We then have the approximate equality

$$
\text{Prob}[NT(i|j)] \approx
\begin{cases}
\dbinom{j}{i} \displaystyle\sum_{\xi=0}^{n_{\text{slack}}} \pi_c(\xi|n_{\text{min}\,i})[\phi(n_{\text{slack}}, \xi, n_{\text{min}\,i})]^i \\
\qquad\qquad [1 - \phi(n_{\text{slack}}, \xi, n_{\text{min}\,i})]^{j-i} & \text{if } i \leq j \\[2ex]
0 & \text{otherwise}
\end{cases}
\tag{8.51}
$$

The approximation stems from the fact that, for tractability, the workload is expressed in integral multiples of miniframes. This is a pessimistic approximation. Suppose that the workload completes at time t_1 in a given miniframe that ends at $t_2 > t_1$, and that the processor then suffers transient failure starting from $t_3 \in (t_1, t_2)$ and lasting beyond the end of the current frame. This will not, in reality, cause a failure to complete the workload. Our model, however, regards such an event as contributing to the probability of failing to complete the critical workload.

$p(i, i) \quad \forall 0 \leq i \leq n_{\text{proc}} - x$ is the probability of no permanent hardware failures during a frame that begins with i permanently failed processors and the probability that at least x of the remaining $n_{\text{proc}} - i$ processors have managed to execute the critical workload. That is,

$$
p(i, i) = (1 - p_{\text{perm}})^{n_{\text{proc}} - i} \sum_{\ell=0}^{n_{\text{proc}} - x - i} \text{Prob}[NT(\ell|i)] \quad \forall 0 \leq i \leq n_{\text{proc}} - x \tag{8.52}
$$

where we denote by p_{perm} the probability of permanent hardware failure over a frame. Clearly, $p_{\text{perm}} = 1 - e^{-\lambda_p t_{\text{frame}}}$.

$p(i, j)$ $\forall 0 \leq i, j \leq n_{\text{proc}} - x$ is the probability that the system survives the current frame and ends it with exactly j permanently failed processors, given that it started the frame with i permanently failed processors, where $0 \leq i \leq j \leq n_{\text{proc}} - x$. This event includes the permanent failure of $j - i$ processors during the current frame. As a conservative approximation, we take these failures to occur at the start of the current frame, i.e., before the critical workload for that frame has been completed. From this, we can immediately write:

$$p(i, j) = \binom{n_{\text{proc}} - i}{n_{\text{proc}} - j} (1 - p_{\text{perm}})^{n_{\text{proc}} - j} \, p_{\text{perm}}^{j-i} \sum_{\ell=0}^{n_{\text{proc}} - x - j} \text{Prob}[NT(\ell | j)]$$

$$\forall 0 \leq i, j \leq n_{\text{proc}} - x \qquad (8.53)$$

The probability that the system makes a transition into the failed state during any given frame is one minus the probability that it makes a transition into some nonfailed state.

We now have a stochastic matrix $P = [p(i, j)]$ defining the rates of transition of the system over a frame. It is easy to use this to compute the probability of the system failing to complete a mission of M frames. Let the initial hardware state of the system be given by the probability vector $\Pi = (\pi_0, \ldots, \pi_{n_{\text{proc}} - x - 1})$, where π_i is the probability that the system state is i failed processors at the beginning of the mission. State $n_{\text{proc}} - x - 1$ corresponds to the failed state. If we always start with a perfect system, we can set $\pi_0 = 1$ and $\pi_i = 0$ $\forall i > 0$. Then an approximation to the failure probability over this mission is given by summing the $(n_{\text{proc}} - x + 1)$th column of the matrix $\mathbf{N} = \Pi P^M$. That is, writing $\mathbf{N} = [n(i, j)]$, the failure probability after M missions is

$$p_{\text{FAIL}} = \sum_{i=0}^{n_{\text{proc}} - x + 1} n(i, n_{\text{proc}} - x + 1) \qquad (8.54)$$

When there is a large number of processors, it may no longer be meaningful to describe the environment as causing a correlated failure that affects every processor. Instead, we might model a hazardous environment as simply raising the rate of individual transient failure. The environment may cycle between being benign (normal individual transient-failure rates) and hazardous (elevated individual transient-failure rates). Such an environment can be characterized by specifying the disruption due to an individual failure in both the benign and hazardous phases π_i^b and π_i^h, respectively, and by specifying the probability $p_M^{\text{mission}}(M_1, M_2)$ that, out of a mission of M frames, M_1 are entirely in a benign environment and M_2 are partially or entirely in a hazardous environment.

It is easy to use this model for such an environment. We can use the model to obtain the stochastic matrices P_h and P_b, which represent the state transitions over a frame under a hazardous environment and under a benign environment, respectively. Then, define **N** as follows:

$$\mathbf{N}(M) = \sum_{\ell=0}^{M} p_M^{\text{mission}}(\ell, M - \ell) \Pi [P_h]^{\ell} [P_b]^{M-\ell} \tag{8.55}$$

Then, writing $\mathbf{N} = [n(i, j)]$, as before, the failure probability after a mission of M frames is given by

$$p_{\text{FAIL}} = \sum_{i=0}^{n_{\text{proc}}-x+1} n(i, n_{\text{proc}} - x + 1) \tag{8.56}$$

8.6 SUGGESTIONS FOR FURTHER READING

Barlow and Proschan [3] and Siewiorek and Swarz [24] are good introductions to the problem of reliability modeling. The generation of errors is modeled in [23]. Packages for reliability evaluation are surveyed in [12].

Software reliability is surveyed in [11]. Discussions of the feasibility of making reliability estimates for software are presented in [4, 16]. Software reliability models are discussed in [1]. The prequential likelihood approach is discussed in [5].

Our discussion of taking time into account in reliability modeling is based on [14].

EXERCISES

8.1. You are given the following sequence of data: 0.35, 0.70, 0.96, 0.95, 0.82, 0.78, 0.05, 0.21, 0.12, 0.27, 0.82, 0.24, 0.01, 0.25, 0.40, 0.09, 0.76, 0.78, 0.99, 0.43. Do these data better fit the uniform distribution over the interval [0,1] or the exponential distribution?

8.2. You are given a lightbulb that fails according to a Poisson process with rate λ_f. All that is known about λ_f is that it could be anywhere in the range (a, b). After c hours of operation, the lightbulb still functions. What is the best estimate of λ_f? (Hint: Compute the probability density function of λ_f conditioned on the fact that the bulb has not failed after c hours).

8.3. What is the hazard rate associated with a three-stage Erlang density function?

8.4. Suppose we have an NMR system with N voters, one per processor. The system is said to fail when a majority of the processors and/or a majority of the voters has failed. Derive an expression of the critical ratio of voter reliabilities.

8.5. We have an NMR system with an unlimited number of backup processors, which purges the system of failed processors. However, every time the purging process is run, it can itself lead to system failure with probability π. Draw a Markov chain for such a system.

8.6. Solve the Markov chain in Figure 8.15 using uniformization.

8.7. Construct a Markov chain similar to that in Figure 8.15 for a system that fails when a majority of the processors is faulty.

8.8. A processor has suffered intermittent failure. The characteristics of this failure are that it is in the failed state for a mean time of $1/x$ and in the nonfailed state for a mean time of $1/y$. Both times are exponentially distributed. At time 0, the processor is in the failed state. What is the probability that it is in the failed state at time t?

8.9. Suppose all the processors of a triplex system have suffered intermittent failure. The parameters of this failure are as in Exercise 8. At time 0, they are all in the nonfailed state. Derive the reliability function $R(t)$, that is, the probability that the triplex will not suffer system failure over $[0, t]$.

8.10. An NMR system is built out of units each of which produces a one-bit output (which can be either 0 or 1). There is a probability p_i that a unit will have its output stuck at i ($i = 0, 1$). Having its output stuck at 0 or 1 is the only failure that the unit can suffer. If the correct output for some computation is 1, what is the probability that the NMR system will deliver that output?

8.11. Suppose processor failure rates are a function $f(u)$ of the processor utilization u. Given seven processors in all, we have the choice of using them either as one 7-MR cluster or as two 3-MR clusters (with one processor as a spare). If two clusters are used, the processor utilization is half that of the single-cluster case. $f(u) = (1 - \exp(-u)) \times 10^{-5}$. For what values of total workload are two clusters better than one, given a mission time of t? The total workload is given in terms of the processor utilization.

REFERENCES

[1] Abdel-Ghaly, A. A., P. Y. Chan, and B. Littlewood: "Evaluation of Competing Software Reliability Predictions," *IEEE Trans. Software Engineering* SE-12:950–967, 1986.

[2] Arlat, J., Y. Crouzet, and J. C. Laprie: "Fault Injection for Dependability Validation of Fault-Tolerant Computing Systems," *Proc. 19th Fault-Tolerant Computing Symposium*, pp. 348–355, IEEE, Los Alamitos, CA, 1989.

[3] Barlow, R. E., and F. Proschan: *Mathematical Theory of Reliability,* Wiley, New York, 1965.

[4] Butler, R. W., and G. B. Finelli: "The Infeasibility of Quantifying the Reliability of Life-Critical Real-Time Software," *IEEE Trans. Software Engineering* 19:3–12, 1993.

[5] Dawid, A. P.: "Statistical Theory: The Prequential Approach," *Journal of the Royal Statistical Society*, Series 147:278–292, 1984.

[6] Dugan, J. B., and K. S. Trivedi: "Coverage Modeling for Dependability Analysis of Fault-Tolerant Systems," *IEEE Trans. Computers* 38:775–787, 1989.

[7] Geist, R.: "Extended Behavioral Decomposition for Estimating Ultrahigh Reliability," *IEEE Trans. Reliability* 40:22–28, 1991.

[8] Heidelberger, P., and A. Goyal: "Sensitivity Analysis of Continuous Time Markov Chains using Uniformization," in *Computer Performance and Reliability*, (G. Iazeolla, P. J. Courtois, and O. J. Boxma, eds.), North-Holland, Amsterdam, 1988.

[9] Heimann, D. I., N. Mittal, and K. S. Trivedi: "Availability and Reliability Modeling for Computer Systems," *Advances in Computers* 31:175–233, 1990.

[10] Hsueh, M. C., R. K. Iyer, and K. S. Trivedi: "Performability Modeling Based on Real Data: A Case Study," *IEEE Trans. Computing* 37:478–484, 1988.

[11] Iannino, A., and J. D. Musa: "Software Reliability," *Advances in Computers* 30:85–170, 1990.

[12] Johnson, A. M., and M. Malek: "Survey of Software Tools for Evaluating Reliability, Availability, and Serviceability," *ACM Computing Surveys* 20:227–270, 1988.

[13] Krishna, C. M., K. G. Shin, and Y.-H. Lee: "Optimization Criteria for Checkpointing," *Communications of the ACM* 27:1008–1012, 1984.

[14] Krishna, C. M., and A. D. Singh: "Reliability of Checkpointed Real-Time Systems Using Time Redundancy," *IEEE Trans. Reliability* 42:427–435, 1993.

[15] Krishna, C. M., and A. D. Singh: "Optimal Configuration of Redundant Real-Time Systems in the Face of Correlated Failure," *IEEE Trans. Reliability* 44:587–594, 1995.

[16] Littlewood, B.: "Predicting Software Reliability," *Philosophical Trans. Royal Society*, Series A, 327:513–528, 1989.

[17] McGough, J., M. Smotherman, and K. S. Trivedi: "The Conservativeness of Reliability Estimates Based on Instantaneous Coverage," *IEEE Trans. Computers* C-34:602–609, 1985.

[18] Meyer, J. F.: "On Evaluating the Performability of Degradable Computing Systems," *IEEE Trans. Computers* C-29:720–721, 1980.

[19] Meyer, J. F., D. G. Furchtgott, and L. T. Wu: "Performability Evaluation of the SIFT Computer," *IEEE Trans. Computers* C-29:501–509, 1980.

[20] Molloy, M. K.: "Performance Analysis Using Stochastic Petri Nets," *IEEE Trans. Computers* C-31:913–917, 1982.

[21] Muppala, J. K., S. P. Woolet and K. S. Trivedi: "Real-Time Systems Performance in the Presence of Failures," *IEEE Computer* 24:37–47, 1991.

[22] Sahner, R., and K. S. Trivedi: "A Software Tool for Learning about Stochastic Models," *IEEE Trans. Education* 36:56–61, 1993.

[23] Shin, K. G., and Y.-H. Lee: "Error Detection Process—Model, Design and its Impact on Computer Performance," *IEEE Trans. Computers* C-33:529–540, 1984.

[24] Siewiorek, D. P., and R. S. Swarz: *Reliable Computer Systems*, Digital Press, Burlington, MA, 1992.

[25] Tomek, L., V. Mainkar, R. M. Geist, and K. S. Trivedi: "Reliability Modeling of Life-Critical, Real-Time Systems," *Proc. IEEE* 82:108–121, 1994.

[26] Tomek, L. A., J. K. Muppala, and K. S. Trivedi: "Modeling Correlation in Software Recovery Blocks," *IEEE Trans. Software Engineering* 19:1071–1086, 1993.

CHAPTER
9

CLOCK SYNCHRONIZATION

9.1 INTRODUCTION

Clock synchronization is vital to the correct operation of real-time systems. Such activities as voting and synchronized rollback assume that the clocks are synchronized fairly tightly. In this chapter, we will look at some algorithms for fault-tolerant synchronization. These ensure that the functional processors remain synchronized despite a few processor or link failures.

We discuss both hardware and software synchronization algorithms in this chapter. Hardware synchronization requires special hardware, which is not required by software synchronization; however, it offers much tighter synchronization. We begin with some background on clocks.

9.2 CLOCKS

Mathematically speaking, clock c_i is a mapping

$$C_i : \text{real time} \rightarrow \text{clock time}$$

That is, at real time t, $C_i(t)$ is the time told by clock c_i. The inverse function $c_i(T)$ is the real time at which clock c_i tells time T. Where it is important to distinguish between real and clock times, we will use the prefixes "r" and "c," respectively. For example, by c-unit we mean a time unit as measured by an actual clock; by r-unit we mean a time unit as measured by a perfect clock. Similarly, the c-interval $[t_1, t_2]$ is the interval of time from when a given clock says the time is t_1 to when it says the time is t_2.

We seek from the clock of a computer essentially what we seek from a wristwatch—accuracy. That is, the clock should not gain or lose time at too high a rate. To put it more formally, it is necessary that the drift rate of a clock c_i

$$\rho = \max_{t, \Delta} \left| \frac{C_i(t + \Delta) - C_i(\Delta)}{\Delta} - 1 \right| \qquad (9.1)$$

be as small as possible. The *drift rate* is the rate at which the clock can gain or lose time.

Conversely, if we specify ρ as the maximum drift rate of a nonfaulty clock, we must have

$$(1 - \rho)(t_2 - t_1) \le C(t_2) - C(t_1) \le (1 + \rho)(t_2 - t_1) \qquad (9.2)$$

The clock is constrained to remain within the cone of acceptability, shown as heavy lines in Figure 9.1. Since $\rho \ll 1$ for all good clocks,

$$1 - \rho \approx (1 + \rho)^{-1}$$
$$1 + \rho \approx (1 - \rho)^{-1}$$

To see this, expand $(1 + \rho)^{-1}$ in a Taylor series:

$$(1 + \rho)^{-1} = 1 - \rho + \frac{\rho^2}{2!} + \cdots + (-1)^n \frac{\rho^n}{n!} + \cdots$$

For $\rho \approx 10^{-6}$, $(1 - \rho) - (1 + \rho)^{-1} \approx 10^{-12}$. Similarly for $(1 - \rho)^{-1}$. Hence, Equation (9.2) is approximately the same as:

$$\frac{t_2 - t_1}{1 + \rho}(t_2 - t_1) \le C(t_2) - C(t_1) \le \frac{t_2 - t_1}{1 - \rho} \qquad (9.3)$$

We will henceforth assume that ρ is such that Equation (9.3) holds for nonfaulty clocks. When we specify the maximum drift of a clock as ρ, we are in effect saying that both Equations (9.2) and (9.3) will hold as long as the clock is nonfaulty.

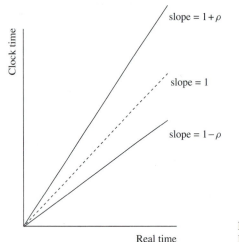

slope = 1 + ρ

slope = 1

slope = 1 - ρ

Clock time

Real time

FIGURE 9.1
Range of permitted clock times.

All this is based on a commodity called real time, which we have not yet defined. By *real time* we mean the time told by a perfect clock in a world that obeys Newtonian physics. All the physical clocks that we construct move so much slower than the speed of light that relativistic effects are negligible and Newtonian physics holds. A perfect clock would, by definition, follow the dashed line in Figure 9.1. Of course a perfect clock has never existed. However, the cesium clock and other clocks used in the bureaus of standards around the world have drift rates about a million times smaller than the drifts of the clocks we shall be considering. For all practical purposes, we can consider these to be perfect clocks, and use them to initialize our clocks and to measure their drift rates.

Why do we want the drift rate to be as small as possible? There are two reasons. Consider how the clock rate of a computer is determined. The speed of a computer is a function of the clock rate. The clock period (the inverse of the clock rate) is chosen to be just long enough for signal propagation along the critical path of a computer circuit (including time for data to settle in the registers). A nominal clock period of T c-seconds is, due to the clock drift, realized as anything in the range $[T - \rho T, T + \rho T]$ r-seconds. If t_{prop} r-units is the time required for signal propagation along the critical path, then to guarantee that there is sufficient time for signals to propagate, we would require $t_{prop} \leq T - \rho T$; that is, we would have to set $T \geq t_{prop}/(1 - \rho)$ c-units. The greater the value of ρ is, the greater the value of T, thus reducing the expected speed of the computer.

The second reason why ρ should be low has to do with clock synchronization. Every T_s c-units, we run some synchronization algorithm to simultaneously adjust the clocks so that they tell roughly the same time after adjustment.[1] What is the maximum *skew* (difference in time told by the clocks) that could occur between the clocks? The fastest clocks could gain up to ρ seconds per second, while the slowest could lose up to ρ seconds per second. Thus, over a period of T_s c-seconds, the fastest and slowest clocks could be up to $2\rho T_s$ r-seconds apart, even if they were perfectly synchronized to begin with. Thus, if we want the clocks to be tightly synchronized, either T_s or ρ (or preferably both) must be small. Indeed, if ρ increases, we will have to decrease T_s to compensate; that is, we will have to resynchronize more often.

All clocks—whether an old-fashioned grandfather clock or a cesium clock—are based on oscillators. The clocks used in computers are square-wave generators, and time is expressed as a multiple of the square-wave periods. Perhaps the simplest digital clock of all consists of an odd number of inverters connected as shown in Figure 9.2. If the total propagation time through the line of inverters is t_{prop}, the output toggles every t_{prop}, thus generating a square wave with a frequency of $1/2t_{prop}$. Unfortunately, the propagation times through gates can vary widely from

---

[1] Such a simultaneous adjustment is, in fact, impossible (since it would assume the ability to measure intervals exactly), but let us assume that it can be done. A very similar argument would hold if the clocks were adjusted not simultaneously but over some small interval of r-time.

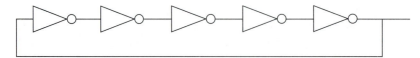

FIGURE 9.2
A simple digital clock.

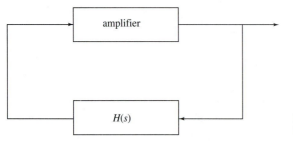

FIGURE 9.3
Using a filter to make an oscillator.

gate to gate (even for gates of the same type), and so the frequency can change from one implementation to another.

Another approach is to use a bandpass filter in the feedback loop of an amplifier, as in the structure in Figure 9.3. The filter essentially gets rid of all the frequencies outside a certain range. If the loop gain is at least one and the amplifier is not saturated, a sine-wave output results; if the amplifier saturates, we have a square-wave output. Sometimes the filter is made out of an inductor and capacitor. A still better clock can be obtained using a quartz crystal as a filter. Such clocks typically have a maximum drift rate of around 10^{-6}, which corresponds to gaining or losing at most 0.087 s per day.

Digital clocks are, as we have said, square-wave generators, and the clock time is simply the number of square waves multiplied by the clock period. For this reason, $C_i(t)$ is really a step function of t. This is analogous to the display in a digital watch or to the second hand in most analog quartz watches, which changes once every second. However, it will sometimes be convenient, in our mathematical analysis, to treat the clock time as a continuous differentiable function, and to treat its digital nature as the consequence of an error in reading the clock.

9.2.1   Synchronization

Two clocks are said to be synchronized if the times they tell are sufficiently close. More precisely, clocks c_i and c_j are synchronized at c-time T if for some given $\delta > 0$,

$$|c_i(T) - c_j(T)| < \delta \qquad (9.4)$$

$|c_i(T) - c_j(T)|$ is the *skew* between clocks c_i and c_j at c-time T.

An alternative definition of synchronization is to define the clock skew at real time t as $|C_i(t) - C_j(t)|$, and to say that clocks c_i and c_j are synchronized

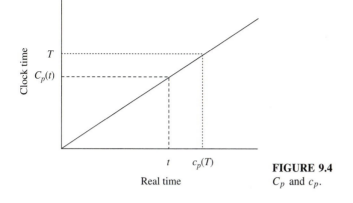

FIGURE 9.4
C_p and c_p.

at real time t if

$$|C_i(t) - C_j(t)| < \delta \qquad (9.5)$$

$|C_i(t) - C_j(t)|$ is the clock skew at real time t. The two conditions are nearly equivalent. In this chapter, we will assume that δ is defined so that both Equations (9.4) and (9.5) hold whenever clocks c_i and c_j are synchronized. Figure 9.4 illustrates these concepts.

Sometimes, synchronization is with respect to an external source of timing signals. For example, the United States National Institute of Standards and Technology broadcasts timing signals on 2.5, 5, 10, 15, and 20 MHz. It is possible for a system to synchronize itself with such an external signal.

The type of synchronization that we will focus on here is internal synchronization. A set of clocks S is said to be internally synchronized at real time t if every pair of clocks $c_i, c_j \in S$ is synchronized at that time, and the time told by each clock lies within the cone of acceptability. The parameters of synchronization are the maximum allowed skew δ, and the maximum allowed system drift rate ρ_{sys}.

Internal synchronization proceeds by the clocks exchanging timing signals, and adjusting themselves appropriately. For the rest of this chapter, unless we say otherwise, by "synchronization" we will mean "internal synchronization." We will assume that each clock sends out timing signals at regular intervals. These timing signals will be called "clock ticks."

9.3 A NONFAULT-TOLERANT SYNCHRONIZATION ALGORITHM

Consider the following simple procedure for synchronization. At regular intervals of T (as measured by itself), each clock sends out its timing signals (clock ticks) to the other clocks. A clock compares its own timing signals with those it receives from the others and adjusts itself appropriately.

For the moment, assume that the signal propagation times are zero and consider a three-clock system. Suppose the timing signals are as shown in Figure 9.5, where t_i is the real time when clock c_i sends its signal. The middle clock is chosen

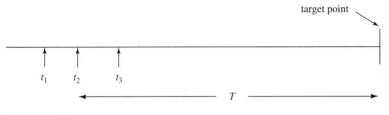

FIGURE 9.5
Three-clock system.

as the correct clock, and the other two try to align themselves with this clock. It is tempting to do this by having each clock correct as soon as it can, by moving clock c_1 back by $t_2 - t_1$ at real time t_2 and clock c_3 forward by $t_3 - t_2$ at real time t_3. However, this is not acceptable, since a process which was using clock c_3 would see time moving backwards (see Figure 9.6b). For example, suppose this process timestamped event X at real time t_x and event Y at real time t_y. Y occurs after X, but due to the clock adjustment, its timestamp will make it appear as if it occurred before X. This illustrates why we should never turn a clock back in the process of synchronization. It is also a bad idea to introduce a jump in the clock time, as in Figure 9.6a. As far as the system is concerned, the interval (A, B) has simply vanished.

Instead of making such immediate, and inadvisable, adjustments, we amortize the adjustments. That is, we adjust the clocks so that at the next comparison point, they try to be aligned. Clock c_1 will slow itself down and clock c_3 will speed itself up so that their next clock ticks will align as closely as possible with the next clock tick of clock c_2 (which, because it delivered its tick between those of clocks c_1 and c_3, is being used as a reference or trigger with which the other clocks align). Clock c_2 is not corrected in any way. In other

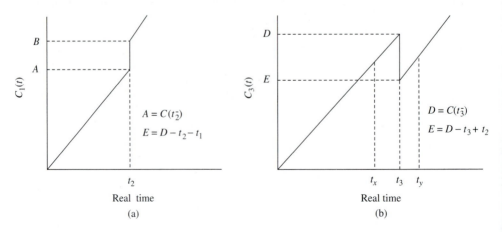

FIGURE 9.6
Inadvisable clock adjustment ($t_i^- = \lim_{\xi \to 0} (t_i - \xi)$): (a) moving c_1 forward at real time t_2; (b) moving c_3 back at real time t_3.

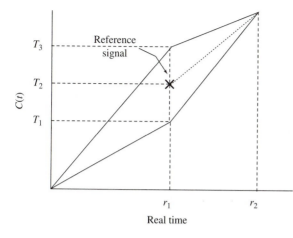

T_3 ---- Reference signal

T_2

$C(t)$

T_1

r_1 r_2

Real time

FIGURE 9.7
Amortized clock adjustment.

words, we will attempt to deliver the next ticks of clocks c_1, c_2, and c_3 at time $R2$, which is T c-seconds after t_2. See Figure 9.7. Of course, since time is being measured by imperfect clocks that can drift up to some value ρ, these times cannot be precisely controlled. Indeed, the best we can do with the clocks is to deliver their next tick sometime in the r-intervals $[T/(1 + \rho)$, $T/(1 - \rho)] \approx [T(1 - \rho), T(1 + \rho)]$, respectively. The clock skew of this system cannot therefore be guaranteed to be less then about $T(1 + \rho) - T(1 - \rho) = 2\rho T$ r-seconds.

All this assumes that the signal propagation times are zero. Suppose this is not the case, and that the propagation times are exactly known. This happens when, for example, there is a dedicated link between each pair of clocks. Then, it is (theoretically, at any rate) possible to correct for the propagation times, and reduce the problem to one where the propagation times are zero.

The skew becomes worse when the propagation times are not exactly known. For example, the clocks could send their clock ticks as messages on a store-and-forward network, and the propagation time then depends on the path chosen and the congestion on that path. Suppose that all we know is that the delay is in some interval $[\mu_{\min}, \mu_{\max}]$ r-seconds. What is the tightest (lowest-skew) synchronization that we can guarantee with this algorithm? Let us return to the order of clock ticks shown in Figure 9.5. Denote by $\mu_{i,j}$ the unknown propagation time from clock c_i to clock c_j. Clock c_i sees the clock tick of clock c_j at real time $t_i + \mu_{j,i}$. Since $\mu_{j,i}$ is unknown, all that c_i can tell from this is that c_j delivered its tick sometime in the interval $[t_i + \mu_{j,i} - \mu_{\max}, t_i + \mu_{j,i} - \mu_{\min}]$.

Consider the case where t_1, t_2, t_3 and the propagation times are such that c_1 and c_3 are both sure that c_2 is the middle clock, and thus is the reference they must synchronize to. Suppose they each estimate the propagation time from c_2 to be x. Let us see what happens with both c_1 and c_3.

c_1 receives the signal from c_2 at real time $t_2 + \mu_{2,1}$. Since it is estimating that the propagation time is x, it thinks that c_2 transmitted that signal at real time $t_2 + \mu_{2,1} - x$. It tries therefore to deliver its next clock tick T c-units after this time. However, this time is being measured by the clock. An interval of nominal duration T c-units may actually be anything in the range $[(1 - \rho)T, (1 + \rho)T]$ r-units. Hence c_1 can deliver its next clock tick in the r-interval

$$I_1 = [(1 - \rho)T + t_2 + \mu_{2,1} - x, (1 + \rho)T + t_2 + \mu_{2,1} - x] \qquad (9.6)$$

By a similar reasoning, c_3 delivers its next clock tick in the r-interval

$$I_3 = [(1 - \rho)T + t_2 + \mu_{2,3} - x, (1 + \rho)T + t_2 + \mu_{2,3} - x] \qquad (9.7)$$

Clock c_2 delivers its next clock tick in the r-interval

$$I_2 = [(1 - \rho)T + t_2, (1 + \rho)T + t_2] \qquad (9.8)$$

What does this do for the clock skew at the next tick? In the worst case, if $\mu_{2,1} = \mu_{min}$ and clock c_1 is running as fast as is legally allowed, the next c_1 tick will occur at r-time $(1-\rho)T + t_2 + \mu_{min} - x$. If $\mu_{2,3} = \mu_{max}$ and c_3 is running as slow as is legally allowed, the next c_3 tick will occur at r-time $(1+\rho)T + t_2 + \mu_{max} - x$. The clock skew will then be

$$[(1 + \rho)T + t_2 + \mu_{max} - x] - (1 - \rho)T + t_2 + \mu_{min} - x = 2\rho T + \mu_{max} - \mu_{min} \qquad (9.9)$$

Uncertainties in the propagation times can therefore have a considerable impact on the skew that can be guaranteed.

How should the algorithm handle the case when the ticks arrive so close together that we cannot tell in which order the clock ticks were originally delivered? This is left for the reader as an exercise.

An alternative to mutual synchronization is to use a master-slave structure. The slave clocks try to align themselves to the master clock. They do this by sending out a `read_clock` request to the master, which responds with a message containing its clock time when it received this request.

Suppose the round-trip real time between sending the `read_clock` request and receiving the answer is r. Let μ_{min} be the minimum time taken to send a message between the master and the slave. Let $t_{s\to m}$ and $t_{m\to s}$ be the respective times taken for a given `read_clock` request to propagate to the master, and for the master's reply (e.g., "Present time is T") to propagate to the slave. By definition, $r = t_{s\to m} + t_{m\to s} > 2\mu_{min}$. See Figure 9.8.

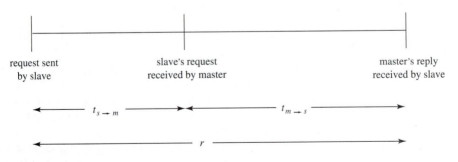

FIGURE 9.8
Slave-master interaction in a `read-clock` request.

When the slave receives the "Present time is T" message from the master, the master clock will tell a time in the interval $I = [T + \mu_{\min}(1 - \rho), T + (r - \mu_{\min})(1 + \rho)]$. The derivation of this is simple. The lower bound is the time when the $t_{m \to s} = \mu_{\min}$ (the minimum possible) and the master clock runs as slow as it is allowed to. The upper bound is computed as follows. The maximum possible value of $t_{m \to s}$ is $r - \mu_{\min}$, for a given value of r. The maximum rate at which the master clock can run is $1 + \rho$.

Suppose for a moment that the slave clock can measure the round-trip delay with perfect accuracy. The duration of the interval I is $r(1 + \rho) - 2\rho\mu_{\min}$. Then, the best estimate of the time told by the master clock when its "Present time is T" message is received by the slave clock is the midpoint of the interval I, that is,

$$T + \frac{r(1 + \rho)}{2} - \mu_{\min}$$

The error in making this estimate is therefore upper-bounded by

$$\frac{r(1 + \rho)}{2} - \mu_{\min}$$

But the slave clock cannot measure the round-trip delay with perfect accuracy; all it has is the round-trip delay as measured by itself. The duration of r, when measured, may be as great as $(1 + \rho)r$. Thus, the interval I may be the interval

$$I' = [T + \mu_{\min}(1 - \rho), T + (r(1 + \rho) - \mu_{\min})(1 + \rho)]$$

and the estimate of the time may be

$$T + \frac{r(1 + \rho)^2}{2} - \mu_{\min}$$

The estimation error is thus upper-bounded by

$$\frac{r(1 + \rho)^2}{2} - \mu_{\min} \approx \frac{r(1 + 2\rho)}{2} - \mu_{\min}$$

If the messages between master and slave clocks pass over a network that is shared by other traffic, r can vary a lot depending on the intensity of that traffic. The slave clock can try to limit the estimation error by simply discarding all the messages that do not arrive within some prespecified round-trip delay. That is, if the clock wishes the estimation error to be upper-bounded by ϵ, it discards all messages with $r > 2(\epsilon + \mu_{\min})/(1 + \rho)^2$. If the network is heavily loaded, it will take many attempts before the slave clock can obtain a clock reading with a sufficiently low estimation error.

9.4 IMPACT OF FAULTS

When faults occur, the simple and obvious algorithm in Section 9.3 will not work. Let us begin by assuming that all signal-propagation times are zero. Suppose, for example, that clock c_2 undergoes malicious failure (see Chapter 7) and delivers its

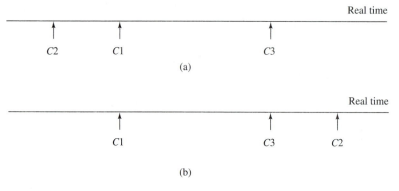

FIGURE 9.9
The result of clock c_2 being maliciously faulty (where Ci = time of receipt of clock c_i's tick): (a) the clocks as seen by clock c_1; (b) the clocks as seen by clock c_3.

ticks to clocks c_1 and c_3 at different times. The situation is illustrated in Figure 9.9. To clock c_1, c_2 appears to be faster than clock c_1; and to clock c_3, c_2 appears to be slower than c_3. As a result, both clocks c_1 and c_3 will think of themselves as in the middle, the reference clock. They will not correct themselves in any way and be free to drift apart indefinitely.

9.4.1   Loss of Synchrony

Synchronization is carried out by clocks exchanging timing messages and adjusting themselves appropriately. There are two ways in which synchrony can be lost as a result of some clocks becoming faulty, when multiple nonoverlapping cliques are formed and when the clocks are driven too fast or too slow.

A *clique* of clocks is defined as follows. Represent each nonfaulty clock c_i by a vertex v_i. Connect vertices v_i and v_j by an edge e_{ij} iff a change in the timing of the kth tick (for $k \in \{1, 2, \ldots\}$) of c_i will cause a change in the timing of the $(k + 1)$th tick of c_j. This results in a synchronization graph with respect to the kth clock tick. We will call each component[2] of a synchronization graph a clique. Two cliques A and B are said to be nonoverlapping with respect to the kth clock tick if every clock in A delivers its kth tick before any clock in B, or vice versa. If the synchronization graph has nonoverlapping cliques, then synchrony cannot be guaranteed.

> **Example 9.1.** Suppose the synchronization graph is as shown in Figure 9.10 for a four-clock system. If the clock ticks are as shown in Figure 9.11a, with clocks c_1, c_2 delivering their kth clock tick before c_3, c_4, then they will form nonoverlapping cliques. Then, there is nothing to prevent the set $\{c_1, c_2\}$ from drifting indefinitely

---

[2]A *component* of a graph is a maximal connected subgraph of the graph. That is, it is a connected subgraph with the property that no point in the subgraph is connected to any point outside it.

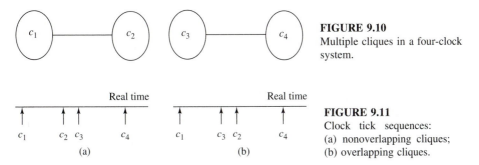

FIGURE 9.10
Multiple cliques in a four-clock system.

FIGURE 9.11
Clock tick sequences:
(a) nonoverlapping cliques;
(b) overlapping cliques.

away from $\{c_3, c_4\}$. On the other hand, if the ticks are as in Figure 9.11b, the cliques are overlapping.

Synchrony can also be lost when clocks are being run at their upper or lower frequency limits. Suppose, for example, that the clocks are trying to catch up with a faulty clock that sends spurious clock ticks at a higher frequency than the good clocks can attain. Then, each good clock will run at its maximum frequency. Since these frequencies vary slightly from one clock to another (e.g., one may be 20.0001 MHz while another is 19.9999 MHz), they will tend to separate over time and synchrony will be lost.

9.5 FAULT-TOLERANT SYNCHRONIZATION IN HARDWARE

To synchronize in hardware, we can use phase-locked loops. These date back to the 1930s, and have been widely used in radio and other forms of communication. The basic structure of a phase-locked loop is shown in Figure 9.12. The objective is to align, as closely as possible, the output of the oscillator with an oscillatory signal input. The comparator puts out a signal that is proportional to the difference between the phase of the input and that of the oscillator. This is passed through a filter, and the resultant signal is used to modify the frequency of a voltage-controlled oscillator (VCO).

Let us carry out a simple analysis of phase-locked loops. The output voltage of the comparator at any time t is proportional to the difference between the phase of the signal input, $\phi_i(t)$, and that of the VCO, $\phi_r(t)$:

$$v_c(t) = K_c\{\phi_i(t) - \phi_r(t)\} \qquad (9.10)$$

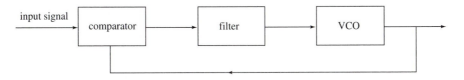

FIGURE 9.12
Structure of a phase-locked loop.

where K_c is the comparator gain factor. The Laplace Transform of the output is thus given by

$$V_c(s) = K_c\{\Phi_i(s) - \Phi_r(s)\} \qquad (9.11)$$

where $\Phi_i(s)$ and $\Phi_r(s)$ are Laplace transforms of the input and oscillator phase, respectively.

Let the Laplace transform of the filter be $L(s)$. The output of the filter has the Laplace transform

$$V_{VCO}(s) = V_c(s)L(s) \qquad (9.12)$$

The output of the filter is applied to the VCO.

The frequency of the VCO is controlled by the applied input voltage. If the voltage applied to the VCO input is $V_c + v_{VCO}(t)$, the frequency of the ideal VCO signal is given by

$$\omega(t) = \omega_c + K_{VCO}v_{VCO}(t) \qquad (9.13)$$

subject to being limited to the range $[\omega_{min}, \omega_{max}]$. See Figure 9.13. K_{VCO} is called the VCO gain factor. In reality, there are usually some random fluctuations (noise) in the VCO output frequency, but we will focus on ideal VCOs for our analysis.

The Laplace transform of the VCO frequency is thus given by

$$\Omega_r(s) = \frac{\omega_c}{s} + K_{VCO}V_{VCO}(s) \qquad (9.14)$$

Since the phase of a signal is the integral of its frequency, we can write

$$\Phi_r(s) = \frac{\Omega(s)}{s} = \frac{\omega_c}{s^2} + \frac{K_{VCO}V_{VCO}(s)}{s} \qquad (9.15)$$

Equations (9.11), (9.12), and (9.13) are three equations with three unknowns $(V_c(s), V_{VCO}(s), \Phi_r(s))$. The other parameters $(\Phi_i(s), K_c, K_{VCO}, L(s))$ are known.

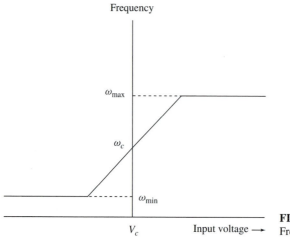

FIGURE 9.13
Frequency control of an ideal VCO.

Solving these equations we have the Laplace transform of the phase of the VCO output

$$\Phi_r(s) = \frac{\omega_c}{s(s + K_c K_{VCO} L(s))} + \frac{K_c K_{VCO} L(s)}{s + K_c K_{VCO} L(s)} \Phi_i(s) \qquad (9.16)$$

The Laplace transform of the difference in phase (the phase error) between the signal input and the VCO output is therefore

$$\Phi_i(s) - \Phi_r(s) = -\frac{\omega_c}{s(s + K_c K_{VCO} L(s))} + \frac{s}{s + K_c K_{VCO} L(s)} \Phi_i(s) \qquad (9.17)$$

Now define $\theta_i(t)$ and $\theta_r(t)$ such that $\phi_i(t) = \omega_c t + \theta_i(t)$ and $\phi_r(t) = \omega_c t + \theta_r(t)$. Let $\Theta_i(s)$ and $\Theta_r(s)$ be the Laplace transforms of $\theta_i(t)$ and $\theta_r(t)$, respectively. Then, we can rewrite Equation (9.17) as

$$\Phi_i(s) - \Phi_r(s) = \frac{s\Theta_i(s)}{s + K_c K_{VCO} L(s)} \qquad (9.18)$$

This is the Laplace transform of the tracking error between the input phase and the VCO output.

Example 9.2. If the input is a unit step at time 0 and there is no filter, we have

$$\Theta_i(s) = \frac{1}{s} \qquad (9.19)$$

$$L(s) = 1 \qquad (9.20)$$

The Laplace transform of the tracking error is then given by:

$$\frac{1}{s + K_c K_{VCO}} \qquad (9.21)$$

In the time domain, this indicates a tracking error that decays exponentially with time; that is, the error is $\exp(-K_c K_{VCO} t)$.

Readers with some prior knowledge of transfer functions should consider what happens when $L(s) = (1 + as)/(1 + bs)$.

9.5.1 Completely Connected, Zero-Propagation-Time System

The purpose of our analysis so far has been to convince the reader that the phase-locked loop has the ability to track input signals and thus synchronize the output with respect to the input. Thus, if we can suitably define a reference (or trigger) input as a function of the outputs of the clocks in the system, we can synchronize the clocks.

Figure 9.14 shows the structure of each of the clocks. Every clock is connected by a dedicated line to every other clock. (See Figure 9.15 for an example of a four-clock system.) We assume, to begin with, that signal-propagation times are zero.

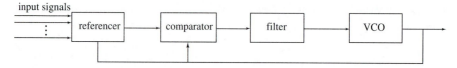

FIGURE 9.14
Structure of a phase-locked loop used in synchronization.

Each clock has a referencer circuit, which accepts as input the clock ticks from the other clocks in the system as well as that of its own VCO. It generates a reference signal to which its VCO tries to align itself. The problem of designing a fault-tolerant synchronizer thus reduces to obtaining a reference signal that will permit the system to remain synchronized in the face of up to a given number of failures.

The obvious approach is to make the reference signal equal to the median of the incoming signals (keep in mind that we are assuming zero-message-propagation times). Unfortunately, this won't work if there are two or more maliciously faulty clocks.

> **Example 9.3.** Consider a system of fifteen clocks $c_1, \ldots c_{15}$. Clocks c_1 and c_2 are maliciously faulty. This means that while the signals of any clock in the set $\{c_3, \ldots, c_{15}\}$ must appear to the others at the same time, c_1 and c_2 can send different signals to different clocks. In particular, let c_1 and c_2 appear to clocks in the set $A\{c_3, \ldots, c_8\}$ as the fastest clocks in the system, and to clocks in the set $B = \{c_9, \ldots, c_{15}\}$ as the slowest clocks in the system (the arrows in Figure 9.16 indicate the order in which the tick of each clock is received). The synchronization graph associated with this state of affairs is shown in Figure 9.17. There are two nonoverlapping cliques in this synchronization graph, since the clocks in A see clock c_8 as the median clock and the clocks in B see clock c_{10} as the median clock. There is now nothing to keep the two sets of clocks from drifting from apart indefinitely, so long as the faulty clocks c_1 and c_2 continue to behave in this manner.

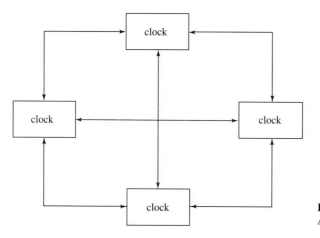

FIGURE 9.15
A four-clock system.

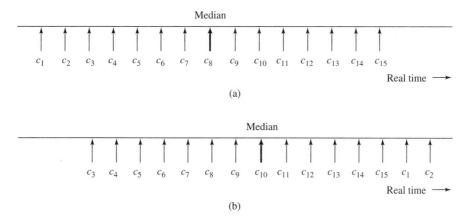

(a)

(b)

FIGURE 9.16
A fifteen-clock system with c_1 and c_2 maliciously faulty: (a) the clocks as seen by clocks c_3 to c_8; (b) the clocks as seen by clocks c_9 to c_{15}.

Let us now construct conditions under which such a loss of synchrony cannot occur. The reason that the median signal does not work in Example 9.3 is that the cliques A and B are nonoverlapping (i.e., every clock in A was faster than any clock in B). Let us now design a clock system where each clock chooses one clock signal as a reference and tries to align itself to it. In particular, let m be the number of faulty clocks that the system has to deal with and N be the total number of clocks. Each clock sees a scenario of the kth tick of clocks in the system in a certain order. Suppose a clock sees itself as the ith fastest clock in the system with respect to the kth tick. Then, let it choose the $f_i(N, m)$th signal (in temporal order) as its reference. We seek to define suitable functions $f_i(N, m)$ for $i = 1, \ldots, N$, such that synchrony can be maintained among the nonfaulty clocks.

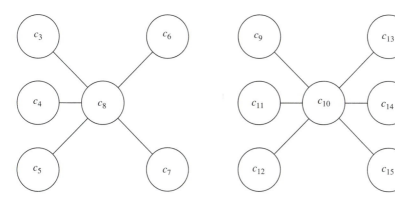

FIGURE 9.17
Synchronization graph of Figure 9.16.

We begin by defining an *ordered partition* $G1, G2$ of the good clocks, with respect to the kth clock tick as any grouping of the good clocks into sets $G1$ and $G2$ such that all clocks in $G1$ deliver their kth tick before any of the clocks in $G2$. Then the clocks will not drift apart if the following two conditions are satisfied for every possible partition $G1, G2$ of the good clocks such that $\|G1\|, \|G2\| > 0$:[3]

C1. If all clocks in $G1$ ($G2$) use as the reference a signal that is faster[4] (slower) than any clock in $G2$ ($G1$), then there must be at least one clock in $G2$ ($G1$) that uses as the reference either the slowest (fastest) clock in $G1$ ($G2$) or a signal faster (slower) than the slowest (fastest) clock in $G1$ ($G2$). This condition ensures that multiple nonoverlapping cliques do not form.

C2. If a good clock x uses as the reference the signal of a faulty clock y, there must exist nonfaulty clocks z_1 and z_2 such that z_1 is faster than or equal to y, and y is faster than or equal to z_2. Either z_1 or z_2 may be x itself.

C1 and **C2** are called the *conditions of correctness*. They may appear to be complicated, but they are really quite simple. Figure 9.18 shows what happens when each of these conditions is violated. If **C1** is violated, then each partition of clocks runs essentially without reference to the other; if **C2** is violated, the faulty clocks can increase or decrease the clock rate of the entire system at will.

Denote by $p(i)$ the position of c_i as seen by itself with respect to the kth tick. That is, c_i sees that $p(i) - 1$ other clocks have delivered their kth ticks before it does so.

Let us begin with how to satisfy **C2**. If $f_{p(i)}(N, m) \leq m$, then **C2** can be violated if the m faulty clocks appear to c_i to be the fastest m clocks in the system. Similarly, if $f_{p(i)}(N, m) > N - m$, **C2** can be violated if the m faulty clocks appear to c_i as the slowest m clocks in the system. To ensure that **C2** is satisfied, we must therefore have

$$m + 1 \leq f_i(N, m) \leq N - m \tag{9.22}$$

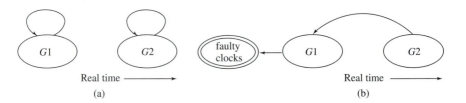

Real time ———→   Real time ———→
(a)   (b)

FIGURE 9.18
Violating the conditions of correctness: (a) condition **C1** is violated (partitions $G1$ and $G2$ both derive references internally, no effect of $G1$ on $G2$ and vice versa); (b) condition **C2** is violated (the clocks are at the mercy of the faulty clocks).

---

[3] $\|X\|$ means the number of elements in X.
[4] We say that signal a is faster than signal b if a occurs earlier than b.

Obtaining conditions to ensure that **C1** is satisfied requires a little more work. If all clocks in $G1$ use as reference a signal faster than any clock in $G2$, $f_{p(x)}(N, m) \leq \|G1\| + m$ for all $x \in G1$. The m on the right-hand side of the inequality is due to the malicious clocks being able to position themselves between $G1$ and $G2$ in the sequence seen by each clock in $G1$. Note that $f_{p(x)}(N, m) \leq \|G1\| + m$ is a sufficient but not necessary condition for all clocks in $G1$ to have the reference faster than any clock in $G2$. (Why?) Similarly, if all clocks in $G2$ use as the reference a signal slower than any clock in $G1$, then $f_{p(y)}(N, m) > \|G1\|$ for all $y \in G2$.

We now have a number of cases to dispose of.

Case 1. $\max_{x \in G1} f_{p(x)}(N, m) \leq \|G1\| + m$: If all the faulty clocks appear to the clocks in $G1$ to be faster than any $G2$ clock, there will be no reference to any clock outside $G1$. Hence, at least one clock in $G2$ must be assured of a reference to a clock in $G1$. This implies that

$$\min_{y \in G2} f_{p(y)}(N, m) \leq \|G1\| \tag{9.23}$$

Case 2. $\min_{y \in G2} f_{p(y)}(N, m) \geq \|G1\| + 1$: By reasoning similar to that in case 1, this requires that there be at least one clock in $G1$ whose reference is drawn from $G2$. But, to be sure of that, we require

$$\max_{x \in G1} f_{p(x)}(N, m) \geq \|G1\| + m + 1 \tag{9.24}$$

Case 3. $\max_{x \in G1} f_{p(x)}(N, m) > \|G1\| + m$ or $\min_{y \in G2} f_{p(y)}(N, m) < \|G1\| + 1$: In such a case, no potential exists for the formation of nonoverlapping cliques.

Our conditions of correctness thus boil down to the following requirements.

- If $\max_{x \in G1} f_{p(x)}(N, m) \leq \|G1\| + m$, then $\min_{y \in G2} f_{p(y)}(N, m) \leq \|G1\|$.
- Otherwise, if $\min_{y \in G2} f_{p(y)}(N, m) \geq \|G1\| + 1$, then $\max_{x \in G1} f_{p(x)}(N, m) \geq \|G1\| + m + 1$.

It follows from these requirements that

$$\max_{x \in G1} f_{p(x)}(N, m) - \min_{y \in G2} f_{p(y)}(N, m) \geq m \tag{9.25}$$

But we require that any reference be neither the first m nor the last m clocks, that is, that any reference lie in the interval of positions $m + 1, \ldots, N - m$. From this observation and Equation (9.25), we obtain the requirement

$$(N - m) - (m + 1) \geq m \Rightarrow N \geq 3m + 1 \tag{9.26}$$

To ensure that conditions of correctness **C1** and **C2** are satisfied for every partition $G1, G2$, it is sufficient to use the following functions f_i.

$$f_i(N, m) = \begin{cases} 2m + 1 & \text{if } i < N - m \\ m + 1 & \text{otherwise} \end{cases} \tag{9.27}$$

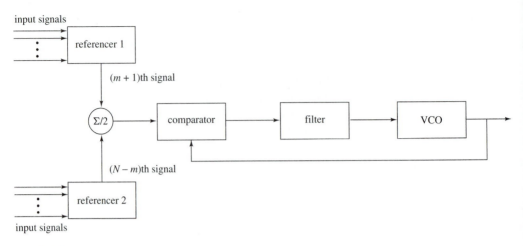

FIGURE 9.19
A system where the reference is the average of the $(m + 1)$th and $(N - m)$th signals.

These are by no means the only functions that will satisfy the constraints in Equations (9.22) and (9.25) (in the exercises, the reader is invited to construct others).

The problem with this scheme is that the reference that a clock c_i chooses is a function of its perceived position $p(i)$ in the sequence of clock ticks. This can complicate the design of the referencer circuitry.

The referencer circuitry can be simplified considerably upon realizing that the average of the times of arrival of the $(m + 1)$th and $(N - m)$th clock ticks ensures that multiple nonoverlapping cliques do not form, and that the clocks are not driven either abnormally fast or abnormally slowly. The structure of this system is shown in Figure 9.19. The proof for this is similar to the preceding discussion and is left as an exercise.

Recall that we have throughout our discussion made two assumptions:

- that the clocks form a completely connected structure, with each clock having a dedicated line to every other clock, and
- that the signal-propagation times are zero.

The first assumption may be difficult to justify if the number of clocks is large, while the second assumption is sometimes not an acceptable approximation. Let us turn now to relaxing these assumptions.

9.5.2 Sparse-Interconnection, Zero-Propagation-Time System

Suppose instead of a completely connected structure, we have clocks organized into multiple clusters. Each clock in a cluster is connected by a dedicated link to every other clock in that cluster. Also, for every pair of clusters, CL_i and CL_j, there is exactly one clock $c_i \in CL_i$ that has a link to the inputs of every clock in CL_j. See Figure 9.20, with links listed in the table below, for a three-cluster example.

From	To	Source
CL_1	CL_2	$v2$
	CL_3	$v6$
CL_2	CL_1	$v3$
	CL_3	$v8$
CL_3	CL_1	$v9$
	CL_2	$v12$

Dense though this interconnect looks, a completely connected network of 13 clocks would be much denser! As before, we assume that the signal-propagation times are effectively zero.

Suppose we have a total of M clusters $CL_1, \ldots, CL_M$. Cluster CL_i has p_i clocks in it. Let $c_{i,j}$ represent the jth clock of cluster CL_i. Define $q(i, k) = (i - 1) \bmod p_k + 1$. Then, clock $c_{k,q(i,k)}$ (i.e., the $q(i, k)$th clock in cluster CL_k) provides clock inputs to every clock in cluster CL_i. For example, consider the case where $M = 7$, and each cluster has exactly four clocks in it. Then, Table 9.1 lists which clocks provide intercluster signals between each cluster pair. Note that because of the way the intercluster connections have been defined, every clock receives signals from the same clocks as every other clock in the same cluster.

Each clock can run the same phase-locked algorithm that we discussed in Section 9.5.1. Using exactly the same arguments, we can show that for a clock to be synchronized with respect to all the nonfaulty clocks that are sending it signals, there must be more than three times as many other clocks sending signals as there are faults. That is, if m is the number of maliciously faulty clocks to be

TABLE 9.1
Intercluster clocking inputs for a seven-cluster system

From	To all clocks in						
	CL_1	CL_2	CL_3	CL_4	CL_5	CL_6	CL_7
CL_1	—	$c_{1,1}$	$c_{1,2}$	$c_{1,3}$	$c_{1,4}$	$c_{1,1}$	$c_{1,2}$
CL_2	$c_{2,1}$	—	$c_{2,2}$	$c_{2,3}$	$c_{2,4}$	$c_{2,1}$	$c_{2,2}$
CL_3	$c_{3,1}$	$c_{3,2}$	—	$c_{3,3}$	$c_{3,4}$	$c_{3,1}$	$c_{3,2}$
CL_4	$c_{4,1}$	$c_{4,2}$	$c_{4,3}$	—	$c_{4,4}$	$c_{4,1}$	$c_{4,2}$
CL_5	$c_{5,1}$	$c_{5,2}$	$c_{5,3}$	$c_{5,4}$	—	$c_{5,1}$	$c_{5,2}$
CL_6	$c_{6,1}$	$c_{6,2}$	$c_{6,3}$	$c_{6,4}$	$c_{6,1}$	—	$c_{6,2}$
CL_7	$c_{7,1}$	$c_{7,2}$	$c_{7,3}$	$c_{7,4}$	$c_{7,1}$	$c_{7,2}$	—

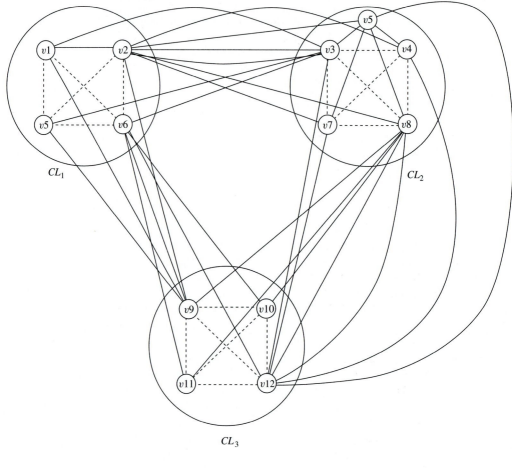

○   Individual clock

——   Directional intercluster link

- - - -   Bidirectional intracluster link

FIGURE 9.20
Example of a sparse interconnection structure.

sustained, the inequality

$$p_i + M - 1 \geq 3m + 1 \tag{9.28}$$

must be satisfied for every cluster CL_i. Is this sufficient to guarantee synchrony? No. Consider, for example, Figure 9.21; if $v1$ and $v2$ fail the two clusters can simply drift apart without check. We therefore need to ensure that despite up to m faulty clocks, there is a link connecting the clusters.

Let δ be the maximum clock skew that results under this algorithm between a clock and all other clocks that send it signals. For example, δ is the maximum

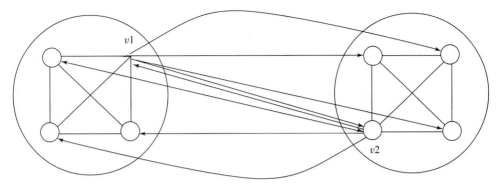

FIGURE 9.21
Counterexample.

clock skew if the entire system is a single completely connected cluster. What is the skew between clocks that are not directly connected? For example, in Figure 9.20, if all the clocks are functional, the skew between $v1$ and $v4$ is at most 2δ, since the skew between $v1$ and $v3$ and that between $v3$ and $v4$ are each at most δ.

Failures can increase the skew between clusters. For example, in Figure 9.20, if both $v2$ and $v3$ fail, the only link between clusters CL_1 and CL_2 is through CL_3. As a result, the maximum skew between the clocks in CL_1 and CL_3 is 3δ. In general, if the only link between two clusters a and b is through k other clusters, the maximum skew between a clock in a and a clock in b will be $(k+2)\delta$. This is a tight upper bound, in that it is possible for the skew actually to be this amount.

In the following, we show that if

- $3m - M + 2 \leq p_i \leq 2M - 2$, for $i = 1, 2, \ldots, M$, and
- $M \geq m + 1$

for every pair of clusters CL_i, CL_j, there will either be a direct link between two clusters or a link through a third cluster. Thus, the skew is no greater than 3δ.

ANALYSIS.* Let us consider what constraints will satisfy the requirement that even if there are m failures, each cluster must be connected to every other cluster through at most one other cluster. Then, the maximum clock skew between any two clocks in the system will be at most 3δ.

Denote by (x, y) the unique clock in cluster CL_x that provides clock signals to cluster CL_y. For example, in Figure 9.20, $v2 = (1, 2)$. Note that the same physical clock can have multiple labels (x, y). For example, in Table 9.1 clock $c_{1,1}$ provides timing signals to all clocks in both CL_2 and CL_6; therefore, both $(1, 2)$ and $(1, 6)$ refer to $c_{1,1}$. We can then define, for each cluster CL_ℓ, the following four sets:

$$IN_\ell = \{CL_s : (s, \ell) \text{ is nonfaulty}\}$$

$$IF_\ell = \{CL_s : (s, \ell) \text{ is faulty}\}$$

$$ON_\ell = \{CL_s : (\ell, s) \text{ is nonfaulty}\}$$

$$OF_\ell = \{CL_s : (\ell, s) \text{ is faulty}\}$$

IN_ℓ is the set of clusters (other than itself) from which CL_ℓ receives nonfaulty clock signals, IF_ℓ is the set of clusters (other than itself) from which CL_ℓ receives faulty clock signals, ON_ℓ is the set of clusters (other than itself) to which the clocks in CL_ℓ provide nonfaulty clock signals, and OF_ℓ is the set of clusters (other than itself) to which the clocks in CL_ℓ provide faulty clock signals. Finally, define $\zeta(x, y)$ to be the skew between clocks x and y.

Lemma 9.1. If $CL_n \in IN_\ell$ or $CL_\ell \in IN_n$ or both, for any c_ℓ, c_n such that $c_\ell \in CL_\ell$ and $c_n \in CL_n$, $\zeta(c_\ell, c_n) \leq 2\delta$.

Proof. Under these conditions, there is a nonfaulty clock signal between CL_ℓ and CL_n. $CL_n \in IN_\ell$ implies a nonfaulty signal from CL_n to CL_ℓ, while $CL_\ell \in IN_n$ implies a nonfaulty signal from CL_ℓ to CL_n. Consider the case in which $CL_\ell \in IN_n$. Then (ℓ, n) is nonfaulty and we have

$$\zeta(c_\ell, c_n) \leq \zeta(c_\ell, (\ell, n)) + \zeta((\ell, n), c_n) \leq \delta + \delta = 2\delta \qquad (9.29)$$

The case in which $CL_n \in IN_\ell$ is similar.   **Q.E.D.**

Lemma 9.2. If $\|OF_\ell\| < \|IN_n\|$ or $\|OF_n\| < \|IN_\ell\|$ or both, the clocks in CL_ℓ and CL_n have a skew of at most 3δ between them.

Proof. If $CL_n \in IN_\ell$ or $CL_\ell \in IN_n$ or both, the result follows from Lemma 9.1. We can thus concentrate on the case in which $(CL_n \notin IN_\ell$ and $CL_\ell \notin IN_n)$.

By definition, $OF_\ell \cup ON_\ell = \{CL_1, \ldots, CL_M\} - \{CL_\ell\}$, and $IF_n \cup IN_n = \{CL_1, \ldots, CL_M\} - \{CL_n\}$.

$\|OF_\ell\| < \|IN_n\| \Rightarrow ON_\ell \cap IN_n \neq \emptyset$. Hence, there is some q such that $CL_q \in ON_\ell \cap IN_n$. This means that there is a path from CL_ℓ to CL_n through CL_q (i.e., that (ℓ, q) and (q, n) are nonfaulty). Figure 9.22 illustrates this. Hence, we have for any $c_\ell \in CL_\ell$, $c_n \in CL_n$

$$\zeta(c_\ell, c_n) \leq \zeta(c_\ell, (\ell, q)) + \zeta((\ell, q), (q, n)) + \zeta((q, n), c_n) \leq 3\delta$$

The proof for the case $\|OF_n\| < \|IN_\ell\|$ is similar.   **Q.E.D.**

Lemma 9.3. If $IN_n \cap ON_\ell = IN_\ell \cap ON_n = \emptyset$, then the number of clusters $M \leq m + 1$.

Proof. From the proof of Lemma 9.2, if $IN_n \cap ON_\ell = IN_\ell \cap ON_n = \emptyset$, we must have $\|OF_n\| \geq \|IN_\ell\|$ and $\|OF_\ell\| \geq \|IN_n\|$. Define $r_i = \lceil (M-1)/p_i \rceil$ for $i = 1, \ldots, M$. There are p_ℓ clocks in CL_ℓ, and each is connected to at most r_ℓ other clusters. If $\|OF_\ell\|$ of these receive faulty signals from CL_ℓ, that means that at least $\lceil \|OF_\ell\|/r_\ell \rceil$ of the clocks in CL_ℓ must be faulty. There are at most m faulty

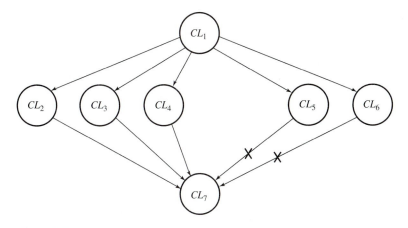

FIGURE 9.22
Condition $\|OF_1\| < \|IN_7\|$; $IN_7 = \{CL_2, CL_3, CL_4\}$; $IF_7 = \{CL_5, CL_6\}$. Unless OF_1 contains $CL_2,$, CL_3, and CL_4, there will be a nonfaulty link from CL_1 to CL_7 through another cluster.

clocks in all, by the definition of m. Hence $\|IF_\ell\| \leq m - \lceil \|OF_\ell\|/r_\ell \rceil$. But, since $\|IF_\ell\| + \|IN_\ell\| = M - 1$,

$$\|IN_\ell\| \geq M - 1 - m + \lceil \|OF_\ell\|/r_\ell \rceil \tag{9.30}$$

Also, we must have

$$\|OF_n\| \leq r_n(m - \|IF_n\|) \tag{9.31}$$

The reason is that, of the up to m faulty clocks, $\|IF_n\|$ are accounted for in clocks supplying signals to cluster CL_n.

Since $\|OF_n\| \geq \|IN_\ell\|$, we have from the inequalities in Equations (9.30) and (9.31),

$$r_n(m - \|IF_n\|) \geq M - 1 - m + \lceil \|OF_\ell\|/r_\ell \rceil \tag{9.32}$$

Let $r = \max\{r_n, r_\ell\}$. Then, from the inequality in Equation (9.32),

$$r(m - \|IF_n\|) \geq M - 1 - m + \|OF_\ell\|/r$$
$$\Rightarrow (r^2 + r)m \geq r(M - 1) + (r^2 - 1)\|IF_n\| + \|IF_n\| + \|OF_\ell\| \tag{9.33}$$

Since $\|OF_\ell\| \geq \|IN_n\|$,

$$\|IF_n\| + \|OF_\ell\| \geq \|IF_n\| + \|IN_n\| = M - 1 \tag{9.34}$$

From Equations (9.33) and (9.34), we have

$$r(r + 1)m \geq r(M - 1) + (r + 1)(r - 1)\|IF_n\| + M - 1$$
$$\Rightarrow m \geq \frac{M - 1 + (r - 1)\|IF_n\|}{r} \tag{9.35}$$

However, $\|IF_n\| \leq m$. Hence, we have from Equation (9.35),

$$m \geq \frac{M - 1 + (r - 1)m}{r}$$
$$\Rightarrow M \leq m + 1 \qquad \text{**Q.E.D.**}$$

Lemma 9.4. If $IN_n \cap ON_\ell = IN_\ell \cap ON_n = \emptyset$, then there exists a cluster CL_i such that $p_i \geq 2M - 1$.

Proof. We have already seen that each clock must be connected to at least $3m$ other clocks if synchrony is to be maintained. Each clock in cluster CL_i is connected to the $p_i - 1$ other clocks in its own cluster, and to one clock per each of the $M - 1$ other clusters. Therefore, we have $p_i - 1 + M - 1 \geq 3m$, and since $m \geq M - 1$ from Lemma 9.3, $p_i \geq 2M - 1$. **Q.E.D.**

Theorem 9.1. If $3m - M + 2 \leq p_i \leq 2M - 2$ for every cluster CL_i, then the skew between any two clocks in the system is upper-bounded by 3δ.

Proof. We have already seen that $p_i + M - 1 \geq 3m + 1$, and this leads immediately to $3m - M + 2 \leq p_i$.

The rest of the proof is by contradiction. Suppose that despite $3m - M + 2 \leq p_i \leq 2M - 2$ for every cluster, there are clocks $c_\ell \in CL_\ell$ and $c_n \in CL_n$ such that $\zeta(c_\ell, c_n) > 3\delta$. Then, $ON_n \cap IN_\ell = \emptyset$, and $ON_\ell \cap IN_n = \emptyset$. But, from Lemma 9.4, that would imply that there was a cluster CL_i such that $p_i \geq 2M - 1$. But we are given that no such cluster exists. Hence the contradiction and the proof. **Q.E.D.**

This theorem leads at once to the following optimization problem.

Given the number of faulty clocks that the system must be able to tolerate and the total number of clocks, minimize the number of clock-to-clock interconnections.

Let us consider the optimization problem for the case where the total of N clocks is divided into M_1 clusters of p_1 clocks each and M_2 clusters of p_2 clocks each. Up to m faults must be tolerated. The total number of clock-to-clock (including the connection of a clock output to its referencer input) interconnections is

$$J(M_1, M_2, p_1, p_2, m) = N(M_1 + M_2 - 1) + M_1 p_1^2 + M_2 p_2^2 \tag{9.36}$$

The optimization problem is to find M_1, M_2, p_1, p_2 to minimize $J(M_1, M_2, p_1, p_2, m)$ subject to the following constraints:

$$M_1 p_1 + M_2 p_2 = N \tag{9.37}$$

$$M_1 + M_2 + p_2 - 2 \geq 3m \tag{9.38}$$

$$p_1, p_2 \leq 2(M_1 + M_2 - 1) \tag{9.39}$$

Table 9.2 shows the optimal configurations for a few cases.

9.5.3 Accounting for Signal-Propagation Delays

So far in this section, we have assumed that signal-propagation times are negligible. This assumption is true if the geographical extent of the system is not large. More concretely, if ϕ is the nominal clock frequency and θ is the minimum phase

TABLE 9.2
Optimal values for a system built out of two cluster types

N	m	M_1	p_1	M_2	p_2	J
20	3	2	3	7	2	206
30		6	5	0	0	300
40		2	6	4	7	468
50		1	8	6	7	658
64		1	8	7	8	960
100		10	10	0	0	1900
20	5	4	2	12	1	328
30		1	2	14	2	480
40		5	2	10	3	670
50		6	3	8	4	832
64		4	6	8	5	1048
100		10	10	0	0	1900
20	7	—	—	—	—	—
30		14	1	8	2	676
40		4	1	18	2	916
50		8	3	13	2	1124
64		4	4	16	3	1424
100		8	5	10	6	2260

Note: From K. G. Shin and P. Ramanathan, "Clock Synchronization of a Large Multiprocessor System in the Presence of Malicious Faults," *IEEE Trans. Computers*, Vol. C-37, 1987. © IEEE 1987. Used with permission.

difference that can be resolved by the referencer circuitry, signal-propagation delays are negligible if they are less than $\theta/2\pi\phi$.

If propagation times are much greater than $\theta/2\pi\phi$, we must design the system to compensate for them. If there is a large variation in the propagation time between the various clock pairs, failure to correct for it can result in the formation of multiple nonoverlapping cliques. For example, the scenario in Figure 9.10 could occur not because c_1 and c_2 are faulty but because the propagation time from c_1, c_2 to clocks $c_3, \ldots, c_8$ is much less than that to clocks $c_9, \ldots, c_{15}$.

Fortunately, if the connections are point-to-point and dedicated to transmitting clock pulses, it is possible to accurately estimate propagation delays between clocks. If these delays can be timed during the design process, the referencer can correct for them.

A second approach involves the estimation of the delays during operation, at the cost of doubling the number of lines interconnecting the clocks. The scheme is shown in Figure 9.23. $d(i, j)$ is the propagation delay from clock c_i to clock c_j. When clock c_j receives a clock tick from c_i, it immediately sends it back to c_i on a special line provided for that purpose. Blocks $R1$ and $R2$ (situated in clock c_i) determine the skew between the signals that they receive. Let c_i^k and c_j^k be

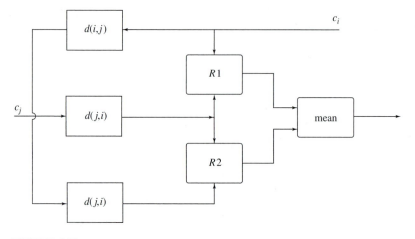

FIGURE 9.23
Correcting for propagation delays. (From K. G. Shin and P. Ramanathan, "Transmission Delays in Hardware Clock Synchronization," *IEEE Trans. Computers*, Vol. C-37, 1988. © IEEE. Used with permission.)

the real times when clocks c_i and c_j deliver their kth ticks. Block $R1$ receives the kth ticks from c_i and c_j at real times c_i^k and $c_j^k + d(j, i)$, respectively, while block $R2$ receives these signals at times $c_i^k + d(i, j) + d(j, i)$ and $c_j^k + d(j, i)$, respectively. The skews as determined by $R1$ and $R2$ are therefore $c_i^k - c_j^k - d(j, i)$ and $c_i^k + d(i, j) + d(j, i) - c_j^k - d(j, i)$, respectively. Averaging them yields

$$c_i^k - c_j^k + \frac{d(i, j) - d(j, i)}{2}$$

If $d(i, j) \approx d(j, i)$, the output of the averager approximates the correct skew, $c_i^k - c_j^k$.

9.5.4   Multiple-Fault Classes

Our discussion in this section has so far assumed that we have to sustain up to m malicious faults. How do the conditions change if we are asked to sustain m malicious faults and b nonmalicious faults (nmf)? Recall that a clock that suffers an nmf cannot send contradictory timing signals to the other clocks. Either it will send the same (possibly wrong) signal to them all, or it will send no signal.

The derivation is similar to what we have done already. As before, consider partitions $G1$, $G2$ of the good clocks. Additionally, define $H1$ as the union of $G1$ and all the nmf clocks that deliver their kth tick before any clock in $G2$. Let $H2$ be the union of $G2$ and all the nmf clocks that deliver their kth tick after some clock in $G2$.

To prevent the clocks from being driven abnormally fast or slow, we have the analog of Equation (9.22),

$$m + b + 1 \leq f_i(N, m) \leq N - (m + b) \tag{9.40}$$

To prevent the formation of multiple nonoverlapping cliques, we have the following requirements for every ordered partition G1,G2.

$$\max_{x \in G1} f_{p(x)}(N) \leq ||H1|| + m \Rightarrow \min_{y \in G2} f_{p(y)}(N) \leq ||H1|| \tag{9.41}$$

$$\min_{y \in G2} f_{p(y)}(N) > ||H1|| \Rightarrow \max_{x \in G1} f_{p(x)}(N) \geq ||H1|| + m + 1 \tag{9.42}$$

From this, we obtain the fault-tolerance requirement

$$N \geq 3m + 2b + 1 \tag{9.43}$$

Note that if $m = 0$, (i.e., if no malicious failure happens), the system will continue to be synchronized as long as the nonfaulty clocks form a majority of the clocks. If $b = 0$ (i.e., all failures are malicious), we have $N \geq 3m + 1$, which is what we derived earlier.

9.5.5 Advantages and Disadvantages of Hardware Synchronization

The chief advantage of hardware synchronization is the very small clock skews that can be attained. Typically, these skews are on the order of nanoseconds. This is due to the frequency with which the resynchronizations are carried out.

Another advantage is that hardware synchronization places no burden on the rest of the system. Unlike software synchronization, it does not consume precious processor resources. Since the clocks are interconnected by dedicated links, the traffic in time signals does not take up any bandwidth on the interprocessor network. It is transparent to both the applications software and the operating system.

The chief disadvantage is the cost of the hardware. For applications where very tight synchronization is not needed, this approach may be too expensive, and software synchronization may be the preferred approach.

9.6 SYNCHRONIZATION IN SOFTWARE

When the extremely tight synchronization that is provided by phase-locking is not needed, synchronization can be carried out in software. In software-based synchronization, we have an underlying hardware clock, and a software-based correction. The clock time is the sum of the hardware time and the correction.

A new correction is calculated at regular resynchronization intervals. It is sometimes helpful to think of the process as starting a new clock at every resynchronization interval, defined by the new correction value.

In what follows, we will frequently encounter very small higher-order terms, that we would like to drop for convenience. For example, consider the following equation,

$$\gamma \geq \alpha + \beta + \alpha\beta \tag{9.44}$$

If α and β are very small quantities, then $\alpha\beta$ is even smaller, and so Equation (9.44) can be rewritten as

$$\gamma \gtrsim \alpha + \beta \tag{9.45}$$

Here, $\gtrsim$ denotes "approximately greater than or equal to." $\lesssim$ is similarly defined.

9.6.1   Interactive Convergence Averaging Algorithm, CA1

The CA1 algorithm assumes a completely connected structure, with a dedicated link connecting every pair of clocks. The time axis is divided into resynchronization intervals, each of duration R c-units. At the end of each resynchronization interval, the clock updates its correction.[5] In particular, let $C_p(t)$ be, as before, the clock time told by the physical (hardware) clock c_p at real time t, and $c_p(T)$ the real time at which it tells clock time T. Denote by $C_p^{(i)}$ the software-based correction applied at the beginning of the ith resynchronization interval. Let $T^{(i)}$ denote the beginning of the ith resynchronization interval. We will model the correction as if the node starts a new logical clock at the beginning of each resynchronization interval. Denote the logical clock started in resynchronization interval i by $c_p^{(i)}$. Then, we have by definition of these symbols that for any $T \in [T^{(i)}, T^{(i+1)})$ (i.e., in the i'th resynchronization interval),

$$c_p^{(i)}(T) = c_p(T + C_p^{(i)}) \tag{9.46}$$

Example 9.4. Figure 9.24 shows an example of four virtual clocks, L_0, L_1, L_2, L_3. L_0 is the physical clock; it is the logical clock used before the first resynchronization point. Between resynchronization points i and $i+1$, we switch to using logical clock L_i. Note that we don't have four physical clocks—each of the logical clocks is just the physical clock with a correction added. To consider an analogy, it is as if we never reset our watches physically, but periodically reevaluated the correction to be applied to it. That is, if the watch says 10:00 AM, and the correction that then applies is 0:13, the time will be read as $10{:}00 + 0{:}13 = 10{:}13$ AM.

Let us now introduce the read error. We will assume in our analysis that the clock function is differentiable. Of course, this is not true; digital clocks are counters. The discrepancy will be accounted for by assuming that the actual clock is continuous and any departures from this clock are the result of a read error.

---

[5]The reader will note that this results in abrupt changes to the clock time at the beginning of each resynchronization interval. We can, as mentioned above, amortize the change instead of making it abruptly. The analysis for the amortized system is almost identical to what we present here.

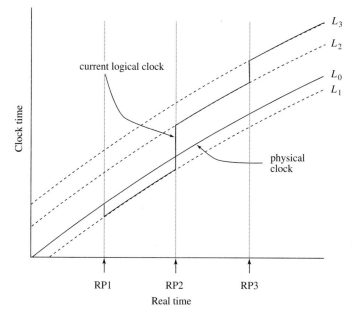

FIGURE 9.24
Virtual clocks (RP stands for resynchronization point).

Example 9.5. In Figure 9.25, the solid line shows the trajectory of a clock, while the dashed line is the trajectory that would have been followed by an equivalent continuous clock. At real time t, the actual clock reads A, while the fictitious continuous clock reads B. The discrepancy of $B - A$ is accounted for as a read error.

Errors in estimating signal-propagation delays can also be included in the read error.

Once every resynchronization interval, at a predefined moment, each clock broadcasts its time to the other clocks in the system. Based on the message it receives from clock c_q, clock c_p can compute the estimated skew between c_p and c_q as Δ_{qp}. This is calculated after correcting for the estimated message transmission time.

The read error ϵ is defined as satisfying the following inequality for nonfaulty clocks c_p and c_q.

$$|c_p^{(i)}(T_0 + \Delta_{qp}) - c_q^{(i)}(T_0)| < \epsilon \qquad (9.47)$$

for some time $T_0 \in [T^{(i+1)} - S, T^{(i+1)}]$. From this, we have $\Delta_{qp} \lesssim \delta + \epsilon$ for synchronized clocks c_p and c_q.

At the end of resynchronization interval i, each nonfaulty clock p computes the correction $C_p^{(i+1)}$ inductively as follows.

$$C_p^{(i+1)} = C_p^{(i)} + \frac{1}{N} \sum_{r=1}^{N} \overline{\Delta}_{rp} \qquad (9.48)$$

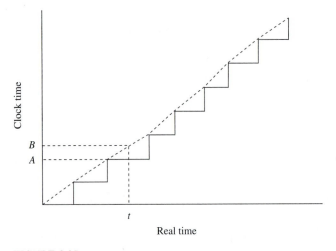

FIGURE 9.25
Read error.

Define $\Delta_p = \frac{1}{N} \sum_{r=1}^{N} \overline{\Delta}_{rp}$ where

$$\overline{\Delta}_{rp} = \begin{cases} \Delta_{rp} & \text{if } r \neq p \text{ and } |\Delta_{rp}| < \Delta \\ 0 & \text{otherwise} \end{cases} \qquad (9.49)$$

and Δ is some constant such that $\Delta > \delta + \epsilon$.

In other words, each clock computes the average of the estimated skew between itself and each of the clocking signals it receives. It ignores signals from clocks that are skewed by more than Δ, and averages the skew associated with the rest. It then corrects itself by this amount. Figure 9.26 summarizes this process. S is the interval over which the timing information is acquired and the correction is computed.

We seek two things from this algorithm. First (and obviously), we want the clock skews to be kept below a given bound. Second, we want the corrections at each resynchronization epoch to be suitably bounded; that is, there must be some acceptably small $\Sigma > 0$ such that $|C_p^{(i+1)} - C_p^{(i)}| < \Sigma$. These are our conditions of correctness.

We show below that if $N \geq 3m + 1$, and the nonfaulty clocks are synchronized to begin with (i.e., at the beginning of system operation) to within a skew

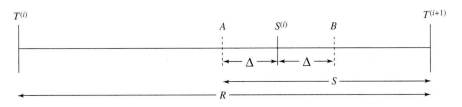

FIGURE 9.26
Resynchronization intervals: the clock sends out its timing signal at $S^{(i)}$; all signals estimated to have been sent by any other clock outside the interval $[A, B]$ will be ignored during this resynchronization.

TABLE 9.3
Upper bound of skews (in ms), under algorithm CA1 (where $S < R$)

					m				
N	0	1	2	3	4	5	6	7	8
4	0.2950								
7	0.1857	0.3250							
10	0.1420	0.2029	0.3550						
13	0.1185	0.1540	0.2200	0.3850					
16	0.1038	0.1277	0.1660	0.2371	0.4150				
19	0.0937	0.1113	0.1369	0.1780	0.2543	0.4450			
22	0.0864	0.1000	0.1188	0.1462	0.1900	0.2714	0.4750		
25	0.0808	0.0918	0.1063	0.1263	0.1554	0.2020	0.2886		
28	0.0764	0.0856	0.0973	0.1126	0.1338	0.1646	0.2140	0.3057	
31	0.0729	0.0807	0.0904	0.1027	0.1189	0.1413	0.1738	0.2260	0.3229

Note: $R = 1$ ms; $\epsilon = 2\,\mu$s; $\rho = 10^{-6}$; $\delta_0 = 1\,\mu$s.

of δ_0, this algorithm will ensure that the clock skews will be upper bounded by δ where

$$\delta \approx \max\left\{\delta_0 + 2\rho R, \frac{2N\epsilon + 2\rho\{2(N-m)S + R\}}{N - 3m}\right\} \qquad (9.50)$$

Also, the magnitude of the correction at each resynchronization epoch is limited to Δ; that is, $|C_p^{(i)} - C_p^{(i+1)}| \le \Delta$.

By definition, $S > 2(\delta + \epsilon)$. In Table 9.3, we list the skew under this algorithm for cases where $S < R$.

Figure 9.27 provides an example of a four-clock system using this algorithm. The figure illustrates a major weakness of this algorithm; once a clock drops out

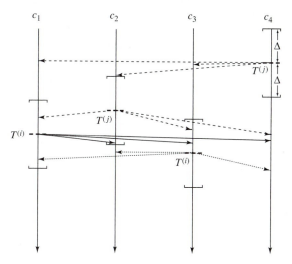

FIGURE 9.27
The CA1 algorithm: tick arrival times are shown corrected for estimated transmission time; all clock ticks arriving outside the bracketed intervals are ignored.

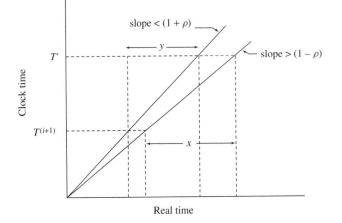

Real time

FIGURE 9.28
Clock skews.

of synchrony (perhaps owing to a transient failure), there is no mechanism for bringing it back to synchrony again. In our example, clock c_4 has dropped out of synchrony with the rest. Because its skew with respect to the other clocks is so large, it ignores all the timing signals from those other clocks, and is ignored by them in return. As a result, there is nothing to force c_4 back to synchrony with the other clocks.

Note that this process may require the clock to instantaneously change its time at the beginning of each resynchronization interval. If this is not allowed—and we have earlier seen why such abrupt changes would be inappropriate—the change in clock time can be amortized over the resynchronization interval.

ANALYSIS. * For what values of the system parameters will this algorithm work? Or, to word it differently, what is the value of δ, as a function of the system parameters, that can be guaranteed?

Let us assume that the clocks are all synchronized to a skew of less than δ_0 to begin with. Also assume that $\delta \ll \min(R, \epsilon/\rho)$, and that $\rho \ll 1$.

If the clocks start (at time 0) with a maximum skew of δ_0, over the next resynchronization interval, they can drift apart by a further $2\rho R$. Hence, $\delta > \delta_0 + 2\rho R$ is a necessary condition.

Suppose the nonfaulty clocks are synchronized to within δ at the end of the ith resynchronization period. Let T' be within the $(i + 1)$th resynchronization period.

As illustrated in Figure 9.28 we have for nonfaulty c_p and c_q

$$x < (1 + \rho)(T' - T^{(i+1)})$$
$$y > (1 - \rho)(T' - T^{(i+1)}) \tag{9.51}$$

where x and y are defined as in Figure 9.28.

$$c_p^{(i+1)}(T') - c_q^{(i+1)}(T') < |c_p^{(i+1)}(T^{(i+1)}) - c_q^{(i+1)}(T^{(i+1)})| + y - x$$

$$< |c_p^{(i+1)}(T^{(i+1)}) - c_q^{(i+1)}(T^{(i+1)})| + (1 + \rho)(T' - T^{(i+1)})$$

$$-(1 - \rho)(T' - T^{(i+1)})$$

$$= |c_p^{(i+1)}(T^{(i+1)}) - c_q^{(i+1)}(T^{(i+1)})| + 2\rho(T' - T^{(i+1)})$$

$$(9.52)$$

$$|c_p^{(i+1)}(T') - c_q^{(i+1)}(T')| < |c_p^{(i+1)}(T^{(i+1)}) - c_q^{(i+1)}(T^{(i+1)})| + 2\rho R$$

$$= |c_p^{(i)}(T^{(i+1)} + \Delta_p) - c_q^{(i)}(T^{(i+1)} + \Delta_q)| + 2\rho R$$

$$\lesssim |c_p^{(i)}(T^{(i+1)}) + \Delta_p - c_q^{(i)}(T^{(i+1)}) - \Delta_q| + 2\rho R$$

$$= \left| \frac{1}{N} \sum_{r=1}^{N} \{c_p^{(i)}(T^{(i+1)}) + \overline{\Delta}_{pr} - c_q^{(i)}(T^{(i+1)}) - \overline{\Delta}_{qr} \} \right|$$

$$+ 2\rho R$$

$$\leq \frac{1}{N} \sum_{r=1}^{N} |c_p^{(i)}(T^{(i+1)}) + \overline{\Delta}_{pr} - c_q^{(i)}(T^{(i+1)}) - \overline{\Delta}_{qr}|$$

$$+ 2\rho R \qquad (9.53)$$

Let us now examine the term

$$\left| c_p^{(i)}(T^{(i+1)}) + \overline{\Delta}_{pr} - c_q^{(i)}(T^{(i+1)}) - \overline{\Delta}_{qr} \right|$$

for nonfaulty c_p, c_q, c_r. We have for $T_0 \in (T^{(i+1)} - S, T^{(i+1)}]$

$$\left| c_p^{(i)}(T^{(i+1)}) + \overline{\Delta}_{pr} - c_q^{(i)}(T^{(i+1)}) - \overline{\Delta}_{qr} \right|$$

$$\approx \left| c_p^{(i)}(T_0 + \overline{\Delta}_{pr} + T^{(i+1)} - T_0) - c_q^{(i)}(T_0 + \overline{\Delta}_{qr} + T^{(i+1)} - T_0) \right|$$

$$\leq \left| c_p^{(i)}(T_0 + \overline{\Delta}_{pr}) - c_q^{(i)}(T_0 + \overline{\Delta}_{qr}) \right| + 2\rho \left| T^{(i+1)} - T_0 \right| \qquad (9.54)$$

$$\leq \left| c_p^{(i)}(T_0 + \overline{\Delta}_{pr}) - c_r^{(i)}(T_0) \right| + \left| c_q^{(i)}(T_0 + \overline{\Delta}_{qr}) - c_r^{(i)}(T_0) \right| + 2\rho S$$

$$\leq 2\epsilon + 2\rho S$$

If, on the other hand, c_r is faulty, we have

$$\left| c_p^{(i)}(T^{(i+1)}) + \overline{\Delta}_{pr} - c_q^{(i)}(T^{(i+1)}) - \overline{\Delta}_{qr} \right|$$

$$\leq \left| c_p^{(i)}(T^{(i+1)}) - c_q^{(i)}(T^{(i+1)}) \right| + \left| \overline{\Delta}_{pr} - \overline{\Delta}_{qr} \right| \qquad (9.55)$$

$$\leq \delta + 2\Delta$$

From (9.53), (9.54), and (9.55), we have

$$|c_p^{(i+1)}(T') - c_q^{(i+1)}(T')| \lesssim \frac{1}{N}[2(N - m)(\epsilon + 2\rho S) + m(\delta + 2\Delta)] + 2\rho R$$

$$(9.56)$$

So, if we define $\delta \gtrsim \frac{1}{N}[2(N-m)(\epsilon + \rho S) + m(\delta + 2\Delta)] + 2\rho R$, the clocks will remain in synchrony. Since we have $\Delta = \delta + \epsilon$, this reduces, after some algebra, to the condition

$$\delta \gtrsim \frac{2N\epsilon + 2\rho((N-m)S + R)}{N - 3m - 2mp} \tag{9.57}$$

This also requires that $N - 3m - 2\rho > 0$. Since $\rho \ll 1$ in practice, this reduces to the condition $N - 3m \geq 1$; that is, $N \geq 3m + 1$, and $N - 3m - 2mp \approx N - 3m$.

To summarize, we have shown that if the clocks are synchronized at the end of the ith resynchronization interval to within a skew of δ and

$$N \geq 3m + 1$$

$$\delta \geq \delta_0 + 2\rho R$$

$$\delta \gtrsim \frac{2N\epsilon + 2\rho((N-m)S + R)}{N - 3m}$$

the nonfaulty clocks will remain synchronized at the $(i+1)$th resynchronization interval to within a skew of δ. Hence, by induction, these clocks will remain within a clock skew of δ so long as these conditions are satisfied.

9.6.2 Interactive Convergence Averaging Algorithm, CA2

Algorithm CA2 differs from CA1 in which clock signals are ignored. In CA1, a clock ignores those time messages that differ from its own by a specified amount, Δ; in CA2, a clock ignores the first m and the last m messages. The clock is aligned with a reference equal to the averaging of the clock signals that are not ignored. Once again, we assume a completely connected network (i.e., there is a dedicated link between every pair of clocks).

More concretely, the CA2 algorithm is as follows. Every time its clock reads a multiple of the resynchronization interval R, a clock transmits its timing message to all the clocks (including itself) in the system. Message-transmission delays range from $\mu_{\min}$ to $\mu_{\max}$. Define the average delay $\mu_{av} = (\mu_{\min} + \mu_{\max})/2$. As before, N is the total number of clocks and m is the maximum number of malicious clocks that this system is designed to tolerate.

Clock c_i receives a time message from c_j at real time $t(i, j)$. It computes the quantities $a(i, j) = t(i, j) - \mu_{av}$, and sorts them in ascending order. Let $A(i, k)$ be the kth element in this sorted list. Then, c_i corrects itself by

$$K_i = \frac{1}{N - 2m} \sum_{i=m+1}^{N-m} a(i, k) \tag{9.58}$$

As with algorithm CA1, we can regard each physical clock as starting a new logical clock at each resynchronization point. This correction happens at the instant a total of $N - m$ signals have been received and K_i has been calculated. Of course, in practice, as we have said before, this correction does not have to be instantaneously applied; it can be amortized over the next resynchronization interval.

This algorithm will work so long as $N \geq 3m + 1 + m\rho$, and will maintain a clock skew of no more than about

$$\frac{N - 2m}{N - 3m - m\rho}\{\mu_{\max} - \mu_{\min} + 2\rho(1 + \rho)R\} + \mu_{\max} - \mu_{\min} \qquad (9.59)$$

Note that an approach similar to this algorithm can be used to reintegrate into synchrony clocks that have undergone transient failure but have now recovered. Such a clock sends no timing messages, but watches the network for timing signals. In a resynchronization interval it throws out the first m and the last m timing signals (corrected for estimated transmission delays), and calculates the midpoint of the remaining ones. It then aligns itself with this midpoint.

ANALYSIS. We will carry out the analysis assuming that a clocks corrects itself instantaneously at the moment it has received $N - m$ messages. The analysis when amortization is used is similar. We will show that if the clocks are synchronized at the beginning of a resynchronization interval, they will remain synchronized throughout that interval. The notation is similar to that used in the proof of CA1.

Let us focus on the ith resynchronization. Let c_p be the nonfaulty clock that begins its ith resynchronization interval soonest (at r-time $t(1)$), and c_q which begins its ith interval last (at r-time $t(2)$). By definition, $t(2) \geq t(1)$. Let $t(3)$ be the r-time when the last $(i + 1)$th resynchronization takes place.

Lemma 9.5. $t(3) - t(2) \leq (1 + \rho)R$.

Proof. Since, for any round of resynchronization, the first m and last m messages are ignored, the only messages that can be used are those from nonfaulty clocks, or from faulty clocks whose messages are sandwiched between those of nonfaulty clocks. The slowest a free-running nonfaulty clock can run is at the rate of $(1+\rho)^{-1}$ c-units per r-unit. Since the messages are sent every R c-units, the last such message must be sent within $(1 + \rho)R$ r-units of $t(2)$. **Q.E.D.**

As in CA1, we assume that we create a new logical clock at each resynchronization point. Let $C_k^{(i)}(t)$ denote the clock time told by logical clock $C_k^{(i)}$ at time t. Logical clock $C_k^{(i)}$ is the clock that is used during the ith resynchronization interval.

Lemma 9.6. The clocks resynchronize by starting a new logical clock at the average of the messages they receive (except for the first and last m signals). The divergence between the c-times to which these logical clocks are initialized is at most $m(\delta + \mu_{\max} - \mu_{\min})/(N - 2m)$.

Proof. Since there are at most m faulty clocks, and these are ignored unless they are sandwiched between the nonfaulty clocks, each faulty clock that does not appear to be in either the m fastest or m slowest clocks must be skewed by at most δ away from any nonfaulty clock. As a result, a faulty clock c_f that is included in the averaging by clocks c_x and c_y must deliver its signals to c_x and c_y no more than δ apart. The maximum difference in transmission time is given by $\mu_{\max} - \mu_{\min}$. Therefore, if c_r

is included by both c_x and c_y in their averaging, it can cause a difference in the average quantity that c_x and c_y compute of no more than $(\delta + \mu_{\max} - \mu_{\min})/(N-2m)$. Since there are at most m faulty clocks, the influence of the faulty clocks in creating a divergence in the computed averages is at most $m(\delta + \mu_{\max} - \mu_{\min})/(N-2m)$.

Q.E.D.

Lemma 9.7. $t(2) - t(1) \leq \frac{m\delta}{N-2m} + \mu_{\max} - \mu_{\min}$.

Proof. The maximum difference in time between when a signal from a nonfaulty clock c_r reaches c_x and when it reaches c_y is $\mu_{\max} - \mu_{\min}$.

From this and the previous Lemma, we have

$$t(2) - t(1) \leq \frac{m\delta}{N-2m} + \mu_{\max} - \mu_{\min} \tag{9.60}$$

Q.E.D.

Theorem 9.2. Algorithm CA2 can maintain a clock skew of no more than

$$\frac{N-2m}{N-3m-m\rho} \{(1+\rho)(\mu_{\max} - \mu_{\min}) + 2\rho(1+\rho)R\}$$

Proof. By the same argument used above,

$$|C_p^{(i+1)}(t(1)) - C_q^{(i+1)}(t(2))| \leq \frac{m\delta}{N-2m} + \mu_{\max} - \mu_{\min} \tag{9.61}$$

We have

$$\left| C_p^{(i+1)}(t(2)) - C_q^{(i+1)}(t(2)) \right| = \left| C_p^{(i+1)}(t(1) + t(2) - t(1)) - C_q^{(i+1)}(t(2)) \right|$$

$$\leq \left| C_p^{(i+1)}(t(1)) - C_q^{(i+1)}(t(2)) \right| + \rho|t(2) - t(1)|$$

$$\leq \frac{m\delta}{N-2m} + \mu_{\max} - \mu_{\min} + \rho|t(2) - t(1)|$$

$$\lesssim (1+\rho) \left\{ \frac{m\delta}{N-2m} + \mu_{\max} - \mu_{\min} \right\} \tag{9.62}$$

For any time $\tau > t(2)$, we have

$$\left| C_p^{(i+1)}(\tau) - C_q^{(i+1)}(\tau) \right| \leq \left| C_p^{(i+1)}(t(2)) - C_q^{(i+1)}(t(2)) \right| + 2\rho(\tau - t(2))$$

$$\leq (1+\rho) \left\{ \frac{m\delta}{N-2m} + \mu_{\max} - \mu_{\min} \right\} + 2\rho(\tau - t(2)) \tag{9.63}$$

Since $t(3) - t(2) \leq (1+\rho)R$, the clocks are synchronized to within δ throughout their resynchronization interval $i+1$ if

$$\delta \geq (1+\rho) \left\{ \frac{m\delta}{N-2m} + \mu_{\max} - \mu_{\min} \right\} + 2\rho(1+\rho)R \tag{9.64}$$

The skew bound is the smallest δ for which Equation (9.64) is true; that is,

$$\frac{N-2m}{N-3m-m\rho} \{(1+\rho)(\mu_{\max} - \mu_{\min}) + 2\rho(1+\rho)R\} \tag{9.65}$$

Q.E.D.

If $N = 3m + 1$, then Equation (9.65) reduces to

$$\frac{m+1}{1-m\rho} \{(1+\rho)(\mu_{\max} - \mu_{\min}) + 2\rho(1+\rho)R\} \qquad (9.66)$$

If $m\rho \ll 1$ (as is almost invariably the case), the maximum skew increases linearly with m. On the other hand, if $N \gg m$ and $m\rho \ll 1$, the maximum clock skew approaches the limit

$$(1+\rho)(\mu_{\max} - \mu_{\min}) + 2\rho(1+\rho)R \qquad (9.67)$$

So far in this section, we have assumed that the interconnection network is completely connected. If this is not the case, we can use the approach of clustering that we described in Section 9.5.2.

9.6.3 Convergence Nonaveraging Algorithm, CNA

The CNA algorithm ensures the synchronization of nonfaulty clocks, regardless of the number of faulty clocks in the system. To do this, it uses encoding to authenticate messages. That is, a clock sends out an encoded timing signal that cannot be altered by any other clock (even if that other clock is maliciously faulty). Also, this algorithm does not require that there be a direct link between two communicating clocks. It is sufficient that there be either a one-hop path (direct link) or a multi-hop path (i.e., one which may pass through other clocks). That is, if we define a graph with the clocks as the nodes and the clock-to-clock connections as directed edges, it is sufficient for the graph to be connected. A clock labels or signs each message that it sends out, so that the recipient knows who the sender is. This signature is encoded so that no other clock can alter it. A message is said to be authentic when neither the message nor the signature has been altered; the encoding is assumed to allow clocks to detect any alterations.

As with the convergence averaging algorithms, resynchronization happens at regular intervals. Each node starts a new logical clock at each resynchronization. If t is some r-time that lies between the ith and $(i + 1)$th resynchronizations (i.e., within the ith resynchronization interval) the c-time told by clock c_k is given by $C_k^{(i)}(t)$.

The algorithm consists of each clock adjusting itself suitably, based on the messages it receives from the other clocks. It can be informally described as follows. Resynchronization happens at least once every interval of length R (as measured in clock time). Unless it has been preempted (by a procedure to be described), each nonfaulty clock c_k waits until its value equals some prespecified waiting point W. At that time, it sends out an encoded signed message saying, "The time is W," to all its neighboring processors. It then defines a new resynchronization-point bound by incrementing W by R. W is a local variable, held at each clock.

The above action can be preempted by c_k receiving a message from another clock saying, "The time is W," that arrives sufficiently close to c_k's waiting point,

W. "Sufficiently close" depends on how many hops this message has gone through on its way to this clock. A message that has passed through s clocks is sufficiently close if it arrives within sD of clock c_k's waiting point, where D is a prespecified constant. If this message is authentic (i.e., has not been altered in transit), clock c_k moves itself forward to W, increments W by R, and forwards the message to all its neighbours after adding its own signature to it.

We have assumed that if a message passes through a number of clocks, the identities of these clocks can be determined. This is done by reading the signatures that they have appended to the message before forwarding them.

Example 9.6. Figure 9.29 contains an example of how this algorithm works. The system consists of four clocks, configured in a ring. To begin with, all the clocks are in their ith resynchronization interval. That is, $W = (i + 1)R$ for each clock. We define w_k, for $k = 1, 2, 3, 4$, such that $C_k^{(i)}(w_k) = (i + 1)R$.

c_1 sends out a time signal at w_1. It arrives before $w_2 - D$, and so it is ignored by c_2. However, due to the placement of w_3, c_3 processes it and moves its own clock value forward to W at the moment it receives the message from c_1. c_3 also sets $W = W + R$ and forwards the message from c_1 (with its own signature added) to c_4. However, since it arrives at c_4 before $w_4 - 2D$, c_4 ignores it. At real time w_2, c_2 issues its time signal to c_1 and c_4. However, since c_1 has already completed that round of resynchronization, it ignores the message. On the other hand, the message arrives in time to cause c_4 to adjust its value to R at real time w_4. c_4 also forwards this message to c_2 and c_3, which ignore it (since they have already completed their adjustment for this round), and sets its next waiting point, $W = W + R$.

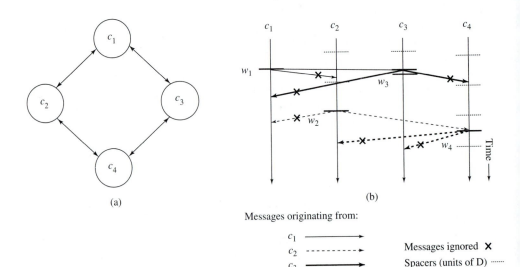

(a)   (b)

Messages originating from:

c_1 ———→

c_2 - - - - - →   Messages ignored ✗

c_3 ———→   Spacers (units of D) ·······

c_4 - - - - - →

FIGURE 9.29
Convergence nonaveraging algorithm in a four-clock system: (a) synchronization graph; (b) timing chart.

A major drawback of this algorithm is that it is possible to have a burst of synchronization-related transmissions on the interconnection network within a relatively short time. This can cause message-delivery times to become large. We show below that this algorithm does indeed synchronize the clocks. Denote by $\mu_{\max}(f_c, f_\ell)$ the maximum message-delivery time if there are f_c and f_ℓ (clock and link failures, respectively). Then, our synchronization proof has the form of deriving the following result. If

- $D \geq (1 + \rho)\mu_{\max}(f_c, f_\ell) + 2\rho(1 + \rho)R$, and
- $R > (1 + \rho)\mu_{\max}(f_c, f_\ell) + f_c D$,

then all nonfaulty clocks will be synchronized to within a skew of D. Furthermore, no clock will need to move itself forward by more than $(f_c + 1)D$ during any resynchronization.

From the two conditions above, the upper bound on the clock skew is given by

$$\frac{(1 + \rho)\mu_{\max}(f_c, f_\ell)}{1 - 2\rho(1 + \rho)f_c}\{1 + 2\rho(1 + \rho)\} \tag{9.68}$$

Recall that this assumes that a message may take from 0 to $\mu_{\max}(f_c, f_\ell)$ to arrive. If we can reduce this uncertainty, we can reduce the maximum clock skew.

ANALYSIS.[*] Let us examine the properties of this algorithm. We begin by defining some terms (see Figure 9.30). $b(i)$ and $e(i)$ are defined as the earliest and latest points, respectively, at which any nonfaulty clock in the system sets its clock to the ith waiting point. In the interval $(e(i), b(i + 1))$, each nonfaulty clock thus has its waiting point R set to iR. We state and prove the following lemmas under the condition that for all nonfaulty clocks c_i and c_j, $|C_k^{(i-1)}(t) - C_k^{(i-1)}(t)| \leq D$ for all $t \in [b(i - 1), e(i - 1)]$.

Lemma 9.8. $e(i) - b(i) \leq \mu_{\max}(f_c, f_\ell)$.

Proof. Let c_k be the earliest nonfaulty clock to set itself to the ith waiting point, that is, to iR. This happens at real time $b(i)$, by definition. Consider any other nonfaulty clock c_j. The time signal from c_k arrives at c_j by real time $t(k, j) = b(k) + \mu_{\max}(f_c, f_\ell)$. If c_j has already set itself to its ith waiting point by $t(k, j)$

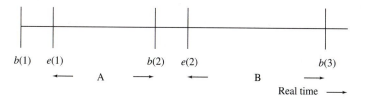

$b(1)$ $e(1)$ $b(2)$ $e(2)$ $b(3)$

$\longleftarrow$ A $\longrightarrow$ $\longleftarrow$ B $\longrightarrow$

Real time $\longrightarrow$

FIGURE 9.30
Waiting points: in range A, the waiting point of all clocks $= 2R$; in range B, the waiting point of all clocks $= 3R$.

(which happens if $C_j^{(i-1)}(t(k, j)) \geq iR$, or if it has received an appropriate time signal from some other clock), there is nothing left to prove. Suppose, therefore, that it has not. For this to be true, we must have $C_j^{(i-1)}(t(k, j)) < iR$ and $e(i-1) > t(k, j) > b(i) > b(i-1)$. We are given that $|C_k^{(i-1)}(t) - C_j^{(i-1)}(t)| \leq D$ for all $t \in [b(i-1), e(i-1)]$. Hence, $C_j^{(i-1)}(t(k, j)) \geq iR - D$, and so c_j sets itself to iR no later than real time $t(k, j)$. But, $t(k, j) - b(i) \leq \mu_{max}(f_c, f_\ell)$. Hence every nonfaulty clock c_j sets itself to the ith waiting point by time $b(i) + \mu_{max}(f_c, f_\ell)$. Hence, $e(i) - b(i) \leq \mu_{max}(f_c, f_\ell)$. **Q.E.D.**

Lemma 9.9. For any two nonfaulty clocks c_k and c_j, $|C_k^{(i)}(e(i)) - C_j^{(i)}(e(i))| \leq (1 + \rho)\mu_{max}(f_c, f_\ell)$.

Proof. The maximum divergence between two clocks will arise if

- one of them is set to iR at real time $b(k)$ and runs at the fastest rate allowed, and
- the other is set to iR at real time $e(k)$.

The divergence is therefore at most $(1 + \rho)(e(i) - b(i))$. But, by Lemma 9.8, $e(i) - b(i) \leq \mu_{max}(f_c, f_\ell)$. Hence, $|C_k^{(i)}(e(i)) - C_j^{(i)}(e(i))| \leq (1 + \rho)\mu_{max}(f_c, f_\ell)$. **Q.E.D.**

Lemma 9.10. Let c_k be the earliest nonfaulty clock to set itself to the ith waiting point (i.e., to iR). Then $C_k^{(i-1)}(b(i)) \geq iR - f_c D$.

Proof. The only way that c_k can set itself equal to its kth waiting point before real time $c_k^{(i-1)}(iR)$ is if it receives a time message from a faulty clock c_m. Moreover, since c_k is the earliest nonfaulty clock to set itself to the kth waiting point, such a time message must have come either directly from c_m, or been forwarded through a set of faulty clocks. There are at most f_c faulty clocks. Hence, the earliest that such a message can arrive and not be ignored by c_i is at real time τ such that $C_k^{(i-1)}(\tau) \geq iR - f_c D$. **Q.E.D.**

Lemma 9.11. No nonfaulty clock c_j reaches its ith waiting point earlier than the r-time when its $(i-1)$th logical clock tells c-time $iR - (f_c + 1)D$.

Proof. By assumption, $|C_k^{(i-1)}(t) - C_j^{(i-1)}(t)| \leq D$, for all $t \in [b(i-1), e(i-1)]$ and all nonfaulty clocks c_k, c_j. This, coupled with Lemma 9.10, yields the result. **Q.E.D.**

Lemma 9.12. $b(i+1) > e(i)$ if $R \geq (1 + \rho)\mu_{max}(f_c, f_\ell) + f_c D$.

Proof. Let c_k be the earliest nonfaulty clock to reach its $(i+1)$th waiting point. From Lemma 9.10, we have

$$C_k^{(i)}(b(i+1)) \geq (i+1)R - f_c D \tag{9.69}$$

Since $e(i) - b(i) \leq \mu_{max}(f_c, f_\ell)$ (Lemma 9.8),

$$C_k^{(i)}(e(i)) \leq (1 + \rho)\mu_{max}(f_c, f_\ell) + iR \tag{9.70}$$

Combining the inequalities in Equations (9.69) and (9.70), we have that $C_k^{(i)}(b(i+1)) \geq C_k^{(i)}(e(i))$ if

$$(i+1)R - f_c D \geq (1+\rho)\mu_{\max}(f_c, f_\ell) + iR$$
$$\Rightarrow R \geq (1+\rho)\mu_{\max}(f_c, f_\ell) + f_c D \tag{9.71}$$

Q.E.D.

Lemma 9.13. For any two nonfaulty clocks c_k, c_j, and $t \in [e(i), e(i+1)]$, $|C_k^{(i)}(t) - C_j^{(i)}(t)| \leq (1+\rho)\mu_{\max}(f_c, f_\ell) + 2\rho(1+\rho)R$.

Proof. From Lemma 9.9, we have

$$|C_k^{(i)}(e(i)) - C_j^{(i)}(e(i))| \leq (1+\rho)\mu_{\max}(f_c, f_\ell)$$

Also, by the definition of ρ,

$$e(k+1) - e(k) \leq (1+\rho)R$$

Two clocks can diverge at a rate of no greater than 2ρ. Hence, over a real time of $(1+\rho)R$, they cannot diverge by more than $2\rho(1+\rho)R$. Hence, $|C_k^{(i)}(t) - C_j^{(i)}(t)| \leq (1+\rho)\mu_{\max}(f_c, f_\ell) + 2\rho(1+\rho)R$.　　　**Q.E.D.**

Lemma 9.14. For any two nonfaulty clocks c_k, c_j and any $t \in [b(i+1), e(i+1)]$, if $b(i+1) > e(i)$, then $|C_k^{(i)}(t) - C_j^{(i)}(t)| \leq (1+\rho)\mu_{\max}(f_c, f_\ell) + 2\rho(1+\rho)R$.

Proof. $b(i+1) \in [e(i), e(i+1)]$. The result follows from this and Lemma 9.13.

Q.E.D.

Lemmas 9.8 to 9.14 lead immediately to the following theorem.

Theorem 9.3. If

$$D \geq (1+\rho)\mu_{\max}(f_c, f_\ell) + 2\rho(1+\rho)R$$
$$R > (1+\rho)\mu_{\max}(f_c, f_\ell) + f_c D$$

are both true, all nonfaulty clocks will be synchronized to within a skew of D. Furthermore, no clock will need to move itself forward by more than $(f_c + 1)D$ during any resynchronization.

9.7 SUGGESTIONS FOR FURTHER READING

An excellent source for phase-locked systems is Gardner [4]. For material on crystal oscillators, the reader can turn, for example, to Matthys [10]. Fault-tolerant phase-locked clocks were first used for the FTMP system, built by the Charles Stark Draper Laboratory under contract to NASA [2]. Our description of phase-locking for synchronization is based primarily on [8, 12, 13, 14, 15]. For another hardware-based synchronization algorithm, see [6].

The CA1 algorithm is described in [9], and the CA2 algorithm in [7]. The source for CNA is [5]. See [11] for a modification of the CA1 algorithm.

In our discussion, we proved the $N \geq 3m + 1$ result individually for systems that do not use authentication. It has been shown that the $N \geq 3m + 1$ is a universal requirement for such systems—see [3].

A good source for a discussion of the effects of message-passing delays on clock synchronization is [1]. Master-slave synchronization is also discussed in detail in this paper.

An excellent bibliography of synchronization and related matters appears in [16].

EXERCISES

9.1. Consider the master-slave arrangement for synchronization. If the round-trip delay r is an exponentially-distributed random variable with parameter μ and the estimation error must be upper-bounded by ϵ, find the probability density function of the worst-case clock skew between the master and the slave. Assume that the round-trip time of any message is independent of the time of any other message, and that $\mu_{\min} = 0$.

9.2. Show that if a phase-locked clocking system is composed of clocks that have a maximum drift rate of ρ when they are good, $\rho_{\text{sys}} \leq \rho$.

9.3. Find ρ_{sys} for the convergence nonaveraging algorithm. (Hint: The clocks are moved forward by no more than $(f_c + 1)D$ during any resynchronization.)

9.4. Find functions $f_i(N, m)$ that satisfy the constraints listed in Section 9.5.1.

9.5. Prove that using the average of the $(m + 1)$th and the $(N - m)$th clock signals (as described in Figure 9.19) will satisfy conditions of correctness, **C1** and **C2**, in Section 9.5.1.

9.6. How should the phase-locked clocks algorithm handle the case when the ticks arrive so closely together that we cannot tell in which order the clock ticks were originally delivered? Assume that message delivery times are zero.

9.7. In algorithm CNA, we assume that message delays can lie within the interval $[0, \mu_{\max}(f_p, f_\ell)]$. Suppose instead that we are given that the message delay per hop is exactly equal to t_m. How would you modify the algorithm to take advantage of this information, and what is skew of the modified algorithm?

9.8. Repeat Exercise 9.7, given that the message delays can lie in the interval $[\mu_{\min}(f_p, f_\ell), \mu_{\max}(f_p, f_\ell)]$.

9.9. Prove that in CNA, the total number of messages sent out on the network is upper-bounded by N^2.

9.10. Suppose we are running the phase-locked clocks algorithm with N completely connected clocks. There are m maliciously faulty clocks, such that $N = 3m - 2$. Show how the malicious clocks must behave so that, given some $\delta_0 > 0$, there exists some T such that for all $t > T$ $|C_i(T) - C_j(T)| > \delta_0$ for every pair of clocks c_i and c_j. That is, not only will all the clocks not be synchronized, but the malicious clocks force every pair of good clocks to be separated by more than δ_0.

9.11. Repeat Exercise 9.10 for the interactive convergence averaging algorithm.

9.12. Suppose c_1 in Figure 9.29 has failed in such a way that it does not put out any signals. Draw a timing chart (like the one in Figure 9.29) that shows the various timing signals.

9.13. Suppose c_1 in Figure 9.29 has failed in such a way that it puts out spurious timing messages every $D/2$ c-units, listing a time of R. Repeat Exercise 9.12 for this case.

9.14. In the convergence nonaveraging algorithm, is there an upper bound on the number of faulty clocks f_c that can be tolerated as a function of ρ?

9.15. In algorithm CA1, consider the case $N = 3m + 1$. If we want all the transmissions associated with the ith resynchronization to take place in the ith resynchronization interval, show that $R \geq S > \max[2(\delta + \epsilon), \delta + \mu_{max}]$. Under this condition, find $\partial \delta / \partial m$, $\partial \delta / \partial R$, and $\partial \delta / \partial \rho$.

REFERENCES

[1] Cristian, F.: "Probabilistic Clock Synchronization," *Distributed Computing* 3:146–158, 1989.

[2] Daly, W. M., A. L. Hopkins, Jr., and J. F. McKenna: "A Fault-Tolerant Clocking System," *Proc. 3rd Symp. Fault-Tolerant Computing Systems*, IEEE, Los Alamitos, CA, 1973.

[3] Dolev, D., J. Y. Halpern, and R. Strong: "On the Possibility and Impossibility of Achieving Clock Synchronization," *Journal of Computer and Systems Science* 32:230–250, 1986.

[4] Gardner, F. M.: *Phaselock Techniques*, Wiley, New York, 1979.

[5] Halpern, J. Y., B. Simons, and R. Strong: "Fault-Tolerant Clock Synchronization," *Proc. 3rd ACM Symp. Principles of Distributed Computing*, pp. 89–102, IEEE, Los Alamitos, CA, 1984.

[6] Kessels, J. L.: "Two Designs of a Fault-Tolerant Clocking System," *IEEE Trans. Computers* C-33:912–919, 1984.

[7] Kopetz, H., and W. Ochsenreiter: "Clock Synchronization in Distributed Real-Time Systems," *IEEE Trans. Computers* C-36:933–940, 1987.

[8] Krishna, C. M., K. G. Shin, and R. W. Butler: "Ensuring Fault-Tolerance of Phase-Locked Clocks," *IEEE Trans. Computers* C-34:752–756, 1985.

[9] Lamport, L., and P. M. Melliar-Smith: "Synchronizing Clocks in the Presence of Faults," *Journal of the ACM* 32:52–78, 1985.

[10] Matthys, R. J., *Crystal Oscillator Circuits*, John Wiley, New York, 1983.

[11] Ramanathan, P., D. D. Kandlur, and K. G. Shin: "Hardware-Assisted Software Clock Synchronization for Homogeneous Distributed Systems," *IEEE Trans. Computers* 39:514–524, 1990.

[12] Shin, K. G., and P. Ramanathan: "Clock Synchronization of a Large Multiprocessor System in the Presence of Malicious Faults," *IEEE Trans. Computers* C-36:2–12, 1987.

[13] Shin, K. G., and P. Ramanathan: "Transmission Delays in Hardware Clock Synchronization," *IEEE Trans. Computers* C-37:1465–1467, 1988.

[14] Vasanthavada, N., and P. N. Marinos: "Synchronization of Fault-Tolerant Clocks in the Presence of Malicious Failures," *IEEE Trans. Computers* C-37:440–448, 1988.

[15] Vasanthavada, N., P. N. Marinos, and G. S. Mersten: "Design and Performance Evaluation of Mutual Synchronized Fault-Tolerant Clocking Systems," *Proc. 16th Symp. Fault-Tolerant Computing Systems*, pp. 206–211, IEEE, Los Alamitos, CA, 1986.

[16] Yang, Z., and T. A. Marsland: "Annotated Bibliography on Global States and Times in Distributed Systems," *Operating Systems Review* 27:55–74, 1993.

APPENDIX

REVIEW OF MODELING TECHNIQUES

This is a brief review of some of the more useful techiques for modeling reliability and performance. It is not meant to be an exhaustive survey of the field, but rather a temporary prop to those without, and a reminder to those with, a prior exposure to the subject. Readers requiring a more encyclopedic—or deeper—coverage of the field can consult one of the many references cited at the end of the Appendix.

We begin this Appendix with a review of some basic laws of probability. We then move on to a discussion of Markov modeling, and provide some examples of its use in reliability and performance modeling. We then briefly discuss some elements of queueing theory.

A.1 REVIEW OF BASIC PROBABILITY THEORY

For each event A of the sample space S we define a number $P(A)$, called the *probability of event* A, that satisfies the following axioms.

1. $0 \leq P(A) \leq 1$

2. $P(S) = 1$

3. If events A_i are mutually exclusive, that is if A_i and A_j cannot simultaneously occur for $i \neq j$,

$$P\left(\cup_{i=1}^{\infty} A_i\right) = \sum_{i=0}^{\infty} P(A_i) \tag{A.1}$$

Two events A and B are said to be *independent* if

$$\text{Prob}(A \cap B) = \text{Prob}(A) \times \text{Prob}(B) \tag{A.2}$$

where $A \cap B$ is the event that both events A and B occur. Informally speaking, if A and B are independent events, knowing that one has occurred tells us nothing about the other. In general, we have

$$\text{Prob}(A \cup B) = \text{Prob}(A) + \text{Prob}(B) - \text{Prob}(A \cap B) \tag{A.3}$$

where $A \cup B$ is the event that either A or B or both occur.

One of the most useful laws in probability theory is Bayes's law. It is a means for computing the conditional probability, $\text{Prob}(A|B)$, of an event A given that another event B is known to have occurred. Bayes's law states that

$$\text{Prob}(A|B) = \frac{\text{Prob}(A \cap B)}{\text{Prob}(B)} \tag{A.4}$$

where the reader will recall that $A \cap B$ is the event that both events A and B occur. The application of Bayes's law to the right-hand side of the above equation yields

$$\text{Prob}(A|B) = \frac{\text{Prob}(B|A)\text{Prob}(A)}{\text{Prob}(B)} \tag{A.5}$$

Recall that, informally speaking, if A and B are independent events, knowing that one has occurred tells us nothing about the other. The application of Bayes's Law confirms this.

$$\text{Prob}(A|B) = \frac{\text{Prob}(A \cap B)}{\text{Prob}(B)} = \frac{\text{Prob}(A)\text{Prob}(B)}{\text{Prob}(B)} = \text{Prob}(A) \tag{A.6}$$

Recall that we denote by $B_1 \cup B_2$ the event that either event B_1 or B_2 or both have occurred. The *law of total probability* states that if $B_1, \ldots, B_n$ are events such that $\text{Prob}(\cup_{i=0}^{n} B_i) = 1$ and $\text{Prob}(B_i \cap B_j) = 0$, for all $i \neq j$, then

$$\text{Prob}(A) = \sum_{i=1}^{n} \text{Prob}(A|B_i)\text{Prob}(B_i) \tag{A.7}$$

Here, n may be either finite or infinite.

A *random variable* is a function that associates each outcome with a real number. If a random variable takes only discrete values (e.g., integers), it is called a *discrete random variable*.

Example A.1. Suppose an experiment consists of tossing coins. We can define an associated random variable as follows. Tossing heads corresponds to a random variable value of 0 and tossing tails to 1. Hence, if we have three coin tosses and obtain a tail, a head, and a tail, the associated random variables form the sequence 1,0,1.

The *probability distribution function* (PDF) of a random variable X is defined as the function

$$F_X(x) = \text{Prob}\{X \leq x\} \tag{A.8}$$

In most instances, $\lim_{x \to \infty} F_X(x) = 1$; however, if there is a nonzero probability that X is infinite, we have $\lim_{x \to \infty} F_X(x) < 1$. Such a distribution is called *improper*.

If the PDF is differentiable, its derivative is the *probability density function* (pdf) of the random variable. That is,

$$f_X(x) = \frac{d F_X(x)}{dx} \qquad (A.9)$$

is the pdf of X. From the definition of the differentiation operation, it is easy to see that

$$f_X(x)dx = \text{Prob}\{x \le X \le x + dx\} \qquad (A.10)$$

If the random variable is *discrete*, that is, if it takes values in some finite or countably infinite set $A = \{a_1, \ldots, a_n\}$ (where the a_i are real numbers), then it does not have a pdf since its PDF is a discontinuous function. Instead, it has a *probability mass function* (pmf), which is given by

$$M_X(n) = \text{Prob}\{X = n\} \qquad (A.11)$$

Quite often, we will drop the subscript X when it is clear from the context which random variable is under discussion.

The *expectation* of a random variable is, in nontechnical terms, its average. The expectation of a discrete random variable X can be computed from its pmf according to the formula

$$E[X] = \sum_{i \in A} a_i M_X(a_i) \qquad (A.12)$$

If the random variable X is continuous and has a pdf, we have

$$E[X] = \int_{-\infty}^{\infty} x f_X(x)dx \qquad (A.13)$$

The expectation can also be determined from the expression

$$E[X] = \int_{x=0}^{\infty} (1 - F_X(x)) \, dx - \int_{-\infty}^{0} F_X(x)dx \qquad (A.14)$$

if at least one of the terms on the right-hand side is finite.

The *n*th *moment* of a random variable is the expectation of the *n*th power of the random variable; that is, $E[X^n]$. The *variance* of a random variable X is given by

$$\text{Var}[X] = E[X^2] - [E[X]]^2 \qquad (A.15)$$

Its *standard deviation* is given by $\sigma(X) = \sqrt{\text{Var}(X)}$.

The expectation of the sum of random variables is equal to the sum of the expectations of the random variables; that is,

$$E[X_1 + \cdots + X_n] = E[X_1] + \cdots + E[X_n] \qquad (A.16)$$

This result holds whether or not the random variables X_i are independent.

A.2 Z-TRANSFORMS AND LAPLACE TRANSFORMS

Z-transforms and Laplace transforms are very useful in probability theory. Here, we provide a brief overview.

The z-transform of any sequence of numbers $S = s_0, s_1, \ldots$ is given by $S(z) = \sum_{i=0}^{\infty} s_i z^i$. Here, z is a complex number. Table A.1 contains some rules for computing z-transforms of functions of the sequence S in terms of $S(z)$. We recommend that the reader verify the entries of the table by simple algebra.

In addition, we have the useful properties:

$$S(1) = \sum_{i=0}^{\infty} s_i \tag{A.17}$$

$$S(-1) = \sum_{i=0}^{\infty} (-1)^i s_i \tag{A.18}$$

$$S(0) = s_0 \tag{A.19}$$

$$\frac{1}{n!} \frac{d^n S(z)}{dz^n} \bigg|_{z=0} = s_n \tag{A.20}$$

$$\lim_{z \to 1} (1 - z) S(z) = s_\infty \tag{A.21}$$

Table A.2 contains the z-transforms of some sequences $S = \{s_1, s_2, \ldots\}$. α and β are any finite constants.

The z-transform of a discrete random variable X that takes only positive integer values is given by

$$g_X(z) = E[z^X] = \sum_{i=0}^{\infty} \text{Prob}\{X = i\} z^i \tag{A.22}$$

TABLE A.1
Some rules for computing z-transforms

Sequence S	$S(z)$
$a s_n + b s_n$	$a S(z) + b S(z)$
$a^n s_n$	$S(az)$
s_{n+1}	$\{S(z) - s_0\}/z$
s_{n-1}	$z S(z)$
s_{n+k}	$S(z)/z^k - \sum_{i=1}^{k} z^{i-k-1} s_{i-1}$
s_{n-k}	$z^k S(z)$
$n s_n$	$z\, d S(z)/dz$
$(n!/m!) s_n$	$z^m d^m [S(z)]/dz^m$

TABLE A.2
Lookup table for
z-transforms

s_n	$S(z)$
$\begin{cases} 1 & \text{if } n = 0 \\ 0 & \text{if } n \neq 0 \end{cases}$	1
$1 \; \forall i = 0, 1, 2, \ldots$	$1/(1 - z)$
$\alpha \beta^n$	$\alpha/(1 - \beta z)$
$(1/n!)$	$\exp(z)$
$n \beta^n$	$\beta z/(1 - \beta z)^2$

The Laplace transform of a function $f(t)$ that takes nonzero values only in the range $t \geq 0$ (i.e., $f(t) = 0$ for $t < 0$) is given by

$$F^*(s) = \int_{t=0-}^{\infty} f(t) \exp(-st) dt \qquad (A.23)$$

where s is a complex number $s = x + \sqrt{-1}\, y$, such that $x > 0$. Table A.3 specifies some rules for computing the Laplace transforms. $\delta_a(x)$ is defined as a delta function at position a. That is, $\delta_a(x)$ is zero for all $x \neq a$ and has magnitude so that $\int_0^{\infty} \delta_a(x) dx = 1$. $u(t)$ is the unit step function, which is 1 for all $t \geq 0$ and 0 elsewhere. In addition, the following properties of the Laplace transform are useful.

$$F^*(0) = \int_{0-}^{\infty} f(t) dt \qquad (A.24)$$

$$\lim_{s \to \infty} s F^*(s) = \lim_{t \to 0} f(t) \qquad (A.25)$$

$$\lim_{s \to 0} s F^*(s) = \lim_{t \to \infty} f(t) \qquad (A.26)$$

Table A.4 contains the Laplace transforms for some commonly encountered functions. Further, we define the function $f(s) = \{(s - a_1)(s - a_2) \cdots (s - a_n)\}^{-1}$, with $a_i \neq a_j$ for $i \neq j$, and define $g(s)$ as any function of s. Finally, we introduce the gamma function,

$$\Gamma(x) = \begin{cases} \int_{t=0}^{\infty} t^{x-1} \exp(-t) dt & \text{if } x > 0 \\ \Gamma(x + 1)/x & \text{if } x < 0 \end{cases} \qquad (A.27)$$

The gamma function is a generalization of the factorial, as can be seen from the recursion

$$\Gamma(1) = 1 \qquad (A.28)$$

$$\Gamma(x) = (x - 1)\Gamma(x - 1) \quad \forall \, x > 1 \qquad (A.29)$$

The Laplace transform of the pdf of a random variable X, $f_X(x)$, is given by

$$F_X^*(s) = \int_{x=-\infty}^{\infty} f(x) \exp(-sx) dx \qquad (A.30)$$

TABLE A.3
Some rules for computing Laplace transforms

Function $y(t)$	Laplace transform, $Y^*(s)$
$af(t) + bg(t)$	$aF^*(s) + bG^*(s)$
$f(t/a)$	$aF^*(as)$
$f(t - a)$	$\exp(-as)F^*(s)$
$t^n f(t)$	$(-1)^n d^n F^*(s)/ds^n$
$\exp(-at)f(t)$	$F^*(s + a)$
$d^n f(t)/dt^n$	$s^n F^*(s) - \sum_{m=0}^{n-1} f^{(k)}(0+)s^{n-m-1}$
$\int_0^t f_1(x)f_2(t - x)dt$	$F_1(s)F_2(s)$
$f(t)\sinh at$	$\{F(s - a) - F(s + a)\}/2$
$f(t)\cosh at$	$\{F(s - a) + F(s + a)\}/2$
$\int_0^t f(t)dt$	$s^{-1}F^*(s)$
$\int_0^t x^{-1}f(x)dx$	$s^{-1}\int_s^\infty F(x)dx$
$\int_t^\infty x^{-1}f(x)dx$	$s^{-1}\int_0^s F(x)dx$
$\partial f(t)/\partial k$	$\partial F^*(s)/\partial k$

TABLE A.4
Laplace transform table

Function $y(t)$ ($y(t) = 0$ for $t < 0$)	$Y^*(s)$
$\delta_a(x)$	$\exp(-as)$
$t^{n-1}/(n - 1)!,\ t \geq 0$	s^{-n}
$\alpha \exp(-\beta t),\ t \geq 0$	$\alpha(s + \beta)^{-1}$
$(t^n/n!)\exp(-\beta t),\ t \geq 0$	$(s + \beta)^{-(n+1)}$
$\cos at$	$s(s^2 + a^2)^{-1}$
$\cosh at$	$s(s^2 - a^2)^{-1}$
$\sum_{\ell=1}^n \{df(s)/ds\|_{s=a_\ell}\}^{-1}\exp\{a_\ell t\}$	$\{f(s)\}^{-1}$
$\sum_{\ell=1}^n g(a_\ell)\{df(s)/ds\|_{s=a_\ell}\}^{-1}\exp\{a_\ell t\}$	$g(s)\{f(s)\}^{-1}$
	$\{\log s\}^{-1}$
$u(t)$ (step function)	s^{-1}

Since $\int_{x=-\infty}^\infty f(x)dx = 1$, $F_X^*(s)$ always converges whenever the real value of s is positive.

The Laplace transforms and z-transforms are extremely useful computational tools, as we shall see. For example, suppose we have two independent random variables $X1$ and $X2$, with pdfs $f_{X1}(x)$ and $f_{X2}(x)$, respectively. It can be shown that the Laplace transform of the pdf of their sum, i.e., of f_{X1+X2} is given by:

$$F_{X1+X2}^*(s) = F_{X1}^*(s) \times F_{X2}^*(s) \tag{A.31}$$

The nth moment of random variable X with pdf $f_X(x)$ can be calculated from the Laplace transform $F_X^*(s)$,

$$E[X^n] = (-1)^n d^n F^*(s)/ds^n \big|_{s=0} \tag{A.32}$$

This expression follows immediately from the definition of the Laplace transform and differentiation.

Analogous results hold for z-transforms. Let $X1$ and $X2$ be discrete random variables taking values only in the set of natural numbers $\{0, 1, 2, \ldots\}$. Then,

$$g_{X1+X2}(z) = g_{X1}(z) \times g_{X2}(z) \tag{A.33}$$

The nth moment of X, taking values only in the set of natural numbers, can be computed from

$$E[X(X-1)\cdots(X-n)] = d^n g_X(z)/dz^n \big|_{z=1} \tag{A.34}$$

The z-transform of a random variable is always finite when $|z| \leq 1$. Also, $g_X(1) = 1$, and $g_X(0) = \text{Prob}\{X = 0\}$. These are extremely useful properties and, as we shall see, lead to a powerful technique for solving complex performance models.

A.3 SOME IMPORTANT PROBABILITY DISTRIBUTION FUNCTIONS

A.3.1 The Uniform Distribution Functions

The PDF of a random variable uniformly distributed in the interval $[a, b]$ is given by

$$F(x) = \begin{cases} 0 & \text{if } x < a \\ \dfrac{x-a}{b-a} & \text{if } a \leq x \leq b \\ 1 & \text{if } x > b \end{cases} \tag{A.35}$$

The corresponding pdf is given by

$$f(x) = \begin{cases} 0 & \text{if } x < a \\ \dfrac{1}{b-a} & \text{if } a \leq x \leq b \\ 0 & \text{if } x > b \end{cases} \tag{A.36}$$

Figure A.1 illustrates the distribution and density functions.

A.3.2 The Exponential Distribution Functions

Perhaps the most widely used PDF in performance modeling is the exponential distribution. It has the form

$$F_X(x) = 1 - \exp(-ax) \tag{A.37}$$

where a is a constant, known as the *parameter of the exponential distribution.* Figure A.2a provides an example. By differentiating the PDF, we arrive at the pdf

$$f_X(x) = -a \exp(-ax) \tag{A.38}$$

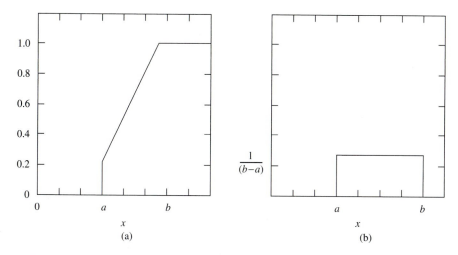

FIGURE A.1
Uniform distribution functions: (a) probability distribution function; (b) probability density function.

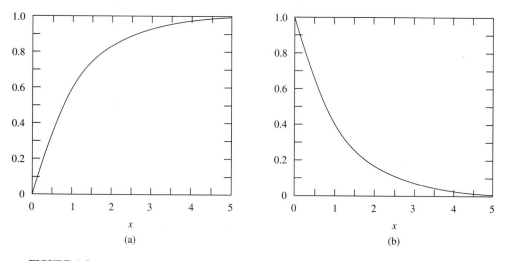

FIGURE A.2
Exponential distribution functions: (a) probability distribution function; (b) probability density function.

See Figure A.2b. The reason that the exponential distribution is so widely used becomes apparent when we use Bayes's law to compute $\text{Prob}(X > x \mid X > y)$ for $x \geq y$.

$$\text{Prob}(X > x \mid X > y) = \frac{\text{Prob}(X > x \cap X > y)}{\text{Prob}(X > y)}$$

$$= \frac{\text{Prob}(X > y \mid X > x)\text{Prob}(X > x)}{\text{Prob}(X > y)}$$

$$= \frac{\text{Prob}(X > x)}{\text{Prob}(X > y)}$$

(A.39)

$$= \exp(-a[x - y])$$

What this shows is that $\text{Prob}(X > x | X > y)$ is independent of the actual values of x and y. It only depends on the difference between them.

> **Example A.2.** The lifetime L of a processor is known to be exponentially distributed with parameter μ. Suppose it is known to be functional at time t. What is the probability that it will not fail before $t + \tau$?
>
> Since L is exponentially distributed,
>
> $$\text{Prob}(L > t + \tau | L > t) = \exp(-\mu[t + \tau - t]) = \exp(-\mu\tau) \qquad (A.40)$$
>
> that is, the probability that the processor will not fail before $t + \tau$, given that it is known to have been functional at t, is independent of t, and is only dependent on τ. So, if the lifetime is exponentially distributed, we do not need to know how long the processor has already been running to determine the probability distribution of its residual lifetime. This is known as the *memoryless* property.

It is possible to show that the exponential distribution is the only one with the memoryless property. The memoryless property makes modeling with exponentially distributed random variables very convenient, as we will see in the next section.

The mean and variance of the exponential distribution are easy to find. Computing them will provide an opportunity for us to use the Laplace transform. From Section A.2, we know that the Laplace transform of the exponential pdf $f_X(t) = a \exp(-at)$ is $F_X^*(s) = a/(s + a)$. The nth moment is given by

$$E[X^n] = (-1)^n \frac{d^n F^*(s)}{ds^n} \bigg|_{s=0}$$

(A.41)

Recall that the mean value is the first moment, and the variance is given by $\text{Var}[X] = E[X^2] - (E[X])^2$. After some calculus, we arrive at the result

$$E[X] = \frac{1}{a}$$

$$\text{Var}[X] = \frac{1}{a^2}$$

(A.42)

A.3.3   The Poisson Process

Consider a sequence of events $S = (s_1, s_2, \ldots, s_n, \ldots)$, and let $t(s_i)$ denote when event s_i happens. The sequence is *temporally ordered* (i.e., $0 < t(s_1) \leq t(s_2) \leq \cdots \leq t(s_n) \cdots$). If S satisfies the following rules,

R1. $\text{Prob}(t(s_i) = t(s_j)) = 0 \ \forall i \neq j$.

R2. The probability that an event occurs in the interval $[t, t + \Delta t)$ is given by $\lambda \Delta t + O(\Delta t^2)^1$ for some constant λ.

it is said to be a *Poisson process*.

What is the probability $P(N, t)$ that there are N events occurring in an interval $[0, t]$; that is, what is the probability that $t(s_N) \leq t$ and $t(s_{N+1}) > t$? We can set up a recursion for this function as follows. From rule **R2**, we can immediately write, neglecting terms of second order and higher in dt,

$$P(N, t + dt) = P(N, t)P(0, dt) + P(N - 1, t)P(1, dt)$$

$$= P(N, t)(1 - \lambda dt) + P(N - 1, t)\lambda dt$$

$$= P(N, t)(1 - \lambda dt) + P(N - 1, t)\lambda dt$$

$$\Rightarrow \frac{P(N, t + dt) - P(N, t)}{dt} = \lambda P(N - 1, t)$$

(A.43)

$$\Rightarrow \frac{dP(N, t)}{dt} = \lambda P(N - 1, t)$$

This is a simple differential equation, and solving it with the initial condition $P(0, 0) = 1$ (we define the time axis so that $t(s_1) > 0$), yields the sought-after result,

$$P(N, t) = \exp(-\lambda t)\frac{(\lambda t)^n}{n!}$$

(A.44)

Note that rule **R2** implies that the probability of an event occurring in some interval is independent of any previous occurrences. This is a memoryless property, and suggests a deep relationship between the Poisson process and the exponential distribution. This is indeed the case.

$$\text{Prob}(t(s_1) > x) = P(0, x) = \exp(-\lambda x)$$

(A.45)

$$\text{Prob}(t(s_n) - t(s_{n-1}) > x) = P(0, x) = \exp(-\lambda x)$$

(A.46)

That is, the interval between successive occurrences of a Poisson process with rate λ is exponentially distributed with parameter λ. Conversely, if some events are separated in time by exponentially distributed intervals of time with parameter λ, their occurrence forms a Poisson process with rate λ.

Example A.3. Suppose that the lifetime of a processor is exponentially distributed, and it is replaced immediately upon failure. Then, the failure events constitute a Poisson process.

Example A.4. A machine takes an exponentially distributed time to complete processing a part. When it finishes processing one part, it immediately starts processing another one. The output of finished parts constitutes a Poisson process.

---

[1] A quantity $q(x)$ is said to be of order $O(f(x))$ if there exists a constant k such that $q(x) < kf(x)$ for all $x > a$, where a is some constant.

Let $N(t)$ be the number of events of a Poisson process with parameter λ that have occurred up to time t. Then, we have

$$
\begin{aligned}
E[N(t)] &= \sum_{n=0}^{\infty} n\mathrm{Prob}(N(t) = n) \\
&= \sum_{n=1}^{\infty} n \exp(-\lambda t)\frac{(\lambda t)^n}{n!} \\
&= \lambda t \exp(-\lambda t)\sum_{n=1}^{\infty}\frac{(\lambda t)^{n-1}}{(n-1)!} \\
&= \lambda t
\end{aligned}
\tag{A.47}
$$

where we have used the fact that

$$
\exp(x) = 1 + x + \frac{x^2}{2!} + \cdots + \frac{x^n}{n!} + \cdots
\tag{A.48}
$$

This is why λ is called the *rate* of the Poisson process.

The moments of the Poisson process can be computed by using z-transforms. The z-transform of the process is given by

$$
\begin{aligned}
S(z) &= \sum_{n=0}^{\infty}\mathrm{Prob}(N(t) = n)z^n \\
&= \sum_{n=0}^{\infty}\exp(-\lambda t)\frac{(\lambda t z)^n}{n!} \\
&= \exp(-\lambda t[1-z])
\end{aligned}
\tag{A.49}
$$

We have the second moment as

$$
\begin{aligned}
E[N^2(t)] &= E[N(t)(N(t)-1)] + E[N(t)] \\
&= \left.\frac{d^2 S(z)}{dz^2}\right|_{z=1} + \lambda t \\
&= (\lambda t)^2 + \lambda t
\end{aligned}
\tag{A.50}
$$

The Poisson process has two remarkable and very convenient properties. The first of these is that the union of several Poisson processes is also a Poisson process; and the rate of the union Poisson process is the sum of the rates of the component Poisson processes. The second property is that if n events of a Poisson process are known to have occurred during an interval $[t_1, t_2]$, then these events are uniformly distributed over that interval.

The Poisson process is the asymptotic limit of a Bernoulli process. Let X_i, $i = 1, 2, \ldots$ consist of a series of mutually independent random variables, each of which can take the value 1 with probability p and the value 0 with probability $1 - p$. The stochastic process consisting of such a series of random variables is called a *Bernoulli process*.

Consider the random variable

$$S_n = \sum_{i=1}^{n} X_i \qquad \text{(A.51)}$$

Its probability mass function is given by

$$\text{Prob}[S_n = i] = \binom{n}{i} p^i (1 - p)^{n-i} \qquad \text{(A.52)}$$

This follows immediately from the fact that all the X_i are mutually independent. The following expressions are easy to derive:

$$E[S_n] = np \qquad \text{(A.53)}$$

$$\text{Var}[S_n] = np(1 - p) \qquad \text{(A.54)}$$

For large n, and for p such that np is finite, a Bernoulli process can be approximated by a Poisson process with arrival rate np. That is,

$$\text{Prob}[S_n = k] \approx e^{-np} \frac{(np)^k}{k!} \qquad \text{(A.55)}$$

This approximation is best for small k.

A.3.4 The Erlangian Distribution

A random variable with the *k-stage Erlang distribution* with parameter μ is the sum of k independent, exponentially distributed random variables, each of parameter $k\mu$. The density of an Erlang random variable $X = X_1 + X_2 + \cdots + X_k$, where the X_i are mutually independent and exponentially distributed, can be found by using Laplace transforms

$$F_X^*(s) = \left(\frac{k\mu}{s + k\mu} \right)^k \qquad \text{(A.56)}$$

and using the Laplace transform table to obtain

$$f_X(x) = \frac{(k\mu)^k x^{k-1}}{(k-1)!} \exp(-k\mu x) \qquad \text{(A.57)}$$

Figure A.3 shows some examples. The Erlang distribution can be found by integrating the density, but it is much easier to compute it directly by exploiting the relationship between the Poisson process and the exponential distribution.

Let $X_1, X_2, \ldots$ be exponentially distributed, mutually independent random variables with parameter $k\mu$, and define a process that occurs at times $X_1, X_1 + X_2, X_1 + X_2 + X_3, \ldots$. Such a process is clearly Poisson, with parameter $k\mu$. The event $X_1 + \cdots + X_k \leq x$ is then identical to the event that there have been at least k occurrences of the Poisson process up to time x. We therefore have

$$\text{Prob}(X_1 + \ldots + X_k \leq x) = \sum_{i=k}^{\infty} P(i, x)$$

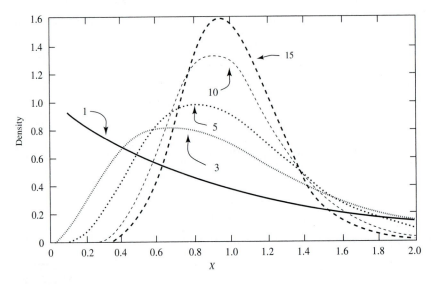

FIGURE A.3
The Erlang density function; line labels indicate number of stages and $\mu = 1$.

$$= 1 - \sum_{i=0}^{k-1} P(i, x) \tag{A.58}$$

$$= 1 - \sum_{i=0}^{k-1} \exp(-\mu x)\frac{(\mu x)^i}{i!}$$

where, as you recall, $P(i, x)$ denotes the probability of i arrivals of the Poisson process over an interval of duration x. Hence,

$$F_X(x) = 1 - \sum_{i=0}^{k-1} \exp(-\mu x)\frac{(\mu x)^i}{i!} \tag{A.59}$$

The mean and variance of an Erlang-distributed random variable X can be found by using the Laplace transform. We leave it for the reader to verify that

$$E[X] = \frac{1}{\mu}$$

$$\mathrm{Var}[X] = \frac{1}{k\mu^2} \tag{A.60}$$

Note particularly that the variance drops as k increases: this fact is apparent from inspection of Figure A.3.

A.3.5 The Weibull Distribution Functions

The Weibull PDF is given by

$$F(x) = 1 - \exp(-[\lambda x]^\alpha) \tag{A.61}$$

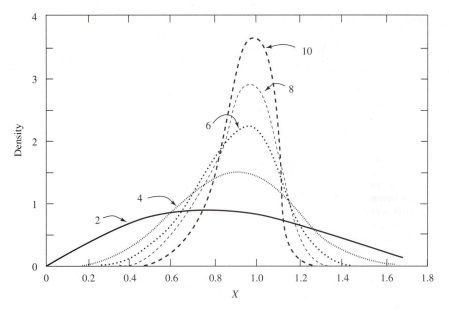

FIGURE A.4
The Weibull probability density function; line labels indicate value of α and $\lambda = 1$.

and the pdf by

$$f(x) = \alpha\lambda^{\alpha}x^{\alpha-1}\exp(-[\lambda x]^{\alpha}) \tag{A.62}$$

where λ and α are constants. When $\alpha = 1$, the Weibull is the same as the exponential distribution.

Figure A.4 contains some Weibull density functions for $\lambda = 1$ and $\alpha = 2, 4, 6, 8, 10$. The mean and variance of this distribution are more complex, and we shall not show their derivation here:

$$E[X] = \frac{\Gamma(1 + 1/\alpha)}{\lambda} \tag{A.63}$$

$$\text{Var}[X] = \frac{\Gamma(1 + 2/\alpha) - \Gamma^{2}(1 + 1/\alpha)}{\lambda^{2}} \tag{A.64}$$

where $\Gamma(x)$ is the gamma function that we encountered earlier.

A.4 BASICS OF MARKOV MODELING

We will begin with an example that will motivate our subsequent foray into Markov modeling techniques.

Example A.5. Suppose that there is a machine that is subject to failures, which arrive as a Poisson process with rate λ. Repair, which begins immediately upon the occurrence of failure, takes an exponentially distributed amount of time, with parameter μ. What is the availability of the machine (i.e., the fraction of time for which it is functional)?

The first step in building our model is to define the states of the machine. There are two obvious ones, up and down. The system cycles between them. Suppose we arrive at a random point in time and find the system is in state up. How much longer is it going to remain in state up before undergoing failure? It will stay in up until the next failure arrives. The time-to-next-failure is independent of how much time the system has already been up since the failures occur as a Poisson process, which is memoryless. The density function of this duration is therefore given by $f_{up}(t) = \lambda \exp(-\lambda t)$. In other words, if we find the system in state up, we can predict the time-to-next-failure without having to know how long the system has been up. This is the memoryless property of the Poisson process asserting itself. A similar observation holds for the down state. If we arrived to find the system down, the time-to-complete-repair is exponentially distributed, and therefore independent of the length of repair it has already undergone.

So, to analyze the system behavior, it is sufficient to know whether the system is up or down at any time, and not how long it has been up or down. In other words, a two-state model is sufficient to describe all the information we need about the current state of the system.

If the system is in state up at time t, what is the probability that it is in state down at time $t + dt$? This is just the probability of the occurrence of an event in the Poisson process of rate λ,

$$P_{up,down}(t, t + dt) = \lambda dt \tag{A.65}$$

Similarly, if the system is in state down at time t, the probability that it is in state up at time $t + dt$ is given by

$$P_{down,up}(t, t + dt) = \mu dt \tag{A.66}$$

$P_{up,down}(t, t + dt)/dt$ and $P_{down,up}(t, t + dt)/dt$ are called *transition rates*; they represent the rate at which the system moves from one state to the other in the model. Define $P_{up}(t)$ and $P_{down}(t)$ as the probability that the system is up and down at time t, respectively. Then, we can invoke Bayes's law to write the equations,

$$P_{up}(t + dt) = P_{up}(t)P_{up,up}(t, t + dt) + P_{down}(t)P_{down,up}(t, t + dt) \tag{A.67}$$

$$P_{down}(t + dt) = P_{up}(t)P_{up,down}(t, t + dt) + P_{down}(t)P_{down,down}(t, t + dt) \tag{A.68}$$

In other words, the probability that the system is up at time $t + dt$ is the probability that it was up at t and does not fail at that time, plus the probability that it was down at t, but its repair was completed at that time. The equation for $P_{down}(t + dt)$ is similar. These equations yield the following differential equations.

$$\frac{dP_{up}(t)}{dt} = -\lambda P_{up}(t) + \mu P_{down}(t) \tag{A.69}$$

$$\frac{dP_{down}(t)}{dt} = \lambda P_{down}(t) - \mu P_{up}(t) \tag{A.70}$$

If we try to solve this system of simultaneous differential equations, we get a shock—they are dependent! That is, since

$$\frac{dP_{up}(t)}{dt} + \frac{dP_{down}(t)}{dt} = 0 \tag{A.71}$$

Equation (A.70) gives us no new information. But we have two unknowns, and need two independent equations to solve them. The second equation is just the fact that the system must be either in state up or down at any time,

$$P_{\text{down}}(t) + P_{\text{up}}(t) = 1 \tag{A.72}$$

Substitute this into one of the differential equations to get

$$\frac{d P_{\text{up}}(t)}{dt} = -(\mu + \lambda) P_{\text{up}}(t) + \mu \tag{A.73}$$

There are many ways of solving this equation; perhaps the simplest is to use Laplace transforms. Apply a Laplace transformation to both sides of this equation and get:

$$s P_{\text{up}}^*(s) - P_{\text{up}}(0) = -(\mu + \lambda) P_{\text{up}}^*(s) + \frac{\mu}{s}$$

$$\Rightarrow P_{\text{up}}^*(s) = \frac{P_{\text{up}}(0)}{s + \lambda + \mu} + \frac{\mu}{s(s + \lambda + \mu)} \tag{A.74}$$

$$= \frac{P_{\text{up}}(0)}{s + \lambda + \mu} + \frac{\mu}{\lambda + \mu} \frac{1}{s} - \frac{\mu}{\lambda + \mu} \frac{1}{s + \lambda + \mu}$$

Referring to our lookup table of Laplace transforms, we can invert the right-hand side to obtain

$$P_{\text{up}}(t) = \left(P_{\text{up}}(0) - \frac{\mu}{\mu + \lambda} \right) \exp(-[\lambda + \mu]t) + \frac{\mu}{\mu + \lambda} \tag{A.75}$$

This equation is worth a moment's reflection. Notice that its right-hand side consists of two parts, one that is a function of t and another that is not. The first part has a factor of $\exp(-[\lambda+\mu]t)$, which decreases as t increases. This is called the *transient* part of the expression, since it dies away with time. It contains the effect of the *initial condition*, namely the state at which the system started at time 0. The rate at which the memory of the initial condition is erased depends on the values of μ and λ, the repair and failure rates. The second part is independent of time, and represents the steady-state value. As $t \to \infty$, this term dominates. Figure A.5 shows this graphically for some values of μ and λ, assuming that we start with the system in the up state.

This example has taught us a few things. First, since we used exponential distributions and Poisson processes, coming up with a state model for the system was not complicated; we did not have to keep track of the length of time for which the system was up or down. Second, there are two parts to the system state trajectory, the transient portion, which dies away with time, and the steady-state portion.

Does the transient portion die away in every system? No, as shown in Example A.6.

Example A.6. A system is in one of two states, S_0 and S_1. It runs in discrete time steps and changes state every time step.

Under such conditions, the memory of the initial state at time 0 will never fade. If the system started in S_0, it will be in S_0 every even time unit; if it started in S_1, it will be in S_1 every even time unit.

We are now ready to formally define a Markov process. A process is called a *Markov process* if it is always in one of a (possibly infinite) number of states, and the state-transition laws depend only on the current state. A formal definition of this is the following.

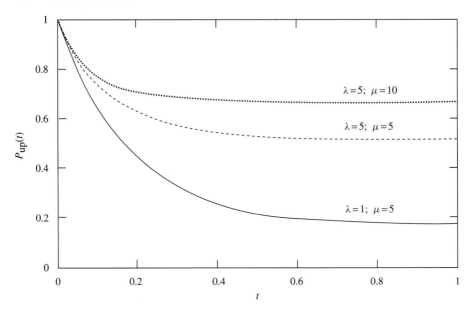

FIGURE A.5
Probability of being in the up state.

Definition A.1. A sequence X that takes value X_t at time t is said to be a Markov process if

$$\text{Prob}(x_k \leq X_t \leq x_m | X_{t1} = x_1, X_{t2} = x_2, \ldots, X_{tn} = x_n)$$
$$= \text{Prob}(x_k \leq X_t \leq x_m | X_{tn} = x_n) \tag{A.76}$$

for $t1 < t2 < \cdots < tn$.

That is, the future of the process depends only on its latest-specified state and not on the past. Alternatively, the latest-specified state has all the information needed to make probabilistic analyses of the future of the system.

A Markov process that consists of discrete states is called a *Markov chain*. Such chains can be either *discrete-time*, with states defined at discrete instants of time, or *continuous*, with states defined for all time.

A.4.1 Discrete-Time Markov Chains

Definition A.2. A sequence of random variables $X_1, X_2, \ldots, X_n, \ldots$ forms a discrete-time Markov chain if

$$\text{Prob}(X_{n+\ell} = x_{n+\ell} | X_1 = x_1, X_2 = x_2, \ldots, X_n = x_n)$$
$$= \text{Prob}(X_{n+\ell} = x_{n+\ell} | X_n = x_n) \tag{A.77}$$

X_i is the state of the chain at discrete time i.

Example A.7. A multiprocessor system consists of two processors and two memory modules connected through a crossbar switch, as shown in Figure A.6. The

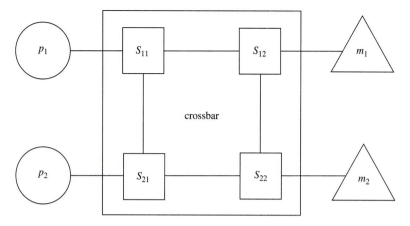

FIGURE A.6
Multiprocessor, Example A.7.

crossbar allows us to connect any combination of processors to the memories, subject to the condition that at most one processor may be connected to any one of the memories.

If its previous request is satisfied, each processor generates a memory request every clock cycle. This memory request is addressed to either memory with equal probability. If both processors request the same memory, one of them, chosen at random, gets through and the other tries again for the same module in the next cycle. All processor-memory transactions take one cycle to complete. What is the average bandwidth of this system; that is, how many memory requests per cycle get through to the memories?

Our first task in solving this problem is to set up a discrete-time Markov chain that captures the behavior of the system. We begin by defining the states of this chain. The states have to be defined in such a way that knowing the state at the end of the previous cycle is sufficient to allow us to compute the probability of being in any state at the end of the current cycle. From the problem statement, we know that the behavior in the current cycle depends on whether each processor has had its previous cycle's request satisfied. Let us define the state $S(i) = (S_1(i), S_2(i))$, where $S(i)$ is the state at the end of cycle i, and

$$S_k(i) \in \{C, U_1, U_2\}, \qquad k \in \{1, 2\} \tag{A.78}$$

where

C denotes that the desired connection to the memory of processor p_k was granted or that there was no request to begin with.

U_k denotes that the desired connection to memory module M_k was blocked by the other processor.

Note that if a connection request is granted, the memory request stream of that processor is independent of which memory module was accessed during that cycle. That is why we do not need to capture in our state descriptions which memory module was accessed.

The state of the system can be one of the following:

(C, C): All requests have been granted.

(C, U_i): Processor p_1's request during this cycle was granted, but processor p_2's request for memory module M_i was rejected during this cycle, $i = 1, 2$.

(U_i, C): Processor p_2's request during this cycle was granted, but p_1's request for memory module M_i was rejected during this cycle, $i = 1, 2$.

We will now consider the transitions from one state to another. Define

$$p_{a,b}(i, i+1) = \text{Prob(State at the end of cycle } i+1 \text{ was } b \mid \text{State}$$
$$\text{at the end of cycle } i \text{ was } a)$$
$$R(\alpha, \beta) = \text{Prob}(p_1 \text{ requested } M_\alpha; \ p_2 \text{ requested } M_\beta$$
$$\text{during cycle } i+1) \tag{A.79}$$

We make extensive use of Bayes's law.

$$p_{(C,C),(C,C)}(i, i+1)$$
$$= \text{Prob}(S(i+1) = (C, C) \mid S(i) = (C, C))$$
$$= \text{Prob}(S(i+1) = (C, C) \mid S(i) = (C, C), \text{ and } R(1, 1)) \text{Prob}(R(1, 1))$$
$$+ \text{Prob}(S(i+1) = (C, C) \mid S(i) = (C, C), \text{ and } R(1, 2)) \text{Prob}(R(1, 2))$$
$$+ \text{Prob}(S(i+1) = (C, C) \mid S(i) = (C, C), \text{ and } R(2, 1)) \text{Prob}(R(2, 1))$$
$$+ \text{Prob}(S(i+1) = (C, C) \mid S(i) = (C, C), \text{ and } R(2, 2)) \text{Prob}(R(2, 2))$$
$$= 0 \cdot \frac{1}{2}\frac{1}{2} + 1 \cdot \frac{1}{2}\frac{1}{2} + 1 \cdot \frac{1}{2}\frac{1}{2} + 0 \cdot \frac{1}{2}\frac{1}{2}$$
$$= \frac{1}{2} \tag{A.80}$$

We can derive the other transition probabilities similarly. We invite the reader to check that

$$p_{(C,C),(U_1,C)}(i, i+1) = \frac{1}{8} \tag{A.81}$$

$$p_{(C,C),(U_2,C)}(i, i+1) = \frac{1}{8} \tag{A.82}$$

$$p_{(C,C),(C,U_1)}(i, i+1) = \frac{1}{8} \tag{A.83}$$

$$p_{(C,C),(C,U_2)}(i, i+1) = \frac{1}{8} \tag{A.84}$$

$$p_{(U_1,C),(C,C)}(i, i+1) = \frac{1}{2} \tag{A.85}$$

$$p_{(U_1,C),(U_1,C)}(i, i+1) = \frac{1}{4} \tag{A.86}$$

$$p_{(U_1,C),(U_2,C)}(i, i+1) = 0 \tag{A.87}$$

$$p_{(U_1,C),(C,U_1)}(i, i+1) = \frac{1}{4} \tag{A.88}$$

$$p_{(U_1,C),(C,U_2)}(i,i+1) = 0 \tag{A.89}$$

$$p_{(U_2,C),(C,C)}(i,i+1) = \frac{1}{2} \tag{A.90}$$

$$p_{(U_2,C),(U_1,C)}(i,i+1) = 0 \tag{A.91}$$

$$p_{(U_2,C),(U_2,C)}(i,i+1) = \frac{1}{4} \tag{A.92}$$

$$p_{(U_2,C),(C,U_1)}(i,i+1) = 0 \tag{A.93}$$

$$p_{(U_2,C),(C,U_2)}(i,i+1) = \frac{1}{4} \tag{A.94}$$

$$p_{(C,U_1),(C,C)}(i,i+1) = \frac{1}{2} \tag{A.95}$$

$$p_{(C,U_1),(U_1,C)}(i,i+1) = \frac{1}{4} \tag{A.96}$$

$$p_{(C,U_1),(U_2,C)}(i,i+1) = 0 \tag{A.97}$$

$$p_{(C,U_1),(C,U_1)}(i,i+1) = \frac{1}{4} \tag{A.98}$$

$$p_{(C,U_1),(C,U_2)}(i,i+1) = 0 \tag{A.99}$$

$$p_{(C,U_2),(C,C)}(i,i+1) = \frac{1}{2} \tag{A.100}$$

$$p_{(C,U_2),(U_1,C)}(i,i+1) = 0 \tag{A.101}$$

$$p_{(C,U_2),(U_2,C)}(i,i+1) = \frac{1}{4} \tag{A.102}$$

$$p_{(C,U_2),(C,U_1)}(i,i+1) = 0 \tag{A.103}$$

$$p_{(C,U_2),(C,U_2)}(i,i+1) = \frac{1}{4} \tag{A.104}$$

Figure A.7 contains a diagram of the Markov chain with the transition probabilities marked. We can write the following as a consequence of Bayes's law.

$$\pi_{i+1}(C,C) = \text{Prob}(S(i+1) = (C,C)) = p_{(C,C),(C,C)}(i,i+1)\pi_i(C,C)$$
$$+ p_{(U_1,C),(C,C)}(i,i+1)\pi_i(U_1,C) + p_{(U_2,C),(C,C)}(i,i+1)\pi_i(U_2,C)$$
$$+ p_{(C,U_1),(C,C)}(i,i+1)\pi_i(C,U_1) + p_{(C,U_2),(C,C)}(i,i+1)\pi_i(C,U_2) \tag{A.105}$$

$$\pi_{i+1}(U_1,C) = \text{Prob}(S(i+1) = (U_1,C)) = p_{(C,C),(U_1,C)}(i,i+1)\pi_i(C,C)$$
$$+ p_{(U_1,C),(U_1,C)}(i,i+1)\pi_i(U_1,C) + p_{(U_2,C),(U_1,C)}(i,i+1)\pi_i(U_2,C)$$
$$+ p_{(C,U_1),(U_1,C)}(i,i+1)\pi_i(C,U_1) + p_{(C,U_2),(U_1,C)}(i,i+1)\pi_i(C,U_2) \tag{A.106}$$

$$\pi_{i+1}(U_2,C) = \text{Prob}(S(i+1) = (U_2,C)) = p_{(C,C),(U_2,C)}(i,i+1)\pi_i(C,C)$$
$$+ p_{(U_1,C),(U_2,C)}(i,i+1)\pi_i(U_1,C) + p_{(U_2,C),(U_2,C)}(i,i+1)\pi_i(U_2,C)$$
$$+ p_{(C,U_1),(U_2,C)}(i,i+1)\pi_i(C,U_1) + p_{(C,U_2),(U_2,C)}(i,i+1)\pi_i(C,U_2) \tag{A.107}$$

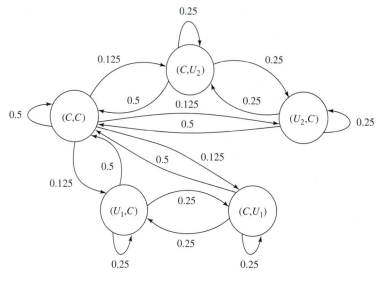

FIGURE A.7
Markov chain, Example A.7.

$$\pi_{i+1}(C, U_1) = \text{Prob}(S(i+1) = (C, U_1)) = p_{(C,C),(C,U_1)}(i, i+1)\pi_i(C, C)$$
$$+ p_{(U_1,C),(C,U_1)}(i, i+1)\pi_i(U_1, C) + p_{(U_2,C),(C,U_1)}(i, i+1)\pi_i(U_2, C)$$
$$+ p_{(C,U_1),(C,U_1)}(i, i+1)\pi_i(C, U_1) + p_{(C,U_2),(C,U_1)}(i, i+1)\pi_i(C, U_2)$$
$$\text{(A.108)}$$

$$\pi_{i+1}(C, U_2) = \text{Prob}(S(i+1) = (C, U_2)) = p_{(C,C),(C,U_2)}(i, i+1)\pi_i(C, C)$$
$$+ p_{(U_1,C),(C,U_2)}(i, i+1)\pi_i(U_1, C) + p_{(U_2,C),(C,U_2)}(i, i+1)\pi_i(U_2, C)$$
$$+ p_{(C,U_1),(C,U_2)}(i, i+1)\pi_i(C, U_1) + p_{(C,U_2),(C,U_2)}(i, i+1)\pi_i(C, U_2)$$
$$\text{(A.109)}$$

This set of equations can be written in matrix form.

$$(\pi_{i+1}(C, C)\ \pi_{i+1}(U_1, C)\ \pi_{i+1}(U_2, C)\pi_{i+1}(C, U_1)\ \pi_{i+1}(C, U_2))$$
$$= (\pi_i(C, C)\ \pi_i(U_1, C)\ \pi_i(U_2, C)\ \pi_i(C, U_1)\ \pi_i(C, U_2))\ \mathbf{P} \quad \text{(A.110)}$$

where

$$\mathbf{P} = \begin{pmatrix} 1/2 & 1/8 & 1/8 & 1/8 & 1/8 \\ 1/2 & 1/4 & 0 & 1/4 & 0 \\ 1/2 & 0 & 1/4 & 0 & 1/4 \\ 1/2 & 1/4 & 0 & 1/4 & 0 \\ 1/2 & 0 & 1/4 & 0 & 1/4 \end{pmatrix} \quad \text{(A.111)}$$

is called the *probability transition matrix*. By induction, it is easy to see that the row-vector

$$(\pi_{i+n}(C, C)\ \pi_{i+n}(U_1, C)\ \pi_{i+n}(U_2, C)\pi_{i+n}(C, U_1)\ \pi_{i+n}(C, U_2))$$
$$= (\pi_i(C, C)\ \pi_i(U_1, C)\ \pi_i(U_2, C)\ \pi_i(C, U_1)\ \pi_i(C, U_2))\ \mathbf{P}^n \quad \text{(A.112)}$$

The expected bandwidth in cycle i is the expected number of requests that succeed (both are successful when the state is (C,C); otherwise, only one succeeds).

$$\text{BW}(i) = 2\pi_i(C, C) + \pi_i(U_1, C) + \pi_i(U_2, C) + \pi_i(C, U_1) + \pi_i(C, U_2) \quad \text{(A.113)}$$

When the system starts functioning at time 0, there are no rejected requests from any previous cycles, so we can use the initial condition $\pi_0(C, C) = 1$.

Let us examine the probability transition matrix, $\mathbf{P}$. If there are n states in the system, it is an $n \times n$ matrix, with the property that each row sums to 1. Such a matrix (i.e., one in which each row sums to 1) is also known as a *stochastic matrix*. As we saw in the above example, $\mathbf{P}^n = [p_{k,\ell}^{(n)}]$ is the n-step transition matrix, that provides the probability $\pi_{i+n}(\ell)$ of being in state ℓ at time $i + n$, given that the state in time i was k. From this definition and Bayes's law, we can write

$$\pi_{i+n}(\ell) = \sum_k \pi_i(k) p_{k,l}^{(n)} \qquad n = 1, 2, \ldots \qquad \text{(A.114)}$$

which is known as the *Chapman-Kolmogorov equation*.

Definition A.3. A discrete-time Markov chain is said to be *periodic* if there exists an integer $m > 1$ such that the probability of being in state i is nonzero only at times $n_i, n_i + m, n_i + 2m, \ldots$, where n_i is any constant. Otherwise it is said to be *aperiodic*.

Theorem A.1. If any state of the chain is periodic, then all its states are periodic with the same period m.

The chain in Example A.6 is a periodic chain with period $m = 2$. The chain in Example A.7 is an aperiodic chain.

A.4.2 Continuous-Time Markov Chains

Definition A.4. A function $X(t)$ is said to form a continuous-time Markov chain if

$$\text{Prob}(X(t) = \alpha | X(t_1) = \beta_1, \ldots, X(t_k) = \beta_k)$$
$$= \text{Prob}(X(t) = \alpha | X(t_k) = \beta_k) \qquad \text{(A.115)}$$

where $t_1 < t_2 \cdots < t_k < t$.

Example A.8. A fault-tolerant system is composed of $N = 2m + 1$ processors, and will continue to work correctly so long as at least $m + 1$ of the processors are functional. For each processor, failure can be modeled as occurring as a Poisson process with rate μ. Failures occur independently (i.e., whether processor x fails or not is not dependent on the health of any other processor y). What is the probability that the system will remain functional over an interval of time $[0, t]$, given that all the processors are functional at time 0? There is no repair.

There are two ways of dealing with this problem. Since the processors fail independently, it is easiest to calculate the probability that an individual processor will

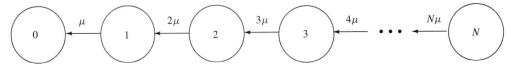

FIGURE A.8
Markov chain, Example A.8.

be up at time t, and from there the probability that at least $m+1$ of them are up. We use another approach here, since our aim is to show how Markov chains are solved.

Our first task in solving this problem is to define a set of states suitably. Let us select the number of functional processors as the system state. Is this a good choice? Does knowing the number of processors that are still functional give us adequate information about the current status of the system? Yes, for the following reasons.

- The failure is a Poisson process, which means that we do not need to keep track of the current time to determine the probability of a processor failing in the next t time units.

- The failure processes of all the processors are identical, so it is sufficient to keep track of how many processors are still functional. We don't need to record exactly which processors are still functional.

- The states are so defined that each corresponds to either a system-functional (number of surviving processors $\geq m+1$) or a system-failed (number of surviving processors $\leq m$) status. We can therefore calculate the probability that the system has failed by computing the probability of being in one of the states that corresponds to system failure.

The Markov chain associated with this system is shown in Figure A.8. The numbers within the circles are the states, and the arrows depict the transitions from one state to another. The labels on the arrows depict the rate of transition, as we shall see below.

Let us write the equations for the probability $\pi_i(t+dt)$ of being in state i $(0 \leq i \leq N)$ at time $t+dt$. To do so, we need to note that if the system state at time t is $i > 0$, the probability that it will make the transition to state $i-1$ over an interval of duration dt is given by $i\mu dt$. This is because there are i functional processors in state i, the failure of each processor is a Poisson process with rate μ, and the aggregate failure process among the i functional processors is the union of the failure processes of each of the individual functional processors. The probability that the system will make the transition from state i to state $i+1$ is 0, since there is no repair. The probability that it will transit from $i \geq 2$ to $i-2$ or a lower state over an interval of duration dt is of order $O(dt^2)$, since this requires two failures. We ignore such terms since dt is infinitesimally small.

We can say all this more formally using Bayes's law. Let us derive, in detail, the equation for $\pi_0(t+dt)$.

$$\pi_0(t+dt) = \text{Prob}(X(t+dt) = 0)$$

$$= \sum_{i=0}^{N} \text{Prob}(X(t+dt) = 0 | X(t) = i)\text{Prob}(X(t) = i)$$

$$= \pi_0(t) + \pi_1(t)\mu dt \tag{A.116}$$

We can therefore write the equations for $\pi_i(t + dt)$, using Bayes's law as in the above equation, to obtain

$$\pi_0(t + dt) = \pi_0(t) + \mu\pi_1(t)dt \tag{A.117}$$

$$\pi_i(t + dt) = \pi_i(t)(1 - i\mu dt) + (i + 1)\mu\pi_{i+1}dt \qquad 0 < i < N \tag{A.118}$$

$$\pi_N(t + dt) = \pi_N(t)(1 - N\mu dt) \tag{A.119}$$

As before, this system of $N + 1$ equations has only N independent equations, since the sum of the equations results in a tautology. The additional equation needed to solve them is the fact that the probabilities must sum to 1,

$$\pi_0(t) + \pi_1(t) + \cdots + \pi_N(t) = 1 \tag{A.120}$$

Some algebra results in the following differential equations.

$$\frac{d\pi_0(t)}{dt} = \mu\pi_1(t) \tag{A.121}$$

$$\frac{d\pi_i(t)}{dt} = -i\mu\pi_i(t) + (i + 1)\mu\pi_{i+1}(t) \qquad 0 < i < N \tag{A.122}$$

$$\frac{d\pi_N(t)}{dt} = -N\mu\pi_N(t) \tag{A.123}$$

We could have written these equations directly from inspection of the Markov chain; the $d\pi_i(t)/dt$ terms represent the rate of change in the probability of being in state i at time t. This is equal to the rate of flow into state i minus the rate of flow out of state i at time t. The rate of flow out of state i is the sum of the failure rates of the i functional processors, $i\mu$. The rate of flow into state i is the rate of flow out of state $i + 1$ for $i < N$, and is zero for $i = N$.

These equations can be solved by using Laplace transforms. Let us solve them for the initial condition $\pi_N(0) = 1$, $\pi_i(0) = 0 \ \forall i \neq N$. This condition captures the requirement that the probabilities must sum to 1. Applying the Laplace transform turns the set of simultaneous differential equations into a set of linear equations.

$$\Pi_0^*(s) = \frac{\mu}{s}\Pi_1^*(s) \tag{A.124}$$

$$\Pi_i^*(s) = \frac{(i + 1)\mu}{s + i\mu}\Pi_{i+1}^*(s), \qquad 0 < i < N \tag{A.125}$$

$$\Pi_N^*(s) = \frac{1}{s + N\mu} \tag{A.126}$$

Substituting the expression for $\Pi_{i+1}^*(s)$ into the equation for $\Pi_i^*(s)$, we arrive at the solution.

$$\Pi_{N-1}^*(s) = \frac{N\mu}{(s + N\mu)(s + [N - 1]\mu)} \tag{A.127}$$

$$\Pi_{N-2}^*(s) = \frac{N(N - 1)\mu^2}{(s + N\mu)(s + [N - 1]\mu)(s + [N - 2]\mu)} \tag{A.128}$$

$$\vdots$$

$$\Pi_1^*(s) = \frac{N(N-1)\cdots 2\ \mu^{N-1}}{(s+N\mu)(s+[N-1]\mu)\cdots(s+\mu)} \tag{A.129}$$

$$\Pi_0^*(s) = \frac{\mu}{s}\ \frac{N(N-1)\cdots 2\ \mu^{N-1}}{(s+N\mu)(s+[N-1]\mu)\cdots(s+\mu)} \tag{A.130}$$

In general,

$$\Pi_i^*(s) = \frac{\mu^{N-i}\prod_{j=1}^{N-i}(i+j)}{\prod_{j=0}^{N-i}s+(i+j)\mu} \tag{A.131}$$

The expression for $\pi_N(t)$ can be obtained by inversion of the Laplace transform. From the expression for $\Pi_N^*(s)$, we have

$$\pi_N(t) = \exp(-N\mu t) \tag{A.132}$$

The expressions for $\pi_i(t)$, $i < N$, are obtained by using partial fractions. In general, we can write

$$\Pi_i^*(s) = \frac{\mu^{N-i}\prod_{j=1}^{N-i}(i+j)}{\prod_{j=0}^{N-i}(s+(i+j)\mu)} = \sum_{j=0}^{N-i}\frac{A(i,j)}{s+(i+j)\mu} \tag{A.133}$$

where

$$A(i,j) = (-1)^j\frac{N!}{i!j!(N-i-j)!} \tag{A.134}$$

We therefore have, by taking the inverse Laplace transform of $\Pi_i^*(s)$,

$$\pi_i(t) = \sum_{j=0}^{N-i}A(i,j)e^{-(i+j)\mu t} \tag{A.135}$$

We are now ready to answer the question we started with: What is the probability of the system failing during an interval of operation $[0, t]$ if it started with all its N processors functional? This is simply the probability of being in any state at time t that has fewer than $m + 1$ processors functional,

$$\text{Prob}\{\text{Failure by time } t\} = \sum_{i=0}^{m}\pi_i(t) \tag{A.136}$$

Figure A.9 contains a plot of the failure probabilities for a five-processor system. We can see that the probability of failure goes to 1 as time increases. This is because the system has no repair. Figure A.10 provides failure probabilities for clusters ranging in size from 3 to 9.

We now introduce the concept of the infinitesimal generator. Recall the differential equations of the process (repeated here):

$$\frac{d\pi_0(t)}{dt} = \mu\pi_1(t) \tag{A.121}$$

$$\frac{d\pi_i(t)}{dt} = -i\mu\pi_i(t) + (i+1)\mu\pi_{i+1}(t) \qquad 0 < i < N \tag{A.122}$$

$$\frac{d\pi_N(t)}{dt} = -N\mu\pi_N(t) \tag{A.123}$$

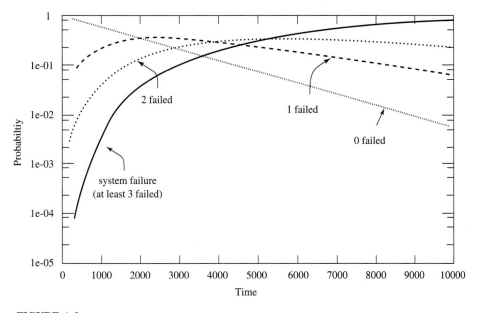

FIGURE A.9
Failure probabilities for a five-processor system ($\mu = 10^{-4}$).

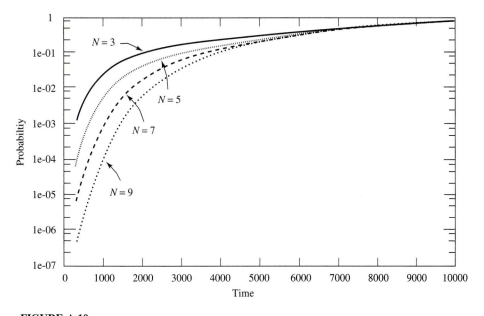

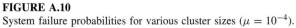

FIGURE A.10
System failure probabilities for various cluster sizes ($\mu = 10^{-4}$).

We can write this using matrix notation as follows:

$$\frac{d\pi(t)}{dt} = \pi(t)\mathbf{Q} \tag{A.137}$$

where $\mathbf{Q}$ is the matrix

$$\begin{pmatrix} 0 & \mu & 0 & 0 & \dots & 0 & 0 \\ 0 & -\mu & 2\mu & 0 & \dots & 0 & 0 \\ 0 & 0 & -2\mu & 3\mu & \dots & 0 & 0 \\ & & & \vdots & & & \\ 0 & 0 & 0 & 0 & \dots & -(N-1)\mu & N\mu \\ 0 & 0 & 0 & 0 & \dots & 0 & -N\mu \end{pmatrix} \tag{A.138}$$

and

$$\pi(t) = (\pi_0(t), \pi_1(t), \dots, \pi_N(t)) \tag{A.139}$$

$\mathbf{Q}$ is called the *infinitesimal generator* of the continuous-time Markov process. Notice that its columns sum to zero, otherwise the sum of the probabilities will not be a constant, as it should.

Define the state-transition probability

$$p_{i,j}(t_1, t_2) = \text{Prob(state at time } t_2 \text{ is } j|\text{state at time } t_1 \text{ was } i) \tag{A.140}$$

Then, Bayes's law allows us to write

$$p_{i,j}(t_1, t_2) = \sum_k p_{i,k}(t_1, \xi) p_{k,j}(\xi, t_2) \tag{A.141}$$

for any ξ such that $t_1 < \xi < t_2$. This is the *Chapman-Kolmogorov equation for continuous-time chains*; compare it with the Chapman-Kolmogorov equation for discrete-time chains, Equation (A.114).

A.4.3   Some Additional Remarks about Markov Chains

Definition A.5. An *irreducible* Markov chain is one where every state can be reached from every other state.

Example A.9. The chain in Example A.7 (See Figure A.7) is irreducible. However, the chain in Example A.8 (see Figure A.8) is not—state i cannot be reached from state j for $j < i$.

Definition A.6. A state i is said to be a *transient* state if the probability of being in that state goes to zero as time increases,

$$\lim_{t \to \infty} \pi_i(t) = 0 \tag{A.142}$$

Otherwise, the state is said to be *recurrent*.

Definition A.7. A recurrent state i is said to be *recurrent non-null* if the expected time between leaving state i and entering it again the next time is finite. If this time is infinite, it is *recurrent null*.

Definition A.8. A state i is said to be an *absorbing* state if the probability of leaving that state is zero.

Definition A.9. A Markov chain is said to be *homogeneous* if the transition probabilities or rates are independent of time.

Example A.10. States $i > 0$ in Example A.8 are all transient, and state 0 is absorbing. All the states in Example A.7 are recurrent non-null. All the chains that we have encountered in this Appendix are homogeneous.

Definition A.10. A state i of a discrete-time Markov chain is said to be *periodic* if the probability of being in that state is nonzero only at times $n\delta$, where $\delta \in \{2, 3, \ldots\}$, and $n = 1, 2, \ldots$. States that are not periodic are called *aperiodic*, and chains consisting of only aperiodic states are called aperiodic Markov chains.

The following theorem, which we state without proof, is the basis of most Markov models.

Theorem A.2. In an irreducible and aperiodic homogeneous Markov chain, the limits

$$\pi_i = \lim_{t \to \infty} \pi_i(t) \tag{A.143}$$

exist, and are independent of the initial state $\pi_i(0)$. These limits are called the steady-state probability of being in state i. If all the states are transient or recurrent null,

$$\pi_i = 0 \tag{A.144}$$

for all states i. If all the states are recurrent non-null, then we have

$$\sum_i \pi_i = 1 \tag{A.145}$$

$$\pi = \pi \mathbf{P} \qquad \text{for discrete chains} \tag{A.146}$$

$$\pi \mathbf{Q} = 0 \qquad \text{for continuous chains} \tag{A.147}$$

where $\mathbf{P}$ and $\mathbf{Q}$ are the transition matrix and the generator matrix of the respective chains.

Example A.11. Let us return to Example A.7, which is an irreducible aperiodic homogeneous Markov chain, and compute the steady-state probabilities. The equations for the steady-state probabilities are

$$\pi_{C,C} = (1/2)\pi_{C,C} + (1/8)\pi_{U1,C} + (1/8)\pi_{U2,C} + (1/8)\pi_{C,U1} + (1/8)\pi_{C,U2} \tag{A.148}$$

$$\pi_{U1,C} = (1/2)\pi_{C,C} + (1/4)\pi_{U1,C} + (0)\pi_{U2,C} + (1/4)\pi_{C,U1} + (0)\pi_{C,U2} \tag{A.149}$$

$$\pi_{U2,C} = (1/2)\pi_{C,C} + (0)\pi_{U1,C} + (1/4)\pi_{U2,C} + (0)\pi_{C,U1} + (1/4)\pi_{C,U2}$$
(A.150)

$$\pi_{C,U1} = (1/2)\pi_{C,C} + (1/4)\pi_{U1,C} + (0)\pi_{U2,C} + (1/4)\pi_{C,U1} + (0)\pi_{C,U2}$$
(A.151)

$$\pi_{C,U2} = (1/2)\pi_{C,C} + (0)\pi_{U1,C} + (1/4)\pi_{U2,C} + (0)\pi_{C,U1} + (1/4)\pi_{C,U2}$$
(A.152)

These equations can be written by inspection of the Markov chain by equating the total probability flow out of each state and the total probability flow into that state. For this reason, they are often called *balance equations*.

These equations are dependent. They can be solved by replacing one of them by the boundary condition that the probabilities sum to 1

$$\pi_{C,C} + \pi_{U1,C} + \pi_{U2,C} + \pi_{C,U1} + \pi_{C,U2} = 1$$
(A.153)

This yields five independent equations in five unknowns (i.e., the state probabilities), which we can solve using standard techniques.

Example A.12.   Consider a continuous-time Markov chain that has the transition rates as shown in Figure A.11. This is the chain of a famous queue, called the M/M/1 queue, which has jobs arriving as a Poisson process with rate λ and served by a single server with rate μ.

It is easy to see that the queue length will go to infinity if $\lambda > \mu$, that is, if the mean service rate is less than the mean interarrival rate. We therefore concentrate on the case where $\lambda \leq \mu$.

The balance equations are

$$\lambda\pi_0 = \mu\pi_1$$
(A.154)

$$(\lambda + \mu)\pi_i = \lambda\pi_{i-1} + \mu\pi_{i+1} \qquad \text{for } i > 0$$
(A.155)

These, together with the boundary condition $\sum_{i=0}^{\infty} \pi_i = 1$, are sufficient to yield the steady-state probabilities π_i.

These balance equations are sufficiently simple to solve by conventional means, but we will take this opportunity to demonstrate how they can be solved using z-transforms. Multiply both sides of the balance equations by z^i for the equation with π_i on the left-hand side, and we get

$$\lambda\pi_0 z^0 = \mu\pi_1 z^0$$
(A.156)

$$(\lambda + \mu)\pi_i z^i = \lambda\pi_{i-1}z^i + \mu\pi_{i+1}z^i \qquad \text{for } i > 0$$
(A.157)

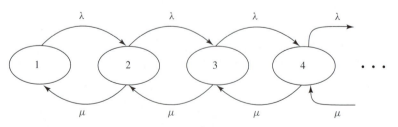

FIGURE A.11
Markov chain, Example A.12.

Add the left-hand sides of the above set of equations, and equate them to the sum of the right-hand sides,

$$\lambda\pi_0 z^0 + \sum_{i=1}^{\infty}(\lambda+\mu)\pi_i z^i = \mu\pi_1 z^0 + \sum_{i=1}^{\infty}\lambda\pi_{i-1}z^i + \sum_{i=1}^{\infty}\mu\pi_{i+1}z^i$$

$$\Rightarrow \sum_{i=0}^{\infty}\{\lambda+\mu\}\pi_i z^i - \mu\pi_0 z^0 = \mu\pi_1 + z\lambda\sum_{i=0}^{\infty}\pi_i z^i + (1/z)\mu\left\{\sum_{i=0}^{\infty}\pi_i z^i - \pi_0 - \pi_1 z\right\}$$

$$\Rightarrow \{\lambda(1-z)+\mu(1-1/z)\}\Pi(z) = \mu\pi_0(1-1/z)$$

$$\Rightarrow \Pi(z) = \frac{\mu\pi_0(1-1/z)}{\lambda(1-z)+\mu(1-1/z)} \tag{A.158}$$

To find π_0, we use the boundary condition that the probabilities sum to one; recall that the sum of the probabilities is given by $\lim_{z\to 1}\Pi(z)$. We will use L'Hospital's rule, which states that if $\lim_{z\to a} f(z) = 0$ and $\lim_{z\to a} g(z) = 0$ for any two functions f and g, then

$$\lim_{z\to a}\frac{f(z)}{g(z)} = \frac{\lim_{z\to a} d^n f(z)/dz^n}{\lim_{z\to a} d^n g(z)/dz^n} \tag{A.159}$$

where n is the smallest number for which at least one of $\lim_{z\to a} d^n f(z)/dz^n$ and $\lim_{z\to a} d^n g(z)dz^n$ is nonzero. For our problem, we have

$$\lim_{z\to 1}\Pi(z) = \lim_{z\to 1}\frac{\mu\pi_0(1-1/z)}{\lambda(1-z)+\mu}$$

$$= \lim_{z\to 1}\frac{[d\mu\pi_0(1-1/z)/dz]}{[d\lambda(1-z)+\mu(1-1/z)/dz]}$$

$$= \frac{\mu\pi_0}{\mu-\lambda} \tag{A.160}$$

$$\Rightarrow \pi_0 = \frac{\mu-\lambda}{\mu}$$

$$= 1 - \frac{\lambda}{\mu}$$

Consider the two cases, $\mu = \lambda$ and $\mu > \lambda$. If $\mu = \lambda$, then $\pi_0 = 0$, and indeed $\Pi(z) = 0$ (resulting in $\pi_1 = \pi_2 = \cdots = \pi_n = \cdots = 0$), which indicates that the chain is not recurrent non-null. If $\mu > \lambda$, we have $\pi_i > 0$ for all $i > 0$, indicating that for such a case the chain is recurrent non-null and that a meaningful steady-state solution exists.

Concentrating on the case for which the chain is recurrent non-null, we have

$$\Pi(z) = \frac{(\mu-\lambda)(1-1/z)}{\lambda(1-z)+\mu(1-1/z)}$$

$$= \frac{\mu-\lambda}{\mu(1-\frac{\lambda}{\mu}z)} \tag{A.161}$$

$$= \left(1-\frac{\lambda}{\mu}\right)\left[1+\left(\frac{\lambda}{\mu}\right)+\left(\frac{\lambda}{\mu}\right)^2 z^2 + \cdots + \left(\frac{\lambda}{\mu}\right)^n z^n + \cdots\right]$$

Since $\Pi(z) = \pi_0 + \pi_1 z + \pi_2 z^2 + \cdots + \pi_n z^n + \cdots$, π_i is just the coefficient of z^i; that is,

$$\pi_i = \left(1 - \frac{\lambda}{\mu}\right)\left(\frac{\lambda}{\mu}\right)^i \qquad i \geq 0 \qquad (A.162)$$

This example has demonstrated how to use z-transforms to solve a set of balance equations. While we could have solved these without recourse to z-transforms, we frequently encounter equations whose complexity is such that a direct solution is impossible and transforms are the only convenient solution tool.

When z-transforms are used to solve equations, we frequently need a result from complex algebra, called Rouche's theorem. We state it here without proof.

Theorem A.3.   Rouche's theorem. Let $f(z)$ and $g(z)$ be functions of a complex variable z. If both $f(z)$ and $g(z)$ are *analytic* (i.e., have a unique derivative) inside and on a closed contour C, and if $|g(z)| < |f(z)|$ on C, then $f(z)$ and $f(z) + g(z)$ have the same number of zeroes inside C (i.e., have the same number of points within C for which they are zero).

Example A.13.   Consider the continuous-time Markov chain shown in Figure A.12. Find the steady-state probability π_i of being in state i. Equating the probability flow out of state i to the probability flow into state i (for $i = 0, 1, \ldots$), we have the following balance equations.

$$\lambda \pi_0 = \mu(\pi_1 + \pi_2) \qquad (A.163)$$

$$(\lambda + \mu)\pi_i = \lambda \pi_{i-1} + \mu \pi_{i+2} \qquad i > 0 \qquad (A.164)$$

Let us solve this by the z-transform method. Multiply the equation with π_i on the left-hand side by z^i and add to get

$$\lambda \pi_0 z^0 + \sum_{i=1}^{\infty}(\lambda + \mu)\pi_i z^i = \mu(\pi_1 + \pi_2)z^0 + \sum_{i=1}^{\infty}\lambda \pi_{i-1} + \sum_{i=1}^{\infty}\mu \pi_{i+2}$$

$$\Rightarrow (\lambda + \mu)(\Pi(z) - \pi_0) = \lambda z \Pi(z) + (\mu/z^2)(\Pi(z) - \pi_0 - \pi_1 z)$$

$$\Rightarrow \Pi(z) = \frac{\mu(\pi_0 + \pi_1 z + \pi_2 z^2) - (\lambda + \mu)\pi_0 z^2}{\lambda z^3 - (\lambda + \mu)z^2 + \mu} \qquad (A.165)$$

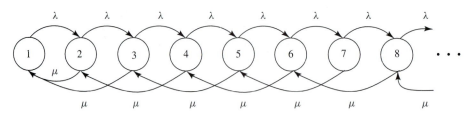

FIGURE A.12
Markov chain, Example A.13.

Consider now the denominator of the right-hand side of the above equation,

$$\lambda z^3 - (\lambda + \mu)z^2 + \mu \tag{A.166}$$

It is a third-order polynomial, so it must have three roots. One root can be seen by inspection to be at $z = 1$. Let us invoke Rouche's theorem, defining $f(z) = \mu - (\lambda + \mu)z^2$, and $g(z) = \lambda z^3$. Then, in the circle $|z| = 1 + \epsilon$, where $\epsilon > 0$, we have

$$|f(z)|_{z=1+\epsilon} \geq \left| \mu - (\lambda + \mu)(1 + \epsilon)^2 \right| \tag{A.167}$$

$$|g(z)|_{z=1+\epsilon} \leq \lambda(1 + \epsilon)^3 \tag{A.168}$$

For small $\epsilon > 0$, it is easy to see from the preceding that $|f(z)| > |g(z)|$ over the circle $C' = |z| = 1 + \epsilon$ if $\mu > \lambda/2$. So, for $\mu > \lambda/2$, $f(z)$ and $f(z) + g(z)$ must have the same number of roots within C'. Since $f(z)$ has two roots inside C', no matter how small the value of ϵ, and one of the roots of $f(z) + g(z)$ has already been identified as 1, a second root must lie somewhere inside the unit circle; that is, $f(z) + g(z)$ must have a root z_0 such that $|z_0| < 1$. The third root z_1 of $f(z) + g(z)$ will then lie outside the unit circle (i.e., $|z_1| > 1$). So we can write the denominator as $L(z - z_0)(z - 1)(z - z_1)$, where L is some constant.

The numerator is a second-order polynomial in z, and must therefore have two roots. One root is at $z = 1$. Since the generating function $\Pi(z)$ is known to converge for all $|z| \leq 1$, the root z_0 of the denominator must coincide with the other root of the numerator; otherwise the generating function will go to infinity for $|z| \leq 1$. So, we can write the numerator as $K(z - z_0)(z - 1)$.

We therefore have

$$\begin{aligned} \Pi(z) &= \frac{K(z - z_0)(z - 1)}{L(z - z_0)(z - 1)(z - z_1)} \\ &= \frac{K}{L(z - z_1)} \end{aligned} \tag{A.169}$$

We have to determine the fraction K/L. To do this, we use the boundary condition $\Pi(1) = 1$ to get $K/L = 1 - z_1$. We therefore have

$$\begin{aligned} \Pi(z) &= \frac{1 - z_1}{z - z_1} \\ &= \frac{1 - 1/z_1}{1 - z/z_1} \\ &= \left(1 - \frac{1}{z_1}\right)\left[1 + \frac{z}{z_1} + \left(\frac{z}{z_1}\right)^2 + \cdots + \left(\frac{z}{z_1}\right)^n + \cdots\right] \end{aligned} \tag{A.170}$$

We can write by inspection of this series,

$$\pi_i = \left(1 - \frac{1}{z_1}\right)\left[\frac{1}{z_1}\right]^i \tag{A.171}$$

Recall that all this is for the case $\mu > \lambda/2$. What happens if $\mu \leq \lambda/2$? In this case, it is impossible to find any root within the unit circle, and the chain is not recurrent non-null.

The transient solution of continuous-time Markov chains (i.e., obtaining the probability of being in state i at time t), $\pi_i(t)$, is usually very difficult to do in closed-form. Numerical techniques must therefore be used. One can either numerically solve the set of differential equations, or use a frequently faster technique called *uniformization*. Let us motivate uniformization with an example.

Example A.14. Consider again the continuous-time chain shown in Figure A.11. Find the probability $\pi_i(t)$ of being in state i at time t, given the initial conditions $\pi_i(0)$.

Denote by $X(t)$ the state of the system at time t, and let $N(t)$ be the number of state-transitions there have been in the interval $[0, t]$. The probability of being in state j at time t, given that the system was in state i at time 0, is given by

$$p_{ij}(t) = \text{Prob}\{X(t) = j \mid X(0) = i\}$$

$$= \sum_{v=0}^{\infty} \text{Prob}\{X(t) = j \mid X(0) = i, N(t) = v\}\text{Prob}\{N(t) = v \mid X(0) = i\} \tag{A.172}$$

Let us examine the problem of computing $\text{Prob}\{N(t) = v \mid X(0) = i\}$. We know that the transitions can be either from state i to $i + 1$ according to a Poisson process with rate λ or from state i to $i - 1$ according to a Poisson process with rate μ for $i > 0$. Since the sum of independent Poisson processes is a Poisson process, the transition rate out of state i is $\mu + \lambda$ for $i > 0$. For $i = 0$, it is different—namely λ, since there are no departures from this state. To compute $\text{Prob}\{N(t) = v \mid X(0) = i\}$ directly, would require us to count the number of departures from state 0 separately from the rest, which would complicate matters a bit.

We get around this difficulty by the following stratagem. Define the transition out of state 0 as having rate $\lambda + \mu$ (i.e., the same rate as out of the other states), but let there be a transition from state 0 back to state 0 with rate μ. This way the transition rates out of all the states are exactly the same. For this reason, the number of transitions that have occurred in the interval $[0, t]$ is independent of $X(0)$. That is, $\text{Prob}\{N(t) = v \mid X(0) = i\} = \text{Prob}\{N(t) = v\}$. Indeed, we can write from our knowledge of the Poisson process

$$\text{Prob}\{N(t) = v\} = \exp\{-(\lambda + \mu)t\}\frac{[(\lambda + \mu)t]^n}{n!} \tag{A.173}$$

We now have a discrete-time Markov chain with the probability-transition matrix:

$$\begin{pmatrix} \dfrac{\mu}{\lambda + \mu} & \dfrac{\lambda}{\lambda + \mu} & 0 & 0 & 0 & 0 & 0 & 0 & \cdots \\[2mm] \dfrac{\mu}{\lambda + \mu} & 0 & \dfrac{\lambda}{\lambda + \mu} & 0 & 0 & 0 & 0 & 0 & \cdots \\[2mm] 0 & \dfrac{\mu}{\lambda + \mu} & 0 & \dfrac{\lambda}{\lambda + \mu} & 0 & 0 & 0 & 0 & \cdots \\[2mm] 0 & 0 & \dfrac{\mu}{\lambda + \mu} & 0 & \dfrac{\lambda}{\lambda + \mu} & 0 & 0 & 0 & \cdots \\[2mm] & & & & & \vdots & & \end{pmatrix} \tag{A.174}$$

This discrete chain is shown in Figure A.13. This chain is the discrete equivalent of the continuous-time chain we aim to solve, in the sense that the probability of

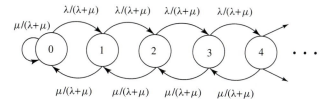

FIGURE A.13
Discrete-time Markov chain, Example A.14.

reaching state j from state i after v transitions is identical in both chains. In other words, the probability $\text{Prob}\{X(t) = j | X(0) = i, N(t) = v\}$ is identical in both cases, and so we can use the discrete-time chain to compute it. Obtaining $\text{Prob}\{X(t) = j | X(0) = i, N(t) = v\}$ numerically is easy—just raise the probability transition matrix to the vth power. Of course, the matrix must be truncated to make it finite (i.e., we do not consider states beyond some number k), but if k is sufficiently large, the numerical errors in truncation will be small. Combining this with the expression for $\text{Prob}\{N(t) = v\}$ and summing (we will have to truncate this sum also) according to Equation (A.172), we can obtain the desired values for $\text{Prob}\{X(t) = j | X(0) = i\}$.

This example shows a way to obtain transient solutions for continuous-time Markov chains when the transition rates are bounded. The procedure is as follows:

1. Let r_i be the total transition rate out of state i. Since r_i is bounded, define some R such that $R \geq r_i$ for all i.
2. Define an equivalent discrete-time Markov chain with the following state-transition probabilities.

$$\hat{p}_{ij} = \begin{cases} 1 - r_i/R & \text{if } i = j \\ \frac{r_i}{R} p_{ij} & \text{otherwise} \end{cases} \tag{A.175}$$

Denote by $\hat{p}_{i,j}^{(n)}$ the probability of reaching state j in the discrete chain n steps after being in state i. $\hat{p}_{i,j}^{(n)}$ can be computed from $\hat{p}_{ij}$.
3. The transition probability, for the continuous-time chain, of getting to state j from state i in time t is given by

$$p_{ij}(t) = \sum_{n=0}^{\infty} \hat{p}_{ij}^{(n)} \exp\{-(Rt)\} \frac{(Rt)^n}{n!} \tag{A.176}$$

Since numerically we can only compute finite sums, the ∞ in the sum can be replaced by N, where N is sufficiently large that the sum from 0 to N is a good approximation to the sum from 0 to ∞. The greater the value of Rt, the greater the value of N will have to be to obtain a good approximation.

The transient solution of some Markov chains can be time-consuming if there is a wide disparity in the transition rates out of the various states. For example, for a system with failures and repair, the failure rate will usually be a small fraction of the repair rate (otherwise the computer system will not be of much use!). In such cases, more advanced techniques such as decomposition must be used to reduce the computational complexity of a transient solution.

A.4.4 The Method of Stages

The method of stages is often a convenient way to model nonexponential holding times. The idea is to express such times as a function of times spent in multiple stages with the time spent in each of the stages being exponentially distributed. For example, consider the chain shown in Figure A.14. The time spent within the dashed box is the sum of the times spent in each of the stages. The time spent in stage i is exponentially distributed with rate μ_i. The Laplace transform of the pdf of this time is given by

$$\prod_{i=1}^{n} \frac{\mu_i}{s + \mu_i} \tag{A.177}$$

Other arrangements of the exponential substates are also useful. The most general is shown in Figure A.15. If the time spent in stage (i, j) is exponentially distributed with rate $\mu_{i,j}$, the Laplace transform of the pdf of the time spent in the dashed box is given by

$$\sum_{i=1}^{m} p_i \prod_{j=1}^{n_i} \frac{\mu_{i,j}}{s + \mu_{i,j}} \tag{A.178}$$

It is evident from inspection of this last equation that this method can represent any service time for which the the Laplace transform of the pdf is a rational function of s. Since any nonrational function can be approximated arbitrarily closely by rational functions, this is a very useful general method for modeling nonexponential holding times.

However, this approach does lead to an increase in the total number of states (as each stage must be treated as a state of the Markov chain), with concomitant increases in the time required to solve for such systems.

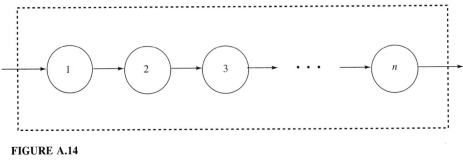

FIGURE A.14
An n-stage system.

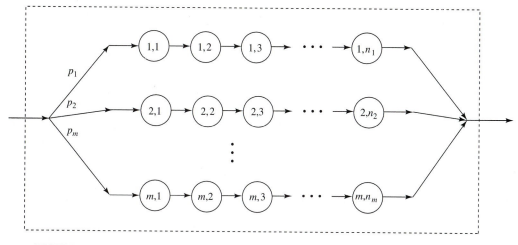

FIGURE A.15
A general system with stages.

A.5 A BRIEF GLIMPSE OF QUEUEING THEORY

In Figure A.16, we display four queueing systems. A *queue* consists of a storage area in which jobs or "customers" awaiting service are held. These jobs are served according to some specified discipline (e.g., first-come-first-served, last-come-last-served, round-robin, etc.) by a server. A queueing system can consist of a single queue, feeding either a single server or a set of multiple servers, an *open queueing network*, where jobs (called *exogenous* jobs) arriving from outside are routed from one queue to another upon service until they leave; a *closed queueing network*, where jobs (called *endogenous* jobs) circulate endlessly through the system; or a partially-open-and-partially-closed network, consisting of some exogenous and some endogenous jobs. The parameters that describe a queue include:

- the number of servers,
- the size of the job population (may be ∞),
- the capacity, in number of jobs, of the queue (may be ∞), and
- the queueing discipline.

One of the most important laws of queueing theory is Little's law.

Theorem A.4. Little's law. The average number of jobs $E[N]$ in a queueing system is equal to the average arrival rate of the jobs into the system, $E[\lambda]$, multiplied by the average time spent in the system, $E[T]$. That is,

$$E[N] = E[\lambda]E[T] \tag{A.179}$$

The queueing system in Little's law can be defined to encompass whichever part of a larger queueing system is the focus of interest. For example, if we wish

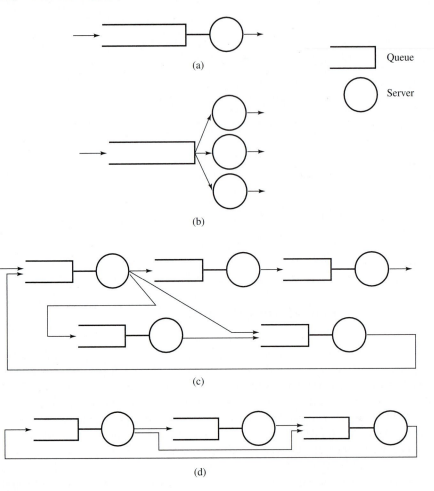

FIGURE A.16
Some queueing systems: (a) single-server queueing system; (b) multiple-server queueing system; (c) open queueing network; (d) closed queueing network.

to consider only the waiting-for-service portion, we will have

$$E[N_q] = E[\lambda]E[T_q] \tag{A.180}$$

where N_q and T_q are the number of jobs awaiting service and the time spent awaiting service.

Example A.15. Consider the queueing network shown in Figure A.17. The labels on the arrows depict the routing probability; for example, half the jobs emerging from server 1 go into the queue of server 2. Jobs arrive at queue 1 according to a Poisson process with rate λ. The service time per job is exponentially distributed with mean $1/\mu_i$ for server i, $i = 1, 2, 3$. We want to find the relationship between the mean number of jobs in the portion of the system enclosed within the dashed box and the mean time spent by a job within the box. The rate out of server 1 must

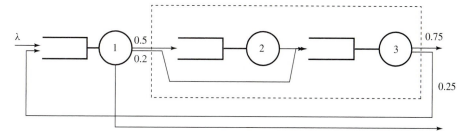

FIGURE A.17
Queueing network, Example A.15.

equal the rate of jobs going in (assuming that the arrival rate does not exceed the service rate). The rate into the box is $(0.5 + 0.2)$ times the rate coming into queue 1; that is, $\lambda_{box} = 0.7\lambda_1$. The rate of jobs coming into queue 1 is computed by adding the rate of jobs arrivals from the outside world to the rate due to feedback,

$$\lambda_1 = \lambda + 0.7 \times 0.25 \times \lambda_1$$

$$\Rightarrow \lambda_1 = 1.212\lambda \tag{A.181}$$

So, we have the equation

$$E[N_{box}] = 1.212\lambda E[T_{box}] \tag{A.182}$$

The standard notation for individual queues is of the form A/B/C/D/E, where

A   represents the arrival process (e.g., M if it is Poisson, D if it is deterministic, and G if it is general).

B   represents the service time (e.g., M if it is exponential, D if it is deterministic, and G if it is general).

C   is the number of servers.

D   is the maximum number of jobs that can be stored in the queue.

E   is the maximum number of jobs in the universe of the queue.

If D or E are infinite, we drop them from the queue description. For example, an M/M/1 queue has Poisson arrivals, exponential service, one server, infinite waiting room, and an unlimited number of jobs. The system D/G/2/30/50 is a system with deterministic arrivals, general service distribution, two servers, a maximum waiting room for 30 jobs in the queue (any who arrive when the queue is full are turned away), and a maximum of 50 jobs in the queueing universe.

Queues can often be solved for their mean waiting time and mean number of jobs using Markov modeling techniques. Solving for the distributions of the waiting time is usually more difficult.

We have already seen in Example A.12 the Markov chain model for the M/M/1 system, with the pmf of the number of jobs in the system. Let us now compute the distribution of the time spent in the system (the system time). To do so, we will use the following result from probability theory.

Theorem A.5. PASTA (Poisson arrivals see time averages). If a queue under steady-state has jobs arriving according to a Poisson process, the probability that an arriving job will find n jobs ahead of it in the system is the probability that there are n jobs in the system at any random moment.

We know π_n, the time-averaged pmf of the number of jobs in the system. Hence, an arriving job will find n jobs ahead of it with probability π_n. Each such job consumes an exponentially distributed amount of service before it can begin to be served. The waiting time is therefore the sum of the service times of these jobs. These service times are independent of each other, and so the Laplace transform of the sum of their pdfs is equal to the product of the Laplace transforms of the pdfs. The transform of the waiting time density is therefore given by

$$
\begin{aligned}
W^*(s) &= \sum_{n=0}^{\infty} \pi_n \left(\frac{\mu}{s+\mu} \right)^n \\
&= \sum_{n=0}^{\infty} \left(1 - \frac{\lambda}{\mu} \right) \left(\frac{\lambda}{\mu} \right)^n \frac{1}{1 - \lambda/(s+\mu)} \\
&= \left(1 - \frac{\lambda}{\mu} \right) \left(\frac{1}{1 - \lambda/(s+\mu)} \right) \\
&= \left(1 - \frac{\lambda}{\mu} \right) \left[1 + \frac{\lambda}{\mu - \lambda} \frac{\mu - \lambda}{s + \mu - \lambda} \right]
\end{aligned}
\tag{A.183}
$$

Let us write $\lambda/\mu = \rho$. Inverting, we obtain the pdf

$$
w(t) = \begin{cases} 1 - \rho & \text{if } t = 0 \\ \lambda(1 - \rho)\exp\{-\mu(1 - \rho)t\} & \text{if } t > 0 \end{cases}
\tag{A.184}
$$

where ρ is the utilization of the server for an M/M/1 system. We can see that, with probability $1 - \rho$, the waiting time is zero (i.e., the job arrives to find the server idle).

Analytical solutions are only available for some queues. M/M/1 is simple to solve because both the arrival and service processes satisfy the memorylessness property. When this is not the case, analysis becomes more complex. Indeed, we do not yet have a solution for M/G/m ($m > 1$), or for G/G/1. Most of the more complex systems can be solved only for the mean waiting times, and not the densities. This is sufficient for general-purpose computer systems, but not for real-time systems, where it is the probability of meeting a deadline that is of interest. This is at least partially why real-time analysts have to focus on developing worst-case timing analyses rather than probabilistic ones.

A.6 SUGGESTIONS FOR FURTHER READING

There is a voluminous literature on probability and modeling. Trivedi [7] and Ross [9] are particularly good starting points. Kleinrock [5, 6] and Gross and

Harris [2] are excellent introductions to queueing theory. Reibman and Trivedi [8] survey numerical methods for the transient analysis of Markov chains. The uniformization technique is also called *randomization*, and its use in transient analysis is treated in depth by Gross and Miller [3]. Queueing networks, which have not been treated in the Appendix, are covered by Walrand [10]. Transform techniques are well covered by Doetsch [1] and Jury [4].

REFERENCES

[1] Doetsch, G.: *Guide to the Applications of the Laplace and z-Transforms*, Van Nostrand, London, 1971.
[2] Gross, D., and C. M. Harris: *Fundamentals of Queueing Theory*, John Wiley, New York, 1985.
[3] Gross, D., and D. Miller: "The Randomization Technique as a Modeling Tool and Solution Procedure for Transient Markov Processes," *Operations Research* 32:343–361, 1984.
[4] Jury, E. I.: *Theory and Application of the z-Transform Method*, John Wiley, New York, 1964.
[5] Kleinrock, L.: *Queueing Systems, Vol. 1: Theory*, John Wiley, New York, 1975.
[6] Kleinrock, L.: *Queueing Systems, Vol. 2: Computer Applications*, John Wiley, New York, 1975.
[7] Trivedi, K. S.: *Probability and Statistics with Probability, Queueing, and Computer Science Applications*, Prentice-Hall, Englewood Cliffs, NJ, 1982.
[8] Reibman, A., and K. S. Trivedi: "Numerical Transient Analysis of Markov Models," *Computers in Operations Research* 15(1):19–36, 1988.
[9] Ross, S.: *Stochastic Processes*, John Wiley, New York, 1983.
[10] Walrand, J.: *An Introduction to Queueing Networks*, Prentice-Hall, Englewood Cliffs, NJ, 1982.

INDEX